THE BUTTERFLIES OF COSTA RICA AND THEIR NATURAL HISTORY

Philip J. DeVries

The Butterflies of Costa Rica

AND THEIR NATURAL HISTORY

VOLUME I

PAPILIONIDAE, PIERIDAE, NYMPHALIDAE

Illustrated by Philip J. DeVries and Jennifer Clark

PRINCETON UNIVERSITY PRESS

Published by Princeton University Press,
41 William Street, Princeton, New Jersey 08540

In the United Kingdom:
Princeton University Press, Chichester, West Sussex

Library of Congress Cataloging-in-Publication Data

DeVries, Philip J., 1952-
The butterflies of Costa Rica and their natural history.
Volume 1.
Bibliography : p.
Includes index.
1. Butterflies—Costa Rica. 2. Insects—Costa Rica. I. Title.
QL553.C67D48 1986 595.78'9'097286 85-28340
ISBN 0-691-08420-3
ISBN 0-691-02403-0 (pbk.)

This book has been composed in Linotron Baskerville

Princeton University Press books are printed on acid-free paper and meet the guidelines for permanence and durability of the Committee on Production Guidelines for Book Longevity of the Council on Library Resources

Printed in the United States of America
by Princeton Academic Press

4 6 8 10 9 7 5

CONTENTS

LIST OF FIGURES

LIST OF COLOR PLATES

PREFACE AND ACKNOWLEDGMENTS

Shortly after beginning my work with butterflies at the Museo Nacional de Costa Rica it was obvious that Costa Rica contained an enormous number of butterfly species, that how many species occurred in Costa Rica was unknown, and that there was no treatment of Central or South American butterflies that was up to date, accessible, or that contained detailed natural history accounts. Equally obvious was that although various authors noisily lamented our lack of knowledge (both taxonomic and ecological), nobody was willing to do a detailed study of the Neotropical butterfly fauna. Hence, as someone who enjoys doing natural history in the field, my reasons for writing this book were very simple: it was something I wanted to do, and I was in a position to devote years to studying butterflies in the field.

The present volume began its life on a rainy night in 1976 within the confines of a very field-worn jeep outside the now extinct Tala Inn in San José, Costa Rica. The work has undergone a number of evolutionary changes since that rainy night, and many people have generously supported me and this project by contributing their time, skills, and materials.

My work on butterflies would never have begun were it not for L. D. Gomez, who was responsible for my employment at the Museo Nacional de Costa Rica and who, against all odds, generously supported and encouraged my field and museum work. Miraculously managing to overlook my naiveté and wild notions, Luis provided the necessary environment at the Museo and the support of its trustees and staff throughout my stay in Costa Rica. My sincere thanks are due to all members of the Museo Nacional for their understanding and help. I am particularly indebted to Dan Janzen, who not only sat inside a leaky jeep listening to the faltering birthing pains of this book, but who has also provided impetus, encouragement, advice, field assistance, and financial support throughout the entire project. Gordon B. Small has supported my work by offering constant encouragement, patiently replying to all my queries (no matter where I happened to be at the time) and sharing with me his unflagging enthusiasm and matchless knowledge of Neotropical butterflies. Throughout my tenure as a graduate student at the University of Texas, Larry Gilbert provided the space to work, encouragement, and support that made writing this book possible.

I have had the good fortune to work with many generous and genuinely interested biologists in a great number of habitats and under a variety of conditions. For field observations and assistance I am particularly grateful to: A. Bien, R. Canet, I. A. Chacon, P. Chai, J. Gamboa, L. E. Gilbert, L. D. Gomez, N. Greig, W. Haber, W. Hallwachs, R. Hesterberg, D. H. Janzen, A. La Rosa, J. Longino, J. Mallet, R. Marquis, R. Ocampos, J. L. Poveda, G. B. Small, M. C. Singer, F. G. Stiles, C. A. Todzia, C. D. Thomas, N. Weintrub, and K. Wolf. I am also grateful to the personnel of Servicios Parques Nacionales de Costa Rica for facilitating my fieldwork in many ways.

To the many people who allowed me free access to the collections and libraries (public and private) in their charge I am deeply grateful. I thank the trustees of the British Museum (Natural History) for allowing me to illustrate specimens from the peerless collection housed there, and for use of an equally superb library. I extend my thanks to the entire staff at the British Museum (Natural History) for assistance and good cheer and, in particular, R. I. Vane-Wright and P. R. Ackery for patience and discussions beyond the call of duty; the staff of the Smithsonian National Museum of Natural History, especially F. G. Clark, W. D. Duckworth, W. D. Field, and R. Robbins; the Carnegie Museum of Natural History, especially the late H. K. Clench; the Allyn Museum of Entomology (L. D. Miller); the Hope Department of Entomology (D. Smith); and the following persons: R. Canet, I. A. Chacon, F. M. Brown, Lt. Col. J. Eliot, T. C. Emmel, L. D. Gomez, D. J. Harvey, R. Hesterberg, A. King, I. J. Kitching, G. Lamas, P. A. Opler, L. San Roman, M. Serrano, G. B. Small, W. H. Wagner, Jr., K. Wolf, and A. M. Young.

The illustrations have benefited from the assistance of a number of people. For generous help, financial assistance, and cheerful banter in setting up the photographic color plates I owe a special debt of gratitude to B. D'Abrera, whose own work on butterflies of the world is testimony to his great determination and artistic skill. I thank B. C. Brodeur for help in transferring color slides to black and white prints, and J. M. Barrs, L. Jost, and K. Winemiller for use of their photos. I am grateful to R. Cubero for his fine drawings of the Brassolinae and his enthusiasm. My deepest appreciation and thanks go to Jennifer Clark for an outstanding contribution of time and energy under all conditions; her superb talent has made the drawings of the early stages come alive.

My work on butterflies has been supported by grants from: the Carnegie Museum, the Smithsonian Institution, a Fulbright-Hayes fellowship, the Smithsonian Peace Corps, the University of Texas at Austin, Sigma-Xi, the Xerxes Society, Partridge Films LTD., L. E. Gilbert, D. H. Janzen, and R. I. Vane-Wright. A special thanks to my parents H. W. and H. M. DeVries for endless patience and help, and to J. J. Bull for financial assistance, access to equipment, encouragement, and for hooking up the dryer.

I would like to thank M. Case, P. R. Ehrlich, T. Emmel, H. Horn, and J. May for editing various drafts of the manuscript, and especially R. I. Vane-Wright whose careful editing and masterful knowledge greatly improved the manuscript. The help of S. Bramblett, E. Bramblett, and the inimitable Sabra Wilson for typing the manuscript onto computer tape is gratefully acknowledged. I dedicate this book to the memory of H. W. Bates, T. Belt, B. Evans, H. Fassl, A. Pepper, D. Reinhardt, and A. R. Wallace, all of whom were artists at the science of interpreting life. Finally, it is my sincere hope that in some small way the present volume can help slow the continual destruction of tropical habitats by providing an access for enjoying certain components of tropical communities through the study of butterflies.

THE CONTENTS AND USE OF THIS BOOK

This book treats, with emphasis on their natural history, nearly 550 species of butterflies in the families Papilionidae, Pieridae, and Nymphalidae that have been recorded from Costa Rica. Members of these butterfly families have been reasonably well collected in Costa Rica, and their taxonomies at the species level are generally worked out; I have amassed a growing body of unpublished field observations on their natural histories. Excluded from this book are treatments of the lycaenoid butterflies, the Lycaenidae, the Riodinidae, and the skippers—Hesperiidae—because there is very little, if any, information on distribution and natural history for most of the species recorded from Costa Rica (see DeVries 1983 for a list). Even more serious is the problem that generic assignment of most lycaenids in the Neotropics is unresolved, new genera require description, and many of the Costa Rican species have not as yet been described. For these reasons it seems unwise to include the lycaenids here until their taxonomy is better understood. The taxonomy of the Riodinidae is better developed, and I am planning a treatment of the Costa Rican fauna in the near future, based on work now in progress.

Area of Coverage

Although it is a small country (approximately 19,600 square miles), Costa Rica contains a great diversity of tropical habitats that occur from sea level to over 3,800 m elevation, and it encompasses more than fifteen distinct life zones. This diversity is reflected in its rich flora and fauna. Costa Rica contains a large percentage of all the butterfly species known from Central America, and a substantial representation of the fauna of the Amazon Basin. For example, 93 percent of the Central American species belonging to the family Papilionidae occur in Costa Rica, and 31 percent of the total Neotropical papilionid fauna occurs in Costa Rica. Likewise, 92 percent of the genera of Central American Pieridae occur in our area, and 66 percent of all Neotropical genera occur here, as well (see also the section on diversity). As a result, the butterfly fauna of Costa Rica appears to be a bridge between the faunas of Central and South America. Hence, although this book is about Costa Rican butterflies, it covers a much larger portion of the Neotropics than national boundaries might suggest.

Informational Content and Sources

Although this is primarily a field guide to the identification of all nonlycaenoid and nonhesperioid butterflies of Costa Rica, I have also included a substantial amount of information on systematics, natural history, and ecology. In the short opening chapters the reader will find introductions to butterfly morphology, biology, diversity, and systematics, and a section on habitats and climates of Costa Rica. These contain references leading to more detailed literature that should aid field biologists and others in their research. At the level of butterfly families and subfamilies, I have provided broad overviews of each group, incorporating information about the group throughout the world. The information provided should allow a researcher to gain an appreciation of each group and immediately have access to key references on its systematics and ecology.

The generic accounts are similar to those covering the families and subfamilies, but concentrate on the Neotropics. For example, under the generic account for *Heliconius*, literature is cited that covers systematics, hostplants and early stages, distribution, adult ecology, and suggestions for further study. Although the literature cited under each generic account is not exhaustive, I have tried to provide references that lead to nearly everything published on the particular group. The generic sections also include illustrations of early stages, which should help with identification of larvae and pupae. The species accounts emphasize identification, and I have summarized field observations on both early stages and adults in Costa Rica.

The information in this book comes from a diffuse literature, most of which is cited under the family, subfamily, generic, and species accounts. The book also contains many field observations made by myself and others. For the distribution of each species, I have relied heavily on the collections of the British Museum (Natural History), National Museum of Costa Rica, U.S. National Museum, Carnegie Museum, Allyn Museum of Entomology, and the private collections of G. B. Small, A. King, R. Canet, L. E. Gilbert, D. H. Janzen, R. Hesterberg, and my own field work. Observations on the natural history and ecology of each species are taken primarily from my own field experience, but have been, in some instances, generously supplemented by the observations of G. B. Small, I. A. Chacon, R. Marquis, L. Gilbert, and D. H. Janzen, to whom I owe debts of gratitude. Due to my predilection for tropical forests, the emphasis in this book is on forest-inhabiting butterflies, at the expense of those species which are most common in severely disturbed habitats. I see no reason to believe that pastures played a significant role in the evolution of most Costa Rican butterfly species, because they are a recent man-made habitat type. Most of the common species typically found in pastures also occur in forests along rivers and in light gaps analogous to small pastures overgrown with weedy plants.

The Color Plates

Each butterfly specimen illustrated in the color plates has a number that corresponds to a line of data found on the facing page. Each line of data gives the name of the butterfly, sex, orientation of the specimen, where the specimen was collected from, and where in the text that species is discussed.

The following abbreviations are used:

♂	male
♀	female
D	dorsal: this means the *upperside* is illustrated
V	ventral: this means the *underside* is illustrated
CR	Costa Rica
[HT]	the holotype is illustrated
[PT]	a paratype is illustrated

I have tried to illustrate only specimens of Costa Rican origin. In some cases this was not possible, however, and some specimens illustrated are from another country. In some instances Chiriqui is given on the collection label as the locality of origin; in such instances, it is impossible to know whether the specimen was in fact from Panama, or, as was common at the turn of the century, from the area around Volcan Chiriqui, which included both Costa Rica and Panama.

Basic Nomenclature Used in This Book

There are entire books devoted to the subject of classification, taxonomy, and nomenclature to which the interested reader may turn (Mayr et al. 1953; Wiley 1981). For our purposes we shall be using the basic binominal or trinominal system of nomenclature to discuss the butterflies of Costa Rica.

Each species in this book has at least a two-part, and in many cases a three-part Latin name. Following the last Latin name is the name of the author, or describer of the species, and a date. Each component part of a butterfly's scientific name is a shorthand method of access to systematic and natural history literature. For example, the butterfly name *Heliconius charitonius* (Linnaeus, 1767) says that this butterfly is in the genus *Heliconius*, its species name is *charitonius*, and it was first described by Linnaeus in 1767. The parentheses around the author's name indicate that *charitonius* was originally described in a different genus (in this case *Papilio*) and later transferred to the genus *Heliconius*. A person searching the literature can look for *charitonius* and be forewarned that information may be found under more than one genus. If there are no parentheses around the author's name, the investigator knows that the species was described in the genus appearing with the species name. In cases where there are three Latin names, the last Latin name refers to a subspecies or geographically distinct form. Breaking down the names of *Anetia thirza insignis* (Salvin, 1869) we know the genus is *Anetia*, the species is *thirza*, and the subspecies is *insignis*, which was described by Salvin in 1869 under a different generic name (hence the parentheses).

How to Use the Species Accounts

As in all field guides, the user matches the specimen in question with the illustration provided, then turns to the text pages that discuss that species. There are diagnostic characters provided under each species to separate it from all others, but because of the extensive mimicry in Costa Rican butterflies, the user should pay particular attention to the notes on similar species to make sure the identification is correct. For example, a specimen may look just like the illustration of *Heliconius ismenius*, but upon closer examination it may turn out to be *Melinaea lilis*, and it may also look similar to several other species. Be sure to compare your specimen to the similar species listed; remember that mimicry really works!

The information provided for each species includes, first, the various names of the butterfly, its wing-length in millimeters (measured from the base of the forewing to the apex), the plate on which the butterfly is illustrated, and the species and subspecies distributions throughout the world. Next the larval hostplants and early stages are described, with a brief description of the egg, mature larva, and pupa; notes of interest are also included. A section on the adult butterfly gives diagnostic characters and similar species that should be referred to; finally, the section on habits tells where the species occurs in Costa Rica by elevation and associated habitat type, summarizes field observations on behavior, feeding, and seasonality, and, whenever possible, gives other information pertinent to its biology. Where available, a reference is provided, but since little is published on the biology of most Costa Rican species, the observations in this section have been taken chiefly from my own field work. I hope that my contributions to the natural history of each species will stimulate more thorough treatments of Costa Rican butterflies in the future.

Classification of Costa Rican Butterflies

In arranging the taxa covered in this book, I have followed, whenever possible, existing classifications (the section on "Systematics and Neotropical Butterflies" traces the history of butterfly systematics in the Neotropics and supplements the material covered in this section). Classification of the Papilionidae and Pieridae poses no serious problems in showing apparent phylogenetic affinities. Within the Nymphalidae, however, the component subfamilies, tribes, and genera have not been examined in detail for phylogenetic affinities. The Nymphalidae must be viewed as a phylogenetically unstudied group of taxa composed of various classifications, and hence the arrangement of many of the genera and the order in which they are listed is arbitrary. The problem of arranging the Nymphalidae is an old one (see Seitz 1913; Ehrlich 1958*a*; Ackery 1984 for reviews and discussion). No one has analyzed the nymphalids in detail below the subfamily level on a global basis, and so we have only a composite picture of their affinities.

Perhaps the most useful classification of the Neotropical Nymphalidae is that of Müller (1886). His work on early stages and their classification is unexcelled and shows piercing phylogenetic insights. Although most modern authors largely ignore Müller's classification, I have incorporated his overall framework for the arrangement of the Costa Rican nymphalid fauna, while adding modifications in the form of more modern generic or subfamilial revisions. This systematic framework and a Costa Rican species list is given in Appendix III.

The following classifications have been used in arranging the families and subfamilies in this book (generic revisions are found under each generic account): *Papilionidae*—Rothschild and Jordan (1906), Munroe (1961), Hancock (1983); *Pieridae*—Klots (1933), Lamas (1979); *Nymphalidae*—Müller (1886), Ehrlich (1958); *Charaxinae*—Comstock (1961), Rydon (1971), DeVries et al. (1985); *Ithomiinae*—Fox (1968); *Danainae*—Ackery and Vane-Wright (1984); *Morphinae*—DeVries et al. (1985); *Satyrinae*—Miller (1968), Forster (1964); *Heliconiinae*—Michener (1942), Emsely (1963); *Nymphalinae*—Müller (1886); *Melitaeinae*—Higgins (1960, 1981).

Butterflies and Habitat Associations

Butterfly collectors, botanists, and field biologists generally tend to associate a species with a habitat within its geographic range. The delineation of a habitat reflects the experience of the biologist in the field,

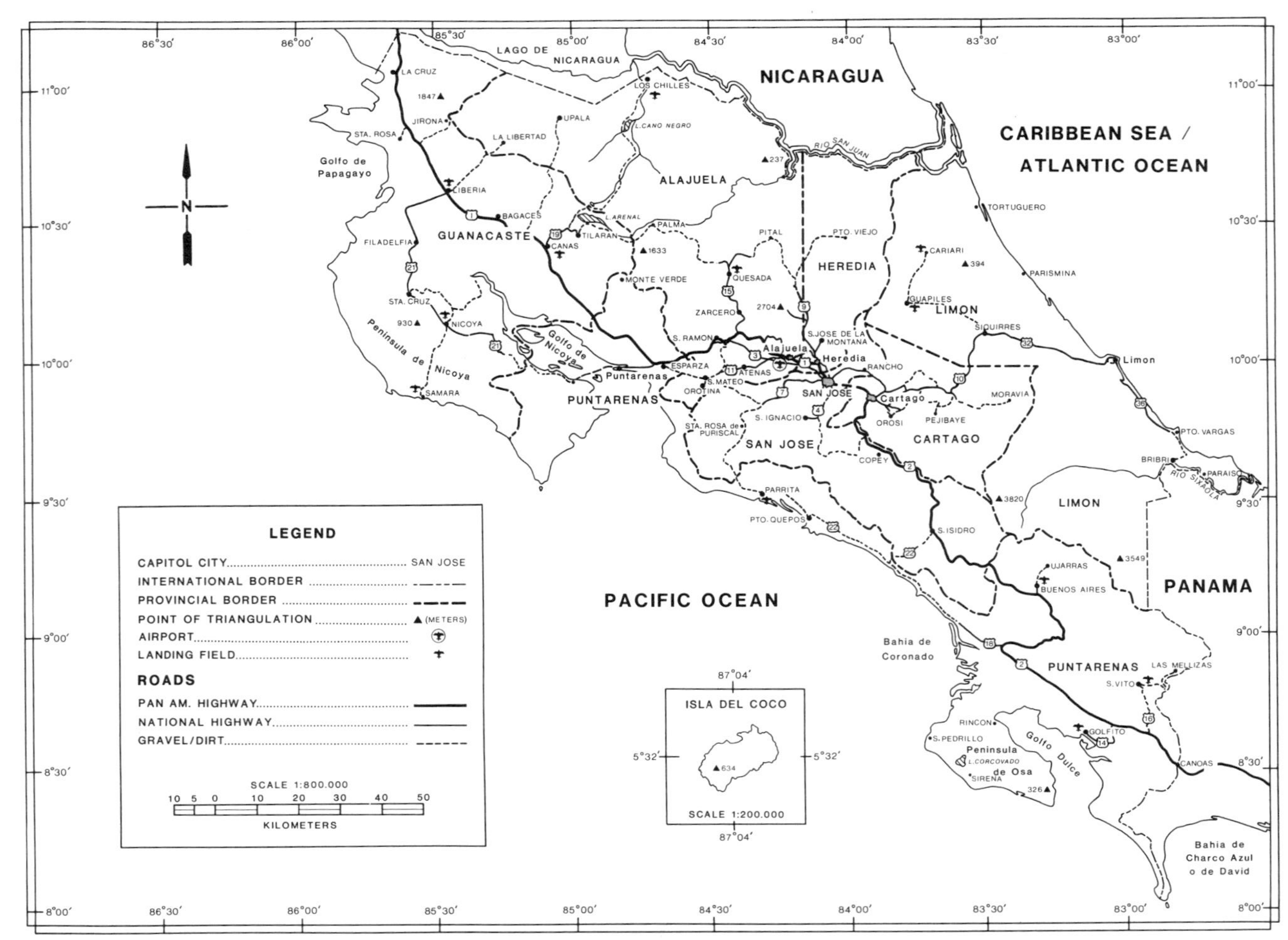

NICARAGUA
LAGO DE NICARAGUA
CARIBBEAN SEA / ATLANTIC OCEAN
PACIFIC OCEAN
PANAMA
GUANACASTE
ALAJUELA
HEREDIA
LIMON
CARTAGO
SAN JOSE
PUNTARENAS
Golfo de Papagayo
Golfo de Nicoya
Peninsula de Nicoya
Golfo Dulce
Peninsula de Osa
Bahia de Coronado
Bahia de Charco Azul o de David
RIO SAN JUAN
RIO SIXAOLA
L. CANO NEGRO
L. ARENAL
L. CORCOVADO
LA CRUZ
STA. ROSA
JIRONA
LA LIBERTAD
UPALA
LOS CHILLES
LIBERIA
BAGACES
FILADELFIA
CANAS
TILARAN
PALMA
MONTE VERDE
STA. CRUZ
NICOYA
SAMARA
PITAL
PTO. VIEJO
QUESADA
ZARCERO
S. RAMON
ESPARZA
Puntarenas
Alajuela
Heredia
S.JOSE DE LA MONTANA
RANCHO
ATENAS
S. MATEO
OROTINA
SAN JOSE
Cartago
OROSI
PEJIBAYE
MORAVIA
S. IGNACIO
STA. ROSA de PURISCAL
COPEY
PARRITA
PTO. QUEPOS
S. ISIDRO
UJARRAS
BUENOS AIRES
TORTUGUERO
PARISMINA
CARIARI
GUAPILES
SIQUIRRES
Limon
PTO. VARGAS
BRIBRI
PARAISO
S. VITO
LAS MELLIZAS
GOLFITO
CANOAS
RINCON
S. PEDRILLO
SIRENA
1847
237
1633
2704
930
394
3820
3549
326
86°30′
86°00′
85°30′
85°00′
84°30′
84°00′
83°30′
83°00′
11°00′
10°30′
10°00′
9°30′
9°00′
8°30′
8°00′
N
LEGEND
CAPITOL CITY .... SAN JOSE
INTERNATIONAL BORDER
PROVINCIAL BORDER
POINT OF TRIANGULATION .... (METERS)
AIRPORT
LANDING FIELD
ROADS
PAN AM. HIGHWAY
NATIONAL HIGHWAY
GRAVEL/DIRT
SCALE 1:800.000
10 5 0 10 20 30 40 50
KILOMETERS
ISLA DEL COCO
87°04′
5°32′
634
SCALE 1:200.000

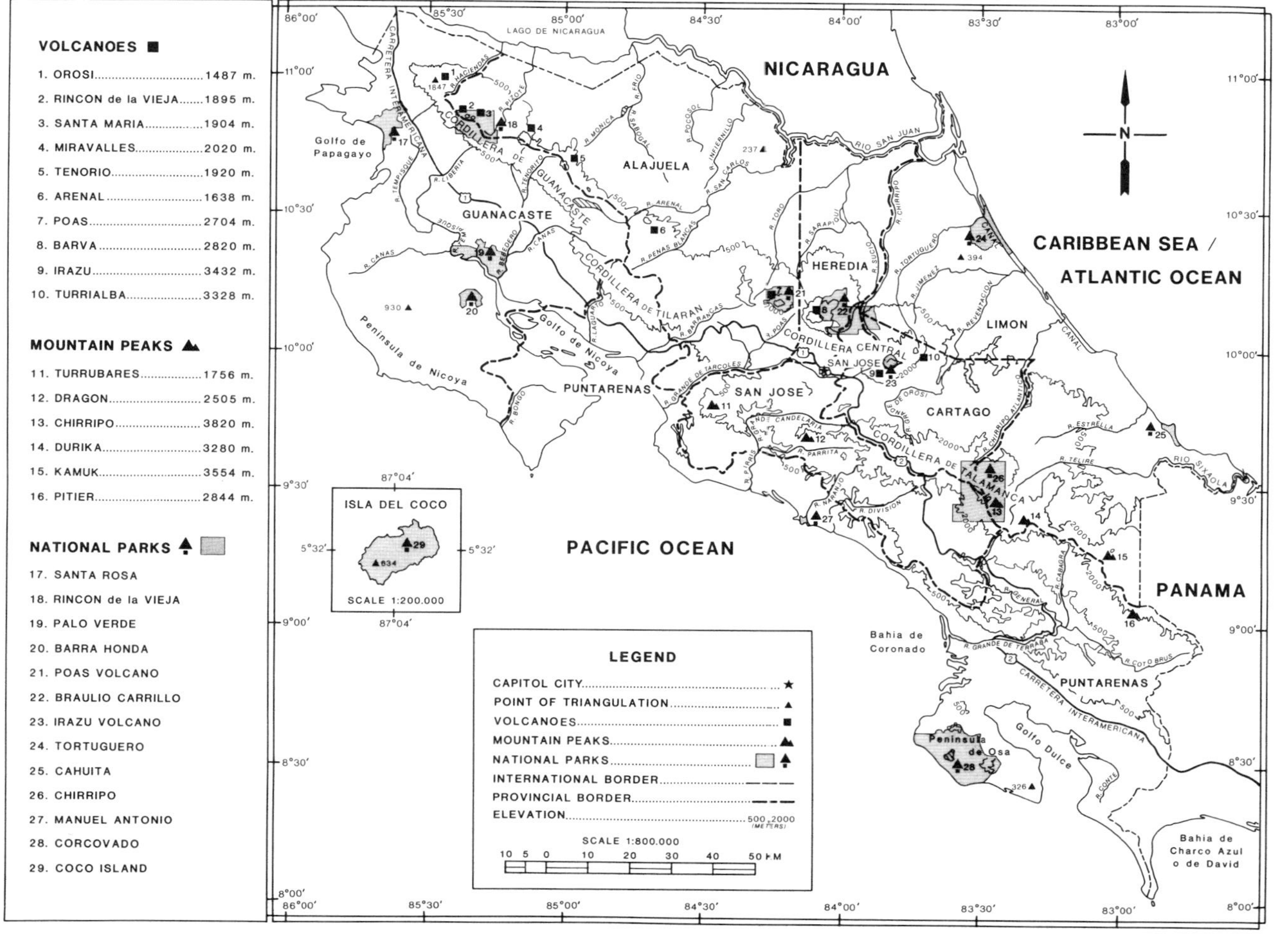
VOLCANOES
1. OROSI....1487 m.
2. RINCON de la VIEJA....1895 m.
3. SANTA MARIA....1904 m.
4. MIRAVALLES....2020 m.
5. TENORIO....1920 m.
6. ARENAL....1638 m.
7. POAS....2704 m.
8. BARVA....2820 m.
9. IRAZU....3432 m.
10. TURRIALBA....3328 m.
MOUNTAIN PEAKS
11. TURRUBARES....1756 m.
12. DRAGON....2505 m.
13. CHIRRIPO....3820 m.
14. DURIKA....3280 m.
15. KAMUK....3554 m.
16. PITIER....2844 m.
NATIONAL PARKS
17. SANTA ROSA
18. RINCON de la VIEJA
19. PALO VERDE
20. BARRA HONDA
21. POAS VOLCANO
22. BRAULIO CARRILLO
23. IRAZU VOLCANO
24. TORTUGUERO
25. CAHUITA
26. CHIRRIPO
27. MANUEL ANTONIO
28. CORCOVADO
29. COCO ISLAND
NICARAGUA
CARIBBEAN SEA / ATLANTIC OCEAN
PACIFIC OCEAN
PANAMA
LAGO DE NICARAGUA
RIO SAN JUAN
ALAJUELA
GUANACASTE
HEREDIA
LIMON
SAN JOSE
CARTAGO
PUNTARENAS
CORDILLERA DE GUANACASTE
CORDILLERA DE TILARAN
CORDILLERA CENTRAL
CORDILLERA DE TALAMANCA
Golfo de Papagayo
Peninsula de Nicoya
Golfo de Nicoya
Bahia de Coronado
Peninsula de Osa
Golfo Dulce
Bahia de Charco Azul o de David
CARRETERA INTERAMERICANA
ISLA DEL COCO
SCALE 1:200.000
LEGEND
CAPITOL CITY
POINT OF TRIANGULATION
VOLCANOES
MOUNTAIN PEAKS
NATIONAL PARKS
INTERNATIONAL BORDER
PROVINCIAL BORDER
ELEVATION....500 2000 (METERS)
SCALE 1:800.000
10 5 0 10 20 30 40 50 KM

the labels on museum specimens, or both. In this sense a species-habitat association is the sum of locality data and a bit of extrapolation on the part of the biologist. Because it is a basic unit of communication among biologists, the methods by which I have associated a species with a habitat type and elevation in this book should be briefly explained.

In the majority of the species accounts, relegating a Costa Rican butterfly species to a strict geographic area has not been possible because individual butterflies move between and across habitats. Such movements may take the form of obvious migrations, as in *Marpesia* or *Phoebis*, or the subtle seasonal movements of the Ithomiinae, or may be grouped under what is known in the literature as individual strays (a species found where it "should not be"). Without doubt there are good and bad years for Costa Rican butterfly populations, and every "good" year has shattered my previous conceptions of where a species was supposed to occur, especially when I found breeding populations. During "bad" years the number of species present in a habitat appears to diminish; things return to "normal" as many of the good year's surprises disappear. However, some species may persist for a few years in a habitat where they had not previously been in evidence. It is important to appreciate that butterfly populations are not static.

Although butterfly movements are poorly understood, some generalizations as to habitat associations can be made. I have associated a species with a habitat type and elevation by amassing all of the locality data I could, and by observing where each species appears to occur most of the time in the course of my repeated visits to the same localities over a number of years. I then calculated a mental average of elevations, localities, and associated life zones.

The bulk of museum locality data comes from material collected by William Schaus or from the Godman and Salvin collections, housed in the United States National Museum of Natural History and the British Museum (Natural History), respectively. My own collections and observations have been supplemented by those of I. A. Chacon, R. Canet, R. Hesterberg, G. B. Small, R. Marquis, D. Janzen, and L. E. Gilbert. The collecting localities and their associated life zones are presented in Appendix I. The reader should bear in mind that the habitat associations presented in the species accounts are in no way definitive, but may serve as general guidelines.

THE BUTTERFLIES OF COSTA RICA AND THEIR NATURAL HISTORY

ONE. BIOLOGY AND SYSTEMATICS OF BUTTERFLIES

The study of butterflies has covered several centuries of human enquiry and has drawn upon a diversity of scientific disciplines. It is not the intention of the present work to cover such a vast subject, but to the interested reader I recommend Vane-Wright and Ackery (1984). This volume covers virtually the whole of butterfly biology and systematics.

The first chapter of the present book is divided into four subsections that treat the life cycle of the butterfly and its morphology, enemies of butterflies and their defenses against them, systematics, and how to study butterflies. These sections, along with the more extensive work of Vane-Wright and Ackery (1984), should provide all readers access to most of the literature and areas of research on butterflies.

Butterfly Life Cycle and Morphology

The development from egg to adult butterfly is called the life cycle, of which there are four distinct stages:

egg: the embryonic stage
larva or *caterpillar*: the feeding and growing stage
pupa or *chrysalis*: the "resting stage," in which larval tissues are first broken down and then redifferentiated to produce an adult
adult butterfly: the sexually mature stage capable of flight

The morphology and behavior of butterflies in these four stages differ between species, and the study of their responses at each stage of the life cycle to environmental influences is called butterfly natural history and ecology. Study of the comparative morphologies of various butterfly life cycles as they respond to the environment through evolutionary time, with the objective of establishing phylogenetic relationship, is called systematics and taxonomy. Both ecology and systematics are disciplines with a basis in evolutionary theory, and they are not mutually exclusive (see the section on systematics). It is important to our understanding of butterflies to see ecology and systematics as complementary, and to take into account all stages of the life cycle.

In this section, a brief overview of each stage of the life cycle is provided, along with basic aspects of morphology. The generalized diagrams depicting morphology will demonstrate the terms used in the sections on identifying butterflies (such as wing areas and venation), and the description of the life cycle should help with natural history studies. I also stress the importance of hostplant relationships to the butterfly's life cycle, which has evolved around the use of appropriate plants.

The Egg

The egg is the fertilized ovum of the female butterfly enclosed in a shell, the *chorion*. The eggs of butterflies are diverse in shape and surface sculpturing among different taxonomic categories, and those of the butterflies treated in this book range from round to barrel- or spindle-shaped, or even hemispherical (Fig. 1). All eggs have a small pore in the "top end," termed the *micropyle*, whereby the sperm enters to fertilize the egg within the body of the female. The micropyle may also be important in egg respiration. Usually a female deposits her eggs on leaves or other vegetative plant parts, attaching them to the plant substrate by means of an adhesive secreted during oviposition. In some butterfly species scales from the female's abdomen adhere to the sur-

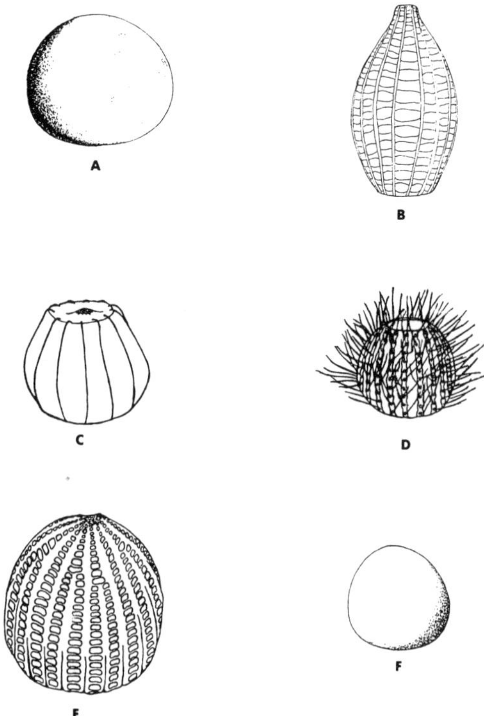

FIGURE 1. Selected eggs of Papilionidae, Pieridae, and Nymphalidae. A: *Papilio birchalli*; B: *Phoebis philea*; C: *Junonia evarete*; D: *Mestra amymone*; E: *Danaus plexippus*; F: *Eretris suzannae* (drawings by P. J. DeVries).

face of the eggs when they are laid. Depending on the species, the eggs may be laid singly or in clusters, or may even be scattered on the ground. The chorion of the egg is often the first meal that a newly hatched caterpillar eats before beginning its life as a herbivore (see *Battus*). The place or the specific plants on which the egg is laid (called the *oviposition site*) is extremely important, and is a major area of research (see Chew and Robbins 1984, Singer 1984, for reviews). The eggs of butterflies are attacked by various parasitic wasps, and are thus a very vulnerable stage in the butterfly's life cycle.

The Larva or Caterpillar

In functional terms, the butterfly larva is a mouth with hard mandibles encased in a head capsule, attached to a long body of soft integument, housing a long digestive tract. This organism is designed to feed, digest its food, and grow. The generalized butterfly larva (Fig. 2) has thirteen segments (T1-3 and A1-10) and a sclerotized head. The head bears a group of simple eyes that are referred to as the ommatidia, ocelli, or stemmata. Near the base of the mandibles are very short antennae that are important to the larva for distinguishing its food. Behind and to the side of the mandibles are the silk-spinning organs. These organs are used throughout larval life for securing the larva to the substrate while walking, escaping from predators, and spinning the "button of silk" for pupal attachment. Every butterfly caterpillar has three pairs of *true legs*, one pair on each of the first three thoracic segments (T1-T3). Each true leg is composed of six segments, like the legs of all insects. Body segments A3-A6 and A10 each bears a pair of

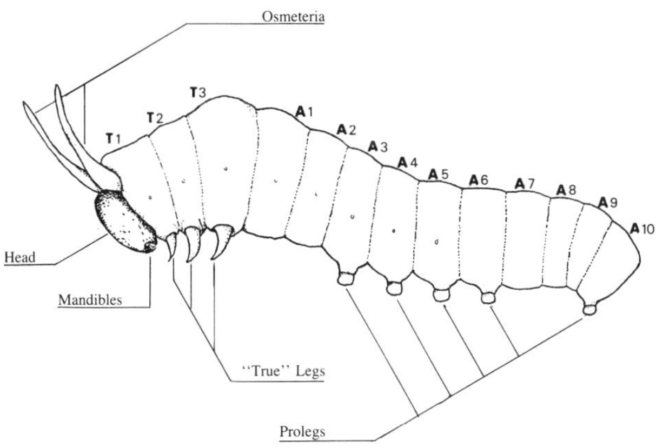

FIGURE 2. Schematic diagram of the butterfly larva showing major morphological features (*Papilio cresphontes*, modified after Klots) (drawing by N. Greig).

prolegs or "sucker-feet." The *prolegs* are extensions of the body wall armed with short hooks (or crotchets), which assist with walking and grasping the substrate; they eventually form the point of attachment of the prepupa to the "button of silk" to which the pupa will be fixed. On either side of segments T1 and A1-5 there is located a *spiracle*, each having an opening from the respiratory system.

To grow, a caterpillar molts or "sheds its skin." The stage between each molt is called an *instar*, and each instar may appear quite different from the preceding stage. For the butterfly families treated in this book, the usual number of molts is five, but it may be four in some Satyrinae, or as many as seven in the Morphinae. At some point during the final instar, the larva stops eating, voids its gut of food, and begins a wandering phase before pupation. This phase of the final instar is called the *prepupa*. It is often very easy to tell when a larva is about to molt to another instar or is ready to pupate: its feces change from the usual dry pellet to a wetter and less solid mass (see Friden [1958] for a treatise on the frass of larvae). The time spent in the larval stage varies according to species. In our Costa Rican fauna it may range from ten to over sixty days. The interested reader is referred to the works of Scudder (1889), Fracker (1915), Snodgrass (1961), and Kitching (1984) for technical aspects of larval morphology.

Although the above description implies that they are a rather dull lot, butterfly larvae show equal or greater diversity of form and behavior than do the adults. The bodies of some larval Nymphalidae are bristling with spines that, in turn, may have accessory spines; the body shape may have bulges or warts, or may be covered in hairs and be patterned with bright red and yellow. Likewise, the head capsule may be round or have diverse accessory spikes, horns, and projections. The behavior of larvae often enhances their looks. For example, certain of our *Adelpha* species have larvae that look like moss, and, indeed, the larvae rest on the upperside of leaves or along stems, as a good bit of moss should. Other examples are certain *Papilio* species that resemble bird droppings, or the early instars of the Charaxinae, which make frass chains to appear like a bit of shredded leaf. Larval morphology is very useful in systematic studies, and can often show relationships that are not evident in the adults (Müller 1896; Singer et al. 1983; DeVries et al. 1985).

Butterfly larvae feed either as solitary individuals or as gregarious groups. As a rule, those larvae that feed as solitary individuals are cryptic (but see *Morpho*) and those that feed in groups are more obvious—and some may even be warningly colored. The reasons for gregarious feeding may be that the young larvae are unable to attack the tough leaf singly, or it may be that there is a better chance of some individuals to attain maturity through protection in numbers. Usually a group of larvae is from one batch of eggs, but in some species larval groups may be the result of egg masses laid by several females (Chew and Robbins 1984). Larvae that feed gregariously are often synchronous in their molts, and for a good reason. If an individual larva delays molting a day or two after the main group molts, that individual is often eaten by the others when it is immobile during the process of shedding its skin. How all individuals in a group time their molting cycles is unknown, but after watching many species molt synchronously, one is left with the impression that there must be a pheromone released that signals a molt. I have noticed that if a different instar from a distinct group of larvae is placed in a container with a group about to molt, the "foreign" individual often wanders about and may molt with the others. Gregarious larvae are known in all families and subfamilies of Costa Rican fauna except the Libytheinae, Charaxinae, and Apaturinae.

Except for some groups of the family Lycaenidae (see Cottrell 1984), butterfly larvae feed on plant material. Because larvae are plant feeders, their digestive systems must be able to process the various secondary chemical compounds contained in the plant tissues—the anti-herbivore compounds or alleochemics (see Rosenthal and Janzen 1979). Butterfly larvae may detoxify such plant compounds, pass them out of their gut with the frass, or store them for their own defense (Brower et al. 1967; Krieger et al. 1971; House 1973). Another method by which butterfly larvae may avoid toxic plant compounds is by cutting the leaf veins, petioles, or other vascular tissues, waiting for a short period, and then feeding on the tissue that has been isolated from the plant's main vascular transport system. Such behavior probably stops the plant from mobilizing chemicals to the area being eaten. Good examples of this type of behavior are found in *Melinaea*, *Lycorea*, *Tigridia*, and *Colobura*. The study of the interactions between plant-feeding insects (including butterfly larvae) and plant compounds has given rise to an enormous area of research, much of which is reviewed in Futuyma and Slatkin (1983).

Butterfly larvae that feed on a restricted set of plant species are termed *monophagous* or specialist feeders. An example would be *Heliconius hewitsoni* or *Melinaea scylax*. Those that are able to feed on various but closely related plant species are termed *oligophagous* feeders. Examples would be *Heliconius cydno* and *Mechanitis isthmia*. Species feeding on a wide range of unrelated plant families (unusual for butterflies) are termed *polyphagous* or generalist feeders. These terms, although widely used in ecological literature, may be misleading because most butterfly species change their breadths of diet (at least the species of plant) from habitat to habitat (see *Adelpha melanthe*) and from place to place. For the best documented cases of changing diet breadth within a single species see Singer (1983, 1984) for accounts of the North American butterfly *Euphydryas editha.*

The Pupa or Chrysalis

When a prepupa settles down for its final molt, the resulting molt is a relatively immobile stage termed the *pupa*, or as it is commonly known, the *chrysalis*. Often described as the resting stage, the pupa is decidedly anything but resting. Within the pupal shell, the tissues of the larva are broken down by biochemical means and reconstructed into an adult butterfly, a process called *metamorphosis*. In the Cost Rican butterflies the time of development of the adult ranges from a week to a month or more. When the butterfly is fully developed, the color of the pupa changes and, after a day or two, the pupal case splits along the ventral surface, where the developing legs, proboscis, and head are formed, and the adult butterfly emerges. After emergence, the adult must hang from the pupal shell and expand its wings. When the wings have fully expanded, the adult expels the metabolic waste products of the pupal stage (termed *meconium*; often colored red or pale brown). Many observations have shown that female butterflies are frequently mated soon after *eclosion* from the pupa; apparently nature abhors a virgin (see also *Heliconius*).

The pupa itself is firmly attached to the substrate by a series of hooks (called the *cremaster*) that are imbedded into the "button of silk" spun by the prepupal larva. Each major group has a characteristic pupal shape and manner of pupation, and pupal characters are useful in butterfly classification. In the Papilionidae and Pieridae, for example, the pupae are attached by the anal segment through the cremaster, with the head directed upward, and a girdle of silk across the back like a safety belt. As a rule, the nymphalid pupae are suspended head downward and attached only by the cremaster. However, this "rule" about nymphalid pupae does not hold for all of the Neotropical species (see *Chloreuptychia, Nessaea, Catonephele, Diaethria, Callicore, Epiphile, Temenis,* and *Pyrrhogyra*). A general morphology of butterfly pupae can be found in Fig. 3, and a more detailed account is in Mosher (1969).

As one might imagine, this sessile stage of the butterfly's life cycle, the pupa, is very susceptible to predation and mechanical injury. Since most injuries to the pupal shell are fatal, butterfly pupae are almost invariably cryptic. Although some of our Costa Rican species pupate gregariously, and the adults are probably distasteful to predators (see *Catasticta, Pereute,* and *Perrhybris*), there are few documented cases of aposematic pupae (Brower 1984). There is a clear case of pupal resemblance to a snake head in one of our species (see *Dynastor*).

Of all the stages in the life cycles of butterflies, the pupal stage is the least known in terms of general biology and ecology.

The Adult Butterfly

The adult stage of the butterfly's life cycle consists of the fully mature insect, which is capable of flight, mating, and reproduction. Every butterfly is composed of three main parts (head, thorax, and abdomen), which are largely covered with scales of various types. The butterfly is the most obvious stage of the life cycle, and has received by far the most attention. In this section I describe general aspects of butterfly morphology and the terminology used in this book. Those concerned with detailed morphological studies may wish to consult Ehrlich (1958*b*). The diagrams in this section are intended to help in using this book as an identification guide (see Fig. 4).

Head. The most obvious features of the butterfly head are the large compound eyes. The eyes are composed of numerous facets (*ommatidia*), and are incapable of focusing but are very sensitive to movement, light, and certain colors. A dorsal pair of *antennae*, each of which terminates in a thickened "*club*," arises from between the eyes. The anten-

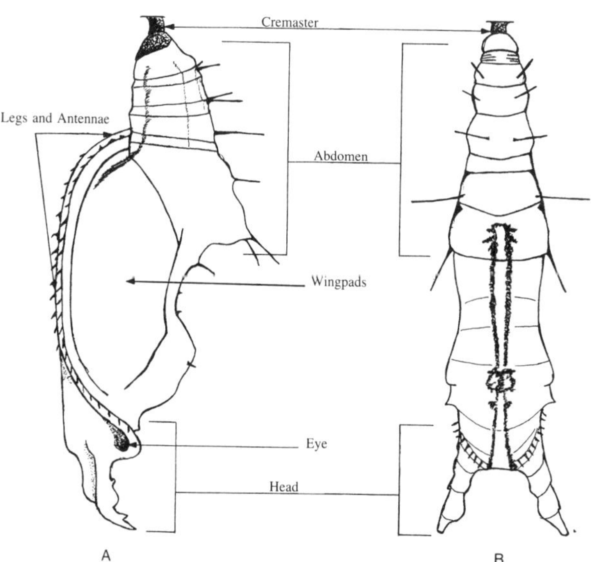

FIGURE 3. Schematic diagram of the pupa of *Heliconius* (Nymphalidae). A: lateral view; B: dorsal view (drawing by N. Weintrub).

nal club varies in thickness and shape according to species or group. The antennae function as sensory organs for finding food, for mating, for balance during flight, and are very sensitive to volatile, airborne chemicals. The chemical receptors are located in pits found predominantly on the antennal club. Ventrally, between the eyes, there is a pair of heavily scaled *palpi*. These structures show considerable variation in form and are often used in classification. Despite this, I can find no reference concerning the function of the labial palps in butterflies. My own observations suggest that these appendages are used, in some species at least, as a cleaning or grooming organ for the eyes. It is quite common to see butterflies brushing the palpi across the eyes while resting or during feeding. The most well-developed palpi are found in those groups that feed as adults on rotting fruits or dung, and in these groups the palpi are capable of passing across the entire surface of the eye like windshield wipers. In obligate fruit feeders (see Charaxinae, Brassolinae, Morphinae) it seems likely that there is a great probability of soiling the eyes or becoming infested with mites (DeVries 1980*b*). However, it remains to be seen whether or not experimental evidence will support this hypothesis.

Between the palpi lies the *proboscis*, a hollow tube composed of two interlocking halves. This feeding organ, coiled like a watch spring

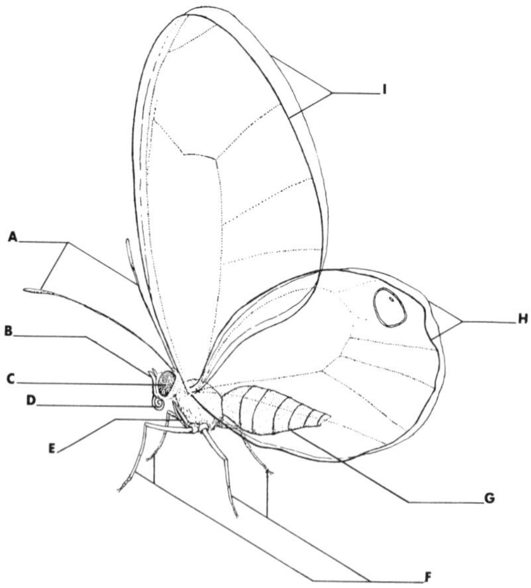

FIGURE 4. Major morphological areas of the adult butterfly (*Cithaerias menander*). A: antennae; B: labial palpi; C: compound eye; D: proboscis; E: forelegs (reduced in all Nymphalidae); F: walking legs; G: abdomen; H: hindwings; I: forewings (drawing by N. Greig).

when not in use, can be extended and inserted into flowers, and may be sufficiently stout to penetrate fruits. By virtue of these "soda-straw" mouth parts, all butterflies are restricted to a diet of liquids, including flower nectar, rotting vegetable juices, carrion, dung, urine, water, or digested pollen.

Thorax. Behind the head is a region composed of three fused segments that bear the wings and legs, and contain the locomotory muscles and various other internal organs. This section is called the *thorax* and is the toughest part of the butterfly. As in all adult insects, the butterfly has six legs (one pair per thoracic segment), but in all of the Nymphalidae the *forelegs* are reduced and modified as chemoreceptors for "tasting," whereas the other four are the *walking legs*.

Attached to the thorax are the all-important wings. A butterfly has four—a pair of *forewings* and a pair of *hindwings*—all of which are usually covered with scales. These scales give butterflies their characteristic patterns and colors. The wings are membranous and are supported by a system of *veins* that run from the *wing base* out to the *distal margins* (see Fig. 5). The forewing *costa*, or leading edge, is heavily reinforced

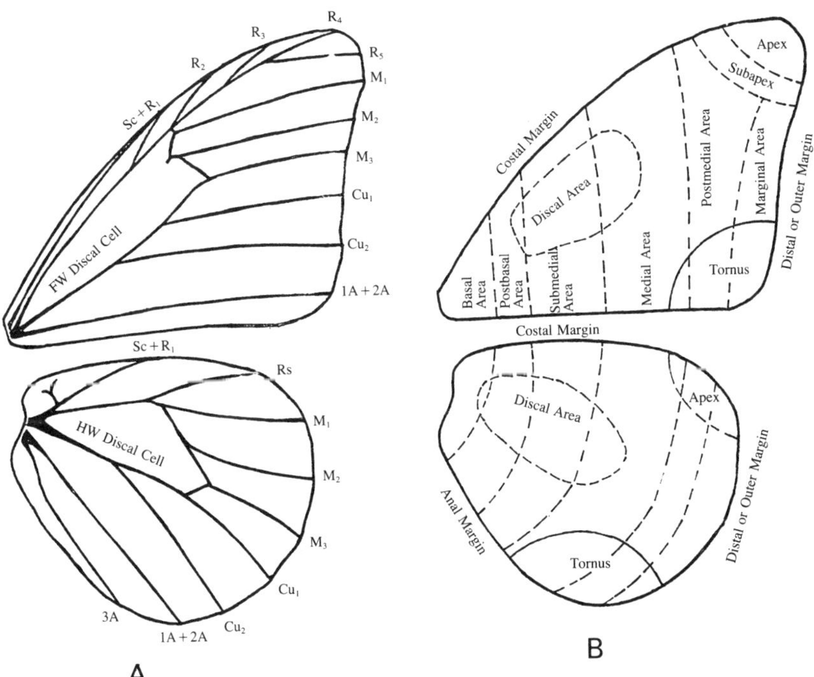

FIGURE 5. A: wing venation of the butterfly, following the modified Comstock system of numbering; B: names of the major wing areas referred to in this book (drawings by P. J. DeVries).

by the confluence of numerous veins. The arrangement of the *venation* has been used extensively in the classification of the butterflies, especially the venation associated with the forewing and hindwing *cells*.

The various color patterns of certain Nymphalidae that often appear radically different have been demonstrated to follow a developmental ground plan (homology system) first described by Schwanwitsch (1924, 1926). Although this ground plan is extremely useful in describing how patterns of many nymphalid butterflies are formed, it does not account well for the patterns seen in the Papilionidae, Pieridae, and most of the tiger-striped ithomiines or the heliconiines. This suggests that there are more ground plans to be discovered. Of great interest is the implication of differing ground plans in relation to models and mimics. One species might be unable to evolve an appearance similar to another species if the two had different ground plans (ontogenetic pathways) controlling their patterns.

The patterns and the colors on the wings of butterflies are mainly the result of a dense covering of scales that are arranged like overlapping roof tiles; in a few species wing membrane colors are also important. Each scale is attached by a thin shaft that is inserted into a socket in the wing membrane, in a fashion analogous to the feathers of birds. The surface of each scale has fine longitudinal ridges cross-linked with finer ridges, and thus has the appearance of a honeycomb. There are three main types of scale: pigmentary scales, structural scales, and the scent scales found in males, termed *androconia*. The pigmentary scales are rather flat and are colored chiefly by deposition of melanin pigments, but may also be colored by pterins (see Pieridae) and other chemicals. The structural scales are found mainly in male butterflies, and normally generate the colors blue, violet, copper, or green by reflecting certain wave lengths of incident light. For a detailed account of colors and scale morphology of butterflies, see Downey and Allyn (1975). Androconial scales may be connected to secretory cells at their bases, and generally store chemical compounds used as *pheromones*, or mating odors. Certain androconial scales appear to be nonsecretory, and are transferred to the female during mating (Vane-Wright 1972). Structurally, androconial scales can be very elaborate, and their biochemistry and function have been recently investigated in certain danaine and ithomiine species (Boppre 1984 and references therein). The androconial scales and their locations on the butterfly are discussed in more detail under the section on secondary sexual characters.

Abdomen. The abdomen contains the digestive and reproductive tracts and terminates in the reproductive organs termed the *genitalia*. The abdomen is composed of ten segments, seven or eight of which form the long portion and the terminal two or three the genitalia. Except for the genitalic segments, the abdomen is capable of stretching when the gut is filled with quantities of liquid food. The distention of the abdomen can be considerable in species that feed on rotting fruits (such as Charaxinae, Brassolinae, and Morphinae).

The genitalia of butterflies are used extensively in systematics and taxonomy, and entire books have been written on their configuration, treatment for study, and homologies (Tuxen 1970). I shall mention only briefly the exterior structures of genitalia to assist the user in determining the sexes. The penultimate segment of the abdomen in the male bears two ventral *valvae* or—the term I have used in the present work—the *claspers*. The claspers open to expose the *aedeagus* (*penis*) and other male organs (see below), and literally clasp the end of the female's abdomen during mating. The female abdomen terminates in three openings: the anus, the egg pore, and the copulatory pore.

Secondary Sexual Characters. The differences between male and female butterflies can often be discerned quite easily without having to examine the genitalic openings. In most species in which the sexes are similar, the female is larger, the forewing apex is rounded, and the coloration is more subdued. However, in many species the males, and to a limited extent females, bear what are termed *secondary sexual characters*. Such characters can be differences in the form of the forelegs, but usually are specialized androconial scales or scent organs. These organs are widespread in butterflies, and can be located on the wings, the forelegs, or within the abdomen (Boppre 1984). The following refers only to the groups treated in this book.

a. *Androconial patches* on the wings or *alar patches* are found in the Pieridae, Heliconiinae, Morphinae, Brassolinae, Satyrinae, and in many Nymphalinae. These patches are usually located on the forewing, near the forewing cell, and stand out from the surrounding scales by being darker or having a "mealy" appearance.

b. *Androconial tufts* are found on the hindwings of the Charaxinae, Satyrinae, Morphinae, and Brassolinae, and can be erected during courtship. They are probably used in concert with androconial patches on the forewings or hindwings. When erected, these tufts resemble the splayed tips of a camel-hair brush (Fig. 6a).

c. *Androconial folds* are found in the Papilionidae (*Parides*) along the inner margin of the hindwing. The long androconial scales within the fold are often white, and are exposed when the fold of the hindwing is opened (Fig. 6b).

d. *Hair pencils* are extrusible abdominal scent organs that are best developed in the Danainae, or long androconial scales found between the wings of the male Ithomiinae (Fig. 6c). These organs often have an

A

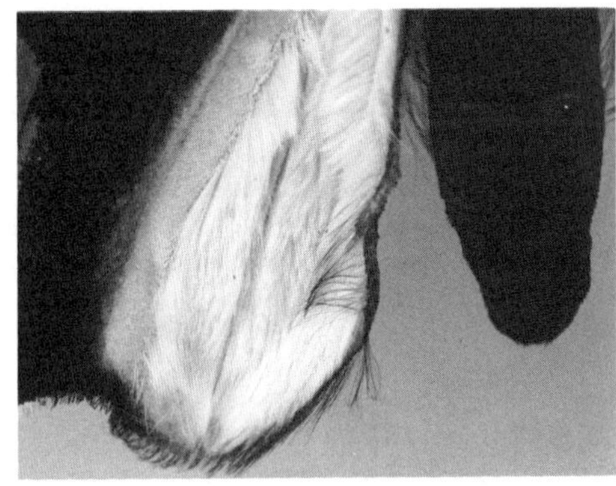

B

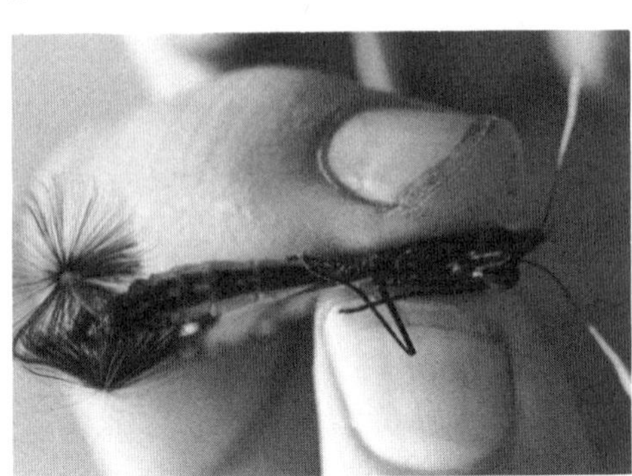

C

FIGURE 6. Secondary sexual characters. A: androconial tuft of *Prepona omphale*; B: androconial fold of *Parides erithalion*; C: hair pencils of *Lycorea cleobaea* (photos by P. J. DeVries).

odor that ranges from sweet to very rancid and is detected by the human nose. Abdominal hair pencils are also found in the Morphinae and Satyrinae; these smell of sweet vanilla.

e. *Stink clubs* are a pair of eversible glands found in the genital openings of females of *Heliconius* and relatives, and in some *Parides* and *Battus*, which are extruded when the live butterfly is handled. In *Heliconius* there is no smell in virgin females, and the odor is thought to be a male antiaphrodisiac (Gilbert 1976). It would be interesting to determine if such antiaphrodisiacs are found in other butterflies, as well.

Hostplant Relationships

Which came first: the butterfly or the egg? To me it was unquestionably the hostplant. The critical aspect of life cycles of the butterflies treated in this book is the ability of the ovipositing female to find and of the larvae to feed upon particular hostplants. Most butterfly species feed on only a few closely related plant species. On a broader evolutionary scale, we find that particular lineages of butterflies are associated with certain lineages of plant, other plants being unacceptable to larvae or ovipositing females. This association is called a *hostplant relationship*.

Extending the work of Brues (1924), Ehrlich and Raven (1965) summarized hostplant relationships of butterflies to develop the idea of coevolution, today a major field of evolutionary biology (Futuyma and Slatkin 1983). The term coevolution has come to have various meanings (Janzen 1980; Futuyma and Slatkin 1983), but with respect to butterflies, it simply means that there are predictable patterns of hostplant relationships observed in all butterflies, which can be used to generate hypotheses about their systematics and ecology. For example, within the papilionid tribe Troidini (see *Parides* and *Battus*) there is a strict hostplant relationship with the Aristolochiaceae. This pattern is so well established that *any* record of a troidine larva feeding on any other plant family is immediately suspect. This relationship can be extended to the theories of mimicry and insect defenses: all troidines are suspected of being unpalatable to vertebrate predators because of poisons derived from their Aristolochiaceae hostplants. In cases where butterfly species have hostplant relationships outside of the "normal" plant family, analysis has shown that the different plant families may contain some of the same chemicals. Examples include pierids using Brassicaceae and Tropaeolaceae (even though distantly related, both contain mustard oils), or heliconiines feeding on Turneraceae, a family very closely related to the Passifloraceae. After all, "herbiverous insects do not feed on Latin binomials, they feed on plants or plant parts" (Janzen 1973*b*), and since butterflies make their living at it, they are extraordinarily good botanists.

Throughout this book I have stressed hostplant relationships because of their great importance in understanding butterfly systematics and ecology. The predictive potential of hostplant relationships allows us to narrow our search for the early stages of species with unknown life histories. For example, *Epiphile grandis* is a rare and peculiar butterfly, yet I would be very surprised if the larvae were not to feed on Sapindaceae. Once the hostplant of a butterfly is found, we are immediately in a much better position to tackle its systematics, and we have a place to start studying its ecology. When the critical importance of the hostplant is appreciated, it is easy to see that considerable effort should be devoted to identifying a plant correctly before reporting it as a hostplant. Incorrect hostplant information leads to incorrect hypotheses, and until a hostplant record is proven, one should be skeptical about any that is far afield from the hostplant relationships of the butterfly's congeners. (See Appendix II and DeVries [1985*a*] for hostplants of Costa Rican butterflies.)

Pathogens, Parasites, Parasitoids, Predators, and Butterfly Defenses against Them

The chance that a newly laid butterfly egg will survive to adulthood in nature is very slim. During all stages of the life cycle, butterflies are at risk from many factors that influence their chances of survival. Like most aspects of the ecology of Neotropical butterflies, little is known about the mortality factors affecting them, and much has been extrapolated from studies carried out in temperate zones. Here I shall outline very briefly the effects of some organisms—parasites, parasitoids, and predators—that affect the lives of butterflies, and put them in the context of the defenses butterflies have evolved against them. This material supplements aspects covered in the section on the butterfly life cycle.

For the purposes here, the reader should bear the following definitions in mind. Pathogens cause diseases that eventually kill the butterfly host. Parasites are organisms that feed on portions of the host but do not directly cause its death. Parasitoids (usually wasp or fly larvae) devour the butterfly host slowly, from the inside, eventually killing it. A predator kills its host by devouring it, and a predator kills many individual hosts during its lifetime.

Pathogens

Anyone who has reared butterfly larvae knows that unless the rearing containers are cleaned regularly the larvae are prone to become moribund, die, and eventually putrefy. This is the effect of viral pathogens that are highly contagious and may rapidly kill all larvae in a particular culture. The best known viral pathogen is a polyhedroses virus that has been studied in the laboratory, but nothing is known of its effects on larvae in the field or how important it may be as a natural mortality factor (Smith 1967).

Fungal pathogens also affect butterflies, especially entomophagous fungi in the genus *Cordyceps*. As reviewed by Evans (1982), it has been shown that *Cordyceps* may attack and kill eggs, larvae, pupae, or adult insects, with the different species of *Cordyceps* appearing to show some host specificity. Although *Cordyceps* has been shown to be an important mortality factor in ants, its importance to butterflies is unexplored. In Costa Rica I have seen live adult *Parides, Taygetis*, and some skippers (Hesperiidae) with fungal infections at the tips of the antennae. I happened to notice them because the individuals behaved oddly for their species: altered behavior is a characteristic of infected hosts. Butterfly defenses against fungal pathogens are not known, but they may well exist.

Parasites

A parasite weakens but does not kill its host, because its own fate is tied to the survival of the host. True parasites have rarely been reported from butterflies. In Costa Rica perhaps the most common are flies in the family Ceratopogonidae or, as they are commonly known, biting midges. These midges feed on the haemolymph of larvae and also from the wing veins of adults (Lane 1984). In Costa Rica they are most frequently seen by the casual observer on *Caligo* larvae or the wing veins of adult ithomiines. The effect of ceratopogonids on their butterfly hosts is unknown, but it is conceivable that they may transmit diseases.

Parasitoids

The term parasitoid is usually applied to certain families of wasps and flies that lay their eggs on or in the early stages of butterflies, and whose larvae devour the internal tissues of the host, eventually killing it. They are important in regulating some butterfly populations in temperate zones (Dempster 1984; Vinson and Iwantsch 1980), but their effects on populations of tropical butterflies are unstudied. (Table 1 lists various parasitoids and predators that are known to affect butterflies in Costa Rica.)

Butterfly egg parasitoids belong to the wasp families Trichogrammatidae and Scelionidae, and as many as sixty individual wasps may emerge from a single butterfly egg. The potential of these parasitoids for regulating butterfly populations, and other aspects of their biology, may be appreciated from Malo (1961) and Salt (1935, 1937).

Parasitoids that attack the larvae or pupae of butterflies include wasps in the families Braconidae, Chalcidae, and Ichneumonidae, and flies of the family Tachinidae. Braconids lay eggs in the body of butterfly larvae (in which the parasitoid larvae subsequently develop). At maturity the wasp larvae emerge from the butterfly host to pupate, frequently leaving a distinctive cottony mass of cocoons on the outside of the shriveled host's body. Perhaps the most important braconid genus to attack butterfly larvae is *Apanteles*. Chalcid wasps lay eggs inside the body of butterfly larvae or pupae immediately after the host has molted, while the skin is still soft. I have on several occasions watched a chalcid wasp wait beside a prepupal larva for hours, until the pupa was complete, at which point the wasp attacked the still soft pupa. Chalcids develop inside the host and, when mature, they chew holes through the side of the host pupa to escape. Many individual braconids or chalcids usually emerge from a single host. In contrast, only one ichneumonid wasp usually develops for each host. See Slansky (1978) and Vinson and Iwantsch (1980) for reviews.

Table 1.
Important Parasitoids and Predators of Costa Rican Butterflies

INSECTA (insects)	
Order	Hymenoptera (wasps)
Family	Formicidae (E,L,P)
	Vespidae (L)
	Sphecidae (L)
	Braconidae (L)
	Chalcidae (L,P)
	Ichneumonidae (L)
	Trichogrammatidae (E)
	Scelionidae (E)
Order	Diptera (flies)
Family	Tachinidae (L,P)
	Sarcophagidae (P)
	Asilidae (A)
Order	Orthoptera (katydids mantids)
Family	Mantidae (A)
	Tettigoniidae (E,P)
Order	Heteroptera (true bugs)
Family	Pentatomidae (L,P)
	Lygaeidae (L,P)
	Reduviidae (L,P,A)
ARACHNIDA (spiders)	
Family	Araneidae (A)
	Uloboridae (A)
	Ctenidae (L,A)
	Lycosidae (L,A)
	Thomisidae (A)
REPTILIA (reptiles)	
Family	Teiidae
Genus	*Ameiva* (A,P)
Family	Iguanidae
Genus	*Anolis* (A)
	Norops (L,A)
MAMMALIA (mammals)	
Order	Primata (primates)
Genus	*Saimiri* (L,P,A)
	Cebus (L,P)
MAMMALIA (cont.)	
Order	Rodentia (rodents)
Family	Muridae
Genus	*Oryzomys* (L,P)
	Nyctomys (L,P)
Order	Marsupialia (marsupials)
Family	Didelphidae
Genus	*Philander* (L,P)
	Marmosa (L,P)
AVIFORMES (birds)	
Family	Cuculidae
Genus	*Piaya* (L)
	Coccyzus (L)
Family	Momotidae
Genus	*Momotus* (A)
Family	Galbulidae
Genus	*Galbula* (A)
	Jacamerops (A)
Family	Bucconidae
Genus	*Notharchus* (L,A)
	Monasa (A)
Family	Capitonidae
Genus	*Eubucco* (L,A)
Family	Cotingidae
Genus	*Pachyramphus* (A)
Family	Tyranidae
Genus	*Tyrannus* (A)
	various genera (A)
Family	Icteridae
Genus	*Cacicus* (L,P)
Family	Corvidae
Genus	various genera (L,A)
Family	Vireonidae (L)
	Parulidae (L)
	Furnariidae (L,A)
	Formicaridae (L,A)

Note: Abbreviations are: E = eggs, L = larvae, P = pupae, A = adults; these correspond to the stage in the butterfly's life cycle most frequently attacked by the parasitoid or predator.

Flies in the family Tachinidae attack butterfly larvae either by laying eggs on larvae or by laying minute eggs on hostplant leaves, which are ingested when the butterfly feeds. The fly maggot feeds on internal tissues until it is ready to pupate. At this time the maggot bores through the body wall of the host and pupates in the ground. Tachinidae are generally considered to be parasitoids, but some tachinid species do not invariably kill their butterfly hosts (DeVries 1984). Records of non-lethal tachinids from Lepidoptera are few, but since we know so little about the life histories of Neotropical Tachinidae, care should be taken not to overlook the possibility that this may be more common than supposed.

Butterfly larvae that contain parasitoids are commonly encountered in casual observation, as witnessed by the number of parasitized larvae found in collections from the field. This may be the result of behavioral changes invoked by the internal parasitoids that make the individual more obvious to the human observer. Shortly before the parasitoids emerge from the host, infected larvae usually go through a wandering phase (similar to prepupation). This has led to the speculation that the larva makes itself more conspicuous to predators in a last attempt to rid itself of the parasitoid.

Predators

Here I define a predator as any organism that kills any stage of a butterfly's life cycle, and depends upon killing more than a single individual to stay alive and reproduce. With such a definition we may distinguish them from parasitoids, which also kill their hosts but depend upon a single host individual to complete their life cycle, and which usually feed internally. Butterflies have both invertebrate and vertebrate predators. Most important among the former are spiders, mantids, ants, wasps, flies, beetles, and some Heteroptera. These arthropods may either suck the juices from their prey (as do spiders and Heteroptera) or consume all or portions of their prey, as do mantids, ants, wasps, and beetles. The major vertebrate predators of butterflies are birds, lizards, and mammals. These may consume all of their prey, or when feeding on adult butterflies, they may eat all but the wings, or eat the gut and discard the body. Although predators are always invoked as important selective forces in butterfly ecology, there are surprisingly few direct observations or studies demonstrating predation rates of Neotropical butterflies by specific predators (see Calvert et al. 1979; Ehrlich and Ehrlich 1982 for summaries). Nonetheless, the major impact that predation has had on the biology of butterflies may be deduced from the evolution of butterfly defense systems.

Butterfly Defenses against Parasitoids and Predators

The defenses of butterflies may result from natural selection brought about by a specific or generalized suite of predators. There are many general defenses (spines on larvae, crypsis, or noxious poisons), but it is only from field observations that we can infer which defenses are possibly directed at specific predators. For example, a spiny nymphalid caterpillar may be equipped to avoid being eaten or killed by predaceous ants, but it will also not be touched by Costa Rican white-faced monkeys, even though it may be palatable and the monkeys insectivorous. However, the same spiny caterpillar may be gobbled up by squirrel monkeys after the spines have been removed. In this example we cannot be sure what promoted the evolution of caterpillar spines. At the moment, too little is known about butterfly defenses to state with any degree of certainty whether they are directed at subsets of predators or at predators in general. Defense by butterflies is undoubtedly complex and involves appearance, physical characteristics, behavior, and chemistry, usually working in concert.

Appearance. There are two major ways in which all stages of butterflies utilize appearance to avoid being eaten: protective resemblance and mimicry. Of the two, mimicry is in concept and evolution the more complex, and is dealt with in a separate section. Protective resemblance may simply be defined as a camouflage that makes the organism blend into its background and, hence, makes its presence difficult to detect: it is cryptic.

The eggs of butterflies are often laid in inconspicuous places on or off the hostplant, and in a certain sense this could be considered a defense against being found. Examples include the placement of *Diaethria* eggs, which are laid at the junctions of leaf veins; the eggs of *Heliconius*, laid at the extremities of the hostplant tendrils; the eggs of *Adelpha*, deposited within damaged portions of leaves; or eggs deposited in leaf litter by certain species of *Cissia*.

On the whole, butterfly larvae show a protective resemblance to their surroundings and exhibit behavior that enhances the protective effect of this camouflage. The resemblance of papilionid larvae to bird droppings (see *Papilio anchisiades* and *P. birchalli*) is enhanced by their habit of resting on the upper surface of leaves. Protective resemblance by countershading plays an important part in the crypsis of many pierid and satyrine larvae. The underside is paler than the upper surface, and under natural illumination such larvae are inconspicuous because they appear uniform with their background. When a countershaded larva is turned over from its normal resting position, the lighting makes the larva stand out against its background. For a discussion of countershading, see Wickler (1968).

In a related form of defense, larvae may also build shelters or structures that further reduce their chances of being detected by visually oriented predators. There are several excellent examples of this in the Costa Rican fauna. The Charaxinae, and the nymphalid genera *Adelpha, Callicore,* and *Diaethria* have larvae that are exceedingly difficult to detect on the hostplant. Not only are they well camouflaged, but they may also rest on frass chains adorned with bits of dead leaf matter, or roll the leaves into a tube and rest inside them (Fig. 20). These cryptic defenses seem to be aimed at such predators as birds and monkeys, but it is not uncommmon to see a mixed flock of foraging birds in which various species of caciques (Icteridae and Oxyruncidae) use their long bills to open leaves sewn together by larvae, and gobble up the hapless caterpillars.

Frass chains seem also to be a method of escaping from predaceous ants in the subfamily Ponerinae, by exploiting the ants' apparent reluctance to walk out on slender threads of vegetation. Another defense that is perhaps analogous and common to almost all Lepidoptera larvae is the habit when molested of dropping off the plant, suspended by a silken thread. However, this does not always work. On several occasions I have watched an ithomiine larva drop off a plant when molested by an individual *Paraponera clavata* (Ponerinae); the ant waited with an antenna on the silken thread until the caterpillar climbed back up, then grabbed it in its large mandibles and carried it away.

Charaxine larvae that hide in rolled leaves and plug the entrance to the tube with their head capsule (such as *Anaea, Memphis, Consul*) may also be avoiding attacks from parasitoids. In such a case, the only direct access that a parasitoid has to the larva is through the head capsule, which is too hard to pierce with an ovipositor; this defense may confer protection from tachinids as well. Indeed, at certain times of the year, leaf-rolling *Memphis* larvae that feed on the local San José *Croton* species may be found with many tachinid eggs attached to the anterior portion of the head capsule, but many of these larvae eventually produce adult butterflies.

Protective resemblance plays an important part in the defenses of adults, and I believe that all adult Costa Rican butterflies are cryptic on the underside of the wings, regardless of whether they are warningly colored. When the butterfly is at rest, the wings are folded and the dull underside blends into the background. Protective resemblance in the Costa Rican fauna ranges from the absolutely stunning resemblance to a dead leaf, complete with herbivore damage, exemplified by *Zaretis,* through a general resemblance to dead leaves in *Memphis* and the dull ocellated patterns of satyrines, morphines, and many nymphalines, to warningly colored genera like *Heliconius* and *Tithorea*; even in the latter, although the two wing surfaces have similar patterns, the underside pattern is always dull colored. The widespread crypsis of the undersides of all Costa Rican butterflies suggests strong selection pressures by visually oriented predators.

In instances when a predator does locate an individual butterfly, however cryptic, patterns on the underside may act as target areas to deflect attacks. A bite taken by a bird or lizard from a butterfly wing where an eyespot is located may result in the predator getting a mouthful of wing while the butterfly escapes with its vital body parts intact. The deflection of attack toward distinct wing markings falls under what is termed the "false-head" hypothesis of escape from predators. Although most extensively studied in the Lycaenidae (Robbins 1981), I commonly find bird and lizard bite marks in the large ocelli of many satyrine, brassoline, and morphine species, as well as the nymphaline genera *Colobura, Baeotus, Vanessa,* and *Junonia*, and I believe these areas are deflection points for predator attacks (see DeVries 1983).

Physical Armaments. Physical means of defense are widespread in many insect groups (wasps, ants, beetles, Hemiptera), but are not generally well developed in butterflies. The most obvious physical defenses are the spines of larvae, which may act as barriers to the attacks of parasitoids, ants, birds, and monkeys. But although some species have irritant spines, on the whole butterfly larvae most likely gain protection through generalized mimicry of the many moth larvae that have violently urticating spines (Janzen 1985). From a few feeding experiments with white-faced monkeys (*Cebus capuchinus*), I know that they will not even touch slightly hairy or spiny larvae, corroborating the Janzen hypothesis. However, S. Boinski (personal communication) has numerous observations on squirrel monkeys (*Saimiri oerstedi*) which demonstrate that these monkeys simply remove spines from larvae through an elaborate processing behavior before eating them.

In adult butterflies there are a few examples of what might be termed physical defense. The Old World genus *Charaxes* (Charaxinae) has a row of teeth along the forewing costa, which may be used to deter attacks by birds, but is most likely used in male-male interactions and for jostling at food resources (Swynerton 1926; Owen 1971). The only analogous system I know of among the Neotropical butterflies is the teeth on the forewing costa of certain *Papilio* species.

Chemical Defenses. Perhaps the most commonly encountered defense systems of butterflies involve "chemical warfare." Noxious chemicals are found in eggs, larvae, pupae, and adults. These may take the form of toxins in eggs, larval regurgitations or chemicals secreted from glands, chemicals stored in the larval body, and chemicals found in the wings and bodies of adult butterflies. It is unclear which enemies these defenses counter in the early stages. They are generally assumed to be directed at insect parasitoids or vertebrate predators. On the other hand, toxins in adult butterflies are probably directed entirely at vertebrate predators. Defensive chemistry in butterflies has been a rich field of enquiry, which has led to many discoveries about the evolution of insects and plants. The vast literature on this complex subject has been elegantly reviewed by Brower (1984).

We may consider chemical defenses in butterflies to be the deployment, by any means imaginable, of noxious chemicals that aid a butterfly at any stage in its life cycle to avoid being killed. Considering the numbers of publications on the distasteful properties of butterflies and the importance of this subject to mimicry, it is surprising that little experimental work and even less chemical work has been done on the majority of butterfly genera. In this section I consider the chemical defenses of larvae and adults.

The larvae of the Papilionidae, Danainae, and Ithomiinae are all considered to be unpalatable to predators, but all areas of this assumption require testing. Perhaps the best studied larval secretions are the various chemicals secreted by the osmeteria of the Papilionidae when the larvae are molested (Eisner and Meinwald 1965; Honda 1983). The larvae of a few Danainae have also been well characterized with regard to their potential for storing cardenolides, a known emetic group of chemicals (Brower 1984). Within the Charaxinae, Morphinae, and Brassolinae, the larvae bear what I have termed "neck-glands." These glands are everted when the larva is molested, and give off a volatile odor. I suggest that such glands are used as a defense against ants (see *Caligo*), but more work is required to characterize the chemistry of the glands. Of interest are the similar and well characterized glands found in the moth family Notodontidae (Weatherston et al. 1979). An additional chemical defense in *Morpho* larvae may be the dorsal gland that secretes a drop of liquid that is combed into the hair tufts (see *Morpho*).

Chemical defenses in adult butterflies are acquired in two ways: active storing of plant compounds or de novo synthesis. The extensive studies by Lincoln Brower on *Danaus plexippus* have demonstrated that these butterflies actively store cardenolides that they acquire from the hostplant through larval feeding. From this it has been inferred that all Danainae use this method of storing up chemicals for defense. However, it is becoming clear that many butterflies obtain their distasteful properties by adult feeding, as in the Ithomiinae and the genus *Heliconius* (Brower 1984; Nahrstedt and Davis 1981, 1983; Brown 1984). A fuller understanding of the relative importance of larval as against adult origin of adult toxicity awaits research on many more species. Additionally, until we know more about the reactions of predators to so-called "palatable species," such as most Nymphalid genera, it is impossible to state with any certainty where a particular butterfly falls within a palatability spectrum. For example, the experimental work of P. Chai (1985) in Costa Rica has demonstrated that such "palatable" genera as *Diaethria, Callicore*, and *Perrhybris* are consistently rejected by the rufous-tailed jacamar (*Galbula ruficauda*), a known butterfly predator. There is no reason to assume that all bird species will treat a set of butterfly species equally. Indeed, in some casual feeding experiments of my own with magpie jays in Guanacaste (DeVries 1983), I found that *Heliconius* were readily eaten by these birds, but that they consistently rejected *Phoebis*. Why this was so is unknown, but it may have been that the *Heliconius* individuals used in the experiment (all field-collected a few hours before the experiment) may not have had access to pollen plants to utilize for defensive chemistry (see Nahrstedt and Davis 1983), or perhaps these birds are not affected by *Heliconius* chemistry. Although there is much already known about adult butterfly defenses, there is clearly an enormous amount of work left to be done.

Mimicry: Mimics Don't Hide, They Advertise

When a *Zaretis* butterfly lands on the forest floor to feed on the juices of rotting fruit, it looks very similar to a dead leaf. While feeding, it appears to melt into the background: this is its *protective resemblance*. But if a bird happens to notice, attack, and subsequently eat the *Zaretis* butterfly, the bird might appear complacent for a few moments, and would probably then give dead leaves more careful scrutiny—at least for a while. If, however, the same bird happens to attack and eat a *Tithorea tarricina* butterfly that is flying lazily past, its reaction will be different. If it swallows the butterfly, the bird will regurgitate the contents of its crop, fluff its feathers, wipe its bill on its perch, and generally give the appearance of having eaten something disagreeable. If another *T. tarricina* then flew past, the bird probably would ignore it. Likewise, the bird would ignore *Heliconius hecale* and any other butterfly that looked like *T. tarricina*. The bird has learned to associate a color pattern and behavior with a nasty experience. Those butterflies that resemble *T. tarricina* gain some immunity from attack by this bird, through their *mimicry*.

Both protective resemblance and mimicry are the result of natural selection, but they are not the same thing, and it is important to bear the distinction in mind. Protective resemblance occurs when an organism resembles its environmental surroundings and gains protection from predators through crypticity (that is, by being overlooked). Protective resemblance can be thought of as a passive defense. Protective mimicry, on the other hand, implies that one species of organism closely resembles another species that is avoided by predators. Mimics thus gain protection from predators by appearing to be unpalatable; mimics do not hide, they advertise. There has been a great deal written on mimicry, and it is a subject that has acquired a great diversity of meanings. In this book I define mimicry in a narrow sense, and the interested reader is referred to the different views of Vane-Wright (1976, 1980), Pasteur (1982), Gilbert (1983), and Turner (1984) for thought-provoking analyses of mimicry theory. In this section I present a brief introduction to mimicry in Neotropical butterflies and give examples from the Costa Rican fauna (see Fig. 7).

Protective mimicry in butterflies may be divided into two general classes: *Batesian mimicry*, where there is an unpalatable model species and a palatable mimic species, and *Müllerian mimicry*, where several unpalatable model species share the same color pattern. Both types of mimicry rely on advertising a conspicuous color pattern. Of the two types, Müllerian mimicry is the more common in Central America, and involves the Papilionidae, Pieridae, and the subfamilies Danainae, Ithomiinae, and Heliconiinae of the Nymphalidae, but may occur in others as well. Batesian mimics occur unambiguously in the Charaxinae and Nymphalinae, and perhaps the Pieridae.

Batesian Mimicry

The first theory of mimicry was presented by H. W. Bates (1862) in an attempt to explain why *Dismorphia* butterflies look and behave like ithomiine and *Heliconius* butterflies. After more than a decade of field observations in the Amazon Basin, Bates concluded that the *Dismorphia* butterflies mimic the warningly colored and unpalatable ithomiine and *Heliconius* butterflies to gain protection from predators. Batesian mimicry, then, involves a palatable species (the mimic) that closely resembles an unpalatable species (the model). Usually, but not always, the model species will be more abundant in a given habitat than the mimetic one, since the model species must be sufficiently common as to educate predators repeatedly of the nasty taste associated with the warning color pattern. If the mimics were too common, predators would not associate the pattern with a nasty taste, and they would quickly begin selecting butterflies with that color pattern until the time came when the models were more common than the mimics. Because the mimic species confers no advantage to the model species, a Batesian mimic can be thought of as a signal-pattern parasite of the model. Defined as such, model species should evolve defenses to rid themselves of their Batesian parasites (see Fisher 1930; Gilbert 1983 for reviews). However, see Turner (1984) for reasons why this may not be possible.

Müllerian Mimicry

In 1879, F. Müller presented a paper on mimicry to explain why so many unpalatable butterfly species look alike. He reasoned that the convergence of color patterns of distasteful species would more effectively serve to educate birds of the nasty taste associated with that color pattern. Müllerian mimicry does not require one species to be more common than another; and, more importantly, protection of one mimetic species does not imply that another species will be put at a disadvantage, although there must certainly be a spectrum of palatability among Müllerian mimics (Turner 1984). Natural selection will favor this association (Poulton 1908; Fisher 1930). In the Neotropics the most common Müllerian color patterns of butterflies are tiger stripes—black and orange, transparent, or blue and white—all of which are found in the ithomiines, danaines, and heliconiines.

Studies of Mimicry in Butterflies

Perhaps the foremost proponent of mimicry in butterflies was E. B. Poulton, who wrote extensively upon the subject and encouraged many naturalists to publish their findings, despite the skeptics of the day. Birds were thus demonstrated to attack butterflies, and were established as important selective agents (see Poulton 1908; Eltringham 1910; Carpenter 1942). Later the experiments of L. P. Brower demonstrated that birds can learn to recognize and avoid color patterns that are associated with a bad taste, and that mimics potentially benefit from resembling bad-tasting models (Brower 1969, and refs. in Brower 1984). Waldbauer and Sternberg (1975) have provided some convincing field evidence for the advantages of mimicry. Selection by predators for Müllerian mimics has been demonstrated by Benson (1972) working with *Heliconius* butterflies in Costa Rica. However, these studies are restricted by their use of a few bird species, and do not account for differences in habitats and feeding biology between entire suites of insectiverous birds within a community. There is no reason to believe that, in nature, blue jays—and even less tanagers—would have the same effect upon, let alone ever encounter, the same species of butterflies as jacamars or kingbirds. There is need for experimental feeding studies to examine the responses of resident birds to butterflies occurring in the same habitat. The selection pressures upon an ithomiine species in a rain forest may be very different from pressures on the same species in montane habitats.

FIGURE 7. Seven examples of Batesian and Müllerian mimicry color patterns common to the Costa Rican butterfly fauna. Except where indicated, the specimens in the outside columns (A and D) are generally considered the unpalatable model species. The taxa involved are: COLUMN A. a1 *Battus belus varus* (Papilionidae), a2 *Parides sesostris tarquinius* (Papilionidae), a3 *Parides iphidamas* (Papilionidae), a4 *Heliconius cydno* (Heliconiinae), a5 *Heliconius sapho* (Heliconiinae), a6 *Ithomia patilla* (Ithomiinae), a7 *Dismorphia theucarilla fortunata* (a palatable mimic?) (Pieridae). COLUMN B. b1 *Papilio birchalli* (Papilionidae), b2 *Eurytides euryleon clusoculis* (Papilionidae), b3 *Papilio rhodostictus* (Papilionidae), b4 *Papilio torquatus tolmides* [female] (Papilionidae), b5 *Eurytides pausanias* (Papilionidae), b6 *Oleria paula* (unpalatable model) (Ithomiinae). COLUMN C. c1 *Perrhybris pyrrha* [female]

(Pieridae), c2 *Consul fabius* (Charaxinae), c3 *Patia orise sororna* (Pieridae), c4 *Dismorphia amphiona praxinoe* (Pieridae), c5 *Lycorea ilione albescens* (unpalatable?) (Danainae), c6 *Consul panariste jansoni* (Charaxinae), c7 *Archonias eurytele* (Pieridae), c8 *Eresia coela* (Melitaeinae). COLUMN D. d1 *Heliconius ismenius clarescens* (Heliconiinae), d2 *Melinaea scylax* (Ithomiinae), d3 *Heliconius ismenius telchinia* (Heliconiinae), d4 *Melinaea lilis imitata* (Ithomiinae), d5 *Eutresis hypereia theope* (Ithomiinae), d6 *Tithorea tarricina pinthias* (Ithomiinae), d7 *Heliconius hecalesia formosus* (Heliconiinae), d8 *Napeogenes peredia hemisticta* (Ithomiinae) (photos P. J. DeVries).

Another area of butterfly mimicry that requires work is the separation of butterflies that are Batesian mimics from those that are unpalatable. *Dismorphia* butterflies are the classic Batesian mimics, yet there are no studies demonstrating their palatability to birds. In fact, there is more evidence indicating that members of the Pieridae are unpalatable than there is of their palatability (see Pieridae). It may be that *Dismorphia* is a Müllerian mimic of ithomiines, as appears to be the case of *Perrhybris pyrrha* in Costa Rica.

From field observations and a few feeding experiments of mine with jays, coupled with the careful feeding experiments of P. Chai with jacamars in Costa Rica, the following genera appear to include the most convincing, palatable Batesian mimics: *Eurytides, Consul, Siproeta, Haetera, Cithaereas*, and *Dulcedo*. The following, often considered to be palatable butterflies, appear to be distasteful to birds: *Biblis, Hamadryas laodamia, Diaethria, Callicore, Chlosyne*, and *Microtia*, and most of the Pieridae, although the key genus *Dismorphia* has not been tested.

Pattern Development and Mimicry

One last area of mimicry that may have theoretical interest involves the pattern elements of the butterfly wings themselves. Because the presence of Batesian mimics is potentially disadvantageous to the models, we might expect natural selection to promote some method by which the models could escape from these parasites. If specimens of warningly colored ithomiine, danaine, and heliconiine butterflies are placed together with their reputed mimics, we find that few of their color patterns conform to the nymphalid ground plan of wing patterns as described by Schwanwitsch (1924, 1926). This ground plan is typified by the genera *Cissia, Smyrna, Memphis*, and *Caligo*, but appears in none of the mimetic butterfly patterns. If we then compare the nymphalid Batesian mimics to their closest nonmimetic relatives, we find that the nonmimetic butterflies conform rather well to Schwanwitsch's ground plan (compare *Eresia* and *Anthanassa, Consul* and *Hypna*, and *Cithaerias* and *Pierella*).

Why, then, do unpalatable butterflies and their reputed mimics not conform to the ground plan when virtually all other nymphalid genera in Costa Rica do? I suggest the following hypothesis: perhaps a divergence from the nymphalid ground plan by a distasteful species allows it to escape from Batesian "parasites" (in this example the palatable mimic is "parasitizing" the model pattern) because the palatable species are unable to generate the developmental pathways to follow changes in warning coloration? Perhaps one reason there are no satyrine mimics of ithomiines is that it is impossible for them to make a tiger-striped pattern, and in only a few instances has natural selection favored the loss of scales to allow genera like *Cithaerias, Dulcedo*, and

Haetera to approach a mimetic pattern. Another consideration is that perhaps all but a very few butterflies with a tiger-striped or clear wing pattern are distasteful and part of a Müllerian mimicry complex that has diverged from the nymphalid ground plan to escape from Batesian "parasites." In other words, it may be that once a species can develop a warningly colored pattern, it also acquires distasteful properties (see also Turner 1984). Here are areas for research on mimicry: describing a ground plan for wing patterns in distasteful butterflies, and testing whether all tiger-striped butterflies are distasteful.

Systematics and Neotropical Butterflies

Systematics and taxonomy are concerned with ordering the natural world into groups or categories, usually by inferred genealogical relationships. The importance of systematics and taxonomy is simply that intelligent comparisons of organisms cannot be conducted in a scientific manner unless their taxonomy has been established (Simpson 1945). When the systematic relationships between organisms have been established, their theoretical genealogy may be expressed as a classification system in which the categories are ordered hierarchically and can be presented as a branching diagram (that is, family-subfamily-genus-species) that resembles an evolutionary family tree. Describing organisms in detail, particularly their morphology, in a manner such that they can be consistently distinguished from and compared with other organisms, is the basis of systematics and taxonomy. Development of systematics and taxonomy depends upon a continual refinement of biological concepts, and their history reflects the development of other areas of biological science (see Mayr et al. 1953; Wiley 1981 for reviews).

Butterflies are probably the most studied group of insects in the world. There have been numerous classifications proposed for them (Ackery 1984) but, oddly enough, their overall classification is still unresolved, especially that for the Nymphalidae. It is beyond the scope of this book to examine all classification systems of butterflies, but it is appropriate to trace certain historic aspects of the subject that are important to Neotropical faunas.

History

The first widely accepted classification of butterflies appeared with the publication of the tenth edition of *Systemae Naturae* in 1758 by Carolus Linnaeus, the creator of the binomial nomenclature system. Although Linnaeus named some South American butterflies, it is to J. C. Fabricius and P. Cramer that we owe many of our Neotropical species names. During this infancy of butterfly systematics, all species were named under the generic name *Papilio*. Roughly fifty years after the first use of the binomial system, generic names other than *Papilio* began to be employed for butterflies, and the relationships of genera to one another became important. Perhaps the single most important worker of the early nineteenth century was Jacob Hübner, who was responsible for many of the generic names of butterflies currently in use. A review of Hübner's work can be found in Hemming (1937), and a catalog of the generic names of butterflies and their type species in Hemming (1967; see also Cowan 1970).

Building upon this framework, workers of the Victorian era produced some of the most valuable contributions to Neotropical butterfly systematics and biology. It was a time when the Neotropics were being explored by British and German naturalists, and when their findings were eagerly published and read by European academic societies. Although seldom in agreement, museum systematists began to be influenced by the ideas of the field naturalists of the period. Most influential of the naturalists were H. W. Bates, T. Belt, C. R. Darwin, W. Müller, F. Müller, and A. R. Wallace, who were responsible for such important concepts as evolution through natural selection, mimicry, pleistocene biogeography, and phylogenetics.

One of the most important landmarks in the study of the Central American butterfly fauna was the publication of the *Biologia Centrali Americana*, volumes 1 and 2, by F. D. Godman and O. Salvin. This exemplary work builds upon systematic studies of A. G. Butler, H. Doubleday, H. Druce, J. O. Westwood, W. C. Hewitson, C. Felder, R. Felder, O. Staudinger, S. H. Scudder, and J. A. Boisduval, all of whom were important pioneers in butterfly systematics. Godman and Salvin's reference to genitalic morphology for separating species foreshadowed the importance of these characters in modern works.

The end of the nineteenth and beginning of the twentieth centuries marks a time strongly influenced by German workers. Volume 5 of the monumental work edited by A. Seitz, *The Macrolepidoptera of the World*, is still, despite problems of nomenclature, the most valuable and wide-ranging treatment of Neotropical butterflies in existence. Of the contributing authors, K. Jordan and H. Fruhstorfer stand out. Jordan's ideas on butterfly systematics are well researched and show many insights into higher classification. Although Fruhstorfer has often been scorned for generating many subspecies names, he consistently brought analyses of genitalia into his generic and species-level treatments, summarized other entomological explorers' observations on butterfly natural history, and brought to bear his own extensive knowledge of butterflies.

Our present knowledge of Neotropical butterflies is the result of the efforts by Victorian explorers who provided systematists and museums with material and observations. A few deserve special comment.

The entomological explorers for the Godman and Salvin project—E. Arce, P. Biolley, G. C. Champion, H. Rogers, and C. F. Underwood—were responsible for most of the new discoveries in Central America included in the *Biologia Centrali Americana*, and their collections form a major part of the British Museum Natural History collection. All of these men were experts in systematic zoology, and contributed systematic revisions on various groups of Neotropical insects, plants, and birds. Another collector working at the same time in South America, distinguished from all others by the abundance of his material and collection localities, is A. H. Fassl. Originally from Germany, Fassl worked for a short time in Central America, and then went to live in South America, where he explored vast areas of the Amazon Basin and the Andes, making his living by sending back specimens to European butterfly dealers. In addition, he always included notes on natural history, and in many instances preserved larvae of the butterflies he collected. Fassl's material is found in every major natural history museum; he wrote a number of important papers on Neotropical butterflies, and contributed important sections to Seitz's *Macrolepidoptera of the World*, volume 5.

After the publication of Godman and Salvin's work, two collectors were particularly important in the further exploration of the butterfly fauna of Costa Rica. William Schaus, best known for the enormous numbers of moth species he described, also described a number of the rarer butterflies of Costa Rica. The large collections he amassed were donated to the Smithsonian Institution, and clearly form one of the most important collections of Neotropical Lepidoptera (see Clark 1974). The Englishman C. H. Lankester was perhaps the greatest naturalist to live in Costa Rica between 1910 and 1950, and his knowledge of insects, animals, and plants made him a major contact for experts collecting in Costa Rica earlier this century. Although Lankester is unknown to most present-day lepidopterists, his influence is evident in the museum specimens from localities well known to him. Hence, we find on the specimens collected by W. Schaus the locality labels: Carrillo, Guapiles, Juan Viñas, Tuis, Peralta, and Lankester's home, Cachi, where Schaus and collectors of all manner of animals, insects, and plants stayed for a time while in Costa Rica (D. Lankester, personal communication). A small but valuable collection of Costa Rican butterflies taken by C. H. Lankester is in the British Museum (Natural History).

Modern Butterfly Systematics

During the time of the great world wars, American authors began to make substantial contributions to the systematics of Neotropical butterflies. A major revision appearing at this time is that of Klots (1933). In a treatment of all the Pieridae, he firmly established the importance of genitalia in butterfly systematics and the importance of phylogeny in classification. Other workers making major contributions to the field were Bates (1935), Brown (1929, 1931), Clark (1947, 1949), and Forbes (1939, 1943, 1945), who wrote generic revisions and regional works, and developed ideas concerned with incorporating phylogeny in butterfly classifications.

Although a number of higher classifications for all butterflies had been proposed over the years (Reuter 1896; Clark 1947), the first widely accepted classification is that of Ehrlich (1958*a*). This classic work was the first to provide an analysis of a large number of characters in a global survey of butterfly genera and, perhaps most importantly, it constituted a real effort to establish a higher classification without group favoritism. Ehrlich's paper established modern criteria for what constituted a family, and to some extent a subfamily, paving the way for more critical thinking and analysis in butterfly systematics.

Within the last thirty years there has been a surge of interest in Neotropical butterflies at the subfamily and generic levels. Much work has appeared as revisions (Fox 1956, 1960, 1967, 1968; Comstock 1961; Munroe 1961; Rydon 1971; Brown 1977; Higgins 1960, 1981) or as catalogs (D'Almeida 1965; Hoffmann 1940; Mielke and Brown 1979). Useful at the species level, many of these contributions have concerned themselves with "cleaning up" the nomenclature of the Seitz volumes (while, paradoxically, describing many new subspecies) and fitting biogeographic concepts into classification schemes. Except for Ehrlich (1958*a*) and Kristensen (1976), almost all of this work has used systematic ideas that, in essence, were developed in the late Victorian period (such as by Rothschild and Jordan 1906).

Although often disregarded by butterfly systematists since the turn of the century, early stages of the butterfly life cycle have proven useful in developing evolutionary theory and highlighting systematic patterns. Building upon the work of Denis and Schiffermüller (1775) and Müller (1886), some recent work has been able to demonstrate systematic affinities at the subfamily, generic, and species levels with the use of early stages, revealing problems in existing classifications (such as Rydon 1971; Muyshondt and Muyshondt 1979 and references therein; Singer et al. 1983; DeVries et al. 1985).

Present Trends in Butterfly Systematics

The entire field of systematics is currently in a state of change that centers on differences of method and philosophy among three schools of systematic theory: evolutionary systematics (Huxley 1940; Mayr 1969), phenetic systematics (Sokal and Sneath 1963), and phylogenetic or cladistic systematics (Henning 1966; Wiley 1981). There is a strong component of emotionalism or even fanaticism in the "war" among the various factions. Although this war has been waged in other areas of systematic zoology for the last fifteen years, cladistic methods are just beginning to affect butterfly systematics, which has traditionally been based almost entirely upon evolutionary or phenetic approaches. Butterfly systematics are now under pressure to question classifications that do not have testable phylogenetic hypotheses. A good introduction to the arguments may be found in the *Journal of Research on the Lepidoptera*, Vol. 21, 1982(83). While it may be some time before the dust settles, it is evident that this is an active period for butterfly systematics, due to the application of cladistic methodology (Kristensen 1976; Ackery and Vane-Wright 1984; DeVries et al. 1985).

Cladistic approaches will probably produce the next era's valuable classifications because of its methods of analysis, and because cladistics can build upon the strengths of evolutionary and phenetic systematics. In butterflies, which have at least two distinct stages acted upon by natural selection, one would expect to find groups in which the larvae are more amenable to morphological analyses than are the adults. A good example is the use of larvae and pupae in separating various groups of *Adelpha* (Aiello 1984) and Old World relatives *Neptis* and *Athyma*, in which the adults are extraordinarily similar. A good classification should ideally be based upon all aspects of the organism amenable to analysis. Such a classification would not only be extremely useful to biologists concerned with ecological and physiological questions, but would further the understanding of systematics in all fields.

The future of Neotropical butterfly classification depends upon doing more Victorian-style natural history (collecting and observing adults and early stages) and applying methods of analysis that allow comparisons between Neotropical groups and their relatives in other parts of the world. We also need to develop methods of analysis that take account of larval hostplant relationships and aspects of adult ecology. Butterfly systematics is proving to be a dynamic and influential field. Its healthy development depends upon spending more time working on the problems, and less time squabbling in the literature.

Collecting and Studying Butterflies

A major part of learning about and studying butterflies is making a collection. It is my hope that the present book will encourage people to collect and study the butterflies of the Neotropics. If it were not for the numerous large collections that I have had access to, it would have been impossible to attempt the present work. From collections and collecting I have been able to develop a list of species for Costa Rica, assess the rarity of species, establish their geographical distributions, compare specimens from various localities, describe new species, and most importantly, develop an eye for watching butterflies in nature. Although there is an ever-increasing number of restrictions upon collecting any natural history specimens, due to the rapidly dwindling habitats (and ever-increasing bureaucracy) throughout the world, the scientific collection and proper preservation of butterfly specimens remains the single most important activity for providing useful information about the conservation of butterflies for the future.

For the serious student of butterflies, making a collection entails hard field work, subsequent exchange of knowledge about butterflies with other students and biologists, and eventually passing collections to museums, where they will be of use for centuries. I do not believe that serious students of butterflies will ever cause a species to become extinct. Strict regulation of commercial collecting and of the "stamp collectors" who keep the dead carcass trade alive is, in my opinion, a considered wisdom. However, to prohibit the study of nature or to hamper scientific research, especially through laws that prohibit collecting butterflies in nature reserves, is absurd. Perhaps the greatest threat endangering butterflies is habitat destruction by commercial development. The fate of all our Costa Rican and Neotropical butterflies remains with the fate of their habitats, and much effort must be put into conserving as many habitats as possible and then studying the butterflies inhabiting them.

I shall not describe in detail the myriad ways and methods used for collecting butterflies. The reader will find thorough accounts and detailed instructions in works devoted to the subject of insect collecting (such as Oldroyd 1958; Borror and DeLong 1971), and I suggest that the beginner start with these sources and experiment. I present here a list of equipment and suggestions that I have found useful for studying butterflies in Costa Rica.

Equipment

Notebooks. The very first habit the student of butterflies needs to cultivate is notetaking. Notes should include the date, place where observations are made, the subject of the notes, and any observations, however trivial, on behavior, hostplants, predators, or thoughts that might be useful in the future. The notebook(s) should be on hand at all times and notes should always be written in indelible ink.

Nets. The material for the net bag should be fine mesh nylon, and the bag should have a depth of at least 90 cm and an opening of 55 cm.

The net should be mounted on a spring steel hoop and *firmly* attached to a lightweight pole measuring at least 100 cm long. I prefer a pole at least 200 cm long, and several extensions of 100 cm each are at times very useful. It is important to make sure that the extensions can be securely attached in a manner that does not bend or break the pole. Butterfly net bags, hoops, and poles can be purchased from entomological supply houses but, with a little diligence and some good materials, nets can be made with few tools.

Traps. Because a substantial fraction (I estimate at least 40 percent) of the butterfly fauna treated in this book feed exclusively upon rotting fruits as adults, traps are very useful for collecting species that one rarely sees by walking around in the forest (such as *Memphis, Prepona, Epiphile, Catoblepia*). Like the net, the material for traps should be of nylon. I find that traps that are at least half again as tall as my forearm work the best: if they are too tall, the butterflies are difficult to remove; if too short, the butterflies escape. It is best to work with about ten traps in each area being studied, and in some cases it is desirable to have more. A practical trap design is shown in Figure 8. The bait for traps can be anything that attracts butterflies, but I find that rotting bananas mixed with sugar or, for certain species, fresh mammal dung works best. These materials are recommended because they are readily available in almost any habitat.

Plastic Bags and Containers. The invention of the plastic bag was a real boon to field biology, and it is a good idea to carry a few with you in the field for larvae and hostplants. Almost all of my field rearing of larvae is done in plastic bags suspended along a clothesline at camp. Plastic containers with tight-fitting lids are very useful for transporting larvae between field sites and for deterring ants. A label placed in each bag or container can always be referred to when taking notes on larval development.

Butterfly Envelopes. I find that glassine envelopes that are commercially sold to stamp collectors are indispensible for storing butterflies. I carry several hundred at all times. The data and notes can be written on each envelope, and there is never a mix-up of notes. Remember either to label your specimens immediately after the day's work, or to do it before you go to sleep. Remember that a specimen without data is completely useless.

Killing the Butterflies. I use different methods of killing butterflies in the field, depending upon the size and behavior of the species. Most medium to large nymphalids, and all pierids and papilionids I kill by a sharp pinch administered to the thorax when the insect's wings are folded over the back. Care should be exercised not to smash the insect—to use only the thumbnail if possible. It will take some practice to be able to judge how much pressure should be used. For all small nymphalids, small Charaxinae, Apaturinae, and all Satyrinae I use a cyanide jar. Remember that only one insect can be left in the killing jar at a time, or the specimens will be badly damaged; so carry at least two. Also do not leave the butterflies in the killing jar too long, or the muscles will set very rigidly. Again, experience is the best teacher. Also remember that all detached legs and antennae should be stored with the specimen from which they came.

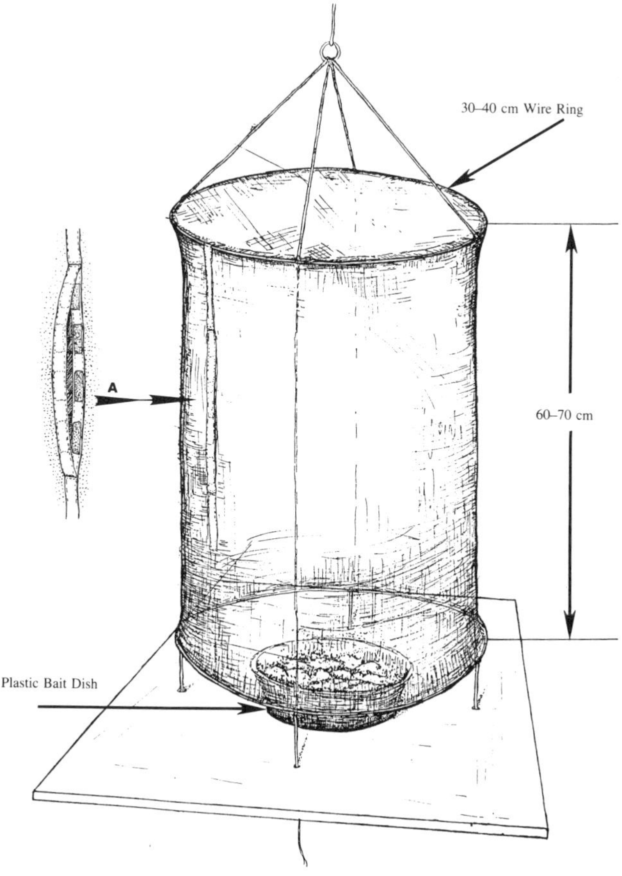

FIGURE 8. A practical design for a butterfly trap. Inset A shows a detail of how Velcro patches may be installed in the seam to facilitate removing specimens. The base should be at least 6 to 10 cm wider than the diameter of the mesh cylinder. For bait, rotting bananas mixed with sugar are effective, but other fruits, carrion, or feces can be used (drawing by N. Greig).

Setting and Pinning. For those who do not know how to set a butterfly, I suggest examining the various methods described in a standard entomology book. I use a flat setting board that will accommodate numerous specimens of varying sizes for everything from a tiny *Euptychia* to a huge *Caligo*. Always use the highest quality insect pins for your specimens. Stainless steel pins have the advantage of not corroding, but bend easily. Standard number 3 insect pins will do fine, provided the specimens are kept dry. I oven-dry specimens at a low heat for twelve to twenty-four hours, although some prefer to leave the specimens on the setting board for a week or more. To relax dry specimens, I use a vacuum jar with a screen to elevate the specimens above wet sand with paradichlorobenzene added. Do not leave specimens in the relaxer too long or they will mold.

Labeling. All specimens need to be labeled with the following information: country, locality, and province, date of capture, and name of the collector. Voucher specimens require labels with more information, and should be cross-referenced to appropriate voucher material. A specimen without a label is hardly worth the pin upon which it is impaled.

Voucher Specimens. A voucher specimen is very special because it is evidence for a fact that you observed. I keep voucher specimens for oviposition records, matings, special behaviors I have observed, and all rearing records. These are the most valuable components of any collection. When rearing butterflies I keep all head capsules, pupae, and a specimen of the hostplant, along with the adult that emerged. Such a specimen will also have a set of notes (and photographs) that describes the larval instars. The voucher specimens, because of the special status, require detailed labels. All serious students should maintain a voucher collection.

Storage. The time and expense in caring for a collection can be considerable, especially if the collection is entirely of set specimens. Set specimens need to be kept in wooden boxes or insect cabinets that have tight-fitting lids, and need to be stored away from light. Light will cause specimens to fade. The collection also needs to be kept dry, or everything will acquire a covering of mold and become damaged. Papered specimens can be stored in airtight tins or boxes, and take up less space. However the butterflies are stored, the specimens must be dry and kept with a chemical preservative to keep other insects and mold from getting in. Although there are health hazards involved (it is a carcinogen), I use paradichlorobenzene because it deters ants, mold, mites, cockroaches, beetles, and all manner of museum pests. Other preservatives can be found in Oldroyd (1958). A collection properly cared for will last several centuries if not longer and, if placed in a museum, will provide a wealth of information for future generations.

Photography. With a little time and patience, anyone is capable of taking very good photographs of butterflies. Such photographs are extremely useful for information retrieval, lectures, articles, and are a pleasure to look at, since they recall the observations made on that particular day. All that is required is a 35 mm camera and a macro lens. An electronic flash is very useful for shots of tiny larvae and small details. No modern automatic, computerized camera equipment is essential; I find that most such gear is a liability in the rain forest.

Field Studies. Because the ecology of most butterflies has not been studied, substantial contributions to this field can be made by anyone patient enough to spend the time. An excellent summary of many of those studies that have been made may be found in Vane-Wright and Ackery (1984). Techniques for field ecology and methods of analysis may be found in Southwood (1978). However, a great deal of valuable information can be gathered by simply watching butterflies, taking detailed notes, and using mark-release-recapture techniques. Butterflies are easily marked by writing a number on their wings and noting the time of day, species, and where the butterfly was captured and released (see also Morton 1984). I would encourage all students of butterflies to try this simple method of studying individual butterflies through time. All that is required is a felt-tipped pen, a notebook, and a watch; in many situations, binoculars are also very useful.

Microscopic Examination. For critical examination of detailed and tiny structures (genitalia, scales, the eyes), additional equipment is necessary. A dissecting microscope is invaluable but expensive. However, with a ten- or greater power hand lens, blunt forceps, needle-nose watchmaker's forceps, and a few probing needles a lot of work can be done. For descriptions of dissections and preparation of small parts see Tuxen (1970) and Borror and DeLong (1971) for techniques.

TWO. FAUNAL REGIONS, HABITATS, AND BUTTERFLY DIVERSITY

Due to its topography and equatorial position (between 8°00″ and 11°9″ north latitude), Costa Rica has an enormous diversity of terrestrial habitats. This diversity is the result of the interactions between the surface wind patterns, the backbone of high, rugged mountains, and the oceans on two sides. Additionally, Costa Rica's location makes it a biological bridge between Central and South America. Consequently, Costa Rica possesses a patchwork of local weather patterns, microhabitats, and elevations each of which supports a high biotic diversity. The climate of Costa Rica is discussed in detail by Coen (1983), and a few examples from his paper will serve to highlight how diverse the climate of Costa Rica can be. The mean annual rainfall ranges from 1.5 meters along the northwest coast of Guanacaste to over 6 meters in the central portion of the Cordillera de Talamanca. Depending upon the locality and month, the number of hours of sunshine per day may range from 2.0 to 9.7. Likewise, depending on the elevation and month, temperatures may range from over thirty degrees centigrade during the day in the lowlands of Guanacaste to zero degrees centigrade on the high peaks of the Talamancas.

The biotic diversity of Costa Rica has been explored by many field biologists over the last century, but D. H. Janzen, more than any other person alive, has made major advances in understanding Costa Rica's diversity of habitats and organisms. Janzen (1983*a*) gives the best overview of the climate, geology, habitats, and flora and fauna of Costa Rica. This is also an important source for access to other literature. In the context of the interaction between climate and biota, Janzen (1967) is particularly useful.

Costa Rica may be divided into Pacific and Atlantic slopes, elevations along these slopes, and their associated life zones as described by Holdridge (1967). Although there are no data that completely correlate life zones and butterfly species (most butterflies move!), the system is useful for making generalizations about where butterfly species are likely to occur within Costa Rica. I have divided the country into six large units that correspond to what may be termed faunal regions, distinguished by characteristic species and butterfly species diversities found in each (see Figs. 9-14). In this section I describe these six major faunal regions in terms of elevation, life zones, butterfly species that are both typical of and peculiar to them, and I highlight certain aspects of the overall biology of butterflies for each region. From my experience, and from comparing notes with other biologists, I further subdivide these regions into what may be termed zones of endemism, boundary zones, and species pockets. I conclude this section by comparing the species diversities of the six faunal regions within Costa Rica, and then compare the total fauna of Costa Rica to that of other tropical areas.

Pacific Slope

The major characteristic of the Pacific slope is its well-defined seasonality. The first rains of the wet season fall in May, and there is an almost daily rainfall until October. By November the dry season has begun in earnest, and little or no rain falls until the following May. The change of seasons acts as a cue for flowering, fruiting, and growth of vegetation (Opler et al. 1976), and is also linked to population fluctuations of insects (Janzen 1973*a*). The severity of the dry season varies along the Pacific slope, with the most clearly pronounced seasonality being found in the lowland deciduous forests of Guanacaste. In this region the habitat fluctuates between a lush green environment with high densities of insects during the wet season, to an almost desert brown with very reduced insect densities. The southeast portions of the lowlands and mid-elevations also exhibit seasonality, but as these regions are generally wetter, the effects of the seasons on the vegetation and the insect populations are much more moderate and less obvious to the casual observer. Butterfly species diversity is correlated with annual precipitation on the Pacific slope, and there is a tendency for all areas in the north to have fewer species than areas in the south.

Pacific Lowland Deciduous Forest (sea level–600 m). This area extends from Nicaragua south to just southeast of the city of Puntarenas, and is composed of tropical dry, tropical dry transition, and some tropical moist forest life zones. I frequently refer to this area as the "Guanacaste" forest. The most salient characteristic of this entire area is the strong dry season when most of the vegetation is leafless, followed by the rainy season with its lush vegetative growth. During the dry season, butterfly diversity and abundance are very reduced, with many resident species passing the dry season in river bottoms (such as *Eurema daira*). The entire area explodes with butterfly diversity and abundance about four weeks after the first rains have fallen (Fig. 9A). As the rainy season progresses there is a noticeable procession in the appearance of species. Some species are most abundant the first two weeks of the rainy season (*Eurytides*), whereas others are most abundant much later (*Archaeoprepona, Zaretis, Memphis*). Resident butterflies in this area exhibit a reproductive diapause in the dry season. Others show regular patterns of seasonal migration (see *Eurema* and *Eurytides*).

B

Figure 9. Pacific lowland deciduous forest. A: early rains of the season sweeping the lowlands; B: ridge forest in dry season, Parque Santa Rosa (photos P. J. DeVries).

On the whole, the deciduous forest habitat has lower butterfly species diversity than any other Costa Rican habitat below 1,600 m. Conspicuously low in diversity are the Ithomiinae, Brassolinae, and Satyrinae. Because this area has been used extensively for agriculture, little forest habitat remains, and this is reflected in an abundance of those butterfly species that thrive in open areas (such as *Eurema daira*, *Phoebis philea*, *Phoebis sennae*, and *Anartia fatima*). Another peculiarity of the deciduous forest is the reduced number of mimetic species, compared to other lowland areas. This is probably due to the paucity of Ithomiinae species in this area.

Butterfly species typical of the lowland deciduous forest are: *Eurytides philolaus, Eurytides epidaus, Itaballia demophile, Kricogonia lyside, Marpesia petreus, Microtia elva, Memphis forreri, Taygetis kerea, Eunica monima,* and *Caligo memnon.* In this region a number of butterflies typical of Central America north of Costa Rica reach their southern limit, including *Parides montezuma, Eurytides epidaus, Myscelia pattenia, Memphis forreri,* and *Kricogonia lyside.*

Pacific Lowland Evergreen Forest (sea level–800 m). This area extends roughly from the Rio Grande de Tarcoles near San Mateo southward to Panama, and is composed of tropical moist, moist transition, premontane wet, premontane wet transition, and tropical wet forest life zones. Although this entire region experiences a dry season (especially in the northern portion), it never completely dries out to the extent that Guanacaste does. This is best exemplified by the forest on the Osa Peninsula (Fig. 10). Although the butterflies occurring in this area do show seasonality, it is not as marked as in the deciduous forest habitats.

This region appears to have two major areas for butterfly species: the drier area north of Punta Quepos, and the more diverse, wetter area to the south. Although there is an overlap of butterfly species, each area has a distinct fauna. Butterflies found in the evergreen forest are involved in extensive mimicry, there is a moderate species diversity, and the region exhibits some degree of endemism.

Butterflies typical of this area include: *Perrhybris pyrrha, Hamadryas iptheme, Marpesia berania, Siproeta superba, Heliconius hewitsoni, Heliconius pachinus, Actinote lapitha, Ithomia celemia, Pteronymia donata, Morpho amathonte, Morpho peleides* (brown form), and *Antirrhea tomasia.* Taken as a whole, this region is a transition zone in which a number of the subspecies change to more southern Panamanian forms, and it has faunal elements representative of South America. Of great interest is the almost boundary effect in the butterfly fauna observed between those areas north and south of San Mateo (see Fig. 15, p. 50). This is best illustrated by the forms of *Morpho peleides*: specimens are blue to the north and very brown to the south (see Plate 38).

Pacific Mid-Elevation (700–1,600 m). This region is very complex with regard to habitats and microhabitats, and is very species rich (Fig. 11). It has various endemic butterflies, and includes the following life zones: tropical moist, premontane belt transition, lower montane moist, lower montane wet, premontane wet, premontane wet-rain transition, and premontane rain forest. The region may be divided into two areas: the drier area of the Cordillera de Guanacaste and the

B

C

FIGURE 10. Pacific lowland evergreen forest. A: interior of flood plain forest, Parque Corcovado; B: trail through interior of Corcovado basin, Parque Corcovado; C: mangrove-estuary forest, Parque Corcovado (photos P. J. DeVries).

Meseta Central, with fewer species; and the very species-rich, wetter areas to the south along the Cordillera Central and Talamanca. These areas differ also in species composition. For example, in the Cordillera de Guanacaste we find populations of *Papilio torquatus, Papilio astyalus, Papilio victorinus*, and *Morpho polyphemus*, whereas in the mountains to the south we find *Taygetis banghaasi, Epiphile grandis, Memphis lankesteri, Pereute cheops*, and different forms of *Morpho peleides, Morpho theseus*, and *Morpho cypris*. The relatively dry areas of the Meseta Central, which is effectively an ecotone between the Guanacaste forest and the wetter mid-elevational forests, appear to be a major migrational corridor between the Atlantic and Pacific slopes. Here we find mix zones where species usually confined to one slope or the other fly together (*Heliconius pachinus, Heliconius cydno, Melinaea lilis, Melinaea scylax*).

A

B C

FIGURE 11. Pacific mid-elevation. A: wind savannas at Ujarraz de Buenos Aires in the Valle General (photo P. J. DeVries); B: forest interior at Parque Rincon de la Vieja (photo J. M. Barrs); C: forest interior in Valle de Copey (photo P. J. DeVries).

Also notable in this respect are the areas around Villa Colón, Santa Rosa de Puriscal, and the Dota Valley.

High-Elevation Pacific and Atlantic (1,600–above 3,000 m). There is a great similarity between the high-elevation faunas of the Atlantic and Pacific slopes, especially above 2,000 m. With few exceptions, all habitats within this region receive daily precipitation and reduced solar radiation compared to other habitats in Costa Rica (some areas may go weeks without sunshine), and freezing temperatures may occur at night. The life zones found in this region include: premontane wet-transition, premontane rain, montane wet, montane rain, and subalpine rain paramo (Fig. 12). The butterfly fauna found here includes a high proportion of Andean genera and species, some endemic to the Talamancas, and some temperate-zone species. Habitats above 2,000 m have the lowest numbers of species in Costa Rica.

An interesting characteristic of the high-elevation butterfly faunas is a drastic reduction in the number of butterflies that feed exclusively upon rotting fruits (probably due to a lack of appropriate fleshy fruits), especially above 1,800 m. Above this elevation there is a shift in the nymphalid species from exclusive fruit feeders to those that feed on dung or, as in the pronophiline satyrids, species that feed as they can on fruits, fungi, and flower nectar. Conspicuously absent from these habitats are the Charaxinae, Apaturinae, Morphinae, and Brassolinae. Another characteristic of the high-elevation butterflies is that, except for transparent-winged ithomiines, there appears to be little mimicry, unless, of course, we assume that the pierid species are distasteful (which they probably are).

Butterfly species typical of all high elevation habitats are: *Papilio garamas syedra, Lieinix nemesis, Catasticta flisa, Catasticta teutila, Pedaliodes dejecta, Cyllopsis rogersi, Cyllopsis argentella, Heliconius clysonimus*, and *Dione moneta*. Butterfly species that appear to be endemic to the Cordillera de Talamanca include: *Lieinix cinerascens, Lieinex viridifascia, Catasticta theresa, Catasticta cerberus*, and *Catargynnis dryadina*.

Atlantic Slope

The major characteristic of the Atlantic slope is that it is always wet. This is due to westerly air masses that move off the Caribbean Sea and come up against the backbone of high mountains. The resultant condensation produces constant high humidity and precipitation. Although the weather patterns are not as predictable as those on the Pacific slope, a general seasonal weather sequence for the Atlantic slope might be described as follows. The driest months (and the ones with most sunshine) are February and March, and at times, a few weeks into

FIGURE 12. High-elevation habitats. A: rain paramo near Cerro Chirripo; B: *Chusquea* thickets on Cerro de la Muerte; C: elfin forest below Cerro de la Muerte; D: Talamancan forest near Madre Selva (photos P. J. DeVries).

April. The rains begin sometime in April (or at the very latest May), and this is followed be a brief dry period that occurs around September and October. This brief dry spell is then followed by the heaviest rains, in November and December. Although the term is misleading, such an equatorial climatic sequence is what has come to be known as the "aseasonal tropics." In my experience, both butterfly abundance and species diversity at Atlantic slope sites are greatest during the dry periods of the year, and the lowest diversity and abundance occur during the period of heaviest rains. However, I know of no ecological studies that have addressed seasonality of insects on the Atlantic slope. Because of the myth of "aseasonality" and the topographic complexity of the Atlantic slope, the habitats and organisms occurring there are some of the least understood in Costa Rica.

Atlantic Lowland (sea level–500 m). This region extends from Nicaragua south to the Panamanian border, and has perhaps the greatest range of all the Central American habitat types between South America and Mexico. This region in Costa Rica contains the following life zones: tropical wet, tropical moist, and premontane wet transition forests, all of which are habitats that never dry out during the year, and that include some areas (such as Tortuguero) which are large tracts of swamp forest (Fig. 13). The butterflies in this region are for the most part wide-ranging species found throughout Central and South

A

B

C

FIGURE 13. Atlantic lowland forest. A: a logging boat on the Río Tortuguero (photo P. J. DeVries); B: aerial view of Tortuguero lowland forests (photo K. Winemiller); C: the Río Sucio in Parque Braulio Carrillo (photo P. J. DeVries).

America. The area around Bribri is peculiar in that here some species exhibit subspecies forms typical of Panama (*Heliconius cydno, Hypothyris lycaste*); it appears to be a genuine biological boundary (see Fig. 15, p. 50). The Atlantic lowlands is species rich, has many mimicry complexes, and although seasonality does occur, it is not well documented for any insect population.

Butterfly species typical of this region include: *Battus belus, Heliconius cydno, Heliconius sapho, Hypothyris euclea, Ithomia bolivari, Morpho peleides* (all-blue form), *Morpho cypris, Antirrhea miltiades*, and *Caligo atreus*.

Atlantic Mid-Elevation (600–1,500 m). This region is very species rich, contains a great diversity of microhabitats, is very wet thoughout the year, and contains the following life zones: tropical wet, premontane transition, premontane wet, and premontane rain forest (Fig. 14). The region exhibits endemism, range disjunctions from northern Central America and the South American Andes, and is one of the most species-diverse areas in Costa Rica. I have termed the portion of this region that extends from the Reventazon Valley along the Cordillera Central and Cordillera de Tilaran the "Carrillo Belt" on account of the number of apparently endemic species that occur there. The steep country that fills this region is the least known of all the Costa Rican habitats, while clearly one of the most interesting.

The butterfly fauna of the Atlantic mid-elevations shows a diversity of mimicry, very clear seasonal movements of certain species (especially ithomiines), and contains some of the rarest butterfly species in Central America. Butterflies that are characteristic of this region include: *Battus laodamas rhipidius, Eurytides pausanias, Dismorphia zaela, Agrias aedon, Memphis lyceus, Memphis aureola, Eunica norica, Epiphile eriopis, Dynamine hecuba, Heliconius eleuchia, Napeopgenes peredia hemisticta, Eresia sticta, Antirrhea pterocopha, Morpho granadensis, Cissia agnata, Cissia drymo*, and *Eretris suzannae*.

Faunal Subzones

Within the six major regions of Costa Rica there are subzones of biological interest. These subzones distinguish themselves from the whole by having elements of endemism or rarity, or they may be boundary zones where the butterflies show apparent mixing of color pattern genes (introgression). The distribution and ecology of Costa Rican butterflies is insufficiently known to say with certainty where all these subzones occur. Such areas surely exist, and in many cases, their peculiarities with respect to the butterfly species is matched by peculiarities of the flora, other insect groups (moths, Orthoptera, ants), birds, reptiles, and amphibians. The reasons why such areas are peculiar are

FIGURE 14. Atlantic mid-elevation. A: La Montura, Parque Braulio Carrillo (photo P. J. DeVries); B: Río Ángel, Colonia del Socorro; (photo P. J. DeVries); C: forest interior at Parque Braulio Carrillo (photo L. Jost).

unknown. Some areas, like rain shadows, appear to be mediated by local climates, whereas other areas may be the result of edaphic features of the forest community. Whatever the reasons, such areas certainly warrant study. I recognize three types of subzones in Costa Rica on the basis of field experience and consideration of the butterfly fauna treated in this book. These are briefly described here with the hope that future studies can examine such areas in detail.

Zones of Endemism. These are fairly sizable areas of Costa Rica with butterfly faunas unique to Costa Rica and western Panama, and they are distinguished on the basis of having a high percentage of butterfly species endemic to them. There are three zones of endemism in Costa Rica: the high montane Talamancan zone, the Carrillo Belt, and the Chiriqui-Talamancan zone, which has two subdivisions. The high Talamancan zone runs from the Cordillera Central south through the Cordillera de Talamanca into Panama, and includes those habitats above 2,400 m. The butterfly fauna of this zone is clearly derived from the South American Andean fauna—the genus *Catasticta*, and most of the satyrine tribe Pronophilini show a very high percentage of species endemic to these mountains. The Carrillo Belt is effectively the Atlantic slope mid-elevation habitat, which follows the Talamancan zone at a lower elevation from 500 to about 1,700 m. Butterflies characteristic of this area are *Eurytides pausanias, Dismorphia zaela oreas, Heliconius eleuchia, Eresia sticta, Ithomia bolivari, Perisama barnesi, Adelpha stilesiana*, and *Antirrhea pterocopha*. The Chiriqui-Talamancan zone is centered around Volcan Chiriqui in Panama. The portion of this zone with higher elevation corresponds fairly well with the Holdridge premontane wet forest, a rain forest transition life zone, and ranges from about 1,000 to 2,000 m elevation. The lower portion of this zone encompasses the Osa Peninsula and surrounding areas, and the area of Panama to the east that at one time was known as "Bugaba" (a legendary forest that has been totally destroyed within the last decade).

Boundary Zones. There are five boundary zones of which I am aware in Costa Rica, and all have the property of being areas where species show a mixture of phenotypes, or where the species composition abruptly changes (Fig. 15). These areas would be of great interest to studies devoted to gene flow. There is a very noticeable boundary effect on the Pacific slope between the areas north and south of the Rio Tarcoles, which is best exemplified by the color changes in *Morpho peleides*. The area northwest and southwest of the Golfo Dulce exhibits a change in phenotypes of several subspecies of the Ithomiinae (among other groups) from Costa Rican to Panamanian forms. The area in the Atlantic lowlands around Bribri also shows a change from phenotypes

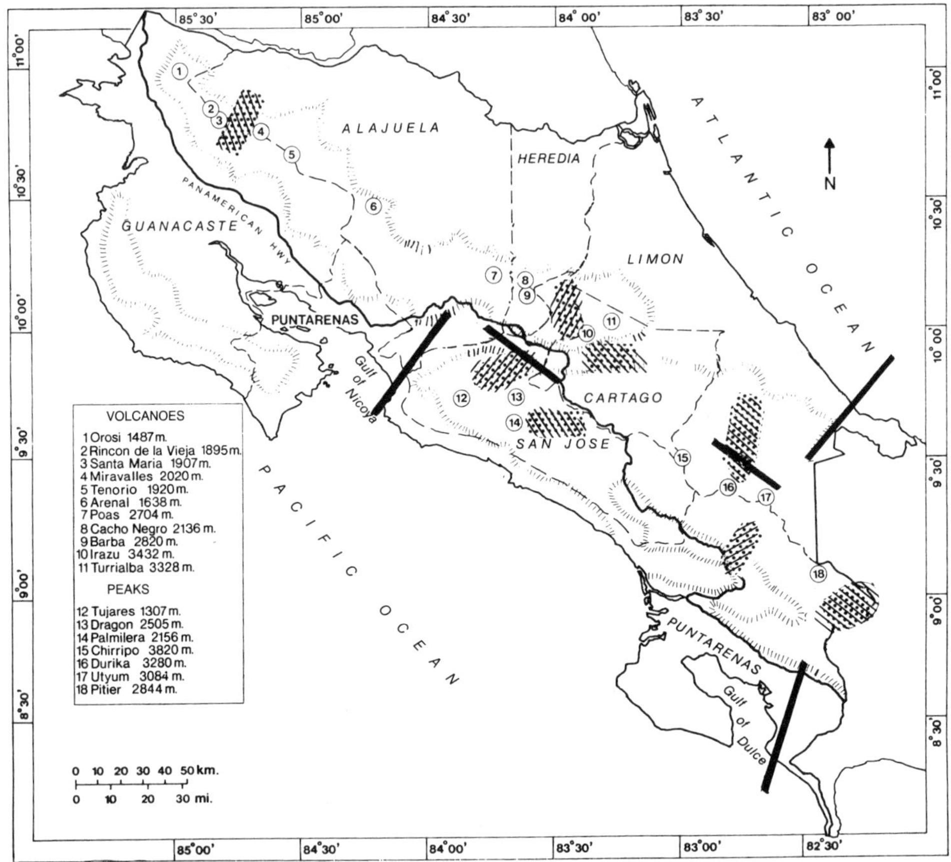

FIGURE 15. Approximate locations of boundary zones (solid black lines) and species pockets (hatched areas) in Costa Rica. As work on the butterflies of Costa Rica continues, more of these subzones will undoubtedly be detected (drawing by P. J. DeVries).

characteristic of Costa Rica to those characteristic of Panama, perhaps best illustrated by *Heliconius cydno*. There is an area on the Atlantic slope between 2,000 and 1,000 m (corresponding to the location of Fila Bugu) where species from high elevations and low elevations mix. Additionally, the species in this region exhibit a great deal of color-pattern variation. The last area is also a mix zone, and is located along the western slope of the Meseta Central. Although this entire area is almost devoid of mature vegetation, there is a mixture of Atlantic and Pacific slope species, and the species occurring there exhibit a phenotypic plasticity.

Species Pockets. There are certain habitats in Costa Rica that have rare or unusual species in them, and hence may be distinguished from the surrounding areas. These species pockets are usually rather small and have unusual climatic patterns: they fall in rain shadows, sun shadows, certain valleys, rivers, or mountaintops. It is unknown how many such areas exist in Costa Rica, but the following is a start toward enumerating them: all habitats classified as subalpine rain paramo; the rain shadows of the Valle de Copey, Las Mellizas, Ujarras de Buenos Aires; the extremely wet areas around Tapanti and the Rio Grande de Orosi; the area around Villa Colon; the mountain passes between Volcan Santa Maria and Volcan Mirravalles; and the pass between Volcan Irazu and Volcan Barba (see Fig. 15).

Diversity

Butterfly Diversity within Forest Habitats. Within any forest habitat there are at least two layers of vegetation: the canopy and the understory. Although more study is needed, it is my general impression that any Costa Rican forest habitat below 1,900 m has a higher butterfly diversity in the canopy than in the understory. This generalization appears to break down in forests that have been severely disturbed and, to some extent, in those at high elevations. In these habitats, the butterflies treat disturbances (light gaps, edges) as if the canopy had come to the ground, and there is a mixture of species between the canopy and the understory; this is why canopy species are best trapped at the forest edge (DeVries 1985*b*).

Why the forest canopy fauna is more diverse is unknown, but it may be simply that the canopy has a greater physical diversity (more nooks and crannies), and hence more organisms live in it. With a series of fruit-traps, pulleys, ropes, and a large supply of rotting fruits, important contributions toward understanding site diversity in Neotropical forests could be made through the study of butterfly species stratification.

Butterfly Diversity within Costa Rica. To compare the species diversities of the six faunal regions, I have selected two sites within each region that I have repeatedly sampled over the course of years; I have then pooled the species lists. The sites I have chosen are as follows:

Pacific Deciduous—Parque Santa Rosa and Cañas area (sea level–300 m).
Pacific Evergreen—Parque Corcovado and Santa Rosa de Puriscal area (sea level–500 m).

Pacific Mid-Elevation—Las Cruces de San Vito and Monte Verde areas (900–1,500 m).

High Elevation— Cerro de la Muerte and Volcan Turrialba areas (2,300–3,500 m).

Atlantic Mid-Elevation—Colonia Virgen del Socorro and La Montura areas (700–1600 m).

Atlantic Lowland—Finca la Selva and Turrialba areas (sea level–600 m).

The comparisons of the families and subfamilies are found in Table 2, along with the total number of species of each family and subfamily found in Costa Rica.

There are several surprising results from this comparison. First,

TABLE 2.
Comparison of Butterfly Diversity between the Six Faunal Regions of Costa Rica by Numbers of Species

	PD	*PE*	*PM*	*HE*	*AM*	*AL*	*Total Species in Costa Rica*
Papilionidae (40)							
Papilioninae	14	17	17	3	21	16	40
Pieridae (70)							
Dismorphiinae	0	3	8	4	9	5	14
Pierinae	15	8	19	9	10	8	30
Coliadinae	16	15	18	5	11	13	26
Nymphalidae (433)							
Nymphalinae	39	63	62	19	62	65	128
Melitaeinae	9	7	8	4	13	11	38
Heliconiinae	14	19	21	3	18	17	27
Acraeinae	1	2	2	1	2	2	5
Ithomiinae	5	27	39	9	41	35	65
Danainae	4	3	5	3	4	4	6
Libytheinae	1	0	1	0	0	1	1
Apaturinae	3	3	4	0	4	6	9
Charaxinae	14	17	20	0	16	30	48
Morphinae	1	5	3	0	5	7	10
Brassolinae	4	8	11	0	10	11	20
Satyrinae	6	20	29	15	30	30	76
Total Species	146	217	267	75	256	261	543

NOTE: Each region is represented by two intensively collected sites: PD = Pacific Deciduous, PE = Pacific Evergreen, PM = Pacific Mid-elevation, HE = High Elevation, AM = Atlantic Mid-elevation, AL = Atlantic Lowland. Numbers in parentheses are the total species in the family known from Costa Rica.

there is an amazingly uniform total species diversity for most groups between all regions except Pacific deciduous and high elevations. The tendency is for the species composition to change but the numbers of species to remain relatively constant. Equally surprising is the uniformity of the numbers in each subfamily between each region (such as Coliadinae, Nymphalinae, Heliconiinae, Ithomiinae, Brassolinae, and Satyrinae). Discrepancies between numbers of each subfamily appear to reflect the amount of precipitation; notice that the Pacific Evergreen region has fewer Dismorphiinae, Ithomiinae, and Satyrinae (groups associated with high precipitation) than the other regions, a trend even more obvious in the drier Pacific deciduous forest. This lower diversity can also be partly explained on the basis of mimicry: there are fewer Ithomiinae models for the Dismorphiinae. Of the four species-rich regions, most of the butterfly diversity of Costa Rica is contained in the Pacific and Atlantic Mid-elevations and the Atlantic Lowlands, each with its own diversity of particular systematic groups. The Atlantic Lowlands are richest in Charaxinae, the Atlantic Mid-elevations in Papilionidae and Ithomiinae, and the Pacific Mid-elevations have a combination of many Heliconiinae, Ithomiinae, and Satyrinae.

The Pacific Deciduous region has fewer species, mostly because of a reduced ithomiine, morphine, brassoline, and satyrine fauna. These groups are found in the greatest diversity in areas of high precipitation, and are apparently unable to withstand the severity of the dry season in the deciduous region. The reduced number of ithomiines is reflected in a reduced number of mimics throughout this region.

Areas of high elevation have the most impoverished species diversity of the six regions. This is certainly a reflection of the low temperatures and low incidence of sunlight. Hence, the high elevations are comparable in species richness to a far-north temperate-zone area. The butterfly fauna present at high elevations is characterized by genera and species groups that have affinities to the Andes of South America, and the overall proportion of endemics is higher than in any of the other faunal regions.

Diversity between Costa Rica and elsewhere in Central America. Because the butterfly faunas of the Neotropics are relatively unstudied, it is difficult to compare accurately the Costa Rican fauna to that of other mainland countries. However, the species lists for Mexico and especially Panama are sufficiently accurate to enable a rough comparison.

To compare the Costa Rican fauna to that of Mexico, I have taken Hoffman (1940), edited out those species that I know are synonyms, counted the number of species listed, and added fifty species to compensate for work done within the last decade (see Revista Sociedad Mexicana De Lepidopterologia, 1979-1983) to come up with a rough estimate of 450 species of butterflies in the families Papilionidae, Pieridae, and Nymphalidae. This is 17 percent fewer species than in Costa Rica. Even if we estimated the butterfly fauna of Mexico to equal that of Costa Rica, the figure would be surprising when we consider that the area of Mexico (761,602 square miles) is almost thirty-nine times greater than that of Costa Rica. From the Hoffman (1940) list it is apparent that although Mexico has a strong component of endemism at the species level, the fauna has a greater affinity to the temperate zone than to South America. Another reason for lower species diversity is most certainly that large areas of Mexico are relatively arid (either semi-desert or tropical deciduous forest). As we have seen, the Costa Rican deciduous forest has fewer species in it than other areas. Whatever the reasons, it is clear that Costa Rica is much more diverse per unit area than Mexico.

From the unpublished work of G. B. Small, I have been able to compare the Costa Rican fauna with that of Panama. Since Panama has a geographical area 1.5 times that of Costa Rica (29,209 square miles) and is connected to Colombia by the Darien Peninsula, its papilionid, pierid, and nymphalid butterfly diversity might be expected to be greater than that of Costa Rica. This appears to be the case, but only marginally so (Panama has about 550 species, as against 543 in Costa Rica). Panama has a greater number of species in the Heliconiinae, Ithomiinae, and Charaxinae, but only a few more species per subfamily. One reason for this very similar species diversity is that although Panama picks up species typical of Colombia, other species typical of Central America range only as far south as Costa Rica. It would be informative to investigate the diversity and relative abundance of butterfly species between eastern Panama, and western Panama and southern Costa Rica. Such a study would be valuable in locating faunal zones and transitional boundaries, and setting the stage for detailed studies on dispersal and gene flow.

Comparative Diversities of Three Tropical Regions. It has been established through comparative studies that the tropics have many more species of plants and animals than the temperate regions (see Owen 1971 for butterflies). However, all tropical regions are not equally diverse. Although it is generally accepted that the Neotropics have more species than the Old World tropics, there are few hard data available on invertebrates that document exactly how much more diverse the Neotropics are. The difficulties lie in finding areas that are biologically comparable (few tropical insect faunas—or floras—are sufficiently well known to estimate the number of species accurately), and in finding areas that are comparable in terms of the habitats they contain. For example, how does one assess a comparison between the butterfly fauna of the eastern slope of the Andes in South America and that of the island of Java in Indonesia? The former contains an unknown number of species, and the latter has no mountains comparable in height to the Andes. This is not to say that such a comparison would not be interesting, but it certainly would be desirable to compare areas that are well known biologically and that are roughly similar in climate and topography. Even so, it must always be remembered that in such comparisons, the areas have very different evolutionary histories, and a direct comparison is limited by the organisms themselves; they represent different evolutionary lineages.

On this cautionary note I compare the butterfly faunas of three distinct tropical regions (Neotropical, Indotropical, and Afrotropical) simply on the basis of numbers of species present and geographical area in square miles. The reason for the comparison is to present hard data for the often-heard statement, "the Neotropics are the most diverse areas in the world." The comparison is made between Costa Rica, the Malay Peninsula and Liberia, all of which are between 11 degrees north latitude and the equator, have (or did have, until recently) areas of extensive rain forest, are influenced by oceans, and have a backbone (or at least a range) of mountains. Moreover, the butterfly faunas are well known (especially those of Costa Rica and Malaysia). My purpose here is to show that, in fact, there are differences in species diversity between tropical regions; it is not to add to the myriad biogeographic theories. Since these regions are not strictly comparable, because of their evolutionary histories, it is appropriate to explain how I compare them (see Table 3).

The data for the Malay Peninsula were taken from Corbet et al. (1978), and I have included only those species known to occur there. The Malayan fauna is so well known that it is unlikely that these estimates will change in the future. The data for Liberia were taken from Fox et al. (1965), and I likewise include only those species positively recorded from there. It is probable that more species will be reported in the future; Fox et al. suggest about twenty. A major problem is how to compare diversities within the Nymphalidae: each of the classifications used for the three countries is different, pointing up the problem of phylogenetic affinities within the Nymphalidae, as mentioned in the section on systematics. To resolve this problem I have collapsed a number of the subfamilies and elevated one tribe to subfamily status, mostly using Ehrlich (1958*a*) as a guide. Hence, the subfamilies Biblidinae, Argynninae, Marpesiinae, Limenitidinae, and Melitaeinae have been collapsed into the Nymphalinae, the Amathusiinae and Brassolinae collapsed into the Morphinae, the Pseudogolinae collapsed into the Apaturinae, and the tribe Charaxini elevated to the Charaxinae. The data for comparison of geographical areas come from Espen-

TABLE 3.
Comparisons Between Butterfly Diversity and Area of Three Equatorial Countries: Neotropical, Indotropical, and Afrotropical

	Costa Rica	*Malaysia*	*Liberia*
Papilionidae	(40)	(44)	(18)
Papilioninae	40	44	18
Pieridae	(70)	(45)	(27)
Dismorphiinae	14	0	0
Pierinae	30	31	20
Coliadinae	26	14	6
Pseudopontiinae	0	0	1
Nymphalidae	(433)	(273)	(188)
Nymphalinae	166	126	109
Heliconiinae	27	3	0
Acraeinae	5	0	28
Ithomiinae	65	0	0
Danainae	6	35	5
Libytheinae	1	2	1
Apaturinae	9	9	0
Charaxinae	48	15	18
Morphinae	30	27	0
Satyrinae	76	56	27
Total	543	362	283
Costa Rican fauna greater by factor of:		1.5	2.33
Area in square miles:	19,600	128,431	43,000
Area greater than Costa Rica by factor of:		6.5	2.2

NOTE: Numbers in parentheses are the total number of species in each family known to occur in each country.
SOURCES: Corbet et al. (1978), Fox et al. (1965), Espenshade (1966). See text for details.

shade (1966) and are straightforward. Costa Rica has an area of 19,600 square miles, the Malay Peninsula 128,431 square miles, and Liberia 43,000 square miles.

Using the data presented in Table 3, we can state that the butterfly diversity of Costa Rica is one and a half times that of the Malayan fauna and over twice that of the Liberian fauna. This is true even though Malaya is 6.5 times, and Liberia over twice the area of Costa Rica. On the basis of the total number of species, the fauna of Malaya is comparable to that of the entire Pacific slope of Costa Rica. Liberia is comparable to the Pacific Evergreen forest.

The Costa Rican fauna has a greater diversity in the families Pieridae and Nymphalidae, whereas the Malayan fauna has a slightly higher diversity of Papilionidae than Costa Rica. Within the Nymphalidae, Costa Rica has a higher diversity of Nymphalinae, Heliconiinae, Charaxinae, and Satyrinae. The Ithomiinae, found only in Costa Rica, is perhaps analogous to the Danainae of Malaya. At all other levels, the diversity of fauna of Costa Rica is most similar to that of Malaya. Liberia's diversity exceeds the other two only in the Acraeinae.

To hazard a guess as to why Costa Rica has so many species, I suggest that the climatic and topographic conditions that form the six faunal regions, as well as the country's position as a biological bridge between Central and South America, give rise to Costa Rica's diverse butterfly fauna. The Malay Peninsula would also seem to be in a position to draw upon the faunal diversities of mainland Indonesia and perhaps the islands that lie in close proximity to it. However, these areas have much less butterfly diversity than the mainland Neotropics. Liberia, although rain forest, is located south of one of the world's greatest geographical barriers, the Sahara desert, and perhaps a better comparison with Costa Rica would be the entire belt of rain forest found in West Africa.

Trying to explain why the Neotropics have so many more species than other regions remains one of the great challenges in evolutionary biology. There have been many theories put forth (see Pianka 1966 and Gentry 1982 for summaries), but none has satisfactorily answered the question, because almost all of them rely on the circular reasoning: greater diversity generates greater diversity.

A GUIDE TO THE BUTTERFLIES OF COSTA RICA

Family **PAPILIONIDAE**

Species of the family Papilionidae are found in almost every type of habitat throughout the world. The adults are distinguished by six walking legs that bear nonbifid tarsal claws; forelegs that bear a spurlike process called an epiphysis; and palpi that are greatly reduced, exposing a broad, hairy frons. In the Neotropics, all of the species are medium- to large-sized butterflies that are conspicuously colored. In Costa Rica, all the species flutter their forewings when visiting flowers, something that no other family of butterflies does when feeding. By far the most comprehensive work on the New World Papilionidae is the revision by Rothschild and Jordan (1906). Although some of the names and systematic ideas have changed since its publication, this work provides a wealth of information. The reader, regardless of interest, is urged to use this revision for access to a much broader literature. A more recent and wide-ranging review is that of Hancock (1978, 1983). In the present work I have followed the basic arrangement of Rothschild and Jordan while incorporating ideas of later workers, especially Munroe (1961).

The hostplant families of importance for the Neotropical Papilionidae are: Aristolochiaceae, Annonaceae, Lauraceae, Cannelaceae, Hernandiaceae, Rutaceae, Apiaceae, Piperaceae, and perhaps Magnoliaceae and Moraceae. The majority of these plant families contain volatile oils, alkaloids, or phenolics, which are potential sources of insect defenses (see Berenbaum 1981, 1983; Cordell, 1981).

All papilionid eggs are round and have little or no sculpturing. The eggs of some species are covered with a waxy material, and the young larvae, upon emerging from the egg, feed on this covering in addition to the eggshell. As Moss (1919) suggested, this covering might be considered a concentrated "meat-essence" to sustain the larva on long walks. I have observed this covering in Central American *Battus* species that oviposit away from the hostplants or on widely separated seedlings. Perhaps the covering represents a form of parental care in species that consistently oviposit away from the hostplant; the tiny larvae need a first meal before searching for a host.

All first instar larvae bear tubercles from which arise numerous setae. Later instars may be without tubercles, or with fleshy ones, as typified by the Troidini. All papilionid larvae have defense organs called osmeteria. These are extrusible fleshy forks that arise from a slit on the dorsum of the prothorax, and are everted when the larvae are molested (Figs. 2, 17). The osmeteria emit a strong odor that contains isobutyric acids (Eisner and Meinwald 1965; Brower 1984). This defense is most likely aimed at parasitic flies and wasps, because it has little effect on vertebrate predators (Common and Waterhouse 1981). Even so, I have observed parasitoids ovipositing on a larva when the osmeteria were everted and in full contact with the parasite. Recently it has been suggested that the osmeterial secretions emit ant alarm pheromones that aid the larvae in keeping ants at bay (Honda 1983).

All pupae of the Papilionidae are fastened to the substrate by a silken girdle that passes across the third thoracic segment and wings. The head area is bifid to some extent, and the coloration of the pupa is invariably cryptic (Figs. 16, 17).

In Costa Rica, the Papilionidae are represented by three tribes. The tribe Troidini contains the genera *Battus* and *Parides*, species without tails that have a black ground color; they are, in effect, the New World representatives of the birdwing relatives in the Indo-Australian region (*Pachliopta* and *Atrophaneura*). The troidines are all considered to be distasteful to predators, and all apparently feed on hostplants belonging to the Aristolochiaceae. In Costa Rica and the rest of the Neotropics, these butterflies are important models in Batesian and Müllerian mimicry complexes involving a number of Lepidoptera families.

The tribe Papilionini, or fluted swallowtails, is a diverse assemblage of species (see Hancock 1983), all included here in the genus *Papilio*. A number of the Neotropical species are sexually dimorphic and some exhibit female-limited polymorphism, but not to an extent comparable with such Old World species as *Papilio dardanus*. The hostplant families that are important in the Neotropics include Rutaceae, Lauraceae, Hernandiaceae, Piperaceae, Apiaceae, and perhaps Moraceae (see *P. cleotas*). Records for the South American species include Magnoliaceae, Cannelaceae, and other plant families that require confirmation. As far as I am aware, there has been no research in the Neotropics to examine chemical defenses of this tribe, even though there are numerous examples of mimicry.

The tribe Leptocircini, or kite swallowtails, are recognized by their short upturned antennae. The Central American genus *Eurytides* is composed of two indefinite groups in Costa Rica. One

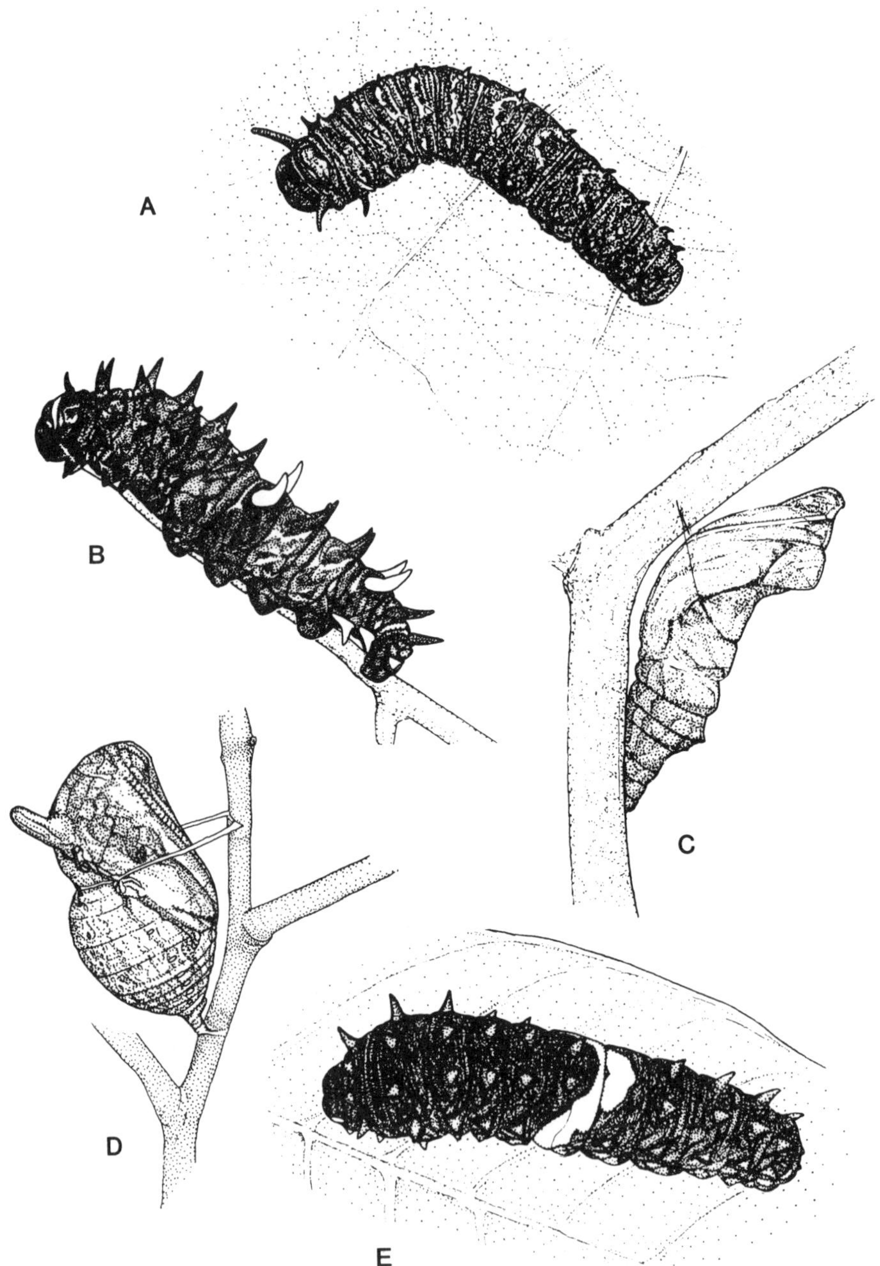

FIGURE 16. Larvae and pupae of the Papilionidae. A: *Battus crassus* mature larva; B: *Parides arcas mylotes* mature larva; C: *Parides arcas mylotes* pupa; D: *Eurytides euryleon clusoculis* pupa; E: *Eurytides branchus* mature larva (drawings by J. Clark).

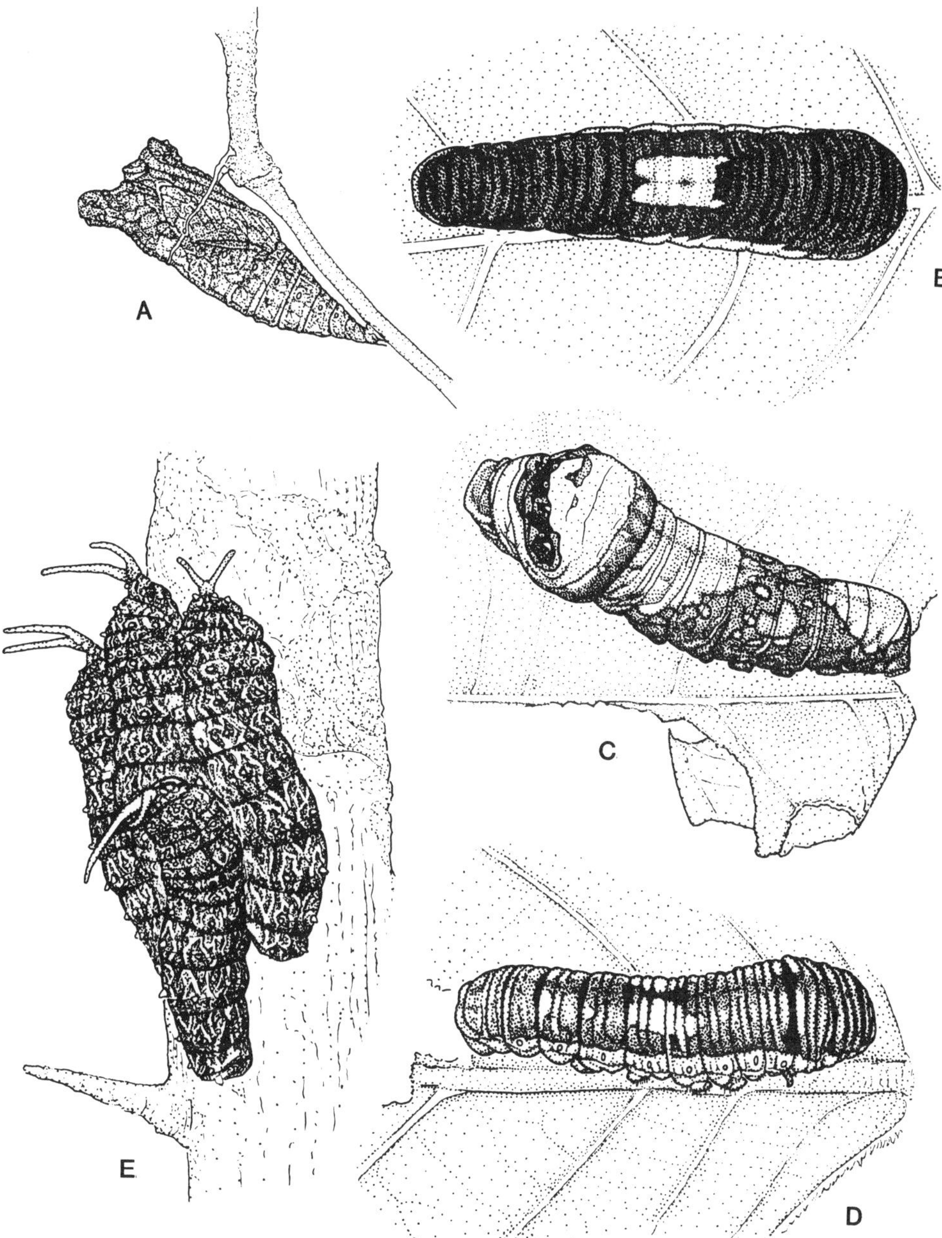

FIGURE 17. Larvae and pupae of the Papilionidae. A: *Eurytides epidaus* pupa; B: *Eurytides epidaus* mature larva; C: *Papilio birchalli* mature larva; D: *Eurytides philolaus* mature larva; E: *Papilio anchisiades* mature larvae (drawings by J. Clark).

group has long tails with black stripes on the wings; the other group does not have tails and mimics other papilionids and certain Nymphalidae. All important hostplants for these butterflies are in the family Annonaceae. Within the two groups, each has a distinctive larva and pupa (Figs. 16, 17).

The Neotropical Papilionidae, diverse as they are, have never been the subject of much research on population dynamics, mimicry, or secondary chemistry, and even their systematic affinities are poorly understood.

Genus **PARIDES** Hübner, 1819

The butterflies in this genus have a black ground color to the wings, a black body with red spots, and asymmetrical tarsal claws. The sexes are dimorphic, with the males usually bearing a green patch on the forewing upperside; the males always have a distinctive androconial fold on the hindwing anal margin, and bear white wooly scales inside the fold. Both sexes have a characteristic red patch on the hindwing, which in some species has an overlay of iridescent violet scales. The females of most species are very similar and form part of an important Müllerian mimicry complex that "drives" associated Batesian mimicry complexes. The great similarity of the female *Parides* species is best appreciated by trying to separate out long series of them from the same locality; it is difficult. To correctly identify them, close attention must be paid to the size and configuration of the white spots on the forewing upperside. Even then there will be problems. There is a need for long series of reared specimens in which the males and females of the same brood can be compared.

Parides hostplants all belong to Aristolochiaceae, known for toxic chemicals that may be incorporated into the insects that feed on them (Rothschild 1972). All Costa Rican *Parides* larvae are solitary feeders. The larvae are darkly colored and may have black, white, or red fleshy tubercles on the dorsum (Fig. 16). The pupae have a distinctive shape and cannot be confused with anything else (Fig. 16). Although many people have reared *Parides* to obtain perfect specimens, there is little reliable information on larvae of certain species (*lycimenes* and *erithalion*). Host specificity and growth rates on different species of hostplants would also be worth studying (see Brown et al. 1981).

In Costa Rica, most *Parides* species inhabit forests, and they are found in elevations ranging from sea level up to 2,000 m in some areas. The butterflies are most frequently seen visiting flowers along forest edges and light gaps, or in the forest canopy. They often visit flowers of *Impatiens sultani* (Balsamaceae), which are abundant along roadsides in montane habitats. In the forest, *Parides* visit flowers of various trees and shrubs in the family Rubiaceae. Individuals from some populations have been reported with pollen loads that are similar to those of *Heliconius* (DeVries 1978). It remains to be demonstrated whether the *Parides* can assimilate nitrogen from the pollen (see *Heliconius*). Population estimates from field data suggest that individuals live a very short time (approximately ten days; Cook et al. 1971; Brown et al. 1981). However, these life-span estimates seem very short for aposomatic butterflies, and a long-term study based across a large area should be done to take into consideration long-distance daily movements by individuals. One thing is clear—the sexes are not only divergent in appearance but in adult ecology, as well. The males spend their time patrolling flower patches engaged in male-male interactions, feeding, or courtship activities. The females spend their time as solitary individuals in forest habitats looking for oviposition sites, and range much further than the males; they are seldom recaptured at the same flower patch. This strongly suggests that population estimates and longevity equations will be different for the two sexes, and future study should take this into consideration. Unlike most other Papilionidae, *Parides* do not visit wet sand, urine, or dung, which helps to separate models from mimics in the field.

Perching or territorial behavior is common in most species. During sunny mornings, males patrol large patches of flowers, and chase and court other butterfly visitors to the patch. During courtship, a male hovers over a female while making repeated dips at her when she has landed. The forewings constantly flutter, while the androconial pouches on the hindwing are exposed. The female may sit with her wings slowly pulsing as the male hovers over her, which most likely signals receptivity, or she may keep the wings shut for a time and then fly away, a rejection signal.

If one examines a recently mated or recently courted female, white scent wool will be found on its antennae and head. This demonstrates that the androconial scales of *Parides* males are transferred during courtship and are important components of mating behavior. It remains to be demonstrated if transfer of androconial scales are necessary for copulation.

Another component of copulation contributed by the male is the *sphragis*. A sphragis (or mating plug) is often found covering the genital pore of recently mated females. Composed of a brown, horny material, the sphragis prevents the female from mating with other males, and hence protects the sperm of the first male. The sphragis will disintegrate after a time, and the female can mate again.

Parides photinus

(Doubleday, 1844)

FW Length: 45-47 mm **Plate 1**

Range: Mexico to Costa Rica

Hostplant: *Aristolochia* (Aristolochiaceae)

Early stages: (Ross 1964*a*) *Egg*—orange, mushroom-shaped with waxy covering, laid singly on young leaves. *Mature larva*—dark black with dull red and white tubercles. In Costa Rica, the larvae are maroon, and bear a collar of pale orange-red tubercles around the head area; the head capsule is black with a white band on the face. They are found most commonly on young hostplants along forest edges. The larvae and pupae are parasitized by braconid wasps.

Adult: Distinguished by the blue sheen on the HW upperside and double row of submarginal spots along the HW margin. See *P. montezuma.*

Habits: Occurs from sea level to 1,000 m on the Pacific slope in deciduous forest habitats. The southern range of this species terminates near the transition to lowland Pacific rainforest near Quepos. Encountered as solitary individuals along forest edges and road cuts, from July to September. Females oviposit from midday until late afternoon. Both sexes visit flowers of *Lantana, Stachytarpheta*, and *Hamelia*. This species is moderately common in the remnant patches of forest, especially from 300-800 m.

Parides alopius

(Godman and Salvin, 1890)

FW Length: Unknown **Not illustrated**

Range: Mexico and Nicaragua

Hostplant: Unreported

Early stages: Unknown

Adult: Distinguished from *P. photinus* by having spatulate tails on the hindwing; submarginal spots on HW are smaller and partly white; HW upperside is less glossy.

Habits: This species has not been reported from Costa Rica to date, and apparently little is known of its habits from anywhere. I include it here as a possibility, since there are some records of it from Nicaragua.

Parides dares

(Hewitson, 1867)

FW Length: Unknown **Not illustrated**

Range: Nicaragua

Hostplant: Unreported

Early stages: Unknown

Adult: According to Rothschild and Jordan (1906), it is distinguished from the similar *P. photinus* by a small white dot in the middle of the FW; the first two anterior HW submarginal spots are not crescent shaped; the femora are scaled.

Habits: This species is apparently known only from a single specimen housed in the British Museum (National History), which may represent an aberration of *P. photinus*. I include it as a possibility for which to search.

Parides montezuma

(Westwood, 1842)

FW Length: 37-42 mm **Plate 1**

Range: Mexico to Costa Rica

Hostplant: *Aristolochia* (Aristolochiaceae)

Early stages: According to Tyler (1975), they are known but undescribed.

Adult: Distinguished from all similar species by having a single row of red spots on the HW margin; tails are very short; HW has no iridescence.

Habits: Occur from sea level to 700 m on the Pacific slope in dry forest habitats. Encountered as solitary individuals, usually flying with *P. photinus*. *P. montezuma* differs from other Costa Rican congeners by flying close to the ground. It visits flowers of *Lantana* and *Stachytarpheta*. Although apparently common north of Costa Rica, it is infrequent to rare in our area. There are breeding populations in Parque Santa Rosa, and in some years it can be locally common during the early part of the rainy season.

Parides sesostris zestos

(Gray, 1852)

FW Length: male 40-44 mm, female 42-48 mm **Plate 2**

Range: Mexico to Bolivia. **Subspecies:** Mexico to Costa Rica

Hostplant: *Aristolochia* (Aristolochiaceae)

Early stages: *Egg*—laid singly. *Mature larva*—Moss (1919). In Brazil there are apparently two forms: the common Brazilian one is mottled dull ochre with black spotting. The other, like the larvae I have reared in Costa Rica, is pale maroon with dark maroon tubercles. The distinctive features of the larvae are the dark dorsal tubercles, except those on segments 8 and 11, which are white; laterally on the same segments the body has dark maroon patches, and the anal segment bears a black triangle. *Pupa*—lime-green with pale yellow wash on abdomen and wings.

Adult: Sexes dimorphic. *Male*—large green patch on FW does not enter cell; no subapical white spot. *Female*—FW has one large white spot that is not fragmented and does not extend beyond the cell. The palpi of both sexes are black. See *P. childrenae.*

Habits: Occurs from sea level to about 1,000 m, mainly on the Atlantic slope, and only reaches the Pacific slope in mountain passes in the Cordillera de Tilaran and Guanacaste. Usually encountered as solitary individuals (occasionally locally common) along forest edges and in light gaps. Both sexes visit flowers in the early morning, and courtship takes place in late mornings. Females are most active from midday to early afternoon along riparian edges and in the forest understory. Although this species can be moderately abundant, it appears to be local, and has not yet been reported from southeast Costa Rica.

Parides childrenae childrenae

(Gray, 1832)

FW Length: male 45-49 mm, female 48-52 mm **Plate 2**

Range: Mexico to Ecuador. **Subspecies:** Guatemala to Panama

Hostplant: *Aristolochia tonduzii* (Aristolochiaceae)

Early stages: *Egg*—yellowish white, laid singly on young plants or developing leaves. *Mature larva*—body mottled dark maroon with grey sides; tubercles on dorsum and sides maroon except for two laterals; two spots on mid-dorsum white, as are two spots on last segment and lateral four on last segment; osmeterial area has a white line where it meets the head. Head is shiny black, osmeteria yellow-orange. *Pupa*—bicolored green with yellow wingpads, head, and last abdominal segment; head flatly bifid.

Adult: Sexes dimorphic. Both sexes have red palpi. *Male*—large green patch on FW and prominent white FW spot. This spot is a reliable field character for distinguishing the species when flying. *Female*—distinguished by the two white patches on the FW, one of which is just outside the cell. See *P. sesostris.*

Habits: Occurs from sea level to 800 m on both slopes, in primary rain forest habitats. Males are very conspicuous, fast fliers that commonly patrol patches of *Hamelia* flowers along forest edges and in light gaps. Patrolling begins in the early morning, and the same flower patch is patrolled by a single male for a few hours, after which he leaves the area and does not return to it. I have found that a marked male may turn up the next day several kilometers from where it was marked, patrolling a different flower patch. Freshly eclosed females are less vigorous fliers, and visit flowers during the early morning; usually they are courted by the patrolling males. Older females fly at midday in the shady forest understory, and are extremely wary. In one area of the Osa Peninsula, both sexes come out of the forest in late afternoon to feed on flowers in open areas, but there is no patrolling or courtship behavior at this time. In some areas of Costa Rica, individuals may collect pollen loads like those of *Heliconius*, although this is rare in most areas. Important nectar sources for both sexes are: *Hamelia, Stachytarpheta, Cephaelis, Lantana, Vouchysia*, and *Warsczewiczia*. Females are very careful where they oviposit; a plant may be inspected for up to twenty minutes before an egg is placed on it. This inspection includes flying out of sight for several minutes and returning to the same plant. It has been my experience that this species is moderately common in primary rain forest, but intolerant of areas without substantial forest cover.

Parides lycimenes lycimenes

(Boisduval, 1870)

FW Length: male 40-42 mm, female 41-44 mm **Plate 2**

Range: Mexico to Ecuador. **Subspecies:** Guatemala to Panama

Hostplant: *Aristolochia pilosa* (Aristolochiaceae)

Early stages: *Larva*—all instars are similar to those of *iphidamas*, but are distinguished by having an isolated white spot near the base of each proleg 1 through 4; its body is a brighter red overall.

Adult: Sexes dimorphic. *Male*—distinguished from similar species by having the green on the FW end broadly along the black inner margin, forming a triangle with a clean-edged base; tibia spinose. *Female*—distinguished by having the white spot of the FW in cell M2 smaller than the one in cell M3. See *P. iphidamas* and *P. erithalion.*

Habits: Due to the confusion in distinguishing the females of this species from those of *P. iphidamas*, I can only make a very general statement on its habits. I have found males to be moderately uncommon, occurring from sea level to 700 m on both slopes, always in association with lowland rain forest. A detailed life history for this and other species will be essential for accurate determinations. At present, it is possible to have a single female specimen determined as any of several species by different experts.

Parides erithalion sadyattes

(Druce, 1874)

FW Length: male 38-43 mm, female 42-44 mm **Plate 2**

Range: Costa Rica to Venezuela. **Subspecies:** Costa Rica and Panama

Hostplant: *Aristolochia* (Aristolochiaceae)

Early stages: Undescribed

Adult: Sexes dimorphic. *Male*—two forms: green patch on FW may be a large patch (Pacific slope) or entirely absent (Atlantic slope). Distinguished by having extracellular FW white spots very reduced; red on HW almost always reduced to three in number. Iridescence may extend beyond the red onto the black discal area. *Female*—white spots generally reduced to a line across the FW cell; red on HW wide, but paler basally. *Note*: it should be borne in mind that all of these characters are variable and that only after a long series of bred specimens are analyzed and the results published will we be able to recognize some good field characters for the separation of the female of this species.

Habits: Occurs from sea level to 700 m, most commonly on the Atlantic slope, and in local populations in the Pacific evergreen forest. This species is usually encountered as solitary individuals in the early morning along forest and riparian edges, but is occasionally common at forest edges where there are abundant flowers. Both sexes visit flowers of *Cephaelis*, *Hamelia*, and *Impatiens*. On both slopes, it is most abundant during July and August, but persistent throughout the year.

Parides iphidamas iphidamas

(Fabricius, 1793)

FW Length: male 38-40 mm, female 39-41 mm **Plate 2**

Range: Mexico to Ecuador and Peru. **Subspecies:** Mexico to Panama

Hostplant: *Aristolochia* (Aristolochiaceae)

Early stages: (Young 1977*a*) *Egg*—yellowish brown, laid singly on young plants. *Mature larva*—head capsule black, body dark glossy purple. A prominent broken white band runs across body at segments 3 and 4; has six white dorsal tubercles, and six white lateral tubercles. *Pupa*—yellowish green.

Adult: Sexes dimorphic. *Male*—green on FW variable, but never ending broadly at anal margin; red area on HW always extends across more than three cells. *Female*—distinguished by having FW white spot in M2 larger than the one in M3, and this spot is cut obliquely at the base. See *P. lycimenes* and *P. erithalion*. Again, as in previous species, all characters are variable and long series must be bred to determine the species with any degree of certainty.

Habits: Occurs from sea level to 1,200 m on both slopes, in all forest habitats. Both sexes visit flowers during the morning and remain active until late afternoon. The female oviposits during midday on hostplants growing along forest edges and in light gaps. Some populations have been found with pollen loads. This species is widespread and common in Costa Rica, and is tolerant of a great many habitat types.

Parides arcas mylotes

(Bates, 1861)

FW Length: male 35-39 mm, female 40-42 mm **Plate 2**

Range: Mexico to Venezuela. **Subspecies:** Mexico to Costa Rica

Hostplant: *Aristolochia* (Aristolochiaceae)

Early stages: (Young 1973*a*) *Egg*—rusty brown, with a red-orange covering, laid singly or in small groups. *Mature larva*—velvety purple-brown with irregular patches of black. Mottled black patches are most extensive on segments with white tubercles; there is a white band along the osmeterial area. The larva of this species is similar to early instars of *P. childrenae*, but smaller. *Pupa*—pale green with a yellow wash on abdomen and wings.

Adult: Sexes dimorphic. Both sexes can be distinguished from all other *Parides* by a pink fringe on the HW. A good field character that can be seen with binoculars is, in the males, dark veins in the HW cell that form a distinct triangle.

Habits: Occurs from sea level to 1,400 m on both slopes in association with all forest habitats, and is the most common and widespread of the Costa Rican *Parides* species. Both sexes fly along forest edges, hedgerows in open areas, or in the forest, and visit a wide variety of flowers. During the dry season in Guanacaste they are present as rare individuals in shady river bottoms; the females, unlike other butterflies, do not exhibit reproductive diapause during this period.

Genus **BATTUS** Scopoli, 1777

The butterflies in this genus are recognized by their black wings, usually with pale green on the hindwing and abdomen, and no red spotting on the body as in *Parides*. The sexes are slightly dimorphic: the dorsum of the male's abdomen is greenish, that of the female is not. Although they are closely related to *Parides*, there is no conspicuous androconial fold on the hindwing in males; the scent scales occur in a narrow strip along the inner margin. The Costa Rican species present no identification problems, and with a little practice they can be identified and sexed while they are on the wing, by using a pair of binoculars. *Battus* is distributed from the southern United States throughout Central and South America, and includes a few isolated species in the West Indian islands.

All of the known hostplants are in the Aristolochiaceae. The eggs are laid in clusters and have waxy coverings. The larvae vary in coloration from grey to black. All have fleshy tubercles, but are distinguished in possessing long motile tubercles on the first segment, unlike *Parides* (Fig. 16). The pupae are similar to *Parides*, but can always be distinguished by the thoracic horn. The early stages of most species are poorly known, and detailed work is needed on the life cycles. *Battus* larvae are gregarious and can be found in groups of up to eighty individual larvae. Although *Battus* are known to be distasteful to vertebrate predators (Brower and Brower 1964), much needs to be investigated concerning hostplant relationships and defensive chemistry.

In general, all of the mainland Neotropical species are forest inhabitants, although a few appear to thrive in open areas. In Costa Rica the genus is found from sea level to almost 2,000 m, on both slopes. All species visit a wide variety of flowers, and may be important pollinators of trees in some Costa Rican rain forests; I have often found individuals of *Battus crassus* with the undersides of the wings heavily covered in the yellow pollen of *Vouchysia* (Vouchysiaceae), a common rain forest tree.

The butterflies are probably protected by toxins sequestered from the hostplants, although this has not been demonstrated. In a few experiments with caged magpie jays in Costa Rica (*Callocitta formosa*: Corvidae), I found that the birds consistently refused to eat *Battus*, and eventually ignored them completely. Although *Battus* is considered a model for some North American butterflies (such as *Papilio glaucus*, *P. troilus*, *Speyeria diana*, and *Limenitis astyanax*), this is generally not noted in Neotropical species. However, I believe from my own observation and inability to distinguish them on the wing that *Battus* may be an important model for certain Neotropical *Papilio* species (*cleotas*, *victorinus*, and *birchalli*).

In the United States, Rausher (1978) has shown that female *B. philenor* use visual search images to locate hostplants, and that the females can assess egg loads laid on plants by other females (Rausher 1979). In Costa Rica, Young (1971*b*) found that *B. polydamas* in Guanacaste lives for over three months during the dry seasons in closed populations. It should be noted, however, that populations in Guanacaste are restricted to the remnant patches of forest, and that although little movement occurs in the dry season, when the rains come in May, most butterflies disperse from these restricted habitats. From the Atlantic slope of Costa Rica, *B. polydamas* and *B. belus* were studied by Young (1972*b*), who concluded that both species are faithful to their nectar sources, and may live for several months.

Battus polydamas polydamas
(Linnaeus, 1758)

FW Length: 43-47 mm **Plate 1**

Range: throughout the Americas and Antilles. **Subspecies:** mainland Americas

Hostplant: *Aristolochia veraguensis* (Aristolochiaceae)

Early stages: (Young 1971*b*) *Egg*—laid in clusters of five to twenty. *Mature larva*—body yellowish grey, bearing many fine black striations on each segment, most prominently on the dorsum; paired tubercles of various lengths, most of which are yellow-brown, with the large motile anterior and posterior ones yellow with black tips (the coloration is variable within the same brood); osmeterial area yellowish. A second morph is common in the Meseta Central that has a velvet black body with yellowish tubercles. The larvae feed gregariously, and may exhibit asynchronous or synchronous molts. *Pupa*—pale tan or brown.

Adult: Distinguished from all other species by the yellow-green submarginal spots on the FW and HW.

Habits: Occurs from sea level to 1,300 m on both slopes in association with disturbed habitats, but may occur in the rain forest canopy in some areas, although it rarely, if ever, enters the forest proper. Both sexes visit flowers in gardens and hedgerows throughout the year, and hence are commonly seen in cities and pastures. Although it varies little throughout its mainland range, this species is highly polytypic on the Caribbean islands, where there are a number of well-defined subspecies.

Battus belus varus

(Kollar, 1850)

FW Length: 44-52 mm **Plate 1**

Range: Mexico to Bolivia. **Subspecies:** Guatemala to Ecuador

Hostplant: *Aristolochia* (Aristolochiaceae)

Early stages: (Moss 1919) *Egg*—small, yellowish, laid in small clusters. The larvae up to the penultimate stage are apparently entirely black, with characteristic tubercles. *Mature larva*—body mottled maroon with regular black marks on the dorsum and sides; the tubercles are whitish with black tips. Prepupa body is yellow with contrasting black areas. *Pupa*—typically has a very prominent brown thoracic horn.

Adult: Sexes dimorphic. *Male*—distinguished by pale green abdomen and large spots on the HW margin. *Female*—apparently two forms: the commoner is similar to the male (without abdominal color), the rare form has a large yellow patch on the FW near cell.

Habits: Occurs from sea level to 1,400 m on both slopes, in association with wet forest habitats, rarely in the deciduous forest. In lowland rain forest this species is a common visitor to flowers of *Warsczewisczia* and *Vouchysia* trees. Throughout the country it is commonly seen visiting *Stachytarpheta* and various Rubiaceae flowers along forest edges. Although present throughout the year in most habitats, it is encountered as solitary individuals and is seldom abundant. Females oviposit during midday on hostplants growing along forest and riparian edges, and may oviposit on vegetation adjacent to the hostplant.

Battus laodamas rhipidius

(Rothschild and Jordan, 1906)

FW Length: male 46-50 mm, female 55-58 mm **Plate 1**

Range: Mexico to Colombia. **Subspecies:** Costa Rica and Panama

Hostplant: Unknown

Early stages: According to Tyler (1975), undescribed

Adult: Sexes dimorphic. *Male*—distinguished by the large greenish area on the HW (I have collected some specimens on which this area was greenish pink). *Female*—green area on HW extensive. See *B. belus*. The green on the HW flashes when the insect is flying, and can be used as a field character.

Habits: Occurs from 500 to 1,200 m on the Atlantic slope, apparently confined to areas within the Carrillo Belt. Although very rare in collections and little known, this subspecies can be moderately common within Parque Braullio Carrillo. The female is active from early morning until midafternoon, flying above the forest canopy and along ridgetops. Males fly in the early afternoon in the forest, and patrol patches of flowers, as *Parides* do. Both sexes visit flowers of *Cephaelus, Inga*, and *Calliandra arborea* that occur along forest edges or in the canopy. This species is extremely local, and I have never found it below 500 m or in any of the forest habitats adjacent to the Carrillo Belt.

Battus lycidas

(Cramer, 1777)

FW Length: 52-55 mm **Plate 1**

Range: Mexico to Bolivia

Hostplant: *Aristolochia* (Aristolochiaceae)

Early stages: (Moss 1919) *Mature larva*—pale gray with maroon tubercles, except for those on segments 3, 5, 8, and 13, which are long and pink; sides of body covered with dark lines; folds below spiracles pale pink; venter black. *Pupa*—pale lemon green, similar in shape to all other *Battus*.

Adult: Sexes dimorphic. *Male*—whitish yellow abdomen with a similar color on the HW inner margin. *Female*—green abdomen, with less color on HW. Both sexes are distinguished by the dark glossy blue-black ground color. See *B. belus* and *B. laodamas*.

Habits: This species is rare in Costa Rican collections, and I have not observed it in the field. Museum specimens are recorded from 300 to 1,400 m, from both slopes. Jordan (1907) states that it is common along rivers, and that the males visit wet sand. This behavior is not characteristic of *Battus* males, and the observer may have been fooled by a *Papilio* species (*birchalli*? or female *androgeus*?) that mimics *Battus*.

Battus crassus

(Cramer, 1777)

FW Length: male 46-49 mm, female 49-52 mm **Plate 1**

Range: Costa Rica to Brazil and Argentina

Hostplant: *Aristolochia veraguensis* (Aristolochiaceae)

Early stages: *Mature larva*—velvety black; tubercles on dorsum and sides short, colored dark maroon. Two tubercles on either side of the osmeterial area are long, black, and project forward; the head is shiny black, divided by a white line across the sutures (Fig. 16). The larvae feed gregariously in groups of up to fifty individuals and molt synchronously, except the prepupae. The prepupa is whitish with black marbling. *Pupa*—dull green-brown with yellow highlights.

Adult: Sexes dimorphic. *Male*—distinguished by the cream color on the HW costal margin; abdomen cream colored. The male has two forms. The name *lepidus* Felder and Felder is applied to the common Costa Rican form, which has no cream color on the FW upperside. In the form *crassus*, the discal area of the FW has a cream-colored patch. I have not seen specimens of this form from Costa Rica. *Female*—always has a creamy patch on the FW discal area, and a black abdomen. See *B. lycidas* and *B. laodamas*.

Habits: Occurs from sea level to 700 m, on both slopes, in association with rain forest habitats. Both sexes fly primarily at the canopy or subcanopy level along trails and in light gaps. Females descend into large light gaps and investigate large hostplants that have lush growth. In the morning, both sexes visit flowers of *Vouchysia* and *Hamelia*. This species is infrequently collected and is usually encountered as solitary individuals or localized populations.

Genus **PAPILIO** Linnaeus, 1757

There are few good characters that can be used to recognize this highly diverse, worldwide genus. There are, however, few difficulties identifying it. In general, the antennae are naked except at the base, but show no grooves (carinae), as do the preceding genera; the inner margin of the hindwing is always curved downward, which gives it a "fluted" appearance when viewed from below—hence the common name "fluted swallowtail." Rothschild and Jordan (1906) divided the group into two sections, both of which are well represented in Costa Rica. One section is characterized by usually having a yellow body and a weak or "soft" forewing costal margin. The second section is characterized by a black body and a hard or rigid forewing costal margin, which on some species bear tiny serrations. Serrations on the forewing costa are characteristic of the nymphalid genus *Charaxes* from the Old World, and are used in that genus for aggressive interactions. In the New World genus *Papilio*, however, there have been no observations concerning the use of the serrations, although their function is possibly similar to those of *Charaxes*. One of our species (*P. ascolius*) belongs to a small group of species intermediate between the two broad systematic groups of Rothschild and Jordan, and also shows characters of color pattern and wing shape not found in any other group of papilionids. It is in this small group of species that we find mimetic species.

Hostplants for *Papilio* are varied and include Apiaceae, Rutaceae, Piperaceae, Lauraceae, Hernandiaceae, and Magnoliaceae. The larvae may be solitary or gregarious, and most have an oily appearance and resemble bird droppings. Others have large eyespots that can be expanded as a defense (Fig. 17). The thoracic area of most of the larvae is expanded and without tubercles. However, in one group of species, represented by *P. torquatus* in Costa Rica, the larvae bear small tubercles on the dorsum in all instars. While in full sunlight, the larvae of some species (*androgeus, anchisiades, rhodostictus*) lift the anterior portion of the body above the substrate, which they do not do in the shade. This suggests behavioral thermoregulation. The pupae of all species are cryptic, have a slight S-curve to them, and generally resemble splinters of wood.

The majority of the *Papilio* species fly in areas where there is bright sunshine. Such areas can either be open pastures or in the canopy of the forest. The mimetic species are found only within the forest and, as one might expect from mimetic species, do not show the powerful flight behaviors that are characteristic of the genus *Papilio*. The genus is distributed from Alaska through North, Central, and South America, and is present in almost all Neotropical habitats. In Costa Rica, *Papilio* is found from sea level to the paramo habitat on Cerro Chirripo. Although *Papilio* is immensely popular with collectors and is perhaps written about more than any other major genus of butterfly, there is disappointingly little known about the biology of the Neotropical species.

The genus *Papilio*, among other genera of butterflies, was instrumental in demonstrating that hilltopping is an important part of the mating biology of North American butterflies. Shields (1967) found that a significant proportion of virgin females visit hilltops, but once they are mated, their behavior changes: they are no longer attracted to hilltops, but fly about searching for oviposition sites. L. E. Gilbert (unpublished) showed that there is an apparent dominance hierarchy of *Papilio* males on a hill, with the dominant male always occupying the top of the hill. This male is therefore in a position to mate more frequently. When two males meet, it is commonplace to see them spiral upward into the sky for some distance; at some point, one of them flies off and the other stays in the general area. This is a territorial contest in which the loser always leaves. The height to which the contending males will spiral is apparently related to the degree of dominance of the individuals involved (Gilbert, unpublished). Butterflies can be manipulated to spiral upward great distances by releasing two males that have never lost a battle (see also Lederhouse 1982). Although this information on mating behavior and male dominance hierarchies is based on North American species, the same probably applies to many Neotropical species. For instance, in Costa Rica all canopy-dwelling *Papilio* species have serrations on the forewing costal margin, and show some spectacular flight abilities. These serrations will probably be shown to play an important part in the male-male interactions of these species.

Both sexes of *Papilio* species visit flowers of many plants, including rain forest canopy trees, and may be important pollinators. The males are commonly encountered visiting wet sand at riverbanks or puddles. This habit is called "puddling," and a "puddle club" may be composed of many individuals and species, all of which are males. The first experimental work on puddling behavior was done by Collenette and Talbot (1928) in the Amazon Basin. They showed that the males are attracted to the salts from sweat. Later, sodium salts were demonstrated to be attractive to North American species (Arms et al. 1974). Why only males visit puddles is unknown, but I favor the idea that the newly emerged males require sodium ions (or associated chemicals) for their mating behavior, as has been demonstrated for male ithomiine butterflies and pyrrolizidine alkaloids (see Ithomiinae section). Whatever the reason, it remains to be demonstrated why only males exhibit this behavior, and this will prove a rewarding area of research.

Papilio polyxenes stabilis

Rothschild and Jordan, 1906

FW Length: 35-40 mm **Plate 4**

Range: Canada through Central and South America. **Subspecies:** Costa Rica and Panama

Hostplant: *Apium leptophyllum, Foeniculum vulgare* (Apiaceae)

Early stages: *Egg*—yellow, laid singly on seedlings or mature plants. *Mature larva*—greenish with black transverse bands overlaid with yellow, orange, and red dots. Larvae are conspicuous on the hostplants and are frequently found crawling across open areas in search of other hostplants.

Adult: Distinguished by the small size and the double row of yellow spots on the FW. The female has a wider and more distinct orange band on the HW.

Habits: Occurs from 500 to 1,800 m, on both slopes, in association with cut-over areas that experience heavy rainfall. Both sexes fly only in bright sunshine and visit flowers of various weeds. Males are strongly territorial on hilltops and patrol from early morning to early afternoon. Populations of this species undergo rapid local extinctions if pastures are not maintained, and this is clearly observable in San José, where there are local year-to-year fluctuations in the numbers of this species. In montane areas of Costa Rica, agriculture and animal husbandry have probably favored *P. polyxenes* by creating suitable habitats (see also Lederhouse 1983).

Papilio thoas nealces

Rothschild and Jordan, 1906

FW Length: 57-61 mm **Plate 4**

Range: Southern United States through Central and South America, Cuba, and Jamaica and Trinidad. **Subspecies:** Nicaragua to Brazil and Ecuador

Hostplant: *Piper* (Piperaceae). *Note*: the larvae of this species feed on at least ten species of *Piper* in Costa Rica and, contrary to other records, I have never found it on Rutaceae.

Early stages: *Egg*—dull amber, laid singly, usually on large plants. *Mature larva*—mottled brown, dull white, drab green, and yellow; resembles a large bird dropping; always has a whitish circular saddle on the thorax (see *P. cresphontes*). *Pupa*—dull brown, resembling a twig, and differing from *P. cresphontes* by having a smaller head and a prominently bulging abdomen.

Adult: There has long been confusion in separating this species from *P. cresphontes*. The males are not a problem, but the females from Costa Rica still present some difficulties in identification. *Male*—has no visible notch at the base of the claspers (see *P. cresphontes*); when viewed from above, the interface of the last abdominal segment and the base of the claspers is smooth and continuous with the claspers (Fig. 18). *Female*—apparently distinguished by having a depression on either side of the vaginal orifice that produces a ridge (Rothschild and Jordan 1906), but this is variable. The only positive way I know of telling the *P. thoas* female in Costa Rica is by observ-

FIGURE 18. Stylized lateral views of male abdomens of *Papilio thoas* and *Papilio cresphontes*. Note that the claspers are smooth in *P. thoas*, whereas those of *P. cresphontes* have a distinctive notch. The notch can be seen with the naked eye in many specimens, and it is easily felt by running a fingernail down the dorsum of the claspers (drawings by P. J. DeVries).

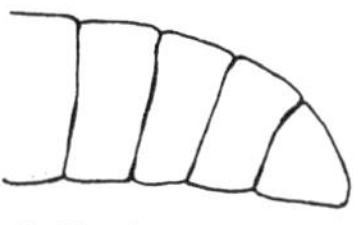

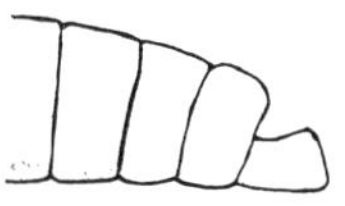

ing one oviposit on *Piper* or by rearing the early stages.

Habits: Occurs from sea level to 1,000 m on both slopes. My observations are based on males or ovipositing females. The species is commonest in areas of high rainfall, although it occurs in Guanacaste during the dry season. Both sexes are very fast fliers, and are encountered as solitary individuals along forest edges and in open areas. Both sexes visit a wide variety of flowers, and some rain forest populations visit flowers of canopy trees. The female oviposits from early morning until late afternoon along forest edges and second-growth forest.

Papilio cresphontes

(Cramer, 1777)

FW Length: 55-62 mm **Plate 4**

Range: Canada to Panama, and Colombia

Hostplant: *Citrus, Zanthoxylum setulosum, Essenbeckia litoralis, Cassimiroa edulis* (Rutaceae). Also reported from other areas, probably incorrectly, on Lauraceae, Salicaceae, Solanaceae, and Piperaceae.

Early stages: *Mature larva*—mottled brown and yellow, with the yellow forming two saddles, one on thorax, the other over end of abdomen. See *P. thoas.*

Adult: Distinguished from *P. thoas* by having a small dorsal notch at the base of the male claspers, which can easily be felt by running a fingernail down the dorsum of the claspers (Fig. 18). *Female*—distinguished by a small tubercle on vaginal orifice at the anterior edge. The best way to tell this from *P. thoas* is by oviposition or by rearing it on Rutaceae.

Habits: Occurs from sea level to 1,000 m on both slopes, but commonest on the Pacific slope. Persistent throughout the year in Guanacaste, but most abundant during the rainy season. A comparative study on this species and *P. thoas* is needed in areas of Costa Rica where the two species are sympatric.

Papilio astyalus pallas

Gray, 1852

FW Length: male 55-57 mm, female 59-61 mm **Plate 4**

Range: Southern United States to Argentina. **Subspecies:** Mexico to Costa Rica

Hostplant: *Citrus* (Rutaceae)

Early stages: (Rothschild and Jordan 1906) Similar to those of *P. thoas* in the egg and larval stages, but *P. astyalus* differs in the pupa by being more slender, and has a longer thoracic tubercle.

Adult: Sexes dimorphic. *Male*—distinguished from *P. androgeus* by the large submarginal yellow spots on the HW, and the spatulate HW tail. *Female*—variable, sometimes with a long tail on HW, sometimes with only a slender tooth projecting beyond other teeth. Distinguished from *P. androgeus* by the large HW submarginal spots. Known in older literature as *P. lycophron pallas.*

Habits: Occurs from sea level to 850 m on the Pacific slope, in deciduous forest habitats. This species flies only just before or during the early part of the rainy season, and is most abundant during June and July. Encountered as rare solitary individuals along forest edges. In the morning, both sexes visit flowers of *Stachytarpheta, Lantana,* and *Cordia,* and are seldom seen in the afternoon. Males are occasionally found as solitary individuals in the midst of a large number of puddling pierids. The female is rare in Costa Rican collections. This subspecies apparently terminates its southern range in northwestern Costa Rica.

Papilio androgeus epidaurus

Godman and Salvin, 1890

FW Length: 63-67 mm **Plate 4**

Range: Mexico to Brazil; West Indies. **Subspecies:** Mexico to Panama

Hostplant: *Zanthoxylum, Citrus* (Rutaceae)

Early stages: (Moss 1919; Ross 1964*b*) *Egg*—pale green when laid, turning deep yellow;

laid singly. *Mature larva*—head pale brown; body dark gray to black with many fine striations and blotches. Knoblike tubercles on all segments have a blue crescent at their bases. Anterior of body expanded into a false head; extensive white patches on head area and posterior segments; overall resemblance to a bird dropping. *Pupa*—similar to *P. thoas*, but with the thoracic horn expanded into a cowl; often there are patches on the body that resemble lichen.

Adult: Sexes dimorphic. *Male*—distinguished from *P. astyalus* by the small submarginal spots; medial band on upperside very broad; HW tail not spatulate. *Female*—distinguished from *P. astyalus* by reduced HW spotting; HW with blue-green color. In South America this species has polymorphic females.

Habits: Occurs from sea level to 1,000 m only on the Pacific slope. Encountered as solitary individuals in open pastures, second-growth forest, and along beaches. Both sexes visit a wide variety of flowers that range from herbs to dominant forest trees. The flight period overlaps with that of *P. astyalus* and is also very seasonal. In areas north of Costa Rica, this species is apparently abundant, but in our area it is uncommon to rare. I have one observation of a tropical kingbird catching, handling, subduing, and then rejecting a female of this species, possibly an indication of unpalatability or effective mimicry.

Papilio anchisiades idaeus

Fabricius, 1793

FW Length: 49-56 mm **Plate 6**

Range: Texas; Mexico to Brazil. **Subspecies:** Mexico to Panama

Hostplant: *Casimiroa edulis, Zanthoxylum, Citrus* (Rutaceae)

Early stages: *Egg*—yellow, laid in clusters of up to forty. Young instar larvae are mottled shiny green and white. *Mature larva*—dull brown with white areas on the dorsum and anal segment; osmeteria orange. All instars are highly gregarious, and feeding and molting are synchronous. When at rest, the larvae form large aggregations on the trunk of the hostplant (Fig. 17). As larvae they are parasitized by braconid and ichneumonid wasps, and by chalcids as pupae. *Pupa*—dull brown, twiglike, with green areas that resemble lichen; the color varies with the pupal substrate.

Adult: Distinguished by having a short FW costa and an elongated distal portion of the HW; tails are absent or present, but always reduced in length. This species is variable with respect to the red-and-white markings. Compare with *P. rhodostictus* and *P. isidorus*.

Habits: Widespread and common from sea level to 1,400 m on both slopes, in association with disturbed habitats. Frequently seen visiting flowers in gardens, pastures, or along forest edges. Probably the most common and abundant swallowtail in Costa Rica, it is present in most habitats throughout the year. An apparent mimic of *Parides* females.

Papilio isidorus chironis

Rothschild and Jordan, 1906

FW Length: 49-53 mm **Not illustrated**

Range: Costa Rica to Bolivia. **Subspecies:** Costa Rica and Panama

Hostplant: Unknown

Early stages: Unknown

Adult: Distinguished from *P. anchisiades* by the distinct, narrow tails and a less elongate HW posterior margin; white on HW reduced. See *P. rhodostictus* and *P. anchisiades*.

Habits: I have never seen this rare species in nature. Judging from data on museum specimens it is apparently montane, occurring above 1,200 m.

Papilio rhodostictus rhodostictus

Butler and Druce, 1874

FW Length: 47-51 mm **Plate 6**

Range: Costa Rica to Ecuador. **Subspecies:** Costa Rica and Panama

Hostplant: *Citrus, Zanthoxylum* (Rutaceae).

Early stages: *Egg*—yellow, laid in clusters. *Larvae*—in all stages quite similar to *anchisiades*, but with greater expanses of white on dorsum and anal segment. *Pupa*—virtually identical to *anchisiades*.

Adult: Distinguished from *P. isidorus* by always having a white patch on the FW that runs across the distal end of the cell; similar in HW shape to *isidorus*, which separates it from *P. anchisiades*.

Habits: I have never seen this species in nature, and it is rare in Costa Rican collections. It has been collected once at Sirena in Parque Corcovado, visiting *Lantana*. R. Canet has reared this species from a female originating from Carrillo.

Papilio torquatus tolmides

Godman and Salvin, 1890

FW Length: male 41-43 mm, female 42-44 mm **Plate 4, Fig. 7**

Range: Mexico to Bolivia. **Subspecies:** Costa Rica and Panama

Hostplant: *Citrus* (Rutaceae)

Early stages: (Moss 1919) *Egg*—greenish yellow, laid singly. *Larva*—similar in all instars to those of *P. thoas*, except that all instars bear prominent dorsal tubercles. *Pupa*—like that of *P. anchisiades*, only more slender and with longer head projections.

Adult: Sexes dimorphic. *Male*—distinguished by the broad transverse yellow bands. *Female*—two forms: one with FW white patch in cell area, one with white patch below FW cell; FW and HW red patch variable. Distinguished from all other species by the HW tail and yellow palpi. See *P. anchisiades*, *P. rhodostictus*, and *P. isidorus*, and *Eurytides ilus*. *Note*: the color illustration (Plate 4) is of a female from Mexico. A Costa Rican specimen is illustrated in the mimicry plate (Fig. 7).

Habits: In Costa Rica this species is known from only three areas, ranging from 400 to 800 m on the Pacific slope: the slopes of Volcan Santa Maria, near Santa Rosa de Puriscal, and Parque Carrara. The males fly very fast along forest edges and in semi-open areas with a swooping, circling flight, and visit flowers of *Stachytarpheta* in the morning and wet sand during late morning. I am informed by R. Canet that in Parque Carrara, the female stays in the shade of the forest, and in appearance and flight mimics a female *Parides*. The flight period is from May to July. This species is very rare in Costa Rican collections, and the female dimorphism warrants further study.

Papilio ascolius zalates

Godman and Salvin, 1890

FW Length: 60-65 mm **Plate 6**

Range: Costa Rica to Colombia. **Subspecies:** Costa Rica and Panama

Hostplant: Unknown

Early stages: Unknown

Adult: This unusual and spectacular species is distinguished from all other Costa Rica congeners by its large size and tiger-striped pattern. From the few specimens I have seen it appears that the amount of black on the FW apex is variable.

Habits: From museum specimens and sight records it is reported along the Cordillera de Talamanca from the city of Cartago southward, at 800 to 1,400 m on both slopes, and is associated with wet forest habitats. With binoculars I have observed males perching high in the forest canopy. They make brief circular sorties around an emergent canopy tree, and then return to the same perch. The flight is slow and gliding, with little flapping of the wings. I am informed by G. B. Small and L. E. Gilbert that the female has a slow, floppy flight. Both have collected the female along trails and streams near San Vito de Java. While flying, the female is apparently an excellent mimic of a large tiger-striped ithomiine or *Lycorea*. Gilbert squeezed an egg from the individual he caught and recorded it as being round, 3 mm in diameter. This species is unusual in our Neotropical fauna because of its ithomiine mimicry. Any observations or early-stage biology of this rare and peculiar *Papilio* species should be reported.

Papilio birchalli godmani

Rothschild and Jordan, 1906

FW Length: 56-59 mm **Plate 5**

Range: Costa Rica to Colombia. **Subspecies:** Costa Rica and Panama

Hostplant: *Hernandia didymanthera* (Hernandiaceae)

Early stages: *Egg*—salmon pink, laid singly. *Larva*—middle instars are shiny olive green with dull white along the middle and last segments; thoracic area is greatly enlarged and bears two black spots behind the head; overall appearance is like a bird dropping. *Mature larva*—pale green with a wide X shape along the back, which bears a number of pink rectangles inside the cross; the swollen thoracic area has a ring of brown along the posterior margin; thoracic area behind the head has a wide brown crescent bearing two false "eyes" that have white and black pupils. When molested, the "eyes" expand, and the larva then resembles a snake (Fig. 17). *Pupa*—similar to *P. thoas* only much rounder, with larger abdomen and rounded head area.

Adult: Distinguished by the green discal area on the HW upperside; FW underside has a postmedial cream-green band. The female has more extensive green on the HW. See *P. cleotas* and *P. victorinus*.

Habits: Occurs from sea level to 1,400 m, on both slopes, in association with rain forest habitats. Males perch in the canopy during the morning, on emergent trees associated with large light gaps. Females fly across the forest canopy and descend into large light gaps, where they oviposit on sapling hostplants, then return to the canopy. Oviposition takes place from morning until early afternoon. Both sexes visit flowers of *Stachytarpheta*, *Vouchysia*, *Inga*, and *Warscewiczia*. While on the wing, this species resembles *Battus belus* or *B. laodamas*. Although widely distributed in Costa Rica, it is seldom collected.

Papilio victorinus vulneratus
Butler, 1872

FW Length: 56-59 mm **Plate 5**

Range: Mexico to Costa Rica. **Subspecies:** Costa Rica and Panama(?)

Hostplant: *Persea americana* (Lauraceae)

Early stages: Described by Schaus (1884) and by Comstock and Vasquez (1961) from Mexico, and more completely by Muyshondt and Muyshondt (1976) from El Salvador. *Egg*—yellow, laid singly. All larval instars except last resemble bird droppings. *Mature larva*—very similar to that described for *P. birchalli*, but differs by the spotting on the thorax, and has darker patterns on the sides. *Pupa*—two color morphs: green with brown bands on the sides that run from cremaster to head, and all brown. Both forms resemble a piece of wood.

Adult: *Male*—distinguished by the submarginal row of cream spots on both wings. *Female*—dimorphic. One form resembles the male, the other has a broad longitudinal olive-green band on the HW upperside. The latter form is the only one I have seen from Costa Rica. See *P. cleotas* and *P. birchalli.*

Habits: Occurs on both slopes in association with cloud forest habitats between 1,000 and 1,300 m, and apparently confined to the Cordillera de Tilaran, Guanacaste, and Central, but does not enter the Talamancas. This rare Costa Rica species is encountered as solitary individuals flying at canopy level. Both sexes visit flowers of *Impatiens, Stachytarpheta*, and *Lantana* during the morning at ground level. This species appears to end its southern range near Volcan Barba, where its ecological replacement (*P. cleotas*) becomes more common and ranges into South America.

Papilio cleotas archytas
Hopffer, 1866

FW Length: 56-58 mm **Plate 5**

Range: Costa Rica to Brazil. **Subspecies:** Costa Rica and Panama

Hostplant: Unknown

Early stages: In Monteverde, W. Haber found a pupa on an isolated tree (*Sorocea* [Moraceae]), which he suggests is the hostplant. This needs confirmation. Unfortunately, there is no description of the pupa.

Adult: *Male*—distinguished by having a serrate FW costa; no spatulate tails; FW has a row of submarginal spots. *Female*—dimorphic; one form similar to male, the other similar to *P. victorinus* but with a blue-green HW discal area. Both forms have been collected from Costa Rica. *Note*: Rothschild and Jordan (1906) point out that there is doubt whether *P. cleotas* and *P. aristeus* Cramer should be considered separate species. It is difficult to separate females of *P. cleotas* and *P. victorinus* from Costa Rica: are they the same species or is this precise mimicry?

Habits: Occurs in cloud forest habitats above 1,300 m, on both slopes, and appears to occur just south of the distribution of *P. victorinus*, principally along the Cordillera Central and Talamanca. Encountered as solitary individuals on sunny days, always flying at canopy level. This species appears to be seasonal in the Meseta Central, occurring during June and July. This species is rare in Costa Rican collections.

Papilio garamas syedra
Godman and Salvin, 1878

FW Length: male 60-64 mm, female 73-75 mm **Plate 5**

Range: Mexico to Panama. **Subspecies:** Costa Rica and Panama

Hostplant: Unknown

Early stages: Unknown

Adult: Distinguished by the enormous size, spatulate tails on HW, and a broad yellow band across both wings, all of which are good field characters.

Habits: Occurs from 1,200 to 2,800 m, on both slopes, in cloud forest habitats. Encountered as solitary individuals flying across the forest canopy. Males perch during the morning on emergent canopy trees. A male will sail in long circles around its perch, return for a few minutes, then begin to sail around again. Perching may occur throughout most of the morning, and I have seen the same perches used for several days (by the same individual?). Although easily identified on the wing with the aid of binoculars, the butterfly usually flies about twenty meters beyond the reach of a net. On occasion, individuals descend to visit flowers of *Fuschia arborea*, or the males will visit mud along rivers. Although certainly not uncommon, this species is seldom collected because of its high-flying habits.

Genus **EURYTIDES** Hübner, 1821

The butterflies in this genus all have short, strongly upcurved antennae, a densely hairy frons, and a short stubby body in relation to the wings. There are two distinctive groups within the genus, which exhibit differences in the early stages as well as in the adults. One group consists of species that, as adults, mimic *Parides* or *Heliconius*, and have a round hindwing and red spots on the body and wing bases. The larvae of this group bear fleshy tubercles and are best considered mimics of *Battus* or *Parides* larvae. The pupae of this group have a peculiarly rotund form (Figs. 16, 17), unusual for the whole of the Neotropical Papilionidae. It is generally thought that all of the mimetic species are Batesian mimics of their various distasteful models. The second group in *Eurytides* involves species that have long, swordlike tails, triangular wings, and are aptly named the "kite swallowtails." The larvae of this group are without tubercles, and the head area is wider than the posterior part, giving them an elongated wedge shape. The pupae are cylindrical and resemble pieces of wood.

In Central America, reliably reported hostplants all belong to the Annonaceae. Other plant families (Lauraceae, Verbenaeceae, and Magnoliaceae) require confirmation.

All of the species of *Eurytides*, especially the kite swallowtails, are capable of fast flight, and most species exhibit a marked seasonality. In Costa Rica, the genus occurs from sea level to 2,000 m, in a variety of habitats. The mimetic species fly in association with forest cover, whereas the kites fly in direct sunshine. All species visit flowers of *Croton* and *Cordia* but, in general, little is known about their feeding habits. The males of some species can form large aggregations at puddles, especially on the Pacific slope in the early rainy season. At these puddles the mimetic species can easily be distinguished from their models because the models do not visit mud. While visiting puddles, the *Eurytides* species jet water up to 3 cm from the anus. Watching them pump water leaves one with a strong impression that the insects are filter feeding. I suggest that this genus would be excellent for studying why papilionid males visit puddles.

Eurytides pausanias prasinus

(Rothschild and Jordan, 1906)

FW Length: 42-45 mm **Plate 3**

Range: Costa Rica to Brazil. **Subspecies:** Costa Rica and Panama

Hostplant: Unknown

Early stages: Unknown

Adult: Distinguished from all other congeners by its mimetic resemblance to *Heliconius cydno*.

Habits: This rare species, confined to the Atlantic slope between 100 and 500 m, is known only from the Carrillo Belt. In a letter to Charles Lankester dated 1919, William Schaus writes, "the species flies along roads and is told from *H. galanthus* (= *cydno*) by visiting mud, which *galanthus* never does." The few times I have observed this species have borne out Schaus's description. It bears a striking similarity to *H. cydno* while flying, even down to the shallow wingbeat that is typical of *Heliconius*. The search for the larva and hostplant of this species has intrigued people for a long time (see Moss 1919), and any information on its habits and biology is worth publishing.

Eurytides phaon

(Boisduval, 1836)

FW Length: 40-42 mm **Plate 2**

Range: Mexico to Ecuador and Brazil

Hostplant: *Annona* (Annonaceae)

Early stages: Undescribed

Adult: Distinguished by the green HW disc and white spots on both wings.

Habits: There are no Costa Rican records, but its range indicates that it is likely to turn up as the fauna becomes better known.

Eurytides euryleon clusoculis

(Butler, 1872)

FW Length: 43-47 mm **Plate 2**

Range: Mexico to Ecuador. **Subspecies:** Costa Rica and Panama

Hostplant: *Annona glabra, Guatteria oliviformis* (Annonaceae)

Early stages: *Egg*—white, laid singly. *Mature larva*—general body color is white to yellow. There are two wide, black, longitudinal bands, interspersed with blue dots and lines, running from head to anus, on either side of a broken yellow dorsal midline; this yellow midline is bisected by a thin black and white stripe. The sides have three broken black lines that break the lateral yellow-white into rectangles; there are two yellow bumps on each segment near the bases of the legs and prolegs; the head capsule is black. Larvae rest on the upper surface of leaves. *Pupa*—pale brown or green, roundly barrel-shaped with a long thoracic horn (Fig. 16). Pupation may take place on the hostplant or associated vegetation, usually at the tips of the branches, where the pupae resemble galls, fruits, or buds. *Note*: the early stages are similar to those described for *E. belesis* (Ross 1964*a*).

Adult: Distinguished from *E. branchus* by the white patch on the FW that enters the cell, usually two spots on the HW outer angle, and a red patch that broadly enters the HW cell. See *E. branchus* and *E. ilus*.

Habits: Occurs from sea level to 1,400 m, on both slopes, in forest habitats. Occasionally this species will move into Guanacaste lowlands during the rainy season. It flies along shaded trails and roadcuts in a fashion similar to *Parides*. The male visits mud. Both sexes visit flowers of *Lantana, Cordia,* and *Croton* during the morning. Females oviposit from morning until midday. Although encountered as solitary individuals, this species is present in most habitats throughout the year.

Eurytides ilus

(Fabricius, 1973)

FW Length: 38-42 mm **Plate 2**

Range: Panama to Venezuela

Hostplant: Unknown

Early stages: Unknown

Adult: Distinguished by the large white patch on the FW located posterior to the cell and reaching almost to the anal margin.

Habits: Not reported from Costa Rica, but collected at the Panamanian border in Chiriqui (where *Papilo torquatus* female is a co-mimic), and will probably be found when the fauna of Parque Amistad becomes better known.

Eurytides branchus

(Doubleday, 1846)

FW Length: 43-45 mm **Plate 3**

Range: Mexico to Costa Rica

Hostplant: *Annona reticulata* (Annonaceae)

Early stages: *Mature larva*—velvet black with eight fleshy, maroon-tinted tubercles per segment; lateral tubercles are bright red warts. Osmeterium is bright yellow, head black. Segments 6 and 7 have a creamy dorsal band in the shape of a V that has the arms directed forward but do not extend to the ventrum. The larva is clearly a mimic of the distasteful *Parides* larva, and it rests on the uppersides of leaves (Fig. 16). *Pupa*—very similar to that of *E. euryleon*.

Adult: Distinguished by the short tails on the HW; the red on the HW forms a curved band located posterior to the cell. The form *belefantes* Godman and Salvin lacks the white patch on the FW, and apparently occurs throughout the range of the species. See *E. euryleon* and *E. ilus*.

Habits: Occurs on the Pacific slope from sea level to 900 m in deciduous forest habitats. The southern range of the species ends just north of the Osa Peninsula. Encountered as solitary individuals along forest edges, from June through August. Apparently common in areas north of Costa Rica, but rare in our area.

Eurytides philolaus

(Boisduval, 1836)

FW Length: 43-45 mm **Plate 3**

Range: Mexico to Costa Rica

Hostplant: *Sapranthus* (Annonaceae)

Early stages: *Mature larva*—in general shape like *E. epidaus* (Fig. 17); dorsum colored a warm pale brown with a white area in the middle and a white lateral band along the spiracles. Larvae feed and rest on upperside of leaves. *Pupa*—I am informed by D. H. Janzen that the pupa is rounder and shorter than that of *E. epidaus*, and that it pupates in the leaf litter, not suspended in any way.

Adult: Distinguished by the black ground color and the transverse white stripes. Apparently there are two female forms: one like the male, the other almost entirely black. As far as I am aware, the latter form has never been collected in Costa Rica.

Habits: Occurs from sea level to 500 m on the Pacific slope in deciduous forest, and ranges as far south as Puntarenas. In Guanacaste, it is present throughout the year, but abundant in May and June and rare for the rest of the year, usually only as individuals in riverbeds and ravines. When the species is abundant, it is commonly seen flying across open pastures, or individuals are found dead on automobile radiators.

Eurytides epidaus epidaus

(Doubleday, 1846)

FW Length: 40-45 mm **Plate 3**

Range: Mexico to Costa Rica. **Subspecies**: Eastern Mexico to Costa Rica

Hostplant: *Annona reticulata* (Annonaceae)

Early stages: *Egg*—white, laid singly on saplings or mature trees. *Mature larva*—velvet black dorsum with a series of white rectangles on mid-dorsum that suggest the rough outline of a castle turret (Fig. 17); white lateral line; pale green ventrum and osmeterium. Larvae rest on upper surface of leaves. This description differs from Ross (1964*a*), who found golden or pale brown larvae (see *E. philolaus*). *Pupa*—two morphs: a brown morph that may remain in pupal diapause for a year, and a green morph from which the adult emerges about two weeks after pupation. Both forms are cylindrical, with a small projection on the head, and resemble a dead twig (see Fig. 17).

Adult: Distinguished by the dark line on the HW that runs from the base almost to the tornus; faint extracellular line on FW; only one short black bar from costa into FW cell. See *E. agesilaus* and *E. protesilaus*.

Habits: Occurs from sea level to 1,200 m on the

Pacific slope in association with deciduous forest. Seasonally abundant at the beginning of the rainy season, then encountered as solitary individuals during the dry season. This species flies in open areas, including above the forest canopy. The pupae in diapause appear to be sensitive to rain, and may react to an unseasonal rain during the dry season. The resulting adults have little chance of survival, since there will be no vegetation and few flowers to feed on. The female oviposits around midday, on new leaves of the hostplant. Although rare in Costa Rican collections, it is very abundant during the early rainy season.

Eurytides agesilaus eimeri

(Rothschild and Jordan, 1906)

FW Length: 37-41 mm **Plate 3**

Range: Mexico to South America. **Subspecies:** Costa Rica and Panama

Hostplant: Unknown

Adult: Distinguished by the short black bars in the FW cell, all of roughly equal length; red medial line on the HW underside is basal to the black submarginal line. See *E. epidaus* and *E. protesilaus*.

Habits: Although it is apparently common in Panama, this species is very rare in Costa Rican collections. It is known in Costa Rica only from the Pacific rain forest habitats centered around the Osa Peninsula. I have collected it only once along a river in Parque Corcovado, and the only specimens I have seen of this species have come from the same area.

Eurytides protesilaus dariensis

(Rothschild and Jordan, 1906)

FW Length: 53-57mm **Plate 3**

Range: Mexico to Paraguay. **Subspecies:** Costa Rica and Panama

Hostplant: *Annona* (Annonaceae)

Early stages: My records are from the Atenas area and are of ovipositions only. Females lay single eggs at the tops of trees growing in remnant patches of riparian forest.

Adult: Distinguished by the large size; second FW costal bar is reduced to a thick triangle; HW margin has a tail and a long tooth. See *E. agesilaus*.

Habits: Occurs from sea level to 1,200 m on both slopes, but commonest on the Pacific side. The flight is very fast and usually near canopy level, and always in bright sunshine. It is most abundant during early rainy seasons in the Meseta Central and, although not uncommon, it is difficult to capture.

Eurytides marchandi panamensis

(Oberthür, 1880)

FW Length: 47-51 mm **Plate 3**

Range: Mexico to Ecuador. **Subspecies:** Costa Rica and Panama

Hostplant: Unknown

Early stages: Unknown

Adult: Distinguished by the golden yellow on the upperside. The yellow has a beautiful pearly sheen that almost glows when the butterfly is flying in sunshine. This sheen is a reliable field character.

Habits: Occurs from sea level to 1,000 m on both slopes in association with rain forest habitats. Encountered as solitary individuals along forest edges or rivers, only in bright sunshine. Males are not infrequently observed visiting wet sand at water crossings.

Eurytides lacandones lacandones

(Bates, 1864)

FW Length: 44-47 mm **Plate 3**

Range: Mexico to Bolivia. **Subspecies:** Mexico to Panama

Hostplant: Unknown

Early stages: Unknown

Adult: Distinguished from *E. calliste* by three round spots in the FW cell and the black tails with yellow tips.

Habits: Occurs from sea level to 900 m, in rain forest habitats. I have collected this species only once, and it is rare in Costa Rican collections. All locality records from Costa Rica indicate that it is a lowland species.

Eurytides calliste olbius

(Rothschild and Jordan, 1906)

FW Length: 45-46 mm **Plate 3**

Range: Mexico to Panama. **Subspecies:** Costa Rica and Panama

Hostplant: Unknown

Early stages: Unknown

Adult: Distinguished from *E. lacandones* by at least three faint yellow bars running across the FW cell, brighter ground color, and yellow along inner margin of tail.

Habits: Occurs from 700 to 1,800 m on both slopes, in association with cloud forest habitats. Encountered as uncommon, solitary individuals, usually along roadcuts or rivers. Individuals fly at canopy level, but occasionally males come to the ground in the morning to visit wet ground. The flight is very fast and erratic, making the butterflies nearly impossible to capture while flying. Costa Rican females are apparently unknown. Although this species is apparently common in Mexico, in Costa Rica it is local and infrequently seen.

Eurytides orabilis
(Butler, 1872)
FW Length: 46-55 mm **Plate 3**
Range: Costa Rica to Colombia; one record from Guatemala requires confirmation
Hostplant: *Guatteria tonduzii* (Annonaceae)
Early stages: *Egg*—white, laid singly on young leaves. The female almost always repeatedly lays many eggs on the same plant. *Larva*—early instars are velvet black with a white V-shaped saddle on the posterior third segment. This description holds for larvae up to the penultimate. *Mature larva*—olive green except for pairs of black spots along the dorsum. The two largest spots on thorax have a yellow-centered dorso-lateral papilla just posterior to the osmeterial fold. The head capsule is olive green, slightly pilose; in shape the thorax is wider than the first two segments, then tapers to the anal segment; the anal segment is elevated from the substrate. All instars rest on the upperside of leaves. *Pupa*—green or brown; shaped like an elongate pupa of *E. euryleon*, but somewhat more rectangular at head, and cremaster very long and stout; thoracic horn somewhat bulbous at tip.
Adult: Immediately recognized by the heavy black FW apex, black wing margins, and FW cell with a heavy black triangle. While flying, this species has a beautiful and characteristic opalescent sheen to the wings, which makes a reliable field character.
Habits: Occurs from sea level to 1,000 m on both slopes, always in association with large tracts of primary forest. Most frequently seen in montane forest habitats on the Atlantic slope, and occasionally in areas below 500 m. Encountered as uncommon solitary individuals that fly along forest edges and rivers, always flying in direct sunshine. The males may be attracted to sand that has been enriched with urine, but are most commonly seen visiting puddles along water courses, making brief stops about every 20 m to test the wet ground. On the Osa Peninsula males may be found visiting sand on beaches where fresh water streams run to the sea. Females oviposit around midday on plants occurring along riparian edges. Each egg is laid singly, but the female may lay up to ten eggs on the same plant. Both sexes have a very fast, sailing flight and may fly close to the ground or over the forest canopy. I have never seen this species abundant in any habitat, but it is persistent throughout the year in many Atlantic slope forests, especially Parque Carrillo, and on the Pacific slope in Parque Corcovado along the coast.

Family **PIERIDAE**

The family Pieridae is composed of a great diversity of species, found in all parts of the world except Antarctica. Although well represented in the temperate regions, the Pieridae is predominantly a tropical family with extensive radiations in Africa and the Neotropics. The butterflies in the Pieridae are recognized by having six walking legs, bifid tarsal claws, and venation. Although the family contains an enormous diversity of colors and patterns, most of the Neotropical species are yellow or white, with or without some mixture of red or black. The coloration of Pieridae is largely due to pterin pigments, which in butterflies are only found in the Pieridae (see Harmsen 1966; Feltwell and Rothschild 1974; and Silberglied 1977 for aspects of pterin chemistry). Klots (1933) provided the classic revisional study of the Pieridae at the tribal and generic levels. This classification has in general been followed, here but the modifications of Ehrlich (1958*a*) and Lamas (1979) have also been incorporated. There is still a need for a phylogenetic classification and work at the species level, especially in the tropical groups. The Pieridae are divided into four subfamilies, three of which (Dismorphiinae, Coliadinae, and Pierinae) occur in the Neotropics; the mysterious Pseudopontiinae, which contains a single species, occurs only in Africa.

The hostplant families of importance to the Neotropical Pieridae are: Mimosaceae to the Dismorphiinae; Fabaceae, Caesalpinaceae, Mimosaceae, and Simaroubaceae to the Coliadinae; and Capparidaceae, Brassicaceae, Tropaeolaceae, and Loranthaceae to the Pierinae. Many of these plant families are known to contain distinct groups of chemical toxins which, in some instances, have been demonstrated to be both important determinants of female oviposition choice and feeding stimuli for larvae (Chew and Robbins 1984; Singer 1984). Work on hostplants and their chemistry has provided information on the apparent unpalatability of some pierid species to predators

(Rothschild 1972). Some experimental evidence on Costa Rican species does indicate that certain pierids are rejected by caged magpie jays and jacamars (DeVries 1983; Chai, 1985). However, much experimental work remains to be done on the Pieridae *and* their predators. Such work could be easily done in the field, and would produce interesting and important information regarding the palatability and mimicry of the Pieridae.

The eggs of all pierid species are spindle-shaped, usually yellow or white, and either laid singly or in neatly spaced clusters. Shapiro (1981) discusses the occurrence of red eggs in the Pieridae and its implications. The larvae are cylindrical, never with spines, though they may have elongate hairs; the round head capsule usually has a granulate surface (Fig. 19). The pupae of the Neotropical pierids are of two general types: one typified by the Coliadinae, with a prominent keel, (Fig. 19), and the other by the Pierinae, which has pupae similar to that of the Dismorphinae (Fig. 19). As in the Papilionidae, the pupae of all pierids have a girdle of silk that attaches the pupa at a 45° angle to the substrate, or holds it against a horizontal surface. All Pieridae pupae are cryptic and either resemble plant parts (buds, new leaves, or flowers) or bird droppings. Depending on the species, pupation may take place singly or as gregarious masses.

All adult Pieridae feed on flower nectar and, as a result, are among the most commonly observed butterflies in the world. Many species have an underside coloration that makes them look like a leaf while they are visiting flowers (see *Anteos*). The males, and to a very limited extent the females, may congregate by the hundreds along riverbanks and puddles. Individuals feed on the waterlogged earth by pumping the water through their gut and expelling drops of water out of the anus. This behavior is especially noticeable during periods of bright sunny weather, but may occur throughout the year. Why the males feed at water seepage is unknown, but since the majority of the butterflies that are found doing this have little wing wear (suggesting recent emergence), it is probable that they get some chemical precursor for mating this way. For certain aspects of this phenomenon, see Collenette and Talbot (1928) and Norris (1936), who provide some interesting ideas that foreshadow work done in recent years.

Migration plays an important part in the biology of the Pieridae. Migrations of "clouds" of pierids have been described from all over the world. Reports of migrations across the seas, over mountain passes, along sea coasts, and far inland are known from virtually all countries (see Williams 1930; Baker 1984, for summaries of butterfly migrations). The best known migrants are the genera *Ascia* and *Phoebis* in the New World, and *Catopsilia* in the Old World. I believe that many, if not all, species of the Coliadinae and many Pierinae will prove to be migratory, even though they may lack the spectacular flights of *Phoebis*. As for most butterfly species, it is not known why they migrate or where individuals go.

Another important aspect of the biology of the Pieridae is the ultraviolet reflectance patterns that are well developed in the Coliadinae. To the human eye, seemingly monomorphic species (such as *Phoebis* and *Eurema*) can be shown to have strongly dimorphic sexes when viewed with the aid of ultraviolet-sensitive film or filters. This can be dramatically demonstrated with the use of ultraviolet-sensitive video cameras; males of some species flash brilliantly in the ultraviolet, like a *Morpho* in normal light. These elaborate patterns are most likely used in courtship displays, and probably in male-male interactions (see Silberglied 1977, 1984, and Vane-Wright 1984 for reviews of coloration in butterflies). These reflectance patterns in butterflies have been studied extensively by the late R. Silberglied, and the interested reader is referred to his work summarized in Silberglied (1984).

Ecological studies on the Pieridae have for the most part been conducted entirely upon temperate zone species. As a result, we must look to studies on North American species and extrapolate to the Neotropics: see Chew (1975, 1977, 1980, 1981) for patterns of host use; Ohsaki (1979) for adult resources; Watt (1968) for thermoregulation and pigment deposition; and Shapiro (1980, 1984) for egg load assessment and aspects of genetics and polyphenisms. Our pierid fauna of Costa Rica is composed of many Central American species, a number of Andean genera, and even a few endemic species, all which should prove interesting subjects for study.

Subfamily **DISMORPHIINAE**

The butterflies in this subfamily present one of the most interesting developments in the evolution of mimicry. Indeed, the studies of H. W. Bates on this subfamly of butterflies over a century ago gave rise to his famous theory of mimicry, which has since become an exciting area of investigation in evolutionary biology (Bates 1862; Fisher 1930; Gilbert 1983). The Dismorphiinae are found en-

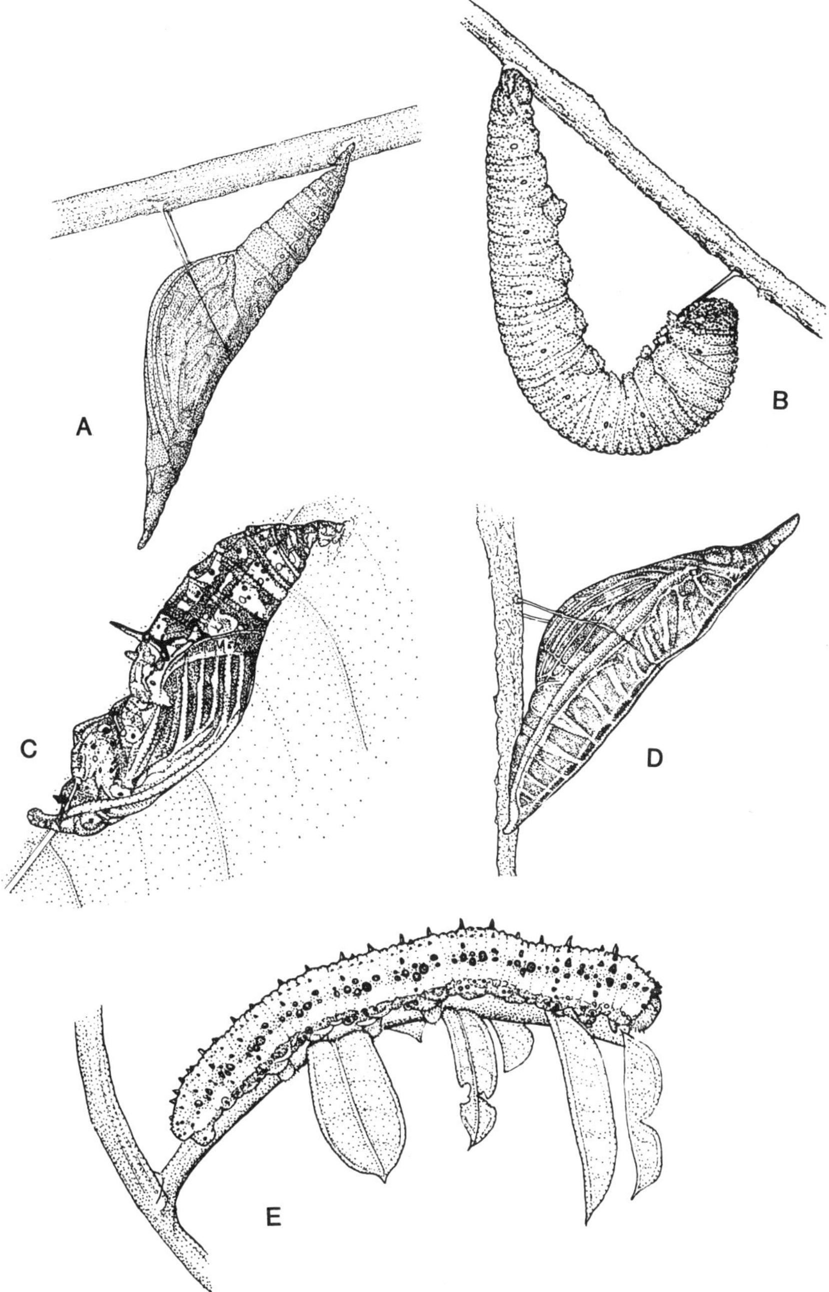

FIGURE 19. Larvae and pupae of the Pieridae. A: *Dismorphia amphiona* pupa; B: *Dismorphia amphiona* prepupal larva; C: *Leptophobia caesia tenuicornis* pupa; D: *Phoebis argante* pupa; E: *Phoebis argante* mature larva (drawings by J. Clark).

tirely in the Neotropics, with the exception of a few species in the Palearctic. They are recognized by the elongate forewing, long narrow antennae (except *Pseudopieris*), and in most species, a resemblance to either an ithomiine or a *Heliconius*. The dismorphiines are, of course, easily separated from their models by having six walking legs. The most recent systematic revision of the subfamily is that of Lamas (1979).

Although the hostplants of most species are unknown, the genus *Inga* (Mimosaceae) is important in Costa Rica. Dismorphiines deposit their eggs singly, and the larvae are dull green and rather similar to those found in the Coliadinae. The pupae resemble a cross between a pupa of a pierine and a coliadinine, with just a hint of a thoracic keel (Fig. 19).

Although the butterflies in this subfamily have engaged the attention of many naturalists, there is remarkably little known about the biology of any species. In Costa Rica the dismorphiines are found from the lowland rain forests to the highest mountains. Some species are endemic to the montane areas of the Talamancas.

Genus **PSEUDOPIERIS** Godman and Salvin, 1889

This genus is best recognized by its short antennae and a wingshape very similar to that of *Leptophobia aripa*. It is considered to be the most primitive genus of the subfamily Dismorphiinae, and is entirely Neotropical in distribution, with one species in Central America and the other in South America. There is nothing known of the early instars of either species. Because *Pseudopieris* may be a key genus to understanding the Dismorphiinae, any information on the early stages would be worth reporting.

Pseudopieris nehemia

(Boisduval, 1836)

FW Length: 24-27 mm **Plate 6**

Range: Mexico to southern Brazil

Hostplant: Unknown

Early stages: Unknown

Adult: Distinguished by the white ground color, short antennae, and a variable black border on the FW apex.

Habits: To date this species has not been collected in Costa Rica, but collections from the Pacific coast of Panama suggest that it will eventually be found in our area. I am informed by G. Small that on the wing it can easily be confused with *Ascia monuste*, both in appearance and flight behavior.

Genus **ENANTIA** Hübner, 1819

This genus is easily recognized by the unusual male wingshape: the forewing is shorter and much narrower than the hindwing. It is distributed from Mexico through Central and South America and probably contains three species. In Costa Rica there are two.

The hostplants and early stages are unknown but they will probably turn out to be similar to those of *Dismorphia*. Although closely related to *Dismorphia*, in Costa Rica, at least, the species do not appear to mimic any distasteful model.

Enantia licinia marion

Godman and Slavin, 1889

FW Length: 25-30 mm **Plate 7**

Range: Mexico to Brazil. **Subspecies:** Mexico to Panama

Hostplant: Unknown

Early stages: Unknown

Adult: Sexes dimorphic. *Male*—distinguished by the black FW apex and underside of HW, with an orange-brown line running from apex to inner margin. *Female*—differs by the blunt FW apex broader black borders.

Habits: Occurs from 50m to 1,200 m on the Atlantic slope, in association with wet forest habitats. I have found it most abundant in the Carrillo Belt. The male flies along forest edges and in light gaps, with a flight not unlike some of the *Eurema* species: fast, zigzag, and close to the ground. Individuals will periodically stop flying and, with wings closed and the forewing set down inside the hindwings, perch on vegetation. In this resting position individuals are very cryptic and can be approached quite closely. When disturbed, the butterfly can escape with an amazingly fast flight. I have observed several males perching on the perimeter of light gaps in the subcanopy, fly about, and return to a different perch in the same light gap. I have never seen the female in nature. The males are encountered as rare solitary individuals, and the species is uncommon in collections.

Enantia melite amalia
(Staudinger, 1884)
FW Length: 22-28 mm **Plate 7**
Range: Mexico to Bolivia, Brazil. **Subspecies:** Nicaragua to Panama
Hostplant: Unknown
Early stages: Unknown
Adult: Sexes dimorphic. *Male*—distinguished by the bright orange upperside with narrow black margins. *Female*—ground color pale yellow, FW black with a short black medial bar, HW without markings.
Habits: Occurs from 500m to 1,600 m in forest habitats. On the Pacific slope this species occurs in all forest types except the Guanacaste deciduous forest in the north. On the Atlantic slope, it is found principally along the Cordillera de Talamanca, and apparently does not go into the lowlands. Both sexes fly along trails, forest edges, and are most often encountered in light gaps. The flight is fast and zigzag, and individuals may fly near the ground or in the subcanopy of the forest. The males perch in the subcanopy along perimeters of light gaps in semibright sunshine, whereas the females are usually found in the forest understory during midday. Usually encountered as solitary individuals. I have found this species to be most common in the much-disturbed Meseta Central in coffee plantations, perhaps a place to look for its hostplant.

Genus **LIEINIX** Gray, 1832

The members of this genus are recognized by the forewing, which is drawn into an acute apex in both sexes, and a glossy sheen on the hindwing underside. The species have been placed in the genera *Dismorphia* and *Acmepteron* in some of the older works on butterflies (see Lamas 1979), and although *Lieinix* is the correct name by priority, I predict that future species lists will exhibit a rich variety of spellings of this genus. The genus is distributed from Mexico through Central and South America, with most species occurring in the mountains of Central America.

The hostplant is known for only one species, which feeds on *Inga* (Mimosaceae) species. The eggs, larvae, and pupae are very similar to those of *Dismorphia*.

In Costa Rica, all species are montane. A few species are endemic to the Cordillera de Talamanca, and some inhabit the highest mountains. Although mimicry is not apparent in museum specimens, when flying in bright sunshine the shiny undersides make the butterflies look like some clear-winged ithomiines.

Lieinix cinerascens
(Salvin, 1871)
FW Length: male 27-32 mm, female 30-33 mm **Plate 7**
Range: Costa Rica and Panama
Hostplant: Unknown
Early stages: Unknown
Adult: Sexes dimorphic. *Male*—distinguished by the black FW with an acute but not falcate apex; HW upperside has pale chalky blue band; HW underside has yellow along anal angle and medial band. See *L. viridifascia*. *Female*—distinguished by the bluntly falcate FW apex. A white unbroken band runs across the FW just outside the cell; the HW upperside is broadly white with narrow black borders. See *L. nemesis*.
Habits: This rare species occurs above 2,500 m along the Cordillera Central and Talamanca. Most specimens in collections are from Volcan Poas, although I have seen some from other high montane localities. The flight is very fast, and individuals dart in and out of the scrubby vegetation associated with volcanic craters and subparamo vegetation in the region of Cerro Chirripo. There is nothing known of adult population biology or early stages, and any such information should be published.

Lieinix viridifascia
(Butler, 1872)
FW Length: 32-35 mm **Plate 7**
Range: Costa Rica and Panama
Hostplant: Unknown
Early Stages: Unknown
Adult: Sexes dimorphic. *Male*—distinguished from *L. cinerascens* by the FW apex, which is elongate and almost falcate; HW upperside has a greenish medial band, HW underside has no yellow. *Female*—FW apex falcate; HW upperside has a restricted whitish medial band, but is not broadly white or yellow. See *L. cinerascens* and L. *nemesis*. According to Lamas (1979), there is a single specimen of this species known from Brazil (*L. christa* [Ressinger]), but there are no other specimens known between Panama and Brazil.
Habits: This rare species is known from the volcanoes in the Meseta Central and a single specimen from the Volcan Chiriqui, perhaps an indication of volcanic endemism. I have never seen this species in nature, and urge that any biological observations be published.

Lieinix nemesis
(Latreille, 1813)
FW Length: 29-39 mm **Plate 7**
Range: Mexico to Venezuela and Peru
Hostplant: *Inga mortoniana, I. densiflora*, other *Inga* spp (Mimosaceae)
Early stages: *Egg*—pale yellow, laid singly on young leaves. *Mature larva*—dark emerald green, including the head capsule; entire body covered with a fine pubescence; each body segment has two to five constrictions. The larvae are extremely cryptic while on the hostplant. *Pupa*—grass green. Wingpads are bowed outward; head is protruded into a tapered cone; venter has pale white diamond shapes along the midline from cremaster to the head; there are two black spots on the venter at the base of the wingpads.
Adult: Sexes dimorphic. *Male*—distinguished by the black FW with pale yellow spots located distal to the cell, and the yellow HW upperside. *Female*—distinguished by the semi-falcate FW apex; FW extracellular band usually broken in two; HW upperside almost entirely pale yellow. See *L. cinerascens*.
Habits: Occurs from 500 to 1800 m on drainages in association with primary and secondary forest habitats, everywhere in Costa Rica except in the Guanacaste dry forest. Encountered as solitary individuals along forest edges, light gaps, and occasionally in open areas in the higher elevations. I have seen this species flying across mountain passes in the Talamancas as well as in coffee plantations on the Pacific drainage during the dry season—an indication of its broad ecological tolerance. The flight is slow and zigzag, which lends to its mimetic resemblance to clear-winged ithomiines. When inactive, both sexes perch on low vegetation or on debris on the ground, with the forewings tucked down inside the hindwings. During cloudy days, or in heavy fog, individuals can be chased from their perches by beating the vegetation. The female will oviposit at any time of the day, provided there is sunshine. This is the most common species of the genus in Central America.

Genus **PATIA** Klots, 1933

Although *Patia* was originally designated by Klots (1933) as a subgenus of *Dismorphia*, I follow Lamas (1979), who elevated it to generic rank and who will define the genus in a future monograph (Lamas, personal communication). In Central America it can be recognized by its large size and bright yellow antennae. There are only three species in the genus, one of which occurs in our area.

There is nothing known of the hostplants or early stages of *Patia* and, judging from the numbers of specimens in museums, it is not commonly collected.

Patia orise sororna
(Butler, 1872)
FW Length: 41-43 mm **Plate 7**
Range: Costa Rica to Bolivia. **Subspecies:** Costa Rica and Panama
Hostplant: Unknown
Early stages: Unknown
Adult: Sexes dimorphic. *Male*—distinguished by the roundly falcate FW; HW bluntly falcate with large shiny white androconial area on upperside. *Female*—FW without falcation, and usually with more orange at the base of the FW. Both sexes are semi-opaque and have the common tiger-striped ithomiine pattern.
Habits: Occurs from sea level to 1,200 m on both drainages in undisturbed rain forest habitats; on the Pacific drainage, restricted to areas above 300 m. Both sexes fly at the subcanopy level in shady, dappled light, and are extremely good mimics of the ithomiine genera *Olyras* and *Eutresis*. The males perch along the perimeters of light gaps with a slow, fluttery flight. I have seen on several occasions individuals visiting the flowers of large *Inga* trees. This species is commonly misidentified in collections as an ithomiine, but it can easily be distinguished by counting the number of walking legs; all pierids have six walking legs. Although this species is somewhat uncommon in collections, I have encountered it in most appropriate forest habitats.

Genus **DISMORPHIA** Hübner, 1816

This diverse genus contains most of the species in the subfamily. These butterflies inspired Henry Bates to write his famous paper on protective mimicry, now called Batesian mimicry. The species of *Dismorphia*, all of which are mimetic, range from Mexico far into the South American forests, and very precisely change their colorations with the changes in coloration of their ithomiine models. For example, in eastern Panama, *D. theucarilla* begins to lose its transparent wings in a transition to the orange subspecies found commonly in Colombia, and looks very different from the Costa Rican populations.

Although this genus is famous for its mimicry and is among the first butterflies that biologists new to the Neotropics want to see, there is nothing known about their adult population biology. This is perhaps because they are usually "good" mimics, being rarer than the models (sensu Brower and Brower 1964). However, the notion that the *Dismorphia* species are all palatable has never been tested, and they may be Müllerian mimics. It is strange that not a single feeding experiment testing their palatability has been performed (but see Haber 1978).

Until recently, hardly any hostplant or early-stage data were known; most of the available early-stage biology has been carried out in Costa Rica. There remains, however, much to do in this respect. In Costa Rica, *Dismorphia* feed on *Inga* (Mimosaceae) species, and certain *Dismorphia* larvae appear restricted more by the plant part than the plant species (DeVries 1985*a*): some are only able to feed on new leaves, others old leaves, but most are not species-specific regarding the hostplant. In general, both the larvae and the pupae are similar to generalized pierids and have no exceptional characteristics (Fig. 19).

Dismorphia eunoe desine

(Hewitson, 1869)

FW Length: male 29-32 mm, female 31-35 mm **Plate 6**

Range: Mexico to Panama. **Subspecies:** Nicaragua and Panama

Hostplant: *Inga* (Mimosaceae) saplings

Early stages: *Egg*—white, elongate, laid singly on saplings. I have not reared the larvae.

Adult: Sexes dimorphic. *Male*—distinguished by the black FW; HW large, with an orange discal half and a prominent white androconial area. *Female*—distinguished by the orange-red HW broken into rays by the black borders.

Habits: Occurs from 600 to 1,900 m usually in association with forest habitats, but also found in coffee plantations in the Meseta Central as well as in experimental conifer plantations. Although I have seen a few ridges in the Carrillo Belt with up to five males in the same light gap, this species is usually encountered along trails and in light gaps in the forest as solitary individuals. The males perch and patrol light gaps in the morning. The perches range from five to fifteen meters above the ground and usually there is a single male per light gap. Some light gaps in Carrillo have had males using them every time I visited over a span of several years. This may indicate that light gap quality plays a part in male displays. The females oviposit around midday and are found flying in the understory. Both sexes have a characteristic slow and lazy flight and, when flying, they resemble *Mechanitis* in pattern, flight behavior, and microhabitat preference.

Dismorphia crisia lubina

Butler, 1872

FW Length: 27-32 mm **Plate 6**

Range: Southern Mexico to Brazil. **Subspecies:** Costa Rica and Panama

Hostplant: *Inga, Pithecellobium brenesii* (Mimosaceae)

Early stages: *Egg*—white, spindle-shaped, laid singly on underside of leaves. Hostplants range from saplings to mature trees. *Mature larva*—dark translucent green, body constricted by many fine rings; last segment lighter green than the rest of the body; head capsule green, sparsely covered with many fine dark granulations and short hairs; dorsum of head has a white line. *Pupa*—grass green with head tapered to a point; dorsum with faint rectangular patches of powdery white, especially on the abdomen; two dark spots on the first abdominal segment near the wingpads.

Adult: Sexes dimorphic. *Male*—distinguished the acute FW apex and the white discal patch on the HW upperside. *Female*—distinguished by the blunt FW apex that has an excavated distal margin. Distinguished from *D. zaela oreas* by the white on the HW upperside and the notch on the FW. See *D. zaela oreas*.

Habits: Occurs from 1,000 to 2,000 m in cloud forest. Found along trails, forest edges, and in light gaps, usually as solitary individuals. The males perch in light gaps and patrol these areas during the morning. The females fly in the understory and are most active from midday to early afternoon. Both sexes visit flowers of *Inga* and various Asteraceae at forest edges and in the canopy. Although present in virtually all cloud forest habitats, the species is met with infrequently unless individuals are started from vegetation.

Dismorphia lua costaricensis

(Schaus, 1913)

FW Length: 31 mm **Plate 6**

Range: Costa Rica to Bolivia. **Subspecies:** Costa Rica

Hostplant: Unknown

Early stages: Unknown

Adult: Sexes dimorphic. Costa Rican female

unknown. Male—distinguished by the narrow black FW; HW large and triangular with a chalky yellow band posterior to cell; HW underside yellow with brown irrorations. *Note*: the specimen figured here is from Colombia. The type is in the Natural History Museum, Washington, D.C., and illustrated in Schaus (1913).

Habits: The solitary specimen known of this subspecies came from Cachi, which at the time of its collection was an area of extensive forest. It is conceivable that this species may be restricted to the area in the Reventazon valley called Tapanti. Any records or notes taken on this species should be published.

Dismorphia zaela oreas

(Salvin, 1871)

FW Length: 29-31 mm **Plate 7**

Range: Costa Rica to Ecuador. **Subspecies:** Costa Rica and Panama

Hostplant: *Inga pittieri*, other *Inga* spp (Mimosaceae)

Early stages: (Young 1972*d*, as *D. virgo.*) *Egg*—white, turning blue-green, laid singly on underside of leaves. *Mature larva*—body dark green covered in a short red pile; spiracles bordered in red; head capsule gray-green. *Pupa*—similar to that described for *D. crisia lubina* but without the dark spots. *Note*: Young (1972*d*) described the life cycle under the misidentification *D. virgo*.

Adult: Sexes dimorphic. *Male*—distinguished by the lemon-yellow discal bar on the FW and white on the HW upperside. *Female*—distinguished by the pale yellow on the upperside. See *D. crisia lubina*.

Habits: Occurs from 500 to 1,000 m on the Atlantic drainage in association with the Carrillo Belt, always in forest. Males are active in light gaps during the morning, females are active and oviposit throughout the day, provided there is sunshine. Both sexes visit fowers of *Inga* and *Calliandra arborea*. Although this species is uncommon in collections and usually encountered as solitary individuals, it can be quite common in the steep ravine forests in Parque Carrillo throughout the entire year.

Dismorphia zathoe pallidula

Butler and Druce, 1874

FW Length: 22-25 mm **Plate 7**

Range: Costa Rica to Ecuador. **Subspecies:** Costa Rica and Panama

Hostplant: *Inga densiflora*, other *Inga* spp (Mimosaceae)

Early stages: *Egg*—white, laid singly on sapling plants. *Mature larva*—similar to that described for *D. zaela oreas*, but much smaller. The larvae feed on the new leaves. *Pupa*—similar to that of *D. zaela oreas* but smaller.

Adult: Sexes dimorphic. *Male*—distinguished by the small size and narrow black FW. *Female*—distinguished by the small size and rounded HW. In some specimens there may be a blush of yellow on the HW upperside.

Habits: Occurs from 700 to 1,900 m on both drainages in cloud forest habitats; very common on the Atlantic side. Encountered along trails, road cuts and water courses, it flies low to the ground and winds in and out of the vegetation. This species flies more like a typical pierid, with a rather fast, nonmimetic flight. Both sexes visit flowers of Asteraceae and *Lantana*. Although not an obvious mimic, in dim light it resembles a clear-winged ithomiine.

Dismorphia amphiona praxinoe

(Doubleday, 1844)

FW Length: male 30-35 mm, female 35-40 mm **Plate 6**

Range: Mexico through South America. **Subspecies:** Mexico to Colombia

Hostplant: *Inga sapindoides*, *I. densiflora*, other *Inga* spp (Mimosaceae)

Early stages: *Egg*—yellow, laid singly on all leaves. *Mature larva*—similar to those described for *D. crisia lubina*. *Pupa*—similar to that described for *D. crisia lubina*. The larvae usually feed on old leaves, and the hostplant is usually a sapling in the forest understory (Fig. 19).

Adult: Sexes dimorphic, but both are distinguished by the tiger-striped pattern without heavy black borders on the HW.

Habits: Occurs from sea level to 1,200 m on both drainages, in association with all forested areas except the Guanacaste dry forest. Encountered as solitary individuals within or along the edges of forest. This common species is one of the more spectacular mimics of the ithomiines *Mechanitis* and *Hypothyris*.

Dismorphia theucharila fortunata

(Lucas, 1854)

FW Length: 25-27 mm **Plate 7**

Range: Mexico to Brazil. **Subspecies:** Mexico to Panama

Hostplant: Unknown

Early stages: Unknown

Adult: Sexes dimorphic. This is the only clear-winged pierid in Central America; the male has a narrower FW than the female. Remember that all pierids have six walking legs, ithomiines only four.

Habits: Occurs from sea level to 1,600 m, on both drainages in wet forest habitats. Encountered along trails, light gaps, and water courses, where it flies slowly in the dappled light. The mimetic resemblance of this species to the clear-winged ithomiines is one of the most astonishing examples of mimicry. The mimetic precision includes coloration, habitat, flight behavior, and I have found aggregations of this species in the forest understory that looked like an ithomiine lek. This species is often placed in collections with ithomiines and misidentified in published photographs. Although not uncommon, this species is seldom, if ever, abundant in any habitat, even though it is usually present throughout the year. In eastern Panama, this species begins to gain some orange coloration on the HW in the transition zone to the entirely orange subspecies *siloe* (Hewitson) of Colombia.

Subfamily **PIERINAE**

The largest number of pierid species belong to this cosmopolitan subfamily, which has extensive radiations in the tropics but is also well represented in all temperate regions. In temperate areas the butterflies are commonly known as whites, orange-tips, or cabbage butterflies. In parts of the Old World tropics the genus *Delias* are known as jezebels. The Neotropical region has almost no established common names for our pierine species. The butterflies in the Pierinae are recognized by their long antennae, well developed palpi, and characteristics of the venation and the integument (see Ehrlich 1958*a*). The systematics of this subfamily were treated by Klots (1933), and his system is followed here.

A great diversity of hostplants have been reported for the New World Pierinae. The plant families of importance to the Neotropical fauna are the Capparidaceae, Brassicaceae, Tropaeolaceae, Loranthaceae, and in one instance, the Euphorbiaceae. In North America, the hostplants include Pinaceae, Papilionaceae, and perhaps Batidaceae and Asteraceae. A number of these plant families are potential sources for chemical defense. Depending upon the species, the eggs may be laid singly or in clusters, and the larvae may be solitary or gregarious. The larvae of the Pierinae range from uniformly green or reddish to some that are quite colorful and polymorphic. Although generally the bodies are unadorned and appear naked, some genera (such as *Catasticta*) have long hairs. The pupae are tapered at either end and bear two short spikes on the head. Depending on the species, the larvae may pupate as solitary individuals or in gregarious groups, and may be positioned vertically or on a horizontal surface (Fig. 19).

Some of the Old World groups (such as *Delias* and *Pieris*) have been demonstrated to be distasteful to vertebrate predators (Brower 1984), and it is clear that some of the Costa Rican species are distasteful, as well. In a series of experiments with captive jacamars (birds known to feed on butterflies) the pierine genera *Ascia, Melete,* and *Perrhybris* have been repeatedly rejected (Chai 1985). These results suggest that there is a lot more to be learned and incorporated into mimicry theory than was previously thought. For example, it is possible that many of the bright color patterns of pierines may in fact represent aposematic coloration, and that those species thought to be Batesian mimics may in fact be part of Müllerian mimicry complexes. While it is unknown what chemicals impart the nasty tastes that certain pierine species clearly possess, *Pieris* species appear to gain some of their unpalatability from carotenoids and mustard oils (Rothschild 1972).

In Costa Rica representatives of the Pierinae are found from sea level to the highest mountains, and occur in all habitat types. Our fauna is composed of some widespread species, a large number of Central American species, and includes some species that are endemic to the Cordillera de Talamanca.

Genus **HESPEROCHARIS** Felder, 1862

The butterflies in this genus are medium sized, white or yellow, with short antennae (which recall the Coliadinae) and a hairy thorax. There are ten species in the genus, with the greatest diversity in South America. Three species occur in Costa Rica, and all inhabit montane areas.

There is little known about any aspect of the biology of *Hesperocharis*. In Costa Rica these butterflies are seldom encountered, and our fauna is composed of wide-ranging Central American species. One of our species feeds as a larva on Loranthaceae and its early stages resemble those of *Catasticta*.

Hesperocharis graphites
Bates, 1864
FW Length: 32-34 mm **Plate 7**
Range: Mexico to Panama
Hostplant: Unknown
Early stages: Unknown
Adult: Distinguished by the scalloped HW margin and the thin black marbling on the HW underside; FW underside may have orange-yellow in cell, but it is variable.
Habits: Occurs locally in small populations in forest, above 1,700 m on both slopes. Usually encountered along road cuts and water courses together with *Catasticta*, for which they are distinguished on the wing by their fast and swooping flight. Both sexes visit flowers of *Cavendishia* (Ericaceae) and *Rubus* (Rosaceae) and, while feeding, are motionless and very cryptic. Although uncommon in collections, this species can be abundant in rain shadow valleys on the Pacific slope of the Talamancas.

Hesperocharis crocea
Bates, 1866
FW Length: 31-33 mm **Plate 7**
Range: Mexico to Panama
Hostplant: *Struthantus* (Loranthaceae)
Early stages: *Mature larva*—head capsule black; body dull maroon, covered in a fine white pile. The larvae are gregarious feeders with about ten individuals in each group. They may pupate in clusters on the trunk of the tree upon which the hostplant grows. *Pupa*—mottled green, white and brown, resembling a bird dropping. In color and shape very similar to *Catasticta*.
Adult: Sexes mildly dimorphic. *Male*—upperside an almost uniform yellow. *Female*—orange on upperside, especially on the HW. Both sexes are immediately distinguished by the small purple spots on the HW underside.
Habits: Occurs from 700 to 1,200 m on both slopes, in disturbed habitats. I have found this species only in the Meseta Central, where it is not uncommon to see solitary individuals flying in the streets of San José or perched on the sides of buildings. While they are flying they remind one of an orange nymphalid rather than a pierid.

Hesperocharis costaricensis
Bates, 1866
FW Length: 25-27 mm **Plate 7**
Range: Nicaragua to Panama
Hostplant: Unknown
Early stages: Unknown
Adult: Distinguished by the faint gray marbling on the underside of both sexes.
Habits: This rare species is known from 1,200 to 2,000 m in Costa Rica, principally along the Cordillera de Talamanca and Cordillera Central. It flies low to the ground across open areas and, while on the wing, strongly resembles *Ascia monuste*. I have seen this species in nature only once, and suspect that its rarity in collections is due to its looking very much like the common white pierid species that inhabit open areas.

Genus **ARCHONIAS** Hübner, 1825

The butterflies in this genus all bear a mimetic resemblance to female *Parides*, *Heliconius*, or tiger-striped ithomiines. The butterflies are recognized by their small size, six walking legs, flattened antennal club, and the slightly scalloped hindwing margin. In some literature, two of the species in *Archonias* were placed under the generic name *Charonias*, although this is usually treated as a synonym. There are five species in *Archonias*, two of which occur in Costa Rica.

The early stages have never been described, but the larva of one South American species is reported to feed on Loranthaceae (Ehrlich and Raven 1965). In Costa Rica both our species occur in mid-elevational rain forest habitats in local populations. In general, little is known about the population biology of the adults. The most extensive observations made on the genus are those of Gilbert (1969*a*), made at San Vito, Costa Rica.

Archonias tereas approximata
Butler, 1873
FW Length: 31-33 mm **Plate 7**
Range: Mexico to Brazil. **Subspecies:** Costa Rica and Panama
Hostplant: Unknown
Early stages: Unknown
Adult: Recognized by resemblance to a miniature *Parides* female. The female has more white on the FW and more red on the HW than the male.
Habits: Occurs in local populations from 300 to 1,000 m on both slopes, in association with forest habitats. Most frequently seen along rivers and streams. The males perch and patrol areas in the morning and are faithful to the same perch from day to day (Gilbert 1969*a*). By midmorning, individuals are seldom seen. Both sexes visit flowers of various Asteraceae that occur along riparian edges. It has been

my experience that this species is intolerant of second-growth forest and requires large areas of forest.

Archonias eurytele

Hewitson, 1852

FW Length: 35-38 mm **Plate 7**

Range: Guatemala to Colombia

Hostplant: Unknown

Early stages: Unknown

Adult: Distinguished by its resemblance to a miniature *Lycorea* or *Melinaea*, without the HW bar. There is usually a round black spot at the distal end of the FW cell. *Note*: There have been many subspecific and aberrational names applied to this species. However, judging from the variety of individuals I have seen in the field, it seems pointless to maintain a multitude of names for them.

Habits: This rare species occurs from 300 to 1,000 m, on both slopes, in association with rain forest habitats. It flies along trails and in the forest understory, and has a slow wing beat similar to that of some ithomiines. Due to this precise mimetic resemblance, it is most frequently collected by accident. The males perch in small light gaps about three meters above the ground, and patrol the light gap during the mornings with a jerky spiraling flight. I once collected an individual visiting flowers of an undetermined Asteraceae.

Genus **MELETE** Swainson, 1832

The butterflies in this genus are recognized by their slightly excavated forewing margin, a black bar that runs through the forewing cell, and their long antennae. The synonym *Daptonoura* has been applied to this genus in some literature, and the reader should be aware of this. The relationship of *Melete* within the Pieridae is uncertain, and hence its placement within a systemic list of genera is arbitrary. According to Klots (1933), the genitalia of *Melete* are very distinct and should be used in revisionary studies, which are badly needed because of the apparent color polymorphisms of most of the species. The genus ranges from Texas throughout Central and South America, where the greatest number of species occur, and there are a few species in the West Indies. Only two species occur in Costa Rica, and they are not difficult to separate.

The larvae have been reported to be Loranthaceae (Ehrlich and Raven 1965), but there are no published descriptions of the early stages.

In Costa Rica, I have had little experience with *Melete*, but have found individuals flying from the interior of rain forests to open pastures. One species that occurs in Guanacaste (*M. isandra*) has, in certain years, large population explosions soon after the start of the rainy season. The individuals remained in the habitat only for a few weeks and then disappeared, suggesting that *Melete* may be migratory.

Melete florinda

(Butler, 1875)

FW Length: 29-33 mm **Plate 10**

Range: Costa Rica to Colombia

Hostplant: Unknown

Early stages: Unknown

Adult: Sexes dimorphic. *Male*—distinguished by the clear yellow ground color; narrow black FW apex and margins; black bar in FW cell, best viewed from underside. *Female*—darker yellow-orange with bolder black markings.

Habits: Occurs as uncommon, solitary individuals from 500 to 1,500 m on both slopes, in association with montane rain forest. Flies along forest edges or in light gaps, sometimes in the subcanopy. I have found this species most common along ridges in Parque Carrillo during February and March. Uncommon in Costa Rican collections.

Melete isandra

(Boisduval, 1836)

FW Length: 28-31 mm **Plate 10**

Range: Mexico to Costa Rica

Hostplant: Unknown

Early stages: Unknown

Adult: Two morphs, either white or yellow. Distinguished by the elongate FW apex and the lack of black wing margins; black bar in the FW cell faint.

Habits: I have only seen this species, which occurs on the Pacific slope, from sea level to about 500 m. In Guanacaste both color morphs fly together and may be found from forest to open habitats. In Parque Corcovado the males patrol forest edges during sunny mornings. An individual will fly along the interface of the forest and open areas for quite some distance (100 m) and then reverse direction and fly back. This patrol lasts until late morning and, although an individual may interact with other males "on patrol," these butterflies invariably fly between two and eight meters from the ground. While patrolling, individuals do not stop to feed.

Genus **LEODONTA** Butler, 1870

The butterflies in this genus are immediately recognized by their distinctive wing shape and color pattern. The genus is closely related to *Pereute* and *Catasticta*, and bears a strong resemblance to the latter in coloration. *Leodonta* ranges from Mexico throughout Central and South America, and is found only in montane habitats. It is unknown how many species there are in *Leodonta*, but it seems likely that there is only one in Central America.

The life history has not been reported for any species, but its relationships to *Catasticta*, general habits, and the large quantities of eggs that can be extracted from females suggest that the Loranthaceae would be a likely place to look for early stages.

In Costa Rica the butterflies are found in virtually all cloud forest habitats, where they can be locally abundant. The butterflies are strong, agile fliers, which makes them difficult to capture.

Leodonta dysoni

(Doubleday, 1847)

FW Length: 25-33 mm **Plate 11**

Range: Costa Rica to Peru

Hostplant: Unknown

Early stages: Unknown

Adult: Distinguished by the white ground color, broad black margins, and short tail on HW margin. The female may have some yellow on the HW discal area.

Habits: Occurs from 900 to 2,800 m, on both slopes, in association with forest habitats. Individuals are commonly encountered along streams and light gaps, flying about five to ten meters above the ground, twisting in and out of the understory vegetation of the subcanopy of the forest. Males perch in light gaps in the subcanopy, and chase other butterflies for long distances through the forest, only to return to the same perch. Both sexes visit flowers of *Cephaelus, Fuschia, Eupatorium,* and *Calliandra* in the forest canopy, understory, or along edges. The most active period of flower feeding occurs during the morning. This species often flies in association with *Catasticta sisamnus*, and the two species closely resemble each other while flying.

Genus **PEREUTE** Herrich-Schaeffer, 1867

The butterflies in this genus are easily recognized by their distinctive black ground color and red or yellow forewing bands. The genus ranges from Mexico to South America, and most species occur in the Andes. In Costa Rica there are two species, both of which are montane. The genus is closely related to *Archonias, Leodonta,* and *Catasticta*. Together these genera form the Neotropical counterpart of the diverse Old World genus *Delias*.

The hostplants of *Pereute* are in the Loranthaceae, and the early stages closely resemble those of *Catasticta*. The larvae are gregarious, and the pupae are found in aggregations on tree trunks where the hostplants are epiphytic parasites.

Most of the species in *Pereute*, especially those in South America, are considered mimics of *Heliconius* butterflies. In Central America, however, there are no suitable *Heliconius* models. In Costa Rica, both species are conspicuous and slow flying, and it seems plausible that *Pereute* have distasteful properties and that their color patterns are convergent upon an established aposematic signal. Old World *Delias* are demonstrated to be unpalatable and warningly colored. This may be the case for some New World pierids, as well. As far as I am aware, there have been no experiments to test the palatability of any montane genus of New World pierid (but see Haber 1978). However, I once observed at Las Alturas an individual streaked flycatcher (*Myiodynastes macutales*: Tyranidae) attack and eat an ovipositing *Pereute charops*.

Pereute charops

(Boisduval, 1836)

FW Length: male 36-40 mm, female 39-42 mm **Plate 11**

Range: Mexico to Peru. **Subspecies:** Mexico to Panama

Hostplant: Loranthaceae

Early stages: I have seen ovipositing females lay large clusters of yellow eggs on, and gregarious larvae feeding upon, the leaves of an undetermined Loranthaceae. The pupae are black and dingy yellow, resembling a bird dropping (much like *Catasticta*).

Adult: Sexes dimorphic. *Male*—upperside washed with gray; underside black with a yellow FW bar; yellow on HW costal margin at least as long as the cell. *Female*—ground color on both sides black with a red medial band on the FW. The antennae of both sexes are white. See *P. cheops*.

Habits: Occurs from 1,200 to 2,200 m in local populations associated with Pacific slope forest habitats. I have not seen specimens from the Atlantic slope, but the species will undoubtedly be found there eventually. This species flies at canopy level with a characteristic flutter-sail behavior that is very conspicuous. In the mornings, males perch in the canopy along the forest edges or in light gaps, and patrol a territory in long, circling flights. Aerial confrontations between males with adjacent territories are frequent and often result in long chases. After the chase, the resident returns to the same area and begins its circling flight again. This lasts until midday. The females are active from morning to midday, when oviposition starts. While ovipositing, the female folds her wings, hangs on the underside of the leaf, and lays a large "mound" of eggs. During this time she may be interrupted by a male that will try to copulate with her. This species is most abundant during the dry season, and is often seen in the streets of San José. Both sexes feed on flowers of *Fuschia arborescens* and *Eupatorium* and other Asteraceae.

Pereute cheops

Staudinger, 1887

FW Length: 33-38 mm **Plate 11**

Range: Costa Rica and Panama

Hostplant: *Antidaphne viscoides* (Loranthaceae)

Early stages: *Egg*—bright yellow, laid in clusters of 20 to 40. The first instar larvae are translucent green with black head capsules, and slightly hairy. The larvae feed gregariously.

Adult: Sexes dimorphic. *Male*—similar to *P. charops* but with indistinct yellow FW band. *Female*—similar to *P. charops*. This species is easily distinguished from *P. charops* by having yellow antennae, a yellow band on the HW costa shorter than the cell, and a number of red dots at the base of the wings.

Habits: This species is known only from two localities in Costa Rica, Copey and Las Alturas, both of which are Pacific slope rain shadow valleys. Historically, this species is rare and is considered an endemic of the Talamanca-Chiriqui habitats. It is likely that *P. cheops* will be found near the Meseta Central, and that it has been overlooked because of its similarity to *P. charops*. The males fly very high over the forest canopy and patrol a territory whose borders may consist of one to four tree canopies; a male will sequentially fly from one canopy, to another, to another, and so on. The patrol flight is a long, gliding circle with little fluttering of wings. A territory owner engages in dogfights with other males, and at this time the flight can be extremely rapid. The winner of the "dogfight" patrols the territory and the loser retreats into the distance. I have seen some individual males patrol a set of treetops for several hours without ever appearing to settle for a rest. The females fly at the subcanopy level, amid the vegetation, from late morning until early afternoon.

Genus **CATASTICTA** Butler, 1870

The butterflies in this genus are recognized by their checkered color patterns, of which white, yellow, and black predominate in the Central American species. *Catasticta* ranges from Mexico through Central and South America, reaching its greatest diversity in the Andes; there are over one hundred species. *Catasticta* is closely related to the Old World genus *Delias*, which also shows both a high species diversity and hostplant relationships with the Loranthaceae. It is surprising that there has not been a biogeographic study examining these two genera in the context of continental drift and speciation events. Although *Catasticta* contains numerous species that can be very confusing (see D'Abrera 1981), there are, for the most part, few problems to be encountered in identifying the Central American species.

The hostplants of *Catasticta*, as far as is known, are all in the Loranthaceae. The larvae are typical of the Pierinae except that they bear long hairs along the body and are highly gregarious (like the larvae of the genus *Delias* in the Old World). If molested, the gregarious larvae react as a unit by rearing their heads and regurgitating a green fluid, which they will smear on the offending stimulus. The pupae are typically pierine and resemble bird droppings. I have found the pupae in gregarious masses on tree trunks, on the undersides of leaves, or nestled in moss or lichen at the base of trees—another similarity to *Delias*. Due to this behavior of pupating on tree trunks, field workers should be careful not to mistake the tree for the hostplant (see DeVries 1982, 1983).

Like most, if not all, pierids, the butterflies in this genus are frequently observed visiting flowers and, in the case of the males, wet sand.

However, the males of *Catasticta* have a peculiar behavior that I have not seen in any other genus (see also P. Hahnel in Seitz 1913, vol. 5). The males fly very close to the surface of streams or the shallows of rivers and literally land in the water. If an individual cannot get a foothold on a stone or other bit of debris and is washed into the water, it flutters out and repeats the process. When an individual butterfly eventually gets a foothold (with its legs and sometimes even the body submerged) the proboscis is uncoiled and it begins to pump water through its system, jetting drops out of its anus much like some of the Papilionidae (see *Eurytides*). In Costa Rica this behavior is observed mostly in *C. theresa*, but occurs in other species as well. Incredible as this behavior seems, along mountain streams in the Talamancas one may encounter up to one hundred individuals of various species lined up on the river sides like so many four-winged ducks.

In Costa Rica, the genus *Catasticta* occurs from middle to high elevations, with most of the species occurring above 1,500 m. Some species show endemism to the Cordillera de Talamanca of Costa Rica and Panama, but most of our fauna is composed of widespread Central or South American species. The males of all species perch and patrol areas for mates at certain times of day. Additionally, the males of different species appear to perch at different levels above the ground. Some of our species appear to be restricted with respect to elevation. For example, *C. cerberus* occurs only on the highest mountain tops, never below 2,500 m. Although mimicry plays a much greater part among the South American species, we have one clear example of *Catasticta* mimicking a distasteful species (*C. strigosa actinotis*).

Although the genus has always been very popular with collectors, and may occur in abundance in many areas, there is very little known about the biology of any *Catasticta*. With its great species diversity and behavioral peculiarities, I would suggest that studies on the population biology of this genus would prove to be extremely rewarding to anyone willing to do the field work.

Catasticta nimbice bryson

Godman and Salvin, 1889

FW Length: 25-29 mm **Plate 11**

Range: Mexico to Panama. **Subspecies:** Costa Rica and Panama

Hostplant: *Struthantus* (Loranthaceae)

Early stages: *Mature larva*—dull red-brown with black granulations and short hairs; black head capsule. The larvae feed gregariously. *Pupa*—dull cream and black with a prominent ridge along the thorax and abdomen; overall, the pupa resembles a bird dropping.

Adult: Distinguished by the straw-yellow ground color and brown wing margins. The brown markings on the female are more pronounced. See *C. theresa*.

Habits: This common species occurs from 1,000 to 2,500 m on both slopes, in association with primary and secondary forest. Individuals are commonly seen along forest edges and streams, and at times in the streets of San José. The males perch in light gaps during the mornings, and wildly chase passing butterflies and engage in swirling dogfights that may spiral over the top of the forest canopy. Both sexes visit flowers of *Fuchsia, Lantana*, and *Senecio*. At times this species can be exceedingly common, especially during the dry seasons.

Catasticta theresa

Butler, 1874

FW Length: 20-22 mm **Plate 11**

Range: Costa Rica and Panama

Hostplant: *Antidaphne viscoides* (Loranthaceae)

Early stages: *Egg*—bright orange-yellow, laid in clusters of thirty or more on the underside of leaves. *Mature larva*—ranges from dull green to greenish brown, somewhat hairy; black head capsule. Larvae are gregarious feeders. *Pupa*—black and white, resembling a bird dropping. Pupae are usually found in small clusters.

Adult: Distinguished by the small size and yellow-orange ground color; both the FW costa and FW margin have a slight indentation. See *C. nimbice*.

Habits: Occurs locally from 1,500 to 2,600 m on both slopes, in montane oak forest habitats. Males are invariably encountered near rivers and streams, where they fly along just above the surface of a shallow and dip down into the water. After repeating this behavior several times, individuals eventually sit on rocks that are just submerged below the surface of the water, drink and jet water out of the anus. Of all the *Catasticta* species in Costa Rica, this is the one most frequently observed attempting to be aquatic. Females oviposit during midday when meandering about the canopies of *Alnus costaricensis* (Betulaceae), where the hostplant frequently grows. Both sexes visit flowers of *Senecio megaphylla* and *Fuchsia arborea*. Usually encountered as solitary individuals, but occasionally locally abundant.

Catasticta flisa

(Herrich-Schaffer, 1854)

FW Length: 27-30 mm **Plate 11**

Range: Mexico to Colombia

Hostplant: Unknown

Early stages: Unknown

Adult: Distinguished by the black ground color, and a narrow white medial band that traverses both wings. FW apex is elongate; HW inner margin often has a small patch of yellow (especially in female). This species is variable.

Habits: Occurs from 1,000 to 2,500 m in association with wet forest habitats throughout the country. The males perch in the subcanopy of the forest along trails and light gaps during the morning. During perching times they engage in long chases with other butterflies. In the Talamancan forests of Las Alturas, I once heard the fighting males before I ever saw them. A pair descended from about twenty feet above the ground, furiously beating their wings together in a tight spiral until both had landed on the ground. Upon ground contact, one male flew straight up to the treetop from which the pair had come, and perched. Seconds later the other flew off the ground and up and away. The sound the two created while beating each other with their wings was like fluttering one's tongue while passing a stream of air across the teeth. I assume that the winner of the bout went back to the perch while the loser left the area. Both sexes visit flowers of *Hamelia, Fuchsia, Psychotria*, and some Asteraceae. This species is at times local, but in the proper habitat it can be very abundant.

Catasticta teutila flavomaculata

Lathy and Rosenberg, 1912

FW Length: 27-31 mm **Plate 11**

Range: Mexico to Colombia. **Subspecies:** Costa Rica and Panama

Hostplant: *Dendropthora costaricensis* (Loranthaceae)

Early stages: *Egg*—yellow, laid in clusters of ten to one hundred. Larvae are gregarious in feeding, defensive behavior (regurgitation), and molting. *Mature larva*—head capsule shiny black; ventrum, anal segment, and legs black; ground color pea green mottled with tiny flecks of brown, with a black dorsal midline; entire body covered with soft green and white hairs. *Pupa*—mottled black, green, and white; five raised plates on dorsum on abdomen, another large plate on thorax. In overall appearance, the pupa resembles a bird dropping. Pupation occurs on treetrunks, leaves, and lichens.

Adult: Sexes dimorphic. *Male*—black above with a fine white transverse band running from FW costa to HW inner margin; orange-yellow on the HW margin of underside. *Female*—black above with a bright orange medial band; orange on HW margin of underside. See *C. flisa*.

Habits: Occurs from 800 to 3,000 m, on both slopes, in association with montane oak and other cloud forest habitats. This species has the broadest elevational distribution of any *Catasticta* species in Costa Rica. It flies along forest edges, forest canopy, or in open areas, with a conspicuous fluttery flight. Males perch in the morning along forest edges, and at times the air can be swirling with many dogfights between rival males and males courting females. The females are commonly seen flying around the tops of isolated trees in pastures and along forest edges, and will oviposit at any time of the day while there is sunshine. Both sexes visit a wide variety of flowers, including those of canopy trees. This species is the commonest *Catasticta* in Costa Rica, and at times it can be extremely abundant.

Catasticta cerberus

Godman and Salvin, 1889

FW Length: 26-28 mm **Plate 11**

Range: Costa Rica and Panama

Hostplant: Unknown

Early stages: Unknown

Adult: Distinguished by black margins and broad white band traversing both wings on the upperside; underside has very little yellow. See *C. flisa*.

Habits: This species appears to be restricted to elevations above 2,500 m in the Cordillera de Talamanca and Cordillera Central. It flies at the summits of mountain tops, at canopy level or through bamboo thickets. The flight is fluttery and erratic, and individuals are most active in the early mornings, about two hours after sunrise. Both sexes bask in bright sunlight to warm up before flying. Males perch in canopy trees and wildly chase passing butterflies and hummingbirds. The females appear most active in late morning, when they can be seen fluttering at the tops of trees. Both sexes visit flowers of *Eupatorium, Senecio*, and *Fuchsia*. This endemic Talamancan species is most common during the dry season of February-April and is rare in Costa Rican collections.

Catasticta strigosa actinotis
(Butler, 1872)

FW Length: 27-31 mm **Plate 11**

Range: Costa Rica, Panama, Peru, and Ecuador. **Subspecies:** Costa Rica and Panama

Hostplant: Unknown

Early stages: Unknown

Adult: Sexes dimorphic. *Male*—distinguished by the dirty gray, striated upperside. *Female*—black ground color with a yellow patch on the FW discal area. *Note*: As pointed out by D'Abrera (1981), there is confusion concerning the correct species name of this insect. It is unclear whether it is *modesta* or *strigosa*, and it is even less clear why this insect has such a patchy distribution. Apparently both species names represent insects with the same geographical range.

Habits: Occurs very locally, from 1,400 to 2,300 m in montane forest along the Cordillera de Talamanca and Cordillera Central. I have found this species mostly in rain shadow valleys (Copey and Las Alturas) where the forest is drier than the surrounding areas. In contrast to other Costa Rican *Catasticta* species, the males perch low in the forest understory, about three to four meters above the ground. Perching and patrolling activities begin early in the morning, and then the butterflies appear to vanish at midday. The females fly slowly along trails and in the shady understory, and resemble *Actinote leucomelas* while on the wing. Both sexes visit flowers of *Fuchsia* and *Cephaelus*. The females are uncommon in collections.

Catasticta prioneris hegemon
Godman and Salvin, 1889

FW Length: 24-30 mm **Plate 11**

Range: Costa Rica to Peru. **Subspecies:** Costa Rica and Panama

Hostplant: Unknown

Early stages: Unknown

Adult: Distinguished from *C. sisamnus* by the narrower black HW margin; small white spot in FW cell; more extensive white on upperside, not sharply delimiting the black margins; yellow spots on underside of the FW and HW discal areas. See *C. sisamnus*.

Habits: Occurs commonly from 1,000 to 2,500 m, in association with wet forest habitats. Often found flying with *C. sisamnus*, especially in the Cordillera Central and Cordillera de Tilaran, where both species can be extremely abundant. Like many of the species in the genus, it is most frequently seen flying in light gaps at the canopy and subcanopy levels.

Catasticta sisamnus sisamnus
(Fabricius, 1793)

FW Length: 28-30 mm **Plate 11**

Range: Honduras to Bolivia. **Subspecies:** Honduras to Venezuela

Hostplant: Unknown

Early stages: Unknown

Adult: Sexes dimorphic. *Male*—distinguished from *C. prioneris* by wide black wing margins that are roundly curved at the interface of the white discal band, especially on the HW; underside has little yellow. *Female*—discal bands are yellow. See *C. prioneris*.

Habits: Occurs commonly from 1,200 to 2,500 m on both slopes, in association with wet forest habitats. The habits of this species are very similar to those described under *C. prioneris*.

Genus **APPIAS** Hübner, 1816

This pantropical genus is represented in Costa Rica by a single species, characterized by two tufts of androconial hairs on the ventral side of the male claspers. The female is recognized by a highly characteristic coloration, and cannot be confused with anything else in Central America.

The hostplants for the genus are Capparidaceae, Brassicaceae, and in some areas Euphorbiaceae. In Costa Rica the genus is found in agricultural and other disturbed areas.

Apparently all species are extremely fast flying, and most are known to migrate. The males form aggregations on damp ground and at times can be extremely common at lower elevations.

Appias drusilla
(Cramer, 1777)

FW Length: 29-34 mm **Plate 12**

Range: Throughout southern United States, Central and South America, and the West Indies

Hostplant: Various Capparidaceae, cultivated Brassicaceae, and *Drypetes* (Euphorbiaceae)

Early stages: *Mature larva*—dark green ground color with lighter grayish green sides and a narrow white lateral line; many granulations on dorsum, which are mostly yellow; yellow-green head capsule.

Adult: Sexes dimorphic. *Male*—upperside entirely pure white, underside shiny. *Female*—two forms: one similar to the male, only with black on FW apex; another, more common form, has black margins and yellowish upperside of the HW discal area. Both forms can easily be determined as *A. drusilla* by the yellowish patch on the FW underside at the base.

Habits: Occurs throughout Costa Rica, from sea level to 1,200 m, in association with open areas and second-growth habitats. Flies along rivers or edges in habitats with forest cover. Both sexes are extremely fast fliers and visit a wide variety of wild and garden flowers. In San José, where the hostplants may be weeds and garden plants, the pupae are often parasitized by chalcid wasps.

Genus **LEPTOPHOBIA** Butler, 1847

The butterflies in this genus have long, slender antennae and either a white or bright yellow ground color to the hindwing underside. The genus ranges from Mexico through Central and South America, and reaches its greatest diversity on the eastern slope of the Andes. In Costa Rica, *Leptophobia* species are found in association with montane habitats, and always near water.

The hostplant families include Capparidaceae, Brassicaceae, and Tropaeolaceae, all of which apparently contain mustard oils and related chemicals. The larvae are slightly hairy, typically pierid in morphology, and colored green, sometimes with blue and orange on the body. They feed singly, but are often found in groups comprising several instars, though larvae are not cannabalistic. Pupation takes place as solitary individuals. The pupa resembles that of *Perrhybris* (Fig. 19). It has been suggested that one of our species (*L. caesia*) may be unpalatable, because it has conspicuous coloration (Young 1972*c*) of the type associated with chemical defense, which seems reasonable in light of evidence from other pierines. Although both species are very common in Costa Rica, little is known about their biology.

Leptophobia aripa
(Boisduval, 1836)

FW Length: 23-27 mm **Plate 12**

Range: Mexico to Brazil

Hostplant: *Nasturtium officionale* (Brassicaceae); *Tropaeoleum maritzianum* (Tropaeolaceae)

Early stages: *Egg*—bright yellow, laid in clusters ranging from four to twenty. Early instars are pale green with darker green heads. *Mature larva*—green body with a yellow lateral line running from head to anus and alternating transverse stripes of black and yellow-green. The larvae are solitary feeders and can walk on the surface film of water between defoliated *Nasturtium* hostplants. *Pupa*—light green with yellow and black spots on the dorsum; head has a darkened spike. Pupation occurs a short distance from the hostplant.

Adult: Distinguished by the white ground color, black FW apex, green eyes, and underside washed a glossy greenish white.

Habits: Occurs from 500 to 2,000 m on both slopes, usually associated with forest habitats but always near water courses. Commonly seen flying along forest and riparian edges with a fast zigzag flight. Both sexes visit flowers of *Impatiens, Lantana, Nasturtium,* various Asteraceae, and numerous Rubiaceae. The female oviposits from late morning to midday. This common species is characteristic of montane wet forest habitats.

Leptophobia caesia tenuicornis
Butler and Druce, 1874

FW Length: 23-31 mm **Plate 12**

Range: Mexico to Ecuador. **Subspecies:** Costa Rica and Panama

Hostplant: *Podandrogyne pulcherrima* (Capparidaceae)

Early stages: (Young 1972*c*) *Egg*—yellow, spindle-shaped, laid singly. All larvae after the first instar have orange head capsule, greenish black body with each segment ringed in pale blue, yellow-orange legs, and orange anal claspers. The larvae may feed on all plant parts, and are found at times in small aggregations of various instars. They do not feed gregariously, however. *Pupa*—pale blue speckled with green, yellow, and white; brown wing-pads. There are three pairs of spines on the first abdominal segments; head has a blunt projection (Fig. 19).

Adult: *Male*—upperside has a pale blue discal area. *Female*—lacks the blue upperside but has white to yellow discal area. Both sexes have a bright yellow HW underside, although this is duller in the female. *Note*: this species has sometimes been referred to the genus *Itaballia*.

Habits: Occurs from 600 to 2,400 m on both slopes, in association with forest habitats. Individuals are commonly encountered along trails and streams within the forest, but usually do not fly in direct sunshine. The rapid, erratic flight and the contrasting yellow and black coloration are very good field characters. Both sexes are commonly found in association with the hostplant, and the females may rest on the flowers of the hostplant, where the males court them. Oviposition takes place throughout the day provided there is sunshine. Both sexes visit flowers of *Lantana, Impatiens, Podandrogyne,* and other red flowers growing along forest edges. This species is present throughout the year in almost all habitats, and is one of the most obvious butterflies in the cloud forest. It has been suggested by Young (1972*c*) that this species may represent a Müllerian co-mimic of *Dismorphia zaela* [not *virgo*] and the ithomiine *Oleria zelica.* He considers *L. caesia* distasteful because it feeds on the Capparidaceae, and suggests that field work should be done to test these hypotheses.

Genus **ITABALLIA** Kaye, 1904

The butterflies in this genus show a close relationship to *Leptophobia, Pieriballia,* and *Perrhybris. Itaballia* is separated on genitalic characters. Locally this genus is recognized by the rounded wingshape and the black and white color patterns. The genus extends from Mexico through Central and South America, and is composed of four species, some doubtful. In Central America there are two species, both of which occur in Costa Rica. Our species appear to be confined to the lowlands, with one species occurring in the dry forest, the other in wet forest.

The hostplants belong to the Capparidaceae. The early stages are similar to those of *Leptophobia.* In Costa Rica, one of the species pupates on the hostplant leaf that it fed from. Very little is known about the biology of this genus.

Itaballia demophile centralis

Joicey and Talbot 1928

FW Length: 25-30 mm **Plate 12**

Range: Mexico to Paraguay. **Subspecies:** Central America

Hostplant: *Capparis indica, C. frondosa* (Capparidaceae)

Early stages: *Egg*—yellow, laid singly on the underside of leaves. *Mature larva*—green with longitudinal rows of yellow and blue tubercles; green head capsule with short black hairs. The larva rests on the upperside of leaves on a silken mat, and feeds on the leaf tip. *Pupa*—white with black spots, similar in morphology to *Perrhybris,* but smaller. Pupation takes place on the same silken mat that the larva rested upon.

Adult: Sexes slightly dimorphic. *Male*—white with black FW apex and margin. A black transverse line runs from end of FW cell to margin; underside is glossy whitish yellow. *Female*—black markings are more prominent, and the ground color is a dirty white.

Habits: Occurs from sea level to 900 m on the Pacific slope, in association with deciduous forest habitats. Encountered as rare solitary individuals along trails, stream beds, and in forest with an open understory. The flight is fluttery, and individuals of both sexes often perch on leaves for a few seconds during a continuing flight. The females oviposit from late morning until midday in dense understory vegetation. Both sexes visit flowers of *Lantana, Psychotria,* and *Hamelia.* This species is uncommon but is present throughout the year in Guanacaste.

Itaballia pandosia kicaha

Reakirt, 1863

FW Length: 20-27 mm **Plate 12**

Range: Honduras to Venezuela. **Subspecies:** Honduras to Panama

Hostplant: Unknown

Early stages: Unknown

Adult: Sexes dimorphic. *Male*—white with black margins except for HW underside, where the distal margin is orange-brown. *Female*—yellow ground color with larger black margins.

Habits: This rare Costa Rican species occurs from 200 to 800 m on both slopes, in association with wet forest habitats. It flies in the forest understory in light gaps and along trails, and has a fairly rapid, bouncing flight, somewhat resembling *Dismorphia.* I have seen this species only twice in nature.

Genus **PIERIBALLIA** Klots, 1933

The butterflies in this genus are recognized by the acute forewing apex, distinct sexual dimorphism, and general color pattern. There are two Central American species, one of which occurs in Costa Rica. Originally Klots (1933) considered *Pieriballia* to be a subgenus of *Itaballia,* separated by distinctive features of the genitalia. I treat *Pieriballia* as a full genus.

The hostplants of *Pieriballia* are in the Capparidaceae. The early stages bear a strong resemblance to *Perrhybris.* The butterfly shows a degree of mimetic resemblance to *Heliconius* species, and aspects of the biology and mimicry of *P. viardi* in Mexico have been discussed by Jordan (1981). None of the other species has been worked on with regard to any biological aspect.

Pieriballia mandela noctipennis
(Butler and Druce, 1872)

FW Length: 35-38 mm **Plate 12**

Range: Costa Rica to Peru. **Subspecies:** Costa Rica and Panama

Hostplant: *Capparis pseudocacao* (Capparidaceae)

Early stages: This species has been reared in Costa Rica from a single late instar larva for which no description is available (Haber, personal communication). The hostplant occurs as a small cloud forest understory tree.

Adult: Sexes dimorphic. *Male*—upperside white with heavy black wing margins; underside has red at base of HW. *Female*—HW almost entirely black above.

Habits: Occurs from 600 to 1,500 m in association with cloud forest habitats and, uncommonly, in the Pacific lowland rain forest. Individuals fly along trails, forest edges, or through the forest, with a rapid and somewhat meandering flight. While flying, the female resembles *Heliconius cydno*. If *P. mandela* is mimicking *H. cydno*, however, it does not have a model on the Pacific drainage, since *H. cydno* is confined to the Atlantic slope. Both sexes visit flowers of *Lantana, Impatiens, Psyguria, Hamelia*, and other red flowers. This butterfly is common in all cloud forest habitats in Costa Rica.

Genus **PERRHYBRIS**
Hübner, 1816

The sexes of this species are strongly dimorphic: the females mimic (Müllerian?) tiger-striped ithomiines and heliconiines, whereas the males are white with a trace of the tiger-stripe pattern on the underside of the hindwing. The genus ranges from Guatemala to South America and is composed of three species, two of which enter our area. All of the species inhabit lowland rain forest areas and can be quite common locally. There are a large number of subspecific names attached to the variations seen in the females. I feel that these names are for the most part unnecessary because of the variation commonly found within single Costa Rican populations.

The confirmed hostplants belong to the Capparidaceae, but the genus has also been doubtfully recorded from the Lauraceae (see Young 1980, 1982*b*; DeVries 1982). The larvae are gregarious feeders and strikingly colored with red, black, and yellow bands. The pupae are also gregarious, and the adults emerge synchronously.

In Costa Rica, populations of *Perrhybris* are usually localized in areas where the hostplant occurs, and individuals show little movement between habitats. The mimetic females fly very differently from the nonmimetic males, and are often chased by tiger-striped males of other species (*Mechanitis, Heliconius*). I have described a lek display by one of the Costa Rican species on the Osa Peninsula (DeVries 1978), but have subsequently been unable to find populations large enough to study this phenomenon again. From experiments with jacamars it has been demonstrated that *Perrhybris* is unpalatable to these birds (Chai 1985).

Perrhybris pyrrha
(Fabricius, 1775)

FW Length: male 36-38 mm, female 40-41 mm **Plate 12**

Range: Costa Rica to Brazil

Hostplant: *Capparis isthmensis, C. pittieri* (Capparidaceae)

Early stages: *Egg*—bright yellow, laid in clusters of twenty to seventy on either surface of the leaf. If an ovipositing female is disturbed while laying, she will return to the same cluster, and then lay more eggs. *Mature larva*—head capsule red, body black, each segment with several rings of yellow; venter and anal claspers bright red; entire body covered with fine whitish hairs. The larvae are highly gregarious and feed and molt synchronously. While the larvae are feeding, the bright red head capsules are visible on the leaf edge and may be aposematical. *Pupa*—ground color creamy tan; dorsum has patches of olive green on thorax and abdomen. There are three pairs of black dorsolateral recurved spines on the first three abdominal segments; each subsequent segment has three short black spines. Head has a bulbous projection, cremaster is orange-yellow. Pupation takes places in aggregations on the upperside of leaves either on or off the hostplant.

Adult: Sexes dimorphic. *Male*—white above with a broad black FW apex; underside of HW has yellow, orange, and black medial stripes, and veins broadly streaked in black. *Female*—highly variable, including occasional forms with entirely black FW, but always with a dentate pattern on the HW where the orange meets the black margin.

Habits: Occurs from sea level to 900 m in localized populations in rain forest habitats on both slopes. The males fly along forest edges and may form aggregations during the morning. I consider these concentrations of males to be leks (DeVries 1978). The males, while in aggregations, chase any tiger-striped butterfly that is near the area. The flight of the male is, like most pierid species, strong and swift. The female stays in the forest understory and flies lazily like ithomiine, and may oviposit from morning until midday. Both sexes visit flowers of *Lantana, Psyguria, Hamelia, Psychotria,* and *Palicourea.* This species is not particularly common, but can be very abundant in local areas where the hostplant occurs.

Perrhybris lypera
(Kollar, 1850)

FW Length: male 33-35 mm, female 35-38 mm **Plate 12**

Range: Costa Rica to Ecuador

Hostplant: *Capparis pittieri* (Capparidaceae), but see Young (1980) for account on Lauraceae

Early stages: *Egg*—bright yellow, laid in clusters of ten to fifty on the same leaf. *Mature larvae*—highly gregarious, as in the preceeding species; mature larvae are similar to *P. pyrrha,* except that the ground color is dark green. *Pupa*—similar to that of *P. pyrrha,* but with the ground color ranging from tan to brown-orange. The pupae are also gregarious, as in *P. pyrrha.*

Adult: Sexes dimorphic. *Male*—white above with broad black margins; HW underside has a broad yellow medial band and an orange patch at the base. *Female*—upperside of FW black with a subapical white patch; HW black with a broad orange medial band.

Habits: Occurs from sea level to 600 m, on the Atlantic drainage, in association with rain forest habitats. The males are more tolerant of bright sunlight than the females, and will occasionally fly across an open pasture. The female stays in the forest understory, usually near ground level, flying along trails and in light gaps. The female is most active from midday until early afternoon, at which time she seeks oviposition sites. The flight behavior differs between the sexes, as in *P. pyrrha,* but both sexes of *P. lypera* fly very fast when disturbed, and both visit flowers of *Hamelia* and *Warscewiczia.* I have found them throughout the year, but in greatest abundance during the dry season. Young (1980) found aggregations of males in the forest understory, and suggested that this behavior may indicate lekking similar to that described for *P. pyrrha* (DeVries 1978). In Costa Rica, populations of this species are very local, and individuals are generally rare in Costa Rican collections.

Genus **ASCIA** Scopoli, 1777

The three species in this genus that occur in our area can all be recognized by having a white ground color with black on the forewing apex, a wing shape that is somewhat angular, and pale blue antennae. The genus ranges from the United States through Central and South America, to the Antilles and Cuba. In Costa Rica the genus occurs from sea level to about 1,500 m and is always associated with open areas.

The hostplant families include Brassicaceae, Capparidaceae, and Tropaeolaceae, all of which contain mustard oils. The larvae are generally green and granulate, and similar to *Itaballia.* The pupae are also similar to *Itaballia.* The larvae of one species is reputed in some areas to be a pest on cabbages and other related crop plants.

All of the species are very strong fliers and some are known to migrate. In a classic paper, Nielsen (1961) described the migratory habits of *A. monuste* in Florida and demonstrated that dark morphs of this species migrate whereas the white morphs remain resident. Apart from this, little has been published on the population biology of *Ascia.* Of interest is that *Ascia* is repeatedly rejected by captive jacamars, suggesting that they are unpalatable.

Ascia monuste
(Linnaeus, 1764)

FW Length: 30-34 mm **Plate 12**

Range: Southern United States through Central and South America and the Antilles

Hostplant: *Lipidium* (Brassicaceae); *Crataeva* (Capparidaceae) (Riley 1975); *Brassica, Cleome* (Brassicaceae); *Tropaeoleum* (Tropaeolaceae).

Early stages: (Riley 1975) *Egg*—white, laid singly. *Mature larva*—pale yellow or yellow-green with dark greenish black longitudinal stripes, and covered with minute black dots that form transverse bands. To my knowledge this species does not do serious damage to crops in Costa Rica.

Adult: Distinguished by the dark wedge-shaped markings centered along the veins on the wing margins. The females are usually darker, and both sexes when alive have a pale blue antennal tip. The darker gray *phileta* forms (not illustrated) are migratory.

Habits: Widely distributed in Costa Rica from sea level to 1,600 m in all disturbed habitats. Most commonly encountered visiting garden flowers or ovipositing on the brassicaceous weeds that grow in San José. As far as I am aware, there has not been a report of this species ever migrating in Costa Rica.

Ascia josephina josepha

(Godman and Salvin, 1868)

FW Length: 40-44 mm **Plate 12**

Range: Southern United States through Central and South America and the Antilles. **Subspecies:** Central America

Hostplant: *Capparis indica, C. odoratissima* (Capparidaceae)

Early stages: *Mature larva*—dark green with a yellow lateral line; dorsum covered with tiny black tubercles; head capsule green with a produced head and two black spines on the wingpads.

Adult: Sexes slightly dimorphic. Distinguished from *A. limona* by always having a distinct black spot in the FW cell and never any black on the FW apex and margins. The female has two forms, one which is like the male; the other (not illustrated) has a series of black spots on the postmedian of the FW upperside, and is often dirty yellow-gray in color. See *A. limona.*

Habits: Occurs from sea level to 1,200 m in Pacific dry forest habitats. This species apparently has its southern limit near the Quepos area on the coast. Individuals fly very fast through open areas, over the forest canopy, and will dip down into light gaps in the forest. In my experience, this species is strongly seasonal and present only during the rainy season (June-September) in most years, although it may persist in local riparian populations. Encountered as solitary individuals.

Ascia limona

(Schaus, 1913)

FW Length: male 35-42 mm, female 45-47 mm **Plate 12**

Range: Mexico to Colombia

Hostplant: Unknown

Early stages: Unknown

Adult: This rare species is distinguished from other congeners by having a very faint black dot in the FW cell; FW apex always has some black (variable), and the female looks like a very large *A. monuste,* with the black HW margin forming a toothlike pattern along the radial veins.

Habits: I have never seen this species in nature but, judging from the series of specimens in the British Museum, it appears to occur only in coastal lowland Atlantic habitats. Any information on this species would be worth reporting, since it has apparently not been seen since Schaus collected it in Costa Rica over eighty years ago.

Subfamily **COLIADINAE**

This cosmopolitan subfamily is composed of a number of butterflies commonly known as "sulphurs." The Coliadinae has its greatest diversity in the tropics, but includes many species in the temperate regions as well, especially the genera *Colias* and *Eurema.* The butterflies in the Coliadinae range from small to medium size, and are recognized by being yellow, orange, white, or a combination thereof, with fairly short antennae (often thickly scaled), and having, in general, a square wing shape. Various aspects of the systematics of this subfamily have been treated by Klots (1928, 1929*b*, 1933), and these have been followed here except for a few modifications made by other authors. The Coliadinae is well represented in the Neotropics, and particularly well represented in Central America.

A number of diverse hostplant families have been reported for the Coliadinae. In the Neotropics, the hostplant families of greatest importance are the Fabaceae, Caesalpinaceae, Mimosaceae, Simaroubaceae, and Zygophyllaceae. As far as I am aware, all coliadinine species lay single eggs and have solitary larvae. The larvae are generally uniform pale green or yellow, but may be striped with green-yellow combinations (Fig. 19), and some are polymorphic (see also *Anteos*). The pupae of most Coliadinae have a prominent keel where the wingpads are located, although this is somewhat reduced in the genus *Colias.* The pupae range in color from green to yellow or pale pink, and resemble new leaves or flower buds when the pupa is on a plant (Fig. 19).

Adult Coliadinae are well known to be migrants, as witnessed by frequent reports of *Anteos, Phoebis* (*Catopsilia* in the Old World), *Aphrissa,* and *Kricogonia* migrating in large numbers across mountains, along sea coasts, and out to sea (see Williams 1930; Leston et al. 1982, for discussions). Many Coliadinae species have two forms: one which is migratory and the other sedentary (see *Zerene* and

Eurema). As one might expect from a subfamily composed of numerous migratory species, the coliadinines, including the small *Eurema* species, are strong and fast fliers.

There is evidence that some species are distasteful to predators (see Brower 1984). This makes intuitive sense, since many Coliadinae are among the most obvious butterflies in open areas. It is even possible that the preponderance of yellow species represents a form of incipient mimicry (especially involving certain Pierinae). There is, however, much research to be done on this aspect of their biology.

The males of some genera, in addition to having well-developed ultraviolet patterns (see Silberglied 1977), possess a row of teeth along the edge of the forewing costa, much like certain of our *Papilio* species (see *Anteos* and *Phoebis*). Although the function of these teeth is unknown, it seems possible that they are used in male-male interactions or as a defense.

In Costa Rica, most members of the Coliadinae occur from sea level to 1,800 meters, with a few species at high elevations. With few exceptions, all species inhabit open areas and fly in bright sunshine, and many are among the most widespread and abundant pierid butterflies in Central America. All species avidly visit flowers, especially red ones. In certain seasons, the males of some genera (such as *Phoebis* and *Eurema*) congregate at puddles and riverbeds by the hundreds. As far as I am aware, there has been no population biology study published on any species in the Neotropics.

Genus **ZERENE** Hübner, 1819

Our single species in this genus is easily recognized by the "dog's head" pattern on the forewing of the male; this is less distinct in the female. The acute forewing apex, the black spot in the forewing cell, and the medium size will separate it from *Eurema*. *Zerene* is considered by some authors a subgenus of *Colias* because of similarities in genitalia and wing venation; I am considering it here as a full genus. The butterflies in *Zerene* are for the most part temperate zone species and barely enter the Neotropics.

The single Central American species is common in areas having a large cattle industry, which is most likely because various legume hostplants grow there.

All female *Zerene* show strong seasonal polyphenism. In Costa Rica, dry-season forms may be white or yellow, and the typical "dog's head" pattern is usually absent. The studies of Silberglied (1977) have demonstrated that ultraviolet reflection patterns play an important part in courtship and mating.

Zerene cesonia centralamericana
(Röber, 1909)

FW Length: 29-34 mm **Plate 8**

Range: Canada to Argentina. **Subspecies:** Guatemala to Panama

Hostplant: *Indigofera, Trifolium, Medicago* (Fabaceae)

Early stages: (Klots 1951) *Mature larva*—variable: some green, thickly covered with small black tubercles, some unmarked; some cross-banded with yellow, orange, and black; others banded lengthwise with yellow and black.

Adult: Distinguished by the "dog's head" on the FW, which is faint in the female; male always bright yellow with black, females pale yellow to white; both sexes have a black spot in the FW cell.

Habits: Occurs from sea level to 1,000 m in association with open areas or second growth. Commonest on the Pacific drainage in Guanacaste. This species is a fast flier that stays close to the ground and is very wary when at rest or visiting flowers. Females oviposit at midday, usually on seedling hostplants. Both sexes visit flowers of *Lantana, Stachytarpheta, Combretum,* and *Malvaviscus*. In Guanacaste it is most abundant in the early rainy season, but is present throughout the year. In Parque Santa Rosa, the white form of the female is most common during the dry season, and these individuals are in reproductive diapause until the rains come in May. In the north temperate regions, this species diapauses as a pupa; in Costa Rica only adult diapause is known.

Genus **ANTEOS** Hübner, 1816

These large butterflies are easily recognized by their distinctive wing shape. Of the three species in *Anteos*, two occur in our area. Both species exhibit female dimorphism correlated with wet and dry seasons. The butterflies in this genus are very fast and powerful fliers, and all inhabit bright, open areas. All species have been recorded as migratory, although little is known about the biology of their migrations. The males bear strong serrations on the forewing costa, which are similar to some *Papilio* species. The females lack these serrations. I am unaware of any work done on the use of these serrations, but I suggest that they will be found to be important in male-male interactions. Indeed, it is common to see a small flock of males swirling around each other as they madly dash along a road cut or forest edge, and they are quite commonly seen visiting mud, where they jostle each other (and other species) in a tight group.

The hostplants for the genus are various species of *Cassia* (Caesalpinaceae). It is unknown whether these butterflies are distasteful as a result of feeding on a hostplant rich in Cassia alkaloids (Rothschild 1972), but they are at times extremely abundant. The larvae can take various forms, depending on whether the egg is laid on the new or old leaves, or on the flowers. This is related to the wet/dry season flowering phenology of the plants themselves, and the cryptic larvae match their foodplant part exceedingly well.

Anteos clorinde

Godart, 1823

FW Length: 38-47 mm **Plate 8**

Range: Mexico to Paraguay

Hostplant: *Cassia emarginata* (Caesalpinaceae)

Early stages: *Egg*—white or yellow, laid singly on new or old leaves, or flower buds. *Mature larva*—at least trimorphic; one morph, entirely yellow, feeds on flowers; one morph, almost entirely pale green, feeds mostly on new leaves. One morph, with a green body, feeds on old leaves; its dorsum is speckled with fine yellow dots; a cream-yellow lateral line runs from head to anus, and the head capsule is green with short hairs. *Pupa*—green, strongly bowed with dorsal keel; white line on side of abdomen.

Adult: Distinguished by the greenish white ground color and large yellow cellular spot on the FW. Some females are without the yellow spot on the FW.

Habits: Occurs from sea level to 1,000 m, principally on the Pacific slope, although occasionally present on the Atlantic slope in some years. A very fast flier commonly seen in open areas, flower gardens, or flying over the forest canopy. While settled, the greenish underside renders it very cryptic and leaflike. Males are common at puddles, often in large aggregations. Females oviposit at midday and often lay from five to ten eggs in succession on the same plant. Both sexes visit flowers of *Malvaviscus, Hibiscus, Combretum, Lantana,* and red flowers in general. This species is most common in Guanacaste during the early portions of the rainy season, and is persistent throughout the year in low numbers, at which time females may be in reproductive diapause.

Anteos maerula

Fabricius, 1775

FW Length: 43-55 mm **Plate 8**

Range: Southern United States to Colombia and Peru

Hostplant: *Cassia emarginata* (Caesalpinaceae)

Early stages: (Riley 1975) *Mature larva*—olive green with two irregular subdorsal rows of yellow blotches, one on either side; a line of minute black tubercles (one to each segment) and a pale yellow spiracular stripe. *Pupa*—similar to that described for *A. clorinde.*

Adult: Distinguished by the lemon-yellow ground color in all males. Females are either yellow, or white with grayish margins.

Habits: Occurs from sea level to 900 m in association with Pacific slope deciduous forest. In flight and feeding habits it is similar to *A. clorinde.* This species differs, however, in having its flight period almost entirely restricted to the rainy season during most years. Both sexes, as in *A. clorinde,* visit a wide variety of red flowers. The female oviposits at midday, and usually lays several eggs on the same plant. Although this species is never as abundant as its congener in Costa Rica, in Guanacaste individuals may be common for several weeks after the rains have begun.

Genus **KRICOGONIA**
Reakirt, 1863

The medium-sized butterflies in this genus are recognized by the short antennae and the yellow at the base of the forewing. There is probably only a single species, which appears to range throughout the subtropical and tropical areas of the Americas and the Antilles, though several other island species have been named. The sexes are somewhat dimorphic, and the coloration of both sexes is also variable. According to Klots (1933) the relationship of *Kricogia* to other pierid genera is not clearly understood.

The hostplants of *Kricogonia, Guaiacum officionale* and *Porlieria* (Zygophyllaceae), are quite unusual for the Pieridae and for butterflies in general. The larvae are apparently typically pierid, as is the pupa. These butterflies are best known for their spectacular migrations, which have attracted the attention of many observers (Williams 1930). Indeed, in Texas I have seen the radiators of automobiles and large trucks so filled with the bodies of these butterflies that the engines overheated and the drivers were forced to stop. In Costa Rica, however, there has never been such a migration reported, and the species has only recently been discovered to live in our area. Although its migrational habits have been known for a long time, there is still no published work on the biology of this phenomenon (but see Gilbert 1985 for a study done in Texas).

Kricogonia lyside

Godart, 1819

FW Length: 24-28 mm **Plate 8**

Range: Southern United States to Venezuela and the Antilles

Hostplant: *Guaicum officionale, Porlieria* (Zygophyllaceae)

Early stages: (Riley 1975) *Mature larva*—dull green with a gray line along the back that is broadly bordered with chocolate brown and silvery lateral lines; green head; varigated yellow and brown sides. The larva is apparently a nocturnal feeder and hides during the day in bark crevices.

Adult: Distinguished by the short antennae and the rather square shape of the FW and the round HW. The male has the base of the FW yellow, and the female may be pale yellow or entirely white. Both sexes have dark spots on the postmedian of the HW.

Habits: As far as I am aware, the only colonies of this species in Costa Rica are closely associated with lignum vitae forests in the Parque Santa Rosa and Palo Verde, Guanacaste. These populations are generally sedentary, and adult activity is confined to these lignum vitae forests. There has never been a Costa Rican migration reported for this species. Although this butterfly is very rare in Costa Rican collections, individuals are present throughout the year as isolated colonies, especially in Parque Santa Rosa. However, it is unknown if these butterflies would persist should the lignum vitae be removed.

Genus **PHOEBIS** Hübner, 1819

The conspicuous butterflies in this genus are easily recognized by their general appearance, medium to large size, yellow or white coloration, and general abundance throughout the Neotropics in all habitats. The sexes are dimorphic, and the female of some species may have up to three forms. The male sex bears a thick mat of androconial scales on the forewing around the forewing cell, readily distinguished from the normal surrounding scales. Many of the species' best characters are found on the undersides, especially in the females. Ultraviolet patterns appear to play an important part in inter- and intraspecific interactions (Silberglied 1977). The genus is entirely Neotropical and in the past has been erroneously considered the same as the Old World genus *Catopsilia* (Klots 1933).

The ecologies of the species are quite similar. All inhabit open areas, whether it be a pasture or above the forest canopy, and all do quite well in areas devastated by humans. All of the species are migrants, although little is known about the biology of their migrations.

The hostplants for the genus are legumes in the families Mimosaceae and Caesalpinaceae, and, in many areas, introduced ornamental plants. The larvae appear to show some dimorphisms that are related to the hostplant part they feed on (see also Anteos), but are in general green with tiny tubercles along the dorsum (Fig. 19). The pupae show the tapered head and pronounced keel, like many other pierids (Fig. 19).

Phoebis rurina

Felder, 1861

FW Length: 38-40 mm **Plate 8**

Range: Mexico to Brazil

Hostplant: *Cassia fruticosa* (Caesalpinaceae)

Early stages: *Mature larva*—body yellow-green, covered with many tiny black and blue warts; head capsule green. The larvae feed only on the new leaves, and a small tree may have many larvae of various instars.

Adult: *Male*—distinguished by the HW being produced into a short taillike process. *Female*—variable, also has HW tail; may be yellow with red-orange on the HW margin or white with a black spot in the FW cell. *Note*: There has been considerable confusion in the literature between this species and *P. cipris* Fabricius, which has been clarified somewhat by Brown (1929).

Habits: Occurs from sea level to 1,000 m on both slopes, in association with a variety of habitat types. I have seen this species flying across mountain passes from Pacific to Atlantic slopes, across lowland rain forest canopy, in pastures in Guanacaste, and in montane forest in Parque Carrillo. The flight of both sexes is very fast and erratic. Both sexes visit *Lantana, Stachytarpheta, Impatiens*, and other red flowers. The female will oviposit at any time of day when there is bright sunshine.

Phoebis philea philea

(Linnaeus, 1776)

FW Length: 40-45 mm **Plate 8**

Range: Throughout Central and South America

Hostplant: *Cassia grandis, C. alata, C. leptocarpa, C. hayesiana, C. fruticosa* (Caesalpinaceae)

Early stages: *Mature larva*—body green with orange patches on either end and along sides and dorsum (variable); dorsum and sides covered with small black tubercles. *Pupa*—green or reddish with prominent keel and tapered head. The pupal coloration appears to be correlated with pupation site.

Adult: Sexes dimorphic. *Male*—distinguished by the lemon ground color with the prominent orange FW medial bar. *Female*—dimorphic: common form has red-orange HW distal margins; another form looks like a very large *P. argante* female, but with more or less evenly black FW distal borders.

Habits: Widespread and common on both slopes, from sea level to 1,500 m. Commonly seen at garden flowers and flying about the streets of San José and other cities. Both sexes visit a wide variety of flowers ranging from herbs to canopy trees. The males of this species are extremely fast flying and rapid in their courtship of females. For example, a female flying overhead while the male is feeding on flowers may be intercepted by the male, bashed around in the air, forced to the ground, and be coupled to the male, all within fifteen to thirty seconds. This is not uncommon during the first rains of the year. Of interest is that both sexes in this species have serrations on the FW costa.

Phoebis argante

(Fabricius, 1775)

FW Length: 34-37 mm **Plate 9**

Range: Mexico to Peru; other subspecies are found on the Antilles (Riley 1975).

Hostplant: *Cassia biflora, C. fruticosa* (Caesalpinaceae); *Pentaclethra macroloba, Inga vera, I. ruiziana* (Mimosaceae)

Early stages: *Egg*—yellow, laid singly on new leaves of all hostplants. The female usually lays several to many eggs on the same plant. *Mature larva*—dimorphic: green or yellow, both with cream-colored granulations on dorsum and sides; there is a dark stripe along the sides, with triangles of the same color above the prolegs; the dorsal midline is light green with pairs of dark green spots on either side; the anal segment is yellow; the head capsule is light green with fine whitish hairs and some warts (Fig. 19). *Pupa*—pale green or with a rosy blush; head produced to a point (Fig. 19) and keel prominent.

Adult: Sexes dimorphic. *Male*—distinguished by having an evenly black FW border, with the transverse medial line on the FW underside broken and set askew. *Female*—highly variable, ranging from white to yellow, with heavy or faint black borders; underside ranges from shiny pale yellow to dark yellow shot with brick red. See *P. agarithe*.

Habits: Occurs from sea level to 1,700 m over the entire country, usually in disturbed habitats. The males form large aggregations at puddles. Both sexes visit a wide variety of red flowers, and are extremely common throughout the year. Individuals of this species can in some years be exceedingly abundant in Guanacaste after the initial rains of the wet season. Individuals are known to migrate long distances.

Phoebis agarithe

Boisduval, 1836

FW Length: 34-36 mm **Plate 9**

Range: Southern United States to Brazil

Hostplant: *Inga vera* (Mimosaceae)

Early stages: (Riley 1975) *Mature larva*—dark green, smooth, covered in a dense, short pile; a yellow lateral line is black-edged below.

Adult: Sexes dimorphic. This species is similar in almost all respects to *P. argante* in both sexes, but is distinguished by the unbroken transverse line on the FW underside. See *P. argante*.

Habits: In my experience, this species appears to be confined to the lowland Pacific forests and coastal margins. It is similar in habits to *P. argante*. In Guanacaste this species is most abundant in the early rainy season, and is either extremely rare or absent during the dry season. Both sexes visit flowers of *Stachytarpheta, Lantana*, and *Malvaviscus*. Although apparently very abundant in some areas, it is rare in Costa Rican collections.

Phoebis sennae

(Linnaeus, 1758)

FW Length: 29-36 mm **Plate 9**

Range: Southern United States to Argentina, with various Antillean subspecies

Hostplant: *Cassia biflora, C. obtusifolia* (Caesalpinaceae)

Early stages: (Riley 1975) *Mature larva*—yellow-green with many black dots; a lateral line of yellow on each side bears blue transverse lines. The larvae are very cryptic and rest on the underside of the leaf petioles when not feeding.

Adult: Sexes dimorphic. *Male*—distinguished from similar species by having a clear lemon yellow ground color with lighter yellow mealy distal margins. *Female*—dimorphic and variable; similar to female *P. argante*, but distinguished by having two spots of roughly equal size in the distal portion of the FW cell.

Habits: Occurs from sea level to 1,200 m, most commonly on the Pacific slope, in association with open areas and bright sunshine. In certain years this species can be the most abundant pierid in Guanacaste, and is certainly one of the most common in the entire country. Its habits and migration patterns are similar to *P. argante*.

Phoebis trite

(Linnaeus, 1758)

FW Length: 32-34 mm **Plate 8**

Range: Mexico to Argentina, with several subspecies on the Antilles

Hostplant: *Pentaclethra macroloba* (Mimosaceae)

Early stages: I have reared one larva from the Atlantic lowlands on the above hostplant and have on numerous occasions seen females inspecting oviposition sites in light gaps in the forest and laying eggs on seedlings. The larva is pale green with many concentric rings at the constrictions between segments.

Adult: Sexes dimorphic. Both sexes of this species are immediately separated from all other congeners by the shiny underside and the straight transverse brown line that runs from the FW apex to the HW inner margin. This character can be used as a field identification mark when there are many puddling butterflies in a dense aggregation.

Habits: Occurs from sea level to 1,000 m, on both slopes, in association with mature wet forest habitats. The male flies along rivers and trails, often in "follow the leader" groups of two to six individuals. Females fly over the forest canopy and high at the forest edge, and come down to ground level in light gaps to oviposit on seedling and sapling plants. Although this species has a very large range, it is localized and not commonly collected in Costa Rica.

Genus **APHRISSA** Butler, 1873

The two species in this genus that enter our area are distinguished by the shiny texture of the undersides of both sexes; the males have the distal one-third of both wings covered in a mealy border of androconial scales. In other respects, including their general biologies, they strongly resemble *Phoebis*. Both the species in our area are reported to be strongly migratory and range throughout Central and South America.

The species are usually reported to feed on Fabaceae, Mimosaceae, and Caesalpinaceae, but there have been several rearings in Costa Rica on Bignoniaceae. The larvae of *A. statira*, depending on which hostplant family they are reared on, are very different, and may actually represent two sibling species that have long been confused under the name *P. statira*.

The adults are common during the early wet seasons in Costa Rica and are frequently seen visiting garden flowers. Unlike *Phoebis*, the males do not have serrations on the forewing costa.

Aphrissa statira

(Cramer, 1777)

FW Length: 32-35 mm **Plate 9**

Range: Southern United States to Brazil and Bolivia; several subspecies on the Antilles

Hostplant: *Callichamys latifolia* (Bignoniaceae), *Cassia (Caesalpinaceae), Dalbergia* (Fabaceae) (Riley 1975); *Calliandra* (Mimosaceae) (Howe 1975)

Early stages: There is a distinct possibility that there are two species under the name *A. statira* because there are two larval forms that feed on different hostplant families. As a result, I will separate the two types here in the hope that future work will shed light on this problem. *Mature larva on legumes*—(Riley 1975) head pale orange; body pale orange with a green tinge; first eleven segments have a blue-black hand along the sides just above the legs; last segment rust colored; spiracles white. *Mature larva on Bignoniaceae*—head green; body pale green with many fine granulations on dorsum and sides; a fine lateral stripe of pale yellow has its ventral edge green. *Pupa*—Each group has a distinct morphology (D. Janzen, personal communication), but I have no details.

Adult: Sexes dimorphic. *Male*—distinguished by the lemon yellow base of the wings, with the distal one-third a mealy yellow. *Female*—lemon yellow with a slightly wavy black FW apex and margin; underside shiny with a slight pink to the FW. See *A. boisduvalii*.

Habits: Occurs from sea level to 1,800 m, and occasionally higher during migrations on both slopes. The flight is very fast and in a straight line, always in open areas. Both sexes visit a variety of red flowers, and the males can be extremely common at puddles. On the Pacific drainage, this species is most common during the early part of the wet season, and is apparently absent from the dry forest habitats during the dry season. This species has been recorded to have huge migrations in South America, where many individuals fly directly out to sea.

Aphrissa boisduvalii

(Felder, 1861)

FW Length: 30-34 mm **Plate 9**

Range: Guatemala to Brazil and Bolivia

Hostplant: I have seen this species oviposit on seedlings of *Mora megistosperma* (Fabaceae) in mangroves on the Pacific coast.

Early stages: Undescribed

Adult: Sexes dimorphic. *Male*—distinguished from *A. statira* by having a tea color on the upperside instead of lemon yellow. *Female*—distinguished from *A. statira* by having a paler ground color and a somewhat wider black FW apex, which is reflected in the pink on the underside.

Habits: Occurs from sea level to 500 m on both slopes. Most commonly associated with mangroves and brackish water, but may be found inland along rivers. The males are frequently seen visiting wet sand on the beaches, forming small aggregations. Both sexes visit flowers on *Inga* and *Hibiscus*. It is frequently quite common, but difficult to capture because of its extremely rapid and wary flight. Uncommon in Costa Rican collections.

Genus **EUREMA** Hübner, 1819

The butterflies in this genus are all small, most inhabit open areas, and are especially common where human disturbance has created pastures and farmlands. *Eurema* butterflies are familiar to anyone who has paused along roadsides or walked in pastures anywhere in Central America. The genus comprises yellow, orange, or white butterflies with black wing margins. The systematics are detailed by Klots (1928, 1929*b*); there are a large number of species. The genus occurs in both the New and Old World. There are thirty-seven species represented in the Neotropics, thirteen of which occur in Costa Rica, and for most of them the sexes are dimorphic and show distinct seasonal polyphenisms.

The hostplants of *Eurema* are in the Fabaceae, Caesalpinaceae, and Mimosaceae, but at least one of our species feeds on Simaroubaceae. The larvae are for the most part dull green with granulations on the body and head, and are very cryptic while feeding. The pupae have the prominent keel typical of the Coliadinae, and may be green or yellow. Although many of the hostplants are known, most species still require detailed work on their life history, particularly in the Neotropics.

In Costa Rica the genus is found from sea level to the highest mountains of the Cordillera de Talamanca. Our fauna is composed of mostly widespread Central American species, and shows no endemism, as in other pierid groups. In an unpublished study, P. Opler has demonstrated that the two morphs of *E. daira* are behaviorally quite different: the dry season form is sedentary and in reproductive diapause, and the wet season form is migratory. His study based in Guanacaste showed that the wet season forms migrate from the lowlands into the mountains and lay eggs on their journey. When the rains come to Guanacaste in May, the dry season forms become reproductive, and their offspring develop into wet season forms. Later in the year, as Guanacaste dries out, more and more dry season forms are produced (which stay in the habitat), while the wet season forms migrate. This important study suggests that as our *Eurema* species become better known, many species may exhibit this behavior.

Eurema proterpia

(Fabricius, 1775)

FW Length: male 19-23 mm, female 23-26 mm **Plate 10**

Range: Southern United States throughout Central and South America and the Antilles

Hostplant: (Riley 1975) reported to be *Desmodium* (Fabaceae)

Early stages: *Mature larva*—uniformly grass-green with a short pile; head capsule somewhat granulate. *Pupa*—green with prominent keel and tapered head.

Adult: Distinguished by the bright orange ground color and the short, wide tails on the HW margin. There are two forms: the dry season form lacks black veins and has shorter tails; wet season form has longer tails, and the black marking is more pronounced. See *E. nicippe*.

Habits: Occurs from sea level to 1,200 m on both slopes, but most commonly on the Pacific side. Individuals fly close to the ground in open areas and disturbed habitats. In Guanacaste, the dry season form is in reproductive diapause and forms torpid aggregations in shady places, feeding very little during the day. The wet season form is much more active, and individuals can be extremely common at the beginning of the wet season. Both sexes visit flowers of a wide variety of herbaceous plants. This species is rejected by rufous-tailed jacamars (P. Chai, personal communication).

Eurema mexicana

(Boisduval, 1836)

FW Length: 22-25 mm **Plate 10**

Range: Southern United States through Central and South America

Hostplant: *Diphysa robinoides, Cassia* (Fabaceae) (Howe 1975)

Early stages: *Mature larva*—pale green to dark green with a granulate head capsule. *Pupa*—green or yellowish green with prominent keel and head.

Adult: Sexes dimorphic. Both sexes distinguished by the pale yellow ground color and the "dog's head" pattern on the FW. *Female*—lacks the heavy black border on the HW. Dry season specimens often have a reddish cast on the underside.

Habits: This common species occurs from sea level to 2,000 m on both slopes, but is much more common on the Pacific drainage above 500 m. Individuals fly in open areas and along forest edges, and may enter highly disturbed patches of forest. Males are commonly observed visiting wet sand, and both sexes visit cattle dung and a wide variety of flowers.

Eurema salome

(Felder, 1861)

FW Length: 23-26 mm **Plate 10**

Range: Southern United States to Colombia and Venezuela

Hostplant: I have seen females oviposit single eggs on *Diphysa robinoides* (Fabaceae), but have not reared the larva.

Early stages: Undescribed

Adult: Sexes dimorphic. Both sexes are distinguished by the lemon yellow ground color and the heavy black FW margins; HW tail more pronounced than in similar species. *Female*—lacks a black margin on HW. See *E. boisduvaliana* and *E. xanthoclora*.

Habits: Occurs quite commonly in areas above 700 m on both slopes, in association with forest habitats. Above 2,000 m it enters open areas but is less common. Individuals fly along forest edges and roadcuts, low to the ground. Both sexes visit a wide variety of flowers.

Eurema xanthochlora

(Kollar, 1850)

FW Length: male 22-24 mm, female 21-25 mm **Plate 10**

Range: Costa Rica to Venezuela, Peru, and Bolivia

Hostplant: Unknown

Early stages: Unknown

Adult: Distinguished by the yellow ground color and black FW apex, which runs from FW costa to where it narrows at the tornus; HW has a slight suggestion of a tail; underside has reddish FW apex and reddish transverse band on HW. The red is variable. *Male*—narrow black HW border. *Female*—has no border. See *E. salome*.

Habits: Occurs from sea level to 1,200 m, on both slopes, in association with disturbed forest habitats. Usually encountered as solitary individuals along forest edges or in open forest. This species is somewhat local but not uncommon.

Eurema gratiosa

(Doubleday and Hewitson, 1847)

FW Length: 19-23 mm **Plate 10**

Range: Costa Rica to Venezuela

Hostplant: (Riley 1975) *Cassia* (Caesalpinaceae)

Early stages: Unknown

Adult: Sexes dimorphic. *Male*—Distinguished by the lemon yellow FW with heavy black border; HW has white ground color and black border, and some orange in the HW apex. *Female*—ground color pale yellow; FW apex black, stops short of the tornus; HW white with an irregular black border. Both sexes have a short tail. See *E. boisduvaliana*.

Habits: Occurs from sea level to 1,200 m on the Pacific slope, in association with deciduous forest habitats and open areas. Encountered as rare solitary individuals along forest edges or in large forest light gaps. This species terminates its northern range in Guanacaste and is uncommon in our area.

Eurema boisduvaliana

(Felder, 1865)

FW Length: 18-23 mm **Plate 10**

Range: Mexico to Costa Rica and the Antilles

Hostplant: Unknown

Early stages: Unknown

Adult: Sexes dimorphic. Similar to *E. gratiosa* except that both wings are yellow. *Male*—heavy black borders. *Female*—no black on HW. See *E. gratiosa*.

Habits: Occurs from sea level to 1,200 m on the Pacific slope. Flies along forest edges or in the forest, close to the ground. In the dry season, individuals are found mostly in the forest, in the wet season they fly in open areas. Common.

Eurema dina westwoodi

(Boisduval, 1836)

FW Length: male 20-26 mm, female 23-27 mm **Plate 10**

Range: Southern United States to Panama and the Antilles. **Subspecies:** Mexico to Panama

Hostplant: *Picramnia alleni, P. quaternaria* (Simaroubaceae)

Early stages: *Egg*—white, barrel-shaped and tapered at the top. *Larva*—early instars are pale yellow, mature larvae are light green with a dark green lateral line running from head to anus. *Pupa*—pale green with prominent keel and tapered head.

Adult: Distinguished by the yellow-orange ground color with a black FW apex; underside usually has a variable orange-red "stain" on HW apex. Female may have stain on FW, as well.

Habits: This species occurs from sea level to 1,200 m on the Pacific slope, in association with deciduous forest habitat. Unlike most other *Eurema* species, *E. dina* flies in the forest understory or in the subcanopy, and rarely in open areas. Females oviposit from late morning to early afternoon, and usually lay a number of eggs on the same plant, after flying around the plant between ovipositions. Both sexes visit flowers of *Lantana, Asclepias*, and a variety of other plants that occur along forest edges. Although most abundant during the rainy season, it is persistent throughout the year.

Eurema albula

(Cramer, 1775)

FW Length: 15-22 mm **Plate 10**

Range: Mexico to Brazil and the West Indies

Hostplant: *Cassia fruticosa* (Caesalpinaceae)

Early stages: *Mature larva*—entirely green except for a white lateral line and a yellow venter. *Pupa*—similar to *E. dina*.

Adult: Distinguished by the pure white ground color with a black FW apex; underside has a wash of bone-yellow and occasional flecks of brown.

Habits: Occurs from sea level to 1,600 m, mostly on the Atlantic slope. When on the Pacific it is always in wet forest habitats. At lower elevations it flies in open areas that have heavy second growth vegetation, or along forest edges. At upper elevations it flies in the forest understory. It is similar to *E. dina* in habits. Encountered as solitary individuals in localized populations.

Eurema nise

(Cramer, 1775)

FW Length: 16-19 mm **Plate 10**

Range: Southern United States to Argentina and the West Indies

Hostplant: (Riley 1975) *Mimosa pudica* (Mimosaceae)

Early stages: *Mature larva*—green with whitish down, faint dorsal stripes, and a white lateral line.

Adult: Distinguished by the clear yellow ground color, with the black pattern on the FW apex roundly curved from costa to tornus. The female has a rounded rusty stain near HW apex. See *E. xanthoclora* and *E. lisa*.

Habits: Occurs commonly from sea level to 1,600 m, on both slopes, in association with disturbed habitat. Its habits are similar to those described for *E. salome*.

Eurema lisa

(Boisduval and LeConte, 1829)

FW Length: 17-18 mm **Plate 10**

Range: United States to Panama and throughout the West Indies

Hostplant: (Riley 1975) *Cassia* (Caesalpinaceae); *Trifolium* (Fabaceae); *Mimosa* (Mimosaceae)

Early stages: *Mature larva*—downy grass green with several white lateral lines.

Adult: Distinguished by the somewhat produced FW apex and pink marginal fringe; FW apex broadly black. Male has black on HW margin, female has less black. See *E. nise*.

Habits: Occurs from 1,200 to 3,000 m on both slopes, in association with open or disturbed habitats. Usually encountered as solitary individuals flying low to the ground near wet grassy areas. At higher elevations it flies in cloudy weather. Both sexes visit flowers of various Asteraceae species. This butterfly is apparently migratory: clouds of individuals have been reported out to sea near Bermuda. Although apparently very common in other areas, in Costa Rica this species is uncommon and local.

Eurema nicippe

(Cramer, 1782)

FW Length: 22-26 mm **Not illustrated**

Range: United States to Costa Rica, West Indies

Hostplant: (Riley 1975) *Cassia* (Caesalpinaceae)

Early stages: *Mature larva*—grayish green covered with a short white pile; orange-spotted lateral band; white spiracles.

Adult: Distinguished by the orange ground color and irregular, heavy black margins; female has less black on HW. HW *without* tails as in *E. proterpia*. Underside has orange specks that are more pronounced during the dry season. See *E. proterpia*.

Habits: This species is known only from the Pacific slopes along the Meseta Central, at 500-1,200 m elevation. It is rare in Costa Rica, and whether this species breeds in our area or occurs as a migrant is unknown. I have never seen it alive in Costa Rica.

Eurema daira

(Godart, 1819)

FW Length: 16-22 mm **Plate 10**

Range: Northeastern United States to Uruguay and the West Indies

Hostplant: *Aeschnemene, Stylosanthes, Desmodium* (Fabaceae)

Early stages: (Riley 1975) *Mature larva*—entirely light green; head covered with minute white dots; lateral line pale yellow, and underside greenish white.

Adult: Sexes dimorphic, with two seasonal forms. *Male*—FW ground color yellow with a black apex; a dark gray bar at inner margin, separated from the inner margin by an orange stripe; HW has black at the apex and at times along entire margin. *Female*—upperside white (or yellowish) with black FW apex; HW margin completely black; underside dirty yellow. The dry season forms of both sexes has more yellow on the FW, HW black margin reduced, and HW underside often washed with yellow to orange that may extend to the fringe. See *E. elathea*.

Habits: Extremely common from sea level to 1,600 m on both slopes, occurring in open areas and agricultural land. The seasonal forms are behaviorally distinct. The wet season form, which is active and mobile, disperses across open areas and mountains. The dry season form is relatively sedentary, is in reproductive diapause, and aggregates in shady spots and river beds during most of the day. Both sexes visit a wide variety of flowers and cattle dung. Males also visit mud puddles in great abundance during the early part of the wet season. Both sexes are rejected by caged jacamars (P. Chai, personal communication).

Eurema elathea

(Cramer, 1775)

FW Length: 14-18 mm **Plate 10**

Range: Nicaragua to Brazil and Bolivia; West Indies and Cuba

Hostplant: (Riley 1975) *Zornia, Stylosanthes* (Fabaceae)

Early stages: Apparently similar to those of *E. daira*.

Adult: Very similar to *E. daira* but distinguished from it by the black bar at the FW inner margin, which is *straight*, not curved, in the male. The female is extremely difficult to separate from *E. daira*, though some individuals may be separated by having the black on the HW more widely separated between the veins and somewhat more yellowish.

Habits: There are very few specimens recorded from Costa Rica (I know of only a few from "Buenos Aires de Terraba") and have never seen it in nature. If it exists in Costa Rica, it has probably been overlooked due to its sympatry with the extremely similar species *E. daira*. Apparently both species have similar habits, but *E. elathea* is always less frequent (Riley 1975).

Family **NYMPHALIDAE**

Most of the butterflies treated in this book belong to the cosmopolitan family Nymphalidae. Without doubt, the Nymphalidae contains the largest number of species, most diverse hostplant relationships, and greatest diversity of larval forms of any nonlycaenoid butterfly family in the world. Nymphalid butterflies are found in virtually every conceivable habitat except Antarctica, and are present in their greatest diversity in the Neotropics. However diverse and varied in appearance, all Nymphalid butterflies can be recognized by the fact that they have only four walking legs, and the forelegs are greatly reduced and, at times, featherlike—hence the common name brush-footed butterflies.

The phylogeny of the Nymphalidae as a whole is unknown. As a result, the number of subfamilies within the family varies, depending upon which authority is consulted. These systematic categories may range from the eight recognized by Ehrlich (1958*a*), to the twenty-five recognized by Clark (1949). For the treatment of the Costa Rican butterfly fauna I have recognized twelve subfamilies, although this number will undoubtedly change once the Nymphalidae have been studied in greater detail. The major systematic references are found under the subfamily accounts. In addition to systematic references, the reader will find there discussions of hostplants, early stages, and adult ecology.

Subfamily **CHARAXINAE**

The Charaxinae include a large number of tropical and very few temperate-region species. All have very stout bodies, large palpi, and a short, stout proboscis; they feed as adults on rotting fruits, carrion, and dung—almost never on flower nectar. Within the subfamily, coloration varies from dull to bright on the upperside, but they are cryptic beneath, resembling dead leaves or wood. Some of the Old World genera (*Charaxes, Euxanthe*) have well-developed teeth on the costa of the forewing, used in defense against predators and in male-male interactions. None of the Neotropical charaxines has such teeth. The greatest number of Neotropical Charaxinae occur in the Amazon Basin of South America; the ranges of over half of all the species, however, include Costa Rica.

The Charaxinae have always been very popular with collectors, and as a result, certain groups are taxonomically well known, but their phylogeny is unexplored. Compared to the Old World fauna, the Neotropical species are very poorly understood. For the Neotropics, the major systematic references are: Fruhstorfer (1916); Stichel (1939); Comstock (1961); and Rydon (1971). However, as will become clear to the user of this literature, most of the species are difficult to identify, and much basic taxonomy remains to be done.

The Charaxinae feed on a diversity of plant families. In the Neotropics, these include Euphorbiaceae, Fabaceae, Mimosaceae, Lauraceae, Annonaceae, Piperaceae, Erythroxylaceae, Convolvulaceae, Monimiaceae, and Quiiniaceae. The eggs are round, with flattened tops and bottoms, and have small ridges on the flattened surfaces. The larvae make frass chains in early instars, and later live freely on the hostplant, or roll tubes from the leaves and hide inside when not feeding. No Neotropical Charaxinae are known to have gregarious larvae. The larvae are generally similar in shape to the apaturines and the satyrines, having bifid tails, no spines on the body, and the head capsule adorned with horns or conspicuous warts (Figs. 20, 21). The Charaxinae may, in fact, be closely related to the Satyrinae (DeVries et al. 1985). The pupa is globose and capsule-like in most of the genera, but may be ovoid and quite similar to the Morphinae in genera such as *Prepona* and *Agrias* (Fig. 20). None of the Neotropical species is known to be unpalatable to predators, but this aspect of their biology is unexplored.

In Costa Rica, charaxines are found in all habitats from sea level to 2,000 meters, with the greatest number of species within forests at 500 to 800 meters elevation. Although many of our Costa Rican species have extensive geographical distributions, many are uncommon to rare in collections, and are seldom seen in the field. Some of our species appear to be restricted to the Cordillera de Talamanca, whereas others show enormous range disjunctions between Costa Rica and South America.

The adults are mainly forest-canopy inhabitants. One relies on luck to make them "magically" appear in traps. Although all species are powerful insects that are nearly impossible to collect while flying, after an individual has been feeding on fermenting fruits, it becomes "intoxicated" and docile. If left to feed, a butterfly may have difficulty flying with its greatly distended abdomen, and can usually be picked up from the fruit with one's fingers. Although the population biology of no Neotropical charaxine species has been studied rigorously in the field, it would not be surprising to find that some species live for several months or longer.

Genus **AGRIAS** Doubleday, 1844

Perhaps the most popular genus of the charaxines, *Agrias* butterflies may be recognized at a glance by their brilliant primary colors. The combination of brilliant coloration and variability in the species has tempted people to give a vast number of names to various forms, few of which appear to relate to any biological concept. Most of the names have been generated by private collectors, to whom the *Agrias* are the most sought-after butterflies in the world (see DeVries 1980). I have followed the arrangement of Fruhstorfer (1915), who took into consideration various observations on living insects and conducted a detailed study of the morphology; he recognized the close relationship

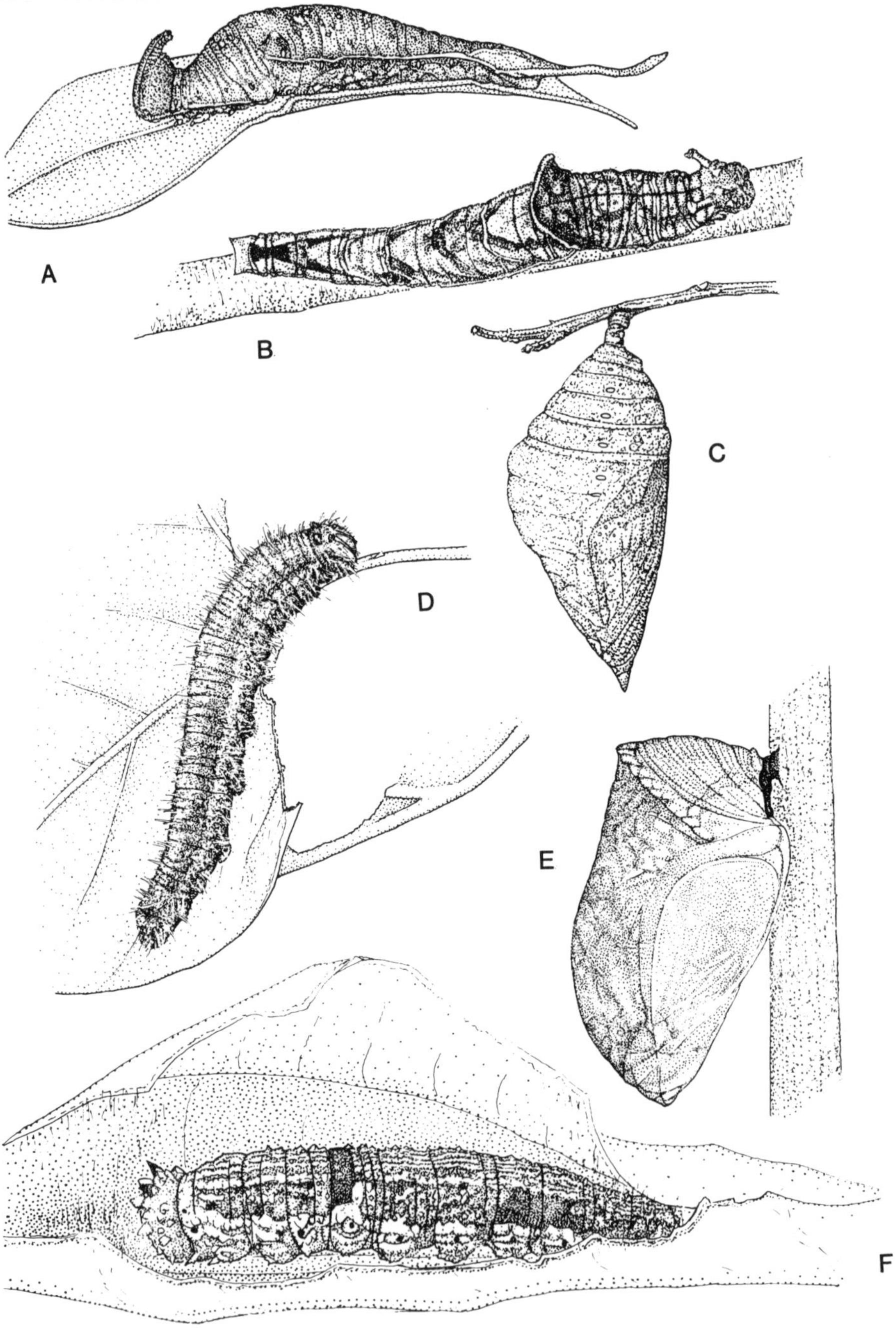

A

B

C

D

E

F

FIGURE 20. Larvae and pupae of the Nymphalidae: Charaxinae. A: *Agrias amydon philatelica* mature larva; B: *Zaretis itys* mature larva; C: *Archaeoprepona demophon centralis* pupa; D: *Memphis morvus boisduvali* mature larva; E: *Memphis eurypyle confusa* pupa; F: *Memphis eurypyle confusa* mature larva in rolled leaf (drawings by J. Clark).

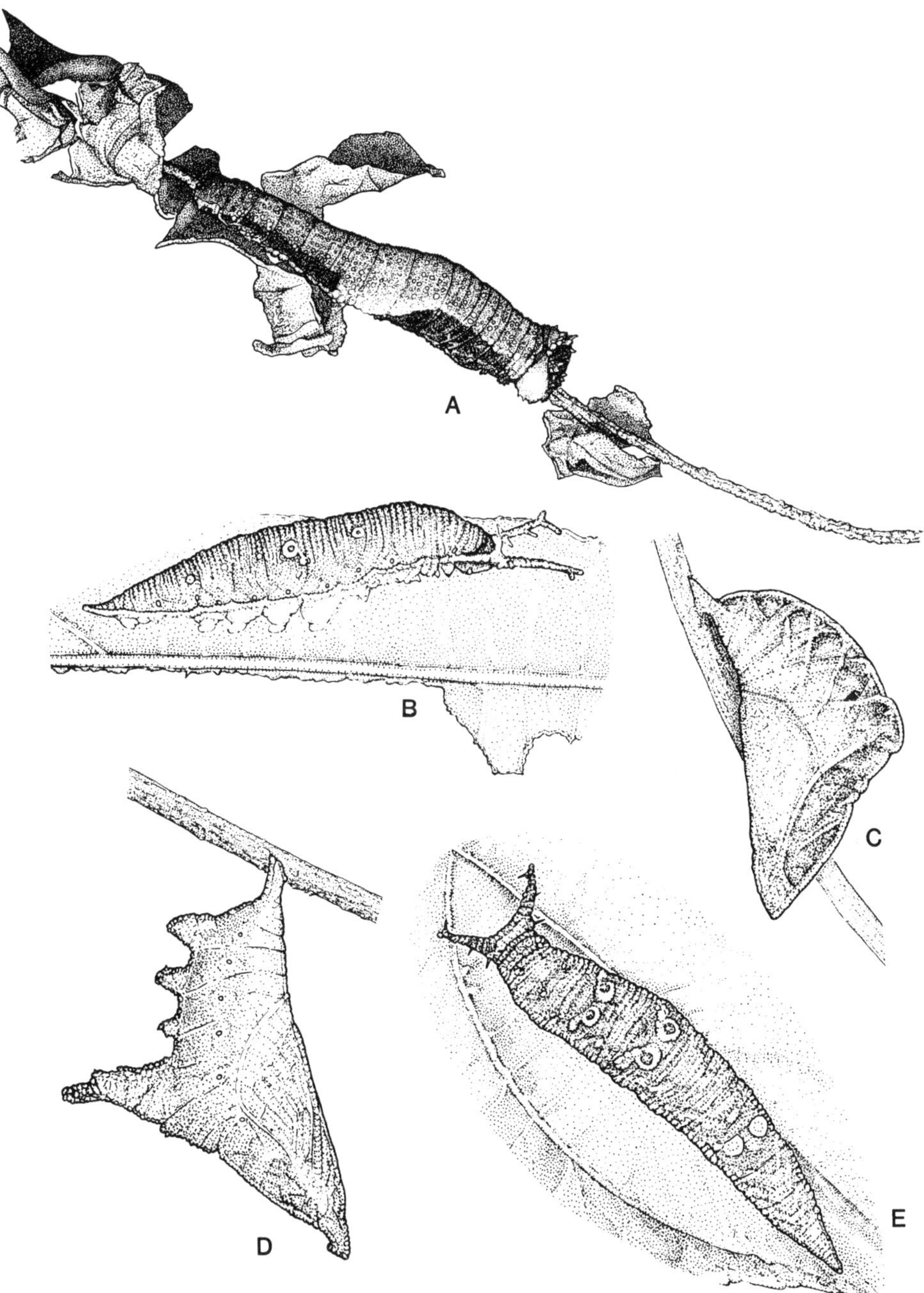

FIGURE 21. Larvae and pupae of the Nymphalidae: Charaxinae and Apaturinae. A: *Memphis beatrix* third instar larva on frass chain; B: *Doxocopa clothilda* mature larva; C: *Doxocopa clothilda* pupa; D: *Doxocopa laure* pupa; E: *Doxocopa laure* mature larva (drawings by J. Clark).

of *Agrias* to *Prepona*—a relationship so close that *Agrias* is dubiously separated from *Prepona*. The genus ranges from Mexico to the Amazon Basin, where the greatest diversity occurs. Of the five species in *Agrias*, two occur in Costa Rica.

The hostplants of *Agrias* are for the most part unknown, although judging from the number of bred specimens in commercial shipments, commercial sources appear to have held hostplant records in secrecy. The only published records are of Erythroxylaceae, Myrtaceae, and Quiinaceae, of which only Erythroxylaceae has been verified. The eggs are round, smooth, and laid singly. The larvae and pupae are, in all respects, like *Prepona* in morphology and behavior (Fig. 20). The secondary chemistry of the hostplants in Erythroxylaceae is moderately well known, and the genus represents an important commercial source of cocaine alkaloids. The other families contain essential oils, phenolics, and alkaloids. It is unknown, however, whether *Agrias* gain chemical defenses of their own from their hostplants, something that should be tested by feeding experiments and subsequent chemical analyses.

Like all charaxines, adult *Agrias* feed on rotting fruits and mammal dung, but nothing is known about their longevity or what foods individuals feed on in nature. The strong resemblance between *Agrias* and *Callicore* has been suggested by Descimon (1976) to represent a mimicry ring in which *Agrias* mimic *Callicore* models. The suggestion, however, is based upon similarity of dead specimens; neither model nor mimic has ever been tested for distasteful properties, and the Descimon hypothesis has been questioned by DeVries (1980*b*). As in *Prepona*, male *Agrias* have a well developed androconial brush on the hindwing upperside, but nothing is known about if and how it is used during courtship.

Agrias amydon philatelica

DeVries, 1980

FW Length: 35-44 mm **Plate 13**

Range: Mexico to Amazon Basin. **Subspecies:** Mexico to Panama

Hostplant: *Erythroxylum havanense*, other *Erythroxylum* spp (Erythroxylaceae)

Early stages: *Mature larva*—body dull pale brown with small lichen-green spots scattered on the dorsum; a pale lateral line runs from behind head to base of caudal tails, which is slightly raised at the interface with the venter; two bumps on the thorax; venter paler brown than dorsum; head capsule pale brown with a darker brown triangular frons; epicranium with two granulate, recurved, tightly appressed horns; entire head capsule conical, as in *Prepona*. *Pupa*—pale shiny green with four dull gray spots on wingpads; tapered at either end, with abdomen produced into a hump; head slightly bifid, and generally the same as *Prepona*. The larvae are solitary, make frass chains in early instars, and later instars rest on the twigs of the plant. The larvae feed at night and have a slow, wobbly gait (see Fig. 20).

Adult: Distinguished by the red and blue on the upperside and the black ground color on the HW underside, which also bears a row of marginal ocelli.

Habits: Occurs locally from sea level to 1,000 m, on both slopes, in association with all forest habitats. Most specimens have been collected on the Pacific slope in the Guanacaste deciduous forest, but individuals have been reared from early stages gathered in lowland forests on both slopes. Individuals generally spend most of their time in the forest canopy and can be baited along forest edges. When not alarmed, individuals have a slow, conspicuous flight that is immediately noticeable up to thirty meters away. This species is rare in collections. In my experience, individuals fly during the dry seasons on the Atlantic slope, and throughout the year on the Pacific.

Agrias aedon rodriguezi

Schaus, 1919

FW Length: 46-51 mm **Plate 13**

Range: Mexico to Amazon Basin. **Subspecies:** Mexico, Guatemala, and Costa Rica

Hostplant: Unknown

Early stages: Unknown

Adult: Distinguished by the purplish hue on the upperside and the broad reddish FW band; underside has a greenish gray ground color.

Habits: This rare species is known in Costa Rica only on the Atlantic slope from two localities: Turrialba at 600 m, and in Parque Carrillo at 900 m. Before 1980, this insect was known from a single specimen collected in Guatemala. The males are canopy insects and chase anything that flies by their perch. Both sexes visit rotting fruits in the late afternoon.

Genus **PREPONA** Boisduval, 1836

The butterflies in this genus are recognized by the bright blue bands on the upperside, usually with well-developed ocelli on the hindwing and, as in *Agrias*, the males have a yellow androconial tuft on the hindwing. Its close affinity to *Agrias* is demonstrated by both the similarities of the male genitalia and the transition species of South America, which have bright red and blue on the upperside like *Agrias*. It is unclear how many species there are in the Neotropics because of the great abundance of named forms, aberrations, and oddities. The interested reader is refered to Stichel (1939). The genus ranges from Mexico south throughout the Neotropics, and has the greatest number of species in the Amazon Basin, at the base of the Andes.

The verified hostplants are Fabaceae and Mimosaceae, of which *Inga* appears to be most important. There are additional records from Sapindaceae, but the plant identifications are uncertain. The egg is round, pale, smooth, and always laid singly. The larvae are similar to those of *Archaeoprepona*, but have a head capsule like that of *Agrias*: conical in shape with two tightly appressed head horns, and twisted tails.

In Costa Rica none of the species is common, although one species (*omphale*) has an enormous geographic range. Like *Agrias*, the butterflies seem to spend most of their time in the forest canopy and seldom come to the ground, except along forest edges. Their undisturbed flight is much slower than that of *Archaeoprepona*, but they rustle when they fly, like sheets of newspaper in the wind. Nothing is known about their longevity or palatability to predators.

Prepona omphale octavia

Fruhstorfer, 1904

FW Length: 50-55 mm **Plate 13**

Range: Mexico to Amazon Basin. **Subspecies:** Central America

Hostplant: *Inga vera, I. ruiziana* (Mimosaceae); *Andira inermis* (Fabaceae)

Early stages: (Muyshondt 1973*e*) *Egg*—white, round, laid singly. *Mature larva*—body pale brown on dorsum, darker brown on venter and prolegs; thorax roundly enlarged with two dark brown warts; dorsum sprinkled with thin black lines; first two body segments constricted into a neck; body tapering markedly on posterior quarter into two long, twisted tails; anal prolegs very reduced; head capsule pale brown, pyramid-shaped, with two tightly appressed, slightly recurved horns that give the head a conical appearance when viewed from the front; entire head granulate. *Pupa*—pale green, ovoid, with a prominent hump across first abdominal segment and thorax; wingpads, head, and spiracles have orange stains; head stoutly bifid. First to third instar larvae make frass chains, later instars rest on twigs. The larvae are very passive and walk with a slow, wobbly gait.

Adult: Distinguished from all other species by the two shades of reflective blue on the FW upperside; FW underside has triangular shapes isolated from the medial line, especially at the apex; HW underside has center of midline straight for a short distance, but angled at 90° basally above and below the straight portion. See *P. gnorima* and *P. lygia*. *Note*: in many publications the names *omphale* and *laertes* have been used for the same insects. I have followed Stichel (1939), who lists the synonymies and the ranges of the two species.

Habits: Occurs from sea level to 1,200 m on both slopes, in all forest habitats. Encountered as uncommon solitary individuals along forest margins and light gaps. The males perch in the canopy and subcanopy during late morning until early afternoon, and chase anything that passes by. While perched, the male holds the wings open at about 45°, with the head toward the ground. Females fly during midday along forest edges and in large light gaps, where they search for oviposition sites. Both sexes feed on rotting fruits, but I have found them to be more attracted to fruits in the canopy than in the understory. Although both sexes can fly unbelievably fast when alarmed, individuals fly rather slowly when approaching rotting fruits or moving through the habitat. This species is the most common *Prepona* in the Neotropics.

Prepona dexamenus

Hopffer, 1874

FW Length: 41-45 mm **Plate 13**

Range: Costa Rica(?), Panama to Amazon Basin

Hostplant: Unknown

Early stages: Unknown

Adult: Distinguished by the small size; distal half of wings on underside brown, basal half white, with a straight interface between the two colors. See *P. lygia*.

Habits: Unknown from Costa Rica, but occurs in Panama in association with lowland rain forest habitats on the Atlantic slope. I include it here as a possibility to be looked for.

Prepona gnorima

Bates, 1875

FW Length: 42-48 mm **Plate 13**

Range: Honduras to Colombia

Hostplant: Unknown

Early stages: Unknown

Adult: Similar to *P. omphale* but distinguished

by the jagged medial line on the HW underside; FW postmarginal line broken into elongated teeth that are not isolated into triangles; basal white of the HW deeply constricted on median. Compare with *P. omphale* and *P. lygia*.

Habits: Very rare in Costa Rica, as well as throughout its range. I have found it in two localities: Las Alturas at 1,600 m in premontane wet–rain forest transition, and in the Talamancas on the Atlantic slope in tropical wet–premontane rain forest transition habitats. For over an hour I watched one male perched during early afternoon in the subcanopy. This male remained on the perch after being approached by *Morpho peleides, M. theseus, Hamadryas amphinome,* and *Adelpha* species, and only left his perch to chase an *Archaeoprepona* on a wild chase, and then return to the same spot. Its flight was less frantic than other *Prepona* and *Archaeoprepona* I have seen.

Prepona lygia

Fruhstorfer, 1904

FW Length: 48-50 mm **Plate 13**

Range: Costa Rica and western Panama

Hostplant: Unknown

Early stages: Unknown

Adult: Distinguished by the intense violet overcast on the FW upperside; HW upperside has blue ocelli along the margin; similar to *P. gnorima* on underside but with distal half of both wings very dark. See *P. gnorima*.

Habits: Extremely rare, known from a few specimens labeled "Chiriqui," and two from Costa Rica taken near Las Alturas at 1,500 m. It is so little known and rare that it is possible that it is a form of *P. gnorima*. I have never seen it alive.

Genus **ARCHAEOPREPONA**
Fruhstorfer, 1915

The butterflies in this genus are similar to *Prepona*, and the group is considered to be a subgenus of *Prepona* by many authors. There is at present sufficient evidence to separate it on the basis of male genitalia, as well as the fact that the male androconial tufts are black (never yellow), and the larvae show differences in the configuration of the head capsule and the shape of the body. The genus *Archaeoprepona* is recognized by the abovementioned characters and also by generally having a somber coloration on the underside, and usually lacking conspicuous ocelli. The genus ranges from Mexico throughout the Neotropics. As in related genera (*Agrias* and *Prepona*), there are many problems with the nomenclature. Most of the present names can be found in Stichel (1939); these may differ considerably from the arrangement by Fruhstorfer (1915, repeated in Seitz 1924). There is one correction of the familiar Fruhstorfer names used in Seitz that applies to the fauna of Costa Rica. The species name *antimache* is a junior synonym of *demophoon*, and hence the correct name becomes confusingly similar to another familiar name, *demophon*.

The hostplants of *Archaeoprepona* include Lauraceae, Malpigiaceae, Annonaceae, Menispermaceae, and Monimaceae. Most of these families contain aromatic oils. The egg is round, smooth, and always laid singly. The larvae differ from *Prepona* by having the head horns widely spaced, the thorax formed almost into a pyramid, and the caudal tails not twisted. The pupa is the same general shape as *Agrias* and *Prepona* (Fig. 20).

In Costa Rica, the adults are very fast fliers, and make a rustling sound that can be heard some meters away. Like *Prepona*, the males perch head-downward on tree trunks and vigorously chase other passing butterflies. It is not unusual to see several racing in long erratic circles around a large tree, only to have each individual return to the same spot where it had previously perched. Although *Archaeoprepona* do spend time in the forest canopy, I have some evidence to suggest that individuals feed most often on the forest floor, the opposite of *Prepona*. In general, *Archaeoprepona* are encountered more commonly than *Prepona*, but there are still some very rare species that occur in our area.

The beak-marks on field-collected specimens and observations on jacamars and other insectivorous birds suggest that adults are palatable to birds. Their defense appears to be the very fast, erratic flight, and the property that the wings tear easily and allow escape. While there has been no formal study on any species, there is some anecdotal evidence that *Archaeoprepona* lives for up to two months and that individuals tend to stay in the same areas for long periods of time (Fruhstorfer 1915; Gilbert 1969; personal observation).

Archaeoprepona demophon centralis

Fruhstorfer, 1905

FW Length: 54-60 mm **Plate 14**

Range: Mexico to Amazon Basin. **Subspecies:** Mexico to Panama

Hostplant: *Annona* (Annonaceae); *Malpigia glabra* (Malpigiaceae)

Early stages: (Muyshondt 1976*b*) *Egg*—round, white, laid singly. *Mature larva*—body brown on thorax and then below spiracles; thorax enlarged, forming a dark brown triangle that has three prominent blue projections at each apex; remainder of dorsum pale brown with a few dark slanting bands; caudal tails dark brown, granulate, with yellow spots, and recurved; many blue spots scattered on the tails and around the spiracles; head capsule pale brown, granulate, with two short, stout, widely spaced, recurved head horns; sides of head have a lateral spine; face has a thin inverted V shape. *Pupa*—bluish green with scattered white irregular spots that resemble lichens; general shape ovoid with stoutly bifid head and prominent thoracic hump. The first three instars make frass chains, later instars rest on the stem of the hostplant (Fig. 20).

Adult: Upperside has greenish blue bands; underside pale brownish gray; HW medial line undulate (not jagged). Compare with *A. camilla* and *A. demophoon.*

Habits: Widespread and common from sea level to 1,600 m on both slopes, in association with all forest and old second-growth habitats, but less frequent in the Guanacaste deciduous forest. In lowland rain forest, this species is persistant throughout the year, most likely as breeding populations, and is occasionally found in Guanacaste during the dry season as very worn individuals.

Archaeoprepona demophoon gulina

Fruhstorfer, 1904

FW Length: 54-58 mm **Plate 14**

Range: Mexico to Amazon Basin. **Subspecies:** Central America

Hostplant: *Persea americana, Nectandra, Ocotea* (Lauraceae)

Early stages: (Muyshondt 1976*b*) Similar to *A. demophon*, but differing as follows: *Mature larva*—thoracic hump more prominent; dorsum posterior to thorax whitish, the remainder of body brown; head capsule less granulate, and a white ridge along sides of horns from tip to base of head. *Pupa*—more slender than *A. demophon.*

Adult: Known in most literature as *A. antimache gulina.* Distinguished by the bluish green bands on the upperside; underside silver-gray; medial line on HW irregular and angular; inner margin of FW has a black patch. See *A. demophon* and *A. camilla.*

Habits: Widespread and common throughout Costa Rica from sea level to 1,600 m on both slopes in all forest habitats; the commonest species in *Archaeoprepona.* Very often found flying with *A. demophon.* Its habits are similar to *A. demophon*, but it is much easier to attract to rotting fruits, and usually found as locally common populations.

Archaeoprepona meander amphimachus

(Fabricius, 1775)

FW Length: 50-58 mm **Plate 14**

Range: Mexico to Amazon Basin. **Subspecies:** Mexico to Colombia

Hostplant: Unknown

Early stages: Unknown

Adult: Distinguished by the contrasting halves of the underside; basal portion of wings white, distal portion brown. *Note*: specimens vary as to the intensity of the brown. The darker brown form that is illustrated is much less common than individuals that have pale brown on the distal half of the wings.

Habits: Occurs from sea level to 1,800 m on both slopes, in all wet forest habitats, and occasionally in Guanacaste during the rainy season. Encountered as rare solitary individuals, but usually present in most forests. I have found that this species is less attracted to rotting fruit than *A. demophon* or *A. demophoon.*

Archaeoprepona camilla

(Godman and Salvin, 1884)

FW Length: 56-60 mm **Plate 14**

Range: Nicaragua to Colombia

Hostplant: Unknown

Early stages: Unknown

Adult: Distinguished by the large size and pale yellowish ground color on the underside; HW margin has a row of small ocelli. See *A. demophoon.*

Habits: Occurs from sea level to 600 m on the Atlantic slope, in rain forest habitats; most common in swamp forest. Encountered as locally abundant populations throughout the year, but found with greatest frequency during the dry seasons. Both sexes visit rotting fruits on the forest floor in large light gaps.

Archaeoprepona phaedra

(Godman and Salvin, 1884)

FW Length: 52-56 mm **Plate 13**

Range: Mexico to Panama

Hostplant: Unknown

Early stages: Unknown

Adult: Distinguished by the produced FW apex and excavated FW margin; upperside has reduced blue bands; the androconial tufts are very reduced; underside has a smoky gray ground color; HW has a row of marginal ocelli. See *A. demophon.*

Habits: Apparently rare throughout its range,

and known from Costa Rica only by a few specimens collected in the Talamancas near Parque Amistad in the premontane wet rain transition forest around the Volcan Chiriqui. I have never seen it alive, and nothing has been published on its habits.

Genus **SIDERONE** Hübner, 1823

This genus is recognized by the elliptical forewing, which always has red coloration, the lobed hindwing distal margin, and a rich brown ground color on the underside. Comstock (1961) treated all of the butterflies in *Siderone* under the species *marthesia* and concluded that all the variations were best placed within this single, highly variable species. In the present accounts I have separated the Central American members of *Siderone* into two species on the basis of their very distinct patterns. The genus ranges from Mexico to the Amazon Basin and the West Indies.

The hostplants are all in the Flacourtiaceae, of which the genus *Casearia* is important. The egg is round, smooth, and laid singly. The larvae and pupae are very similar to *Zaretis*. The larvae make frass chains on leaf tips and rest on these when not feeding. In Costa Rica the larvae are attacked by chalcid wasps.

In Costa Rica, *Siderone* is found in all habitats below 1,000 m throughout the country, although on the Pacific slope one species is more common than on the Atlantic. The butterflies are infrequently seen in the forest, but occasionally may be found in numbers at rotting fruits. In the Guanacaste deciduous forest, the genus is very seasonal, being most abundant during the rainy season. While flying, the red on the upperside makes individuals very conspicuous. It is unknown if this bright coloration is linked to unpalatability.

Siderone marthesia

(Cramer, 1777)

FW Length: 34-39 mm **Plate 13**

Range: Mexico to Brazil

Hostplant: *Casearia sylvestris, Zuelania quidonia* (Flacourtiaceae)

Early stages: (Muyshondt 1976*b*) Similar to *Zaretis itys*, but differs as follows: larger in all stages; mature larva has a conspicuous white patch on the mesothorax; head horns are very thick and knobbed; entire head is covered in granules and setae. The larvae behave like *Zaretis*. *Pupa*—green with dark areas near the spiracles and edges of wingpads; wingpads conspicuously indented.

Adult: Variable; distinguished by a dark oblique band that splits the red on the FW upperside; HW upperside usually has red near costa. See *S. syntyche*.

Habits: Occurs from sea level to 1,000 m on the Pacific slope, in all forest habitats, and occasionally on the Atlantic slope in lowland disturbed forest. Individuals are found mostly in forests, but occasionally will fly around isolated trees in pastures. The flight is fast and sailing, and similar in many respects to that of *Archaeoprepona*. When not feeding on rotting fruits, individuals perch for long periods in the canopy. The females oviposit during midday, usually on small plants along forest edges. This species is less common in Costa Rican collections than in collections from other parts of its range.

Siderone syntyche

Hewitson, 1853

FW Length: 35-37 mm **Plate 13**

Range: Mexico to Costa Rica

Hostplant: Unknown

Early stages: Unknown

Adult: Distinguished from *S. marthesia* by the violet-blue FW upperside with a single wide red medial band that runs from costa to cell. See *S. marthesia*.

Habits: This rare Costa Rican species is known from the Atlantic slope in the Valle de Turrialba at 700 m, and on the Pacific slope at 1,200 m near San Vito de Java. Both localities are premontane wet forest habitats. I have not seen this species alive, and include it here as distinct from *S. marthesia* to call attention to the very different pattern, in the hope that the habits and status of both species can be compared in the future.

Genus **ZARETIS** Hübner, 1819

This genus is immediately recognized by the striking resemblance to dead leaves on both upper and undersides of the wings. This resemblance is especially striking, since in all species there are several transparent spots on the forewing that appear to be "rot holes." There are four species, three of which occur in Costa Rica. The genus ranges from Mexico throughout Central and South America, and all of the species apparently show seasonal variation with respect to forewing apex and patterns.

The hostplants belong to the Flacourtiaceae and include a number of genera, *Casearia* being most important. The egg is round, smooth, and laid singly. The larvae show a transition from *Archaeoprepona* by having an enlarged thorax, a stout head with two widely spaced horns, and a short bifid tail (Fig. 20). The pupa is angularly compressed, with the abdominal segments greatly compacted. The larvae, which are frequently parasitized by chalcid wasps, make frass chains on leaf tips and rest on these when not feeding.

In Costa Rica, *Zaretis* is found from sea level to 1,000 m in all forest habitats. The adults show marked seasonality, and in some years can be exceedingly common; at other times, individuals are extremely rare. From observations on caged birds and beak-marks on their brittle wings, there is little evidence to indicate that *Zaretis* are anything but very palatable to predators.

Zaretis ellops

(Felder, 1869)

FW Length: 29-35 mm **Plate 14**

Range: Mexico to Colombia

Hostplant: *Casearia* (Flacourtiaceae)

Early stages: (Muyshondt 1976*b*) *Mature larva*—body dark brown with a conspicuous thoracic hump that is truncated anteriorly, and is darkest brown on this face; dorsum posterior to hump has dark rhomboid shapes that are outlined in white; a white line runs from apex of hump, along sides to the last segment; segments anterior to hump constricted; head capsule blocky, dark brown, with two stout, widely spaced, black peglike head horns; epicranium and sides have a scattering of granulations. All instars rest on frass chains. *Pupa*—pale green or brown with an elaborate red-brown cremaster; abdomen very compressed; head squared off; general shape roundly angular.

Adult: Sexes dimorphic: *Male*—dull orange on upperside, with variable FW apex. *Female*—yellowish with a dark FW apex; underside of both sexes pale yellow-brown, looking like a dead leaf. See *Z. itys*.

Habits: Occurs in seasonally and locally abundant populations from sea level to 800 m on the Pacific slope, in all forest habitats. Present throughout the year in most habitats, but in some years abundantly, in others as rare individuals. In the dry season all the dark markings are reduced in the Guanacaste forms. Individuals fly in the canopy of the forest and only descend to feed on rotting fruits, and males occasionally visit mud and dung. When settled, individuals hold their tails to the substrate and, in fact, appear to be dead leaves.

Zaretis itys

(Cramer, 1777)

FW Length: 33-36 mm **Plate 14**

Range: Southern Mexico to Brazil

Hostplant: *Casearia, Ryanea, Laetia* (Flacourtiaceae)

Early stages: Similar to those of *Z. ellops*, but differ slightly as follows: mature larva has the thoracic hump and the rhomboid shapes on the dorsum highlighted in green; last segment is splayed into a short fan; head horns curve inward toward each other, and the entire head is dotted in green granules (Fig. 20). All instars rest on frass chains at the leaf tip.

Adult: Sexes dimorphic. *Male*—upperside dark brownish orange with excavated FW margin. *Female*—upperside yellow-orange with a broad, elliptical FW; underside has a conspicuous tan area on the FW that looks like a skeletonized leaf. See *Z. ellops*.

Habits: Locally and seasonally abundant from sea level to 600 m on the Atlantic slopes, in all forest habitats. In some years individuals are exceedingly common, whereas in other years they are scarce in the same locality. Both sexes are active throughout the day, with peak activity during late morning. Females oviposit on seedling to mature hostplants occurring along forest edges and in light gaps. Both sexes feed on rotting fruits in the forest canopy and along forest edges at the ground level. I have found this species to be most common during the dry season, February to April.

Zaretis callidryas

(Felder, 1869)

FW Length: 35-42 mm **Plate 14**

Range: Mexico to Panama

Hostplant: *Casearia sylvestris* (Flacourtiaceae)

Early stages: (Muyshondt 1976*b*) *Mature larva*—similar to *Z. ellops* (as *itys* in Muyshondt) but differs by being lighter on the dorsum; head smoother and the head horns strongly curved posteriorly.

Adult: Sexes dimorphic; male has dark wing margins, female has no dark margins. Both sexes are distinguished from anything else by the opalescent sheen on the upperside and the greenish cast to the underside.

Habits: Rare and apparently very local in Costa Rica, known from three localities: Monte Verde and San Vito de Java on the Pacific slope, and Virgen del Socorro on the Atlantic slope. These localities are between 700 m and 1200 m elevation and in transition cloud forest habitats. I have collected this species on one occasion, from a trap.

Genus **HYPNA** Hübner, 1819

This genus is composed of a single species that is recognized by the broad wing shape, spatulate tails on the hindwings, and a broad creamy band on the forewings. The genus ranges from Mexico throughout Central and South America, and the West Indies.

The hostplant of *Hypna* is *Croton* (Euphorbiaceae). The egg is round, smooth, and laid singly. The larvae are similar to *Zaretis* in general shape, but are peculiar in having long bristles on the body and the head capsule.

Hypna clytemnestra clytemnestra

(Cramer, 1777)

FW Length: 40-45 mm **Plate 15**

Range: Mexico to Amazon Basin. **Subspecies:** Nicaragua to Brazil

Hostplant: *Croton* (Euphorbiaceae)

Early stages: (Based on unpublished paintings by M. Fountaine in the British Museum [Natural History]) *Larva*—body pale brown with general shape like *Zaretis*, but with a more developed thoracic hump; ten reddish tubercles on dorsum from which arise numerous long black bristles; dorsal midline black; head capsule pale brown with a corona of eight bristled tubercles; face has white warts.

Adult: Distinguished by the cream band on the FW and silver spots on the underside. The FW apex has a variable shape.

Habits: Occurs locally from 100 to 700 m on the Atlantic slope in rain forest habitats, mainly at the base of the mountains. Encountered as rare, solitary individuals, mostly on rotting fruits and sap flows, but occasionally seen flying in the forest understory. When flying, individuals resemble a medium-sized *Opsiphanes*. In my experience, individuals are seldom found with the wings intact: most have bird-beak marks or shredded tails.

Genus **CONSUL** Hübner, 1807

The butterflies in this genus are recognized by the broad wing shape, spatulate tails, lobed hindwing anal angle, and fine, almost transparent scales on the underside (best seen when a specimen is held up to a light). The genus embraces about five species, in some of which the sexes are similar, in others dimorphic. *Consul* contains the only Neotropical charaxine species that are mimetic, both in pattern and in behavior. The genus occurs throughout the mainland Neotropics in forest habitats.

The hostplants are all *Piper* (Piperaceae). The genus seems to include species that are generalist herbivores on many species of *Piper*, while others are apparently specialists. The egg is round and laid singly. The larvae are cylindrical, without projections, and the rounded head capsules bear numerous short tubercles. The pupa is compressed, as in *Zaretis*, and has the same general shape. The larvae make frass chains in early instars, and later roll the leaves into a tube and hide inside when not feeding.

In Costa Rica, *Consul* is found in all forest habitats from sea level to 1,500 m, and flies in both understory and canopy microhabitats. The flight of the nonmimetic species differs from relatives by sailing, like a *Papilio*. This form of flight is probably due to the relatively slender thorax of *Consul*. There is no evidence to suggest that *Consul* is unpalatable to predators. The adult ecology has never been studied.

Consul fabius cecrops

(Doubleday, 1849)

FW Length: 36-40 mm **Plate 15**

Range: Mexico to Amazon Basin. **Subspecies:** Mexico to Bolivia

Hostplant: Numerous species of *Piper* (Piperaceae)

Early stages: (Muyshondt 1976*b*) *Egg*—pale green, smooth, round, laid singly. *Mature larva*—body dark green (black in previous instars) with dark red stains on dorsum; spiracles yellow; head capsule black with black and yellow warts on epicranium and sides; frons has yellow bands; there are two stubby, granulate head-horns. *Pupa*—green with a shiny black cremaster; abdomen tapers sharply from wingpads, giving the appearance of a rounded wedge. The mature instars are frequently found by searching for the rolled tubes at the ends of the leaves. When confined in a plastic container, the larvae do not rest in the tubes.

Adult: Distinguished by the tiger-striped pattern, long tails, and falcate FW.

Habits: Occurs from sea level to 1,200 m on both slopes in all forested habitats. Most frequently seen flying along forest edges or rivers during the morning or at midday. The flight is slow and deliberate, like that of *Heliconius ismenius* or *Melinaea lilis*. This slow flight and tiger-striped color pattern represent the only clear example of mimicry in all the Neotropical Charaxinae. The coloration has the property that while the butterfly is flying in sunlight, the tiger-striped pattern is visible from above and below. When the wings are held together while it is feeding, only the dead-leaf pattern is shown and the tiger-striped pattern is not visible. In the early mornings I have seen males maintain perches in the subcanopy of the forest. They settle in a sunny spot with the wings held apart at about 45° (revealing the tiger stripes) and occasionally chase tiger-striped butterflies. The females are active during midday, searching for oviposition sites along forest edges and in large forest light gaps. I have been fooled on numerous occasions into thinking that the females were *Melinaea* or *Heliconius*, especially since both genera also appear to oviposit during midday, and occur in the same habitats. Both sexes feed on rotting fruits at any time during the day, but not fruits that are in the canopy. Although the typical flight is slow, when alarmed, individuals can fly very fast, like a typical charaxine.

Consul electra

(Westwood, 1850)

FW Length: 42-45 mm **Plate 15**

Range: Mexico to Panama

Hostplant: *Piper* (Piperaceae)

Early stages: (Muyshondt 1976*b*) Similar to *C. fabius* but differs by having the head capsule mostly green, and black horns on the head and different yellow bands on the face.

Adult: Distinguished by the pale tan ground color and dark FW apex. The dry season populations have a more pronounced hook to the FW apex.

Habits: Occurs from 500 to 1,400 m on both slopes in all forest habitats. The males perch in the canopy and the subcanopy during the morning, and chase almost all passing butterflies, returning to the same perch. Perching usually lasts about one hour. Females are active during midday along forest edges. This species is moderately common, but local.

Consul panariste jansoni

(Salvin, 1871)

FW Length: 39-49 mm **Plate 15**

Range: Guatemala to Colombia. **Subspecies:** Guatemala to Panama

Hostplant: *Piper reticulatum* (Piperaceae)

Early stages: Almost identical to those of *C. fabius*, but differs slightly in the lines on the face of the larval head capsule.

Adult: Sexes dimorphic; *Male*—FW upperside dark brown; HW upperside has a wide yellow band on the costa. *Female*—FW upperside dark brown with a series of yellowish spots; HW upperside orange-brown. *Note*: Comstock (1961) considered *C. jansoni* and *C. panariste* separate species. Recently G. Small has found that in the Darien peninsula of Panama, populations of the two species have identical females. As a result, *jansoni* becomes a subspecies of the older name, *panariste*. He feels the change in subspecies is due to the changing appearance of the distasteful ithomiine models. This observation is clearly worth investigating in detail.

Habits: Occurs as rare individuals from 100 to 800 m on both slopes, in association with rain forest habitats. The males are rare in collections, and I have only seen one in nature. The females are occasionally taken at rotting fruits, but this species is by no means common.

Genus **ANAEA** Hübner, 1819

The butterflies in this genus are very similar to those in *Memphis*, but are consistently separated from *Memphis* by the position of the vein R1 (see Comstock 1961). In Costa Rica, the genus is recognized by the square wing shape and the orange upperside coloration. *Anaea* ranges from the southern United States through Mexico to Panama, and all of the West Indies. There are nine species in the genus, one of which occurs in our area.

The hostplants are all in the Euphorbiaceae, and the eggs, larvae, and pupae show a strong similarity to *Memphis*. The larvae make frass chains in early instars, and later roll a tube and hide inside when not feeding.

In Costa Rica, the genus is found only on the Pacific slope, and is generally associated with disturbed habitats. *Anaea* may well be migratory, since it has managed to populate all of the Caribbean islands and is also occasionally found far north into the United States. There have been no studies on the ecology of any *Anaea* species.

Anaea aidea

(Guerin-Meneville, 1844)

FW Length: 37-40 mm **Plate 16**

Range: Mexico to Costa Rica

Hostplant: *Acalypha macrostachya* (Euphorbiaceae)

Early stages: *Egg*—white, round, laid singly.

Mature larva—body pale green, unmarked except for some pale whitish granulations and two dark reddish spots on mid-dorsum and a dark "stain" on dorsum near last segment; head capsule black with two stubby wartlike horns, and sides and face covered with white warts. *Pupa*—pale green to dark brown; cremaster black; white trim on wingpads and first abdominal segment; general shape compressed. First instars make frass chains on leaf tips, later instars roll tubes. Larvae are parasitized by tachinid flies and chalcid wasps.

Adult: Distinguished from similar species by having the distal FW margin straight; a pale, indistinct band on FW upperside runs partially onto the HW. The dry season forms have falcate FW apices. See *Memphis glycerium* and *M. eurypyle confusa*.

Habits: Occurs from sea level to 800 m on the Pacific slope, in association with deciduous forest habitats, very occasionally in wet forest. The southern range of *A. aidea* stops on the Pacific slope of the Meseta Central near Villa Colon. In Guanacaste there are some years when individuals are very common, followed by years when they are almost completely absent. Flies in the forest canopy and, when abundant, in the understory. The females oviposit during midday and may lay eggs on vegetation associated with the hostplant. Both sexes visit rotting fruits and dung, and males visit mud.

Genus **MEMPHIS** Hübner, 1819

The butterflies in this large genus bear a strong resemblance to *Anaea*, of which they were considered a subgenus by Comstock (1961). However, the third radial vein always arises distal to the fifth radial vein (as it does in *Consul*). *Memphis* includes the greatest number of species of Neotropical Charaxinae. The species range from small to medium in size. Depending on species, the sexes are similar or dimorphic, tailed or tailless, and all have a dead-leaf pattern on the underside. In total there are about one hundred species in *Memphis*, thirty of which occur in Costa Rica. The genus ranges from Mexico through the entire mainland Neotropics and the islands of Trinidad and Tobago.

Identification of *Memphis* to species is not easy, especially for some of the blue forms. The difficulty is due to the variation of upper and underside patterns, and also to the fact that quite a few species are known from only one or few specimens. When identifying *Memphis*, close attention must be paid to both the upper and underside patterns, making some allowance for known variation. In the color plates I have tried wherever possible to illustrate type specimens, or typical Costa Rican material. Even with all the literature and a large museum collection available to me, I have found certain specimens exceedingly difficult to identify. I suggest in ecological studies, where the identity of a species is very important, that the genitalia be examined and compared to the figures in Comstock (1961), or sent to a specialist who is in a position to assess all of the characters. In such situations, the more specimens from the same locality that are sent to a specialist, the better the chances are that the identifications will be correct. More than perhaps any other genus, *Memphis* requires material to be reared from long series, with a careful comparison between the adults and the early stages. After the majority of the species have been reared, we may then be able to enumerate and separate the species with confidence.

Memphis hostplants include Piperaceae, Euphorbiaceae, Lauraceae, and perhaps Monimaceae and Annonaceae. The egg is round, smooth, and laid singly. The larvae are cylindrical, without projections, usually covered in small granulations, have bifid tails, and a round head capsule with tubercles (Figs. 20, 21). The pupa is generally the same as *Anaea*. The early instar larvae make frass chains at the leaf tips; later instar larvae roll tubes and hide inside the tube when not feeding, and a single larva may make more than one tube during the course of its life (Figs. 20, 21). I have found most larvae along forest and especially riparian edges, although some species appear to be more common on isolated trees in open areas (*M. glycerium, M. arginussa, M. xenocles*). The larvae are attacked by tachinid flies and chalcid wasps. Although the leaf tube presumably protects the larvae from being attacked by parasitoids, it is not uncommon to find eggs of Tachinidae stuck on the front of the head capsule as it sits in its tube. Whether these eggs are able to hatch and the fly larvae to bore into the *Memphis* larva is unknown. The eggs of the Tachinidae are also frequently found on the body, just behind the head. As far as I am aware, all of the larvae have a well-developed neck gland that produces a range of odors, depending on the species. Perhaps this gland comes into play as a defense against parasitoids when the larva is rolled into its tube.

Throughout the Neotropics as a whole, *Memphis* occurs in all forest and second-growth habitats. The genus includes widespread and common species as well as some that occur in restricted areas, or show strange geographical disjunctions. In general, most species fly in the forest canopy, and certain species appear to be restricted to this habitat (DeVries 1985*b*). As a result, the general biology, courtship behaviors, and population ecologies have proved impossible to study. Hence there are few observations on any aspect of the adult biologies aside from the fact that they feed on rotting fruits, dung, or sometimes carrion; they look like leaves when at rest; and they fly very fast when alarmed. Collecting *Memphis* involves luck: one cannot predict which species will come to the traps—they just appear.

In the markedly dry habitats it is apparent that species are seasonal, but whether or not any migrate is unknown. Certainly in the Guanacaste forests there are greater numbers of species and individuals during the rainy season, but it is unknown how many species are actually resident in a given habitat throughout the year.

From a few feeding experiments with caged birds, and from many field-caught specimens with beak-marks on their brittle wings, it appears that *Memphis* (like other Charaxinae) rely entirely upon crypsis and fast flight as a defense.

Memphis titan peralta

(Hall, 1929)

FW Length: male 34-35 mm, female 38-40 mm **Plate 15**

Range: Costa Rica to Peru. **Subspecies:** Costa Rica and Panama

Hostplant: Unknown

Early stages: Unknown

Adult: Sexes dimorphic: *Male*—distinguished by the pinkish violet sheen on the upperside; dark brown FW margins and apex; concave FW margin; reddish brown underside ground color. *Female*—upperside has reddish brown base to both wings, wide yellowish HW margins; underside ground color is straw yellow and pale brown.

Habits: Very rare, known in Costa Rica from Coronado, Cachi, and Las Alturas, all which are classified as premontane wet forest habitats and are situated on volcanic soils. It is also reported from Volcan Chiriqui in Panama. The elevational range of the localities is 1,200-1,500 m. I have never seen this species in nature.

Memphis eurypyle confusa

(Hall, 1929)

FW Length: male 28-30 mm, female 31-34 mm **Plate 15**

Range: Mexico to Bolivia. **Subspecies:** Mexico to Panama

Hostplant: *Croton reflexifolius, C. jalapensis* (Euphorbiaceae)

Early stages: (Muyshondt 1974*b*) *Egg*—white, round, laid singly. *Mature larva*—green body with pale green longitudinal stripes and transverse rows of yellow tubercles; irregular white band on sides; dark reddish patches on sides and across thorax. Head capsule is green with two black stubby horns and yellow tubercles on the sides; face has alternate green and yellow vertical bands. *Pupa*—pale green or brown with yellow on edge of wingpads; shape like that of *Consul*. The early instars make frass chains, later instars roll tubes and hide inside (see Fig. 20).

Adult: Sexes dimorphic. *Male*—reddish orange on upperside; black FW subapical bar; HW squared, with tail; underside ground color reddish brown with a thin medial line on FW that curves basally, enters HW, then breaks and continues in a more distal position. *Female*—upperside yellow-orange, with irregular pale area near submargin; underside has medial line bowed basally on both wings. See *M. ryphea* and *M. chrysophana*.

Habits: Occurs from 100 to 700 m on both slopes, in rain forest habitats. Numerous collections of this species have been made in Turrialba, San Vito de Java, and Palmer Norte. In these habitats, it is not infrequently taken in traps placed along a forest edge.

Memphis ryphea ryphea

(Cramer, 1775)

FW Length: male 27-30 mm, female 30-34 mm **Plate 15**

Range: Mexico to Amazon Basin. **Subspecies:** Mexico to Peru

Hostplant: Unknown

Early stages: Unknown

Adult: Sexes dimorphic. *Males*—with or without tails; distinguished by the dark blue bar across the distal end of the FW cell on the upperside. *Female*—tailed; upperside golden brown; FW upperside has dark brown margins and apex; underside of FW has a straight line running from apex to inner margin; ground color brownish. See *M. eurypyle confusa* and *M. chrysophana*.

Habits: In Costa Rica, apparently confined to the Atlantic slope below 700 m, in rain forest habitats. Most of the specimens I have seen are from the Turrialba Valley. Uncommon.

Memphis chrysophana
(Bates, 1866)

FW Length: 25-29 mm **Plate 15**
Range: Costa Rica and Panama
Hostplant: Unknown
Early stages: Unknown
Adult: Sexes dimorphic. *Male*—distinguished by the violet-pink overcast to the upperside; FW extracellular bar dark blue. *Female*—ground color on upperside yellow-orange; FW cell bar and apex black. Both sexes have straight FW margin and no scalloping to the HW margin. See *M. eurypyle confusa* and *M. ryphea*.
Habits: Occurs as uncommon local populations from sea level to 900 m on both slopes in rain forest habitats. I have found it at La Selva, Guapiles, Turrialba, and San Vito.

Memphis glycerium
(Doubleday, 1850)

FW Length: 32-35 mm **Plate 16**
Range: Southern United States to Colombia
Hostplant: *Croton jalapensis* (Euphorbiaceae)
Early stages: *Egg*—white, laid singly. *Mature larva*—similar to *M. eurypyle confusa*.
Adult: Distinguished by the excavated FW margin; dark FW margins and distinct FW extracellular band. See *Anaea aidea*.
Habits: Widespread and common on the Pacific slope from sea level to 1,000 m, less common on the Atlantic slope from 800 to 1,000 m, and apparently not in the lowlands. Flies in areas of disturbed forests and is commonest during May to October. Males fly along forest edges from ground to canopy level, and are active from morning until early afternoon. The females are active in the forest understory and along forest edges during midday, when they are searching for oviposition sites, usually on sapling plants.

Memphis aureola
(Bates, 1866)

FW Length: male 32-34 mm, female 36-38 mm **Plate 16**
Range: Guatemala to Colombia
Hostplant: Unknown
Early stages: Unknown
Adult: Sexes dimorphic: *Male*—distinguished by the pale green band across the FW, which continues along the HW margin. *Female*—tailed; FW upperside has a prominent white to pale greenish white band.
Habits: Rarely collected in Costa Rica. It occurs very locally from 100 to 700 m on the Atlantic slope, in rain forest and premontane rain forest. In my experience, both sexes inhabit the forest canopy, and may be taken at ground level only at the edges of ravines.

Memphis lankesteri
(Hall, 1935)

FW Length: 30-35 mm **Plate 16**
Range: Costa Rica
Hostplant: Unknown
Early stages: Unknown
Adult: Distinguished by the black upperside ground color with a trace of blue at the bases of the wings; FW underside has pale brown and silver markings; FW apex slightly produced and curved outward.
Habits: This rare species is apparently endemic to Costa Rica, occurring locally from 1,000 to 1,500 m in the southwestern Meseta Central, in association with premontane wet forest habitats. Virtually all specimens have come from the mountains near Tres Rios and Patarra. I am informed by I. Chaon that the species is locally abundant in Patarra from the end of the dry season through the mid-rainy season in the remnant patches of forest in that area. This species is very rare in Costa Rican collections.

Memphis herbacea
(Butler and Druce, 1872)

FW Length: 29-32 mm **Plate 16**
Range: Mexico to Costa Rica
Hostplant: Unknown
Early stages: Unknown
Adult: Known only from males. Distinguished by a subapical blue-green spot on FW upperside; basal portion of wings blue-green; underside similar to *M. lankesteri*, but with a dark area (band) near base of wings.
Habits: This rare species is known in Costa Rica from the Pacific slope wet forest habitats ranging from 500 to 1,000 m, and from one locality on the Atlantic slope. The localities are San Mateo, Atenas, San Vito, and Juan Viñas.

Memphis ambrosia
(Druce, 1874)

FW Length: male 34-35 mm, female 39 mm **Plate 16**
Range: Costa Rica and Panama
Hostplant: Unknown
Early stages: Unknown
Adult: Sexes dimorphic. *Male*—tailless; upperside is blue with a distinct rectangular patch on FW subapex; FW and HW margins have sparse light blue scaling; there are three

round blue spots on posterior of HW margin; underside is mottled reddish brown; there is a line of light scales from FW apex to midwing, and a round patch of scales around excavated inner margin; HW shape is rounded. *Female*—spatulate tail; colors and rectangular FW spots more distinct on upperside; HW tornus lobate; underside paler brown with narrow dark line on FW and two dark oblique lines on HW.

Habits: Rare, known from 1,000 to 1,500 m on both slopes from Orosi, Carrillo, and Talamancas near Valle de Talamanca, all of which are premontane rain forest habitats.

Memphis beatrix

(Druce, 1874)

FW Length: male 35-38 mm, female 37-40 mm **Plate 16**

Range: Costa Rica and Panama

Hostplant: *Piper* (Piperaceae)

Early stages: *Mature larva*—body dark brown with whitish hairs, head capsule rounded with a corona of yellowish, black, and reddish tubercles; face black (Fig. 21).

Adult: Sexes dimorphic. *Male*—tailed; general HW shape squarely angular; blue on HW upperside runs broadly to distal margin without a distinct blue margin, as in *M. ambrosia*; underside ground color washed gray-brown. *Female*—upperside of FW has rectangular blue spot in subapex; underside ground color gray-brown; some green scales in HW tornus; a white spot in middle of HW near costa and a white spot near inner margin of FW that is usually covered by the HW costa. See *M. ambrosia* and *M. proserpina*.

Habits: This characteristic montane species is met with throughout Costa Rica and is widespread and common from 700-1,600 m. Individuals are easily attracted to rotting bananas.

Memphis proserpina

(Salvin, 1869)

FW Length: male 35-37 mm, female 42-44 mm **Plate 17**

Range: Mexico to Costa Rica

Hostplant: Unknown

Early stages: Unknown

Adult: Sexes dimorphic. *Male*—tailless; upperside dark blue with a pale blue FW band and light blue scaling on HW distal margin; HW shape slightly angular; underside pale reddish brown with sparse white scaling at FW apex, base of costa, and whitish round spots similar to *M. beatrix*. *Female*—HW broader than FW; underside mottled reddish brown with a wide submarginal area on HW lighter in color than the rest of the ground color; basal half of both wings sprinkled with black spots; base of tail with white and green scaling. See *M. ambrosia* and *M. beatrix*.

Habits: Occurs from 600 to 1,600 m on both slopes. I have records of this species from Santa Maria, Miravalles, Turrialba, Ricon de la Vieja, and Orosi volcanoes. It is unclear whether this is distinct from *M. beatrix* or *M. ambrosia*, but a large series from Turrialba is very consistent in the patterns of the underside.

Memphis chaeronea indigotica

(Salvin, 1869)

FW Length: male 27-29 mm, female 30-32 mm **Plate 17**

Range: Costa Rica to Colombia. **Subspecies:** Costa Rica and Panama

Hostplant: Unknown

Early stages: Unknown

Adult: Sexes dimorphic. *Male*—tailed; blue on upperside; underside pattern distinct. *Female*—upperside brown with a prominent orange FW band; underside distinct.

Habits: Occurs from 400 to 1,200 m on both slopes in all forest types except the Guanacaste dry forest. Most frequently found along rivers, where the female will fly up and down the river during midday. The males perch in the canopy and the subcanopy during the morning and chase other blue butterflies. The same perch may be used over a period of several weeks.

Memphis centralis

(Röber, 1916)

FW Length: 30-33 mm **Plate 17**

Range: Costa Rica and Panama

Hostplant: Unknown

Early stages: Unknown

Adult: Distinguished by the shiny pale brown ground color on the underside. Variations include one to several black spots on distal margin of HW near base of tail; one, two, or no whitish spots on median of HW; male has tail of variable length. See *M. xenocles*.

Habits: Occurs locally on both slopes, from 100 to 600 m, in association with rain forest habitats. I have found it at Turrialba, La Selva, Palmar Sur, and Rincon de Osa. Uncommon.

Memphis xenocles

(Westwood, 1850)

FW Length: 29-32 mm **Plate 17**

Range: Mexico to Brazil

Hostplant: *Croton* (Euphorbiaceae)

Early stages: *Egg*—white, laid singly

Adult: Sexes dimorphic. *Male*—distinguished

by row of square blue-green spots on the upperside which run across the subapex to FW margins, then along the HW margin; usually one or two white dots at base of tail; underside pale gray-brown with a straight line running from FW apex to inner margin; HW has a dark line running obliquely from distal margin to inner margin; white spot at base of tail. *Female*—upperside black with basal portion of wings blue; FW with usually three, sometimes two, white subapical spots; underside similar to male. See *M. centralis* and *M. arginussa*.

Habits: Occurs from 100 to 1,400 m on both slopes, in all forest habitats except the Guanacaste dry forest. Present in most habitats throughout the year, and can be very common on the Atlantic slope.

Memphis niedhoeferi

(Rotger, Escalante, and Coronado, 1965)

FW Length: 28-31 mm **Plate 17**

Range: Mexico and Costa Rica

Hostplant: Unknown

Early stages: Unknown

Adult: Distinguished from all other species by the heavily scalloped HW margin and the variable but distinctly mottled underside.

Habits: This species is somewhat of a puzzle. Recently described from Mexico, and thought to be endemic to that country, this species can be quite common in Turrialba, Costa Rica. As far as I am aware, it occurs at 600 m in the forests around Turrialba as localized populations during the dry seasons. It is unknown between Mexico and Costa Rica.

Memphis arginussa eubaena

(Boisduval, 1870)

FW Length: 29-32 mm **Plate 17**

Range: Mexico to Amazon Basin. **Subspecies:** Mexico to Panama

Hostplant: *Croton* (Euphorbiaceae)

Early stages: Undescribed

Adult: Distinguished by an excavated FW margin and the distinctly mottled underside pattern on the HW. The name *onophis* is given to specimens with a reduced number of blue spots on the FW upperside. This species is variable. See *M. pithyusa* and *M. xenocles*.

Habits: Occurs commonly from sea level to 1,500 m on both slopes, in all forest types except the Guanacaste lowland dry forest. This species is very common around the major cities in the Meseta Central and does very well in second-growth habitats where pioneer *Croton* species are grown in hedgerows. It is present throughout the year in all habitats and appears to have about four or five major broods annually.

Memphis morvus boisduvali

(Comstock, 1961)

FW Length: male 29-32 mm, female 32-34 mm **Plate 18**

Range: Mexico to Amazon Basin. **Subspecies:** Mexico to Panama

Hostplant: *Nectandra, Ocotea* (Lauraceae)

Early stages: (Muyshondt 1975*b*) *Egg*—pale green, smooth, laid singly. *Mature larva*—body dark brown with olive-red blush; covered with numerous pale bristles; head capsule rounded, black, with pale vertical bands on the face; entire head covered with tiny pale tubercles, each bearing pale bristles; tubercles on sides are largest. *Pupa*—marbled pale and dark brown; generally rounded with compact abdominal segments, giving the impression of a small snail shell. First to third instars make frass chains; later instars roll tubes and hide inside when not feeding (Fig. 20). This species apparently lacks an eversible neck gland and emits no scent when molested; this requires verification. Larvae are attacked by tachinid flies and an entomophagous fungus.

Adult: Sexes dimorphic. Both sexes tailed. *Male*—FW apex and HW tornus acute; FW margin excavated; underside ground color mottled dark brown with lighter scaling on FW margin and above the excavated inner margin. *Female*—pale blue on upperside with wide black margins; HW tail and tornus lobate; underside ground color light brown with white scaling at base of tail and along median of HW. Variable.

Habits: Widespread and common throughout Costa Rica on both slopes, from sea level to 700 m, in association with wet and rain forest habitats, and occasional in the Pacific lowland tropical moist forest near Puntarenas. On the Atlantic slope this species is much more commonly trapped in the canopy than in the understory.

Memphis lyceus

(Druce, 1877)

FW Length: male 29-31 mm, female 34-35 mm **Plate 18**

Range: Costa Rica, Colombia to Ecuador and Bolivia

Hostplant: Unknown

Early stages: Unknown

Adult: Sexes dimorphic. *Male*—tailless; wingshape in general similar to *M. proserpina*; underside coloration reddish brown overshot with silvery scales that form a dark transverse line on FW and two oblique lines on the HW across the posterior third. *Female*—upperside has dark margins and blue base; HW tornus lobate; underside paler than male with more silvery scales, but with the distinctive lines across the HW. See *M. elara, M. proserpina,* and *M. ambrosia.*

Habits: Occurs from 700 to 1,700 m on the Atlantic slope in association with premontane rain forest. Comstock (1961) mentioned this species as perhaps occurring in Costa Rica on the strength of an old specimen collected at Orosi by A. H. Fassl. I have found this species at Bajo la Hondura, La Montura, Moravia de Chirripo, and on the Penas Blancas side of Monte Verde. It has not been found in Panama, and hence represents yet another curious range disjunction between the mountains of Colombia and the Carrillo Belt.

Memphis elara

(Godman and Salvin, 1897)

FW Length: male 34-35 mm, female 39-42 mm **Plate 18**

Range: Costa Rica and western Panama

Hostplant: Unknown

Early stages: Unknown

Adult: Sexes dimorphic. *Male*—wing shape in general like *M. proserpina*; dark blue on upperside with variable amount of light blue-green on FW subapex and HW margin; underside reddish brown with white scaling; one or two prominent whitish spots on postmedian of HW near cell; HW tornus slightly produced. *Female*—tailed; upperside has conspicuous pale blue band on FW; underside similar to male but has more scaling at base of tail. See *M. proserpina* and *M. laura.*

Habits: Occurs locally from 600 to 1,700 m on both slopes in lower and premontane wet forest habitats. I have watched males perching high in the canopy along road cuts and ravines, from mid-morning until early afternoon. The same perch was maintained by an individual for the entire day. Individuals fly extremely fast, with a short glide followed by a burst of wing-flapping. Both sexes feed on fruits in the canopy, and will also descend to feed on rotting fruits at the forest edge. This species is uncommon in collections.

Memphis laura laura

(Druce, 1877)

FW Length: male 34-35 mm, female 39-42 mm **Plate 18**

Range: Costa Rica to Colombia. **Subspecies:** Costa Rica to Colombia

Hostplant: Unknown

Early stages: Unknown

Adult: Very similar to *M. elara* but distinguished as follows: *Male*—upperside coloration dark blue (not greenish blue); HW tornus elliptically produced; underside similar but usually with only one white spot on HW median. *Female*—upperside dark blue; FW has a prominent whitish band; underside has fewer markings than *M. elara,* usually with one white spot on HW median.

Habits: Although this species is apparently not uncommon in Panama, it is only known from two specimens from Costa Rica. These I collected at Finca La Selva, in canopy traps.

Memphis oenomais

(Boisduval, 1870)

FW Length: male 25-30 mm, female 28-32 mm **Plate 18**

Range: Mexico through Central and South America

Hostplant: *Croton* (Euphorbiaceae)

Early stages: Undescribed

Adult: Sexes dimorphic; both are highly variable. *Male*—tailed; upperside black with blue at wing base; FW apex acute; FW margin excavate; underside reddish brown with a pale triangular shape or transverse line. *Female*—wing shape similar to male but broad; tail spatulate; underside pale brown, mottled, but always with a white spot in mid-HW near costa. See *M. forreri, M. orthesia, M. cleomestra,* and *M. morvus.*

Habits: Occurs from sea level to 1,000 m on both slopes, in association with all forest habitats except the Guanacaste dry forest. I have found it most commonly on the Pacific slope. This is one of the few *Memphis* species that will fly in open areas, and is commonest in disturbed areas that have extensive second growth.

Memphis artacaena

(Hewitson, 1869)

FW Length: 27-31 mm **Plate 18**

Range: Mexico to Colombia

Hostplant: *Croton schiedianus* (Euphorbiaceae)

Early stages: *Egg*—white, round, laid singly. *Mature larva*—body dull olive-green, finely pilose, with a black band across dorsum that bears a white spot on either side; a wide lateral band of black on last three segments, ending with white on anal segment; dorsum of anal segment black; head capsule black with highly ornate corona of five stubby warts colored orange and yellow; frons with dull yellow vertical bands and inverted V shapes; epicranium with stubby black horns; eversible scent gland. *Pupa*—pale brown speckled with dark brown; very compressed and lycaenidlike. First three instars make frass chains, later instars roll tubes.

Adult: Distinguished by the blue ground color

on upperside and the prominent white band on the FW.

Habits: Occurs from sea level to 800 m on both slopes, in rain forest habitats (mostly primary vegetation). Both sexes stay mainly in the forest canopy. During the morning, males perch along riparian edges and in large light gaps at the subcanopy level and chase other butterflies. During midday the females descend to the ground level and search for oviposition sites along rivers and trails in the forest. I have found this species to be present in all rain forest habitats, but it is seldom seen because individuals tend to stay in the canopy.

Memphis pithyusa

(Felder, 1869)

FW Length: 27-32 mm **Plate 19**

Range: Southern United States, through Central America to Bolivia

Hostplant: *Croton* (Euphorbiaceae)

Early stages: (Muyshondt 1975*a*) *Egg*—translucent green, round but flat on bottom and top. *Mature larva*—body green or brown with a black band on thorax, which is bordered posteriorly with white; black anal plate, black continuing anteriorly along sides, leaving the dorsum greenish brown; head capsule black with many yellow-orange tubercles; epicranium has two stubby black horns; face has yellow lines. *Pupa*—purple-brown with dark band on the fifth abdominal segment; compressed and rounded. First to third instars make frass chains, later instars roll tubes. Larval defenses include a pungent smell from the neck gland, or regurgitation of green fluid from the mouth. The eggs are parasitized by trichogrammatid wasps and the larvae by tachinid flies.

Adult: Both sexes are variable and tailed but distinguished by the darker basal portion of both wings on the underside and, usually, five spots on the FW upperside.

Habits: Widespread and common on both slopes in all primary and secondary forests from sea level to 1,500 m. On the Pacific slope individuals can be very common during the rainy season, and on the Atlantic slope it is common in secondary forest habitats and occasional in primary rain forest.

Memphis forreri

(Godman and Salvin, 1884)

FW Length: male 26-28 mm, female 30-32 mm **Plate 19**

Range: Mexico to Costa Rica

Hostplant: *Ocotea veraguensis* (Lauraceae)

Early stages: Undescribed

Adult: Sexes dimorphic. *Male*—tailless; upperside dark blue with lighter blue on FW apex and wing bases; FW apex produced; FW margin excavated; HW tornus elliptical; underside mottled pale brown and white, with a whitish triangular shape on FW near excavation on inner margin. *Female*—tailed; upperside has blue on FW and a dull dark brown on HW; FW shape broadly elliptical; FW subapex has a broad pale blue band (sometimes reduced to spots); underside mottled sandy brown with black spots on medial area of both wings. See *M. oenomais, M. centralis, M. cleomestra*, and *M. orthesia*.

Habits: Occurs from sea level to 800 m on the Pacific slope, in association with deciduous forest habitats and, rarely, in wet forest. In Guanacaste it can be very common in some years during the rainy season; other years it is infrequent, though persistent throughout the year. Most abundant from San Mateo northward but, occasionally, it may be found along the coast southward to the Osa Peninsula.

Memphis orthesia

(Godman and Salvin, 1884)

FW Length: male 27-29 mm, female 30-33 mm **Plate 19**

Range: Mexico to Panama

Hostplant: Unknown

Early stages: Unknown

Adult: Sexes dimorphic. *Male*—tailless; dark blue on upperside with lighter blue at base of wings; FW has a faint blue submarginal band; FW apex acute; underside shiny, dark brown with whitish scales prominent above the excavated FW inner margin. *Female*—tailed; similar to *M. forreri* but with a single white subapical FW spot, and without black mottling on underside.

Habits: Occurs from sea level to 700 m on the Atlantic slope, in rain forest habitats. I found this species by trapping in the forest canopy or at forest edges at the tops of steep ravines. Uncommon in Costa Rican collections.

Memphis cleomestra

(Hewitson, 1869)

FW Length: male 30-31 mm, female 35-37 mm **Plate 19**

Range: Costa Rica to Colombia

Hostplant: *Piper* (Piperaceae)

Early stages: *Egg*—pale green, round, laid singly. *Mature larva*—body velvet black with many white spots on dorsum from which arise white bristles; a white spot on side near venter at the interface of each segment; head capsule black with four short knobs on epicranium; face has white vertical bands. Earlier instars are two-tone, light and dark brown. *Pupa*—marbled white and brown; compressed and rounded, giving the impression of a snail shell. First to third instars make frass chains, later instars either sit on a frass chain, along the stem of the plant, or roll tubes. The host-plant is an epiphytic vine that grows on tree trunks.

Adult: Sexes dimorphic. *Male*—without tails; dark blue on upperside with a FW submarginal band of squarish spots; HW margin has conspicuous pale blue bands; fringe white; underside reddish brown sprinkled with white; a dark line from FW apex to HW cell; two oblique dark lines, one across the distal submargin, the other just outside the cell. *Female*—tailed; distinguished by two-tone blue on upperside, dark blue basally and pale blue distally, and broad black margins. See *M. aulica.*

Habits: I have found this species locally from 100 to 600 m on the Atlantic slope. It is rare in Costa Rican collections and infrequent in canopy traps.

Memphis aulica

(Röber, 1916)

FW Length: 31-32 mm **Plate 19**

Range: Costa Rica and Panama

Hostplant: Unknown

Early stages: Unknown

Adult: Female is unknown. *Male*—similar to *M. cleomestra* but distinguished by the more extensive pale blue on FW and HW margin; HW shape more rounded; FW margin not excavate, and FW apex not acute. See *M. cleomestra.*

Habits: Extremely rare and known from Costa Rica by a few specimens collected in the Talamancas near San Vito and Las Alturas, from 1,000 to 1,500 m. It is unclear whether this species is distinct from *M. cleomestra*, but the elevation and the apparently constant wing shape suggest that they are distinct. It will be important to describe the female of this species when it is discovered, and compare it with that of *M. cleomestra.*

Subfamily **APATURINAE**

The classification of this group of butterflies has long been controversial. Most often, the butterflies are given subfamily status or tribal status (Apaturidi), whereas some authors place the butterflies in a separate family (Howe, 1975). Since little is known about the group as a whole, and because they form a discrete global unit, they are treated here as a subfamily. The butterflies are recognized by having the discal cell in the hindwing open and a stout thorax; the sexes are dimorphic, the males usually having brilliant reflective purple, blue, or green on the upperside, whereas the female is more somberly colored. The subfamily is found in Europe, Asia, the African region, and throughout the Americas. There are about fifteen genera in the world; two occur in the New World, and only one genus occurs in the Neotropics.

It appears that the apaturines may be related to the Charaxinae and Satyrinae because of the similarities of the early stages (DeVries et al. 1985). The host plants are apparently all in the Ulmaceae, of which *Celtis* is the most important. The eggs are round with fine vertical ridges, and are usually laid singly, although some species lay eggs in clusters (*Sasakia* and *Asterocampa*). The larvae have the body smooth or rough, without spines, and the head capsule bears two prominent head horns and sometimes some lateral spikes (Fig. 21). The pupa is reminiscent of the satyrines by being elongate, smooth, flat on the venter and bowed on the dorsum, tapering to either end, and with the head bifid (Fig. 21).

In the Neotropics there is little known about the biology of the adults. In general, they are extremely fast fliers, and impetuous, mostly spending their time high in the forest canopy. Both sexes are occasionally taken at puddles enriched with urine or mammal dung, but for the most part their habits and population biology are a mystery.

Genus **DOXOCOPA** Hübner, 1819

The butterflies in this genus are often treated in older literature under the name *Chlorippe.* The butterflies are recognized by the iridescent, reflective coloration of blue, green, or purple in the males, and green forelegs in almost all species. The forewing apex is squared off and the underside has a pearly sheen. All species are sexually dimorphic; many have females that look like the genus *Adelpha. Doxocopa* ranges from the southern United States (as strays) throughout Central and South America.

There are about thirty species, nine of which occur in Costa Rica (D. W. Jenkins is planning a revision of this group).

Few species of *Doxocopa* have been reared, and like other apaturines, they feed on Ulmaceae, of which *Celtis* seems most important. The early stages are similar to the North American genus *Asterocampa* (see Scudder 1889; Howe 1975). Although the life history of one species (*D. laure*) has been known for almost a century (Müller, 1886), no other species has had its life history published (see Fig. 21).

In Costa Rica, the genus occurs from sea level to 1,200 m on both slopes in a variety of forest habitats. Most of the species are rarely seen, some are known from a single or a few specimens, and others are known only from one sex. Males are more frequently encountered than the females, and when the males fly, some resemble small *Prepona*. The females are seldom seen, apparently because they spend most active periods in the forest, and when they are seen they are often mistaken for *Adelpha*. I believe that both sexes, when fugitive, are capable of flying faster than any other Neotropical butterfly.

Although they are not common, *Doxocopa* are most frequently found along a road cut through a forest where a stream runs across the bare soil, especially where there is a source of sewage effluent. River banks where tapirs or peccaries have been are also good places to look for them. If one is fortunate enough to find a place where there is an abundance of *Doxocopa*, observations are frustrated by their incredibly quick, nervous flight; collecting them can be difficult enough, let alone watching them. Outside of noting that some species feed on flower nectar, I have been able to add little to our knowledge of their habits.

Doxocopa clothilda

(Felder, 1866)

FW Length: 30-33 mm **Plate 19**

Range: Costa Rica to Colombia

Hostplant: *Celtis* (Ulmaceae)

Early stages: *Mature larva*—body green, covered with minute granulations; five pairs of indistinct yellow-white dorsal blotches; a yellow-white dorsal midline runs from head to tips of caudal tails; head capsule has two stout horns that are black on anterior face and yellowish on posterior; face broadly striped with white, green, and black. Larvae rest with the face appressed to the leaf surface and the horns projecting forward. *Pupa*—pale green with minute white granulations; head and thoracic areas fused into a wedge shape (Fig. 21).

Adult: *Male*—upperside deep iridescent blue; underside reddish brown. *Female*—upperside brown with a broad orange band on FW; underside similar to male.

Habits: Occurs locally, and uncommonly, from 100 to 700 m on the Atlantic slope, and from sea level to 1,000 m on the Pacific slope. Individuals are generally found along riparian edges in rain forest. While flying, the female may be confused with *Adelpha melanthe*.

Doxocopa pavon

(Latreille, 1805)

FW Length: 24-30 mm **Plate 19**

Range: Mexico to Bolivia

Hostplant: *Celtis* (Ulmaceae)

Early stages: *Mature larva*—similar to *clothilda* but with more dorsal spots; green head horns.

Adult: *Male*—upperside iridescent violet with an orange spot on FW subapex. *Female*—upperside has white transverse band; resembles *Adelpha*, and bears a prominent orange spot on FW.

Habits: Occurs from sea level to 1,000 m on both slopes in association with all forest types, but only occasionally in the Guanacaste dry forest. Males visit wet sand, dung, and wet laundry. During the morning they perch about five meters above the ground, along forest edges. Females are visibly active from midday until early afternoon. Both sexes visit flowers of *Cordia* and *Croton*. On the Pacific slope it is present during the rainy season, and on the Atlantic slope during the dry seasons. Encountered as uncommon solitary individuals, but found throughout Costa Rica.

Doxocopa callianira

(Menetries, 1855)

FW Length: 25-32 mm **Plate 19**

Range: Mexico to Costa Rica

Hostplant: Unknown

Early stages: Unknown

Adult: *Male*—upperside iridescent purple with several hyaline spots on the FW subapex; underside pale brown. *Female*—brown on upperside with a broken white band on the FW; some reddish on disc of HW.

Habits: This very rare species is known from our area by a single specimen labelled "Costa Rica." Judging by collections from other countries, it is also rare outside of Costa Rica. This species requires confirmation.

Doxocopa felderi

(Godman and Salvin, 1884)
FW Length: male 21-25 mm, female 25-27 mm **Plate 19**
Range: Costa Rica to Bolivia
Hostplant: Unknown
Early stages: Unknown
Adult: *Male*—Distinguished by the purple upperside with a double row of spots running from FW costa to tornus; FW underside reddish brown at base. *Female*—round wing shape; upperside green-brown with pale green on FW and HW; underside reddish with a black postmedial band. See *Perisama* and *Diaethria.*
Habits: This rare species is known from a few individuals collected on the Atlantic slope at 1,000 to 1,500 m, all from the Talamancas south of the Valle de Reventazon. Once I observed a female perched about three meters above the ground in a large light gap. The flight was similar to *Diaethria* or *Perisama* but somewhat slower. Apparently no males have been collected in Costa Rica.

Doxocopa cherubina

(Felder, 1866)
FW Length: male 31-33 mm, female 34-37 mm **Plate 20**
Range: Mexico to Colombia
Hostplant: Unknown
Early stages: Unknown
Adult: *Male*—Distinguished from similar species by the iridescent blue-green band on the upperside, well developed on both wings but not extending to the HW margin; HW upperside has a small lunule just distal to the iridescent band, near the tornus. *Female*—distinguished by the white band on upperside that is bordered by pale blue on both wings, and a small red lunule on HW upperside that is more distinct than in the male. See *D. excelsa* and *D. cyane.*
Habits: Occurs from 400 to 1,600 m on both slopes, in association with forest habitats. The males perch on vegetation at the forest and riparian edges about five meters above the ground, and chase other butterflies in a manner that is similar to *Prepona* or *Adelpha.* During sunny mornings males visit wet sand, frequently taking flight and patrolling the wet sand with a fast circling flight, alighting for a few moments, then repeating the patrol. The female will feed on rotting fruits along riparian edges, but is rarely seen on the wing. Individuals are most frequently seen during the dry seasons, though I have never seen this species abundant.

Doxocopa cyane

(Latreille, 1833)
FW Length: male 30-31 mm, female 32-33 mm **Plate 20**
Range: Mexico to Peru
Hostplant: *Celtis spinosa* (Ulmaceae)
Early stages: Undescribed
Adult: *Male*—Distinguished from similar species by the iridescent blue-green on the upperside, confined mostly to the HW, with a small amount at base of FW; base of FW underside is a conspicuous orange, which can be used as a field character. *Female*—distinguished by the fact that the orange band on the FW upperside is thin; white band bordered by pale blue is confined to the HW; FW underside has three distinct black submarginal spots. See *D. cherubina* and *D. excelsa.*
Habits: Occurs from 200 to 1,500 m on both slopes in a wide variety of habitations, particularly where sewer drains run into a stream or river. The males perch along forest edges from 2 to 10 m above the ground, often in small groups that perform whirling aerial displays and then return to the same general area. The female is seldom seen outside of the forest, and is generally rare in collections. I found females to be active during late morning until early afternoon along rivers that run through the forest, but they were by no means common. Both sexes feed on fresh mammal dung, but I have never seen them feed on rotting fruit. This is the most commonly seen *Doxocopa* species in Costa Rica.

Doxocopa excelsa

(Gillot, 1927)
FW Length: male 33-34 mm, female 35-38 mm **Plate 20**
Range: Nicaragua and Costa Rica
Hostplant: Unknown
Early stages: Unknown
Adult: *Male*—distinguished from similar species by the extensive iridescent blue on the upperside, which extends to HW tornus and the HW margin. *Female*—distinguished by the wide orange band on the FW upperside; no red lunule on HW upperside; FW underside with one distinct black spot with a blue center, bordered on either side by two indistinct ones. See *D. cherubina* and *D. cyane.*
Habits: Occurs very locally on the Atlantic slope, so far known only from Turrialba at 600 m. The species is highly seasonal—present as adults only during June and July (A. King, personal communication) and totally absent the rest of the year. Males perch along forest edges about 8 to 10 m above the ground, and

vigorously chase each other and passing insects. The female perches close to the ground and apparently does not chase other insects. Both sexes visit flowers of a *Mikania* vine that flowers at the time of their emergence, and the female will feed on rotting fruits. This species is very rare in Costa Rican collections, and is otherwise known only from a single specimen collected in Nicaragua.

Doxocopa laure

(Drury, 1773)

FW Length: male 31-33 mm, female 36-38 mm **Plate 20**

Range: Mexico to Colombia, Venezuela, and Brazil

Hostplant: *Celtis* (Ulmaceae)

Early stages: (Comstock and Vasquez 1961) *Mature larva*—body pale green (three pairs of red-white spots on dorsum in Panamanian specimens) with tiny yellow granulations; tapered to a conical point on anterior segments, and terminated in a bifid tail; head capsule green with a corona of short green spines on sides, and two prominent, widely spaced epicranial horns that are slightly bifid at the tip. *Pupa*—pale green with a powdering of white; in lateral view it has a triangular shape; a short recurved horn arises from the dorsum and is directed posteriorly; wingpads smooth and without ridges. While at rest, the larva keeps the face down to the substrate and the horns directed forward (see Fig. 21).

Adult: Sexes slightly dimorphic, and both resemble the genus *Adelpha*. *Male*—distinguished by the overcast of iridescent purple bordering the white band on the upperside; FW has orange band extending almost to inner margin. *Female*—upperside has prominent white band on both wings and an isolated subapical orange spot on FW. See *D. plesaurina*.

Habits: Occurs from sea level to 800 m, most commonly on the Pacific slope in association with deciduous forest, and occasionally on the Atlantic slope in areas where there is extensive secondary forest. I have found that both sexes visit wet sand, fresh mammal dung, and flowers of *Cordia* and *Croton*. In Guanacaste this species is persistent throughout the year but in greatest abundance during the early rainy season; on the Atlantic slope it is found during the dry seasons.

Doxocopa plesaurina

(Butler and Druce, 1872)

FW Length: male 30-31 mm, female 32-33 mm **Plate 20**

Range: Costa Rica and Panama

Hostplant: Unknown

Early stages: Unknown

Adult: *Male*—Distinguished from *D. laure* by the configuration and greater expanse of orange on the FW upperside and lack of iridescent blue on HW. *Female*—distinguished by the extensive orange on the FW upperside. See *D. laure*.

Habits: This rare species is known from very few specimens. The type came from "Cartago," and the female illustrated here is from Bugaba, Panama. The status of this insect is unsettled; some feel it to be the South American species *D. griseldis* (Felder), others a separate species. I include it here to draw attention to the question of its status and to suggest that it be looked for.

Subfamily **LIBYTHEINAE**

This cosmopolitan subfamily is composed of relatively few species and contains only two genera: *Libythea* in the Old World, and *Libytheana* in the New World. The butterflies are medium to small and can be recognized immediately by their enormous palpi, which project forward and resemble a snout or a beak (hence the common name "snout butterflies"). All species have a falcate forewing that is squarely produced at the apex. At times considered a separate family (Ehrlich 1958*a*), the "snouts" are now treated as a subfamily of the Nymphalidae (Kristensen 1976). The systematics and relationships within the subfamily have never been elucidated, and it is unclear exactly how many species there are in the world. In the Americas there are two, perhaps three, species, one of which enters our area.

All hostplants of the Libytheinae are species of *Celtis* (Ulmaceae). The eggs are deposited singly and are rather elongate in shape. The larvae strongly resemble the subfamily Pierinae: the body is cylindrical, without spines, covered with minute hairs, and has a round, unadorned head capsule. The pupae are suspended and resemble those of certain Satyrinae or Apaturinae species.

To the field biologist, perhaps the most notable thing about the butterflies in the subfamily is the spectacular mass migrations reported for a number of the species (Williams 1930; Collenette and Talbot 1928; Gilbert 1985). During certain years very large populations can build up in areas where the hostplants are abundant. Prior to migration, the adults rest by the thousands on trees and other vegetation and, usually after heavy rain, the migration then begins. As far as I am aware, no migrant activity has been reported in the Costa Rican species.

Genus **LIBYTHEANA** Michener, 1943

The butterflies in this genus are recognized by their long, snoutlike palpi, falcate forewing, and dull brown-orange upperside with black on the forewing apex. The genus ranges throughout the United States, Central and South America, and occurs in the West Indies and Jamaica. There are approximately ten species in the genus (although it is not known for certain), one of which occurs in Central America.

The hostplants, like those of the other members of the subfamily, are species of *Celtis* (Ulmaceae). The early stages have never been described in detail for any of the Central American populations.

Libytheana carinenta mexicana Michener, 1943

FW Length: 26-29 mm **Plate 20**

Range: Southern United States to Brazil. **Subspecies:** Central America

Hostplant: probably *Celtis iguanae* (Ulmaceae)

Early stages: Undescribed, but probably similar to those of *L. bachmanii* from the United States.

Adult: Immediately distinguished from all other butterflies in Costa Rica by the long palpi and the form of the forewing apex.

Habits: Encountered as solitary individuals in certain years on the Pacific slope, from sea level to 800 m. Although they are rare, I have seen a few specimens from the Atlantic lowlands. I have most frequently found this species as occasional individuals visiting mud puddles, along with other nymphalids such as *Marpesia* and *Eunica*, during the rainy season in Guanacaste. The butterflies are quite impetuous and difficult to approach. Furthermore, when at rest, the forewing is folded down into the hindwing and the cryptic underside coloration then makes them very difficult to detect. The periodic occurrence of this species in Costa Rican habitats suggests that our populations may be part of a larger migration from elsewhere in Central America.

Subfamily **NYMPHALINAE**

Of all the subfamilies of the Nymphalidae, the most heterogeneous and least understood phylogenetically is the Nymphalinae. The Nymphalinae is a general dumping ground for all nymphalid genera that do not fit nicely into other subfamilies. As treated in this book, this diverse group is composed of the Nymphalinae, Limenitidinae, and Marpesiinae of Müller (1886) and, I am sorry to admit, these butterflies must be recognized on negative grounds—there is no easy set of characters that will always identify this group of butterflies. However, the reader should have no trouble placing a butterfly in this group with the aid of the color plates and the species accounts.

The hostplants of the Nymphalinae as treated here include: Acanthaceae, Burseraceae, Ericaceae, Euphorbiaceae, Melastomaceae, Moraceae, Rubiaceae, Sapindaceae, Tiliaceae, Ulmaceae, Urticaceae, and Verbenaceae. The early stages are amazingly diverse and the reader is directed to Figures 22, 23, and 24, and the generic accounts of *Nessaea, Epiphile, Hamadryas, Siproeta, Vanessa, Historis, Adelpha,* and *Marpesia* to appreciate this.

In Costa Rica members of the Nymphalinae are found in every habitat, and some are among our most common species. The butterflies may be palatable or unpalatable to vertebrate predators, depending on the species, and correspondingly may be cryptic or aposematically colored. The group includes butterflies that feed entirely on flower nectar, and some that feed on juices of rotting fruits. The males of many species are frequently seen visiting wet sand along rivers or at puddles (see *Eunica* and *Marpesia*), rather like members of the Papilionidae and Pieridae.

Genus **COLOBURA** Billberg, 1820

The butterflies in this genus are immediately recognized by the fine black and white "zebra stripes" on the underside and the conspicuous forewing band. The genus is considered monotypic, with a single species that ranges from Mexico to the Amazon Basin, and is common everywhere. There are, however, in Costa Rica

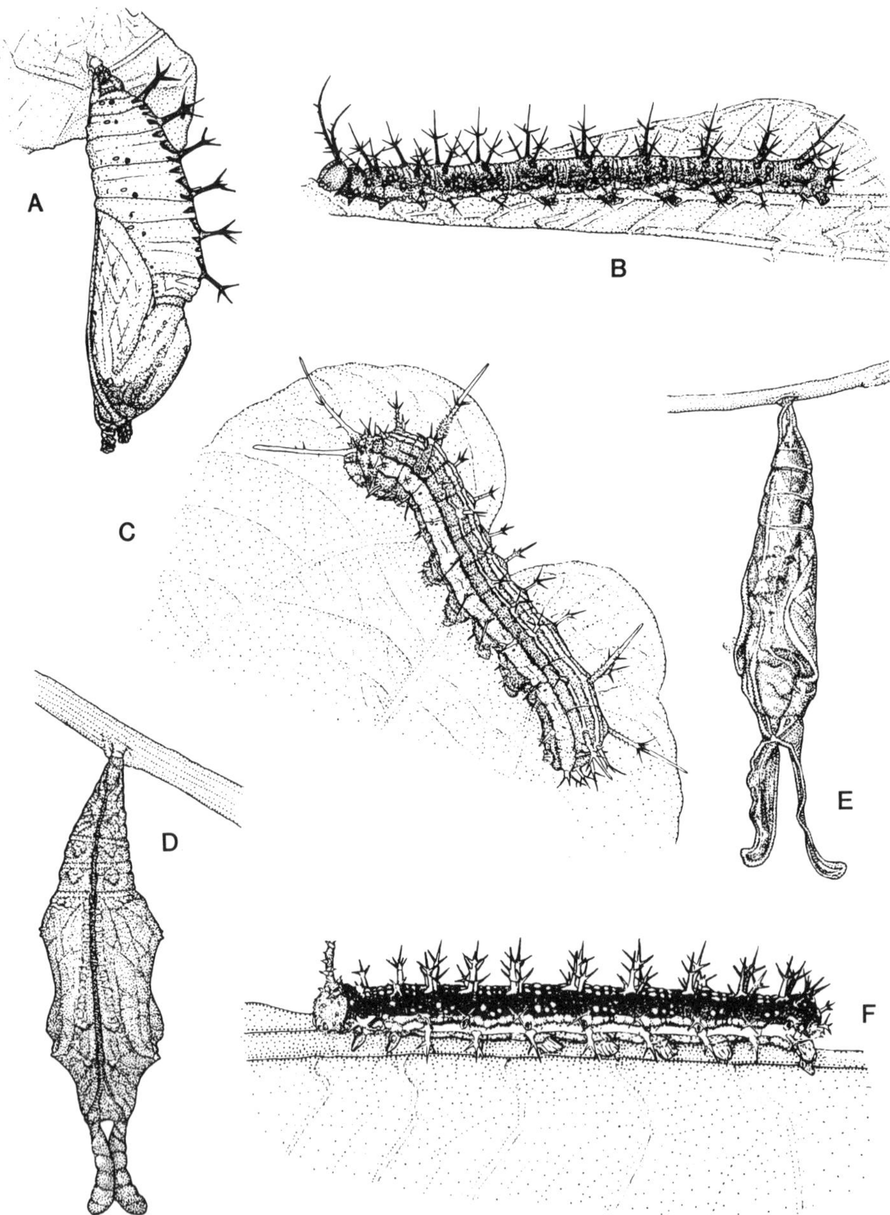

FIGURE 22. Larvae and pupae of the Nymphalidae: Nymphalinae. A: *Baeotus baeotus* pupa; B: *Tigridia acesta* mature larva; C: *Hamadryas laodamia saurites* mature larva; D: *Hamadryas februa* pupa; E: *Hamadryas amphinome mexicana* pupa; F: *Smyrna blomfildia datis* mature larva (drawings by J. Clark).

and areas in South America, two distinctive forms of larvae. This difference in larvae convinced Sepp (1848) to describe a second species, *dircoides*. I have examined the genitalia of a few reared specimens from both larval types and find nothing substantially different, but am still curious if this genus is like related genera, and has two species. More biological work is required.

Throughout its range, the hostplant for *Colobura* is Cecropia (Moraceae). The commonest larval form is velvet black, very spiny, and has two prominent head horns. The pupa is wonderfully cryptic, resembling a snapped-off splinter of wood.

In Costa Rica the adults are found from sea level to 2,000 m wherever the hostplant grows. *Cecropia* is a common secondary succession plant species and, as a result, *Colobura* is a familiar sight near human habitations. The butterflies are very tame and will visit anyone who cares to share his mango or banana with a butterfly.

Colobura dirce

(Linnaeus, 1764)

FW Length: 35-37 mm **Plate 21**

Range: Mexico throughout Central and South America, and the West Indies.

Hostplant: *Cecropia* (Moraceae)

Early stages: (Muyshondt and Muyshondt 1976) *Egg*—white, laid in small clusters of two to ten. Early instars make frass chains along the edges of the leaf. *Mature larva*—body velvet black with several rows of white rosetted spines on dorsum; spines on sides are yellow; head capsule shiny black with two prominent, recurved white horns with brown tips; a corona of short black spines on sides of head. The larvae feed in loose aggregations on the leaf. A second larval morph found in Costa Rica differs as follows: all spines bright yellow; a series of eight transverse bands on dorsum of most segments; horns on head capsule bright yellow. Larvae have been found in gregarious masses composed of all instars on canopy-sized *Cecropia* trees. *Pupa*—cylindrical, elongate, and looks like a dead broken twig.

Adult: Immediately distinguished by the yellowish FW band or, when in the field, by the zebra pattern on the underside.

Habits: Occurs from sea level to 1,500 m on both slopes, in association with all habitat types, especially second-growth forest. Essentially a canopy species, but feeds anywhere from the ground level upward on rotting fruits, carrion, dung, and can be baited with wet laundry. Both sexes perch around midday on tree trunks, head down, about three to eight meters above the ground, where they are most frequently encountered. The females oviposit throughout the day on seedling to mature canopy trees. It appears that juvenile plants without *Azteca* ant colonies in them are most frequently used. Even so, many *Cecropia* plants with thriving ant colonies in them have larvae feeding on the leaves. In some cases, the larvae cut the leaf veins like *Tigridia, Lycorea*, and *Melinaea*, and feed on the drooping leaf tips. In my experience, the adults are found throughout the year in all habitats, but at low population densities.

Genus **TIGRIDIA** Hübner, 1819

This close relative of *Colobura* is recognized by the orange zebra-striped pattern on the underside, and the orange disc on the hindwing upperside. There is a single species that ranges from Costa Rica through South America.

Seitz (1914) records the larval hostplant to be *Theobroma* (Sterculiaceae), which I feel is an error, even though his description of the larva seems to fit. In Costa Rica, *Tigridia* feeds on *Cecropia* and *Paruma* (Moraceae) and will not eat cocoa (*Theobroma*) leaves if offered. The larvae are very spiny, and the head capsule bears two recurved head horns; all of the spines have accessory spines on the shafts (Fig. 22). The pupa, as in *Colobura*, resembles a splinter of wood, but differs by having the head area more produced and toothed on the outside edges of the head horns.

The habits are similar to those of *Colobura* except that they are less tolerant of highly disturbed areas and are intolerant of areas that experience a severe dry season.

Tigridia acesta

(Linnaeus, 1758)

FW Length: 28-30 mm **Plate 21**

Range: Costa Rica to the Amazon Basin

Hostplant: *Cecropia, Paruma aspera* (Moraceae)

Early stages: *Egg*—white, laid singly, but a female usually lays several eggs on the same plant. Early instars occasionally make frass chains. *Mature larva*—body a "rotten meat" purple; each segment bears six black spines, each of which has one whorl of accessory spines about one-third of the way down the shaft; there is a black square on body at base of each spine; the dorsal midline is composed of black squares; the head capsule is a dull yellow-orange and bears two recurved horns with white tips; the horns have many small spines and granules on shafts (Fig. 22). *Pupa*—resembles a piece of wood that is tapered at each end; overall color tan, mottled with green, with a dark isoceles triangle on the first abdominal segment; head has a pair of flatly appressed horns that are toothed on the outer edges. The larvae cut through leaf veins, which causes the leaf tip to droop into a tent. After the leaves have drooped, the larvae feed on the leaf tips.

Adult: Distinguished by the orange upperside and the orange zebra stripes on the underside. The female has a darker orange FW band.

Habits: Occurs from sea level to 1,500 m on both slopes, in association with wet forest habitats; not entering the Guanacaste dry forest. The males, especially, are most frequently found in light gaps in the forest, perched head-down on tree trunks. The females are most active at midday along forest edges and in light gaps, when they inspect sapling hostplants. Both sexes feed on rotting fruits. Present in most forests, but at low densities.

Genus **HISTORIS** Hübner, 1819

The butterflies in this genus strongly resemble species in the subfamily Charaxinae with respect to general morphology and habits. They are, however, only distantly related and represent a remarkable case of evolutionary convergence. There are a number of generic names that have been used for the butterflies in *Historis*, most of which apparently are still potentially valid (see Muyshondt and Muyshondt 1979). There are two species in *Historis* that are recognized by the black wing margins and orange forewing base on the upperside, and a dead-leaf pattern on the underside. The genus ranges from the southern United States through Central and South America, and occurs in the West Indies.

The hostplants are various species of *Cecropia* (Moraceae). The larvae are very spiny and bear no resemblance to the Charaxinae, even though the adults do. The pupae have a peculiar ridge of rosetted spines on the dorsum, and the head is strongly bifid.

In Costa Rica, the species are found from sea level to 1,400 m in all habitats. The wide distribution is probably due to the fact that its hostplant thrives in disturbed areas. The adults feed entirely on rotting fruits and dung, and are very sensitive to small quantities of fruit on the forest floor. This is best demonstrated by placing a small quantity of banana on the ground in a light gap and returning about one hour later. If there are *Historis* in the area, they will be sure to find it. The flight powers of *Historis* are remarkable. It is not uncommon to hear males crashing about in the forest canopy as they chase other butterflies or birds for long distances at great speed, then return to the same perch. During midday, both sexes are frequently associated with the hostplant, either flying around it or perching on it. It is not known whether the hostplant plays a role in courtship.

Historis odius

(Fabricius, 1775)

FW Length: 50-55 mm **Plate 21**

Range: Southern United States and throughout Central and South America and Cocos Island

Hostplant: *Cecropia* (Moraceae)

Early stages: (Muyshondt and Muyshondt 1979) *Egg*—pale brown, laid singly along the midvein of the leaf. Early instar larvae make frass chains at the leaf edges, most likely to stay away from the ants that usually inhabit the hostplant. Later instars rest on the terminal meristem and are not bothered by ants. *Mature larvae*—body brown to tan with yellowish transverse stripes; dorsum sparsely covered with orange rosetted spines; sides sparsely covered with rosetted yellowish spines; head capsule squarish with prominent lobes on top of head; each lobe bears a short, stout, spiny horn with a terminal rosette of spines; base of horns are set into an orange area on the head. *Pupa*—sandy pink with six prominent, reddish, rosetted spines on abdominal segments; body curved dorsolaterally; head bears two appressed, rodlike, recurved horns with a granular surface. The pupa wriggles like a fish out of water if molested, hence the Costa Rican name "pescadillo."

Adult: Distinguished by the single white spot in the FW apex, no tail on HW margin, and underside without angled midline. See *H. acheronta*.

Habits: Widespread and common in all habitats in Costa Rica, including Isla del Coco, from sea level to 1,500 m. Although frequently seen near human habitations feeding on garbage, this species spends a good deal of time in the forest canopy, where it feeds on ripening and damaged fruits. Persistent in all areas throughout the year, commonest in

Guanacaste during the rainy season, and during the dry seasons in rain forest habitats.

Historis acheronta
(Fabricius, 1775)
FW Length: 35-47 mm **Plate 21**
Range: Mexico to the Amazon Basin and the West Indies
Hostplant: *Cecropia* (Moraceae)
Early stages: (Muyshondt and Muyshondt 1979) Early instars make frass chains on the leaf edges, probably for the same reason that *H. odius* does. *Mature larva*—body black, dotted with spots of blue; dorsum has three conspicuous orange patches; dorsum sparsely covered with white rosetted spines; head capsule (variable in Costa Rica) black or red with two short rosetted head horns. *Pupa*—similar to *odius* but differs in that the head horns are recurved and divergent, not appressed.
Adult: Distinguished by the five to seven white spots on the FW apex, short, spikelike tail on HW margin, and angled midline on underside. *Note*: there is a great amount of variability in size of this species; some individuals are quite small.
Habits: Occurs from sea level to 1,200 m on both slopes, in association with all forest habitats. Its habits are similar to those of *H. odius*, but this species is decidedly less common, and it may be rare in many areas.

Genus **BAEOTUS** Hemming, 1939

The butterflies in this genus are recognized by their white underside with many fine black lines, and the hindwing margin with toothlike projections. The genus ranges from Costa Rica to the Amazon Basin. There are two species, one of which enters our area.

The hostplants are unknown, but the pupa of our Costa Rican species (Fig. 22) strongly resembles that of *Historis*, suggesting that Moraceae or Urticaceae are likely candidates when searching for larvae.

In Central America the genus is extremely rare. From observations in Peru, the adults show all of the characteristics of *Historis*, including rapid flight and fruit feeding.

Baeotus baeotus
(Doubleday, 1849)
FW Length: 42-47 mm **Plate 21**
Range: Costa Rica to the Amazon Basin
Hostplant: Unknown
Early stages: *Pupa*—very similar to that of *Historis acheronta*, but differs by being chalky white, with the dorsal spines black and the head horns reddish (Fig. 22).
Adult: Sexes dimorphic. *Male*—upperside black with a broad blue medial band; HW margin sharply dentate; underside checkered white with black. Although the Central American *female* is unknown, it would appear from Colombian material that it differs from males by having an orange instead of blue medial band on the upperside.
Habits: From the few specimens of Costa Rican origin, it appears to occur from sea level to about 500 m on the Atlantic slope in association with primary rain forest, and recently a single specimen was collected at sea level in Parque Corcovado. I have encountered it only at Finca la Selva. Details of the early stages or the female should be published.

Genus **SMYRNA** Hübner, 1816

These butterflies are recognized by the rounded wing shape and the zebra-striped pattern of the underside. The genus contains two species, one of which ranges from Mexico to the Amazon Basin, the other from Mexico to Nicaragua.

The hostplants are in the Urticaceae, the larvae are very spiny, including the head capsule, and are polymorphic (Fig. 22). Unlike *Colobura* or *Historis*, the pupae are rounded, without sharp projections, and show similarities to *Euptoieta* or *Vanessa*. These differences suggest that this genus is incorrectly placed in the Coloburini (Muyshondt and Muyshondt 1979).

The adults feed on rotting fruits and dung, and the males can be baited with wet laundry. Both sexes are very fast fliers and males are somewhat territorial. In El Salvador, *S. karwinskii* has been shown to roost gregariously during the dry season in a state of reproductive diapause (Muyshondt and Muyshondt 1974). This behavior has not been noted in the Costa Rican species.

Smyrna blomfildia datis
Fruhstorfer, 1908
FW Length: 34-41 mm **Plate 21**
Range: Mexico to Peru. **Subspecies:** Mexico to Panama
Hostplant: *Urrera baccifera* (Urticaceae)

Early stages: (Muyshondt and Muyshondt 1978) *Egg*—pale green, laid singly. *Mature larva*—apparently polymorphic. In Costa Rica the body is black and bears many white branched spines; the dorsal midline is broken into small white speckles; the head capsule is bright orange and bears two stout recurved horns; there are many short spines and warts all over the head (Fig. 22). *Pupa*—light or dark brown with a single black dot on the wing pads, otherwise identical to those described in El Salvador.

Adult: Sexes dimorphic. *Male*—golden brown upperside. *Female*—upperside brown with cream colored FW band. Both sexes have the FW apex black with white spots. See *S. karwinskii*.

Habits: Occurs from sea level to 1,200 m on both slopes in all forest habitats, and especially common in some years on the Pacific slope. The habits are similar to *Historis*, but they tend to stay in the understory up to subcanopy levels. In most habitats it is persistent throughout the year, and in some years this species undergoes large population explosions. For example, in Parque Santa Rosa this species was so abundant during the 1978 rainy season that I was getting about fifty individuals a day in a single butterfly trap. Interestingly, in the following years there were virtually none of this species present. This is a pattern similar to that of migratory species such as *Eunica monima*, and suggests that *S. blomfildia* may in some years have mass migrations.

Smyrna karwinskii

Hübner, 1816

FW Length: 32-38 mm **Not illustrated**

Range: Mexico to Nicaragua

Hostplant: *Urrera* (Urticaceae)

Early stages: (Muyshondt and Muyshondt 1978) Apparently the larva of this species is not polymorphic, and differs from that of *S. blomfildia* by being lighter on the dorsum and having a white pattern on the face. The pupa differs by bearing a short angular protrusion on the abdomen and a slightly bifid head.

Adult: Distinguished from *S. blomfildia* by not having the HW anal angle produced into a tail; the patterning on the underside is smeared and indistinct. See *S. blomfildia*.

Habits: From Nicaragua northward, this species is apparently very common, usually flying with *S. blomfildia*. It has never been reported from Costa Rica; I include it here as a possibility to be searched for.

Genus **PYCINA** Westwood, 1849

The two species in this genus are recognized by the elongate forewing apex, extremely hairy eyes, short palps, brushy forelegs, and the peculiar underside pattern. The genus ranges from Mexico to the Amazon Basin, with one species Central American, the other South American.

The hostplants are in the Urticaceae, and the early stages are similar to those of *Smyrna* in some respects and *Historis* in others (Muyshondt and Muyshondt 1979).

Little is known about the habits of this genus. In Costa Rica and Panama, the adults are not known to visit rotting fruits or the flowers of any plant. In Costa Rica, adults are usually crepuscular and very local, which makes observation difficult.

Pycina zamba zelys

Godman and Salvin, 1884

FW Length: 44-47 mm **Plate 21**

Range: Mexico to Peru. **Subspecies:** Mexico to Panama

Hostplant: *Urrera* (Urticaceae)

Early stages: In Costa Rica I have several oviposition records from Monte Verde, all from a solitary female. A single pale green egg is laid on the underside of the hostplant leaf. In this instance, the female laid only one egg per plant. According to Muyshondt and Muyshondt (1979), the early stages resemble those of *Smyrna*.

Adult: Distinguished by the elongate, square FW apex; HW margin scalloped; HW underside marbled gray and black; forelegs densely hairy. See *Historis*.

Habits: Occurs from 800 to 1,700 m on both slopes, in association with cloud forest habitats. In Costa Rica it is most active at dusk or dawn, when it is almost dark. At this time, males perch in tree falls and on ridge tops in the forest, and fly extremely rapidly around light gaps, occasionally perching on low vegetation. The single observation I have on the female was at midday, during cloudy weather. She flew very quickly along a forest edge, ovipositing on the *Urrera* that grew there, and flew into the forest. As far as I am aware, this species has never been taken at rotting fruits or flowers. It is generally rare in collections, although at dusk in Parque Carrillo during the dry season I have seen numerous individuals. The rarity of this butterfly in collections is certainly due to its fast flight and crepuscular habits, and the consequent difficulties of netting it.

Genus **BIBLIS** Fabricius, 1807

These butterflies are immediately recognized by the round wing shape, black ground color, and a bright red stripe on the hindwing. The males have extrusible abdominal hair pencils and androconial patches on the underside of the forewing. Another curious feature of this genus is the almost spatulate form of the palpi. It would be of interest to see how the male scent organs and the palpi are used. The genus is distributed from Mexico throughout Central and South America, and to the islands of the West Indies. There is apparently a single species.

The hostplant records indicate that *Tragia* (Euphorbiaceae) is the only plant used by *Biblis*, although other related genera probably are used. The larvae have been reared a number of times, but a good published account of the life cycle does not exist. In shape the larvae resemble *Hamadryas* to a remarkable degree. The pupa differs slightly from *Hamadryas* by having a pronounced thoracic keel and lacking long head processes.

In most references to this genus, it is described as being very common. In Costa Rica, however, this genus is quite rare in collections, and is infrequently seen in the field. In countries where it is common it is apparently found only in open areas. The adults are said to feed on rotting fruits.

Biblis hyperia

(Cramer, 1782)

FW Length: 30-35 mm **Plate 21**

Range: Mexico to the Amazon Basin and the West Indies

Hostplant: *Tragia volubilis* (Euphorbiaceae)

Early stages: The following description is taken from the unpublished paintings of M. Fountaine in the British Museum (Natural History). *Mature larva*—dorsum densely streaked with fine brown and black lines; sides streaked with gray; dorsum and sides have many finely branched spines with terminal rosettes of tiny spines, and all spines are reddish; head capsule is reddish gray(?) with two prominent recurved horns that bear many finer spines on the shaft. *Pupa*—brown or green with a rose-colored blush; edges of wing pads project away from the body; thoracic keel prominent, as is area posterior to it. *Note*: In the manuscript, the host is given as *Urtica destuans* (Urticaceae). The partial drawing looks to me like *Tragia*.

Adult: The red band on the HW margin separates this species from all others. The male has a dark androconial patch on the FW underside.

Habits: Occurs infrequently from sea level to 1,000 m on both slopes in association with disturbed habitats, but is most often seen on the Pacific slope. The insect is readily identified while on the wing; it has a slow and steady wing beat that shows the red band. In contrast to other areas, this species is rare in Costa Rica. As with *Mestra*, the distribution of the hostplant *Tragia* probably influences the abundance of the butterfly, although *Biblis* larvae most likely will feed on other plants, as well.

Genus **MESTRA** Hübner, 1825

The genus is composed of small butterflies that are recognized by their elongate wing shape and generally grayish ground color with golden brown margins; the base of the subcostal vein is swollen. The genus is composed of about seven species, one of which enters Central America; most of the species are distributed across the Antilles and West Indian islands.

Mestra of Central American origin have never been reared, but in all other areas the genus *Tragia* (Euphorbiaceae) is the recorded hostplant. The larvae show similarities to *Hamadryas* with respect to the arrangement of the spines and the head capsule, as does the pupa.

The adults fly in open areas and are inhabitants of disturbed areas. The flight is reminiscent of a slow-flying *Dynamine* and, like that genus, individuals tend to stay in close association with the hostplant.

Mestra amymone

Menetries, 1857

FW Length: 22-24 mm **Plate 22**

Range: Southern United States through Central America

Hostplant: *Tragia volubilis* (Euphorbiaceae)

Early stages: (Summarized from Brown and Heineman [1972] on *M. dorcas* and from my observations on Texas populations of *M. amymone*.) *Egg*—pale yellow, covered with pile, laid singly. *Mature larva*—head capsule reddish with black on the crown; two prominent head horns, each terminating in a knob and thickest in the middle; body brown with green diamond shapes on the dorsum; last three segments brown; there are eight rows of spines, four of which are composed of spines larger than the rest. *Pupa*—brown or green with a prominent thoracic hump, and in general shape like *Hamadryas* without the elongate head horns.

Adult: Distinguished by gray ground color with golden brown FW apex.

Habits: This species is known from Costa Rica by a single specimen collected near Upala on the Atlantic slope in an open pasture. The insect was visiting *Lantana* flowers (L. D. Gomez, personal communication). In most literature, this species is cited to be "everywhere common," yet it is one of the rarest butterflies in Costa Rica. This fact was remarked upon by Godman and Salvin: "We have not yet received specimens from Costa Rica or further south." Perhaps one reason for this species' great rarity in Costa Rica is that *Tragia* is not known to occur in Costa Rica, imposing ecological restrictions on the butterfly's range.

Genus **HAMADRYAS** Hübner, 1806

The butterflies in *Hamadryas* are recognized by their spotted "calico" pattern on the uppersides. The genus ranges from the southern United States throughout Central and South America, and half of the known species occur in Costa Rica. Known from many years under the name *Ageronia* Hübner, the basic systematic reference is Fruhstorfer (1916), and the recent revision of *Hamadryas* by Jenkins (1983) provides a synthesis of current information.

The genus is apparently quite uniform and contains two sections, or subgenera, which are separated upon dubious differences in venation (Jenkins 1983). The two groups also differ by generally having the sexes either monomorphic or dimorphic.

Reliable hostplant records of *Hamadryas* are either *Dalechampia* or *Tragia* (Euphorbiaceae), although there are some records from Mexico of Moraceae, which sound plausible but require confirmation (see Comstock and Vasquez 1961). Depending on the species, the eggs are deposited either singly or in pendant chains with the eggs end-to-end. The larvae are very spiny, bear two spined, recurved, knobbed headhorns, and feed gregariously or as solitary individuals, depending on the species (Fig. 22). In Costa Rica, I noticed that gregarious larvae will feed on all plant parts, whereas the solitary feeders feed only on leaves. The pupae are quite distinct in shape (Fig. 22), and all bear two flattened headhorns that show affinities to *Ectima*.

In Costa Rica, *Hamadryas* is commonly encountered in all habitats below 1,500 m, and may show vertical stratification by species in some forests (DeVries 1985*b*). The genus is most famous for the crackling noises that individuals produce during interactions with congeners. The mechanism and the function of the crackling noise is unknown, but it seems very likely that it is part of male-male or courtship behavior. Ross's (1963) Mexican study on three species concluded that individuals do not have territories or home ranges. It would be interesting to reexamine this hypothesis with other species and in other habitats. It will also be important to demonstrate whether females make sounds or keep territories. Both sexes of all species perch head-down on tree trunks with the wings open against the substrate, and in most habitats it is common to find one or two trees that invariably have some numbers of *Hamadryas* perching on them.

All species visit rotting fruits and are easily collected in traps, and individuals occasionally visit mammal dung. I found some of the rarest Costa Rican species to be quite common in the forest canopy, suggesting specializations in dietary ecology. Except for Ross (1963), there is nothing known about the adult ecology or population biology of any of the species in the Neotropics. Of interest is that three of our species (*arinome, laodamia*, and *amphinome*) are unpalatable to caged jacamars, whereas species without red and black on the wings (*feronia, februa*) are readily eaten (P. Chai, personal communication).

Hamadryas februa ferentina

(Godart, 1824)

FW Length: 33-39 mm **Plate 21**

Range: Southern United States to Brazil. **Subspecies:** Mexico to Brazil

Hostplant: *Dalechampia scandens* (Euphorbiaceae)

Early stages: (Young 1974*a*; Muyshondt and Muyshondt 1975*a*) *Egg*—white, laid singly. Early instars make frass chains at the leaf edges; later instars do not. *Mature larva*—body black with light green spines and six yellow longitudinal lines running from thorax to anal segments; two orange spots on either side of the lateral spines; head capsule reddish brown with two long, recurved, knobbed horns and tiny white spines on side of head. *Pupa*—variable in color, from pale green to dark brown; body thickens from cremaster to wingpads; small dorsal keel; head terminates in two flat, partially fused, then diverging head horns (Fig. 22).

Adult: Distinguished from similar species by having red crescents in the distalmost ocelli on the HW margins. See *H. feronia*.

Habits: Occurs from sea level to 1,200 m on both slopes, but most common in association with disturbed Guanacaste forest. This is the commonest species in Costa Rica, and is persistent throughout the year in all habitats, sometimes passing the Guanacaste dry season in reproductive diapause.

Hamadryas glauconome glauconome

(Bates, 1864)

FW Length: 31-39 mm **Plate 21**

Range: Mexico to Panama(?). **Subspecies:** Central America

Hostplant: *Dalechampia scandens* (Euphorbiaceae)

Early stages: *Egg*—white, laid singly along stems and leaf petioles.

Adult: Distinguished from all other species by the white apical area on the FW.

Habits: Occurs from sea level to 900 m on the Pacific slope, in association with dry forest habitats. This species terminates its southern range in Costa Rica near Puntarenas, although it should be looked for in western Panama. Encountered as solitary individuals in open forest, usually in light gaps. In Guanacaste it is persistent throughout the year, but in the dry season it is rare and in reproductive diapause.

Hamadryas feronia farinulenta

(Fruhstorfer, 1916)

FW Length: 35-38 mm **Plate 21**

Range: Southern United States to Brazil. **Subspecies:** Central America

Hostplant: *Dalechampia* (Euphorbiaceae)

Early stages: Undescribed

Adult: Distinguished from similar species by the HW ocelli, which are without red crescents as in *H. februa*; pupils on the HW underside are smaller and less gray than in *H. guatemalena*. Compare with *H. guatemalena*.

Habits: Occurs from sea level to 1,400 m on both slopes, in all forest habitats. The habits are similar to *H. februa*, but I have no detailed notes on its behavior in Costa Rica because of the difficulty in identifying live individuals. Although apparently common in most other Central American countries, it is local and uncommon in Costa Rican collections.

Hamadryas guatemalena guatemalena

(Bates, 1864)

FW Length: 35-45 mm **Plate 21**

Range: Mexico to Brazil. **Subspecies:** Mexico to Costa Rica

Hostplant: *Dalechampia scandens* (Euphorbiaceae)

Early stages: (Muyshondt and Muyshondt 1975*b*) *Egg*—white, laid singly. *Mature larva*—body black with prominent yellow patches forming a wide, irregular dorsal band; covered with spines, but with two spine clusters on segment three, one cluster on segment four, and then another on segment eight; head capsule black with two knobbed horns. *Pupa*—differs from *H. februa* by having widely separated head horns; two dark green stripes run from cremaster to head.

Adult: Distinguished from *H. feronia* by the large size, larger submarginal ocelli on both wings, and large pale area on HW underside. See *H. feronia*.

Habits: Occurs from sea level to 1,000 m on the Pacific slope, in association with all forest habitats, although commonest in deciduous forests, where it can be very abundant during the rainy season. In Guanacaste individuals are persistent throughout the year, but may be in reproductive diapause during the dry season.

Hamadryas ipthime ipthime

(Bates, 1864)

FW Length: 33-36 mm **Plate 21**

Range: Mexico to Brazil. **Subspecies:** Costa Rica to Brazil

Hostplant: *Dalechampia* (Euphorbiaceae)

Early stages: See Müller (1886) under *Ageronia* "sp. ign." (species undetermined), where all stages are described (fide Jenkins 1983).

Adult: Distinguished from all other species by the brown submarginal line on the HW underside. See *H. feronia*.

Habits: Occurs from 300 to 1,000 m on both slopes, in association with wet forest habitats, and especially common near San Vito de Java. Encountered as uncommon solitary individuals along trails and in light gaps. Uncommon in Costa Rican collections, but may be locally abundant during some years.

Hamadryas fornax fornacalia

(Fruhstorfer, 1907)

FW Length: 36-39 mm **Plate 21**

Range: Southern United States to Brazil and Bolivia. **Subspecies:** Central America

Hostplant: *Dalechampia scandens* (Euphorbiaceae)

Early stages: Undescribed

Adult: Distinguished from all other species by the orange-brown HW underside.

Habits: Occurs infrequently from sea level to 1,000 m on both slopes, in wet forest habitats. I have found it along trails and light gaps near rivers and streams. Uncommon in Costa Rican collections.

Hamadryas amphinome mexicana

(Lucas, 1853)

FW Length: 36-40 mm **Plate 22**

Range: Mexico to Amazon Basin. **Subspecies:** Mexico to Colombia

Hostplant: *Dalechampia scandens* (Euphorbiaceae)

Early stages: (Muyshondt and Muyshondt 1975*c*) *Egg*—white, laid in pendant chains on the underside of leaves. *Mature larva*—gregarious feeders; body black with yellow pattern resembling the letters OTO on dorsum; body covered with rosetted spines, of which the anterior and posterior are black and the spines on the middle half of the body orange; head capsule shiny black with two prominent head horns. *Pupa*—differs from that of *H. guatemalena* by having flat head horns that are very slightly curved; color varies from green to brown (Fig. 22).

Adult: Distinguished by the blue-gray upperside; FW has a jagged white medial band; HW underside has a red-ray pattern. See *H. arinome*.

Habits: Widespread and common on both slopes from sea level to 1,500 m, but most abundant on the Pacific slope. Often associated with second-growth habitats, this species can become extremely abundant during the rainy season on the Pacific slope and in the Meseta Central. In the Atlantic lowland rain forests, it is found at low densities, and may be found in the rain forest canopy as rare individuals along with the similar *H. arinome*. Certain individuals of this species are rejected by jacamars, indicating a variable unpalatability.

Hamadryas arinome ariensis

(Godman and Salvin, 1883)

FW Length: 35-38 mm **Plate 22**

Range: Mexico to Amazon Basin. **Subspecies:** Costa Rica to Bolivia

Hostplant: *Dalechampid triphylla* (Euphorbiaceae)

Early stages: *Mature larva*—body yellow-orange with a fine netting of black lines on dorsum; spine arrangement differs from that of other congeners: the thoracic spines have very stout shafts and are encased in a dense tuft of fine spines; the posterior spines are similar except that they are located centrally, not laterally; lateral spines have velvet red at bases; head capsule shiny black and similar to *H. amphinome*.

Adult: Sexes dimorphic. Distinguished by the jagged FW white band, distinct in *female*, indistinct in *male*. HW upperside has elongate marginal blue ocelli; HW underside black with red spots. Compare with *H. amphinome* and *H. laodamia*.

Habits: Occurs from sea level to 600 m in association with Atlantic lowland primary forest habitats, but in the canopy. Costa Rican specimens are quite rare in collections (and Panamanian as well), though it is one of the commonest butterflies in the rain forest canopy in the Sarapiqui and Carrillo Belt forests. Individuals rarely come to the ground level, even along the forest edge. Such behavior suggests that adults may be specialists on canopy fruits. At Finca la Selva I found individuals present throughout the year, but commonest during the dry seasons. This species is most likely a comimic of *H. laodamia* and *H. amphinome*, and unpalatable to birds.

Hamadryas laodamia saurites

(Fruhstorfer, 1916)

FW Length: 34-37 mm **Plate 22**

Range: Mexico to Amazon Basin. **Subspecies:** Mexico to Colombia

Hostplant: *Dalechampia triphylla* (Euphorbiaceae)

Early stages: *Mature larva*—body warm brown with a pale green band on dorsum, bisected by a fine brown one; a wide, white dorsolateral band bordered on either side with black; each segment has several short whorled spines; segments 3 and 10 have pairs of large spines with long white terminal shafts, segment (4?) has a similar, solitary dorsal spine; head capsule brown with two long, green sparsely spinose head horns. The larva rests on upperside of leaves. *Pupa*—similar to *H. februa*, only pale brown; cremaster very broad (Fig. 22), and the flattened head processes are curly and at 90° to the body.

Adult: Distinguished from other species by the rounded wing shape; both sexes have velvet black upperside with blue spots and iridescent blue-black underside with submarginal red spots. Female has a white band on the FW, the male does not. Compare with *H. arinome*. The coloration of this species makes me suggest the common name "starry night" after van

Gogh's painting. *Note*: this species was known in most literature as *H. arethusa* (a homonym).

Habits: Occurs from sea level to 1,000 m on both slopes, in all forest habitats but commonest in the Atlantic lowlands. Both sexes fly in the canopy and subcanopy, occasionally coming to ground level along forest edges. Males perch and patrol in light gaps from late morning until late afternoon. Females are usually encountered in light gaps near dense tangles of branches that have fallen from the canopy. Although both sexes will visit rotting fruits along forest edges, this species is commonly taken in canopy traps at Finca la Selva. This species is always rejected by caged jacamars (P. Chai, personal communication), indicating that it is unpalatable.

Genus **PANACEA** Godman and Salvin, 1883

The butterflies in this genus are recognized by the reflective blue upperside and in some species with the red or yellow underside. Closely related to *Hamadryas*, this genus ranges from Costa Rica to South America, where it is common. In Central America it is extremely rare, with only four specimens known from Panama and the Chiriqui region combined.

There is apparently nothing known about the hostplants or early stages of any species, and it will be of great interest to see how the early stages differ from those of *Hamadryas*.

The adults behave like *Hamadryas*, but are apparently found only in montane habitats. From observations in South America, I found that males are easily attracted to rotting fruit and dung. When approaching the food, they "flutter-glide" in circles around the bait, often perching on a tree trunk with the wings open before settling down to feed.

Panacea procilla lysimache

Godman and Salvin, 1883

FW Length: 42-45 mm **Plate 22**

Range: Panama to the Amazon Basin. **Subspecies:** Panama and (Costa Rica?)

Hostplant: Unknown

Early stages: Unknown

Adult: Upperside of FW metallic blue at base with a greenish medial band and black FW apex; HW metallic blue with many fine black markings; Underside light brown with a submarginal row of ocelli on HW.

Habits: Although this species has not been recorded from Costa Rica, its collection in recent years from the mountains of Chiriqui suggests that eventually it will turn up in the Talamancas, probably in the Parque Amistad area. Any biological information, especially on the early stages, should be published.

Genus **ECTIMA** Doubleday, 1849

The butterflies in this genus are recognized by the dark gray upperside and the tan forewing band. All of the species look very similar. The genus ranges from Mexico through Central and South America, where most of the species occur. One species enters our area.

The hostplants are *Dalechampia* (Euphorbiaceae), and the early stages resemble those of the allied genus, *Hamadryas*, in miniature.

The adults feed on rotting fruit and are behaviorally very similar to *Hamadryas* although they do not, to my knowledge, have the ability to make crackling sounds with the wings. All are forest inhabitants and, in general, little is known about their biology. I have found that many people confuse this genus with "some odd type of Riodinidae" and it is not infrequently found in collections under that family.

Ectima rectifascia

Butler and Druce, 1874

FW Length: 23-26 mm **Plate 22**

Range: Nicaragua to Panama

Hostplant: *Dalechampia triphylla* (Euphorbiaceae)

Early stages: *Egg*—white, laid singly on the new growth leaves. *Mature larva*—body black with many black, branched spines; anal segment and venter orange; head capsule with two recurved, spiny horns on the crown. *Pupa*—pale brown, slight thoracic hump, suspended; head has two flattened horns that are widely divergent and have distally toothed margins.

Adult: Immediately distinguished by the FW band, small size, and the tan-colored underside. In the field its size and tree-trunk perching are good identification marks.

Habits: Occurs from sea level to 800 m on both slopes, in association with forest habitats except those with severe disturbance or in the lowlands of Guanacaste. Encountered as solitary individuals in light gaps, especially in recent tree falls, behaving like a miniature *Hamadryas* that perches head-down on a tree trunk. Very occasionally attracted to rotting fruits. The females oviposit from midday until early afternoon, often remaining in the presence of a particular plant for several hours, and periodically ovipositing on it. It is uncommon in Costa Rican collections, and although found in a diversity of habitats, never common. See also Jenkins (1985*b*).

Genus **MYSCELIA** Doubleday, 1849

This genus is composed of medium-sized butterflies that are recognized by the blue banding on the upperside, a hooked forewing apex, and a nondescript cryptic underside. The genus ranges from the southern United States through Central and South America. Of the ten species in the genus, about half are found in Central America. A recent revision is provided by Jenkins (1984).

Little is known about the early stages. Hostplant records indicate that *Dalechampia* and *Tragia* (Euphorbiaceae) are important, although only one South American species has ever been fully described. The larvae of *M. orisis* from Brazil show affinities to *Eunica* and other members of the Catonephele series (see also Jenkins 1984). The head capsule bears two large horns that have whorled spines along the shaft; the body is covered with white warts, and has several spines on the posterior segments. The pupa is similar to *Hamadryas*, but the head is much more flattened and has long processes (Müller 1886).

In Costa Rica the genus is found in all habitats below 1,000 m. The adults feed on rotting fruits on the ground and in the forest canopy. The sexes are slightly dimorphic, with the females less brightly colored than the males. One of the species in Costa Rica is found only in the Pacific deciduous forest in Guanacaste.

Myscelia cyaniris cyaniris
(Doubleday, 1848)

FW Length: 30-32 mm **Plate 22**

Range: Mexico to Peru. **Subspecies:** Mexico to Panama

Hostplant: *Dalechampia triphylla* (Euphorbiaceae)

Early stages: On several occasions I have seen females oviposit single eggs on the new leaves of a canopy vine. The early stages need full description (see Jenkins 1984).

Adult: Immediately distinguished by the iridescent blue upperside. The female is less iridescent.

Habits: Occurs from sea level to 700 m on the Atlantic slopes in association with rain forest habitats. The males are found perching about 4 to 8 meters above the ground on tree trunks in light gaps and along forest edges. Females are active at midday. As in other species, both sexes are often found in association with the hostplant. While at rest, the butterfly folds the FW down into the HW, which in profile looks like an isosceles triangle. In this position the butterfly is almost invisible. Infrequently collected at rotting fruits in the understory and in the canopy, and occasionally the males will visit wet sand.

Myscelia leucocyana smalli
Jenkins, 1984

FW Length: 27-29 mm **Plate 22**

Range: Nicaragua to Venezuela. **Subspecies:** Nicaragua to Costa Rica

Hostplant: Unknown

Early stages: Unknown

Adult: Distinguished by the large white spots on the FW; blue on upperside not iridescent; HW upperside has three wide bands. See *M. pattenia*.

Habits: Occurs from sea level to 1,000 m on both slopes, in association with all forest habitats except the lowland deciduous forest in Guanacaste. Found flying in full sunlight along forest edges and in second-growth vegetation. Both sexes visit rotting fruits in the understory and forest canopy, and occasionally dung and carrion. This common species is present throughout the year on the Atlantic slope and in the rain forests around the Osa Peninsula.

Myscelia pattenia
Butler and Druce, 1872

FW Length: 34-36 mm **Plate 22**

Range: Guatemala to Costa Rica

Hostplant: Unknown

Early stages: Unknown

Adult: Distinguished from *M. leucocyana* by having four blue bands on the HW upperside; HW underside has much darker discal area, although this varies seasonally. Compare with *M. leucocyana*.

Habits: Restricted to the Pacific slope deciduous habitats, from sea level to 500 m, from Parque Santa Rosa south to San Mateo. Although usually very common in these habitats, this species is poorly represented in Costa Rican collections. Both sexes feed on rotting fruits, dung, and carrion. Present throughout the year, some populations pass the dry season in reproductive diapause, whereas those near rivers do not.

Genus **DYNAMINE** Hübner, 1816

The butterflies in this genus are all small-sized and generally recognized by their metallic markings, either on the hindwing underside or on the upperside of both wings. There are two major sections in the genus: those species that have the upperside white and the sexes similar, and those species that have metallic coloration on the upperside and the sexes dimorphic. The latter section can be subdivided further into one group with ocelli on the hindwing underside and the other group without ocelli. *Dynamine* contains about thirty species, and ranges from the southern United States throughout Central and South America, where the greatest species diversity is in the Amazon Basin. Central America has about fourteen species, twelve of which occur in Costa Rica.

The hostplants are in the genera *Tragia* and *Dalechampia* (Euphorbiaceae), although there are few published life histories. Depending on the group, the larvae may feed on flower parts, or bore into the developing ovary, or feed on bracts and developing leaves. In this respect, *Dynamine* is a specialist feeder that, much like the larvae of the Lycaenidae, can be classified as bud predators. Although it is certain that the larvae kill developing flowers and seeds, the full effect on the plant's reproductive output is unstudied. The unique larvae are sluglike with tiny rosettes of spines on the back. The pupae look like miniature *Diaethria* pupae with the dorsal keel more pronounced, and can often be found on the hostplant by careful searching.

Aside from a few generalities, there is little known about this genus. In Costa Rica the adults are found in all habitats below 1,200 m. Most of the species are rarely collected, some are extremely local, and some are only known from a few specimens. *Dynamine* exhibits endemism and curious range disjunctions in the Carrillo Belt, highlighting the special importance of this area in Costa Rica. The males visit wet sand along rivers, puddles in road cuts, and occasionally visit dry mammal dung. The females, especially those of the *mylitta* group, appear to stay in close association with the hostplants, and the hostplants also appear to be important in adult courtship behavior.

Dynamine agacles

Dalman, 1823

FW Length: 13-15 mm **Plate 24**

Range: Costa Rica to the Amazon Basin

Hostplant: *Dalechampia triphylla* (Euphorbiaceae)

Early stages: *Egg*—white, laid singly on leaf axils.

Adult: Sexes similar; upperside white with black margins; distinguished from *D. theseus* by the rounded wing shape; the white portion of the FW is roundly curved where it meets the black margins, not tapered. See *D. theseus*.

Habits: This species is rare in Costa Rican collections, and known only from lowland Pacific rain forest habitats centered around the Osa Peninsula. Both sexes fly from mid-morning until early afternoon in bright sunshine. In my experience, this butterfly stays close to patches of its hostplant.

Dynamine theseus

Felder, 1861

FW Length: 15-17 mm **Plate 24**

Range: Mexico to Colombia and Venezuela

Hostplant: Unknown

Early stages: Unknown

Adult: Similar to *D. agacles* but distinguished from it by the broader black margins and a more elongate wingshape. See *D. agacles*.

Habits: Very rare in Costa Rican collections, and known only from the Pacific slope around San Mateo. I have not seen it alive.

Dynamine ate

(Godman and Salvin, 1883)

FW Length: 16-18 mm **Plate 24**

Range: Guatemala and Costa Rica

Hostplant: Unknown

Early stages: Unknown

Adult: Sexes similar; distinguished from all other species by the narrow purple band that intrudes into the white areas of the wings; the HW underside has two small marginal ocelli.

Habits: Occurs from sea level to 500 m on the Atlantic slope of Volcan Turrialba. In museums it is known only from two localities in Guatemala and Guapiles in Costa Rica. The species is found as solitary individuals along riparian edges, in association with primary rain forest. This rare species is probably in danger of extinction when the last remnants of the Guapiles forest are logged.

Dynamine salpensa

Felder, 1862

FW Length: 16-18 mm **Plate 24**

Range: Costa Rica to the Amazon Basin

Hostplant: *Dalechampia triphylla* (Euphorbiaceae)

Early stages: *Egg*—laid singly on developing flower buds. *Mature larva*—body dull red-brown, sluglike and sparsely spinose; head capsule dull orange without spines. The larva feeds on the inside of the flower on the bracts and flower parts. The color of the larva and the damaged flower parts are identical, providing excellent crypsis for the larva. In a related species Müller (1886) reported that the larva fed on pollen and then bored into the ovaries. This habit would be worth investigating.

Adult: Sexes generally similar. Distinguished from all other Costa Rican species by the reflective blue upperside; FW has five subapical white spots; no ocelli on the HW underside.

Habits: Occurs from sea level to 600 m on both slopes, in association with rain forest habitats. I have only found individuals in southern Costa Rica, on the Osa Peninsula and from the Sarapiqui southward. Solitary males are found along rivers, where they visit wet sand. Although generally rare, occasionally I have found groups of 8 to 10 individuals of both sexes swarming around a tangle of the hostplant.

Dynamine hecuba

Schaus, 1913

FW Length: 22-24 mm **Plate 24**

Range: Costa Rican endemic

Hostplant: Unknown

Early stages: Unknown

Adult: Sexes dimorphic. *Male*—entire upperside reflective green. *Female*—large white spots on the FW, and FW apex broadly black. Both sexes are distinguished from *D. hoppi* by the white distal margin of the HW underside, no metallic blue surrounding the HW submarginal band, and a brown distal margin on the FW underside. See *D. hoppi.*

Habits: Occurs at 200 to 900 m on the Atlantic slope, in association with the Carrillo Belt, and is apparently endemic to Costa Rica. A curious aspect of its distribution is that it appears to occur in habitats slightly higher in elevation than its close relative *D. hoppi*, yet the two species do not overlap. However, this requires study. Usually found as solitary individuals along forest edges and along rivers. The flight is fast and zigzag, and unlike many of the other species, *D. hecuba* tends to fly high above the ground and occasionally in the canopy. The females are encountered more often than the males. The species is local, uncommon in collections, and flies from April to July.

Dynamine hoppi gillotti

Hall, 1930

FW Length: female 26-28 mm **Plate 24**

Range: Colombia and Costa Rica. **Subspecies:** Costa Rica

Hostplant: *Dalechampia triphylla* (Euphorbiaceae)

Early stages: Single eggs are oviposited on new leaves and flowers. The early stages beyond this oviposition record are unknown.

Adult: Sexes dimorphic. *Male*—(from Colombian material) upperside reflective blue-green. *Female*—large white spots on the FW. Distinguished from *D. hecuba* by the four white spots in the FW tornus, reflective blue surrounding the brown medial bands on the HW underside, and HW distal margin brown. See *D. hecuba.* The male is unknown in Costa Rica.

Habits: This very rare species is known from Costa Rica by three specimens, all female. Originally described from a single specimen as a new species, I have compared it with Colombian material and consider that our material represents a well-defined subspecies of the South American *D. hoppi.* I collected this species once during a six-month residency at Finca La Selva. The following year, J. Mallet collected another in the same light gap. Both specimens were collected during July. This species appears to replace *D. hecuba* at lower elevations, and to date the two species have not been taken together.

Dynamine chryseis

Bates, 1865

FW Length: 18-20 mm **Plate 24**

Range: Nicaragua to the Amazon Basin

Hostplant: Unknown

Early stages: Unknown

Adult: Sexes dimorphic. *Male*—metallic green upperside with broadly black FW apex; HW underside has four fine golden-brown transverse bands. *Female*—has white spots on the FW upperside. Compare with *D. sosthenes.*

Habits: In Costa Rica, known only from a few specimens collected on the Pacific slope near San Mateo. I have not seen it in nature.

Dynamine sosthenes

Hewitson, 1869

FW Length: 18-20 mm **Plate 24**

Range: Nicaragua and Costa Rica

Hostplant: Unknown

Early stages: Unknown

Adult: Similar to *D. chryseis*, but distinguished from it by black tornal HW margin and reduced black FW apex on the upperside of the male; the underside has fewer white spots on the disc of the FW; HW has narrower bands on disc.

Habits: As in *D. chryseis*, this species is known from Costa Rica from a few specimens, all taken on the Pacific slope. I have not seen it alive.

Dynamine thalassina
Boisduval, 1870

FW Length: 18-21 mm **Plate 24**

Range: Mexico to Colombia

Hostplant: Unknown

Early stages: Unknown

Adult: Sexes dimorphic. *Male*—metallic green above with black on HW margin. *Female*—white and black above; similar to *D. mylitta* but distinguished from it by having more white spots on the disc of the FW underside, and the configuration of the ocelli on the FW underside. See *D. mylitta.*

Habits: Very rare in Costa Rican collections. From the small number of museum specimens, it appears that this species is found in the lowland Atlantic around Limon. There is, however, one record from Palmar on the Pacific slope. I have not seen it alive.

Dynamine mylitta
(Cramer, 1782)

FW Length: 15-23 mm **Plate 24**

Range: Mexico throughout Central and South America

Hostplant: *Dalechampia* (Euphorbiaceae)

Early stages: *Egg*—white, laid singly on flower bracts or leaf axils. *Mature larva*—pale green, bearing several rows of short rosetted spines on the dorsum; a few black warts on thorax; smooth head capsule. Larvae feed on buds, flowers, and young leaves. While not feeding, the larvae rest in the leaf axils and resemble buds.

Adult: Sexes dimorphic. *Male*—blue-green on upperside; HW underside has ocelli ringed in yellow; between HW medial bands there is a metallic blue cast. *Female*—upperside white and black with two indistinct blue ocelli at HW margin. See *D. thalassina.*

Habits: The most common of the Central American species, occurring from sea level to 1,400 m on both slopes in association with disturbed forest habitats, and markedly common on the Pacific slope. Found in bright sunlight along forest edges where tangles of the hostplant occur. Females seldom leave the hostplant and, at midday, they are frequently seen perched there even when not ovipositing. I have seen females oviposit throughout the day. Both sexes visit flowers of various Asteraceae, and the males visit wet sand.

Dynamine glauce
Bates, 1865

FW Length: 14-16 mm **Plate 24**

Range: Mexico throughout Central and South America

Hostplant: *Dalechampia* (Euphorbiaceae)

Early stages: Very similar to those described for *D. mylitta.*

Adult: Sexes dimorphic. *Male*—upperside metallic green; FW apex black with a green crescent near the tip; HW underside has two distinct ocelli that are melted into a wide postmedial band. *Female*—upperside white and black with three subapical white spots on the FW. Compare with *D. dyonis.*

Habits: Occurs at 400-1,200 m on both slopes, in association with rivers and swampy areas in the forest. Found as uncommon, solitary individuals feeding on various types of Asteraceae flowers. Uncommon in Costa Rican collections.

Dynamine dyonis
Hübner, 1837

FW Length: 18-22 mm **Plate 24**

Range: From Texas south throughout Central America

Hostplant: *Dalechampia* (Euphorbiaceae)

Early stages: Very similar to those of *D. mylitta.* The female usually lays three to six eggs on the same plant, each in a leaf axil.

Adult: Sexes dimorphic. *Male*—upperside pale green with a narrow black FW apex and a black spot near end of cell; underside of HW has two distinct ocelli that are ringed in yellow. *Female*—upperside black and white. Compare with *D. glauce.*

Habits: Occurs at 400 to 1,000 m on the Pacific slope, in association with forest habitats, but does not enter the Guanacaste coastal forest. Encountered as solitary individuals along forest edges in association with the hostplant. Both sexes feed on various Asteraceae flowers in open areas, and the males visit wet sand and dung. Common.

Genus **MARPESIA** Hübner, 1818

The genus *Marpesia* is composed of a rather uniform group of butterflies, all of which are recognized by long tails on the hindwing, and are thus known as "dagger-wings." Although *Marpesia* has an entirely New World distribution, a close relative, *Cyrestis* Boisduval, is found in the Old World tropics, and together they form what some authors have considered to be a subfamily of the Nymphalidae, the Marpesiinae (Müller 1886; Brown and Heineman 1972; Howe 1975). *Marpesia* ranges from the southern United States throughout Central and South America (where the most species occur), to the West Indies, where there are a number of well-differentiated species. The names

Megalura and *Timetis* are synonyms (Hemming 1967).

The hostplants are all in the family Moraceae, and the larvae are very distinct from other nymphalids. Usually brightly colored, they are immediately recognized by having a single row of spines along the back and a pair of spines on the head (Fig. 24). The pupae are likewise very distinct, and have several stiff processes projecting from the thorax and along the abdomen (Fig. 24). *Marpesia* and *Cyrestis* share these peculiarities of the early stages.

In Central and South America, these butterflies are often encountered in great numbers at mud puddles and along rivers, where the males form large aggregations. Collecting at these puddles can be difficult because the butterflies are extremely fast and agile fliers. In some of the species, the sexes are dimorphic and, in most cases, the females are rarely collected. In my experience this is because the females stay within the forest, at times in the canopy, and are not nearly as obvious as the impetuous males. Both sexes feed on flowers, but again males are most frequently seen. A few of the species will visit rotting fruits and fresh mammal dung but, in general, little is known about most of the species and what they feed upon. One species in Costa Rica (*Marpesia berania*) is known to form gregarious nocturnal roosts and to return to the roost for several months (Benson and Emmel 1972). In the same study, these authors calculated that *berania* can live up to five months. Although *Marpesia chiron* is known to migrate (Williams 1930), this habit is not recorded for most of the other species, even though in Costa Rica some of them have been observed migrating with *M. chiron* or the moth *Urania fulgens* (Uraniidae).

Marpesia petreus

(Cramer, 1778)

FW Length: 39-41 mm **Plate 23**

Range: Southern United States, Central and South America

Hostplant: *Anacardium* (Anacardiaceae); *Ficus* (Moraceae)

Early stages: (Comstock and Vasquez 1961) *Egg*—white, laid singly. *Mature larva*—head capsule reddish brown with two stiff recurved horns; top of head deeply invaginated; body covered with spots of brick red and yellow, and black; very wide dorsal yellow band is composed of triangular shapes; sides reddish, then black at the interface with the yellow dorsal band; four stiff spines on dorsum at segments 4, 6, 8, and the anal plate; legs black (see Fig. 24). *Pupa*—white with black patches on abdomen; thorax and head have thin black spines on dorsum of abdomen, a large black bifurcated spine on thorax, and two black spines on the head (Fig. 24). Parasitized pupae are yellowish. The larvae are easily seen, since they rest on the upperside of the hostplant leaves.

Adult: Immediately recognized by the falcate FW apex and dull orange color. The sexes are similar.

Habits: Occurs from sea level to 1,500 m on both slopes in all habitats. This species flies in open areas and resembles *Dryas iulia* and *Dione moneta*, perhaps gaining from protective mimicry. In some years the adults can be very common in the Pacific deciduous forest, and in a subsequent year they will be virtually absent from the habitat. Both sexes visit flowers of *Cordia, Croton, Lantana*, and *Mikania*; males also visit mud.

Marpesia coresia

(Godart, 1823)

FW Length: 33-37 mm **Plate 23**

Range: Southern United States through Central and South America

Hostplant: Unknown

Early stages: Unknown

Adult: Distinguished by the chocolate brown upperside; underside sharply divided, basal half white, distal half brown. This is an obvious and reliable field character. The sexes are similar.

Habits: Occurs in all habitats from 500 to 2,500 m on both slopes, usually in association with forest habitats, but will enter open areas as well. The males are commonly found visiting puddles along forest edges and along rivers, sometimes in very large aggregations. The female is uncommon in collections. Both sexes visit flowers of *Cordia* and *Croton*, and occasionally the males visit mammal dung. In Costa Rica this widespread and common species is frequently seen in mass migrations of *M. chiron*.

Marpesia chiron

(Fabricius, 1775)

FW Length: 28-30 mm **Plate 23**

Range: Southern United States, Central and South America, and West Indies

Hostplant: *Brosimum, Artocarpus, Chlorophora, Ficus* (Moraceae)

Early stages: (Brown and Heineman 1972) *Egg*—yellowish, laid singly. *Mature larva*—dorsum of body yellow-orange with reddish streaks and two black lines; sides yellow with red and black longitudinal lines; spiracles and

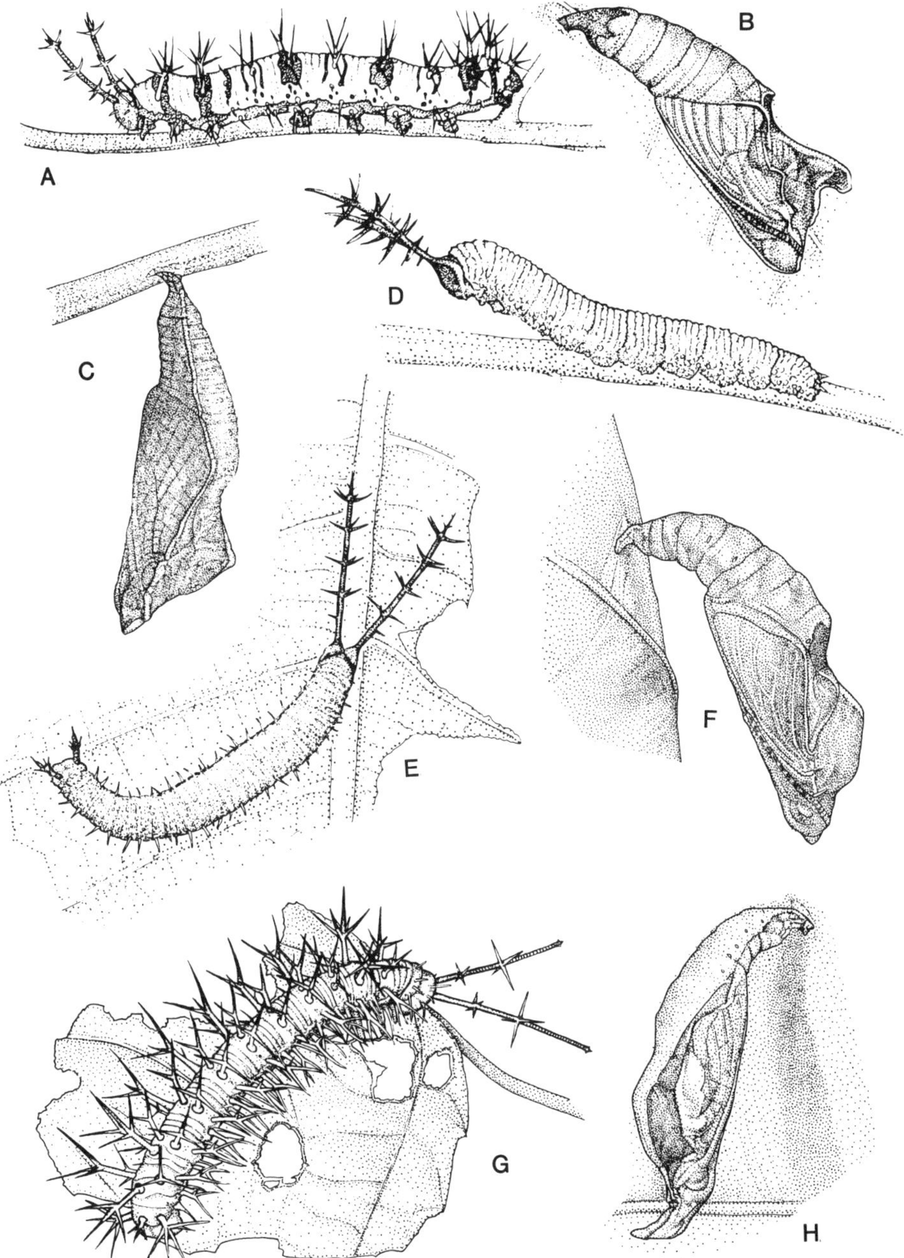

FIGURE 23. Larvae and pupae of the Nymphalidae: "Nymphalinae." A: *Pyrrhogyra neaerea hypsenor* mature larva; B: *Pyrrhogyra neaerea hypsenor* pupa; C: *Diaethria astala* pupa; D: *Diaethria astala* third instar larva in resting position; E: *Callicore atacama manova* mature larva; F: *Callicore atacama manova* pupa; G: *Nessaea aglaura aglaura* mature larva; H: *Temenis laothoe* pupa (drawings by J. Clark).

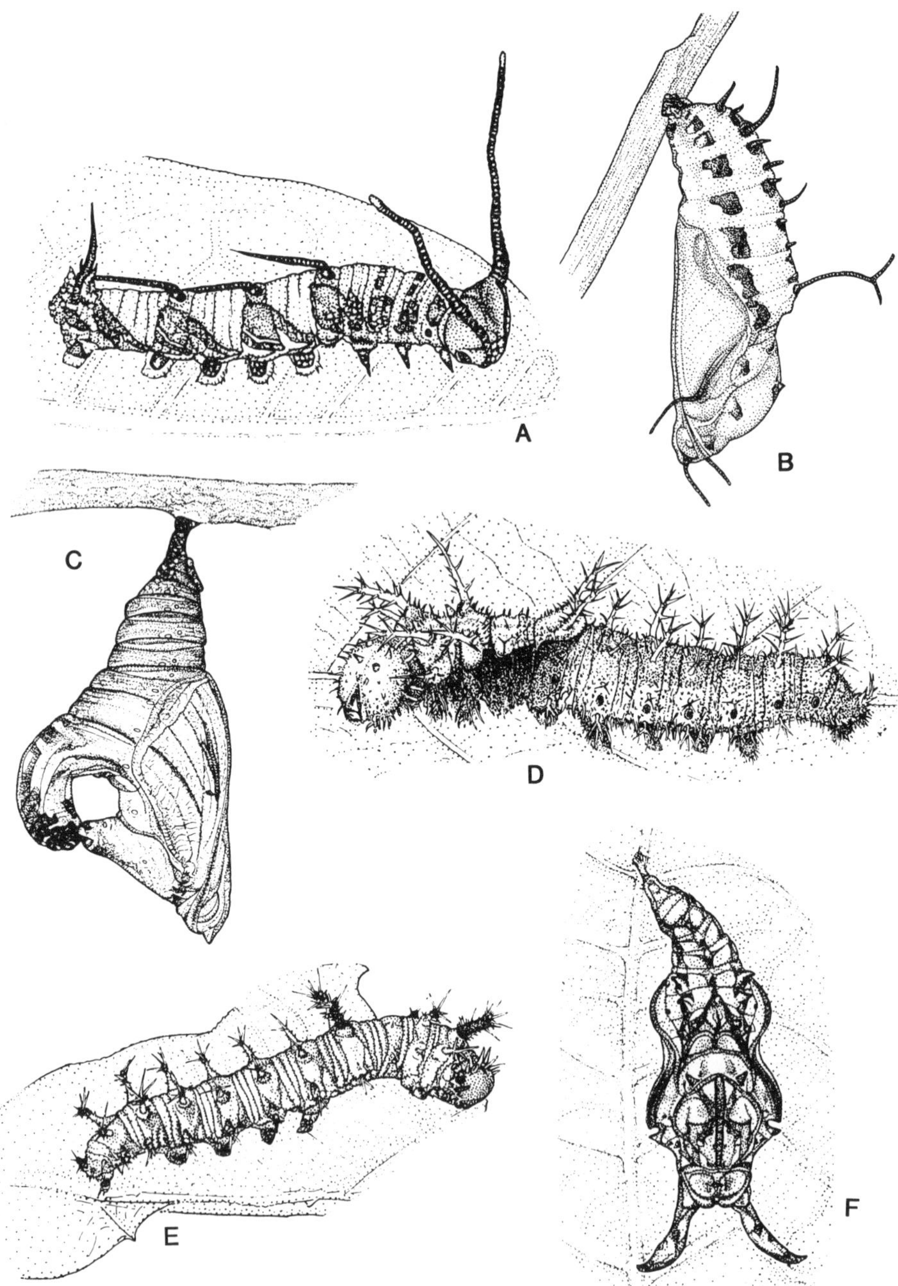

FIGURE 24. Larvae and pupae of the Nymphalidae: "Nymphalinae." A: *Marpesia petreus* newly molted mature larva; B: *Marpesia petreus* pupa; C: *Adelpha melanthe* pupa; D: *Adelpha melanthe* mature larva; E: *Adelpha heraclea* mature larva; F: *Adelpha celerio* pupa (drawings by J. Clark).

dorsal spines black and placed as in *M. petreus*; head capsule yellow-green with two black spots at base of head horns. *Pupa*—similar to *M. petreus*, only colored red-brown with a gray head.

Adult: The entire upperside brown and similar to that of *M. alcibiades* and *M. berania*.

Habits: The males of this common and widespread species are a familiar sight at any puddle or river bank, from sea level to 2,800 m, but especially common above 500 m. During population explosions, males visit wet sand by the hundreds, and resemble a great gray-violet cloud as they swirl around each other. The female is seldom collected, and is usually found as single individuals along ridge tops or in the forest understory at midday. Both sexes visit flowers of *Cordia, Lantana*, and *Croton*. I have seen riverside roosts of this species composed of 10 to 15 individuals located about 10 meters above the ground. As noted previously, this species is well known for mass migrations. The size of the migrations seems to vary from year to year, and their occurrence is often associated with the migrations of *Urania fulgens* (Uraniidae).

Marpesia alcibiades

(Staudinger, 1876)

FW Length: 34-37 mm **Plate 23**

Range: Mexico to Panama

Hostplant: Unknown

Early stages: Unknown

Adult: Very similar to *M. chiron* on the upperside and *M. berania* on the underside, but distinguished from both by not having a short, square tooth on the HW anal angle. See *M. chiron* and *M. berania*.

Habits: From the few Costa Rican records in museums, it appears to be known only from the Pacific slope. I have never seen this species alive. Its apparent rarity is possibly due to its similarity with the two common species *M. chiron* and *M. berania*, because of which it may seldom be collected. Observations and biological information on this species would be worth publishing.

Marpesia merops

(Boisduval, 1836)

FW Length: 29-33 mm **Plate 23**

Range: Guatemala throughout Central and South America

Hostplant: *Brosimum* (Moraceae)

Early stages: I have found late instar larvae on the above plant, looking for a place to pupate. This record needs to be substantiated and the early stages described. The pupa is similar to that of *M. chiron* except it is pale green.

Adult: Immediately distinguished by the gray-white upperside; FW has white spots; underside white with brown streaks. The sexes are similar.

Habits: Occurs from sea level to 3,000 m on both slopes in all forest habitats except the Pacific deciduous forest of Guanacaste. Occasionally found in great abundance along rivers in the Talamancas, where many hundreds of males cloud about one particular spot on a river bank or puddle in the road. The males become active as soon as the sun warms the canopy in the morning. First they descend from their night perches and then, after a few minutes basking, start to suck at the wet sand. The greatest activity in males is seen early in the morning. I have never seen this species feed on anything else. The rarely collected female can be observed early in the morning in the forest canopy. In various areas of Costa Rica I have seen small nocturnal and diurnal roosts of this species, always along river banks. This species is frequently seen in the mass migrations of *M. chiron*.

Marpesia marcella

(Felder, 1861)

FW Length: 31-34 mm **Plate 23**

Range: Guatemala to Peru

Hostplant: Unknown

Early stages: Unknown

Adult: Sexes dimorphic. *Male*—HW upperside has reflective purple discal area; FW upperside has a broad orange medial band that extends to the HW margin. *Female*—upperside ground color black with a broad white FW medial band.

Habits: Occurs at 500 to 2,800 m on both slopes, in association with forest habitats. Except for the area in the Talamancas near Parque Amistad, where it is usually very common, this species is encountered as solitary individuals. Where it is common, the crowds of males visiting wet spots along river banks form purple clouds that swirl in the sunshine. As in *M. marcella*, the males' activity begins in the morning when they descend from the canopy to wet spots. The females fly in the canopy during the morning, and in the forest and along ridgetops during midday. I have no flower records for this species. It is commonest on the Pacific slope during March through June, when there are weeks of brilliant sunshine.

Marpesia iole

(Drury, 1782)

FW Length: 29-33 mm **Plate 23**

Range: Nicaragua to Peru and Bolivia

Hostplant: Unknown

Early stages: Unknown

Adult: Sexes dimorphic. *Male*—FW apex acute; upperside of wing margins dark brown, basal portion intense violet-blue; underside nut brown with many wavy medial lines and margins with a satin sheen. *Female*—upperside golden brown with dark brown FW apex and margin, and five subapical white spots; underside as in male.

Habits: Occurs from sea level to 1,400 m on both slopes, in association with wet forest habitats. This species is uncommon. I have not found aggregations of males as in other species, only solitary individuals.

Marpesia berania

(Hewitson, 1852)

FW Length: 30-32 mm **Plate 23**

Range: Mexico through Central and South America

Hostplant: Unknown

Early stages: Unknown

Adult: Distinguished by the pale orange upperside and a dull yellow underside, which has a gloss, and six to eight transverse bands. The female is paler on the upperside and at times almost a pale brown. See *M. chiron* and *M. alcibiades*.

Habits: Occurs from sea level to 1,000 m on both slopes, in all habitats. Most frequently found along rivers or in swampy areas in rain forests, and much less common in the deciduous Pacific forest. Both sexes visit flowers of *Cordia* and *Croton*. This species is known to roost in nocturnal aggregations of over fifty individuals and remain faithful to the roost for many months (Benson and Emmel 1972). The sex ratio on the roost is 1:1, and both sexes are known to live up to three months. I watched one roost on the Osa Peninsula intermittently for over one year. Some members of the roost did not leave either in the morning or when they were jostled by the comings and goings of others during the day. Common and widespread throughout all of Costa Rica.

Note: The following series of genera—*Catonephele, Nessaea, Callicore, Cyclogramma, Diaethria, Haematera, Temenis, Pyrrhogyra, Eunica* and *Epiphile*—all show a great similarity of form in eggs, larvae, and pupae. Additionally, the behavior of both adults and early stages, and the affinities of their hostplants, seem to point to a close evolutionary relatedness. In his numerous papers on the life cycles of Neotropical butterflies, Alberto Muyshondt has proposed the use of the subfamily name Catonephelinae Orfilia (1952)—a replacement name of the invalid Epicaliinae of Müller (1886)—to delimit this group. Future revisionary work should provide necessary insights into the phylogenetics of this group so that it can be either accepted or rejected.

Genus **EUNICA** Hübner, 1819

Eunica is a diverse genus whose members may be recognized by the cryptic brown underside marked with ocelli, and an inflated forewing cubitus. The sexes are dimorphic; males usually show reflective blue, purple, or white on the upperside, and females are usually brown with a white band on the forewing. The genus is distributed from the southern United States through Central and South America and the Antilles, with greater diversity in the Amazon Basin. Costa Rica and Panama have the most species in Central America, some being very rare. There are upwards of sixty species of *Eunica* which, based on larvae and secondary sexual characters, probably represent several genera (Brown and Heineman 1972). The species vary geographically and, like most brightly colored butterflies, have an abundance of subspecific names.

The hostplants and early stages are poorly known. In Costa Rica and Panama there are at least two plant families used by *Eunica*: Euphorbiaceae and Burseraceae. Some South American species are reported to use Euphorbiaceae, as well (Müller 1886; Miles Moss, unpublished manuscripts in British Museum [Natural History]). The standard reference of Rutaceae by Dyar (1912) requires confirmation. The larvae show affinities to *Callicore* and *Epiphile* in general shape and configuration of the spines, but differ in having three erect dorsal spines on the posterior segments. The head capsule bears two prominent horns that vary in size according to the species. The pupa also shows differences in length and configuration of the head processes.

In Costa Rica the adults are usually found as solitary individuals, and are generally rare. The females are very rare in collections, and in some species the female is unknown. Occasionally, a species will be found along a riverbank or landslip in groups of five to ten males feeding on water seepage. This may last for several days, after which the species may not be seen again for several years. The rarity of most *Eunica* species is probably due in part to the tendency to stay within the forest at the canopy level and seldom descend to the ground. I have observed a number of our rarer species in the canopy. Another factor that influences the rarity of some species (such as the *E. monima* group) is mass migration. During years of migrations, *E. monima* can be exceedingly common, and in later years very rare (or abundant in some other part of the country). However, most *Eunica* species are not known to mass migrate.

The feeding habits of most species are unknown. As noted previously, males can be found feeding at water seepage, but it is unknown whether this provides any nutrition. None of the species is known to visit flowers. A few feed at rotting fruits—only males in some species, both sexes in others. One thing is certain about the biology of most *Eunica* species: they are intolerant of areas under intensive agriculture and seem to require tracts of primary forest.

Eunica tatila caerula

Godman and Salvin, 1887

FW Length: 27-30 mm **Plate 22**

Range: Southern United States to Amazon Basin. **Subspecies:** Mexico to Colombia

Hostplant: Unknown

Early stages: Unknown

Adult: Distinguished by the squared-off FW apex, FW upperside with many white spots; HW margin scalloped. The male is suffused with purple, the female with reflective blue.

Habits: This species is known from a few specimens of Costa Rican origin collected by C. Lankester. In Mexico and Guatemala it is apparently abundant at times. Unknown from south of Guatetmala except for the few Costa Rican records (but see Opler and Krizek 1984), it then reappears in Colombia as a common species. *E. tatila* is known to make mass migrations, but it is unclear why a portion of Central America is unpopulated by this species. Information on migrations or captures from Costa Rica should be published.

Eunica monima modesta

Bates, 1864

FW Length: 22-24 mm **Plate 22**

Range: United States, Antilles, Bahamas, Mexico, Central and South America. **Subspecies:** Central America

Hostplant: *Bursera simaruba* (Burseraceae). *Note*: the record of *Zanthoxylum* (Rutaceae) requires confirmation (Dyar 1912).

Early stages: *Egg*—white, laid singly on developing leaves. *Mature larva*—(from Costa Rica) body olive drab; eight pairs of short spines laterally over a longitudinal black stripe running from head to anus; a yellow lateral stripe just above the leg, running the length of the body; three erect black spines above posterior three segments, one centrally located, the others to either side of midline; anal plate black; head capsule bicolored: dorsal half orange, ventral half black; two short, stout horns on top of head. *Pupa*—pale green, shaped similarly to *Nica*, with head area slightly bifid. In some years the larvae can defoliate entire trees in Guanacaste early in the rainy season. During outbreak years, emergence from the pupa appears to be somewhat synchronous.

Adult: Variable in size, but all small; males have a dull purple sheen, and females dull brown above; FW has white spots. *Note*: this species can be confused with some Satyrinae.

Habits: Occurs from sea level to 1,200 m on both slopes, but rare on the Atlantic side. During outbreak years, this species is very common in Guanacaste during the early rainy season, then later mass migrates across the Cordillera de Guanacaste to the Atlantic slope. During such times, the migrations are observed all along the Pacific slope, but their final destination is unknown. See Williams (1930) for more details on migration. On the Pacific slope and especially in Guanacaste, this species is present throughout the year as occasional individuals. In the dry season females are in reproductive diapause. Both sexes feed on rotting fruits and fresh mammal dung.

Eunica malvina

Bates, 1864

FW Length: 29-31 mm **Plate 22**

Range: Mexico to the Amazon Basin

Hostplant: *Mabea occidentalis* (Euphorbiaceae)

Early stages: Undescribed

Adult: Sexes dimorphic. *Male*—dull brown on upperside; HW underside has light gray ground color and ocelli ringed in pale yellow with blue pupils. *Female*—similar to male, but with medial band of white spots on FW. See *E. mygdonia*.

Habits: Occurs from sea level to 700 m on Pacific slope, in association with all forest habitats. Encountered as rare individuals along forest edges, where males visit water seepage and both sexes visit rotting fruits. Present throughout the year, though in reproductive diapause in the dry season.

Eunica mygdonia

Godart, 1823

FW Length: 28-31 mm **Plate 22**

Range: Mexico to the Amazon Basin

Hostplant: *Mabea occidentalis* (Euphorbiaceae)

Early stages: Undescribed

Adult: FW apex squared off. *Male*—uniform brown above with an indistinct band of five white spots on FW; underside suffused with various shades of brown, purple, and white; ocelli indistinct. *Female*—distinct FW band with two subapical FW spots. See *E. malvina*.

Habits: Occurs from sea level to 1,200 m on the Pacific slope in all forest habitats, and rarely on the Atlantic slope. Habits very similar to *E. malvina*, and often found flying with that species. In South America this species apparently shows fluctuations between scarcity and great abundance, which suggests a migratory habit. In Central America this species is always found as rare, solitary individuals.

Eunica mira

Godman and Salvin, 1877

FW Length: 25-27 mm **Plate 22**

Range: Costa Rica and Panama

Hostplant: *Mabea occidentalis* (Euphorbiaceae)

Early stages: *Egg*—white, laid singly on developing leaves or inflorescence. *Mature larva*—body shiny brick red, encircled on all segments with rings of dull yellow; dorsal line red bordered on either side by yellow; dorsal spines black, lateral spines yellow, both types short and branched at the tips; head capsule reddish brown with two prominent horns on top of the head. *Pupa*—pale green with powdery white lines along segments and dorsum; head has a pair of long, tightly appressed horns that are separated by a small space near the head. Larvae seem to prefer to feed on the male flowers and spin a web around the flowers as they are eaten; the female flowers are not eaten. When there are no flowers, only the young leaves are eaten.

Adult: Sexes dimorphic. *Male*—velvet black on upperside with a light metallic green band on the HW. *Female*—no green on HW; white FW band. Both sexes have metallic ocelli on the HW underside and a dull red medial band that is widest at base, constricted at median, then broadly extended to the margin. The female can be determined in the field by the fact that the FW underside may look like a smeared watercolor.

Habits: Occurs from sea level to 500 m on both slopes, in association with primary rain forest habitats and most common in swamp forest. The males are found along riparian edges and light gaps. During the morning they perch about five to ten meters above the ground. Around midday the males dart about in the forest understory, and later in the afternoon perch on tree trunks, sometimes in the canopy. Females oviposit at midday and fly in the forest understory. Although this species is rarely collected, an isolated *Mabea occidentalis* in the forest rarely fails to attract a female around midday. I have never collected this species feeding on rotting fruits or at water. In Costa Rica, populations tend to be localized around stands of the hostplant.

Eunica norica

Hewitson, 1852

FW Length: 28-30 mm **Plate 22**

Range: Costa Rica to Bolivia

Hostplant: Unknown

Early stages: Unknown

Adult: Sexes dimorphic. *Male*—deep metallic blue on HW distal margin; HW underside has a distinct, black, pupillate figure 8 in the tornus. *Female*—upperside entirely black except for an oblique white FW band that is broken near the cell. *Note*: specimens from Costa Rica differ from the South American phenotype by having the blue reduced in the males and the white FW band larger in the females.

Habits: Recently discovered in Costa Rica, this species occurs at 800 to 1,300 m on both slopes, in association with cloud forest habitats. It is seasonal and local, flying during April and May in the Carrillo Belt and other Talamancan areas. I have never seen this species at any other time. Males visit wet sand at water crossings, and perch in the canopy and subcanopy along edges and in gaps. Both of these activities take place from early morning until midday. The rare females are found along ridges and mountain passes. This species is rare in collections and very seldom seen in nature, in contrast to its apparent abundance in South America.

Eunica caresa

Hewitson, 1857

FW Length: 37-40 mm **Plate 22**

Range: Guatamala to Peru

Hostplant: Unknown

Early stages: Unknown

Adult: Sexes dimorphic. *Male*—velvet black above with a dull violet-blue area on FW; FW apex squared off and produced. *Female*—dark brown above with an oblique white FW band and two or three white spots between the band and the apex. (The female is unknown from

Central America, and this description is based on South American material.)

Habits: This very rare species is reported from Costa Rica by very few individuals collected at the following localities: San Mateo, Carrillo, and Turrialba. In South America this species is apparently easily baited with rotting fruits. I have never seen *E. caresa* in the field.

Eunica venusia

Felder and Felder, 1867

FW Length: 36-39 mm **Plate 23**

Range: Costa Rica to Colombia

Hostplant: Unknown

Early stages: Unknown

Adult: Sexes dimorphic. *Male*—velvet black above with a dull metallic blue band on the HW; FW apex squared off; HW underside has a reflective blue spot near the margin that is visible at certain angles; HW has several ringed ocelli with blue pupils; FW tornus has a greenish cast. *Female*—Judging from Colombian material, the female has a white FW band, and the entire upperside ground color is a dull metallic green, quite unlike the females of other species. The female is unknown from Costa Rica and Panama.

Habits: Occurs from sea level to 600 m on both slopes, in association with primary rain forest habitats. This rare Costa Rican species is known only from the forests of the Osa Peninsula and those of the Carrillo. Encountered along rivers that have large areas of beach where the males visit wet sand intermittently between very rapid, short flights. This species is very difficult to capture because of its erratic flight.

Eunica excelsa

Godman and Salvin, 1877

FW Length: 36-39 mm **Plate 23**

Range: Costa Rica to Ecuador

Hostplant: Unknown

Early stages: Unknown

Adult: Sexes dimorphic. *Male*—upperside has deep reflective blue at FW base and HW distal margin; underside ground color mottled brown, violet, and tan; HW has three medial ocelli, the posterior one greatly reduced. *Female*—brown on the upperside with a white FW band that is broken into three parts and bordered by reflective aquamarine. Compare with *E. venusia* and *E. caresa*.

Habits: Similar to *E. venusia* in habits and distribution. I have observed solitary males, perched in the forest canopy along rivers, fly out to chase passing butterflies. The flight, as in *E. venusia*, is very fast. This species is rare in Costa Rican collections.

Eunica augusta

Bates, 1866

FW Length: 31-34 mm **Plate 23**

Range: Mexico to Colombia

Hostplant: Unknown

Early stages: Unknown

Adult: Sexes dimorphic. *Male*—FW upperside deep blue with irregular white FW band; HW margin scalloped; HW underside a dull calico pattern. *Female*—upperside dull gray-blue; FW band very distinct. This species is easily identified in the field with the aid of binoculars.

Habits: Occurs from sea level to 1,300 m on both slopes in a wide variety of habitats, but as rare, solitary individuals. I have seen this species migrating with *E. monima* through mountain passes in the Cordillera de Guanacaste. Both sexes visit wet sand at rivers in Talamancan cloud forests. In Guanacaste it can be confused with *Myscelia* when it is perched on a tree trunk with the wings closed. Although it is apparently common in northern areas, in Costa Rica this species is rarely collected.

Eunica alcmena amata

Druce, 1874

FW Length: 33-35 mm **Plate 23**

Range: Mexico to Peru. **Subspecies:** Costa Rica and Panama

Hostplant: Unknown

Early stages: Unknown

Adult: Sexes dimorphic. *Male*—velvet black above with deep blue FW costal margins and HW distal margins; HW underside has two medial ocelli, the ocellus near costa having a double pupil, and both ocelli are ringed in yellow. *Female*—brown on upperside with a white FW band that is broken at the radial veins. See *E. pomona*.

Habits: Occurs from sea level to 1,200 m on both slopes, but most common along the southern portion of the Talamancas on the Pacific slope. Usually found as solitary males visiting water seepage along rivers and landslips. As in other species, the female is rarely seen. I have only seen them flying at midday along water courses within the forest, searching for oviposition sites in the understory. Both sexes feed on fresh mammal dung, and occasionally the males are attracted to rotting fruits. Although wide ranging, this species is infrequently encountered in Costa Rica.

Eunica pomona
Felder, 1862
FW Length: 31-35 mm **Plate 23**
Range: Costa Rica to Venezuela
Hostplant: Unknown
Early stages: Unknown
Adult: Very similar to *E. alcmena*, of which it is considered a subspecies by some authors, but differs by having blue along the FW distal margin, and the HW underside bears a doubled ocellus with two pupils. The female is unknown.
Habits: Occurs from sea level to 500 m on both slopes, in association with primary rain forest. The males are similar in habits to *E. alcmena*, but I have not taken them at rotting fruits. Both species fly together on the Osa Peninsula. Rare in Costa Rican collections.

Genus **TEMENIS** Hübner, 1816

One of the two species in this genus is honey yellow, while the other bears red on its wings. In the latter, the females may either be similar to the male or show a color pattern similar to *Callicore*. The genus is closely allied to *Epiphile* and *Nica*, and is separated from those genera by details of the larvae and pupae. The genus is found everywhere in the Neotropics except in desert habitats, and is highly variable geographically.

The hostplants are in the Sapindaceae, of which *Serjania* and *Paullinia* are important. The larvae show characteristics of *Epiphile, Cantonephele*, and related genera in terms of general morphology and habits (Muyshondt 1973*c*). The larvae have a curious arrangement of dorsal spines and, at each molt, the body color changes. The pupa is similar to *Epiphile* but with the head more deeply bifid (Fig. 23).

In Costa Rica the genus occurs from sea level to 1,600 m in association with all forest habitats. The adults of both sexes feed on dung. It has been suggested that *Temenis* and other related Sapindaceae feeders are unpalatable to vertebrate predators (Muyshondt 1975*c*). This hypothesis requires confirmation through feeding experiments.

Temenis laothoe agatha
(Fabricius, 1787)
FW Length: 27-29 mm **Plate 24**
Range: Mexico to the Amazon Basin. **Subspecies:** Guatemala to Colombia
Hostplant: *Serjania, Paullinia, Cardiospermum, Urvillea* (Sapindaceae)
Early stages: (Muyshondt 1973*c*) *Egg*—white, truncated cone shape, laid singly on mature leaves. Early instars make frass chains and are generally brown in color. *Mature larva*—dorsum dull green; there is a velvet brown area behind head, from which arise two stout rods, each bearing a whorl of spines, to form a V shape; anterior to the rods is a dull green stripe; behind the brown dorsal saddle a dull green area is interrupted by thin black rectangles; the posterior two segments bear one black rod with spines; the lateral line is velvet black with intrusions of green rhomboid shapes; the venter is black; the head capsule is black with two stout, recurved horns that bear three whorls of spines on the shafts. *Pupa*—similar to that described for *Catonephele*, but with head more bifid and colored a two-tone green (Fig. 23). The larval behavior is similar to that of *Catonephele* and *Diaethria*.
Adult: Distinguished by the ground color, square FW apex, and elongate HW anal angle. See *Nica flavilla*.
Habits: Occurs from sea level to 1,600 m on both slopes, in association with forest habitats. Much more common in wet forest than in Guanacaste dry forest. Encountered as solitary individuals along forest edges and in light gaps. The flight is rapid and nervous, with the butterfly settling on vegetation momentarily and then flying again to another sunny spot. I have found this species to feed on fresh mammal dung. Common and widespread throughout Costa Rica and Central America.

Temenis pulchra
Hewitson, 1816
FW Length: 25-27 mm **Plate 24**
Range: Costa Rica to the Amazon Basin
Hostplant: Unknown
Early stages: Unknown
Adult: Sexes dimorphic or similar. *Male*—distinguished by the black ground color on the upperside, with red FW and HW bases and FW medial band; HW underside has two blue ocelli along the median. *Female*—two forms: one similar to the male; the other has a yellow FW band, and the HW discal area has a patch of reflective blue on upperside, an apparent mimic of *Callicore*; underside as in the male. Both female forms occur in Costa Rica, but I only have experience with the form looking like *Callicore*.
Habits: This rare Costa Rican species is known from a few widely separated localities that range from Atlantic lowland rain forest in the San Carlos Valley, south to Carrillo, and into the Reventazon valley, and from sea level at

Corcovado to 1,400 m on the Pacific slope of the Talamancas near San Vito de Java. Individuals stay in the forest canopy unless feeding. Males visit mammal dung or urine at bare ground along forest edges or river banks. The female also feeds on the urine-soaked ground. The mimetic female form flies along forest edges or in large light gaps, and behaves like a female *Callicore* when investigating plants. The female has an ambling, flutter-sail flight interspersed with brief alightings on vegetation. In one instance a female was observed patrolling the same light gap for two consecutive days. Males fly more rapidly and erratically.

Genus **EPIPHILE** Doubleday, 1849

The butterflies in this genus are easily recognized by the presence of a triangular spot on the costa of the hindwing underside that contrasts with the ground color, and all have conspicuous forewing bands. The sexes are dimorphic in all species, and the differences between the sexes can be considerable. *Epiphile* is entirely Neotropical and ranges from Mexico through Central and South America, being most diverse in Colombia. For a recent revision see Jenkins (1986).

The larvae feed on the Sapindaceae and show affinities to other sapindaceous feeders in morphology and arrangement of the spines. The pupa is similar to that of *Catonephele*.

In Central America all of the species are essentially montane, and in Costa Rica the genus occurs from 500 to 2,000 m. Depending upon the species and the sex, the adults feed on rotting fruits and mammal dung. In Costa Rica some of the species are very rare and restricted in their distributions.

Epiphile adrasta
Hewitson, 1861

FW Length: 26-29 mm **Plate 24**

Range: Mexico to Panama

Hostplant: *Serjania, Paullinia, Cardiospermum, Urvillea* (Sapindaceae)

Early stages: (Muyshondt 1973*b*) *Egg*—white truncated cone, laid singly on mature leaves. Early instars make frass chains. *Mature larva*—head capsule brown with reddish tinge, and whitish spines surrounding the head; a triangular spot on face; two large recurved horns that bear four whorls of spines along shafts of each; tip of horn drawn to a point, body green with yellow longitudinal stripes at sides of thoracic segments; narrow yellow, lateral lines with slanting bands of white-green near prolegs; dorsum has short orange spines with black forks; base of dorsal spines and spiracles yellow-orange. *Pupa*—Similar to that of *Catonephele*, but with a silver spot on wingpad and a light green abdomen contrasting with the dark green thorax. Pupa is suspended horizontally to substrate.

Adult: Sexes dimorphic. *Male*—orange FW band running from costa to tornus; orange HW band; black inner margin. *Female*—cream FW band; FW apex has prominent white subapical spot; orange HW disc.

Habits: Occurs commonly from 500 to 1,600 m on both slopes and occasionally at sea level, in association with wet forest habitats and very rarely in the Guanacaste dry forest. Persistent throughout the year in cloud forest. Unlike most butterflies, the female of this species is more frequently collected. Both sexes feed on fruit and dung.

Epiphile orea plusios
Godman and Salvin, 1883

FW Length: 26-29 mm **Plate 24**

Range: Costa Rica to Brazil. **Subspecies:** Costa Rica and Panama

Hostplant: *Serjania, Paullinia* (Sapindaceae)

Early stages: *Mature larva*—body dark emerald green; ten pairs of orange-yellow warts on either side of the dorsum, each with a pair of short black spines; penultimate segments have one wart centrally located with a rosette of spines; a fine wavy yellow lateral line just above the legs; head capsule broad and flat at the face; frontal half dark blue with two turquoise crescents on the face; clypeus white; posterior half of head brown; sides of head have short spines that are most dense at the mandibles; a pair of prominent head horns with four whorls of spines on the shaft; venter of body waxy white. *Note*: the larvae I have reared in Costa Rica appear to be different from those described by Müller (1886) from Brazil. *Pupa*—same as *E. adrasta*.

Adult: Sexes dimorphic. *Male*—distinguished by the double orange medial FW bands and the reflective blue on the HW disc. *Female*—upperside brown with a single orange medial FW band.

Habits: Occurs from 1,000 to 1,800 m on both slopes in association with cloud forest habitats in the Cordillera de Talamanca and the volcanoes in the Carrillo Belt. I have found this species most commonly in rain shadows and in semi-dry mountain passes, where both sexes fly at canopy level. The males perch in the canopy along forest edges or light gaps and chase other butterflies, returning to the same perch day after day. The females are active in the canopy during the mornings, and then at ground level in light gaps at midday. Both sexes are extremely impetuous, flitting rapidly from leaf to leaf. The males appear to feed only on fresh mammal dung or carrion, whereas the females are occasionally attracted to rotting fruits. This species is uncommon and local, and in my experience, active from January until June.

Epiphile eriopis devriesi

Jenkins, 1986

FW Length: 26-28 mm **Plate 24**

Range: Nicaragua to Colombia. **Subspecies:** Nicaragua to Panama

Hostplant: Unknown

Early stages: Unknown

Adult: Sexes dimorphic. *Male*—distinguished by the white FW band and purple cast on the HW discal area. *Female*—upperside entirely dull black with a white FW band running from costa to tornus.

Habits: Very poorly known from Central America, this species is known in Costa Rica from 600 to 1,400 m on the Atlantic slope, in association with the Carrillo Belt. The males are attracted to fresh mammal dung in the forest interior. The female flies with, and can be confused with, *Eunica norica* females. The subspecific differences between our populations and those of Colombia are the greater expanse of purple on the HW inner margin of the males and a wider white band in the female.

Epiphile grandis

Butler, 1872

FW Length: 36-39 mm **Plate 24**

Range: Costa Rica and Panama

Hostplant: Unknown

Early stages: Unknown

Adult: Sexes dimorphic. *Male*—distinguished by the dark purple bands across the orange FW and the almost entirely dark purple HW disc. *Female*—ground color on HW upperside almost entirely brown except for distal margins; FW has orange medial band and subapical white spot. Compare with the *Opsisphanes* species.

Habits: Occurs very locally at 1,600 to 2,200 m on the Pacific slope, in association with cloud forest habitats in the Talamancas centered around Cerro Echandi-Volcan Chiriqui. This area is geologically and climatogically distinct from the surrounding habitats and is classified as a transition zone between various forest types. The males perch during the early morning on tree trunks and branches that intrude into light gaps about five to fifteen meters above the ground. By midday the males are found only in the high forest canopy. The same perches are used day after day. This can be demonstrated by removing a succession of males through the course of a week: a new male will take up residence when the previous one is removed. Until quite recently, the male of this species was unknown, and the female, on the basis of which the species was described, is still only known from the holotype. Although still very rare in collections, the males can be quite abundant in the canopy. I have observed over twenty individuals in one day, but capture is another matter. Shooting them out of the canopy with bird shot can result in the very tedious task of finding the insect after a fall of twenty meters to the forest understory, and the method is not recommended. During the mornings males are attracted to fresh mammal dung. I have observed only one female, perched high in the canopy at midday with its wings held open against the trunk of a tree. From its history, it seems clear that this Costa Rican-Panamanian endemic species is dependent upon the special forest type found in the Talamancas, and it seems unlikely that it would survive much deforestation.

Genus **NICA** Hübner, 1816

The butterflies in this genus are small, have a honey yellow ground color, and bear metallic ocelli along the median of the underside and have slightly scalloped hindwing margins. The genus ranges from Guatemala through Central and South America and contains a single species.

The larvae feed on various genera of Sapindaceae, and are similar in appearance to *Epiphile* and *Catonephele* in the arrangement of the spines and larval resting behavior. The pupa is also quite similar to those genera.

In Costa Rica the species is widespread and present in most habitats below 1,500 meters. The behavior of the adults is also similar to that of related genera.

Nica flavilla canthara
Doubleday, 1849

FW Length: 18-23 mm **Plate 24**

Range: Mexico to the Amazon Basin. **Subspecies:** Mexico to Panama

Hostplant: *Cardiospermum, Serjania, Paullinia* (Sapindaceae)

Early stages: (Muyshondt 1973*d*) *Egg*—a white truncated cone, laid singly on the central portion of mature leaves. Early instars make frass chains. *Mature larva*—brown head capsule with orange areas on the frons and sides; two orange, straight, head-horns bearing whorls of brown spines; green body with a brown lateral stripe bordered above with a fine pink line; dorsum with a pair of rosetted spines on each segment; spines on thorax much stouter than the rest; dorsum with three conspicuous brown transverse bands. *Pupa*—green with brown speckles, very similar to *Diaethria*.

Adult: Distinguished by the ground color, small size, and the two metallic ocelli on the underside of the HW. See *Temenis laothoe*.

Habits: Occurs from sea level to 1,500 m on both slopes, in association with wet forest habitats and occasionally in the Guanacaste dry forest. Flies along forest edges and in light gaps, and occasionally in the forest canopy. Although widespread and encountered in most habitats, it is seldom abundant. Females oviposit around midday and are most frequently seen along trails and in large light gaps.

Genus **PYRRHOGYRA** Hübner, 1816

The genus is recognized by pale green or white medial bands on both wings, bordered in red on the underside. The genus ranges from Mexico through Central and South America; most of the species occur in the northeast part of South America. In Central America there are four species, all of which occur in our area.

The larvae feed on Sapindaceae and show affinities to *Temenis* and *Epiphile* in both morphology and behavior. The pupae likewise are allied to other sapindaceous-feeding species (Fig. 23).

In Costa Rica the genus occurs from sea level to 2,000 m, in all forest habitats. Some of the species feed on rotting fruits as adults, and others appear to be only attracted to mammal dung. All of the species are very fast fliers and are most often found in brightly sunlit light gaps or in the forest canopy.

Pyrrhogyra neaerea hypsenor
Godman and Salvin, 1884

FW Length: 31-33 mm **Plate 28**

Range: Mexico to the Amazon Basin. **Subspecies:** Mexico to Panama

Hostplant: *Paullinia* (Sapindaceae)

Early stages: (Muyshondt 1974*c*) *Egg*—bright yellow, truncated cone-shaped, laid singly on new growth leaves. Early instars make frass chains. *Mature larva*—body brown-orange with yellow dorsum and wide red bands across segments 2 and 3; three black dorsal stripes posterior to segment 3; head capsule heart-shaped, reddish, with two prominent horns that bear three rosettes of accessory spines on each shaft; dorsum has spines arising from all segments plus a row of lateral spines near venter (Fig. 23). *Pupa*—bright lime green with dull brown trim on cremaster and last abdominal segments; head slightly bifid (Fig. 23). The larvae behave in the way described for *Catonephele* and *Diaethria*.

Adult: Distinguished from all other Central American species by having the medial bands on both wings white, not green.

Habits: Occurs from sea level to 1,000 m, mostly on the Pacific slope, and is especially common in Guanacaste dry forest habitats. I have seen museum specimens from the Atlantic slope, but have not myself seen this species there. Most commonly encountered as small groups of males in the forest canopy at forest edges or in light gaps, swirling around a central perch. In Guanacaste this species is persistent as adults during the dry season, when some females are in reproductive diapause, others are not. Both sexes feed on rotting fruits and dung. Most abundant during the late Pacific slope rainy season.

Pyrrhogyra otolais otolais
Bates, 1864

FW Length: 24-27 mm **Plate 28**

Range: Mexico to Bolivia. **Subspecies:** Mexico to Panama

Hostplant: Unknown

Early stages: Unknown

Adult: Distinguished from the very similar *P. crameri* by having a red line along the posterior margin of the FW cell and some red at the base of the HW, both seen on the underside. Compare with *P. crameri*.

Habits: Occurs from sea level to 700 m on both slopes, in association with lowland rain forest habitats. Encountered in light gaps and along rivers where the males perch during the mornings, about five to fifteen meters above the ground. I have never collected this species with baits, and it is rare in Costa Rican collections.

Pyrrhogyra crameri
Aurivillius, 1882
FW Length: 25-27 mm **Plate 28**
Range: Nicaragua to the Amazon Basin
Hostplant: *Paullinia* (Sapindaceae)
Early stages: *Egg*—white truncated cone, laid singly upon the red new growth of sapling understory plants. Early instars make frass chains. *Mature larva*—body dull reddish amber that matches the new leaves exactly; dorsal spines black; head capsule amber with two prominent black horns that bear whorled spines on the shafts and terminate in a rosette. *Pupa*—bright lime green with dull brown on wingpads and thorax; head slightly bifid and a prominent thoracic keel; general shape as in *Catonephele*; the silk spun by the prepupa is red, the same color as the new leaves of the hostplant. *Note*: Seitz (1913, p. 475) suggests that the larvae of *P. crameri* and *P. neaerea* are identical. According to my observations they are distinct.
Adult: Very similar to *P. otolais*, but distinguished by the distinct subapical FW spot and the FW underside red line that runs along the costa but does not continue to the posterior margin of the cell or to the base. Compare with *P. otolais*.
Habits: Occurs from sea level to 900 m on both slopes in association with rain forest habitats, and most common in areas of swamp forest. The males perch in small groups of three to five individuals in light gaps that border swampy areas and rivers. These perches are used over the course of several months. I do not know if they are used by the same individuals or a succession of individuals through time. While perching, males behave like large lycaenids: chasing each other in wild zigzag flights, then returning to the same perch, waiting for a time, then racing off again. The females are found at midday, searching for oviposition sites in tree falls and light gaps. The males will occasionally feed on fruit and dung, but I have never been able to trap this species. Although the older literature mentions that this species is rare in Costa Rica, I have found it to be quite common in swamp forests, especially on the Atlantic slope during the dry seasons, and in Parque Corcovado throughout the year.

Pyrrhogyra edocla aenaria
Fruhstorfer, 1908
FW Length: 28-33 mm **Plate 28**
Range: Mexico to the Amazon Basin. **Subspecies:** Mexico to Panama
Hostplant: *Paullinia, Serjania* (Sapindaceae)
Early stages: *Mature larva*—body pale green, densely covered with black spines, all of roughly the same length; head capsule rose-red and bearing a pair of black recurved horns; head horns granulate with four whorls of spines along the shafts; each shaft terminates in a rosette of spines; sides of head near mandibles have two short black spines directed downward. *Pupa*—similar to that of *Catonephele* but with scaly brown wingpads and base of abdomen.
Adult: Immediately distinguished by the elongate FW apex and the highly visible green medial bands; FW apex has a prominent subapical spot, which is a useful field identifier; HW has no short tail, as in other congeners.
Habits: Occurs at 900 to 1,500 m on both slopes, in association with cloud forest habitats. Most commonly encountered along the Cordillera Central and Talamanca. Flies with an impetuous start-stop action along breaks in the forest canopy and riparian edges. The males perch as solitary individuals along forest edges during early mornings, and visit mammal urine along rivers from late morning until midday. The females are rare in Costa Rican collections, and males are rarely seen at puddles in groups of more than two individuals. Most abundant during February to June, and often in local populations.

Genus **CATONEPHELE**
Hübner, 1816

The genus is easily recognized by the highly dimorphic sexes: males have a black ground color with a bright orange pattern, and females have a black ground color with yellowish cream-colored transverse bands. In general, males of different species are distinct, but females of most species look alike. Within the genus there are two groups based on male androconial patches. In one group there are conspicuous scent hairs on the posterior margin of the hindwing; the other group lacks these structures. Although almost certainly connected with courtship, the use of these organs has never been observed, and it would be of interest to see how such seemingly awkward structures could function (see Boppré 1984 for possibilities). However, Jenkins (1985*a*) recognizes four groups based on a variety of characters. The genus ranges from Mexico through Central and South America and, in general, inhabits lowland forests. In Costa Rica one of our species is entirely montane.

The hostplants of *Catonephele* belong to the Euphorbiaceae, of which the genera *Alchornea* and *Dalechampia* are most important. In Costa Rica some species will occasionally use plants of other genera, as well. The larvae are solitary and very spiny. The head capsule bears two prominent spines that are usually metallic blue. The body of the larva is colored velvet black or deep green, and can be conspicuous when seen in the typical S-shaped resting position on the dorsal surface of leaves. The pupa is dark green and attached to the substrate in such a manner as to hold the body horizontally, like the pupae of *Epiphile*, *Temenis*, and *Diaethria*.

The adults feed entirely upon rotting fruits. In Costa Rica I have found that *C. orites* is generally restricted to the rain forest canopy, but the females oviposit on hostplant seedlings in light gaps. The larvae of *C. orites* are easily found, but the adults are seldom seen, and then only females.

Catonephele mexicana

Jenkins and de la Maza, 1985

FW Length: 28-31 mm **Plate 25**

Range: Mexico to Costa Rica

Hostplant: *Alchornea latifolia, Veconcibea pleistemona, Dalechampia triphylla, D. scandens* (Euphorbiaceae)

Early stages: (Muyshondt 1973*b*) *Egg*—a white truncated cone with a yellow zone around the micropyle. *Mature larva*—body olive green; all segments have seven orange, branched spines; dorsal body spines have black forks, lateral spines in late instar are green with black forks; head capsule reddish orange except lateral margins, which are black; two prominent head spines bear three rosettes of spines on the shaft. *Pupa*—various shades of green with brown wingpads and orange spiracles and portion of the thorax.

Adult: Male distinguished by the orange band running from FW apex to HW inner margin. Female has the FW spots visible through to the underside. The small size of both sexes distinguishes it from all other species.

Habits: Occurs from sea level to 1,200 m on both slopes, in association with wet forest habitats, or very occasionally in the Guanacaste gallery forest. Unlike all other Central American species, *mexicana* is tolerant of disturbed habitats and can persist in second growth. As a result, it is the most common and widespread species in Costa Rica. Conversely, it is infrequently found in areas of primary forest. The males perch in light gaps or along forest edges on tree trunks about 3 or 4 meters above the ground. The females fly low to the ground in dense vegetation during midday. Both sexes commonly visit rotting guavas, mangos, and bananas. *Note*: In all previous literature this butterfly has been referred to under the name *nyctimus* Westwood, a species that apparently ranges from Panama southward (Jenkins 1985). I follow the Jenkins revision here with reservations as to the specific differences between these two taxa; they are probably the same species.

Catonephele numilia esite

(Felder, 1869)

FW Length: male 34-36 mm, female 38-40 mm **Plate 25**

Range: Mexico to S. Brazil and Argentina. **Subspecies:** Mexico to Colombia, Ecuador, Venezuela, and Trinidad

Hostplant: *Alchornea costaricensis, A. latifolia* (Euphorbiaceae)

Early stages: (Muyshondt 1973*a*) *Egg*—white, barrel shaped, laid singly. *Mature larva*—head reddish orange except for lateral edges and spines, which are black; two prominent head spines bear three black rosettes of spines along the green shaft; body entirely green mottled with white spots, and covered with short branched spines; dorsal spines orange with black forks, the rest green with black forks. The larvae swing the head back and forth violently when molested or when one larva comes in contact with another. This may result in puncturing the body wall and eventual death of one or both larvae. *Pupa*—similar to *C. mexicana*, only larger.

Adult: Sexes dimorphic. *Male*—distinguished by the six round orange spots on the velvet black dorsal surface, a characteristic easily seen in the field. *Female*—distinguished by the cream-colored medial band on the FW and no bands on the HW. This cannot be confused with any other Central American species.

Habits: Occurs from sea level to 1,000 m on both slopes, where it is most common in wet forest habitats, less common in montane forests, and very rare in the Guanacaste dry forest. Encountered as solitary individuals in a diversity of microhabitats that include deep shade, forest canopy, and forest edges. The males perch in light gaps high in the forest subcanopy on tree trunks from morning until early afternoon. The females fly during midday, searching for hostplants along water courses and trails in the forest. Although in

Costa Rica *C. numilia* is present throughout the year in most habitats, it is seldom abundant.

Catonephele orites
Stichel, 1898
FW Length: male 32-34 mm, female 38-40 mm **Plate 25**
Range: Costa Rica to Colombia and northwest Ecuador
Hostplant: *Alchornea costaricensis* (Euphorbiaceae)
Early stages: *Egg*—yellow-green, barrel shaped with a sculptured crown, laid singly on seedling hostplants along riparian edges. *Mature larva*—velvet black with a maroon lateral line that bears many white warts; maroon dorsal saddle above the prolegs; shiny black head with two recurved knobbed horns that bear two whorls of spines on the shaft. When the larva is at rest, the head is held face down on the leaf surface and the body is in an S shape (but see also description in Jenkins 1985). When molested, the larvae show the same violent reaction as that described for *C. numilia. Pupa*—jade green with a pale silver area on the wingpads; in general outline it resembles the head of a small lizard.
Adult: Sexes dimorphic. *Male*—distinguished by the transverse orange band running from the FW cell to the HW inner margin; underside dull brown with conspicuous scent hairs between the wings. *Female*—distinguished from *C. chromis* by not having the subapical FW spot, HW underside whitish with a wavy brown transverse line running from costa to inner margin, and a transverse row of four submarginal brown spots on the HW. See *C. chromis*.
Habits: Occurs from sea level to 600 m in association with lowland swamp forest on the Atlantic slope, and is most common in the Carrillo Belt. In the past this species was considered an erroneous record from Costa Rica and very rare in Panama. I have found it to be one of the most common butterflies in the rain forest canopy in the Sarapiqui and Carrillo forests. This species is very rarely attracted to rotting fruits in the forest understory but is extremely responsive to fruits in the canopy (DeVries 1985*b*). Females are occasionally encountered during midday in light gaps or along riparian edges, searching for oviposition sites at ground level. The males perch and patrol areas of the forest canopy from mid-morning until afternoon. This species appears to be present throughout the year, but is in greatest abundance during the Atlantic slope dry seasons.

Catonephele chromis godmani
Stichel, 1901
FW Length: male 34-36 mm, female 41-43 mm **Plate 25**
Range: Honduras to Bolivia(?). **Subspecies:** Costa Rica and Panama
Hostplant: *Alchornea poasana* (Euphorbiaceae)
Early stages: *Egg*—white, barrel shaped, highly sculptured on crown, laid singly on seedling hostplants. The early stages have not been described in detail, but see Jenkins (1985).
Adult: Sexes dimorphic. *Male*—distinguished by the semi-falcate FW apex, which bears a rectangular orange spot; transverse orange bands wide and run from FW cell to HW inner margin. *Female*—distinguished from *C. orites* by having the base of the HW underside cream colored, the distal half reddish brown.
Habits: Occurs from 900 to 1,800 m on both slopes in association with cloud forest habitats. It is distributed principally along the Cordillera de Talamanca, and is uncommon and quite local. I have observed this species in the cloud forest canopy, where the males behave similarly to *C. orites*. The females are more common in collections because they are easily attracted to fruits placed on the ground, whereas the males are not. This species appears to be present throughout the year in most habitats surrounding the Cartago valley, and reaches greatest abundance during the dry season. In general it is an uncommon species in collections which, I believe, reflects its local nature.

Genus **NESSAEA** Hübner, 1819

Closely related to *Catonephele*, this genus is easily identified by the green coloration on the underside and the presence of a pigmentary blue band on the forewing (Vane-Wright 1979). The genus ranges from southern Mexico throughout Central and South America, and is composed of five species, one of which occurs in Central America.

As in *Catonephele*, the larvae feed on *Alchornea* and related Euphorbiaceae, and the early stages are extremely similar in all respects to that genus (Fig. 23). It is conceivable that *Nessaea* will prove to be part of *Catonephele* (Vane-Wright, personal communication).

In Costa Rica, the genus is confined to primary rain forest and is intolerant of disturbed areas. The adults are fast fliers and very wary of any movement. The green coloration provides highly effective crypsis. All of the species feed on rotting fruits, and apparently all are confined to swamp forest habitats.

Nessaea aglaura aglaura

(Doubleday, 1848)

FW Length: 24-39 mm **Plate 25**

Range: Southern Mexico to Colombia. **Subspecies:** Mexico to Panama and Ecuador

Hostplant: *Alchornea costaricensis, Plukenetia volubilis* (Euphorbiaceae)

Early stages: *Egg*—yellow-green as in *Catonephele orites*, laid singly on seedling hostplants occuring in light gaps. *Mature larva*—body a beautiful jade green with three spines per segment, each bearing five branches; spines amber; head the color of blue steel on the anterior half, amber on the posterior half; two long head horns bearing three sets of whorled spines on the shaft; posterior half of horns amber, the anterior half blue (Fig. 23). As in *Catonephele*, the larvae rest on the dorsal surface of leaves with the face down and the horns projecting forward, and react violently when molested. *Pupa*—dark green, mottled with scaly brown on the wingpads. Pupation takes place on the dorsal surface of leaves, with the body held horizontal to the substrate.

Adult: Sexes slightly dimorphic. This species is immediately distinguished by the green underside and the blue on the FW upperside. *Male*—darker than the female, with an orange patch on the costal margin of the HW.

Habits: Occurs from sea level to 600 m on both slopes, only in association with swampy areas in primary rain forest. Encountered as solitary individuals in the forest along trails and in light gaps. Males perch on vegetation 1 to 5 meters above the ground, with the wings held slightly apart, exposing the blue bands. When disturbed, the wings are immediately snapped shut and the insect melts into the surrounding greenery of the forest. The females are most active during midday, when they are ovipositing on seedlings of *Alchornea*, which occur in light gaps and along riparian edges. On the Pacific side, this species is rare and is distributed from Punta Quepos south to the Osa Peninsula. Conversely, on the Atlantic side, especially along the Rio Tortuguero and Sarapiqui, it can be very common. At Finca la Selva it is present throughout the year, but undergoes wild fluctuations of abundance from month to month. This species is local and intolerant of disturbed habitats.

Genus **HAEMATERA** Doubleday, 1849

This monotypic genus is closely related to *Cyclogramma*, but is easily distinguished by the dull coloration of the HW underside, and it does not have the characteristic "88" pattern of *Cyclogramma*. The genus *Haematera* ranges from Costa Rica to South America, where it seems to be common in most habitats. In Central America it is very rare.

The hostplant for the genus in South America is *Urvillea* in the Sapindaceae, and the early stages seem to resemble strongly those of *Diaethria* and *Callicore*. The hostplant and the larvae are unknown in Central America.

Haematera pyramus thysbe

Doubleday, 1849

FW Length: 20-22 mm **Plate 25**

Range: Nicaragua to the Amazon Basin. **Subspecies:** Nicaragua to Colombia

Hostplant: *Urvillea ulmacea* (Sapindaceae)

Early stages: (Müller 1886) In Brazil the mature larva is pale green, covered with tiny white warts and dark spiracles; the head bears two large spines with three rosettes of spines projecting forward.

Adult: Distinguished by the red wing bases with purple margins; underside mottled grayish pink.

Habits: I have seen only two authentic records from Costa Rica, both from near the Guapiles area at the base of the mountains. G. B. Small informs me that in Panama this species flies and behaves like *Diaethria*: it is a fast, erratic flier with frequent stops on vegetation and tree trunks. In South America this species is found in association with second growth and bright sunshine, and males will visit wet sand along roadsides. Very rare in Costa Rican collections.

Genus **CYCLOGRAMMA** Doubleday, 1847

The butterflies in this genus are recognized by reddish base to the forewing underside and the faint outline of the figure 88 on the hindwing underside. There are only two species in the genus, one of which occurs in our area, the other confined to Mexico. The genus is entirely Central American. Both adult and early stages are very similar to *Diaethria*, and there has long been uncertainty as to its generic validity.

The hostplants for the genus are in the Sapindaceae, of which the genera *Serjania* and *Paullinia* are important. In Costa Rica and Panama, this genus is confined to montane forest habitats, and is commonly encountered along rivers where the males come to drink at wet sand.

Cyclogramma pandama

Doubleday, 1847

FW Length: 22-23 mm **Plate 25**

Range: Mexico to Panama

Hostplant: *Serjania* (Sapindaceae)

Early stages: (Muyshondt 1975*c*) Apparently all the early stages are identical to those described for *Diaethria astala*.

Adult: Distinguished by the orange medial band, which is easily visible in the field; FW apex has a prominent white spot; HW underside with a faint figure 88.

Habits: Occurs from 800 to 2,500 m on both slopes, in association with cloud forest habitats. Encountered as solitary individuals on areas of exposed ground, especially along land slips and cliff faces where there is water seepage. The flight is very fast and erratic, with wild sweeping movements close to the ground; then the individual quickly settles after a few moments. Capturing this species takes patience, since it is disturbed at the slightest movement. The males visit wet sand and dung, and can be attracted by enriching bare soil with urine. The females, uncommon in collections, are found along forest edges or in light gaps at midday, as they look for oviposition sites. This species is present throughout the year in all cloud forest areas. It is typical of the Talamancan butterfly fauna, but rarely are more than two individuals found per day at a single locality.

Genus **DIAETHRIA** Billberg, 1820

This genus is easily recognized by the very distinct figure 88 on the HW underside, set upon a white ground color, and by the upperside coloration of either blue or green. In many of the older works on tropical butterflies, the species were referred to under the name *Callicore*, which now refers to another, related genus. *Diaethria* is entirely Neotropical and ranges from southern Texas (as strays) throughout Central and South America. The greatest number of species occur in the Amazon basin, where these butterflies can be exceedingly common. Several of the Central American species have dimorphic sexes; one of these occurs in Costa Rica.

The hostplants for *Diaethria* are Sapindaceae and Ulmaceae. Although the latter has been disputed, the Ulmaceae is unquestionably the hostplant for one of our Costa Rican species. The eggs and larvae are similar to *Callicore*, but the larvae lack some of the spines on the dorsum (Fig. 23). The pupae are also similar to *Callicore*, and have the general shape seen in *Catonephele*, *Nessaea*, *Epiphile*, *Temenis*, and *Pseudonica*, a point previously noted by Muyshondt (1975*c*).

The adults are found at all elevations in Costa Rica, except the paramo vegetation in the high Cordillera de Talamanca above 3,000 m. Some of the species are familiar sights along sandy freshwater beaches and some are "anthropophilic." Perhaps as a result of this fondness for human habitations, it is considered a sign of luck to find one of these butterflies in your house; one should then run out and buy a lottery ticket with the number 88 or 89 on it. The Costa Rican countryside abounds with campesinos who have assured me that fortunes have been gained in this way.

All of the species feed on rotting fruits and dung, and the males are highly attracted to bare soil enriched with urine. In some years, the montane dry seasons will produce huge numbers of all species, and a particular spot along a river will be swarming with individuals intermingled with other nymphalid genera. This is especially true in the Talamancas at 1,000 to 1,700 meters, and it is a remarkable sight.

Diaethria eupepla

(Godman and Salvin, 1874)

FW Length: 22-25 mm **Plate 25**

Range: Guatemala to Colombia

Hostplant: *Serjania* (Sapindaceae)

Early stages: *Egg*—white, highly sculptured, laid singly on new growth. The first and second instars are similar to those described for *D. astala*; later instars and the pupae need description.

Adult: Distinguished by the brilliant metallic green FW band; HW upperside has a large patch of iridescent blue-green; HW underside ground color shiny white with a distinct figure 88; HW underside has no red submarginal line. See *D. astala*.

Habits: Occurs at 700 to 1,600 m on both slopes in association with cloud forest habitats; especially common on the Pacific slope of the Cordillera de Talamanca. Usually encountered along rivers or land slips where there is water seepage, in small groups of five to ten males. Occasionally very common in some of the Talamancan rain shadow valleys. The flight is extremely fast and wary, with low swoops to the ground and circling back and forth. Although the males can be very common, females are rare in collections, and I have never seen one in nature. Perhaps the female spends most of her time in the forest canopy.

Diaethria anna

(Guérin-Méneville, 1844)

FW Length: 22-25 mm **Plate 25**

Range: Mexico to Costa Rica

Hostplant: Unknown

Early stages: Unknown

Adult: Very similar to female *D. astala*, but distinguished by a metallic green band on the FW upperside; HW underside ground color pure white with a distinct figure 88 and red costa margin. Compare with *D. astala*.

Habits: Although this species is apparently very common in parts of Mexico, I have only seen a handful of specimens in the British Museum (Natural History) collected by C. F. Underwood and labeled "Costa Rica." Because of its great similarity to the female of *D. astala* and general color pattern of *D. marchalii*, it has probably been overlooked by most collectors.

Diaethria marchalii

(Guérin-Méneville, 1844)

FW Length: 22-25 mm **Plate 25**

Range: Nicaragua to Brazil

Hostplant: *Trema micrantha* (Ulmaceae)

Early stages: *Egg*—white, highly sculptured, laid singly along a major leaf vein on the underside of leaves. *Mature larva*—body light green with two rows of yellow spots along the dorsum; two short spines on either side of the anal segment; head bears two long green spines that have whorled spines along the shaft. The face is held appressed to the leaf while the larva is at rest. The first two instars make frass chains; later ones do not. When the larva is molested, the head is swung violently from side to side. *Pupa*—dull greenish brown with two short head horns. The pupa is suspended.

Adult: Distinguished from all other Costa Rican congeners by the dirty gray ground color on the HW underside, with a distinct figure 88; FW underside red from base to subapex. See *Perisama barnesi*.

Habits: Occurs from sea level to 2,000 m on both slopes, in all forest habitats except the lowland dry forests of Guanacaste. Most commonly encountered near human habitations, where it is a familiar sight to see individuals perched head down on buildings. Its association with human habitations is most likely due to the fact that the hostplant (*Trema*) is a common secondary-succession tree species with a very wide distribution in Costa Rica. Although the butterfly is widespread and common in Costa Rica, away from human habitations it is found as solitary individuals and never with the great abundance seen in other species. Females oviposit on hostplants ranging from seedling to mature forest trees, and appear to oviposit at any time there is sunshine. Both sexes feed on the juices of rotting fruits and sewage, and the males visit water seepage and wet laundry.

Diaethria astala

(Guérin-Méneville, 1844)

FW Length: 23-25 mm **Plate 25**

Range: Mexico to Colombia

Hostplant: *Serjania, Paullinia, Cardiospermum* (Sapindaceae)

Early stages: (Muyshondt 1975*c*) *Egg*—pale green with light green ribs, laid singly. *Mature larva*—body pale green with many white granules over entire body and three rows of yellow granules along the sides. Head capsule brown with two large spines: the shafts are alternately colored reddish brown and white, and bear three whorls of spines that are reddish at the base; sides of head reddish. While at rest the larvae make frass chains in the first two instars, and in later instars rest on the leaf with the face downward and the head held above the substrate (Fig. 23). If the larva is molested, the head and spines are swung around and may puncture the body wall of another larva, should it be on the same leaf. *Pupa*—green with brown lateral lines running from cremaster to wingpads and head area; shape expands from cremaster to wingpads, and the thorax is keeled; head slightly bifid; pupation is suspended (see Fig. 23).

Adult: *Male*—rich blue ground color on upperside with a subapical white dot on FW; HW underside similar to that of *D. eupepla* but with a submarginal red line. *Female*—upperside similar to *D. anna* and *D. marchalii*, but distinguished by the subapical white spot on the FW and the submarginal red line on the HW underside. Compare with *D. anna* and *D. marchalii*.

Habits: Occurs at 800 to 1,600 m on both slopes, in association with cloud forest habitats. In habits it is similar to *D. eupepla*, but appears to be more tolerant of disturbed habitats. As a result, it is much more common in the Meseta Central and areas that have been used for agriculture. The males are encountered in bright sunshine as solitary individuals along rivers and landslips, and are often found in company with *D. eupepla* and *D. marchalii*. While at rest, all of these species can be separated by the marks on the HW underside. The females fly along ridge tops or in the canopy during midday. Both sexes will feed on rotting fruits and occasionally dung. This species is present in most localities throughout the year, but is most abundant during dry seasons.

Genus **CALLICORE** Hübner, 1819

The butterflies in this genus are small to medium-sized, all have primary colors to some extent, and can be recognized by their "numerical" patterns, usually with figures of 69, 66, 88, or 89 on the underside of the hindwing. For many years, species in this genus were referred to the genus *Catagramma*, which has now been placed in synonymy. The species impress one as being like miniature *Agrias*, a fact that prompted Descimon (1976) to propose a mimicry system with *Callicore* species as models. As a result of their highly colorful patterns, these butterflies have always been great favorites with collectors, and have inspired some to increase the commercial trade of butterflies. The *Callicore* species are used in construction of placemats, coasters, dinner plates, and wall hangings.

Callicore is entirely Neotropical, and distributed from Mexico throughout Central and South America, reaching greatest local diversity on the eastern slope of the Andes in the Amazon Basin. Costa Rica once again shows its biogeographical affinities with South America in this genus; some species end their northern range in our area, other species are apparently endemic to Costa Rica, and still others end their southern range in our area, along the Atlantic slope.

Considering the size and popularity of the genus, it is surprising that few species have had their early stages described. Of those known, the hostplants of importance are in the Sapindaceae. The larvae are very similar to those described for *Diaethria*, but have slightly more spines on the dorsum, and the head capsule bears relatively enormous spines: "antlers" that rival those found on the extinct Pleistocene Irish Elk for comparative size (Fig. 23). The pupae are also similar to those described for *Diaethria* (see Fig. 23).

In Costa Rica, most of the species are found in the lowland rain forests, but a few species do occur above 700 meters. All the species feed on rotting fruits, the males will visit mud, and some are components of the rain forest canopy and seldom descend to the ground.

Callicore lyca aerias

(Godman and Salvin, 1883)

FW Length: 25-28 mm **Plate 25**

Range: Mexico to Colombia. **Subspecies:** Guatemala to Panama

Hostplant: *Serjania, Allophylus* (Sapindaceae)

Early stages: *Egg*—white, laid singly on new growth of *Paullinia*, old leaves of *Allophyllus*. *Early instars*—similar to those described for *C. atacama* but with some reflective coloration on the dorsal spines and a red area on the sides of the head. The mature larva has not been described.

Adult: Distinguished by the yellow FW band directed anterior to the tornus; configuration of blue dots on the HW underside form two offset lines. The female has more extensive blue on HW and broader orange on the FW.

Habits: Occurs from sea level to 1,600 m on both slopes in association with wet forest habitats; enters Guanacaste only in mountain passes. Encountered as solitary individuals in light gaps and along water courses in the forest. Males perch in the subcanopy of the forest and chase other butterflies from the perches. These perches may be maintained by the same individual for several days. Females are rarely collected, and fly at midday in the shady understory of the forest or in the subcanopy, where they search for oviposition sites. Occasionally, this species is taken on rotting fruits, and males may visit water seepage along landslips. Although present in all wet forest habitats in Costa Rica, it is seldom abundant.

Callicore brome

(Boisduval, 1836)

FW Length: 25-26 mm **Plate 25**

Range: Costa Rica to Ecuador

Hostplant: Unknown

Early stages: Unknown

Adult: Distinguished by the small size; FW yellow band is constricted near the costa and inflated at the tornus; blue on HW almost reaches the base; dull yellow ring on HW underside broadly ovate, containing four staggered blue and white dots. The female is more broadly marked than the male.

Habits: Until recently, this species was unknown in Costa Rica. It is known from only two localities, both of which are within the rain forest habitats that occur near the Osa Peninsula and north to Punta Quepos, from sea level to 500 m. I observed the species only once in a remnant tract of forest near Parrita, where two males were perching in the morning about two meters from the ground along a shady forest edge. Compared with Colombian material, the Costa Rican specimens have a wider FW band and less extensive blue on the HW. Since this species is very rare in Costa Rica, and probably only occurs in the remnant Pacific rain forest habitats, any information on its habits or biology should be made available.

Callicore atacama manova

(Fruhstorfer, 1916)

FW Length: 25-27 mm **Plate 25**

Range: Costa Rica to Peru and Bolivia. **Subspecies:** Costa Rica and Panama

Hostplant: *Allophyllus* aff. *psilospermus* (Sapindaceae)

Early stages: *Egg*—white, laid singly on damaged leaf tips of old leaves. First to third instar larval make frass chains, later instars rest on the uppersides of leaves in a manner reminiscent of *Nessaea. Mature larva*—body pale emerald green covered with tiny white granulations; at interface of venter and sides (above prolegs) arise two rows of short yellow spines that are rosetted at tips; spines in dorsal row are thicker and directed anteriorly, ventral row are slender and directed posteriorly and downward; anal segment has two stout orange spines with tiny black accessory spines on the shafts; head capsule amber colored on face, black on sides and epicranium; a pair of very large, maroon head horns bear five rosettes of spines on their shafts, and have two white rings on shaft between rosettes 1, 2, and 3 (Fig. 23). *Pupa*—similar to *Epiphile* (Fig. 23).

Adult: Distinguished by the yellow FW band being directed *basad* to the tornus; HW underside has six separate yellow bands where the posterior portion of the central band terminates as three blue and white dots. The female has a reduced blue patch on the HW. See *C. faustina*.

Habits: This rare Costa Rican species is known from the Pacific lowland rain forests near the Osa Peninsula, where it can be quite common. Encountered as solitary individuals along trails and in shady light gaps from morning until just after midday. Females oviposit around midday on seedling to mature shrubs. Both sexes visit rotting fruits. These butterflies are persistent throughout the year in Parque Corcovado.

Callicore faustina

(Bates, 1866)

FW Length: 25-28 mm **Plate 25**

Range: Costa Rica and Panama

Hostplant: Unknown

Early stages: Unknown

Adult: Similar to *C. atacama*, but distinguished by having a central line of blue dots on the HW underside that runs from the costa to the tornus. The female has a wider FW band and reduced blue on the HW.

Habits: In Costa Rica, this species is apparently confined to the Reventazon Valley and the Atlantic slope of the Talamancas, from 500 to 700 m elevation. Every specimen from Costa Rica I have seen, alive or dead, has come from this area. Encountered as solitary individuals in the forest along light gaps and trails, where the males perch from late morning until early afternoon about five meters from the ground. The same perches are used by several males over a succession of time. This is best demonstrated by removing one male a day over a period of time from the same perch. When one is removed, the next day another individual is usually found on the same perch. Because I have found this species along ridge tops, I suspect that it may be more common in the forest canopy. This species will occasionally feed on rotting fruits and dung placed in traps. Uncommon.

Callicore texa titania

(Salvin, 1869)

FW Length: 27-30 mm **Plate 25**

Range: Mexico to Colombia. **Subspecies:** Guatemala to Colombia

Hostplant: *Serjania* (Sapindaceae)

Early stages: (Muyshondt 1975*c*) Apparently, in El Salvador, the early stages are almost identical to those described for *Diaethria astala*, and differ by having spines on the eighth abdominal segment and reduced subdorsal spines.

Adult: Distinguished by the red base of the FW and the HW upperside with a deep violet patch; HW underside has a crude figure 8 bordered heavily in pale yellow. Compare with *C. patelina*. *Note*: near the Panamanian border in the Talamancas, some populations of this species have a red patch on the HW upperside.

Habits: Occurs from sea level to 1,000 m on the

Pacific slope in association with either deciduous forest or disturbed wet forest habitats. Encountered as solitary individuals along forest edges, light gaps, and occasionally in open areas. The males perch on tree trunks or vegetation from late morning until early afternoon. Males visit wet sand and can be baited with wet laundry. The flight period is restricted mainly to the Pacific rainy season between July and August, but in some years rare individuals can be found during the dry season in dry river bottoms. Uncommon.

Callicore patelina

(Hewitson, 1853)

FW Length: 29-31 mm **Plate 25**

Range: Southern Mexico to Costa Rica

Hostplant: Unknown

Early stages: Unknown

Adult: Distinguished by the deep red base of the FW; the entire upperside is cast with an intense blue-violet; the figure 8 on the HW underside is narrowed anteriorly and bears only one blue-white dot in the most anterior ring. See *C. texa titania.*

Habits: This rare species is known in Costa Rica only from the Atlantic lowland rain forest, from sea level to 500 m. Its known Costa Rican distribution is in general concordance with the lower edge of the Carrillo Belt, and I have found it only in the rain forest canopy. In contrast, I have seen this species in Belize at ground level, in the swamp forests that are so common in that country. In the past, it has been thought to be most common in Nicaragua. Although there is little known of this species in Costa Rica, it may be that it is restricted to the forest canopy and hence difficult to observe or collect.

Callicore pitheas

(Latreille, 1811)

FW Length: 26-30 mm **Plate 25**

Range: Mexico to Venezuela and Ecuador

Hostplant: Sapindaceae

Early stages: (Muyshondt 1975*c*) Apparently similar to *Diaethria astala*, but in need of formal description.

Adult: Distinguished by the bright red and black upperside; HW underside has two separate black patches that bear a single pupil in each. According to Dillon (1948), this species is variable.

Habits: Occurs from sea level to 1,200 m on the Pacific slope in association with dry forest habitats, and is most common in Guanacaste. Encountered as solitary individuals along trails and in well-lighted forest interiors. This species is most abundant at the beginning of the rainy season, but is persistent as rare individuals along riverbeds during the dry season. Males perch head down on tree trunks about three meters above the ground and make sorties from the perch, usually encircling the tree. While at rest, the forewings are folded down into the hindwing and the insect is surprisingly cryptic. As would be expected, the red and black pattern make this butterfly conspicuous (aposematic?) when it is flying. Both sexes feed on rotting fruits and fresh dung, and the males visit wet sand and laundry. Although not uncommon in some years, this species can be highly localized within a tract of forest.

Callicore peralta

(Dillon, 1948)

FW Length: 20-22 mm **Plate 26**

Range: Costa Rica and Panama

Hostplant: Unknown

Early stages: Unknown

Adult: Distinguished from *C. pacifica* by the orange line at the base of the HW near the costa; the orange lines on the underside are narrower. Compare with *C. pacifica*.

Habits: Few specimens of this species are known from Costa Rica, and fewer still from Panama. In Costa Rica all specimens have come from the Atlantic slope near the Guapiles area, and range in elevation from 200 to 500 m. I have not seen this species in nature, but would guess that it is similar in behavior to *C. pacifica*.

Callicore pacifica bugaba

(Staudinger, 1875)

FW Length: 20-22 mm **Plate 26**

Range: Guatemala to Panama. **Subspecies:** Costa Rica and Panama

Hostplant: Unknown

Early stages: Unknown

Adult: The orange-yellow band on the FW is of uniform width across its length; HW underside with distinct figure 8; no orange spot on HW costa, as in *C. peralta*.

Habits: Occurs from sea level to 1,400 m on both slopes, but much more common on the Pacific side of the Cordillera de Talamanca, and especially common near the Panamanian border. Commonly found along rivers and forest edges in small groups of up to ten individuals, or as solitary individuals near human dwellings. Males perch along forest edges and chase any insect that passes by, and are attracted to bare soil enriched with urine. Females fly at midday in light gaps or along shady forest edges. Present throughout the year in montane habitats.

Genus **PERISAMA** Doubleday, 1894

Of the fifty or more species in this genus, all but two are confined to South America. One occurs in Costa Rica and another in Mexico; both are endemic. The genus is easily recognized by having the same wing shape and color pattern as *Diaethria* and *Callicore*, but without the numerical figures on the hindwing underside. The discal area is uniformly colored, with a few small spots along the median.

Although *Perisama* is a great favorite with collectors, there is absolutely nothing known about its hostplants or early stages. All of the species, including the Central American ones, are restricted to montane regions, where they can be very abundant. However, the Central American species are two of the rarest butterflies known, being represented in collections by very few specimens. In South America the males are known to visit wet sand and form large aggregations, but there are no such observations on the Central American species.

Perisama barnesi

Schaus, 1913

FW Length: 25-27 mm **Plate 26**

Range: Endemic to Costa Rica

Hostplant: Unknown

Early stages: Unknown

Adult: Distinguished by the gray-black ground color of the HW underside; FW underside has a red base and white margins; upperside similar to *Diaethria marchalii*, but with a blue-green submarginal band on both wings. See *Diaethria marchalii, D. astala*, and *D. anna*.

Habits: This rare endemic species is known from 300 to 1,000 m on the Atlantic slope, in association with the Carrillo Belt. I have seen a forewing in the C. Lankester collection in the British Museum (Natural History) labelled Cachi, which may indicate that the species' distribution extends into the Talamancas as well. It flies along forest edges at ridge tops about one meter above the ground and, when flying, resembles *Diaethria marchalii* or the aposematic species *Eumaeus godarti* (Lycaenidae). All of the specimens I have seen, and my own experience with it in the field, suggest that it flies during the dry periods, in May to June. The great rarity of this species is most likely a reflection of the habitat where it occurs: steep forested mountain ravines. Any biological observations should be published, particularly any indication of its larval hostplants.

Genus **ADELPHA** Hübner, 1816

The butterflies that compose the genus *Adelpha* are, in my opinion, the most difficult and trying taxonomically of all the nymphalids. There are several reasons for this: the adults can be extremely similar (including the male genitalia); although the larvae have proven to be reliable for separating species (see Moss 1933*b*; Aiello 1984); relatively few life histories are known; and the nomenclature of *Adelpha*, that is, the identity of type-specimens and the spellings, is chaotic. These difficulties have added to about a century of misidentifications in the literature (see Hall 1938), and hence misidentification in museum collections. In my treatment of *Adelpha*, I have tried to consult every type specimen, original figure, and description, and have examined most of the genitalia before committing a name to paper. The reader will find that names given here, in many cases, will be different than those found in the standard Neotropical reference works and from my own previous work (DeVries 1983). The changes here reflect misidentifications in the literature and the deletion of subspecies names I felt were not useful or fell within the range of variation in Costa Rica. For example, the familiar name *iphicla* is here presented with the original Linnaean spelling *iphiclus*.

The butterflies in *Adelpha* are recognized at a glance by their brown upperside ground color, forewing with subapical orange patch, and in some species a medial white band that traverses both wings or just the hindwing. The only genus it can be confused with is *Doxocopa*, where in certain species the females look like white-banded *Adelpha*. When identifying *Adelpha* species, close attention must be paid to seemingly insignificant spots, angles, and colors. I have found that the shape of the hindwing medial band as it enters the tornus, the position and angle of the forewing band as it crosses the cell, and the configuration of the subapical spots have been useful characters. Although the male genitalia are very similar, some differences will be seen in the harpes and the shape of the claspers. The major references for the taxonomy of *Adelpha* are: Godman and Salvin 1884, Fruhstorfer 1915, Moss 1933*b*, Hall 1938, Chermock 1950, and Aiello 1984. Our understanding of *Adelpha* would be greatly improved by a much-needed revision that takes into consideration early stages, hostplants, and long series of bred specimens. An excellent start is Aiello (1984). Any portion of a life history that has an associated adult should be saved and made available to a museum; this is an area where amateurs can make substantial contributions to butterfly biology.

The genus is entirely Neotropical, but has close relatives (*Limenitis*) in North America, and other members of the tribe Limenitini are found throughout all temperate and tropical regions in the Old World. There are upwards of seventy species of *Adelpha* in the Neotropics, thirty of which occur in Costa Rica. There are well over 250 named forms and geographical races in the Neotropics, many of dubious validity, but others will without doubt be found to be distinct species.

The hostplants of *Adelpha* are diverse and include Rubiaceae, Moraceae, Urticaceae, Ulmaceae, Verbenaceae, Melastomaceae, Bombacaceae, Icacinaceae, Piperaceae, Tiliaceae, and Ericaceae. Of these families, Rubiaceae and the Ulmales (Moraceae, Urticaceae, and Ulmaceae) appear to be the most important. From rearing records in the literature (Moss 1933) and my own work in Costa Rica, it seems that some species are restricted to a specific plant family, while others have been recorded on widely different families. When the latter is observed, it seems probable that, at least in some cases, there are two *Adelpha* species involved, although some species may be extreme generalist herbivores. I cannot stress enough the importance of rearing the *Adelpha* species and maintaining a collection that has voucher specimens of hostplants, adults, and the cast skins and head capsules properly keyed to individual adult specimens.

The eggs of *Adelpha* are, as far as is known, always laid singly, either on new leaves or old and damaged leaves. All of the species make frass chains in the early instars, and many of the mature larvae have areas on a particular leaf that are covered with frass, silk, and bits of dead leaf material where they rest. The larvae of all species are spiny, and have conspicuous spines, directed laterally, on the dorsum of the thorax. The head capsule is adorned with a single or double corona of spines, and small head horns may be present. No larvae are aposematic; all rely entirely upon crypsis for protection, and may take a form resembling a bird dropping, a bit of dead leaf, or a small twig covered with moss (Fig. 24). Although the larvae are generally very difficult to find in the field, none of the species hides under cover; all sit on top of leaves or in exposed places. And although they all bear a general morphological resemblance to one another, they provide one of the best methods of separating the species. The pupae are also helpful in this regard. In general there are two types of pupae, one with a prominent dorsal keel, the other without (Fig. 24). All species appear to have pupae with bifid heads, but these may range from slight projections to large processes that recall *Hamadryas*. The pupal coloration ranges from shades of brown and green to a mirrorlike chrome color. See Aiello (1984) for a good summary.

In Costa Rica, *Adelpha* occurs from sea level to the highest mountains, and is found in all habitats and microhabitats. Many of the rain forest species spend much of their adult lives in the forest canopy, while other species (*A. cytherea*) stay at ground level. Most of the species are uncommon to rare, and are not well represented in collections—especially those species that occur only in the high montane habitats. I have found that a number of the species are very local, while others are found in almost all habitats but are taken as solitary individuals. The males perch along forest edges, in light gaps, or in the canopy, and chase other insects as they fly past. In general, an individual male stays on a perch for only a few minutes, and after a few sorties, moves to another perch some distance away. The females are generally active during midday, and from what little is known, appear to oviposit on plants along forest edges and in light gaps. The searching female stops every few meters to test a plant by drumming its forelegs on the surface, and then moves on. Once she has found an appropriate plant, she may circle around it and keep testing it, flying off, returning and testing again for some time before an egg is laid (for example, *A. heraclea*, *A. cocala*, and *A. leucophthalma*). Other species, like female *A. cytherea*, spend little time away from the hostplant and generally display little ritual when ovipositing.

Both sexes feed on rotting fruits on the forest floor, and fruits that are still on trees high in the canopy. Both sexes, especially of those species occurring at higher elevations, will also feed on flower nectar. The males that have very recently emerged from the pupa visit wet sand and mud. There is absolutely nothing known about how long individuals live or about other aspects of their population biology, although *A. cytherea* is common enough in some localities to be used for such a study.

Why many different species have very similar color patterns is unknown. Mimicry theory can

PLATES

PLATE 1 · PAPILIONIDAE

1. **Battus polydamas polydamas** ♂, D: Guapiles, CR, p. 68
2. **Battus belus varus** ♂, D: Chontales, Nicaragua, p. 69
3. **Battus belus varus** ♀, D: CR, p. 69
4. **Battus laodamas rhipidius** ♂, D: Carrillo, CR, p. 69
5. **Battus laodamas rhipidius** ♀, D: Carrillo, CR [HT], p. 69
6. **Battus lycidas** ♂, D: San Mateo, CR, p. 69
7. **Battus lycidas** ♀, D: San José, CR, p. 69
8. **Battus crassus** ♂, D: Carrillo, CR, p. 69
9. **Battus crassus** ♀, D: Carrillo, CR, p. 69
10. **Parides photinus** ♂, D: CR, p. 65
11. **Parides montezuma** ♂, D: CR, p. 65

1
2
3
4
5
6
7
8
9
10
11

PLATE 2 · PAPILIONIDAE

1. **Parides sesostris zestos** ♂, D: Guapiles, CR, p. 65
2. **Parides sesostris zestos** ♀, D: Juan Viñas, CR, p. 65
3. **Parides childrenae childrenae** ♂, D: Guapiles, CR, p. 66
4. **Parides childrenae childrenae** ♀, D: Carrillo, CR, p. 66
5. **Parides lycimenes lycimenes** ♂, D: Carrillo, CR, p. 66
6. **Parides lycimenes lycimenes** ♀, D: Carrillo, CR, p. 66
7. **Parides erithalion sadyattes** ♂, D: CR [HT], p. 67
8. **Parides erithalion sadyattes** ♀, D: Carrillo, CR, p. 67
9. **Parides erithalion** subspecies ♂, D: Carrillo, CR, p. 67
10. **Parides erithalion** subspecies ♀, D: Cartago, CR, p. 67
11. **Parides iphidamas iphidamas** ♂, D: CR, p. 67
12. **Parides iphidamas iphidamas** ♀, D: Carrillo, CR, p. 67
13. **Parides arcas mylotes** ♂, D: Sixaola, CR, p. 67
14. **Parides arcas mylotes** ♀, D: Sixaola, CR, p. 67
15. **Eurytides ilus** ♀, D: Summit, Canal Zone, Panama, p. 77
16. **Eurytides euryleon clusoculis** ♂, D: Carrillo, CR, p. 76
17. **Eurytides phaon** ♂, D: Vera Paz, Mexico, p. 76

1
2
3
4
5
6
7
8
9
10
11
12
13
14
15
16
17

PLATE 3 · PAPILIONIDAE

1. **Eurytides branchus** ♀, D: CR, p. 77
2. **Eurytides pausanis prasinus** ♂, D: Carrillo, CR, p. 76
3. **Eurytides philolaus** ♂, D: CR, p. 77
4. **Eurytides epidaus epidaus** ♀, D: CR, p. 77
5. **Eurytides agesilaus eimeri** ♂, D: CR, p. 78
6. **Eurytides protesilaus dariensis** ♂, D: CR, p. 78
7. **Eurytides orabilis** ♂, D: CR [HT], p. 79
8. **Eurytides marchandi panamensis** ♂, D: CR, p. 78
9. **Eurytides calliste olbius** ♂, D: Chiriqui, p. 78
10. **Eurytides lacandones lacandones** ♂, D: Vera Paz [HT], p. 78

1
2
3
4
5
6
7
8
9
10

1. **Papilio cresphontes** ♂, D: CR, p. 72
2. **Papilio thoas nealces** ♂, D: CR, p. 71
3. **Papilio astyalus pallas** ♂, D: Peralta, CR, p. 72
4. **Papilio astyalus pallas** ♀, D: Nicaragua, p. 72
5. **Papilio androgeus epidaurus** ♂, D: Calobre, Panama [HT], p. 72
6. **Papilio androgeus epidaurus** ♀, D: Bugaba [HT], p. 72
7. **Papilio polyxenes stabilis** ♂, D: San José, CR, p. 71
8. **Papilio torquatus tolmides** ♂, D: La Gloria, CR, p. 73
9. **Papilio torquatus tolus** ♀, D: Tampico, Mexico [HT], p. 73

1
2
3
5
4
6
7
8
9

PLATE 5 · PAPILIONIDAE

1. **Papilio garamas syedra** ♂, D: La Estrella, CR, p. 75
2. **Papilio cleotas archytas** ♂, D: CR, p. 75
3. **Papilio cleotas archytas** ♀, D: Volcan Chiriqui, Panama, p. 75
4. **Papilio cleotas archytas** ♀, D: Chiriqui, p. 75
5. **Papilio victorinus vulneratus** ♂, D: Matagalpa, Nicaragua, p. 75
6. **Papilio victorinus vulneratus** ♂, D: Matagalpa, Nicaragua, p. 75
7. **Papilio birchalli godmani** ♂, D: Bogotá, Colombia [HT], p. 74
8. **Papilio birchalli godmani** ♂, V: CR, p. 74
9. **Papilio birchalli godmani** ♀, D: Peralta, CR, p. 74

1
2
3
4
5
6
7
8
9

PLATE 6 · PAPILIONIDAE - PIERIDAE

1. **Papilio rhodostictus rhodostictus** ♂, D: CR, p. 73
2. **Papilio rhodostictus rhodostictus** ♀, D: Cachi, CR, p. 73
3. **Papilio anchisiades idaeus** ♂, D: CR, p. 73
4. **Papilio anchisiades idaeus** ♀, D: Carrillo, CR, p. 73
5. **Papilio ascolius zalates** ♂, D: Bugaba, Panama [HT], p. 74
6. **Papilio ascolius zalates** ♀, D: Las Concavas, CR, p. 74
7. **Pseudopieris nehemia** ♂, D: Zapote, Guatemala [PT], p. 82
8. **Pseudopieris nehemia** ♀, D: Nicaragua, p. 82
9. **Dismorphia lua idae** ♂, D: Colombia, p. 85
10. **Dismorphia lua idae** ♀, D: Colombia, p. 85
11. **Dismorphia amphiona praxinoe** ♂, D: Guapiles, CR, p. 86
12. **Dismorphia amphiona praxinoe** ♀, D: Pejivalle, CR, p. 86
13. **Dismorphia eunoe desine** ♂, D: Pejivalle, CR, p. 85
14. **Dismorphia eunoe desine** ♀, D: Peralta, CR, p. 85
15. **Dismorphia crisia lubina** ♂, D: Irazu, CR, p. 85
16. **Dismorphia crisia lubina** ♀, D: CR, p. 85

1
2
3
4
5
6
7
8
9
10
11
12
13
14
15
16

1. **Dismorphia zaela oreas** ♂, D: Carrillo, CR, p. 86
2. **Dismorphia zaela oreas** ♀, D: Carrillo, CR, p. 86
3. **Dismorphia theucharila fortunata** ♂, D: Carrillo, CR, p. 86
4. **Dismorphia theucharila fortunata** ♀, D: Cachi, CR, p. 86
5. **Dismorphia zathoe pallidula** ♂, D: CR, p. 86
6. **Dismorphia zathoe pallidula** ♀, D: CR, p. 86
7. **Lieinix nemesis** ♂, D: CR, p. 84
8. **Lieinix nemesis** ♀, D: Cartago, CR, p. 84
9. **Lieinix cinerascens** ♂, D: Chiriqui, p. 83
10. **Lieinix cinerascens** ♂, V: Volcan Chiriqui, Panama, p. 83
11. **Lieinix cinerascens** ♀, D: Potrero Cerrado, CR, p. 83
12. **Lieinix viridifascia** ♂, D: Volcan Chiriqui, Panama, p. 83
13. **Lieinix viridifascia** ♂, V: Volcan Irazu, CR, p. 83
14. **Lieinix viridifascia** ♀, D: CR, p. 83
15. **Patia orise sororna** ♂, D: Chiriqui, p. 84
16. **Patia orise sororna** ♀, D: Chiriqui, p. 84
17. **Enantia licinia marion** ♂, D: Carrillo, CR, p. 82
18. **Enantia licinia marion** ♀, D: Carrillo, CR, p. 82
19. **Enantia melite amalia** ♂, D: Juan Viñas, CR, p. 83
20. **Enantia melite amalia** ♀, D: Juan Viñas, CR, p. 83
21. **Hesperocharis graphites** ♀, V: Rio Sucio, CR, p. 88
22. **Hesperocharis costaricensis** ♂, V: Barberena, Guatemala, p. 88
23. **Hesperocharis crocea** ♂, D: Mexico, p. 88
24. **Hesperocharis crocea** ♂, V: Mexico, p. 88
25. **Archonias eurytele** ♂, D: Chiriqui, p. 89
26. **Archonias tereas approximata** ♂, D: San Carlos, CR, p. 88
27. **Archonias tereas approximata** ♂, V: Bugaba, Panama, p. 88

PLATE 8 · PIERIDAE

1. **Zerene cesonia centralamericana** ♂, D: San José, CR, p. 100
2. **Zerene cesonia centralamericana** ♀, D: San José, CR, p. 100
3. **Zerene cesonia** ♀, D: CR (dry season form), p. 100
4. **Anteos clorinde** ♂, D: San José, CR, p. 101
5. **Anteos maerula** ♂, D: Chontales, Nicaragua, p. 101
6. **Anteos maerula** ♀, D: Caracas, Venezuela, p. 101
7. **Phoebis rurina** ♂, D: CR, p. 102
8. **Phoebis rurina** ♀, D: CR, p. 102
9. **Phoebis rurina** ♀, D: CR, p. 102
10. **Kricogonia lyside** ♂, D: Matagalpa, Nicaragua, p. 102
11. **Kricogonia lyside** ♂, D: Nicaragua, p. 102
12. **Phoebis trite** ♂, D: CR, p. 104
13. **Phoebis trite** ♂, V: New Grenada, p. 104
14. **Phoebis philea philea** ♂, D: CR, p. 103
15. **Phoebis philea philea** ♀, D: CR, p. 103
16. **Phoebis philea philea** ♀, D: Santa Clara, CR, p. 103

1
2
3
10
4
7
11
5
8
12
6
9
13
14
15
16

PLATE 9 · PIERIDAE

1. **Phoebis sennae** ♂, D: CR, p. 103
2. **Phoebis sennae** ♀, D: CR, p. 103
3. **Phoebis sennae** ♀, V: CR, p. 103
4. **Aphrissa statira** ♂, D: Calobre, Panama, p. 104
5. **Aphrissa statira** ♀, D: CR, p. 104
6. **Aphrissa statira** ♀, V: CR, p. 104
7. **Phoebis argante** ♂, D: CR, p. 103
8. **Phoebis argante** ♂, V: San José, CR, p. 103
9. **Phoebis argante** ♀, V: CR, p. 103
10. **Phoebis argante** ♀, D: Rio Sucio, CR, p. 103
11. **Phoebis argante** ♀, D: Cachi, CR, p. 103
12. **Phoebis agarithe** ♂, D: CR, p. 103
13. **Phoebis agarithe** ♂, V: Volcan Santa Maria, Guatemala, p. 103
14. **Phoebis agarithe** ♀, D: Polochic Valley, Guatemala, p. 103
15. **Phoebis agarithe** ♀, D: CR, p. 103
16. **Aphrissa boisduvalii** ♂, D: Santa Clara, CR, p. 105
17. **Aphrissa boisduvalii** ♂, V: Santa Clara, CR, p. 105
18. **Aphrissa boisduvalii** ♀, D: San Pedro, Honduras, p. 105
19. **Aphrissa boisduvalii** ♀, V: Chontales, Nicaragua, p. 105

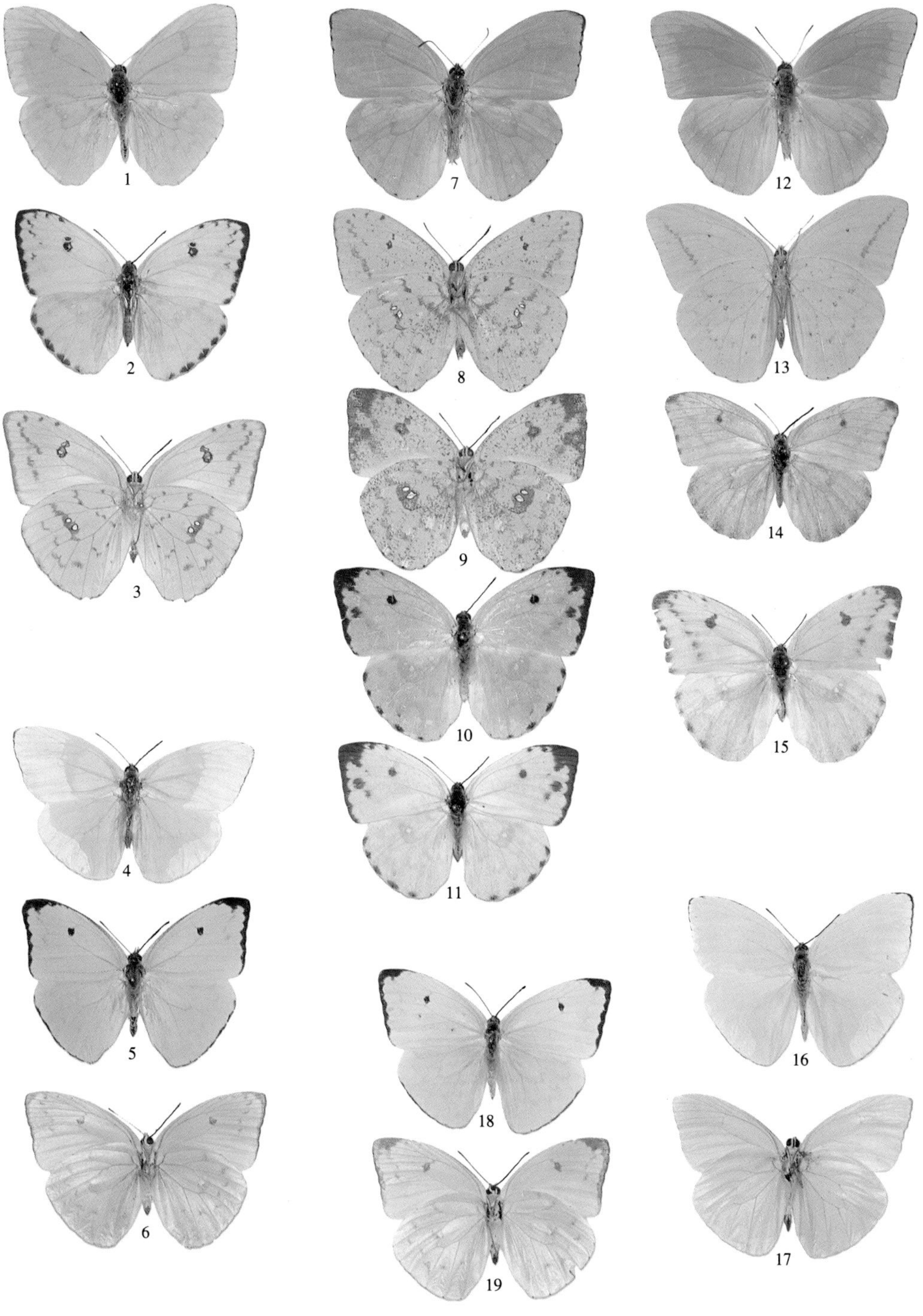
1
7
12
2
8
13
3
9
14
10
15
4
11
5
18
16
6
19
17

1. **Eurema proterpia** ♂, D: Rio Sucio, CR, p. 105
2. **Eurema proterpia** ♀, D: CR, p. 105
3. **Eurema proterpia** ♂, D: CR, p. 105
4. **Eurema proterpia** ♀, D: San Francisco, CR, p. 105
5. **Eurema mexicana** ♂, D: San José, CR, p. 106
6. **Eurema mexicana** ♀, D: Cachi, CR, p. 106
7. **Eurema salome** ♂, D: CR, p. 106
8. **Eurema salome** ♀, D: CR, p. 106
9. **Eurema xanthochlora** ♂, D: Volcan Chiriqui, Panama, p. 106
10. **Eurema xanthochlora** ♂, V: CR, p. 106
11. **Eurema xanthochlora** ♀, D: Turrialba, CR, p. 106
12. **Eurema xanthochlora** ♀, V: Cachi, CR, p. 106
13. **Eurema gratiosa** ♂, D: Veraguas, Panama, p. 106
14. **Eurema gratiosa** ♀, D: Panama, p. 106
15. **Eurema boisduvaliana** ♂, D: Turrialba, CR, p. 106
16. **Eurema boisduvaliana** ♀, D: Guapiles, CR, p. 106
17. **Eurema dina westwoodi** ♂, D: San José, CR, p. 107
18. **Eurema dina westwoodi** ♀, D: San José, CR, p. 107
19. **Eurema dina westwoodi** ♀, V: CR, p. 107
20. **Eurema albula** ♂, D: CR, p. 107
21. **Eurema albula** ♂, V: CR, p. 107
22. **Eurema nise** ♂, D: David, Panama, p. 107
23. **Eurema nise** ♀, V: Chiriqui, p. 107
24. **Eurema nise** ♂, D: Guapiles, CR, p. 107
25. **Eurema nise** ♀, D: San Francisco, CR, p. 107
26. **Eurema nise** ♀, V: El Alto, CR, p. 107
27. **Eurema lisa** ♂, D: Cachi, CR, p. 107
28. **Eurema lisa** ♂, V: San José, CR, p. 107
29. **Eurema daira** ♂, D: CR, p. 108
30. **Eurema daira** ♀, D: San Francisco, CR, p. 108
31. **Eurema daira** ♀, V: Bugaba, Panama, p. 108
32. **Eurema daira** ♂, D: Cachi, CR, p. 108

Nos. 33-42 continue following Plate 50

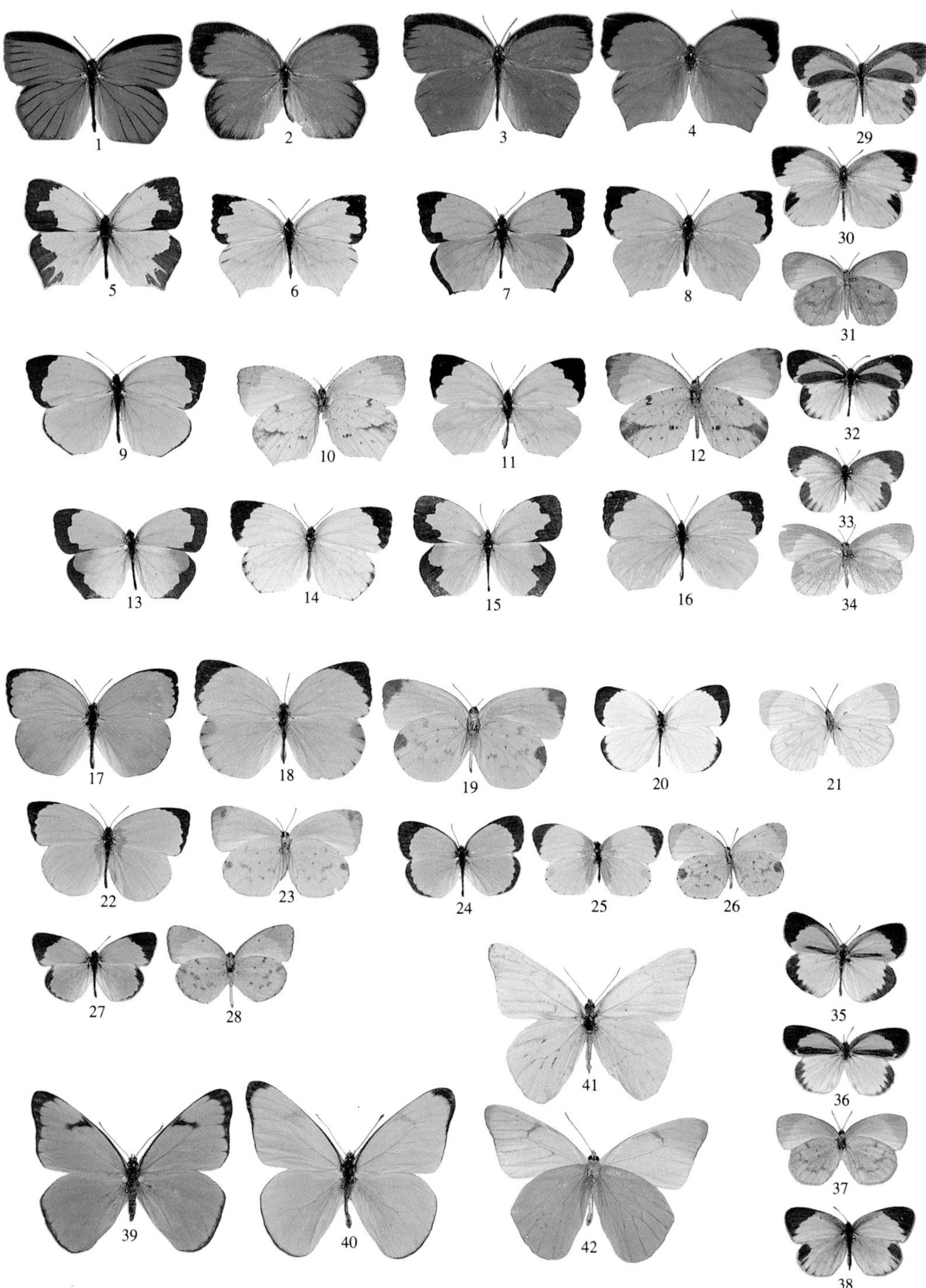
1
2
3
4
29
5
6
7
8
30
31
9
10
11
12
32
13
14
15
16
33
34
17
18
19
20
21
22
23
24
25
26
27
28
35
41
36
39
40
42
37
38

PLATE 11 · PIERIDAE

1. **Catasticta nimbice bryson** ♂, D: Cachi, CR, p. 92
2. **Catasticta nimbice bryson** ♂, V: Chiriqui, p. 92
3. **Catasticta theresa** ♂, D: Chiriqui, p. 92
4. **Catasticta theresa** ♀, V: Volcan Irazu, CR, p. 92
5. **Catasticta flisa** ♀, D: Cachi, CR, p. 93
6. **Catasticta flisa** ♂, V: Cachi, CR, p. 93
7. **Catasticta teutila flavomaculata** ♂, D: Volcan Irazu, CR, p. 93
8. **Catasticta teutila flavomaculata** ♂, V: Volcan Irazu, CR, p. 93
9. **Catasticta teutila flavomaculata** ♀, D: Volcan Irazu, CR, p. 93
10. **Catasticta cerberus** ♂, D: Volcan Irazu, CR, p. 93
11. **Catasticta cerberus** ♂, V: Volcan Irazu, CR, p. 93
12. **Catasticta strigosa actinotis** ♂, D: Cachi, CR, p. 94
13. **Catasticta strigosa actinotis** ♀, D: Chiriqui, p. 94
14. **Catasticta prioneris hegemon** ♂, D: Cachi, CR, p. 94
15. **Catasticta prioneris hegemon** ♂, V: Volcan Chiriqui, p. 94
16. **Catasticta prioneris hegemon** ♀, D: CR, p. 94
17. **Catasticta sisamnus sisamnus** ♂, D: Cachi, CR, p. 94
18. **Catasticta sisamnus sisamnus** ♂, V: Cachi, CR, p. 94
19. **Catasticta sisamnus sisamnus** ♀, D: Pitana, CR, p. 94
20. **Leodonta dysoni** ♂, D: Volcan Irazu, CR, p. 90
21. **Leodonta dysoni** ♀, V: Volcan Chiriqui, p. 90
22. **Pereute charops** ♂, D: Cachi, CR, p. 90
23. **Pereute charops** ♀, D: Cachi, CR, p. 90
24. **Pereute charops** ♂, V: Cachi, CR, p. 90
25. **Pereute cheops** ♂, D: no data [PT], p. 91
26. **Pereute cheops** ♀, D: Chiriqui, p. 91
27. **Pereute cheops** ♂, V: Chiriqui, p. 91

1
2
5
6
3
4
7
8
9
10
11
12
13
14
15
16
20
17
18
19
21
22
23
24
25
26
27

1. **Appias drusilla** ♂, D: San José, CR, p. 94
2. **Appias drusilla** ♀, D: Cachi, CR, p. 94
3. **Appias drusilla** ♀, D: CR, p. 94
4. **Leptophobia aripa** ♂, D: Cartago, CR, p. 95
5. **Itaballia demophile centralis** ♂, D: Abangares, CR, p. 96
6. **Itaballia demophile centralis** ♀, D: Abangares, CR, p. 96
7. **Itaballia pandosia kicaha** ♂, V: Pozo Azul, CR, p. 96
8. **Itaballia pandosia kicaha** ♀, D: David, Panama, p. 96
9. **Pieriballia mandela noctipennis** ♂, D: no data, p. 97
10. **Pieriballia mandela noctipennis** ♀, D: Bugaba, Panama, p. 97
11. **Leptophobia caesia tenuicornis** ♂, D: Carrillo, CR, p. 95
12. **Leptophobia caesia tenuicornis** ♂, V: Carrillo, CR, p. 95
13. **Leptophobia caesia tenuicornis** ♀, D: Carrillo, CR, p. 95
14. **Perrhybris pyrrha** ♂, D: Chontales, Nicaragua, p. 97
15. **Perrhybris pyrrha** ♀, D: R: CR, p. 97
16. **Perrhybris lypera** ♂, D: Colombia, p. 98
17. **Perrhybris lypera** ♂, V: New Grenada, p. 98
18. **Perrhybris lypera** ♀, D: Colombia, p. 98
19. **Ascia limona** ♂, D: Limon, CR, p. 99
20. **Ascia limona** ♀, D: CR, p. 99
21. **Ascia josephina josepha** ♂, D: CR, p. 99
22. **Ascia josephina josepha** ♂: V: CR, p. 99
23. **Ascia monuste** ♀, D: Veraguas, Panama, p. 98

1
2
3
4
5
6
7
8
9
10
11
12
13
14
15
16
17
18
19
20
21
22
23

PLATE 13 · CHARAXINAE

1. **Agrias aedon salvini** ♂, D: Muzo, Colombia, p. 112
2. **Agrias aedon salvini** ♂, V: Muzo, Colombia, p. 112
3. **Agrias aedon salvini** ♀, D: no data, p. 112
4. **Agrias aedon rodriguezi** ♀, D: Turrialba, CR, p. 112
5. **Agrias amydon philatelica** ♀, D: Volcan Santa Maria, CR [PT], p. 112
6. **Prepona omphale octavia** ♂, V: Panama, p. 113
7. **Prepona omphale octavia** ♂, D: San Pedro Sula, Honduras [HT], p. 113
8. **Prepona dexamenus** ♂, V: Puntamayo, Colombia, p. 113
9. **Prepona gnorima** ♂, V: Bogotá, Colombia [HT], p. 113
10. **Archaeoprepona phaedra** ♀, V: Chiriqui [HT], p. 115
11. **Prepona lygia** ♀, V: Chiriqui [HT], p. 114
12. **Siderone syntyche** ♂, D: Turrialba, CR, p. 116
13. **Siderone marthesia** ♀, D: San Mateo, CR, p. 116
14. **Siderone marthesia** ♂, V: Juan Viñas, CR, p. 116

1
2
3
4
8
12
9
5
13
6
10
14
7
11

PLATE 14 · CHARAXINAE

1. **Archaeoprepona demophon centralis** ♂, D: San Pedro Sula, Honduras [HT], p. 114
2. **Archaeoprepona demophon centralis** ♀, V: San Pedro Sula, Honduras [HT], p. 114
3. **Archaeoprepona demophoon gulina** ♂, V: San Pedro Sula, Honduras [HT], p. 115
4. **Archaeoprepona camilla** ♂, V: Veraguas, Panama [HT], p. 115
5. **Archaeoprepona meander amphimachus** ♂, V: CR, p. 115
6. **Archaeoprepona meander amphimachus** ♂, D: CR, p. 115
7. **Zaretis callidryas** ♂, D: Chiriqui, p. 117
8. **Zaretis callidryas** ♂, V: Chiriqui, p. 117
9. **Zaretis ellops** ♂, D: Calobre, Panama, p. 117
10. **Zaretis ellops** ♀, V: Calobre, Panama, p. 117
11. **Zaretis ellops** ♀, D: Vera Paz, p. 117
12. **Zaretis itys** ♂, D: Chontales, Nicaragua, p. 117
13. **Zaretis itys** ♀, V: Chontales, Nicaragua, p. 117
14. **Zaretis itys** ♀, D: New Grenada, p. 117

3
5
14
1
6
13
2
7
12
8
11
4
9
10

PLATE 15 · CHARAXINAE

1. **Hypna clytemnestra clytemnestra** ♂, D: Peralta, CR, p. 118
2. **Consul fabius cecrops** ♂, D: no data [HT], p. 118
3. **Consul fabius cecrops** ♂, V: Las Concavas, CR, p. 118
4. **Consul panariste jansoni** ♂, D: Chiriqui, p. 119
5. **Consul panariste jansoni** ♀, D: Volcan Chiriqui, Panama, p. 119
6. **Consul electra** ♂, D: San Geronimo, Guatemala, p. 119
7. **Memphis titan peralta** ♂, D: Chiriqui [HT], p. 121
8. **Memphis titan peralta** ♀, D: CR [PT], p. 121
9. **Memphis ryphea ryphea** ♂, D: Lion Hill, Panama, p. 121
10. **Memphis ryphea ryphea** ♀, V: no data, p. 121
11. **Memphis ryphea ryphea** ♀, D: Calobre, Panama, p. 121
12. **Memphis eurypyle confusa** ♂, D: CR, p. 121
13. **Memphis eurypyle confusa** ♂, V: Bugaba, Panama, p. 121
14. **Memphis eurypyle confusa** ♀, D: CR, p. 121
15. **Memphis chrysophana** ♂, D: Carrillo, CR, p. 122
16. **Memphis chrysophana** ♂, V: Lion Hill, Panama, p. 122
17. **Memphis chrysophana** ♀, D: Veraguas, Panama [HT], p. 122
18. **Memphis chrysophana** ♀, V: Veraguas, Panama, p. 122

1
2
3
4
5
6
7
8
9
10
11
12
13
14
15
16
17
18

1. **Memphis glycerium** ♂, D: CR, p. 122
2. **Memphis glycerium** ♀, D: CR, p. 122
3. **Anaea aidea** ♂, D: CR, p. 119
4. **Anaea aidea** ♀, D: CR, p. 119
5. **Memphis ambrosia** ♂, D: Bugaba, Panama, p. 122
6. **Memphis ambrosia** ♂, V: Carrillo, CR, p. 122
7. **Memphis ambrosia** ♀, V: CR, p. 122
8. **Memphis ambrosia** ♀, D: Chiriqui, p. 122
9. **Memphis aureola** ♀, V: Volcan Chiriqui, Panama, p. 122
10. **Memphis aureola** ♀, D: Finca la Selva, CR, p. 122
11. **Memphis aureola** ♂, V: Chiriqui, p. 122
12. **Memphis aureola** ♂, D: Muzo, Colombia, p. 122
13. **Memphis lankesteri** ♂, D: Azahar de Cartago, CR, p. 122
14. **Memphis lankesteri** ♂, V: Azahar de Cartago, CR [PT], p. 122
15. **Memphis herbacea** ♂, D: CR [HT], p. 122
16. **Memphis herbacea** ♂, V: CR, p. 122
17. **Memphis beatrix** ♂, D: Volcan Chiriqui, Panama, p. 123
18. **Memphis beatrix** ♂, V: Volcan Chiriqui, Panama, p. 123
19. **Memphis beatrix** ♀, D: Chiriqui, p. 123
20. **Memphis beatrix** ♀, V: Volcan Chiriqui, p. 123

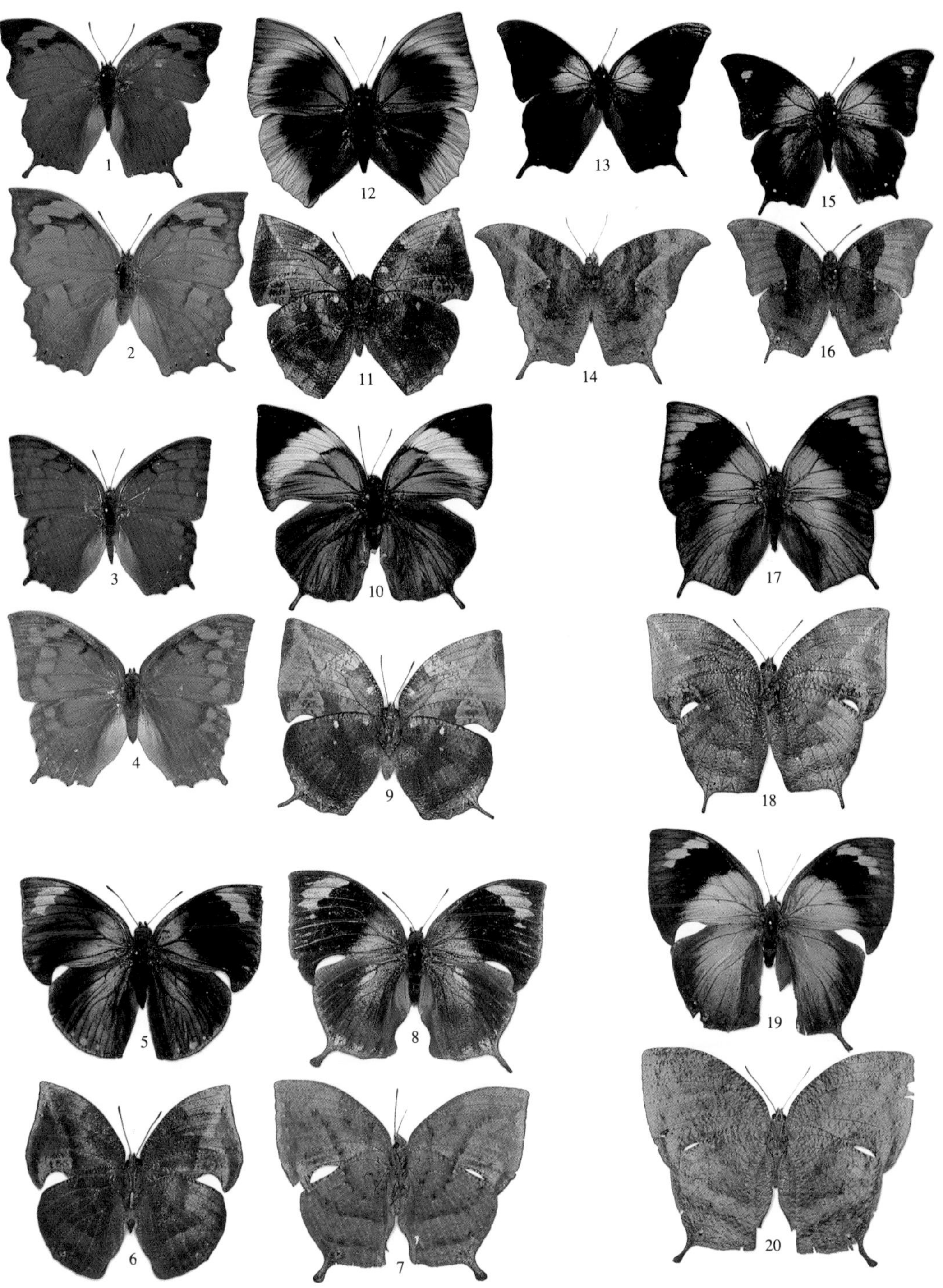
1
12
13
15
2
11
14
16
3
10
17
4
9
18
5
8
19
6
7
20

PLATE 17 · CHARAXINAE

1. **Memphis proserpina** ♂, D: Vera Paz, p. 123
2. **Memphis proserpina** ♂, V: Vera Paz, p. 123
3. **Memphis proserpina** ♀, D: Coban, Guatemala, p. 123
4. **Memphis proserpina** ♀, V: Vera Paz, p. 123
5. **Memphis chaeronea indigotica** ♂, D: CR, p. 123
6. **Memphis chaeronea indigotica** ♂, V: Chiriqui, p. 123
7. **Memphis chaeronea indigotica** ♀, D: San Vito de Java, CR, p. 123
8. **Memphis centralis** ♂, D: Finca la Selva, CR, p. 123
9. **Memphis centralis** ♂, V: Chiriqui, p. 123
10. **Memphis centralis** ♀, D: Veraguas, Panama, p. 123
11. **Memphis xenocles** ♂, D: no data, p. 123
12. **Memphis xenocles** ♂, V: Bugaba, Panama, p. 123
13. **Memphis xenocles** ♀, D: Chiriqui [HT], p. 123
14. **Memphis xenocles** ♀, V: Chiriqui, p. 123
15. **Memphis niedhoeferi** ♀, D: CR, p. 124
16. **Memphis niedhoeferi** ♀, V: Orizaba, Mexico, p. 124
17. **Memphis niedhoeferi** ♂, D: Turrialba, CR, p. 124
18. **Memphis arginussa eubaena** ♀, V: Carrillo, CR, p. 124
19. **Memphis arginussa eubaena** ♀, D: Mexico, p. 124
20. **Memphis arginussa eubaena** ♂, V: Cachi, CR, p. 124
21. **Memphis arginussa eubaena** ♂, D: Irazu, CR, p. 124

1
2
3
4
5
6
7
8
9
10
11
12
13
14
15
16
17
18
19
20
21

PLATE 18 · CHARAXINAE

1. **Memphis morvus boisduvali** ♂, D: Carrillo, CR, p. 124
2. **Memphis morvus boisduvali** ♂, V: CR, p. 124
3. **Memphis morvus boisduvali** ♀, D: San Pedro Sula, Honduras, p. 124
4. **Memphis morvus boisduvali** ♀, V: San Pedro Sula, Honduras, p. 124
5. **Memphis lyceus** ♂, D: CR, p. 124
6. **Memphis lyceus** ♂, V: CR, p. 124
7. **Memphis lyceus** ♀, D: Colombia, p. 124
8. **Memphis lyceus** ♀, V: Colombia, p. 124
9. **Memphis elara** ♂, D: Puriscal, CR, p. 125
10. **Memphis elara** ♀, V: Puriscal, CR, p. 125
11. **Memphis laura laura** ♀, V: Colombia, p. 125
12. **Memphis laura laura** ♂, V: Colombia, p. 125
13. **Memphis laura laura** ♂, D: Bogotá, Colombia, p. 125
14. **Memphis oenomais** ♀, V: Nicaragua, p. 125
15. **Memphis oenomais** ♀, D: Chiriqui, p. 125
16. **Memphis oenomais** ♂, V: Chontales, Nicaragua, p. 125
17. **Memphis oenomias** ♂, D: Peralta, CR, p. 125
18. **Memphis artacaena** ♂, V: Bugaba, Panama, p. 125
19. **Memphis artacaena** ♂, D: Chiriqui, p. 125

1. **Memphis orthesia** ♂, D: Turrialba, CR, p. 126
2. **Memphis orthesia** ♂, V: Turrialba, CR, p. 126
3. **Memphis orthesia** ♀, D: Tabasco, Mexico, p. 126
4. **Memphis orthesia** ♀, V: Coatapec, Mexico, p. 126
5. **Memphis forreri** ♂, D: Parque Santa Rosa, CR, p. 126
6. **Memphis forreri** ♂, V: Coatapec, Mexico, p. 126
7. **Memphis forreri** ♀, D: Coatapec, Mexico, p. 126
8. **Memphis forreri** ♀, V: Coatapec, Mexico, p. 126
9. **Memphis pithyusa** ♂, D: Turrialba, CR, p. 126
10. **Memphis pithyusa** ♂, V: Turrialba, CR, p. 126
11. **Memphis pithyusa** ♀, D: Turrialba, CR, p. 126
12. **Memphis pithyusa** ♀, V: Turrialba, CR, p. 126
13. **Memphis cleomestra** ♂, D: Turrialba, CR, p. 126
14. **Memphis cleomestra** ♂, V: Turrialba, CR, p. 126
15. **Memphis cleomestra** ♀, D: Turrialba, CR, p. 126
16. **Memphis aulica** ♂, R: Cerro Campana, Panama, p. 127
17. **Doxocopa callianira** ♂, D: Vera Paz, p. 128
18. **Doxocopa clothilda** ♂, D: Bugaba, Panama, p. 128
19. **Doxocopa clothilda** ♂, Veraguas, Panama, p. 128
20. **Doxocopa pavon** ♂, D: Chontales, Nicaragua, p. 128
21. **Doxocopa callianira** ♀, D: Central Valley, Guatemala, p. 128
22. **Doxocopa clothilda** ♀, D: Reventazon, CR, p. 128
23. **Doxocopa clothilda** ♀, V: Reventazon, CR, p. 128
24. **Doxocopa pavon** ♀, D: CR, p. 128
25. **Doxocopa felderi** ♂, D: Cauca, Colombia, p. 129
26. **Doxocopa felderi** ♂, V: Cauca, Colombia, p. 129
27. **Doxocopa felderi** ♀, D: Bogotá, Colombia, p. 129

1
2
5
6
3
4
7
8
9
10
13
14
11
12
15
16
17
18
19
20
21
22
23
24
25
26
27

PLATE 20 · APATURINAE - LIBYTHEINAE

1. **Doxocopa cherubina** ♂, D: Bugaba, Panama, p. 129
2. **Doxocopa cherubina** ♂, V: Chiriqui, p. 129
3. **Doxocopa cherubina** ♀, D: Volcan Chiriqui, Panama, p. 129
4. **Doxocopa cherubina** ♀, V: Volcan Chiriqui, Panama, p. 129
5. **Doxocopa cyane** ♂, D: Volcan Chiriqui, Panama, p. 129
6. **Doxocopa cyane** ♂, V: Volcan Chiriqui, Panama, p. 129
7. **Doxocopa cyane** ♀, D: CR, p. 129
8. **Doxocopa cyane** ♀, V: CR, p. 129
9. **Doxocopa excelsa** ♂, D: El Libano, CR [HT], p. 129
10. **Doxocopa excelsa** ♀, D: Chontales, CR, p. 129
11. **Doxocopa excelsa** ♀, V: Turrialba, CR, p. 129
12. **Doxocopa laure** ♂, D: Bugaba, Panama, p. 130
13. **Doxocopa laure** ♀, D: San Pedro Sula, Honduras, p. 130
14. **Doxocopa plesaurina** ♂, D: CR [HT], p. 130
15. **Doxocopa plesaurina** ♀, D: Bugaba, Panama, p. 130
16. **Libytheana carinenta mexicana** ♂, D: CR, p. 131
17. **Libytheana carinenta mexicana** ♂, V: CR, p. 131

1
2
12
3
4
13
5
9
14
6
10
15
7
11
16
8
17

1. **Tigridia acesta** ♀, V: Carrillo, CR, p. 133
2. **Colobura dirce** ♂, D: Santa Clara, CR, p. 133
3. **Historis odius** ♂, D: Muzo, Colombia, p. 134
4. **Historis acheronta** ♂, D: Volcan Chiriqui, Panama, p. 135
5. **Smyrna blomfildia datis** ♂, D: Chontales, Nicaragua, p. 135
6. **Smyrna blomfildia datis** ♀, D: Chontales, Nicaragua, p. 135
7. **Baeotus baeotus** ♂, D: Colombia, p. 135
8. **Baeotus baeotus** ♂, V: Colombia, p. 135
9. **Pycina zamba zelys** ♂, D: Volcan Chiriqui, Panama [PT], p. 136
10. **Biblis hyperia** ♂, D: Colombia, p. 137
11. **Hamadryas glauconome glauconome** ♂, D: Matagalpa, Nicaragua, p. 139
12. **Hamadryas februa ferentina** ♂, D: Calobre, Panama, p. 138
13. **Hamadryas feronia farinulenta** ♂, D: Guapiles, CR, p. 139
14. **Hamadryas feronia farinulenta** ♂, V: Santa Clara, CR, p. 139
15. **Hamadryas guatemalena guatemalena** ♂, D: CR, p. 139
16. **Hamadryas guatemalena guatemalena** ♂, V: Matagalpa, Nicaragua, p. 139
17. **Hamadryas ipthime ipthime** ♂, V: Chiriqui, p. 139
18. **Hamadryas fornax fornacalia** ♂, V: CR, p. 139

1
2
3
4
5
6
7
8
9
10
11
12
13
14
15
16
17
18

1. **Hamadryas amphinome mexicana** ♂, V: Bugaba, Panama, p. 140
2. **Hamadryas arinome ariensis** ♂, D: Colombia, p. 140
3. **Hamadryas arinome ariensis** ♀, V: Colombia, p. 140
4. **Hamadryas laodamia saurites** ♂, D: Bugaba, Panama, p. 140
5. **Hamadryas laodamia saurites** ♀, V: Bugaba, Panama, p. 140
6. **Panacea procilla lysimache** ♂, D: Chiriqui [HT], p. 141
7. **Myscelia cyaniris cyaniris** ♂, D: Chontales, Nicaragua, p. 142
8. **Myscelia cyaniris cyaniris** ♀, D: San Isidro, CR, p. 142
9. **Myscelia pattenia** ♀, V: Volcan Santa Maria, Guatemala, p. 142
10. **Ectima rectifascia** ♂, D: CR [HT], p. 141
11. **Myscelia leucocyana smalli** ♀, V: Chontales, Nicaragua, p. 142
12. **Myscelia leucocyana smalli** ♂, D: Bugaba, Panama, p. 142
13. **Mestra amymone** ♂, D: Chontales, Nicaragua, p. 137
14. **Myscelia pattenia** ♂, D: Nicaragua, p. 142
15. **Eunica tatila caerula** ♂, D: Juan Viñas, CR, p. 151
16. **Eunica tatila caerula** ♀, D: CR, p. 151
17. **Eunica monima modesta** ♂, D: Irazu, CR, p. 151
18. **Eunica malvina** ♂, V: Volcan Santa Maria, Guatemala, p. 151
19. **Eunica norica** ♂, D: Colombia, p. 152
20. **Eunica norica** ♀, D: Carrillo, CR, p. 152
21. **Eunica norica** ♀, V: Carrillo, CR, p. 152
22. **Eunica mira** ♀, V: San Ramon, Nicaragua, p. 152
23. **Eunica caresa** ♂, D: Azahar de Cartago, CR, p. 152
24. **Eunica caresa** ♂, V: Colombia, p. 152
25. **Eunica mygdonia** ♂, V: Zapote, Guatemala, p. 152

1
2
3
4
5
6
7
8
9
10
11
12
14
13
15
16
17
18
19
20
21
22
23
24
25

1. **Eunica venusia** ♂, D: Bugaba, Panama, p. 153
2. **Eunica venusia** ♀, D: no data, p. 153
3. **Eunica excelsa** ♂, D: Bugaba, Panama, p. 153
4. **Eunica excelsa** ♂, V: Bugaba, Panama, p. 153
5. **Eunica alcmena amata** ♂, D: San Mateo, CR, p. 153
6. **Eunica alcmena amata** ♀, V: Orizaba, p. 153
7. **Eunica augusta** ♂, D: Vera Paz, p. 153
8. **Eunica augusta** ♀, V: San Geronimo, Guatemala, p. 153
9. **Eunica pomona** ♂, D: San Mateo, CR, p. 154
10. **Marpesia alcibiades** ♂, D: Chiriqui, p. 149
11. **Marpesia alcibiades** ♀, D: Veraguas, Panama, p. 149
12. **Marpesia coresia** ♂, D: Volcan Chiriqui, Panama, p. 146
13. **Marpesia merops** ♂, D: CR, p. 149
14. **Marpesia berania** ♂, D: Santa Clara, CR, p. 150
15. **Marpesia berania** ♀, D: CR, p. 150
16. **Marpesia marcella** ♂, D: Cachi, CR, p. 149
17. **Marpesia iole** ♂, D: Bugaba, Panama, p. 150
18. **Marpesia petreus** ♂, D: CR, p. 146
19. **Marpesia chiron** ♀, V: San Geronimo, Guatemala, p. 146
20. **Marpesia marcella** ♀, D: CR, p. 149
21. **Marpesia iole** ♀, D: Bugaba, Panama, p. 150

1
2
3
4
5
6
7
8
9
10
11
12
13
14
15
16
17
18
19
20
21

1. **Dynamine agacles** ♂, D: Veraguas, Panama, p. 143
2. **Dynamine agacles** ♂, V: Volcan Chiriqui, p. 143
3. **Dynamine theseus** ♂, D: CR, p. 143
4. **Dynamine salpensa** ♂, D: Rio Estrella, CR, p. 143
5. **Dynamine mylitta** ♂, D: Santa Clara, CR, p. 145
6. **Dynamine mylitta** ♀, V: Chontales, Nicaragua, p. 145
7. **Dynamine hecuba** ♂, D: Carrillo, CR, p. 144
8. **Dynamine hoppi gillotti** ♀, D: Finca la Selva, CR, p. 144
9. **Dynamine dyonis** ♂, D: San Francisco, CR, p. 145
10. **Dynamine glauce** ♂, D: Cachi, CR, p. 145
11. **Dynamine thalassina** ♂, D: Veraguas, Panama, p. 145
12. **Dynamine hecuba** ♀, D: Carrillo, CR, p. 144
13. **Dynamine chryseis** ♂, D: Bogotá, Colombia, p. 144
14. **Dynamine dyonis** ♀, V: San Francisco, CR, p. 145
15. **Dynamine glauce** ♀, V: Cachi, CR, p. 145
16. **Dynamine thalassina** ♀, D: CR, p. 145
17. **Dynamine hecuba** ♀, V: Carrillo, CR, p. 144
18. **Dynamine chryseis** ♀, V: Chontales, Nicaragua, p. 144
19. **Dynamine sosthenes** ♂, D: Chontales, Nicaragua, p. 144
20. **Dynamine sosthenes** ♀, V: Chontales, Nicaragua, p. 144
21. **Dynamine sosthenes** ♀, D: Chontales, Nicaragua, p. 144
22. **Dynamine ate** ♂, D: Guapiles, CR, p. 143
23. **Temenis laothoe agatha** ♂, D: CR, p. 154
24. **Temenis pulchra** ♂, D: Colombia, p. 154
25. **Temenis pulchra** ♀, V: Upala, CR, p. 154
26. **Nica flavilla canthara** ♂, V: CR, p. 157
27. **Epiphile adrasta** ♂, D: CR, p. 155
28. **Epiphile adrasta** ♀, D: CR, p. 155
29. **Epiphile grandis** ♂, D: Las Alturas, CR, p. 156
30. **Epiphile orea plusios** ♂, D: CR, p. 155
31. **Epiphile eriopis devriesi** ♂, D: Chitaria, CR [PT], p. 156
32. **Epiphile grandis** ♀, D: CR [HT], p. 156
33. **Epiphile orea plusios** ♀, D: Chiriqui, p. 155
34. **Epiphile eriopis devriesi** ♀, D: Carrillo, CR [PT], p. 156

1. **Catonephele mexicana** ♂, D: Volcan Chiriqui, Panama, p. 159
2. **Catonephele numilia esite** ♂, D: Bugaba, Panama, p. 159
3. **Catonephele chromis godmani** ♂, D: Rio Sucio, CR, p. 160
4. **Catonephele mexicana** ♀, D: Bugaba, Panama, p. 159
5. **Catonephele numilia esite** ♀, D: Bugaba, Panama, p. 159
6. **Catonephele chromis godmani** ♀, D: Azahar de Cartago, CR, p. 160
7. **Catonephele orites** ♂, D: Bogotá, Colombia, p. 160
8. **Nessaea aglaura aglaura** ♀, V: Guapiles, CR, p. 161
9. **Haematera pyramus thysbe** ♂, D: Peralta, CR, p. 161
10. **Haematera pyramus thysbe** ♂, V: Peralta, CR, p. 161
11. **Catonephele orites** ♀, V: New Grenada, p. 160
12. **Cyclogramma pandama** ♂, D: Chiriqui, p. 162
13. **Diaethria anna** ♀, D: Venezuela, p. 163
14. **Diaethria anna** ♂, V: CR, p. 163
15. **Diaethria marchalii** ♂, V: Chiriqui, p. 163
16. **Diaethria eupepla** ♂, D: no data, p. 162
17. **Diaethria astala** ♂, D: Chiriqui, Panama, p. 163
18. **Diaethria astala** ♂, V: CR, p. 163
19. **Diaethria astala** ♀, D: Honduras, p. 163
20. **Callicore pitheas** ♂, V: Veraguas, Panama, p. 166
21. **Callicore lyca aerias** ♂, V: Volcan Chiriqui, Panama, p. 164
22. **Callicore atacama manova** ♂, D: Veraguas, Panama, p. 165
23. **Callicore atacama manova** ♂, V: Pozo Azul de Piris, CR, p. 165
24. **Callicore faustina** ♂, V: Peralta, CR, p. 165
25. **Callicore brome** ♂, V: Pozo Azul de Piris, CR, p. 164
26. **Callicore texa titania** ♂, V: Veraguas, Panama, p. 165
27. **Callicore patelina** ♂, V: Turrialba, CR, p. 166

1
2
3
4
5
6
7
8
9
10
11
12
13
14
15
16
17
18
19
20
21
22
23
24
25
26
27

1. **Perisama barnesi** ♂, D: Estrella de Cartago, CR, p. 167
2. **Callicore peralta** ♂, V: CR, p. 166
3. **Callicore peralta** ♂, D: CR, p. 166
4. **Callicore pacifica bugaba** ♂, V: Turrialba, CR, p. 166
5. **Callicore pacifica bugaba** ♀, D: Turrialba, CR, p. 166
6. **Perisama barnesi** ♀, V: Carrillo, CR, p. 167
7. **Adelpha melanthe** ♂, V: Irazu, CR, p. 169
8. **Adelpha zalmona sophax** ♂, D: Cachi, CR, p. 169
9. **Adelpha zalmona sophax** ♂, V: Bugaba, Panama, p. 169
10. **Adelpha boreas opheltes** ♂, D: Bugaba, Panama, p. 169
11. **Adelpha boreas opheltes** ♂, V: Bugaba, Panama, p. 169
12. **Adelpha salmoneus salmonides** ♂, D: Honduras, p. 169
13. **Adelpha salmoneus salmonides** ♂, V: Chontales, Nicaragua, p. 169
14. **Adelpha leucopthalma** ♂, D: Cachi, CR, p. 170
15. **Adelpha zina** ♂, V: Bogotá, Colombia, p. 170
16. **Adelpha justina lacina** ♂, D: Chontales, Nicaragua, p. 171
17. **Adelpha cytherea marcia** ♂, D: Limon, CR, p. 171
18. **Adelpha cocala lorzae** ♂, D: Finca la Selva, CR, p. 171
19. **Adelpha cocala lorzae** ♀, V: Chiriqui, p. 171
20. **Adelpha heraclea** ♂, D: Finca la Selva, CR, p. 171
21. **Adelpha heraclea** ♂, V: Canal Zone, Panama, p. 171
22. **Adelpha boeotia boeotia** ♂, D: Honduras, p. 172
23. **Adelpha boeotia boeotia** ♂, V: Irazu, CR, p. 172
24. **Adelpha erymanthis** ♂, D: Volcan Irazu, CR, p. 172
25. **Adelpha basiloides** ♂, D: Chiriqui, Panama, p. 172

1
2
3
4
5
6
7
8
9
10
11
12
13
14
15
16
17
18
19
20
21
22
23
24
25

1. **Adelpha iphiclus** ♂, D: Cachi, CR, p. 173
2. **Adelpha iphiclus** ♂, V: Irazu, CR, p. 173
3. **Adelpha erotia** ♂, D: Chiriqui, p. 173
4. **Adelpha erotia** ♀, V: Cauca, Colombia, p. 173
5. **Adelpha lerna aeolia** ♂, D: Bugaba, Panama, p. 173
6. **Adelpha lerna aeolia** ♀, V: Chiriqui, p. 173
7. **Adelpha phylaca** ♂, D: Turrialba, CR, p. 173
8. **Adelpha phylaca** ♀, V: Turrialba, CR, p. 173
9. **Adelpha naxia** ♂, D: Bugaba, Panama, p. 174
10. **Adelpha naxia** ♂, V: San Pedro Sula, Honduras, p. 174
11. **Adelpha ixia leucas** ♂, D: Turrialba, CR, p. 174
12. **Adelpha ixia leucas** ♂, V: Turrialba, CR, p. 174
13. **Adelpha leuceria** ♂, D: Rio Sucio, CR, p. 174
14. **Adelpha tracta** ♂, D: Volcan Chiriqui, Panama, p. 174
15. **Adelpha demialba** ♂, R: Cachi, CR, p. 174
16. **Adelpha diocles** ♂, D: Cascajal, CR, p. 175
17. **Adelpha diocles** ♂, V: CR [HT], p. 175
18. **Adelpha celerio** ♂, D: Panama, p. 175
19. **Adelpha celerio** ♀, V: Chontales, Nicaragua, p. 175
20. **Adelpha fessonia** ♂, D: San Antonio, CR, p. 175
21. **Adelpha stilesiana** ♂, D: La Montura de Carrillo, CR [HT], p. 170
22. **Adelpha zea paraeca** ♂, D: Cordova, Mexico, p. 175
23. **Adelpha zea paraeca** ♀, V: Rio Sucio, CR, p. 175
24. **Adelpha felderi** ♂, D: CR, p. 176
25. **Adelpha felderi** ♂, V: Polochic Valley, Guatemala, p. 176

1
2
3
4
5
6
7
8
9
10
11
12
13
14
15
16
17
18
19
20
21
22
23
24
25

1. **Pyrrhogyra neaerea hypsenor** ♂, D: Bugaba, Panama, p. 157
2. **Pyrrhogyra crameri** ♂, V: Bugaba, Panama, p. 158
3. **Pyrrhogyra otolais otolais** ♂, V: Zapote, Guatemala, p. 157
4. **Pyrrhogyra edocla aenaria** ♂, V: CR, p. 158
5. **Hypanartia lethe** ♂, D: CR, p. 176
6. **Hypanartia godmani** ♂, D: CR, p. 176
7. **Hypanartia arcaei** ♂, D: CR, p. 177
8. **Hypanartia kefersteini** ♂, D: CR, p. 177
9. **Siproeta stelenes biplagiata** ♂, D: Bugaba, Panama, p. 178
10. **Siproeta epaphus epaphus** ♂, D: San José, CR, p. 177 Boquete, Volcancito Arriba Panamá Dec 30, 2008
11. **Siproeta superba eunoe** ♂, D: CR, p. 178
12. **Anartia jatrophae** ♂, D: Belize, p. 179
13. **Anartia fatima** ♂, D: San Francisco, CR, p. 178
14. **Junonia evarete** ♂, D: CR, p. 180
15. **Vanessa cardui** ♂, D: CR, p. 180
16. **Vanessa cardui** ♂, V: Cerro Chirripo, CR, p. 180
17. **Hypolimnas misippus** ♂, D: Dominican Republic, p. 181
18. **Vanessa virginiensis** ♂, D: CR, p. 179
19. **Vanessa virginiensis** ♂, V: CR, p. 179
20. **Hypolimnas misippus** ♀, D: CR, p. 181

1
2
3
4
5
6
7
8
9
10
11
12
13
14
15
16
17
18
19
20

PLATE 29 · MELITAEINAE

1. **Chlosyne lacinia** ♀, D: CR, p. 201
2. **Chlosyne lacinia** ♂, V: San Pedro Sula, Honduras, p. 201
3. **Chlosyne lacinia** ♀, V: Irazu, CR, p. 201
4. **Chlosyne lacinia** (form *saundersi*) ♂, D: CR, p. 201
5. **Chlosyne lacinia** (form *saundersi*) ♂, V: CR, p. 201
6. **Chlosyne lacinia** (form *quetala*) ♂, D: Bugaba, Panama, p. 201
7. **Chlosyne lacinia** (form *quetala*) ♂, V: Calobre, Panama, p. 201
8. **Chlosyne janais** ♂, D: Limon, CR, p. 199
9. **Chlosyne janais** ♂, V: Cachi, CR, p. 199
10. **Chlosyne melanarge** ♂, D: El Salvador, p. 200
11. **Chlosyne melanarge** ♀, V: Chontales, Nicaragua, p. 200
12. **Chlosyne hippodrome** ♂, D: Guatil, CR, p. 199
13. **Chlosyne hippodrome** ♂, V: Puriscal, CR, p. 199
14. **Chlosyne poecile** ♂, D: San Mateo, CR, p. 201
15. **Chlosyne poecile** ♀, V: San Mateo, CR, p. 201
16. **Chlosyne erodyle** ♂, D: Chontales, Nicaragua, p. 201
17. **Chlosyne erodyle** ♂, V: San Ramon, Nicaragua, p. 201
18. **Chlosyne gaudealis** ♂, D: Tuis, CR, p. 200
19. **Chlosyne gaudealis** ♀, V: Guapiles, CR, p. 200
20. **Chlosyne narva** ♂, D: Bugaba, Panama, p. 200
21. **Chlosyne narva** ♀, V: Panama, p. 200
22. **Thessalia ezra** ♂, D: Limon, CR, p. 202
23. **Thessalia ezra** ♀, V: Chiriqui, p. 202
24. **Thessalia theona** ♂, D: Abangarez, CR, p. 202
25. **Thessalia theona** ♂, V: Matagalpa, Nicaragua, p. 202
26. **Thessalia theona** ♀, D: CR, p. 202
27. **Microtia elva** ♂, D: Matagalpa, Nicaragua, p. 205
28. **Tegosa anieta anieta** ♂, D: Cachi, CR, p. 209
29. **Tegosa nigrella** ♂, D: Cachi, CR, p. 209
30. **Tegosa nigrella** ♂, V: Cachi, CR, p. 209
31. **Eresia nigripennis** ♂, D: Cachi, CR, p. 207
32. **Eresia nigripennis** ♂, V: Cachi, CR, p. 207

Nos. 33-36 continue following Plate 50

1
2
3
4
5
6
7
8
9
10
11
12
13
14
15
16
17
18
19
20
21
22
23
24
25
26
27
28
29
30
31
32
33
34
35
36

1. **Eresia coela** ♂, D: CR, p. 206
2. **Eresia coela** ♀, D: Guapiles, CR, p. 206
3. **Eresia coela** ♀, V: Limon, CR, p. 206
4. **Eresia mechanitis** ♂, D: Guapiles, CR, p. 207
5. **Eresia mechanitis** ♂, V: Rio Estrella, CR, p. 207
6. **Eresia mechanitis** ♀, D: CR, p. 207
7. **Eresia eutropia** ♂, D: Panama [HT], p. 206
8. **Eresia eutropia** ♀, D: Santa Fe, Panama, p. 206
9. **Castilia eranites** ♂, D: Juan Viñas, CR, p. 208
10. **Castilia eranites** ♂, V: Cachi, CR, p. 208
11. **Castilia eranites** ♀, D: Carrillo, CR, p. 208
12. **Eresia sticta** ♂, D: Rio Estrella, CR, p. 207
13. **Eresia sticta** ♂, V: Carrillo, CR, p. 207
14. **Eresia sticta** ♀, D: Carrillo, CR, p. 207
15. **Eresia poecilina** ♂, D: CR [HT], p. 207
16. **Eresia poecilina** ♀, V: Santa Fe, Panama, p. 207
17. **Eresia clara** ♂, D: Guapiles, CR, p. 206
18. **Eresia clara** ♀, V: San Pedro Sula, Honduras, p. 206
19. **Castilia ofella** ♂, D: Nicaragua, p. 208
20. **Castilia ofella** ♀, V: San Mateo, CR, p. 208
21. **Janatella leucodesma** ♂, D: Panama, p. 209
22. **Janatella leucodesma** ♂, V: Panama, p. 209
23. **Anthanassa drusilla lelex** ♂, D: Juan Viñas, CR, p. 203
24. **Anthanassa drusilla lelex** ♂, D: Alajuela, CR (dark form), p. 203
25. **Anthanassa drusilla lelex** ♂, V: CR, p. 203
26. **Anthanassa drusilla lelex** ♀, D: Juan Viñas, CR, p. 203
27. **Anthanassa tulcis** ♂, D: Nicaragua, p. 205
28. **Anthanassa tulcis** ♂, V: no data, p. 205
29. **Anthanassa tulcis** ♀, D: San Antonio, CR, p. 205
30. **Anthanassa atronia** ♂, D: Chiriqui, p. 204
31. **Anthanassa atronia** ♂, V: Chiriqui, p. 204
32. **Anthanassa atronia** ♀, D: Chiriqui, p. 204

Nos. 33-56 continue following Plate 50

1
2
3
4
5
6
7
8
9
10
11
12
13
14
15
16
17
18
19
20
21
22
23
24
25
26
27
28
29
30
31
32
33
34
35
36
37
38
39
40
41
42
43
44
45
46
47
48
49
50
51
52
53
54
55
56

1. **Philaethria dido** ♂, D: Panama, p. 187
2. **Dione moneta poeyii** ♂, D: Irazu, CR, p. 189
3. **Dione juno** ♂, D: San Mateo, CR, p. 188
4. **Agraulis vanillae** ♂, D: San Mateo, CR, p. 189
5. **Dryadula phaetusa** ♂, D: Santa Clara, CR, p. 188
6. **Dryas iulia** ♂, D: Carrillo, CR, p. 189
7. **Eueides lineata** ♂, D: Rio Sucio, CR, p. 190
8. **Eueides aliphera** ♂, D: San Carlos, CR, p. 190
9. **Eueides procula vulgiformis** ♂, D: Rio Sucio, CR, p. 191
10. **Eueides isabella** ♂, D: Orosi, CR, p. 192
11. **Heliconius ismenius telchinia** ♂, D: Guapiles, CR, p. 196
12. **Eueides vibilia vialis** ♂, D: CR, p. 191
13. **Heliconius doris** ♂, D: Juan Viñas, CR, p. 193
14. **Heliconius ismenius clarescens** ♂, D: Orosi, CR, p. 196
15. **Eueides vibilia vialis** ♀, D: CR, p. 191
16. **Heliconius doris** ♂, D: Santa Clara, CR, p. 193
17. **Heliconius hecale zuleika** ♂, D: San José, CR, p. 196
18. **Eueides lybia olympia** ♂, D: Carrillo, CR, p. 191
19. **Eueides lybia libioides** ♂, D: Pozo Azul de Piris, CR, p. 191
20. **Heliconius doris** ♂, D: San Mateo, CR, p. 193
21. **Heliconius hecale zuleika** ♂, D: CR, p. 196

1
2
3
4
5
6
7
8
9
10
11
12
13
14
15
16
17
18
19
20
21

PLATE 32 · HELICONIINAE - ACRAEINAE

1. **Heliconius melpomene rosina** ♂, D: no data, p. 194
2. **Heliconius cydno galanthus** ♂, D: Guapiles, CR, p. 194
3. **Heliconius cydno chioneus** ♂, D: Sixaola River, CR, p. 194
4. **Heliconius pachinus** ♂, D: Pozo Azul de Piris, CR, p. 195
5. **Heliconius erato petiverana** ♂, D: Escazu, CR, p. 195
6. **Heliconius hecalesia formosus** ♂, D: Turrialba, CR, p. 195
7. **Heliconius sara fulgidus** ♂, D: Sixaola River, CR, p. 197
8. **Heliconius sara theudela** ♂, D: CR, p. 197
9. **Heliconius charitonius** ♂, D: CR, p. 193
10. **Heliconius clysonymus montanus** ♂, D: Orosi, CR, p. 196
11. **Heliconius sapho leuce** ♂, D: Cachi, CR, p. 197
12. **Heliconius hewitsoni** ♂, D: Pozo Azul de Piris, CR, p. 197
13. **Heliconius eleuchia eleuchia** ♂, D: Carrillo, CR, p. 198
14. **Euptoieta claudia poasina** ♂, D: Zarcero, CR, p. 182
15. **Euptoieta claudia poasina** ♀, V: Volcan Poas, CR, p. 182
16. **Euptoieta hegesia hoffmanni** ♂, D: CR, p. 182
17. **Actinote leucomelas** ♀, D: CR, p. 183
18. **Actinote leucomelas** ♂, D: CR, p. 183
19. **Actinote anteas** ♂, D: Navarro, CR, p. 185
20. **Actinote melampeplos** ♂, D: CR [PT], p. 185
21. **Actinote leucomelas** ♀, V: CR, p. 183
22. **Actinote lapitha** ♂, D: Colombia, p. 185
23. **Actinote guatemalena** ♂, D: Santa Clara, CR, p. 185
24. **Actinote melampeplos** ♀, D: Juan Viñas, CR, p. 185

1
2
3
4
5
6
7
8
9
10
11
12
13
14
15
16
17
18
19
20
21
22
23
24

PLATE 33 · DANAINAE

1. **Anetia thirza insignis** ♀, D: Azahar de Cartago, CR, p. 214
2. **Lycorea ilione albescens** ♀, D: Cachi, CR, p. 213
3. **Danaus plexippus** ♂, D: Patarra, CR, p. 212
4. **Lycorea cleobaea atergatis** ♂, D: Las Concavas, CR, p. 213
5. **Danaus gilippus thersippus** ♂, D: Tres Rios, CR, p. 212
6. **Danaus eresimus montezuma** ♂, D: Patarra, CR, p. 212
7. **Eutresis dilucida** ♀, D: Carrillo, CR, p. 216
8. **Eutresis hypereia theope** ♀, D: Chiriqui, p. 217
9. **Olyras crathis staudingeri** ♂, D: Tres Rios, CR, p. 217
10. **Olyras insignis insignis** ♂, D: Guapiles, CR, p. 217

1
2
3
4
5
6
7
8
9
10

1. **Tithorea tarricina pinthias** ♂, D: Guapiles, CR, p. 218
2. **Tithorea harmonia helicaon** ♂, D: San Mateo, CR, p. 218
3. **Thyridia psidii melantho** ♂, D: Guapiles, CR, p. 220
4. **Melinaea scylax** ♂, D: Panama, p. 219
5. **Melinaea ethra lilis** ♀, D: Guapiles, CR, p. 218
6. **Mechanitis polymnia isthmia** ♂, D: Juan Viñas, CR, p. 221
7. **Mechanitis lysimnia doryssus** ♂, D: Colombiano, CR, p. 220
8. **Mechanitis lysimnia doryssus** ♀, D: Irazu, CR, p. 220
9. **Mechanitis polymnia isthmia** ♀, D: CR, p. 221
10. **Mechanitis menapis saturata** ♀, D: Carrillo, CR, p. 221
11. **Scada zibia xanthina** ♀, D: Veraguas, Panama, p. 221
12. **Mechanitis polymnia isthmia** ♀, D: CR, p. 221
13. **Hyalyris excelsa decumana** ♂, D: Tres Rios, CR, p. 225
14. **Hypothyris lycaste callispila** ♀, D: Chontales, Nicaragua, p. 223
15. **Hypothyris lycaste callispila** ♂, D: Cachi, CR, p. 223
16. **Hypothyris euclea valora** ♂, D: Guapiles, CR, p. 223
17. **Napeogenes peredia hemisticta** ♂, D: Peralta, CR, p. 222
18. **Napeogenes tolosa amara** ♂, D: Guapiles, CR, p. 222
19. **Hypothyris euclea valora** ♂, D: Sixaola River, CR, p. 223
20. **Napeogenes cranto paedaretus** ♂, D: Cachi, CR, p. 222
21. **Napeogenes cranto paedaretus** ♀, D: Cachi, CR, p. 222

1
2
3
4
5
6
7
8
9
10
11
12
13
14
15
16
17
18
19
20
21

1. **Ithomia bolivari** ♂, D: Carrillo, CR, p. 224
2. **Ithomia bolivari** ♀, V: Carrillo, CR, p. 224
3. **Ithomia celemia plaginota** ♂, D: no data, p. 225
4. **Ithomia diasa hippocrenis** ♂, D: Colombiana, CR, p. 224
5. **Ithomia heraldica** ♂, D: Colombiana, CR, p. 224
6. **Ithomia patilla** ♂, D: Turrialba, CR, p. 224
7. **Ithomia patilla** ♀, V: Santa Clara, CR, p. 224
8. **Ithomia terra vulcana** ♂, V: Cachi, CR, p. 225
9. **Ithomia xenos** ♂, D: El Alto, CR, p. 225
10. **Ithomia xenos** ♀, D: CR, p. 225
11. **Aeria eurimedia agna** ♂, D: CR, p. 226
12. **Hyposcada virginiana evanides** ♀, D: Volcan Chiriqui, Panama, p. 226
13. **Oleria paula** ♂, D: Bugaba, Panama, p. 228
14. **Oleria rubescens** ♂, D: Volcan Chiriqui, Panama, p. 227
15. **Oleria vicina** ♂, D: Cachi, CR, p. 227
16. **Oleria zelica pagasa** ♀, D: Chiriqui, p. 227
17. **Callithomia hezia hezia** ♂, D: Colombiana, CR, p. 228
18. **Callithomia hydra megaleas** ♂, D: Pozo Azul de Piris, CR, p. 229
19. **Callithomia hydra megaleas** ♀, D: Venecia, CR, p. 229
20. **Ceratinia tutia dorilla** ♂, D: Colombiana, CR, p. 228
21. **Dircenna chiriquensis** ♂, D: CR, p. 229
22. **Dircenna dero euchytma** ♂, D: CR, p. 230
23. **Dircenna dero euchytma** ♀, D: CR, p. 230
24. **Dircenna klugii** ♂, D: San Francisco, CR, p. 230
25. **Dircenna klugii** ♀, D: CR, p. 230
26. **Dircenna relata** ♂, D: Sixaola River, CR, p. 229
27. **Godyris zavaleta sorites** ♂, D: Peralta, CR, p. 230
28. **Godyris zavaleta sorites** ♀, D: Juan Viñas, CR, p. 230
29. **Dircenna relata** ♀, D: Pejivaye, CR, p. 229

1
2
3
4
5
6
7
8
9
10
11
12
13
14
15
16
17
18
19
20
21
22
23
24
25
26
27
28
29

1. **Godyris zygia** ♂, D: CR, p. 231
2. **Godyris zygia** ♀, D: Abangares, CR, p. 231
3. **Greta oto** ♀, D: CR, p. 231
4. **Greta polissena umbrana** ♂, D: Volcan Chiriqui, Panama, p. 232
5. **Greta polissena umbrana** ♀, V: Volcan Chiriqui, Panama, p. 232
6. **Greta nero** ♀, D: CR, p. 231
7. **Greta nero** ♀, V: Chiriqui, p. 231
8. **Greta andromica lyra** ♂, D: CR, p. 232
9. **Greta andromica lyra** ♂, V: CR, p. 232
10. **Greta anette** ♂, D: CR, p. 231
11. **Greta anette** ♀, V: El Alto, CR, p. 231
12. **Hypoleria cassotis** ♂, D: Colombiana, CR, p. 232
13. **Hypoleria cassotis** ♂, V: CR, p. 232
14. **Pseudoscada utilla pusio** ♂, D: CR, p. 233
15. **Pseudoscada utilla pusio** ♀, V: Cachi, CR, p. 233
16. **Episcada salvinia** ♀, D: Colombiana, CR, p. 233
17. **Episcada salvinia** ♂, V: CR, p. 233
18. **Pteronymia agalla** ♂, D: Bugaba, Panama, p. 235
19. **Pteronymia artena artena** ♂, D: CR, p. 234
20. **Pteronymia cotytto** ♂, D: Lion Hill, Panama, p. 236
21. **Pteronymia donata** ♀, D: Finca el Rodeo, CR, p. 234
22. **Pteronymia notilla** ♂, D: Cachi, CR, p. 235
23. **Pteronymia notilla** ♀, D: Rio Sucio, CR, p. 235
24. **Pteronymia fulvescens** ♂, D: CR, p. 235
25. **Pteronymia fulvimargo** ♀, D: CR, p. 235
26. **Pteronymia parva** ♂, D: CR, p. 235
27. **Pteronymia fumida** ♀, D: CR, p. 236
28. **Pteronymia simplex simplex** ♂, D: CR, p. 236
29. **Pteronymia simplex simplex** ♂, V: Volcan Chiriqui, Panama, p. 236
30. **Pteronymia simplex simplex** ♀, D: CR, p. 236
31. **Pteronymia lonera** ♀, D: San Vito, CR, p. 236
32. **Heterosais edessa nephele** ♂, D: Sixaola River, CR, p. 237
33. **Heterosais edessa nephele** ♀, V: CR, p. 237

1
2
3
4
5
6
7
8
9
10
11
12
13
14
15
16
17
18
19
20
21
22
23
24
25
26
27
28
29
30
31
32
33

PLATE 37 · MORPHINAE

1. **Antirrhea miltiades** ♂, D: CR, p. 239
2. **Antirrhea miltiades** ♀, V: Sixaola, CR, p. 239
3. **Antirrhea tomasia** ♂, D: no data, p. 241
4. **Antirrhea tomasia** ♀, V: Bugaba, Panama, p. 241
5. **Antirrhea pterocopha** ♂, D: Chiriqui, p. 239
6. **Antirrhea pterocopha** ♂, V: Cariblanco de Sarapiqui, CR, p. 239
7. **Antirrhea pterocopha** ♀, D: Cachi, CR, p. 239
8. **Antirrhea pterocopha** ♀, V: Cachi, CR, p. 239

1
3
2
4
5
6
7
8

PLATE 38 · MORPHINAE

1. **Morpho granadensis polybaptus** ♂, D: Peralta, CR, p. 244
2. **Morpho granadensis polybaptus** ♂, V: CR, p. 244
3. **Morpho peleides limpida** ♀, D: CR, p. 244
4. **Morpho peleides marinita** ♂, D: CR, p. 244
5. **Morpho peleides marinita** ♂, D: CR, p. 244
6. **Morpho peleides limpida** ♀, V: CR, p. 244

1
2
3
4
5
6

PLATE 39 · MORPHINAE

1. **Morpho amathonte** ♂, D: Bugaba, Panama, p. 245
2. **Morpho amathonte** ♀, D: Chiriqui, p. 245
3. **Morpho polyphemus catarina** ♂, D: no data, p. 243
4. **Morpho theseus aquarius** ♂, V: CR, p. 243
5. **Morpho theseus aquarius** ♀, D: Chiriqui, p. 243
6. **Morpho theseus aquarius** ♂, D: Cachi, CR, p. 243

1
2
3
4
5
6

PLATE 40 · MORPHINAE

1. **Morpho cypris** ♂, D: Colombia, p. 244
2. **Morpho cypris** ♂, V: Colombia, p. 244
3. **Morpho cypris** ♂, D: Chiriqui (form *bugaba*), p. 244
4. **Morpho cypris** ♀, D: Chiriqui, p. 244
5. **Morpho cypris** ♀, D: New Grenada (form *cyanites*), p. 244
6. **Caerois gerdrudtus** ♂, D: Ecuador, p. 241
7. **Caerois gerdrudtus** ♀, V: Ecuador, p. 241

1
2
3
4
6
7
5

PLATE 41 · SATYRINAE - BRASSOLINAE

1. **Cissia alcinoe** ♂, V: Chiriqui, p. 276
2. **Cissia calixta** ♂, V: Cachi, CR, p. 276
3. **Cissia hermes** ♂, V: Limon, CR, p. 277
4. **Cissia polyphemus** ♂, V: Rio Sucio, CR, p. 277
5. **Dynastor darius stygianus** ♂, D: Veraguas, Panama, p. 250
6. **Narope cyllastros testacea** ♂, D: Santa Anna, CR, p. 256
7. **Narope cyllastros testacea** ♂, V: Pozo Azul de Piris, CR, p. 256
8. **Brassolis isthmia** ♂, D: Peralta, CR, p. 249
9. **Brassolis isthmia** ♀, D: Limon, CR, p. 249
10. **Opsiphanes tamarindi tamarindi** ♂, D: San Mateo, CR, p. 250
11. **Opsiphanes tamarindi tamarindi** ♂, V: CR, p. 250
12. **Opsiphanes tamarindi tamarindi** ♀, D: CR, p. 250

1
2
3
4
5
6
7
8
9
10
11
12

PLATE 42 · BRASSOLINAE

1. **Opsiphanes invirae cuspidatus** ♂, D: Panama [HT], p. 251
2. **Opsiphanes invirae cuspidatus** ♂, V: Sixaola River, CR, p. 251
3. **Opsiphanes invirae cuspidatus** ♀, D: Sixaola River, CR, p. 251
4. **Opsiphanes cassina chiriquensis** ♂, D: Chiriqui [HT], p. 252
5. **Opsiphanes cassina fabricii** ♂, V: Peralta, CR, p. 251
6. **Opsiphanes cassina chiriquensis** ♀, D: Chiriqui [HT], p. 252
7. **Opsiphanes quiteria quirinus** ♂, D: Honduras, p. 251
8. **Opsiphanes quiteria panamensis** ♂, V: Chiriqui, p. 251
9. **Opsiphanes quiteria panamensis** ♀, D: Las Alturas, CR, p. 251
10. **Opsiphanes quiteria quirinus** ♀, V: Honduras, p. 251

1
2
3
4
5
6
7
8
9
10

PLATE 43 · BRASSOLINAE

1. **Opsiphanes bogotanus** ♂, D: Cariblanco, CR, p. 251
2. **Opsiphanes bogotanus** ♂, V: CR, p. 251
3. **Opsiphanes bogotanus** ♀, D: Monte Verde, CR, p. 251
4. **Opoptera staudingeri** ♀, D: Chiriqui, p. 252
5. **Opoptera staudingeri** ♂, V: Chiriqui, p. 252

1

2

3

PLATE 44 · BRASSOLINAE

1. **Catoblepia xanthicles xanthicles** ♂, D: Veraguas, Panama [HT], p. 253
2. **Selenophanes josephus josephus** ♂, D: New Grenada, p. 253
3. **Catoblepia orgetorix championi** ♂, D: Bugaba, Panama [PT], p. 253
4. **Catoblepia orgetorix championi** ♂, V: Bugaba, Panama [PT], p. 253
5. **Catoblepia orgetorix championi** ♀, D: CR, p. 253
6. **Eryphanis polyxena lycomedon** ♂, D: Sabanillas, CR, p. 254
7. **Eryphanis polyxena lycomedon** ♂, V: CR, p. 254
8. **Eryphanis polyxena lycomedon** ♀, D: Veraguas, Panama, p. 254

1
2
3
4
5
6
7
8

PLATE 45 · BRASSOLINAE

1. **Eryphanis aesacus buboculus** ♂, D: Volcan Chiriqui, Panama, p. 254
2. **Eryphanis aesacus buboculus** ♀, D: CR, p. 254
3. **Caligo eurilochus sulanus** ♂, D: Bugaba, Panama, p. 256
4. **Eryphanis aesacus buboculus** ♂, V: CR, p. 254
5. **Caligo eurilochus sulanus** ♀, V: CR, p. 256

1
2
3
4
5

PLATE 46 · BRASSOLINAE

1. **Caligo memnon memnon** ♂, D: CR, p. 256
2. **Caligo illioneus oberon** ♂, D: Peralta, CR, p. 255
3. **Caligo atreus dionysos** ♂, D: Peralta, CR, p. 256
4. **Caligo illioneus oberon** ♂, V: Peralta, CR, p. 255
5. **Caligo illioneus oberon** ♂, D: CR, p. 255
6. **Caligo illioneus oberon** ♀, D: Peralta, CR, p. 255

1
2
3
4
5
6

PLATE 47 · SATYRINAE

1. **Haetera macleannania** ♂, D: Peralta, CR, p. 260
2. **Cithaerias menander** ♂, D: CR, p. 260
3. **Dulcedo polita** ♂, D: Esperanza, CR, p. 262
4. **Pierella helvetia incanescens** ♂, D: Rio Estrella, CR, p. 262
5. **Pierella luna luna** ♂, D: CR, p. 262
6. **Manataria maculata** ♂, D: Parque Santa Rosa, CR, p. 264
7. **Cyllopsis hedemanni hedemanni** ♀, V: CR, p. 265
8. **Cyllopsis rogersi** ♂, V: CR, p. 265
9. **Cyllopsis argentella** ♂, V: Volcan Chiriqui, Panama, p. 266
10. **Cyllopsis philodice** ♂, R: Volcan Chiriqui, Panama, p. 265
11. **Cyllopsis philodice** ♀, V: Cascajal, CR, p. 265
12. **Cyllopsis pephredo** ♂, V: Volcan Chiriqui, Panama, p. 266
13. **Oressinoma typhla** ♂, D: CR, p. 264
14. **Taygetis kerea** ♂, V: Chisoy, Guatemala, p. 268
15. **Taygetis mermeria excavata** ♂, V: CR, p. 267
16. **Taygetis xenana godmani** ♂, V: Bugaba, Panama, p. 267
17. **Taygetis celia keneza** ♂, V: Bugaba, Panama, p. 267
18. **Taygetis salvini** ♂, V: Veraguas, Panama, p. 268
19. **Taygetis salvini** ♀, V: Bugaba, Panama, p. 268
20. **Taygetis virgilia rufomarginata** ♂, V: Volcan Chiriqui, Panama, p. 267

1
2
3
4
5
6
7
8
9
10
11
12
13
14
15
16
17
18
19
20

1. **Taygetis andromeda** ♂, V: CR, p. 267
2. **Taygetis andromeda** ♂, V: Santa Clara, CR, p. 267
3. **Taygetis penelea** ♂, V: Bugaba, Panama, p. 268
4. **Taygetis zimri** ♂, V: Finca la Selva, CR, p. 268
5. **Taygetis lineata** ♂, V: Las Concavas, CR, p. 269
6. **Cissia gigas** ♂, V: Irazu, CR, p. 275
7. **Cissia gigas** ♀, V: CR, p. 275
8. **Cissia satyrina** ♂, V: Volcan Chiriqui, Panama, p. 275
9. **Cissia satyrina** ♂, V: Volcan Chiriqui, Panama, p. 275
10. **Cissia tiessa** ♂, V: Nicaragua, p. 275
11. **Megeuptychia antonoe** ♂, V: Bugaba, Panama, p. 271
12. **Euptychia westwoodi** ♂, V: CR, p. 270
13. **Euptychia jesia** ♂, V: La Estrella, CR, p. 269
14. **Euptychia mollis** ♂, V: Parque Corcovado-Sirena, CR, p. 270
15. **Euptychia hilara** ♂, V: New Grenada, p. 271
16. **Euptychia insolata** ♂, V: Bugaba, Panama, p. 270
17. **Euptychia insolata** ♀, V: Parque Corcovado-Sirena, CR, p. 270
18. **Chloreuptychia arnaea** ♂, D: Irazu, CR, p. 271
19. **Chloreuptychia arnaea** ♂, V: Bugaba, Panama, p. 271
20. **Cissia similis** ♂, V: CR, p. 272
21. **Cissia similis** ♀, V: CR, p. 272
22. **Cissia usitata** ♂, D: Bugaba, Panama, p. 272
23. **Cissia usitata** ♂, V: Bugaba, Panama, p. 272
24. **Cissia confusa** ♂, V: Finca la Selva, CR, p. 273
25. **Cissia pseudoconfusa** ♂, V: Parque Corcovado-Sirena, CR, p. 273
26. **Cissia joycae** ♂, V: Finca la Selva, CR [HT], p. 274
27. **Cissia labe** ♀, V: Finca la Selva, CR, p. 273
28. **Cissia palladia** ♂, V: Atenas, CR, p. 274
29. **Cissia terrestris** ♂, V: David, Panama, p. 274
30. **Cissia drymo** ♂, V: Guapiles, CR [PT], p. 274
31. **Cissia agnata** ♂, V: La Estrella, CR, p. 274
32. **Cissia gomezi** ♂, V: CR [HT], p. 274

Nos. 33-39 continue following Plate 50

1
2
3
4
5
6
7
8
9
10
11
12
13
14
15
16
17
18
19
20
21
22
23
24
25
26
27
28
29
30
31
32
33
34
35
36
37
38
39

1. **Amphidecta pignerator** ♂, V: San Pedro Sula, Honduras, p. 277
2. **Dioriste tauropolis** ♂, D: CR, p. 278
3. **Dioriste cothon** ♂, D: CR, p. 279
4. **Dioriste cothonides** ♀, D: Cartago, CR, p. 279
5. **Dioriste tauropolis** ♀, V: Guatemala, p. 278
6. **Dioriste cothon** ♀, V: Cartago, CR, p. 279
7. **Drucina leonata** ♂, D: CR, p. 278
8. **Eretris hulda** ♂, V: Rio Sucio, CR, p. 280
9. **Eretris suzannae** ♂, V: Carrillo, CR [PT], p. 280
10. **Eretris subrufescens** ♂, V: "CR" [HT], p. 280
11. **Pedaliodes dejecta** ♂, V: CR, p. 281
12. **Pedaliodes manis** ♂, V: Carrillo, CR, p. 282
13. **Pedaliodes triaria** ♂, D: Volcan Irazu, CR, p. 282
14. **Pedaliodes triaria** ♀, V: Volcan Irazu, CR, p. 282
15. **Pedaliodes perperna** ♂, Volcan Chiriqui, Panama, p. 281
16. **Pedaliodes perperna** ♀, V: Cartago, CR, p. 281
17. **Pedaliodes petronius** ♂, V: CR, p. 281
18. **Pedaliodes petronius** ♀, V: CR, p. 281
19. **Pedaliodes ereiba cremera** ♀, V: CR, p. 282
20. **Oxeoschistus puerta submaculatus** ♂, D: CR, p. 279
21. **Oxeoschistus puerta submaculatus** ♂, V: Cachi, CR, p. 279

1
2
3
4
5
6
7
8
9
10
11
12
13
14
15
16
17
18
19
20
21

PLATE 50 · ADDENDA: SATYRINAE, NYMPHALINAE, MELITAEINAE

1. **Taygetis banghassi** ♀, V: La Estrella de Cartago, CR, p. 268
2. **Oxeoschistus euriphyle** ♂, Cartago, CR, p. 279
3. **Oxeoschistus euriphyle** ♀, V: Volcan Irazu, CR, p. 279
4. **Lymanopoda euopis** ♂, D: Azahar de Cartago, CR, p. 283
5. **Lymanopoda euopis** ♂, V: CR, p. 283
6. **Lymanopoda euopis** ♀, D: CR, p. 283
7. **Lymanopoda euopis** ♀, V: Volcan Irazu, CR [HT], p. 283
8. **Catargynnis dryadina** ♂, D: Cascajal, CR, p. 283
9. **Catargynnis dryadina** ♂, V: Cascajal, CR, p. 283
10. **Catargynnis rogersi** ♂, D: Azahar de Cartago, CR, p. 282
11. **Catargynnis rogersi** ♀, V: Cartago, CR, p. 282
12. **Pronophila timanthes** ♂, D: Volcan Irazu, CR, p. 283
13. **Eresia melaina** (eutropia?) ♀, D: San Vito, CR, p. 207
14. **Eresia melaina** (eutropia?) ♂, D: San Vito, CR, p. 207
15. **Eresia eutropia** ♂, D: San Vito, CR, p. 206
16. **Eresia eutropia** ♀, D: San Vito, CR, p. 206
17. **Eresia eutropia** ♀, D: San Vito, CR, p. 206
18. **Eresia eutropia** ♀, D: San Vito, CR, p. 206
19. **Adelpha delinita uta** ♂, D: CR, p. 172
20. **Adelpha delinita uta** ♂, D: Cachi, CR, p. 172

1
2
3
4
5
6
7
8
9
10
11
12
13
16
19
14
17
15
18
20

PLATE 10 CONTINUED

33. **Eurema daira** ♀, D: CR, p. 108
34. **Eurema daira** ♀, V: CR, p. 108
35. **Eurema elathea** ♂, D: Puerto Limon, CR, p. 108
36. **Eurema elathea** ♂, D: CR, p. 108
37. **Eurema elathea** ♀, V: Cachi, CR, p. 108
38. **Eurema elathea** ♀, D: Veraguas, Panama, p. 108
39. **Melete florinda** ♀, D: Chiriqui, p. 89
40. **Melete florinda** ♂, D: Chiriqui, p. 89
41. **Melete isandra** ♂, D: Caldera, CR, p. 89
42. **Melete isandra** ♂, V: Nicaragua, p. 89

PLATE 29 CONTINUED

33. **Eresia nigripennis** ♀, D: Carrillo, CR, p. 207
34. **Eresia alsina** ♂, D: Cachi, CR, p. 206
35. **Eresia alsina** ♂, V: Rio Sucio, CR, p. 206
36. **Eresia alsina** ♀, D: Carrillo, CR, p. 206

PLATE 30 CONTINUED

33. **Castilia myia** ♂, D: Guapiles, CR, p. 208
34. **Castilia myia** ♀, V: Guatemala, p. 208
35. **Anthanassa otanes sopolis** ♂, D: Volcan Poas, CR, p. 204
36. **Anthanassa otanes sopolis** ♀, D: Poas, CR, p. 204
37. **Castilia fulgora** ♂, D: Carrillo, CR, p. 208
38. **Castilia fulgora** ♂, V: CR, p. 208
39. **Castilia fulgora** ♀, D: Volcan Irazu, CR [HT], p. 208
40. **Anthanassa fulviplaga** ♂, D: Juan Viñas, CR, p. 205
41. **Anthanassa fulviplaga** ♂, V: Cachi, CR, p. 205
42. **Anthanassa fulviplaga** ♀, D: Juan Viñas, CR, p. 205
43. **Anthanassa fulviplaga** ♀, V: Cachi, CR, p. 205
44. **Anthanassa sosis** (form *dora*) ♀, D: CR, p. 204
45. **Anthanassa sosis** (form *dora*) ♀, V: Escazu, CR, p. 204
46. **Anthanassa crithona** ♂, D: Juan Viñas, CR, p. 204
47. **Anthanassa crithona** ♂, V: CR, p. 204
48. **Anthanassa crithona** ♀, D: Juan Viñas, CR, p. 204
49. **Anthanassa ardys** ♂, D: Irazu, CR, p. 203
50. **Anthanassa ardys** ♂, V: Irazu, CR, p. 203
51. **Anthanassa ardys** ♀, D: Cachi, CR, p. 203
52. **Anthanassa sosis** ♂, D: Volcan Irazu, CR [HT], p. 204
53. **Anthanassa sosis** ♂, V: Honduras, p. 204
54. **Anthanassa sosis** ♀, D: Azahar de Cartago, CR, p. 204
55. **Anthanassa ptolyca** ♂, D: Nicaragua, p. 203
56. **Anthanassa ptolyca** ♀, V: Nicaragua, p. 203

PLATE 48 CONTINUED

33. **Cissia gomezi** ♀, V: Parque Corcovado-Sirena, CR [PT], p. 274
34. **Cissia libye** ♂, V: CR, p. 275
35. **Cissia metaleuca** ♂, V: CR, p. 275
36. **Cissia hesione** ♂, V: CR, p. 276
37. **Cissia renata** ♀, V: Volcan Chiriqui, Panama, p. 276
38. **Cissia renata** ♂, V: Matagalpa, Nicaragua, p. 276
39. **Cissia gulnare** ♂, V: CR, p. 276

only be invoked if we assume that to a predator, *Adelpha* represents a food item that must be strenuously pursued, and when caught does not offer much nutritional value. The chemical defenses of the adults are unknown, but I think that it can be reasonably assumed that *Adelpha* is palatable; all species offered to jacamars are readily eaten. However, even invoking mimicry theory, it is still unclear why certain riodinid (*Thisbe*) and *Doxocopa* species fit into the common white-banded *Adelpha* color pattern. Clearly, there is much to be learned from the study of this genus (see also Aiello 1984).

Adelpha melanthe
Bates, 1864.
FW Length: 35-40 mm **Plate 26**
Range: Mexico to Ecuador
Hostplant: *Trema micrantha* (Ulmaceae); *Urera, Myriocarpa* (Urticaceae); *Cecropia* (Moraceae)
Early stages: *Egg*—white, laid singly. *Mature larva*—body pale brown; saddle area on thorax has eight transparent, whorled spines that project horizontally; there is a pair of spines, rosetted at tips, along the dorsum of each segment; lateral spines are bristlelike; the head capsule is pale brown with a double corona of short spines and warts on the face. First to third instars make frass chains, later instars rest on the upper surface of the leaf in an elongate N shape, looking like dead leaf matter. *Pupa*—dark brown with dull, shiny bronze wing pads; there is a large recurved lobe on the thorax; head bifid (Fig. 24).
Adult: Distinguished by the broad yellow-orange on FW upperside and the dull yellow ray pattern on the underside. See *Doxocopa clothilda.*
Habits: Occurs from sea level to 1,400 m on both slopes in virtually all forest habitats, but encountered as uncommon solitary individuals. During late morning, males perch in sunny spots in the subcanopy and chase other *Adelpha* species. The ray pattern is easily seen with binoculars. Females oviposit during midday. Both sexes feed on rotting fruits and mammal dung, and the males visit wet sand on river banks. The wide distribution of this species probably reflects its ability to use a variety of plants in the Urticales, most of which are second-growth weeds. I found that this species uses *Trema* in the Pacific deciduous forest, *Urera* and *Myriocarpa* in the Atlantic lowlands, and *Cecropia* in the montane regions. These data suggest that *A. melanthe* uses hostplants according to habitat type. All of the hostplant genera have sympatric distributions.

Adelpha zalmona sophax
Godman and Salvin, 1878
FW Length: 34-37 mm **Plate 26**
Range: Costa Rica to Colombia. **Subspecies:** Costa Rica and Panama
Hostplant: *Sabicea aspera* (Rubiaceae)
Early stages: *Egg*—pale green, laid singly. *Mature larva*—body mottled dark and pale brown; spine arrangement as in *A. cytherea*; head capsule dark brown with a double corona of short spikes. First to third instars make frass chains, later instars rest on the damaged portions of the leaf. *Pupa*—as in *A. cytherea.*
Adult: Distinguished by the orange band on the FW upperside, with wavy inner and outer margins; HW underside has a dark medial band with its edges lighter brown than the surrounding ground color, and a gray-violet band basal to it. See *A. boreas, A. salmoneus,* and *A. stilesiana.*
Habits: Occurs from 500 to 1,200 m on the Atlantic slope, in cloud forest habitats, mostly along the Cordillera Central and Talamanca. Encountered as solitary individuals along forest and riparian edges during sunny mornings, and occasionally in the forest. Males perch along forest edges from early morning until about ten o'clock. This species is uncommon in collections, although in the Carrillo Belt during the February-March dry season it can be locally abundant.

Adelpha salmoneus salmonides
Hall, 1938
FW Length: 28-31 mm **Plate 26**
Range: Mexico to Venezuela and Colombia. **Subspecies:** Central America
Hostplant: *Sabicea* (Rubiaceae)
Early stages: *Mature larva*—similar to *A. zalmona*
Adult: Orange band on the FW upperside runs from costa to tornus, with a slight notch on the inner margin; underside overcast with pale reddish brown; medial band faint, silver-gray, with two short bands basal to it in the sub-basal area. See *A. boreas, A. zalmona,* and *A. stilesiana.*
Habits: Occurs from sea level to 1,000 m on the Atlantic slope, in rain forest. Encountered as rare solitary individuals during the dry seasons. This species is rare in collections, but can be locally abundant during February and March in the Carrillo Belt.

Adelpha boreas opheltes
Fruhstorfer, 1915
FW Length: 29-30 mm **Plate 26**
Range: Costa Rica to Bolivia. **Subspecies:** Costa Rica and Panama

Hostplant: *Satyria* (Ericaceae)

Early stages: *Egg*—white, laid singly. *Mature larva*—mottled brown and green, with spines as in *A. cocala*; head capsule brown with a corona of short spikes. *Pupa*—pale brown with general shape as in *A. leucophthalma*, but without flanges on the bifid head.

Adult: Orange band on the FW upperside runs from the costa into the tornus, curved at the inner margin; underside has a violet-gray ground color; HW shape generally rounded with dentate margin. Compare with *A. zalmona, A. salmoneus*, and *A. stilesiana.*

Habits: Occurs as rare, solitary individuals from 100 to 1,000 m on the Atlantic slope in association with rain forest and cloud forest habitats. This species is seldom collected and is generally rare in collections. In Bolivia it is apparently restricted to montane habitats; in Costa Rica, however, it occurs in the lowland rain forest, where it breeds. The record of *Satyria* as a hostplant is unusual for the Nymphalidae, and this plant family is generally very rare in tropical lowland forests. *Satyria* is an epiphyte occurring high in the forest canopy.

Adelpha stilesiana

DeVries and Chacon, 1982

FW Length: 32-34 mm **Plate 27**

Range: Costa Rica

Hostplant: Unknown

Early stages: Unknown

Adult: Distinguished from all other similar species by the broad orange band on the FW upperside, which terminates broadly on the distal margin. See *A. boreas, A. salmoneus*, and *A. zalmona.*

Habits: Occurs from 800 to 1,100 m on the Atlantic slope in the Carrillo Belt. At the time of writing, only two specimens have been collected, but individuals have been seen within Parque Braulio Carrillo along the old oxcart trail that runs down to the Rio Sucio. Individuals have been observed from May to June, although it is unknown whether the species is persistent throughout the year. The species can be identified easily with binoculars, and separated from *A. zalmona* and *A. salmoneus*, which fly in the same habitats.

Adelpha leucophthalma

(Latreille, 1811)

FW Length: 27-31 mm **Plate 26**

Range: Nicaragua to Colombia and (?)Peru

Hostplant: *Pentagonia* (Rubiaceae)

Early stages: (Young 1974*b*) *Egg*—pale green, highly sculptured, fuzzy, laid on old leaves. *Mature larva*—body dull mottled green and brown, covered in green rosetted spines; largest spines arise from thorax and posterior quarter; overall appearance like a moss-covered twig; head capsule brown with vertical cream bands on the face; a double corona of short spikes; two black cones on the epicranium, and two white warts on the face. *Pupa*—dark brown; dorsal keel prominent, but not as large as in *A. melanthe*; a ridge on the dorsum of abdominal segments; head bifid with flat flanges directed distally. First to third instars make frass chains, later instars rest on the damaged portion of the leaves.

Adult: Distinguished at once by the round white spot in the middle of the HW; no orange subapical spots on HW upperside. See *A. zina* and *A. justina. Note*: the subspecies *mephistopheles* Butler and *tegeta* Fruhstorfer show almost no difference from the nominate form and are here considered synonyms (see Hall 1938).

Habits: Occurs from 500 to 1,800 m on both slopes in all forest habitats, but especially cloud forest. Young (1974*b*) considers this a rare species. On the contrary, I find it to be locally common in virtually all montane forest habits and characteristic of such habitats throughout Costa Rica. The males perch from early morning until early afternoon along forest edges. Females oviposit during midday on juvenile hostplants growing along trails, and forest and riparian edges. Both sexes visit rotting fruits, and the males are commonly found visiting wet sand and dung along road cuts or where there is water seepage. On the Atlantic slope this species is most abundant during the dry seasons, frequently being observed in small groups of three or four individuals. During the rainy seasons individuals are uncommon, but the species is persistent throughout the year in virtually all of its habitats.

Adelpha zina

Hewitson, 1867

FW Length: 25-28 mm **Plate 26**

Range: Guatemala to Peru

Hostplant: Unknown

Early stages: Unknown

Adult: Distinguished from the similar *A. leucophthalma* by having the white spot on the HW slightly elongate; FW upperside has a few subapical orange spots; borders of the orange FW band are even. See *A. justina* and *A. leucophthalma.*

Habits: It is uncertain whether this species is distinct from *A. leucopthalma*, but *A. zina* occurs as rare individuals in Costa Rica at 800 to

2,000 m in cloud forest habitats. It is found in association with either *A. justina* or *A. leucophthalma*. The early stages may help to establish the status of *A. zina*.

Adelpha justina lacina

(Butler, 1872)

FW Length: 24-28 mm **Plate 26**

Range: Guatemala to Peru. **Subspecies:** Guatemala to Colombia

Hostplant: Unknown

Early stages: Unknown

Adult: Distinguished by the elongate white band on the HW; orange band on the FW reaches the inner margin. See *A. leucophthalma* and *A. zina*.

Habits: Occurs from 700 to 2,000 m on both slopes in rain-shadow habitats. Encountered as rare, solitary individuals along forest edges and rivers, usually in localized, small populations. The males perch in the subcanopy of the forest on sunny mornings, most often in light gaps. This species can be identified with binoculars. Uncommon.

Adelpha cytherea marcia

Fruhstorfer, 1915

FW Length: 22-25 mm **Plate 26**

Range: Mexico to Amazon Basin. **Subspecies:** Guatemala to Colombia

Hostplant: *Sabicea villosa* (Rubiaceae)

Early stages: *Egg*—white, laid singly; female often lays several separate eggs on the same plant. *Mature larva*—body dark brown; thorax has four large, rosetted spines, two directed anterior, two posterior; head capsule darker brown than body with a double corona of short spikes; the entire body is covered with short spines or bristles. *Pupa*—similar to *A. boreas*. First to third instars make frass chains covered with bits of dead leaf material; later instars rest on damaged leaf parts.

Adult: Distinguished by its small size and by the FW upperside with a broad orange band, which is intruded upon by a white triangle near the inner margin; underside overcast with pale orange.

Habits: Widespread and common from sea level to 900 m on both slopes in all forest habitats except the lowland Guanacaste dry forest. This species can be abundant in areas of second growth where its hostplant is an early successional weed. Ecotones such as forest edges, beaches, and large treefalls in the forest are good places to find this butterfly. Both sexes are found in association with the hostplant, and are frequently found perching on the tangles of *Sabicea* low to the ground. Both sexes visit rotting fruits and flowers of *Cephaelis* and various Asteraceae. It is persistent throughout the year in all habitats, and larvae are most abundant during the dry seasons.

Adelpha cocala lorzae

Boisduval, 1870

FW Length: 24-29 mm **Plate 26**

Range: Mexico to Amazon Basin. **Subspecies:** Honduras to Panama

Hostplant: *Pentagonia, Psychotria, Calycophyllum, Chomelia, Uncaria, Genipa* (Rubiaceae)

Early stages: *Egg*—gray, laid singly on damaged edge of leaf. *Mature larva*—body dull green with many short brown rosetted spines, looking like a moss-covered twig; eight of the dorsal spines are large and resemble papillae, especially on the thorax, head capsule light brown with a double corona of short, stout spikes. Early instars make frass chains along the veins of the leaves; later instars rest on the upperside of the leaf but on a small soggy mass of detritus assembled by the larva. *Pupa*—dull green; large dorsal keel; bifid head with flat flanges directed laterally as in *A. leucophthalma*.

Adult: Distinguished by the orange band on the FW upperside having a straight edge, not angled as it crosses the cell; FW has no subapical orange spots; no white on the FW upperside; FW underside washed with orange, but with white band visible. See *A. boeotia* and *A. delinita*.

Habits: Occurs commonly on both slopes, from sea level to 700 m, in association with rain forest habitats. I have found individuals to be most abundant in areas of swamp forest or along riparian edges, and less abundant in upland forest. The males perch in light gaps and along forest edges, from early morning until late afternoon during the dry seasons, and when there is bright sunshine during the rainy seasons. The female is active ovipositing on seedlings and small saplings around midday, usually in the shade of the forest or along rivers. Both sexes feed on rotting fruits, and males visit fresh mammal dung.

Adelpha heraclea

(Felder, 1867)

FW Length: 25-28 mm **Plate 26**

Range: Nicaragua to Venezuela

Hostplant: *Vitex cooperi* (Verbenaceae)

Early stages: *Egg*—white, laid singly on mature trees growing along forest edges and along rivers. *Mature larva*—body light green; each segment has a pair of terminally whorled spines except the second segment, which has four; a distinct creamy green spot on sides of fifth segment; head capsule pale brown with a double corona of toothlike spines, which are black at their bases. *Pupa*—opalescent white with dull black markings on wing pads, abdomen, and cremaster; thorax without keel but with laterally flattened flaps; head broadly bifid with recurved horns (Fig. 24). Early instars make frass chains; later instars rest on leaf damage. The larva and pupa of our Costa Rican populations strongly resemble the early stages of *A. jordani* described in Moss (1933*b*), and *jordani* may in fact be the same species, in which case the name *heraclea* has priority.

Adult: Distinguished by the 90° angled "notch" on the orange band of the FW as it crosses the cell; HW shape somewhat rounded. See *A. cocala, A. boeotia*, and *A. erymanthis*.

Habits: Occurs from 100 to 700 m on the Atlantic slope and, in areas around the Osa Peninsula, on the Pacific slope from sea level to 400 m in rain forest habitats, especially in swamp forest. Encountered as solitary individuals along forest and riparian edges. During the morning, males perch five to ten meters above the ground. Females oviposit at midday and fly along forest edges and in light gaps. Although not common, this species is persistent throughout the year and can be locally abundant during the dry seasons.

Adelpha boeotia boeotia

(Felder and Felder, 1867)

FW Length: 25-29 mm **Plate 26**

Range: Guatemala to Amazon Basin. **Subspecies:** Costa Rica to Colombia

Hostplant: *Cecropia* (Moraceae); *Luhea seemani* (Tiliaceae)

Early stages: *Mature larva*—body brown, spiny as in *A. melanthe*; head capsule pale brown with spines arranged as in *A. leucophthalma*.

Adult: Distinguished by the gradual angle (no notch) of the orange band on the FW upperside as it crosses the cell; outer margin of the orange band is blurred, without sharp definition; FW subapex has a dark square spot where the orange band is interrupted; white band on the HW upperside is wide at costal margin and terminates as a long taper following the inner margin. *Note*: specimens that have white intruding into the FW orange have been called subspecies *oberthuri*, but both forms occur in Costa Rican populations. See *A. cocala, A. heraclea, A. erymanthis*, and *A. delinita*.

Habits: Occurs from sea level to 700 m, mainly on the Atlantic slope, but also in the lowland rain forest on the Pacific slope around the Osa Peninsula. It is unknown whether the Atlantic populations use solely *Cecropia* as hostplants, but on the Pacific side the populations appear only to use *Luhea*. Encountered as uncommon solitary individuals, mostly during the dry seasons, along forest edges and in large light gaps.

Adelpha erymanthis

Godman and Salvin, 1884

FW Length: 30-32 mm **Plate 26**

Range: Costa Rica to Colombia

Hostplant: Unknown

Early stages: Unknown

Adult: Distinguished by the produced FW apex; orange on FW similar to *A. boeotia*, but the orange intrudes into the white on the HW as a fine line along distal margin of white band; the HW white band tapers to a point near inner margin. Compare with *A. boeotia* and *A. delinita*.

Habits: Very rare throughout its range, this species is known from only a handful of specimens found on the Atlantic slope of Costa Rica at 800 to 2,000 m. It has been taken on Volcan Irazu, Volcan Poas, Carrillo, and La Virgen del Socorro. I have collected it only once. The individual was flying along a ridge top above the forest canopy.

Adelpha delinita uta

Fruhstorfer, 1915

FW Length: 25-27 mm **Plate 50**

Range: Honduras to Ecuador. **Subspecies:** Honduras to Panama

Hostplant: Unknown

Early stages: Unknown

Adult: Distinguished from *A. boeotia* by the orange FW band having its basal and distal margins wavy and indistinct, especially when viewed on the underside; subapical portion of the FW orange band is more sharply angled across the cell; white HW band is constricted near the costa. See *A. boeotia* and *A. cocala*.

Habits: Occurs from sea level to 700 m on the Atlantic slope, in rain forest habitats. I have found it most common around Turrialba and Guapiles. Its habits are similar to *A. boeotia*. This species has been considered a subspecies of *boeotia*, but was correctly separated by Fruhstorfer (1915) in his treatment of *Adelpha*. I have compared the genitalia and found them to be distinct.

Adelpha basiloides

(Bates, 1865)

FW Length: 24-30 mm **Plate 26**

Range: Mexico to Panama

Hostplant: *Alibertia edulis, Faramea, Ixora* (Rubiaceae)

Early stages: Not described

Adult: Distinguished by the white band on the FW upperside, which enters the cell as a white triangle. See *A. iphiclus.*

Habits: Occurs from sea level to 1,000 m on the Pacific slope, in all forest habitats. Most frequently found flying with *A. iphiclus,* but is much less common. In Guanacaste, *A. basiloides* is most abundant during the rainy season. Both sexes feed on rotting fruits of *Genipa, Alibertia, Guazuma,* and mammal dung. In the lowland rain forest it is found only in association with second-growth habitats and overgrown pastures. In the deciduous and drier forest habitats, *A. basiloides* will enter the forest where there is sufficient sunlight filtering in from the canopy. At one time (Hall 1938), this species was considered a subspecies of *A. iphiclus,* but the hostplants and larvae prove that it is separate. It is curiously rare in Costa Rican collections, yet is persistent throughout the year in many Pacific slope habitats.

Adelpha iphiclus

(Linnaeus, 1758)

FW Length: 26-29 mm **Plate 27**

Range: Mexico to Amazon Basin

Hostplant: *Calycophyllum, candidissimum, Isertia, Uncaria* (Rubiaceae)

Early stages: (Moss 1933*b*) *Mature larva*—in general very similar to *A. cytherea,* but slightly larger and with a dark brown band along the sides. In Costa Rica, first to third instars make frass chains, later instars may rest on the frass chains or on the damaged portion of the leaves where the larva has previously fed. *Pupa*—similar to *A. cytherea,* only larger.

Adult: Distinguished from similar species by the white band on the FW, which begins at the posterior edge of the FW cell; FW upperside has a square, orange subapical spot. The white band is variable in width; some females in particular have a wider band. See *A. basiloides, A. fessonia, A. naxia,* and *A. ixia.*

Habits: Perhaps the most familiar species in all of the Neotropics. It is widespread and common in Costa Rica from sea level to 1,000 m, and most abundant on the Pacific slope. Frequently found in small groups along forest edges, where the males perch and chase passing butterflies, including each other. In the Pacific slope dry forest, it is also frequently found around human habitations where there are fruit trees. Both sexes visit fruits of mango, *Guazuma, Genipa,* and fresh mammal dung. On the Atlantic slope I have collected this species in the rain forest canopy visiting flowers of *Vouchysia* and *Paullinia.*

Adlepha erotia

(Hewitson, 1847)

FW Length: 30-34 mm **Plate 27**

Range: Costa Rica to Colombia and Venezuela

Hostplant: Unknown

Early stages: Unknown

Adult: Distinguished by its large, robust build; FW upperside has a wide orange band, with a "notch" in the cell and with a small area of white near FW inner margin. See *A. phylaca* and *A. lerna. Note*: as originally pointed out by Hall (1938) and by my subsequent study of the type specimens, this species has been confused in the literature for a long time under the names *A. delinita* and *A. aeolia.*

Habits: This rare species is known from both slopes, at 700 to 1,500 m, in montane wet forest habitats. I have found it only in Carrillo and at San Vito de Java. Judging from museum collections, this species is apparently common in Colombia.

Adelpha lerna aeolia

(Felder, 1862)

FW Length: 30-35 mm **Plate 27**

Range: Nicaragua to Amazon Basin.

Subspecies: Nicaragua to Panama

Hostplant: Unknown

Early stages: Unknown

Adult: Distinguished by stocky build; white band on FW crosses three cells; orange on FW has a distinct "notch" at the subapex. See *A. erotia* and *A. phylaca.*

Habits: Encountered as rare solitary individuals on both slopes, in rain forest habitats. Recorded from sea level to 800 m in collections. I have found it upon a few occasions on the Atlantic slope, at 800 m in the Carrillo Belt. Rare in Costa Rican collections.

Adelpha phylaca

(Bates, 1860)

FW Length: 27-33 mm **Plate 27**

Range: Guatemala to Bolivia. **Subspecies:** Guatemala to Panama

Hostplant: *Cecropia peltata* (Moraceae)

Early stages: *Undescribed*

Adult: Distinguished by the sharply angled orange patch on the FW upperside as it crosses the cell; distal margins of the orange are blurred, and it blends with the white on the FW. The specimens illustrated in Plate 27 differ from the Guatemalan type by having a more blurred interface between the orange and the white on the FW, but do not resemble the subspecies *pseudaethalia* described by Hall (1938). The Costa Rican populations are variable, and I do not feel they require a subspecific name.

Habits: Known from rain forest habitats on both slopes, from 300 to 800 m. This species is rare in Costa Rican collections and infrequently seen in nature. Both sexes will visit rotting fruits placed in light gaps and along forest edges, especially the fruits of guava (*Psidium suave*: Myrtaceae). On the Osa Peninsula, this species is persistent throughout the year, but most common during the dry season (March-April).

Adelpha naxia
(Felder and Felder, 1867)
FW Length: 29-32 mm **Plate 27**
Range: Mexico to Amazon Basin
Hostplant: Unknown
Early stages: Unknown
Adult: FW upperside has a white band that crosses four wing cells but does not enter the discal cell; FW has an elongate orange rectangle and an isolated spot in the apex; underside similar to *A. iphiclus*. See *A. ixia, A. iphiclus*, and *A. basiloides*.
Habits: Occurs from 300 to 1,200 m on both slopes in association with most forest habitats. Encountered as solitary individuals along forest edges and old second growth along rivers. Both sexes visit rotting fruits and are active from late morning until early afternoon. Most frequently seen during the dry seasons.

Adelpha ixia leucas
Fruhstorfer, 1915
FW Length: 28-31 mm **Plate 27**
Range: Mexico to Venezuela. **Subspecies:** Mexico to Panama
Hostplant: Unknown
Early stages: Unknown
Adult: Distinguished by the white band on the FW upperside, which crosses only three cells; orange spot on FW apex crudely T-shaped. See *A. naxia, A. phylaca*, and *A. iphiclus*.
Habits: Occurs from sea level to 800 m on both slopes, in rain forest. Widespread and common; habits similar to *A. iphiclus*.

Adelpha leuceria
(Druce, 1874)
FW Length: 26-31 mm **Plate 27**
Range: Guatemala to Panama
Hostplant: Unknown
Early stages: Unknown
Adult: Distinguished by the orange band on the upperside, which traverses both wings. This is a good field character. See *A. tracta*.
Habits: Occurs at 900 to 2,000 m on both slopes in association with cloud forest. Encountered as rare solitary individuals, usually localized within a portion of a forest habitat. The males perch high in the canopy and are active during the morning, most frequently in light gaps on ridge tops, and occasionally along forest edges. The female is rare in collections. I have collected males on bright sunny mornings visiting wet sand enriched with urine, and have seen this species flying in misty weather.

Adelpha tracta
(Butler, 1872)
FW Length: 28-34 mm **Plate 27**
Range: Costa Rica and Panama
Hostplant: Unknown genus of Rubiaceae
Early stages: Unknown
Adult: Distinguished by the broken orange band on the FW upperside, which extends from costa to inner margin. See *A. leuceria*.
Habits: Widespread and common in all forest habitats, from 800 to 3,000 m, on both slopes. Encountered as solitary individuals along road cuts and forest edges whenever there is sunshine. In the mornings males perch on vegetation one to three meters above the ground, and remain there until early afternoon. On the Atlantic slope, individuals are most abundant during the dry seasons. Both sexes feed on rotting fruits of Melastomaceae and Lauraceae, and the males visit wet sand and mammal dung.

Adelpha demialba
(Butler, 1872)
FW Length: 30-38 mm **Plate 27**
Range: Costa Rica and Panama
Hostplant: *Rhondeletia* (Rubiaceae)
Early stages: *Pupa*—morphologically very similar to *A. melanthe* except with some silvery spotting on the wing pads.
Adult: Distinguished by the broad white-checkered FW apex and dark ground color on the upperside. This is a good field character.
Habits: Occurs from 700 to 2,300 m on both slopes, in association with cloud forest habitats, although it is distributed mainly along the Cordillera de Talamanca. Encountered as solitary individuals along landslips and water courses, where the males visit water seepage on the bare soil. The flight is very fast and wary, and when on the wing it may be mistaken for *Marpesia chiron*. However, once perched, it can be easily identified. Both sexes visit flowers of *Mikania* and *Senecio megaphylla* (Asteraceae). Although never abundant, and somewhat rare in collections, during the dry seasons on the Atlantic slope or in rain shadow habitats, it is not unusual to see ten individuals per day. In Parque Braulio Carrillo, between

May and August, this species flies from early morning until it rains, continuing on the wing even in the fog. The females oviposit around midday, along forest edges or roadsides.

Adelpha diocles

Godman and Salvin, 1878

FW Length: 24-26 mm **Plate 27**

Range: Costa Rica and Panama

Hostplant: Unknown

Early stages: Unknown

Adult: Distinguished by the pearly sheen on the underside; HW has a short lobe on tornus. See *A. cytherea*.

Habits: Occurs at 2,000 to 3,000 m on both slopes, in montane rain forest habitats, mostly along the Cordillera de Talamanca. Individuals fly at the canopy level and seldom descend to the ground. With the aid of binoculars it can be identified easily. From the experience of G. B. Small, I. Chacon, and myself, it appears that this species is very local and highly seasonal, but certainly can be abundant during the main dry season (February-March). This butterfly is very rare in collections, most likely because individuals seldom descend within reach.

Adelpha celerio

Bates, 1864

FW Length: 28-33 mm **Plate 27**

Range: Mexico to Amazon Basin

Hostplant: *Urera, Myriocarpa* (Urticaceae); *Ochroma* (Bombacaceae)

Early stages: *Mature larva*—body green, resembling a moss-covered twig; head capsule elongate, black with two vertical lines on face; a corona of short spines and two larger ones on epicranium. *Prepupa*—the larva changes color to a beautiful lemon yellow with black spines; dark spot on the dorsum. *Pupa*—general shape like a small *Hamadryas*: elongate with two flat head horns; the body is chrome color divided by black lines, and has a geometrical appearance, like an M. C. Escher woodcut (Fig. 24).

Adult: Distinguished by the greenish bands traversing both wings and the FW subapical, spot which is regularly shaped but clearly divided by the veins. *Note*: this taxon probably harbors a number of distinct species that will only be separated and revised when the early stages of all are known.

Habits: Occurs from sea level to 1,000 m on both slopes in all forest habitats, but rarely in the Guanacaste dry forest. Individuals feed on rotting fruits, but, as noted above, there are probably several species masquerading under this name.

Adelpha fessonia

Hewitson, 1847

FW Length: 25-32 mm **Plate 27**

Range: Mexico to Panama

Hostplant: *Randia* (Rubiaceae)

Early stages: Undescribed

Adult: Distinguished from all other similar species by the white band on the FW running from costa, across the cell, to the HW inner margin.

Habits: Occurs from sea level to 900 m on the Pacific slope, in deciduous forest habitats, and is commonest in the lowlands of Guanacaste. In Parque Santa Rosa it is persistent throughout the year, commonest in the rainy season, and in reproductive diapause during the dry season. Both sexes visit flowers of *Cordia* and *Croton*, and feed on rotting fruits. The geographic range of *A. fessonia* terminates in Panama just south of the Osa Peninsula, being rare in the rain forest and common in the deciduous forest.

Adelpha zea paraeca

Bates, 1864

FW Length: 27-32 mm **Plate 27**

Range: Mexico to Amazon Basin. **Subspecies:** Guatemala to Panama

Hostplant: Unknown

Early stages: Unknown

Adult: Distinguished from the similar *A. celerio* by the orange patch on the FW, which bears a small spot that touches or is very close to the white band; the white band is in general without a greenish cast; underside has a reddish cast to the submarginal markings. See *A. celerio*.

Habits: I have collected and seen specimens of this species from montane rain forest habitats on both slopes, between 900 and 1,500 m. Individuals are rare in collections. This butterfly's relationship to *A. celerio* is unknown, and the possibility of several species being included within *A. zea* unresolved.

Adelpha serpa sentia

Godman and Salvin, 1884

FW Length: 26-31 mm **Not illustrated**

Range: Mexico to Amazon Basin. **Subspecies:** Central America

Hostplant: (Moss 1933*b*) *Miconia* (Melastomaceae)

Early stages: Unknown

Adult: Distinguished from *A. zea* and *A. celerio* by having a white medial band, and the FW subapical orange spot is like an elongate rectangle; the medial band tends to be wide; HW underside has a silvery submargin.

Habits: In collections there are always specimens of *serpa* mixed with *A. celerio and A. zea*, all with the same localities, and I assume that the habitats and habits of these three species are similar. I have not seen *serpa* in nature.

Adelpha felderi

Boisduval, 1870

FW Length: 23-27 mm **Plate 27**

Range: Mexico to Costa Rica

Hostplant: Unknown

Early stages: Unknown

Adult: Distinguished by the narrow white medial bands traversing both wings, and the underside ground color washed in reddish brown. See *A. iphiclus*.

Habits: Although the type-locality of this species is Costa Rica, I have only seen a few specimens in the British Museum (National History), which are labeled "Costa Rica," but I have never seen it in the field or in other collections. It is apparently quite common north of our area, and I include it here as a species that requires confirmation.

Genus **HYPANARTIA**
Hübner, 1821

Medium-sized butterflies recognized by the toothlike tail on the hindwing and dark ground color. It has been suggested that this genus is closely related to a fossil butterfly from the Miocene (see Brown and Heineman 1972). *Hypanartia* is apparently close to the Old World genus *Antanartia*—so close, in fact, that there has been some doubt as to their distinctness. The genus ranges from Mexico throughout Central and South America and the West Indies. Of the eight species in *Hypanartia*, four occur in our area.

The hostplants recorded for *Hypanartia* include Urticaceae and Ulmaceae. The larvae are black and spiny. The head capsule is unadorned with spines, and the larva in general shows affinities to genera like *Vanessa* and *Anartia*. The larvae build small shelters on the hostplant of leaves sewn together with silk, and rest in these; they may even pupate in them. The pupae are pale green with reflective silver markings, and have the general shape of *Vanessa*.

In Costa Rica this genus is found from sea level to 2,800 m, always in association with forest habitats. The butterflies are rarely observed at flowers and are not attracted to rotting fruits. The males will visit cattle urine and wet sand along rivers.

Hypanartia lethe

(Fabricius, 1793)

FW Length: 28-30 mm **Plate 28**

Range: Mexico to Brazil

Hostplant: *Phenax, Boehmeria* (Urticaceae); *Celtis* (Ulmaceae)

Early stages: *Egg*—white, very small, laid singly on new leaves. *Early instars*—entirely black and slightly spined; they make a silk-lined tube from the leaf and rest inside, feeding on the epidermis of the leaf tube and other leaves. *Mature larva*—body a dull cream yellow with black spines; head capsule dull orange. The mature larva forms a tent out of the leaves and rests, and may even pupate, in this tent. *Pupa*—pale green, slightly wedge-shaped toward the head, with a single row of yellow spines on the dorsum.

Adult: Distinguished by the orange spots on the black FW apex and a black bar on the HW inner margin. The FW apex is a good field character. See *H. godmani*.

Habits: Most frequently occurs from 300 to 1,300 m on both slopes, in association with disturbed forest habitats and second growth. Rarely found in the Guanacaste deciduous forest. Commonly encountered along forest edges and on rotting fruits on the forest floor, and males are frequently seen along landslips and at water seepage. Both sexes will occasionally visit flowers of the Asteraceae. Common and widespread throughout Central America.

Hypanartia godmani

(Bates, 1864)

FW Length: 29-31 mm **Plate 28**

Range: Mexico to Colombia

Hostplant: Unknown

Early stages: Unknown

Adult: Immediately distinguished by the black FW apex, which is very visible while butterfly is on the wing. See *H. lethe*.

Habits: Occurs infrequently from 900 to 1,800 m on both slopes, in association with cloud forest habitats. Encountered as solitary individuals along forest edges and rivers, often flying with *H. lethe*. Males visit wet riverine sand, and can be baited by enriching the sand with urine. Although much less common than *H. lethe*, *H.*

godmani is typical of the Costa Rican cloud forests.

Hypanartia kefersteini

(Doubleday, 1847)

FW Length: 26-29 mm **Plate 28**

Range: Mexico to Peru

Hostplant: *Pilea* (Urticaceae)

Early stages: (Young 1976*a*) *Egg*—white, laid singly. *Mature larva*—head capsule dull orange covered in a fine pile; body glossy black with olive green spiracles; dorsum has black spines on segments 1, 2, and 9-11, white spines on segments 3 and 5-8, and a black spine with a white base on segment 6. *Pupa*—bluish gray with doublets of silver spots on the thoracic region; general shape as in *Vanessa.*

Adult: Distinguished by the excavated FW margin, the white spotting on the FW apex, and the reddish ground color. *Note*: as pointed out by Godman and Salvin (1883), the specimens from Ecuador (the type locality) differ in the size and placement of the hyaline spots.

Habits: Occurs from 800 to 1,900 m on both slopes, in association with cloud forest habitats, especially along rivers. Males visit water seepage at landslips and along riverbanks, and during the morning they perch high in the forest canopy. Young (1976*a*) comments that the female has a very rapid oviposition behavior, stopping only momentarily at a plant to oviposit, then rapidly moving on. This impetuous behavior is characteristic and can make observations on this species difficult.

Hypanartia arcaei

(Godman and Salvin, 1871)

FW Length: 28-30 mm **Plate 28**

Range: Costa Rica and Panama

Hostplant: Unknown

Early stages: Unknown

Adult: Distinguished by the yellowish band and the hyaline spots on the FW. *Note*: some authors consider this to be a subspecies of the South American *H. dione* Latr., a relationship that will be clarified by a future revision of the genus.

Habits: Occurs from 1,200 m to over 2,000 m on both slopes, in association with cloud forest habitats centered around the Cordillera de Talamanca. Encountered as solitary individuals along rivers and other constantly wet places, where the males visit water seepage or perch along the vegetation overhanging rivers. Occasionally found visiting flowers of *Senecio megaphylla* and other Compositae. Unlike other congeners, this species will fly when it is cloudy. The females are rare in collections.

Genus **SIPROETA** Hübner, 1823

As pointed out by Fox and Forbes (1971), the butterflies in this genus have been placed under various generic names that have either been misapplied or are synonyms. The butterflies are recognized by being medium- to large-sized, the forewing apex is slightly produced, and the hindwing margin is dentate. The genus ranges from the southern United States throughout Central and South America and the West Indies. Of the five species in the genus, three occur in our area.

Host plants are all in the Acanthaceae, and all the larvae are spiny, have knobbed horns on the head, and show many similarities to *Anartia.* The pupae are elongate and somewhat egg-shaped, and are adorned with golden spikes.

All of the species fly in bright sunlight and are associated with disturbed habitats. All species visit flowers as well as rotting fruits, carrion, and dung. One species, *S. stelenes,* is considered to be a Batesian mimic of at least one or two distasteful species in the Heliconiinae (Brown and Heineman, 1972); *epaphus* has been the subject of a study on ecology, longevity, and parasitization in Costa Rica (Young, 1972*a*). The larvae appear to mimic the caterpillars of distasteful *Battus* and *Parides* swallowtails.

Siproeta epaphus epaphus

(Latreille, 1811)

FW Length: 48-50 mm **Plate 28**

Range: Mexico to Peru. **Subspecies:** Central America

Hostplant: *Ruellia, Blechum* (Acanthaceae)

Early stages: (Young 1972*a*) *Egg*—dark green with yellow ribs, laid in loose clusters on the new leaves. *Mature larva*—body velvety maroon, bearing three pairs of yellowish orange spines per segment; head capsule shiny black with two recurved, knobbed horns. *Pupa*—pale green, elongate egg-shaped, flecked with many tiny black spots on thorax and abdomen; and two prominent orange-based black spots on dorsum of first and second abdominal segments.

Adult: Immediately distinguished by the split brown coloration on the wings. This makes an excellent field identification mark.

Habits: Occurs commonly from 400 to 1,500 m on both slopes, in association with wet forest habitats that do not have a pronounced dry season. Frequently seen along forest edges and rivers, where they parade back and forth across the edge vegetation about 1 or 2 meters above the ground. Males visit wet sand at landslips and river crossings. Both sexes visit flowers of *Cordia, Stachytarpheta, Impatiens, Lantana*, and *Croton*. The females oviposit during midday on young plants growing at forest edges. Oviposition is rapid and is often repeated again and again along the same patch of plants during a single oviposition bout. Frequently found with clear bird-beak marks, and occasionally seen to be chased by birds while visiting flowers.

Siproeta stelenes biplagiata

(Fruhstorfer, 1907)

FW Length: 45-48 mm **Plate 28**

Range: Southern United States to the Amazon Basin. **Subspecies:** Central America

Hostplant: *Ruellia, Justicia, Blechum* (Acanthaceae)

Early stages: *Egg*—dark green, laid singly on new leaves. *Mature larva*—similar to *S. epaphus*, but differs by having the body velvety greenish black; only dorsal spines are reddish yellow; head horns even more prominent; anal claspers dull purple. *Pupa*—as in *S. epaphus* but with fewer black spots and a longer, recurved cremaster.

Adult: Pale green upperside with broad brown margins; rusty brown margins and marking on underside. There is a great variability in the brown margins, which seems to depend on seasons and habitat. See *Philaethria dido*.

Habits: Occurs commonly from sea level to 1,400 m on both slopes, in a variety of habitat types but commonest in open second growth. Frequently seen in open areas visiting flowers, dung, carrion, or rotting fruits, and a familiar visitor to domestic gardens. Although considered a mimic of *Philaethria dido* by some, in Costa Rica these two species occupy very different microhabitats. I agree with Brown and Heineman (1972), who consider it a mimic of *Heliconius charitonius*. This is clearly seen in the Pacific slope deciduous forest, where both species commonly fly together in the same forest edge habitat. This species is perhaps one of the most familiar butterflies in all Central America.

Siproeta superba eunoe

Fox and Forbes, 1971

FW Length: 48-50 mm **Plate 28**

Range: Mexico to Costa Rica. **Subspecies:** Costa Rica

Hostplant: Unknown

Early stages: Unknown

Adult: Distinguished by the broad white medial bands set against the blue and brown of the upperside; a very distinctive field character.

Habits: This rare endemic subspecies occurs from 300 to 900 m on the Pacific slope, in the transition zone to tropical moist forest near Atenas-San Mateo. Encountered as rare, solitary individuals from January to April along forest and riparian edges. Both sexes visit flowers of *Cordia, Croton*, and *Lantana*. It appears that this species is restricted to a specialized habitat that is one of the most endangered by agriculture in all of Costa Rica. While the small patches of habitat remain, a study of this species would certainly repay the efforts involved.

Genus **ANARTIA** Hübner, 1819

The four species in this genus are recognized by their medium size, undulate hindwing margins, and a small bumplike tail on the hindwing tornus. The genus ranges from the southern United States throughout Central and South America and the West Indies. Two species occur in Central America north of the Darien Peninsula of Panama, and a third, *A. amathea*, replaces *A. fatima* in South America. The fourth species is endemic to the island of Hispaniola in the Caribbean.

Hostplants are in the Acanthaceae, and perhaps Verbenaceae and Scrophulariaceae. The larvae are spiny and show a similarity to *Siproeta* (Silberglied et al. 1979). In Central America the genus is common everywhere that forest cover is absent, and is found in forest areas only along rivers. *Anartia* is certainly one of the first genera of butterflies a visitor will see when entering the Neotropics for the first time, and the biology of Costa Rican and Panamanian species has been intensively studied (see Silberglied et al. 1979).

Anartia fatima

Godart, 1820

FW Length: 27-30 mm **Plate 28**

Range: Southern United States through Central America to eastern Panama

Hostplant: *Blechum, Justicia, Dicliptera, Ruellia* (Acanthaceae)

Early stages: (Silberglied et al. 1979) *Egg*—yellowish green, variably ribbed, laid singly. *Mature larva*—body black with reddish brown spots and spines; body covered with finely branched spines; head capsule black has two straight, knobbed horns with fine spines on the shaft. *Pupa*—translucent jade green, spindle shaped and without protuberances, and a few dark spots.

Adult: Distinguished by the white or cream bands traversing both wings on the upperside. *Note*: this condition is variable (Aiello and Silberglied 1978*b*).

Habits: In Costa Rica this species is very common in all disturbed habitats from sea level to 1,500 m on both slopes. In extensive tracts of forest it occurs as small populations in landslips or along riparian edges, suggesting that individuals may disperse over long distances. Both sexes are active throughout the day, and visit a great variety of second growth flowers while there is direct sunshine. The males perch on low vegetation and, from late morning until early afternoon, chase other males and females. The females oviposit with greatest frequency during midday, but will lay eggs from late morning until early afternoon if they have direct sunshine. This species is often found with bird and lizard beak marks, and also forms the diet of a great many anthropod predators in second-growth areas (Silberglied et al. 1979). Even though the adults only live for about two weeks under field conditions, it is certainly the commonest butterfly in Costa Rica and most of Central America, present throughout the year. Due to the transient nature of their favored habitats (human-caused disturbance), populations can become extremely abundant and then undergo radical local extinctions. In Guanacaste during the dry season, most females are in reproductive diapause, but along rivers they are reproductive. The color variation of the bands on the dorsal wing surface has been treated from different viewpoints, and it appears that part of the yellow-white polymorphism is due to genetic causes (and is subject to both natural and sexual selection), and in part is due to aging (see Silberglied et al. 1979 for review).

Anartia jatrophae

(Linnaeus, 1763)

FW Length: 28-30 mm **Plate 28**

Range: Southern United States through Central and South America and the West Indies

Hostplant: *Blechum, Ruellia* (Acanthaceae); *Lippia* (Verbenaceae); *Bacopa, Lindernia* (Scrophulariaceae)

Early stages: Undescribed

Adult: Distinguished by the whitish-gray upperside with golden hindwing margins. There is a great variability in the reddish on the underside, which depends on seasonality and habitat.

Habits: Commonly occurs from sea level to 1,200 m on both slopes in the same habitats as *A. fatima*, but is seldom as abundant. Areas of high abundance do occur on the Pacific slopes in association with costal lowland rain forest. The behavior and ecology is similar to that of *A. fatima* except that it flies a bit faster, and is apparently better at persisting after the open areas grow over than is *fatima*. This is probably due to its wider hostplant spectrum (Silberglied et al. 1979).

Genus **VANESSA** Fabricius, 1807

The genus *Vanessa* is found throughout the tropical and temperate regions of the world, and is composed of species that usually have enormous geographical distributions. In Costa Rica, the so-called "painted ladies" are recognized by their triangular wing shape, a reddish area on the forewing underside, and the presence of several blue ocelli on the hindwing underside. Two species occur in Central America.

The hostplants of *Vanessa* include Asteraceae, Urticaceae, Scrophulariaceae, and Malvaceae, of which Asteraceae is probably most important to the Central American species. The larvae are variably colored and bear many short spines of varying lengths on the body. The pupae are usually somber gray or brown and have flecks of reflective gold. Pupation usually takes place on the hostplant (in the United States), in a silken web or nest. The life histories for the Central American species are undescribed.

In southern Central America, the genus is restricted to montane regions and inhabits the highest mountain ranges. All species feed on flower nectar, and occasionally visit rotting fruits and dung. In the United States some species exhibit periodic migrations that result in yearly fluctuations of abundance; other species have been reported to migrate across open seas. Migrations are, however, unknown in the Central American species.

Vanessa virginiensis

(Drury, 1773)

FW Length: 26-29 mm **Plate 28**

Range: Southern Canada, through North America, Central American montane regions, montane Colombia, and the West Indies; Hawaiian Islands, Azores, Madeira and Canary Islands, and occasionally Europe, including Great Britain.

Hostplant: *Gnapthalium, Antennaria, Artemesia, Senecio* (Asteraceae); *Antirrhinnum* (Scrophulariaceae); *Malva* (Malvaceae)

Early stages: (Howe 1975) *Egg*—white, laid singly on all stages of the hostplant. *Mature larva*—body black with many short spines that are mostly black; head capsule black; dorsum cross-banded with narrow yellow bands; sides have a row of white spots. The larvae feed solitarily in a "nest" of spun silk that is usually near the top of the plant. Pupation may take place in this nest.

Adult: Distinguished from the very similar *V. cardui* by only having two prominent blue ocelli on the HW underside. See *V. cardui.*

Habits: Occurs uncommonly from 1,200 to over 3,000 m on both drainages, in association with open ground, roadsides, or pastures. Most frequently seen sitting on the ground with the wings pulsing open and shut. If disturbed, individuals fly very fast and erratically, and soon land on the ground again. Both sexes visit flowers of *Lantana, Asclepias,* and various roadside weeds. The males visit wet sand along rivers and in puddles, and occasionally rotting fruits and mammal dung. Although seldom abundant, this species is present throughout the year in all appropriate habitats.

Vanessa cardui

(Linnaeus, 1761)

FW Length: 28-31 mm **Plate 28**

Range: Everywhere on the continents in the temperate and tropical regions, except Australia and New Zealand

Hostplant: *Cirsium, Carduus, Centaurea, Arctium, Artemesia,* and other genera of the Asteraceae

Early stages: (Howe 1975) *Egg*—white, laid singly on all stages of hostplants. *Mature larva*—body yellow-green mottled with black; spines black except the lateral ones, which are yellowish; head capsule black. The larvae construct nests on various portions of the hostplant and feed in these structures. Pupation takes place within these nests.

Adult: Distinguished from *V. virginiensis* by having a row of four or more small blue ocelli on the HW underside (*virginiensis* has only two larger ocelli).

Habits: This species is rare in Costa Rican collections and occurs only on the highest mountain regions of the Talamancas or Cordillera Central. I have found it only in association with the Paramo vegetation in Parque Chirripo, where it occurs as uncommon solitary individuals. Its behavior is very similar to *V. virginiensis.* Activity is restricted to mornings when there is sunshine, usually only a few hours a day. It is unknown whether this species shows seasonal abundance, migration, or even if it is a resident of the Talamancas.

Genus **JUNONIA** Hübner, 1816

The butterflies in this genus are immediately recognized by the large eyespots on the upperside, which give them the common name of "the Buckeye." In many reference works the genus *Precis* has been applied to the New World species as well as the Old World species, but it is now generally considered that the American members are placed in *Junonia.* The genus is distributed from southern Canada throughout the United States, Central and South America, and most of the islands of the West Indies. It is unknown exactly how many species there are, and as pointed out by Harvey (1985), much remains to be done in unraveling the puzzle of what constitutes a species.

The genus has been reported to feed on a variety of hostplant families that includes Plataginaceae, Onagraceae, Scrophulariaceae, Verbenaceae, Crassulaceae, and Rhizophoraceae. It may turn out that the species-level taxonomy will follow lines of hostplant relationships. The larvae are generally black with many short, finely branching spines, and a pair of spines on the head capsule; the larvae apparently show good species characters (Harvey 1985). The pupae are similar in morphology to *Vanessa.*

The adults all feed on nectar, and males visit mud. There are records indicating that the species migrate (Williams 1930). In Costa Rica (and Central America in general) it is unknown exactly how many species there are, and the problem deserves study. The butterflies are most often found along the coastlines and in pastures.

Junonia evarete

(Cramer, 1782)

FW Length: 26-29 mm **Plate 28**

Range: Southern United States throughout the American tropics

Hostplant: Reported on Verbenaceae of various genera but unknown in Costa Rica

Early stages: Unknown due to the problems at the species level

Adult: Distinguished by the orange upperside and the two prominent ocelli. There appears to be considerable variation between wet- and dry-season forms; some have more distinct markings than others. However, it may be that there are two or more species in our area (*coenia* and *incarnata*), since there appear to be two types of males: one with pale antennal tips, the other with dark antennal tips. The confusion is compounded by the fact that the females are apparently identical in several species known in the United States. The populations in Costa Rica need to have a careful comparison made of their early stages and then a comparison of the adult behaviors.

Habits: Occurs commonly from sea level to 1,200 m on both slopes, only in association with disturbed habitats that have bare ground. As a consequence, this species is most commonly found in Pacific slope cattle pastures and along beaches. The flight is very fast and erratic, and individuals are difficult to catch.

Genus **HYPOLIMNAS**
Hübner, 1819

This essentially Old World genus is represented in the Neotropics by a single species that may have been introduced by the slave trade from West Africa and the West Indies (Corbet et al. 1978). The reasoning for this is simple: in all Old World countries where *Hypolimnas* occurs, the females are close mimics of the danaine model *Danaus chrysippus*. In the New World there is no model that closely resembles *Hypolimnas*, and they still look like the Old World *D. chrysippus*. The single species occurring in our area has dimorphic sexes: the palpi are projected forward into a beak, and have an undulating hindwing margin. It is found sporadically from as far north as New York, along the coast of Central America, South America, and the West Indies.

The hostplants of the single species occurring in the New World are exceedingly varied (Vane-Wright et al. 1977) and include Convolvulaceae, Malvaceae, Acanthaceae, Amaranthaceae, Portulacaceae, Moraceae, and Arecaceae. The larvae are dark and have numerous finely branched spines and a pair of longer spines on the head. The pupa is angular with a dorsal row of pointed processes on the abdomen. The early instars in general show affinities to *Junonia* and *Vanessa*.

There are very few records of this species from Central America, but it appears that in some years there may be local abundance because of migrations. Although in Africa the species is known to show highly distorted sex ratios and very rapid population increases in the rainy season (Smith 1976), these aspects of their biology are unstudied in the New World.

Hypolimnas misippus
(Linnaeus, 1764)

FW Length: male 35-38 mm, female 40-46 mm **Plate 28**

Range: Pantropical and occasionally North America

Hostplant: Convolvulaceae in the New World

Early stages: The larvae are gregarious; body black with gray bands and many finely branched, whitish spines; head capsule reddish or black with two prominent spines. *Pupa*—pale brown with a row of dorsal tubercles.

Adult: Sexes strikingly dimorphic. *Male*—blackish purple with four prominent white spots on the upperside, one on each wing. *Female*—dull orange above with a black FW apex and a white apical band.

Habits: This species is known from Costa Rica by a single specimen collected in the Atlantic lowlands at Cairo, Limon Province, by Charles Lankester (1918). This specimen is the female illustrated on Plate 28. G. Small informs me that occasionally he has seen small migrations of this species in Panama near the Canal Zone.

Genus **EUPTOIETA**
Doubleday, 1848

This genus is composed of two wide-ranging species that are distributed throughout the Americas and West Indies. The genus is recognized by the large eyes, blocky wing shape, and orange ground color. This genus is closely allied to *Argynnis* of the Old World and *Speyeria* of the New World, and forms a transition to the Heliconiinae, both in adult and early stage morphology.

The hostplants recorded for *Euptoieta* are varied and include Violaceae, Turneraceae, and Passifloraceae. These familes are chemically similar, and support the idea that *Euptoieta* forms a transition between North American *Speyeria* and the Neotropical heliconiines. The larvae have short body spines, and short spines on the head. The pupae are somewhat angular, brightly colored, and have reflective gold on the wingpads and abdomen.

In Costa Rica and Central America, the genus is found from sea level to 3,000 m, but the two species seem to separate into lowland and highland habitats, without much in the middle. The adults are extremely wary and fast flying, feed on nectar and occasionally fresh mammal dung, and the males visit puddles.

Euptoieta hegesia hoffmanni
Comstock, 1944

FW Length: 30-34 mm **Plate 32**

Range: Southern United States throughout Central America and the West Indies. **Subspecies:** United States to Panama

Hostplant: *Turnera ulmnifolia* (Turneraceae)

Early stages: *Egg*—yellow, laid singly on seedlings to mature plants. *Mature larva*—body bright shiny red with many short, black, bristly spines in parallel rows; head capsule red without spines; dorsal and lateral lines silver, edged with black. *Pupa*—dull burgundy with reflective gold areas on the wingpads and abdomen; thorax and abdomen have numerous square protrusions. The larvae are frequently found wandering on the ground looking for a hostplant. This is especially true in Guanacaste during the beginning of the rainy season, when eggs have been laid on seedling plants.

Adult: Distinguished by the dull orange upperside and the brown dots on the HW upperside.

Habits: Occurs commonly from sea level to 1,200 m, on both slopes, in association with open ground choked with weeds, especially in cattle pastures. Both sexes are active from early morning until late afternoon while there is bright sunshine. They fly very fast and nervously, flitting in a zigzag course, across the tops of low vegetation, and often interacting with the butterflies *Anartia* and *Junonia*. Both sexes visit flowers of *Lantana, Stachytarpheta,* and *Turnera*. According to Brown and Heineman (1972), this species is apparently migratory in Mexico and the southern United States. This requires confirmation in Costa Rica. Present throughout the year in all appropriate habitats.

Euptoieta claudia poasina
Schaus, 1913

FW Length: 26-31 mm **Plate 32**

Range: Canada throughout Central and South America and the West Indies. **Subspecies:** Costa Rican and Panamanian mountaintops(?)

Hostplant: *Viola* (Violaceae); *Passiflora* (Passifloraceae)

Early stages: The Costa Rican subspecies has never been reared, and the hostplant and early stages are unknown. The following description pertains to North American populations. *Mature larva*—body shiny red with a pair of long, blunt spines immediately behind the head; remainder of body spines shorter and of staggered length; dorsal midline composed of white rectangles; lateral lines composed of small white spots; dorsum flecked with white spots.

Adult: Distinguished by the dull, washed-out orange upperside that is densely marked with brown lines and spots; underside has a dull wash on HW.

Habits: This rare Costa Rican species is known from very few specimens, all taken between 2,000 and 2,500 m, and known only from Volcan Poas and associated mountains. I have seen it alive only once in an open pasture above Zarcero, where it behaved like *E. hegesia*. When at rest, the underside coloration renders the insect very cryptic. It is not known whether the populations in Costa Rica are the same "species" as *E. bogatana* Staudinger from Colombia. In the United States, this butterfly migrates from the southern states northward into Canada, but a return migration is unknown.

Subfamily **ACRAEINAE**

The butterflies in this entirely tropical subfamily are small- to medium-sized; they have sparsely scaled antennae with well-developed flattened antennal clubs; both wing cells are closed by tubular veins, and they generally have a roundly elongate forewing. The Acraeinae includes five or six genera, with greatest diversity in Africa. The Neotropics has a single genus that contains approximately fifty species and over one hundred subspecies. The systematics of the Neotropical acraeines has not been studied since Jordan's (1913) treatment. Although the subfamily is quite diverse in South America, there are only a few species in Central America, none of which presents problems in identification.

The hostplants of the Acraeinae are predominantly the Passifloraceae in the Old World and the Asteraceae in the Neotropics. The eggs are usually yellow and laid in large clusters. The larvae are tubular with six or more rows of short bristly spines, and recall the genus *Chlosyne* in appearance (Fig. 25). Certain Neotropical species have mildly urticating properties to sensitive human skin. The pupae are similar to those of *Chlosyne* and are usually pale yellow whitish in color, highlighted by black lines.

The adult acraeines are involved in extensive Müllerian and Batesian mimicry complexes, and are probably the most important models for the African butterfly faunas. In the Neotropics the acraeines are also involved in mimicry, but to a lesser extent than in the Old World. All acraeines have tough rubbery bodies, fly with a slow fluttery flight, and some of the African species are known to secrete cyanide (Rothschild 1972; Narhstedt and Davis 1981; see also Müller 1879). All of these characteristics are typical of a warningly colored, distasteful butterfly. Although there has been much attention paid to the African species within the last century, very little has been done with the Neotropical species regarding their biology and aposematic properties. One of the African species (*Acraea encedon*) is known to produce entirely female populations: all eggs develop into females. See Owen (1966) and Owen and Chanter (1969) for a discussion of the genetics and the population biology. One further aspect of African acraeines is that a number of them are clearly migratory as the seasons change (see Owen 1971). Although at present little is known about the adult biology of most Neotropical Acraeinae, it seems highly probable that many of the phenomena known from studies on African *Acraea* will eventually prove to be similar in *Actinote*.

Genus **ACTINOTE** Hübner, 1816

This entirely Neotropical genus is closely allied to the large Old World genus *Acraea*, but is separated by characters of the legs, venation, and scaling (Jordan 1913). *Actinote* species are recognized by the roundly elongate wing shape, flattened antennal club, and dark wing venation that is especially noticeable on the hindwing. *Actinote* ranges from Mexico through Central and South America, and includes a few species on the islands of Trinidad and Tobago. There are many species and forms known from the eastern slope of the Andes and the Amazon Basin in South America, but only five species occur in Costa Rica.

The hostplants apparently include *Boehmeria (Urticaceae)* and *Eupatorium, Vernonia, Mikania (Asteraceae)*, of which *Mikania* is most important for the Central American species. The larvae are densely spiny, without spines on the head capsule, and in general dull colored (Fig. 25). The larvae of all species appear to be gregarious until the last instar, when the group breaks up. The pupae are generally chalky white or yellow with black wing veins, spots, and spines on the abdomen. Of interest is that the early stages are virtually identical to those of the African genus *Acraea*.

The adults in Costa Rica are found from sea level to the highest areas on the Cordillera de Talamanca, and all our species have a conspicuously slow, fluttery flight. Although expressed very little in Central America, mimicry is extremely important in the South American species. On the eastern slope of the Andes, *Actinote* fits into mimicry complexes with heliconiines, ithomiines, and with apparent Batesian mimics such as *Castilia* and *Eresia*. Simple field observations suggest that *Actinote* is chemically defended from predators. The body is rubbery and resistant to crushing, some species exude brown (or green) drops of liquid from the thorax when handled, and in general most species have an evil smell. Although the chemistry of how they derive their defenses is unknown, the hostplants are all within a section of Asteraceae that contains pyrolizidine alkaloids. One of our species (*A. lapitha*) has been demonstrated to be distasteful to caged jacamars (P. Chai, personal communication). Little is known about their population biology and how long individuals may live, and these aspects are in need of study. In Costa Rica, most of the species are very local and show great abundance during certain times of the year. All of the species fly in open areas in bright sunlight, and are usually associated with disturbed habitats.

Actinote leucomelas

(Bates, 1864)

FW Length: male 24-28 mm, female 28-33 mm **Plate 32**

Range: Mexico to Panama

Hostplant: *Mikania* (Asteraceae)

Early stages: *Egg*—yellow, barrel-shaped, laid in clusters of 50 to 100. *Mature larva*—ground color dull olive-green; many fine black spines cover the body; head capsule shiny black. The

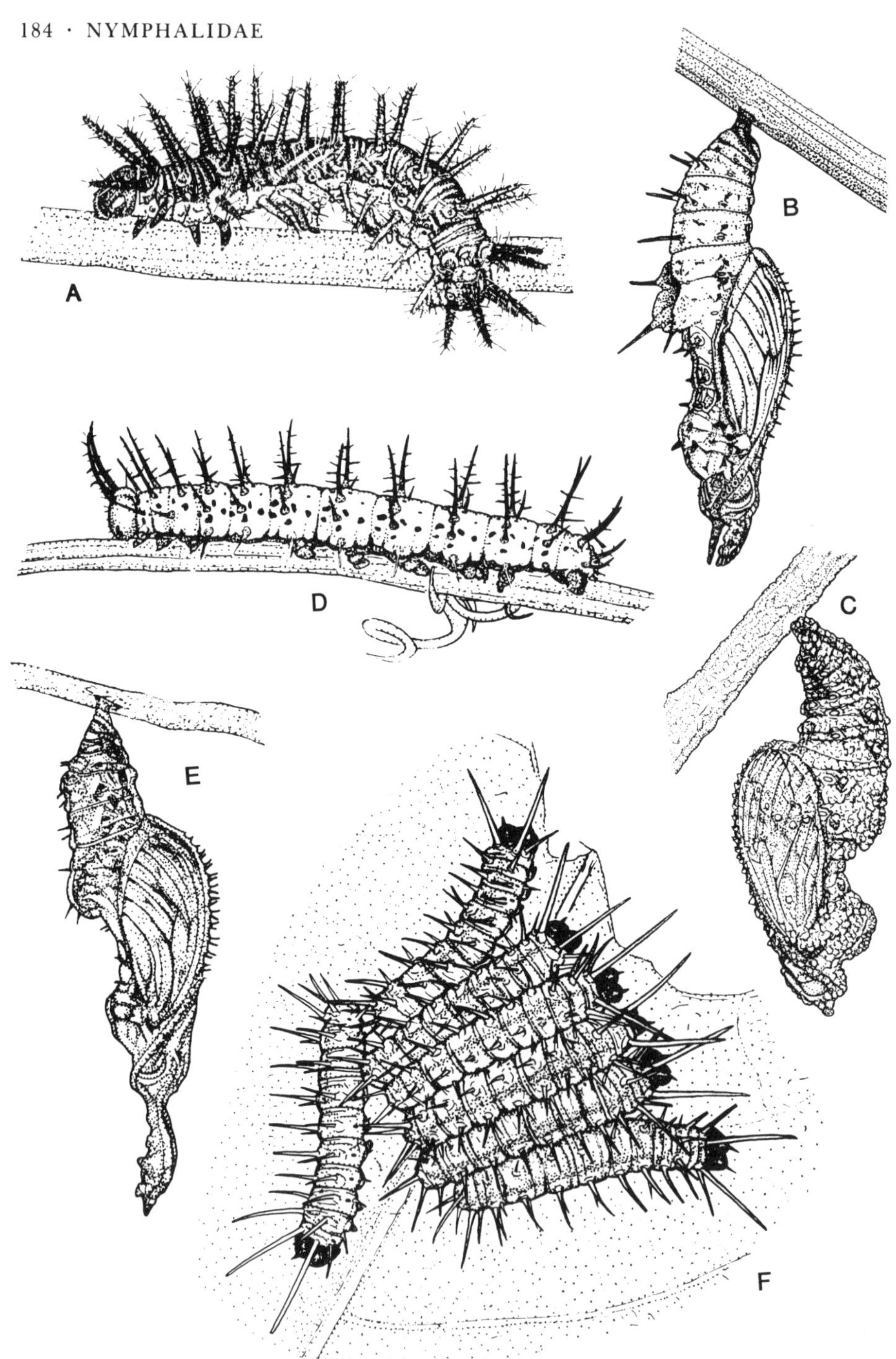

FIGURE 25. Larvae and pupae of the Nymphalidae: Acraeinae and Heliconiinae. A: *Actinote anteas* fifth instar; B: *Heliconius sara* pupa; C: *Dione juno* pupa; D: *Heliconius erato* fifth instar; E: *Heliconius erato* pupa; F: *Heliconius hewitsoni* fifth instars (drawings by J. Clark).

larvae are very gregarious and, in many instances, totally defoliate numerous hostplants in large areas. The later instars are frequently found wandering, looking for food. *Pupa*—chalky white with fine black striations on wingpads; a double row of short black spines on the thorax and abdomen; black cremaster.

Adult: Sexes dimorphic. *Male*—inky black on upperside; FW underside has a yellow-white area in the cell. *Female*—larger than the male and with much more streaking on the underside; the FW upperside has yellow in the cell.

Habits: Occurs from 700 to 3,000 m on both slopes in association with cloud forest habitats, and is especially common in disturbed forest. Most frequently found along forest edges in abundant local populations. The flight is distinctly fluttery and, in combination with the color pattern, provides an excellent field identification mark. On the Pacific slope this species is most abundant during the dry season, when individuals are familiar sights in the streets of Jan José. On the Atlantic slope, although it is most abundant in dry seasons, it is present throughout the year. Courtship usually takes place at *Inga* flowers in the canopy, where at times hundreds of individuals swarm over the blossoms. Males hover over a female and the female responds by either fluttering about in a dance with the male, or by closing her wings, dropping through the air, and escaping his courtship. In addition to *Inga*, both sexes visit a variety of roadside weeds in the Asteraceae. If provided sufficient hostplants, *A. leucomelas* does well in the insectary and should prove to be a useful species for laboratory studies (see Harvey 1983).

Actinote anteas

(Doubleday, 1847)

FW Length: male 26-31 mm, female 32-35 mm **Plate 32**

Range: Mexico to Venezuela

Hostplant: *Mikania* (Asteraceae)

Early stages: *Mature larva*—black and dark brown at the base of the many black spines; some yellowish striation on the sides; head capsule shiny black (Fig. 25). *Pupa*—similar to *A. leucomelas* but yellower and less chalky.

Adult: Distinguished by the orange ground color and the very fine black striations on the HW upperside. See *Eueides vibilia.*

Habits: Occurs from 400 to 1,500 m on both slopes, in association with disturbed forest habitats and old second-growth forest. Commonly found visiting flowers of *Lantana* and *Asclepias* along forest edges and in pastures. Most common during the dry seasons, and most frequently encountered on the Pacific slope of the Meseta Central.

Actinote guatemalena

(Bates, 1864)

FW Length: male 26-30 mm, female 28-33 mm **Plate 32**

Hostplant: Unknown

Range: Guatemala to Costa Rica

Early stage: Unknown

Adult: Distinguished by the broad black FW apex and reduced yellow band at the subapex; FW cell has a tiny black spot; HW discal area pale orange with many fine black striations. Compare with *A. anteas* and *A. melampeplos.*

Habits: This rare species is known only from the Atlantic drainage in association with rain forest habitats. I have seen this butterfly only in local populations at Finca la Selva in second-growth areas. Like most *Actinote* species, it has a weak fluttery flight, and is associated with *Lantana* and other open-area weedy flowers. It is unknown whether this species and *A. melampeplos* are the same; the early stages should provide important information.

Actinote melampeplos

Godman and Salvin, 1881

FW Length: male 24-26 mm, female 28-32 mm **Plate 32**

Range: Costa Rica to Ecuador

Hostplant: Unknown

Early stages: Unknown

Adult: Very similar to *guatemalena* but distinguished from it by being more transluscent, almost pale yellow on the HW disc; the FW subapical band apparently does not reach the costa; black striations around the HW cell are more pronounced. See *A. guatemalena.*

Habits: From the few specimens I have seen in museums, it appears that this species is confined to the Atlantic slope, from sea level to about 600 m elevation, but I have never seen it alive. It is unknown if it is biologically distinct from *guatemalena.*

Actinote lapitha

(Staudinger, 1885)

FW Length: 23-28 mm **Plate 32**

Range: Costa Rica and Western Panama

Hostplant: *Mikania riparia* (Asteraceae)

Early stages: *Mature larva*—dull yellow-orange; dorsum has many black branched spines; base of the spines chitinous brown; head capsule dark brown and densely spined (unlike other species); there is a faint lateral black line on the body. The larvae are semigregarious and very sluggish. *Pupa*—suspended; body pale cream with black veins on the wingpads and two rows of short black spines on the abdomen; cremaster black.

Adult: Distinguished by the pale, semi-translucent yellow ground color and black striations.

Habits: Occurs from sea level to 300 m on the Pacific slope, in association with the rain forest habitats centered around the Osa Peninsula. Occurs only in open areas that have been clear-cut for cattle pastures, and does not enter the forest or old second growth. Very rare in Costa Rican collections, but local populations can be very abundant during February-March and sometimes into June, although absent the remainder of the year. Both sexes visit flowers of *Lantana* and sit for long periods of time on the blossoms, with their wings open. The flight is almost ridiculously slow. Caged jacamars will not eat either sex, even if the birds are in a state of starvation.

Subfamily **HELICONIINAE**

Except for some Old World genera such as *Cethosia*, the Heliconiinae is composed of almost entirely Neotropical species. All of the species are brightly colored, well collected, and represent one of the most studied groups of butterflies in the world. The systematics of the group have remained essentially unchanged since the generic revision of Michener (1942) and the later analysis by Emsley (1963, 1964). Extensive bibliographies and reviews are found in Turner (1977) and Brown (1981) that cover both systematics and biology. The heliconiines are recognized by the elongate forewing, large eyes, and long antennae. They are distributed from the southern United States throughout Central and South America and the West Indies, with the greatest diversity found in the Amazon Basin of Peru and Brazil. There are currently about seventy species recognized, twenty-four of which occur in Costa Rica.

The hostplants for the subfamily are almost exclusively in the Passifloraceae, and to a limited extent, in the Turneraceae. The restricted hostplant relationships have given rise to the name "passion flower butterflies." The close association of heliconiines and Passifloraceae has been instrumental in refining thoughts on coevolution between insects and plants (Gilbert 1975, Benson et al. 1976), and in assessing the roles of plant defenses against herbivores (Gilbert 1971). These ecological studies show that subgroups within the heliconiines tend to feed on subgroups within the Passifloraceae. For example, using Killip (1938) for subgroups in the Passifloraceae, Benson et al. (1976) showed that members of the *sappho* group of *Heliconius* tend to feed on the *Astrophea* group of *Passiflora*, and also show attendant behaviors, feeding damage, and adult morphologies. Likewise, other closely related heliconiines were shown to exhibit patterns of relationships to the Passifloraceae.

The larvae of all heliconiines are spiny, have two spines on the head capsule, and feed either solitarily or gregariously. Many species have irritant spines that probably deter predators (Fig. 25). This latter point is interesting, since some people break out in a rash if they handle *Heliconius* larvae, others do not. The placement of eggs by ovipositing females is correlated with systematic subdivisions within the Heliconiinae: some lay single eggs on tendrils, stipules, leaf tips, or leaves, whereas others lay egg masses, and only on old leaves. Such oviposition behavior is thought to have influenced the leaf shape in *Passiflora* (Gilbert 1975) and given rise to egg mimics produced on the stipules of some *Passiflora* species. These plant-evolved egg mimics inhibit ovipositing females from using the plant for oviposition. Although the species group of *Passiflora* that produces the egg mimics occurs in Costa Rica, in our area these species do not express this characteristic.

The pupae of the heliconiines are spiny in so-called advanced groups and nonspiny in the primitive groups (Fig. 25). They are suspended either with the body held horizontal to the pupation substrate or with the body vertical.

The brightly colored adults are conspicuous components of virtually all Neotropical habitats below the paramo vegetation type, and are found in all microhabitats in tropical forests, although most are clearly more abundant in second growth and disturbed forest. All species feed on flower nectar, and the genus *Heliconius* is the only group of butterflies demonstrated to have developed a highly specialized pollen-feeding behavior. Unlike most butterflies, *Heliconius* is able to utilize the nutrients in pollen in addition to nectar (Gilbert 1972). The pollen-feeding behavior centers around a group of vines in the Cucurbitaceae, *Psiguria* and *Gurania*. Since these vines flower continuously over many years and produce mostly male flowers, it has been suggested that the vines utilize *Heliconius* as major pollinators. In essence, the adult heliconiines are as tightly associated with a restricted set of hostplants as the larvae are. This close association between adults and pollen sources allows an investigator to assess accurately how many species of heliconiines are in a habitat simply by first finding *Psiguria* flowers, and then waiting for the heliconiine species to arrive. This simple technique has proved enormously useful for studying population biology of *Heliconius* (Ehrlich and Gilbert 1973), and has led to advances in our knowledge of community ecology (Gilbert 1984) and population dynamics of tropical butterflies (Ehrlich 1984).

Impressed by the great diversity and apparent similarity of heliconiine species, Henry Bates (1862) was able to formulate portions of his famous theory of mimicry. Today, the heliconiines still provide rich ground for testing mimicry theory and genetics (Benson 1972; Turner 1971, 1984; Gilbert 1983) and for the development of refugia theory to explain race formation during the Pleistocene glaciation (Brown et al. 1974). The refugia theory is particularly popular among biogeographers, and has generated much research in biogeography and systematics (see Brown 1981 for review). However, it is of interest that the essential details of this theory were proposed over a century ago by Thomas Belt (1874). Although it is known that some heliconiines are distasteful to birds, and that this factor certainly must drive the evolution of certain mimicry complexes, there is no hard chemical evidence that the butterflies derive their defenses from their hostplants. In fact, it appears that the defenses are manufactured by the adults by as of yet, unknown means (Nahrstedt and Davis 1981, 1983). It is clear that heliconiines will provide many interesting questions for the next century, as they have for the past.

Studies on the physiology of heliconiines have revealed that they have exceptionally good eyesight and are able to learn by color association (Swihart 1971; Swihart and Swihart 1970). This explains why a free-flying heliconiine is able to home in on a small *Psiguria* flower in the rain forest canopy. Other studies have shown that nutrients in the pollen diet of *Heliconius* are used for egg production and maintenance of ovaries (Dunlap-Pianka et al. 1977; Dunlap-Pianka 1979), and that females are able to use male spermatophores to nourish egg development, and hence mate a number of times.

Many heliconiines roost gregariously. The roosts are composed of many individuals of the same species, occasionally with some of other mimetic species, and the individuals return every night to the same spot to sleep. The roosting habit has provided yet another means by which to study heliconiine biology (Benson et al. 1976, Waller and Gilbert 1982), but why they roost is unknown. The most widely held theory is that it is advantageous to roost gregariously if all the members of the roost are distasteful, but this is far from well studied and documented.

Genus **PHILAETHRIA** Billberg, 1820

There are apparently three species in this genus, all of which are recognized by the green pattern on the upperside and the typical heliconiine elongate forewing. The genus ranges from Mexico throughout Central and South America, with all three species represented in the Amazon Basin and one in Central America.

The genus feeds on several subgroups of the genus *Passiflora*, and the larvae utilize the older leaves in all instars. The larvae appear very much like *Heliconius*, but the pupae lack spines and resemble a bird dropping. The utilization of old leaves by the larvae, the pupal morphology, and the morphology of the adult place *Philaethria* as the most primitive member of the heliconiines.

The adults are almost entirely restricted to the forest canopy, and do not feed on pollen. Conversely, adults are occasionally seen visiting fresh mammal dung, a trait not seen in other heliconiines.

Philaethria dido
(Linnaeus, 1763)

FW Length: 49-54 mm **Plate 31**

Range: Mexico to the Amazon Basin

Hostplant: *Passiflora vitifolia, P. edulis, P. ambigua* (Passifloraceae)

Early stages: (Young 1974*b*) *Egg*—laid singly on the underside of older leaves, usually on plants growing along the ground level. *Mature larva*—body pale green with blackish red marking on the dorsum and sides; dorsal and lateral spines red with an orange base, and some with black tips; head capsule shiny beige with two prominent head spines. *Pupa*—mottled brown and gray, covered with warts; abdomen and thorax have keels; generally resembles a bird dropping or a splinter of wood.

Adult: Immediately distinguished by the green markings with dark brown wing margins. Compare with *Siproeta stelenes*.

Habits: Occurs from sea level to 1,200 m (in some areas), on both slopes, in association with rain forest habitats. The adults are rarely seen because they fly above the forest canopy. The females are most often collected because they descend at midday to oviposit along edges and in light gaps. The flight is fast and agile, often in a zigzag path across the canopy. Both sexes visit flowers of *Cissus* and other canopy plants. Although seldom seen, this species is a frequent member of the butterfly fauna in all lowland rain forest habitats in Costa Rica.

Genus **DRYADULA** Michener, 1942

The genus is recognized by having shorter and broader wings than other heliconiines, comparatively short antennae, and an androconial patch in the males. The genus ranges from Mexico throughout Central and South America, and is composed of a single species.

The early stages and hostplant affinities are not well known. The larvae look, in general, like those described for *Dione*, with slightly larger head horns. The genus is an inhabitant of disturbed areas in the lowlands, and is seldom found in association with forests. The butterflies do not collect pollen loads as in other heliconiines, and individuals are in general uncommon.

Dryadula phaetusa

(Linnaeus, 1758)

FW Length: 40-41 mm **Plate 31**

Range: Mexico to Brazil

Hostplant: *Passiflora talamacensis* (Passifloraceae)

Early stages: *Mature larva*—body dull purple with many short bristly spines; head capsule dark purple with two semi-knobbed head horns.

Adult: Immediately distinguished by the broad black HW margin and discal bar.

Habits: Occurs infrequently from sea level to 1,200 m in open areas throughout Costa Rica. On the wing, this species can be confused with *Danaus*, and both visit *Asclepias* flowers. Occasionally found to roost gregariously at night, but in general little is known about its habits, palatability, or general biology.

Genus **DIONE** Hübner, 1818

The butterflies in this genus are recognized by the orange upperside, reflective silver spots on the underside, and the shape of the antennal club. The genus ranges from the United States throughout the mainland and island Neotropics. In Central America there are two very widespread species.

The hostplants are all members of the Passifloraceae. *Dione* is able to utilize a great number of species and subgroups of *Passiflora*. The eggs are laid in large rafts on old leaves, and the larvae can be agricultural pests in passion flower farms. The larvae are almost unicolored, spiny, and gregarious feeders. The pupae are not spined, and in general are dull and cryptic (Fig. 25).

In Costa Rica, the adults are found in virtually every habitat, from primary rain forest to pasture and the high montane paramo. They all fly in bright sunshine and seem to flourish in the aftermath of complete deforestation. The adults feed on flower nectar but do not collect pollen loads.

Dione juno

(Cramer, 1779)

FW Length: 35-40 mm **Plate 31**

Range: Throughout Central and South America and the Lesser Antilles

Hostplant: *Passiflora vitifolia, P. alata, P. platyloba, P. edulis* (Passifloraceae)

Early stages: (Muyshondt et al. 1973) *Egg*—bright yellow, eventually turning dark red, laid in large clusters on old leaves, petioles, and stems. *Mature larva*—body mottled light brown, covered with short bristly spines; head capsule dark brown with two short head horns. Larvae feed gregariously and show synchronization of molts. *Pupa*—dark brown with a darker brown cremaster and spiracles; wingpads strongly bowed, with an indentation between abdomen and thorax (Fig. 25).

Adult: Distinguished from similar species by the excavated FW margin; FW upperside has a dark bar across the cell; HW upperside has dark margins. See *D. moneta* and *Agraulis vanillae*.

Habits: Occurs from sea level to 1,200 m on both slopes, usually in association with open areas and disturbed habitats, but also found in primary rain forest areas, in the canopy. Flies in bright sunshine, usually with *D. moneta, Dryas iulia*, and *Agraulis vanillae*. These four species often swirl together around flowers, either at ground level or in the canopy. On the Pacific slope, *D. juno* is persistent throughout the year but most abundant during the rainy season. On the Atlantic slope, it is most often seen during periods of dry weather, and is usually not as abundant except where the host plant is grown commercially.

Dione moneta poeyii
Butler, 1873
FW Length: 35-38 mm **Plate 31**
Range: Southern United States throughout Central and South America. **Subspecies:** Central America
Hostplant: *Passiflora adenopoda, P. capsularis, Tetrastylis lobata* (Passifloraceae)
Early stages: *Egg*—yellow turning dark red, laid singly. *Mature larva*—body dark brown with many orange and gray spots; body covered with short bristly spines; head capsule dark brown with horns, as in *D. juno. Pupa*—similar to *D. juno.*
Adult: Distinguished from similar species by having much more silver on the underside; upperside has dark bases and medial area on FW. Compare with *Agraulis vanillae.*
Habits: Occurs sporadically from sea level to 500 m, and commonly from 500 to over 3,500 m, on both slopes. A fast flier found as solitary individuals in open areas, in bright sunshine. Both sexes visit a wide variety of flowers that range from roadside weeds to canopy trees. On the wing it is easily confused with *Agraulis vanillae*, but is distinguished by the greater number of silver spots on the underside and a faster flight. The enormous geographical and altitudinal range of this species is undoubtedly due to its migratory habits (see Gilbert 1969*b*).

Genus **AGRAULIS** Boisduval and LeConte, 1833

There is a single species in this genus, which is closely allied to *Dione* but separated by a sexual dimorphism in wing venation, by the hindwing margin that is not undulate, and by the presence of scaling on the femora of the mid- and hind legs. In much of the literature, *Agraulis* is made synonymous with *Dione*. The genus ranges from the southern United States throughout Central and South America and the West Indies.

The hostplants appear to be those species of *Passiflora* that are not used by many other species of heliconiines. The larvae are very similar to *Dione*. The adults visit flowers but do not collect pollen loads.

Agraulis vanillae
(Linnaeus, 1758)
FW Length: 31-38 mm **Plate 31**
Range: Southern United States throughout the Neotropics
Hostplant: *Passiflora foetida, P. quadrangularis, P. ligularis, P. costaricensis, P. auriculata* (Passifloraceae)
Early stages: All stages are very similar to *Dione moneta*, but the larva varies in body color from gray to black.
Adult: Distinguished from similar species by the two silvery spots in the FW cell and the triangular shape of the HW; few silver spots on HW underside. Compare with *Dione juno.*
Habits: Occurs from sea level to 1,400 m in all open areas, disturbed habitats, and montane rain shadows. Often found in the presence of *D. juno* and *D. moneta*, which it resembles in appearance and habits.

Genus **DRYAS** Hübner, 1807

Recognized by the elongate wing shape and the bright orange upperside, the single species in this genus is widespread and common from the southern United States throughout all the Neotropics. The larvae and pupae have an appearance somewhat intermediate between *Heliconius* and *Dione*. In Costa Rica, the larvae feed on various subgroups in the Passifloraceae.

Dryas iulia
(Fabricius, 1775)
FW Length: 41-45 mm **Plate 31**
Range: Southern United States throughout the Neotropics
Hostplant: *Passiflora* species in the *Plectostemma* group, but also *Passiflora vitifolia* and *P. platyloba*
Early stages: (Beebe et al. 1960) *Egg*—laid singly, usually on tendrils and occasionally on associated vegetation. *Mature larva*—multicolored; generally beige body with variably red to dark brown patches on dorsum, which are finely dissected with black lines; dorsum covered with long bristly black spines and three pairs of white ones; spines denser on thorax; head capsule beige with variable amounts of black and reddish spotting; head horns fairly short but longer than head is high. *Pupa*—similar to *Dione juno* but with a few reflective spots, and generally more rounded shape.
Adult: Immediately distinguished by the orange upperside; black markings on FW and HW variable. A good field character is the distinctive fluttery "dragonflylike" flight.
Habits: Commonly occurs from sea level to 1,500 m, and less frequently from 1,500 to 1,800 m on both slopes in association with

open areas or in the forest canopy. Usually found along forest edges, flying about three meters from the ground, in association with the hostplants. Both sexes visit a wide variety of flowers that include herbs and canopy trees and vines. Adults are persistent and common throughout the year on the Pacific slope, and locally abundant throughout the year on the Atlantic slope: essentially a "weedy" species. The female may lay eggs on tendrils and leaves or even lay off the hostplant on the adjacent vegetation. Although very common, this species can be difficult to capture because of its alertness and rapid flight.

Genus **EUEIDES** Hübner, 1816

The butterflies in this genus are similar to *Heliconius* but are recognized by the smaller size, a relatively short body, and short antennae. The species exhibit mimicry, polymorphisms, and in a few species, sexual dimorphism. The genus ranges from Mexico through Central and South America and the West Indies. Most are found in the Amazon Basin, and of the six species in Central America, all occur in our area.

The hostplants are in the Passifloraceae and the Turneraceae, and include vines and trees. The larvae are similar to *Heliconius*, except that they are more colorful and feed only on mature leaves. The larvae are solitary in some species, gregarious in others, and seem to show indications of larval mimicry in at least one species. The pupae are highly distinctive, with four dorsal spines that are usually spread out into an X shape, and a strong curve to the abdomen that causes the suspended pupa to be held horizontally to the substrate.

In Costa Rica, all but one of the species are essentially canopy-flying insects and tend to live in localized populations near the hostplants. The color patterns show mimetic resemblance to tiger-striped species, *Heliconius* and *Actinote*, and others that seem to form mimicry complexes with *Dryas* and other *Eueides* species. In general there is little known about their adult biology.

Eueides aliphera

(Godart, 1819)

FW Length: 27-32 mm **Plate 31**

Range: Mexico to Brazil

Hostplant: *Passiflora oerstedi, P. vitifolia, P. auriculata* (Passifloraceae)

Early stages: (Beebe et al. 1960) *Egg*—laid singly. *Mature larva*—dorsum black covered with long, finely bristled spines; spines on posterior two-thirds of dorsum are black with whitish distal halves, while the remainder of spines are entirely black; side has a broad yellowish or pure white stripe that runs from head to anus; venter colorless; head capsule shiny black with white markings on face and sides, and two long, recurved head spines. *Pupa*—greenish white with black markings on the wingpads and short spines on dorsum that are tipped in black.

Adult: Distinguished from similar species by the small size, narrow black bar on the FW upperside, and fine black veins on the HW upperside. See *Dryas iulia* and *Eueides lineata*.

Habits: Occurs from sea level to 1,400 m on both slopes, in association with disturbed habitats adjacent to forests, or as a canopy species. Most frequently seen along forest edges visiting flowers of *Cissus, Lantana*, and other small red flowers; it is also a common canopy species in primary rain forest. The females descend to the ground at midday to oviposit, or will oviposit on canopy vines. In lowland Guanacaste this species is rare, probably because of its intolerance of a severe dry season.

Eueides lineata

Salvin, 1868

FW Length: 30-36 mm **Plate 31**

Range: Mexico to Panama

Hostplant: *Passiflora microstipula* (Passifloraceae)

Early stages: (Mallet and Longino 1982) *Egg*—greenish white, laid singly on the underside of mature leaves. (The hostplant of this species appears to be a *Passiflora* that is not eaten by any other heliconiine.) *Mature larva*—body white with four black and white transverse stripes on dorsum of each segment except segment 8, which is orange dorsally; sides are white with a black spiracle; the body is covered with black spines; the head capsule is orange, with black and white markings, and two prominent black head spines; venter colorless. *Pupa*—white with olive-green and brown markings, black spots on the spiracles and cremaster, and with the four typical *Eueides* anteriorly directed spines.

Adult: Distinguished from similar species by the dark black margins and FW bar on the upperside, and its small size. See *Dryas iulia* and *Eueides aliphera*.

Habits: Occurs as rare solitary individuals, from sea level to 1,600 m on both slopes, usually in association with cloud forest habitats, but occasionally in rain forest (as strays?). Flies along forest edges and in large light gaps, and is extremely similar to *E. aliphera* while on the wing. In general this species is rare in collections and appears to have a very patchy distribution.

Eueides lybia lybioides
(Fabricius, 1793)
Eueides lybia lybioides
Staudinger, 1876

FW Length: 29-31 mm **Plate 31**

Range: Nicaragua to the Amazon Basin. **Subspecies:** *olympia*—Atlantic slope from Nicaragua to Colombia; *lybioides*—Pacific slope of Costa Rica and Panama.

Hostplant: *Passiflora vitifolia* (Passifloraceae)

Early stages: *Mature larva*—similar to *E. aliphera* but distinguished from it by the almost solid black dorsum broken by white on the thorax and some round spots on the dorsal midline; the entire anal plate is white; all spines are black. *Pupa*—as in *E. aliphera.*

Adult: Distinguished from similar species by the heavy black FW apex and HW margins; *olympia* has the FW spot clear white, whereas *lybioides* has this same spot washed out and almost orange. See *E. lineata* and *E. aliphera.*

Habits: Occurs from sea level to 900 m on both slopes in association with rain forest habitats. The subspecies *olympia* is confined to the Atlantic slope and *lybioides* to the Pacific slope. Encountered most frequently along shady forest edges and in light gaps, flying 2 to 30 m above the ground. Both subspecies spend a large portion of their time flying above the forest canopy. Both sexes visit flowers of *Lantana, Cissus, Serjania, Psiguria,* and various canopy trees and shrubs. Both subspecies are known to sleep gregariously, although very little is known about their biology and population dynamics. One thing appears certain: this species is intolerant of large tracts of second growth vegetation and is rarely found flying in the direct sunlight of deforested areas.

Eueides vibilia vialis
Stichel, 1903

FW Length: 31-38 mm **Plate 31**

Range: Mexico to Brazil. **Subspecies:** Guatemala to Panama

Hostplant: *Passiflora pittieri* (Passifloraceae)

Early stages: (Mallet and Longino 1982) *Mature larva*—gregarious feeders with synchronous molts, feeding on old leaves that show skeletonized damage from the feeding of early instars; body is olive-green with black patches on the dorsum; a creamy yellow lateral line runs the entire length of the body; venter translucent yellow-green; all spines black; head capsule shiny black, with two head spines. *Note*: all stages up to fifth instar appear to mimic the gregarious larvae of *Heliconius hewitsoni*, and can be distinguished from them principally by having the head spines shorter and by the old-leaf feeding damage. *Pupa*—similar to *E. lineata* except that the dorsal four spines are roughly the same length.

Adult: Sexes dimorphic. *Male*—distinguished by heavy black FW with two broken yellow-orange bars; discal area of HW has no black venation; antennae black. *Female*—heavier black markings and black venation on the HW, mimicking *Actinote*. See *Eueides procula* and *Actinote anteas.*

Habits: Occurs from sea level to 800 m on both slopes, in association with all forest habitats except the lowland Guanacaste deciduous areas. This species is rare and has a very patchy distribution in Costa Rica, suggesting that it occurs in highly localized populations that exhibit pronounced seasonality. I have never seen more than one individual at a time in nature, and it is generally rare in collections.

Eueides procula vulgiformis
Butler and Druce, 1872

FW Length: 32-38 mm **Plate 31**

Range: Guatemala to Brazil. **Subspecies:** Costa Rica and Panama

Hostplant: *Erblichia odorata* (Turneraceae)

Early stages: (Janzen 1983*b*) *Egg*—yellowish green laid singly, or occasionally in loose clusters on the underside of old leaves. *Mature larva*—body grayish white with many black spots on the dorsum; covered in black spines that meet the body at black dots; penultimate segment orange-yellow dorsally; head capsule shiny black with white marks surrounding the bases of the two prominent head horns. Prepupa has a bright yellow body and white head capsule. *Pupa*—shaped as other *Eueides*; white overall, with black spots and black tips to abdominal spines; spines on head yellow-tipped.

Adult: Immediately distinguished from all similar species by the bright yellow antennae and the almost entirely black FW. See *Heliconius hecale* and *H. hecalesia.*

Habits: Occurs from sea level to 1,000 m on both slopes, in association with forest habitats. As in *E. vibilia*, this species is generally rare but it can be very common in localized populations where its hostplant occurs. For example, this species was not present for several years in Parque Santa Rosa; then one year it became very abundant in a small patch of forest where the hostplant is moderately abundant. The butterflies were frequent in this locality for several years but, since 1982, have greatly fluctuated in abundance. The adults glide in circles at the canopy level, usually above the hostplant, and engage in aerial dogfights. Both sexes visit flowers of *Lantana* and *Cissus*. This is the only true heliconiine known to feed on plants outside the Passifloraceae.

Eueides isabella

(Cramer, 1781)

FW Length: 37-42 mm **Plate 31**

Range: Mexico to the Amazon Basin and the West Indies. *Note*: there are various named forms of this species, and the tiger-striped form that occurs in Costa Rica is identical to the form that occurs throughout Central America and the West Indies (form zoracon)

Hostplant: *Passiflora platyloba, P. ambigua* (Passifloraceae)

Early stages: (Beebe et al. 1960) *Egg*—creamy white, laid singly, sometimes off the hostplant. *Mature larva*—similar to *E. aliphera* but differing as follows: yellow lateral body stripe; a conspicuous orange patch on segments 8 and 9; the dorsal markings are white narrow bands; head capsule entirely black, or with a few white spots, and head spines all black; body spines are all pale with a black base except for those on the posterior orange patch. *Pupa*—similar to *E. aliphera.*

Adult: Distinguished from similar species by the white dots on the upperside of the HW margin; FW upperside has an almost circular black dot near end of cell; antennae short. *Note*: the males usually have black antennae and the females yellow. In Costa Rica there are some populations in which the FW is almost entirely black. See *Heliconius ismenius, Melinaea lilis, Lycorea cleobaea.*

Habits: Commonly occurs from sea level to 1,500 m on both slopes, in association with forest habitats and second growth. Encountered as common, solitary individuals along forest edges, light gaps, and occasionally in open areas where there is high second-growth vegetation. Both sexes visit a wide variety of flowers ranging from ground level herbs to canopy trees and vines. A common visitor to garden flowers, and occasionally seen in the streets of San José.

Genus **HELICONIUS** Kluk, 1802

One of the most conspicuous butterfly genera in the Neotropics, *Heliconius* is recognized by the large eyes, long antennae, characteristic elongate wing-shape, and distinctive color pattern. The genus is found from the southern United States throughout Central and South America and the West Indies, with the greatest diversity of species and subspecies in the Amazon Basin. Of the fifteen species known to occur in Central America, thirteen occur in Costa Rica.

The hostplants are all Passifloraceae, and there is a correlation between species groups of *Passiflora* and the group of *Heliconius* species that feed on them (Benson et al. 1976). The early stages have been elegantly described by Alexander (1961*a*, 1961*b*), who originally pointed out the correspondence of morphology and behavior to the now accepted species groupings.

In Costa Rica, *Heliconius* occurs from sea level to 2,800 m, in virtually all habitat types. The genus exhibits a spectrum of species from the cosmopolitan ones to those restricted to certain elevations and specific geographical areas. Our understanding of the biology of Central American *Heliconius* comes mainly from the work of L. E. Gilbert, who has made many contributions to Neotropical butterfly ecology and insect/plant interactions. The interested reader is referred to Gilbert (1979, 1983, 1984) for detailed accounts of *Heliconius/Passiflora* biology.

Heliconius butterflies are known to live up to nine months, and an individual butterfly will usually spend its entire life in a restricted area. One reason for this probably has to do with resources: *Heliconius* has been shown to be very closely associated with *Psiguria* (Cucurbitaceae) flowers, from which the butterflies collect pollen. The pollen is processed by the butterflies in such a way as to extract amino acids. The amino acids aid in nutritional requirements and defensive chemistry (Nahrstedt and Davis 1983). The result of pollen feeding is that the butterflies are able to live a very long time, and the females in particular are able to maintain a steady daily output of eggs (Dunlap-Pianka 1979; Boggs et al. 1981). The *Psiguria* plants appear to reinforce this behavior by maintaining a constant source of flowers. Through population studies and marking of individual butterflies and flowers, it has been demonstrated that individual butterflies "trapline" flowers on a daily basis, and tend to spend their lives visiting the same flowering plants (Ehrlich and Gilbert 1973) on a regular circuit within their home range (see also Gilbert 1984). However, when flower resources are limited, individual *Heliconius* tend to be stationary, visiting a single or a few *Psiguria* plants and defending them from other butterflies (Murawski and Gilbert, 1986).

The mating biology of *Heliconius* has some

peculiar twists to it. In certain groups, male butterflies will actually mate with a female while she is still in the pupa. Furthermore, two males will sometimes mate with the same female pupa, at the same time, which leads inevitably to the death of the female. It is also known that a mated female *Heliconius* produces a stronger odor from her characteristic scent glands ("stink clubs")—live ones readily extrude these when handled—which is thought to represent an anti-aphrodisiac that deters other males from mating with the same female (Gilbert 1976). This effectively ensures that the first male's spermataphore will fertilize at least a substantial number of eggs.

The occurrence of mimicry in *Heliconius* needs no introduction to most entomologists, but of special interest are the mimetic pairs, *cydno-sapho* and *pachinus-hewitsoni*, as they occur in Costa Rica. Each pair is composed of one species from a particular group and another species from a different group. For example, *H. cydno* uses a wide variety of larval hostplant species, whereas *H. sapho* is an extreme specialist in using a single species of *Passiflora. Heliconius cydno* females lay single eggs, whereas *H. sapho* females lay clusters. This same phenomenon is true for *H. pachinus* and *H. hewitsoni*, respectively. Indeed, there are great similarities in the early stage morphologies and in the response of their comimic species, *H. sara*, to the color patterns expressed by *cydno-sapho* on the Atlantic slope and *pachinus-hewitsoni* on the Pacific slope. This effectively indicates that the only real difference is that one group of species is found on the Atlantic slope and the other on the Pacific. From data gathered in insectary studies concerned with hybridization between *cydno* x *pachinus* and *sapho* x *hewitsoni*, L. E. Gilbert believes that in Costa Rica there are in reality only two species (*cydno* and *sapho*), and that *pachinus* and *hewitsoni* are merely expressions of different wing-pattern genes that have become fixed in the Pacific slope populations. The genes for color pattern are maintained by restriction of gene flow by suitable habitat and the high Cordilleras. In support of this are sightings and captures of *cydno* x *pachinus* hybrids in the Meseta Central, an area that unites the two slopes. The comimic *H. sara* is influenced by the changes in model coloration through selection by predators.

Heliconius doris

(Linnaeus, 1771)

FW Length: 35-45 mm **Plate 31**

Range: Mexico to the Amazon Basin

Hostplant: *Passiflora ambigua* (Passifloraceae)

Early stages: (Beebe et al. 1960) *Egg*—small, yellow, laid in clusters that may be composed of groups of up to two hundred. *Mature larva*—body is greenish yellow with ten transverse black bands on dorsum; the dorsal black spines are shorter than other *Heliconius* species; head is black with two very short horns; prothorax, anal plate, spiracles, and outside of prolegs are shiny black. *Pupa*—of general *Heliconius* shape but without spines or protuberances, and general color reddish brown. The larvae are highly gregarious and feed on old leaves, and at times one can find large aggregations of pupae on tree trunks where the larvae have descended from the canopy hostplant.

Adult: The HW ray pattern distinguishes this species from all others in Costa Rica; the color of the pattern is highly variable and can be yellow, red, blue, green, or any mixture of these colors. Although there are numerous subspecific names applied to these color forms, it appears that all colors can arise from the same clutch of eggs.

Habits: Found from sea level to 1,200 m on both slopes, in association with all forest habitats. Generally encountered during the morning as solitary individuals along forest edges and in light gaps, but the insect can be very common in the forest canopy. Some authors consider *H. doris* to represent a subgenus (*Laparus*) of *Heliconius* because it has a different chromosome number, and is behaviorally somewhat different from other species. Although *H. doris* is often said not to collect pollen, in Costa Rica this species is frequently found with the largest pollen loads of any *Heliconius*. It is of interest that *H. doris* does not fit into any particular mimicry pattern, unlike all the other species. This species appears to be seasonally abundant during dry periods, and although widespread, breeding populations appear to be very local.

Heliconius charitonius

(Linnaeus, 1767)

FW Length: 39-47 mm **Plate 32**

Range: Southern United States throughout Central and South America and the West Indies

Hostplant: *Tetrastylis lobata* (Passifloraceae)

Early stages: (Young et al. 1976) *Egg*—yellowish, laid in small clusters on new growth and meristems. *Mature larva*—body bluish white with a pale yellow head capsule; spines black; venter and anal claspers dull orange; body covered with many dark reddish brown spots. *Pupa*—very similar to *H. erato*. This species is apparently the only *Heliconius* able to feed on *Tetrastylis*, and in the Meseta Central it occasionally feeds on *Passiflora adenopoda*, a hostplant that other species are unable to feed on because of the hooked trichomes on the leaves.

Adult: Distinguished immediately by the zebra-striped pattern, which gives it the common name of the "zebra."

Habits: Commonly occurs from sea level to 1,200 m on both slopes in association with second-growth habitats; rarely found in primary forest. Frequent along forest edges and in old second-growth areas, visiting flowers of *Lantana, Hamelia*, and *Stachytarpheta*. This widespread and common species is apparently unable to compete with the forest *Heliconius* for adult resources (Gilbert 1984) and is confined to disturbed areas. It is interesting to note that the larvae of *H. charitonius* are able to utilize hostplants that are deadly to other *Heliconius* species, yet are apparently ecologically unequipped to compete for pollen and nectar as adults. *Heliconius charitonius*, like *H. doris*, appears isolated in its color pattern and is not part of a mimetic pair, like other species. This species exhibits pupal mating behavior, and it is thought that the female pupae emit a pheromone to attract males. This still remains to be demonstrated. There have been a number of studies on the nocturnal roosting behavior and population biology (Young et al. 1976; Waller and Gilbert 1982).

Heliconius melpomene rosina
Boisduval, 1870

FW Length: 35-39 mm **Plate 32**

Range: Mexico to Brazil. **Subspecies** Mexico to Panama

Hostplant: *Passiflora oerstedii, P. menispermifolia* (Passifloraceae)

Early stages: (Beebe et al. 1960) *Egg*—yellow, laid singly on stipules and young leaves of hostplant. *Mature larva*—body white with black spots and spines; prothoracic segment black; anal plate and head capsule yellow-orange with two prominent black head horns. *Pupa*—brown with gold spots on the dorsum; thorax strongly bowed; many short black spines on the antennae; five pairs of black spines on abdomen, the most anterior being longest; head horns short.

Adult: Distinguished from its comimic species, *H. erato*, by the yellow line on the HW which, when viewed from the underside, the distal ends curve toward the posterior, not to the margin; at the base of the FW underside there are three red dots; red patch on FW is blurred where it is bordered by the black. Compare with *H. erato*.

Habits: Occurs uncommonly from sea level to 1,000 m on both slopes in association with second-growth areas. Encountered as solitary individuals along forest edges and old second growth, flying with its comimic, *H. erato*, but tends to stay away from direct sunshine (whereas *H. erato* flies in direct sunlight). This species collects pollen mainly from *Psiguria*, but also visits flowers of *Hamilia, Lantana*, and *Cissus*. Although this species is apparently well known in areas of South America, in Costa Rica we know little about its habits and why it is rare. The study by Benson (1972) provides some interesting data concerned with the mimicry between *H. erato* and *H. melpomene* and the possible consequences on evolution and population structure.

Heliconius cydno galanthus
Bates, 1864

Heliconius cydno chioneus
Bates, 1864

FW Length: 38-43 mm **Plate 32**

Range: Mexico to Colombia and Ecuador. **Subspecies:** *galanthus*—Mexico to Costa Rica; *chioneus*—southeast Costa Rica to Colombia

Hostplant: *Passiflora vitifolia, P. biflora*, and most other *Passiflora* spp (Passifloraceae)

Early stages: (Young 1973*d*) *Egg*—yellow, laid singly on tendrils and stipules. Early instar larvae have a white body, all black spines. *Mature larva*—body pinkish brown; head capsule yellow-orange with two black head horns; all body spines black; a few black spots on all segments. *Pupa*—dark brown with two rectangular gold patches on the thorax; antennae with long spines, and five pairs of long spines on the abdomen.

Adult: Distinguished from its comimic *H. sapho* by the straight distal margins on the FW white patch; HW underside with a double red discal band (in some specimens the disc is entirely red). Compare with *H. sapho* and *Eurytides pausanias*.

Habits: Occurs from sea level to 1,400 m on the Atlantic slope, and as rare migrant individuals on the Pacific slope and the Meseta Central. Very occasionally, individuals are captured in the lowland Guanacaste forest. The subspecies *chioneus* is found only to the southeast near the Panamanian border, and usually in the presence of *galanthus*. In Panama the situation is reversed; *galanthus* is rare. This species is most commonly found in forest habitats, but is not infrequent in second growth if there is a forest nearby. Its obvious coloration and slow fluttery flight make this one of the most noticeable species in Costa Rica. Both sexes collect large pollen loads from *Psiguria* and appear to be the most defensive toward other species when they are sitting on the flowers. The roosts of this species are seldom seen, usually because they are in the forest subcanopy. The specimens from the Carrillo Belt sometimes have more red and white on the HW and have been shown to carry color pattern genes typical of South American races (L. E. Gilbert, in prep.). A good field character to distinguish *cydno* from *sapho* is that the eversible abdominal glands of *cydno* have a strong pungent smell, whereas *sapho*'s smell is fragrantly sweet.

Heliconius pachinus

Salvin, 1871

FW Length: 38-43 mm **Plate 32**

Range: Costa Rica and Panama

Hostplant: *Passiflora costaricensis, P. vitifolia,* and many other Passiflora spp (Passifloraceae)

Early stages: *Egg*—yellow, laid singly on tendrils and new leaves. *Mature larva*—all of the early stages are very similar to (if not the same as) *H. cydno.*

Adult: Distinguished from its comimic *H. hewitsoni* by having the basalmost yellow FW bar on the outside of the FW cell, and from *H. sara* by having the yellow HW bar pass through the disc. See *H. hewitsoni* and *H. sara.*

Habits: Occurs from sea level to 1,600 m on the Pacific drainage in association with rain forest habitats, and rarely as a migrant into the Guanacaste deciduous forest. In Costa Rica the general range of *pachinus* is from San Mateo up into remnant patches of montane forest near Villa Colon on the edge of the Meseta Central, and southward in all rain forest habitats. In general ecology, *H. pachinus* is extremely similar to the Atlantic slope species, *H. cydno.* The two species breed freely in the insectary, and in Villa Colon both species fly together, occasionally hybridizing. Like *H. cydno,* the live insects have a pungent smell that arises from the abdominal glands. This smell may be used as a field character.

Heliconius erato petiverana

Doubleday, 1847

FW Length: 31-37 mm **Plate 32**

Range: Mexico to the Amazon Basin. **Subspecies:** Mexico to Panama

Hostplant: *Passiflora talamancensis, P. coreacea, P. biflora* (Passifloraceae)

Early stages: *Egg*—yellow, pointed apex, laid singly on the tips of developing leaf clusters. *Mature larva*—similar to *H. melpomene* but differing by having a buff-colored head capsule and shorter head and body spines. *Pupa*—similar to *H. melpomene* but with long head horns and short abdominal spines (Fig. 25).

Adult: Distinguished from its comimic *H. melpomene* by the yellow bar on the HW underside, which has the distal ends curved toward the costal margin, sometimes touching the margin; the red patch on the FW upperside has the margins sharply cut where it borders the black; base of the FW underside has four red spots. Compare with *H. melpomene.*

Habits: Occurs commonly from sea level to 1,600 m on both slopes, in association with disturbed forest and second-growth habitats. Frequently found flying low to the ground along forest edges, in coffee plantations, and in open pastures. This species is able to utilize a wide range of pollen species for food, and hence is able to supplement the usual *Psiguria* pollen with many other species. This species is the commonest *Heliconius* in Costa Rica, and is a familiar visitor to garden flowers. The nocturnal roosts are usually low to the ground along rivers or in second growth, and composed of up to ten individuals.

Heliconius hecalesia formosus

Bates, 1863

FW Length: 45-48 mm **Plate 32**

Range: Mexico to Colombia and Venezuela. **Subspecies:** Costa Rica and Panama

Hostplant: *Passiflora biflora, P. lancearea* (Passifloraceae)

Early stages: *Mature larva*—body dark green-brown with black spines and head capsule, very similar to *H. erato. Pupa*—slate gray with black markings, with a streamlined *H. erato* appearance.

Adult: Distinguished from its comimics *H. hecale* and *Tithorea tarricina* by the black HW apex, which has a row of spots within it, and a rounded FW apex. Compare with *H. hecale* and *Tithorea tarricina.*

Habits: Occurs very locally from sea level to 1,400 m on both slopes in association with wet forest habitats. Commonest in premontane and cloud forest areas and absent in the Guanacaste deciduous forest. This seldom-collected species is usually encountered in small, very local populations in association with its hostplant. Both sexes fly in the subcanopy of the forest and are uncommon at most flowers, although during the morning *H. hecalesia* is frequently seen at *Psiguria* flowers. The largest population I know of is near the base of La Carpintera in the Meseta Central, an area destined for destruction by housing developments. The basic biology and life cycle of this species are essentially unknown and require documentation.

Heliconius hecale zuleika
Hewitson, 1854

FW Length: 42-50 mm **Plate 31**

Range: Mexico to the Peruvian Amazon. **Subspecies:** Nicaragua to Panama

Hostplant: *Passiflora oerstedii, P. vitifolia, P. auriculata, P. platyloba* (Passifloraceae)

Early stages: (Young 1975*a*) *Egg*—large, orange, laid singly on tendrils or leaves. *Mature larva*—body chalky white; head capsule orange; all spines, spiracles, and dots on dorsum black. In general appearance, very similar to *H. cydno. Pupa*—similar to *H. melpomene* but with three gold spots on the abdomen.

Adult: Distinguished from similar species by the wide, rounded FW apex; HW apex is not widely black. This species is highly variable, with some populations in Guanacaste showing yellow and black HW bands, and variation in number and color of FW spots, some being almost black. See *H. hecalesia, Tithorea tarricina,* and *T. harmonia.*

Habits: Widely distributed from sea level to 1,700 m on both slopes, this species is found in literally all habitats from primary rain forest to open pastures. It shows an enormous range of variation and subspeciation within the Neotropics, and is one of the most common *Heliconius* species in Central and South America. I have watched individuals fly from Pacific to Atlantic slopes through mountain passes, and do not doubt that this species is migratory. Just as *H. cydno* is highly successful at utilizing numerous species of *Passiflora* as larval hostplants, *H. hecale* also has a broad range. Both sexes visit various types of flowers, but are commonest at *Psiguria* and *Gurania* flowers, where individuals aggressively defend a flower against other butterflies. The nocturnal roosts are usually found in the subcanopy of the forest and are difficult to spot unless carefully searched for at dusk.

Heliconius ismenius telchinia
Doubleday, 1847

Heliconius ismenius clarescens
Butler, 1875

FW Length: 38-48 mm **Plate 31**

Range: Mexico to Ecuador. **Subspecies:** *telchinia*—Mexico to Panama; *clarescens*—Costa Rica and Panama

Hostplant: *Passiflora alata, P. pedata, P. ambigua, P. platyloba* (Passifloraceae)

Early stages: All stages are similar to *H. hecale*; the mature larva differs by having larger black spots on sides and dorsum.

Adult: Distinguished from all similar species by the large eyes, and the presence (or suggestion of) a black HW medial band. See *Melinaea lilis* and *M. scylax.*

Habits: Occurs from sea level to 1,200 m in association with forest habitats. Subspecies *telchinia* is mostly confined to the Atlantic slope, although it occurs on the Pacific slope of the Meseta Central. Subspecies *clarescens,* on the other hand, occurs on the Pacific slope, commonly in rain forests and as rare individuals in the Guanacaste deciduous forest. This species is commonest in primary rain forest habitats, and is most frequently seen along forest edges and in light gaps. Its greatest period of activity is from dawn until midday. Although it visits numerous types of flowers, it is most commonly seen at *Psiguria* and *Gurania,* where individuals collect large loads of pollen. The nocturnal roosts are usually found in the subcanopy of the forest or along forest edges.

Heliconius clysonymus montanus
Salvin, 1871

FW Length: 37-42 mm **Plate 32**

Range: Honduras to Colombia and Ecuador. **Subspecies:** Costa Rica and Panama

Hostplant: *Passiflora apetala, P. biflora* (Passifloraceae)

Early stages: *Egg*—large, yellow, laid singly on the surface of leaves. *Mature larva*—very similar to *H. erato* but with the body slightly more yellowish. *Pupa*—similar to *H. erato.*

Adult: Distinguished from all other species by the broad red medial band on the HW.

Habits: This species, confined to montane forest habitats at 800 to 1,800 m, occurs on both slopes, and is the only *Heliconius* species restricted to montane areas. Commonly seen along forest edges and in light gaps at any time of the day when it is sunny. Both sexes visit a wide variety of flowers, but are most frequently found visiting *Gurania,* and to a lesser extent *Psiguria.* Both sexes collect large pollen loads. The female is most active around midday and is frequently seen ovipositing on seedling hostplants that occur in light gaps and along forest edges. Indeed, it is very easy to collect numerous eggs by inspecting seedlings, and yet it is apparent that the seedling will not support one larva through five instars. This suggests that *H. clysonymus* larvae must either have a high mortality rate from starvation, or that the larvae wander across the ground searching for more hostplants when the plant on which the egg was laid has been consumed.

Heliconius sara fulgidus
Stichel, 1906
Helionius sara theudela
Hewitson, 1874

FW Length: 30-35 mm **Plate 32**

Range: Mexico to the Amazon Basin. **Subspecies:** *fulgidus*—Guatemala to Panama; *theudela*—Costa Rica and Panama

Hostplant: *Passiflora auriculata* (Passifloraceae)

Early stages: *Egg*—small, yellow, laid in clusters (10-50) on a shoot-tip of developing leaves. *Mature larva*—body black with yellow bands (similar to *H. doris*); all spines and head capsule are black; two spines on head capsule are short and almost converge at tips; the spines on the prothorax are longer than the rest. *Pupa*—pale brown with black spines and black veins on the wingpads; head horns short; a few gold spots (Fig. 25).

Adult: Distinguished from all similar species and comimics by the most basal FW bar, which crosses the wing well inside the cell, and by its small size. See *H. pachinus, H. hewitsoni*, and *H. doris*. The two subspecies are separated geographically by the continental divide. *H. sara theudela* enters into a mimicry complex with the above species on the Pacific slope, and to some extent *H. sara fulgidus* mimics the *H. cydno-sapho* complex on the Atlantic slope. There are no known intermediate forms between the two subspecies.

Habits: Occurs locally, but commonly, from sea level to 700 m on both slopes, in association with rain forest habitats (each slope has a different subspecies). Most commonly found along forest edges or in second growth vegetation, and invariably in association with its specific hostplant. The hostplant specificity is undoubtedly an important factor in limiting its distribution, and is certainly one of the reasons why some populations are very local. Both sexes visit flowers of *Hamelia, Palicourea, Lantana*, and *Psiguria*, and are able to collect pollen from all these genera. The nocturnal roosts are usually found along forest edges low to the ground or along streams.

Heliconius sapho leuce
Doubleday, 1847

FW Length: 38-42 mm **Plate 32**

Range: Mexico to Colombia and Ecuador. **Subspecies:** Mexico to Costa Rica

Hostplant: *Passiflora pittieri* (Passifloraceae)

Early stages: *Egg*—whitish, laid in clusters of up to thirty on developing apical meristem. The eggs are laid in a tight cluster that separates when the meristem grows. *Mature larva*—body yellowish green; spines and venter yellowish, which turn black; head capsule black with two short head horns. The larvae feed gregariously and require soft, new leaves in early instars. Later instars will feed on old leaves. All molts are synchronous. *Pupa*—pale yellow to pale brown, with well-marked black wing veins and black spines. Pupation often takes place in groups.

Adult: Distinguished from its comimic *cydno* by the FW white patch, which has a narrow, tooth-shaped extension on vein M3; underside has red at the base of both wings and no reddish discal bands. Compare with *H. cydno* and *Eurytides pausanias*.

Habits: Restricted to the Atlantic slope, from sea level to 500 m, in association with primary rain forest habitats. This rare species flies only in the shaded understory and subcanopy, and is intolerant of disturbed forest. Very seldom seen at *Psiguria* or other flowers, although both sexes collect large pollen loads. In the field, live specimens have a sweet, ambrosial smell that is emitted from the abdominal glands and serves as an excellent field character to separate it from *H. cydno*. Clusters of pupae are attractive to males, which wait on the female pupae and eventually mate with either the emerging adult or the pupa. In general, there is little known about the population biology of this species.

Heliconius hewitsoni
Staudinger, 1875

FW Length: 34-41 mm **Plate 32**

Range: Costa Rica and Panama

Hostplant: *Passiflora pittieri* (Passifloraceae)

Early stages: *Egg*—pale yellow, laid in clusters of twenty or more on developing apical meristem. As in *H. sapho*, soon after the female lays a tight cluster of eggs, the shoot-tip grows very rapidly, spreading the egg cluster out. This implies that the female assesses a shoot-tip for vigor before she lays her eggs. *Mature larva*—body yellow-green with yellowish spines; or the body may have black on it and the spines may turn black; head capsule black with two large head horns (see also *Eueides vibilia*). *Pupa*—similar to *H. sapho*. The larvae feed gregariously on new, then older leaves (Fig. 25). All molts are synchronous, and pupation is often gregarious.

Adult: Distinguished from its comimic *H. pachinus* by having the most basal yellow FW band cross the wing within the cell. Compare with *H. pachinus* and *H. sara*.

Habits: Occurs from sea level to 1,100 m on only the Pacific slope, in association with rain forest habitats. Its present range is from the Rio Grande de Tarcoles south into the Osa Peninsula, but it is essentially restricted to remnant patches of rain forest. Although generally uncommon, in Parque Corcovado at Sirena in the early 1980s, there was an abundance of hostplants (resulting from thinning the forest) which were all saplings with vigorous shoot-tips, and as a result, the butterfly was very common. Both sexes visit *Psiguria* and other flowers and collect large pollen loads. The males sit on female pupae and either mate with them immediately upon eclosion, or mate with the pupa. Often two males will mate with the same pupa, which results in the death of the female butterfly. Pupal mating invariably takes place during the early morning, and the presence of pupae can be detected by encountering several males swirling around a low piece of vegetation, trying to knock the older males from the female pupae. As in *H. sapho*, individuals fly in the understory of the forest, and very seldom in open sunlight (see Longino 1985).

Heliconius eleuchia eleuchia
Hewitson, 1853

FW Length: 35-41 mm **Plate 32**

Range: Costa Rica to Ecuador and Colombia. **Subspecies:** Costa Rica to Colombia

Hostplant: Unknown, but most probably *Passiflora tica*, which is a medium-sized tree with a very restricted but sympatric distribution

Early stages: Unknown in Costa Rica, but almost certainly very similar to either *H. sapho* or *H. hewistoni*.

Adult: Distinguished immediately by the yellow bands on the FW and the white marginal band on the HW; almost appears to be a hybrid of *H. sapho* and *H. hewitsoni*.

Habits: This rare Costa Rican species is restricted to 100 to 700 m elevation on the Atlantic slope, in association with the Carrillo Belt, a type of tropical wet forest in the transitional premontane belt. The present known distribution is from La Virgen del Socorro on the Rio Sarapiqui, south to the floodplain of the Valle de Turrialba, and it seems likely that the species extends further south along the Cordillera de Talamanca. Most frequently seen flying along rivers and ridge tops during the morning. Both sexes visit flowers of *Psychotria*, along riparian edges. It is unknown to what extent this species uses pollen of *Psiguria*, and nothing is known about its general biology. In Ecuador, it is known that males mate with female pupae.

Subfamily **MELITAEINAE**

The butterflies in the Melitaeinae (sensu Higgins 1981) form a group of nymphalids with a worldwide distribution, which range in size from small to medium, and can be recognized by having the antennal club well developed and flattened at the tip. It seems doubtful that the group will stand as a separate subfamily of the Nymphalidae, but I am using it here as a convenient way of treating the various genera occurring in our area.

There are two tribes (sensu Higgins) that occur in the Neotropics: the Melitaeini, composed of *Chlosyne, Thessalia*, and *Microtia* (Higgins 1960), and the Phyciodini, composed of *Anthanassa, Tegosa, Eresia, Castillia*, and *Janatella* (Higgins 1981).

Closely related to *Euphydryas* of the United States, the Neotropical species should prove to be useful in studies aimed at population dynamics, genetics, and gene flow, as studied for *Euphydryas* (see Ehrlich 1984 for review); however, not a single study has been done on this group in the Neotropics. In an analogous fashion, one might predict that some of the species (notably *Chlosyne*) may prove to be unpalatable from chemicals sequestered from the larval hostplants, as has been recently documented for *Euphydryas* (Bowers 1981), a supposition based mostly on the conspicuous behavior of the species in this genus.

Perhaps more than any other nymphalid group, the butterflies in the Melitaeinae subfamily show a great deal of variation, polymorphism, and apparent temperature-sensitive colorations. These variations have added to the complexity of the systematics and taxonomy of the group, and I stress this when making comparisons between the ecologies of related species. Although there have been many works devoted to these butterflies, the research has barely begun.

Tribe **MELITAEINI** Higgins, 1960

This tribe is relatively straightforward, and it is easy to identify the species in our area. The standard reference for the group is Higgins (1960), which summarizes the literature. I follow his arrangement in the following treatments of *Chlosyne, Thessalia*, and *Microtia*, except that I have eliminated, for the purposes of this work, some of the numerous names given to the forms of *Chlosyne*.

Genus **CHLOSYNE** Butler, 1870

The butterflies in this genus are recognized by having black and orange ground colors, a slightly excavated forewing margin, and conspicuously flattened antennal clubs. The genus ranges from the southern United States through Central and South America, with greatest diversity in Mexico.

The hostplants are various genera of Asteraceae, Acanthaceae, and Amaranthaceae. The eggs are laid in very large clusters, and are mature inside the female upon eclosion. A fresh female can barely fly due to the enormous weight of the eggs in her abdomen. The larvae are gregarious feeders, are dull-colored, and bear short spines on the body. The pupae are pale colored (often waxy), marked with fine black lines on the wingpads and abdomen, and are similar to those of genera in the tribe Phyciodini.

Some of the species (notably *C. lacinia*) show a great deal of variation within and between populations, and many form names have been generated. Since one can find most of the forms within the same population, I have disregarded the "subspecific" names applied by Higgins (1960). The genetics and ecology of some of the forms can be found in Neck (1974). As the genus enters southern Central America, mimicry begins to affect species. Hence we find species like *C. narva* entering mimicry complexes with ithomiines and perhaps into Batesian mimicry with *Eresia*.

Although generally considered a palatable group of butterflies, aspects of the behavior and the chemistry of the hostplants suggest that at least some species may be distasteful to birds. A case in point is *C. lacinia*, which is obvious, slow flying, and feeds as a larva on *Helianthus* (Asteraceae), which contains numerous poisonous compounds. Certainly more research using *Chlosyne* species in feeding experiments is needed to assess their palatability to vertebrate predators. On the whole, it is assumed from studies on *C. lacinia* done in Texas that adults are short-lived and fairly sedentary. Again, other species need to be investigated and findings compared with studies made in the temperate zone, especially on some of the rain forest species. In Costa Rica, the genus is found from sea level to 1,400 m, and although most of the species tend to be associated with open pastures and second growth, a few are found within the rain forests. All species feed on flower nectar, and the males visit puddles. In the deciduous forest habitats of Guanacaste, some species show marked seasonality, and have local population explosions at the start of the rainy season but are almost absent during the height of the dry season.

Chlosyne janais

(Drury, 1782)

FW Length: 21-30 mm **Plate 29**

Range: Mexico to Colombia

Hostplant: *Odontonema* and related Acanthaceae

Early stages: (Ross 1964*b*) Body dull metallic gray-green; many black spines at whose base the body is black; head capsule bicolored, orange on dorsum, black on venter. The larvae feed gregariously in all instars and are semi-synchronous feeders. *Pupa*—grayish green with black lines on wingpads and small black warts on the abdomen and thorax; black on the head.

Adult: Distinguished from similar species by the scattered white spots on the black FW, which do not form a band; discal patch on the HW upperside is reddish orange; HW underside has a reddish orange medial band. Compare with *C. lacinia* and *C. erodyle*.

Habits: Occurs from sea level to 1,200 m on both slopes, in association with disturbed, open areas that have a moderate amount of second-growth vegetation. Encountered as locally abundant populations during the dry seasons on the Atlantic slope and at the beginning of the rainy season on the Pacific slope. In the Meseta Central, individuals are present throughout the year and are common garden flower visitors. The freshly eclosed females are usually so heavy that they can barely fly, and characteristically fly with the heavy abdomen hanging down. Both sexes visit a variety of flowers, and while feeding open and close the wings.

Chlosyne hippodrome

(Geyer, 1837)

FW Length: 24-31 mm **Plate 29**

Range: Mexico to Colombia

Hostplant: *Melanthera aspera* (Asteraceae)

Early stages: *Mature larva*—body black with white markings, densely covered with fine spines. The larva are semi-gregarious. *Pupa*—similar to *C. janais* but with a yellower cast.

Adult: Distinguished by the round wing shape; upperside black with a white FW band and HW margin; underside has yellow HW margin and red spots on the HW medial area. See *C. melanarge*.

Habits: Occurs from sea level to 1,000 m on the Pacific slope, in association with disturbed deciduous forest and open pastures. It is unknown if it occurs on the Atlantic slope, but this seems likely. In Guanacaste this species is found in seasonal populations at the start of the rainy season, in open pastures and along forest edges. It disappears during the dry season during most years, or is present in low numbers along rivers. Most frequently found flying with other species of *Chlosyne*, but differs in flight behavior by being a somewhat more agile and faster flier. Although uncommon in Costa Rican collections, individuals can be very common in certain years, especially in northwestern Guanacaste.

Chlosyne melanarge

(Bates, 1864)

FW Length: 21-26 mm **Plate 29**

Range: Mexico to Costa Rica

Hostplant: *Aphelandra deppiana* (Acanthaceae)

Early stages: *Mature larva*—body dull olive-green with eleven rows of black, finely branched spines; three rows of white dots along back and sides; head capsule orange. Larvae are gregarious feeders. *Pupa*—ground color white, covered with small black dots.

Adult: Distinguished by the dull yellow spots on the FW that form a subapical band; HW underside margin has dull yellow spots. See *C. hippodrome*.

Habits: Occurs from sea level to 830 m on the Pacific slope, in association with deciduous forest habitats, ranging as far south in Costa Rica as San Mateo. It can be seasonally abundant in some years, and is only present during the rainy season. The larvae are sometimes the most obvious clue that this species is present in a particular habitat: the conspicuous hostplant can be covered with larvae, whereas the adults may not be in evidence. This species flies in the open as well as in the forest interior. Surprisingly rare in Costa Rican collections.

Chlosyne gaudealis

(Bates, 1864)

FW Length: 20-29 mm **Plate 29**

Range: Guatemala to Panama

Hostplant: *Justicia* (Acanthaceae)

Early stages: *Egg*—bright yellow, laid in small clusters, usually on small or immature hostplants. *Mature larva*—similar to *C. janais* but with more black markings. *Pupa*—as in *C. janais* but with a rosy yellow ground color. Larvae are usually found in groups of two or three on small hostplants growing in the forest understory or along riparian edges.

Adult: Distinguished from all other species by the bright reddish patch on the jet black FW upperside and the bright yellow discal area on the black HW upperside.

Habits: Occurs from sea level to 800 m on the Atlantic slope, in association with rain forest habitats, usually along rivers. Encountered as uncommon solitary individuals throughout the year, flying along forest and riparian edges with a slow, obvious flight. When flying, the species resembles several *Heliconius* species (such as *H. melpomene* and *H. erato*). Both sexes visit flowers of *Psychotria, Justicia*, and various Asteraceae during sunny mornings, and activity will continue even in a slight rain. The males perch on low vegetation along trails and streams and chase other slow-flying butterflies. Although these butterflies fly very slowly, if alarmed they can take off with an amazingly fast, erratic flight, usually high into the subcanopy of the forest.

Chlosyne narva

(Fabricius, 1893)

FW Length: 27-35 mm **Plate 29**

Range: Nicaragua to Venezuela

Hostplant: I have upon several occasions reared this species on *Amaranthus* (Amaranthaceae), which is an unusual record and requires confirmation.

Early stages: *Mature larva*—pale yellow-green with black spines and head capsule. *Pupa*—similar to *C. gaudealis*

Adult: Distinguished by the elongate FW; orange patch on the HW upperside and two black medial hands on the FW upperside. The name *C. bonplandi* (Latréillé) is given to some of the Costa Rican and more southern populations, and refers to those individuals with an orange cast to the HW patch. Since there is complete intergradation in Costa Rica, the name is given here only as a point of access to the literature.

Habits: Occurs from sea level to 1,000 m on the Atlantic slope, in association with rain forest habitats. Encountered as uncommon solitary individuals along forest edges, riparian edges, and on cloudy days, in open areas and second growth. Its habits are similar to *C. gaudealis*, but it tends to fly in more open, conspicuous microhabitats, and hence is more readily noticed. The flight is very similar to the ithomiine genera *Mechanitis* and *Hypothyris*, and can easily be mistaken for such while flying in dappled light. Both sexes visit flowers of various Asteraceae, *Lantana*, and *Psychotria*. Present throughout the year in most Atlantic lowland areas, but more common during the dry seasons.

Chlosyne erodyle

(Bates, 1864)

FW Length: 23-28 mm **Plate 29**

Range: Mexico to Costa Rica

Hostplant: Unknown

Early stages: Unknown

Adult: Distinguished by the yellow patch on the base of the HW upperside and the reddish band near the HW margin on the underside. Compare with *C. janais* and *C. poecile*.

Habits: Occurs as rare individuals from sea level to 300 m on the Pacific drainage, in association with the Guanacaste deciduous forest habitats, and most frequently in open pastures. Rare in Costa Rican collections, and present only during the beginning of the rainy season.

Chlosyne poecile

(Felder, 1867)

FW Length: 20-25 mm **Plate 29**

Range: Costa Rica to Venezuela

Hostplant: Unknown

Early stages: Unknown

Adult: Distinguished by yellow patches interspersed with black on the upperside of both wings. Compare with *C. erodyle*.

Habits: Occurs from sea level to 900 m on the Pacific slope, in association with semi-deciduous forest, from San Mateo southward to Panamanian border. Rare in Costa Rican collections. Its habits are similar to *C. erodyle*.

Chlosyne lacinia

(Geyer, 1837)

FW Length: 21-33 mm **Plate 29**

Range: United States south to Bolivia and Peru

Hostplant: *Helianthus, Verbesina, Ambrosia* (Asteraceae)

Early stages: *Eggs*—bright orange-yellow, laid in large clusters on any stage of the hostplant. *Mature larva*—polymorphic; ranges from black to orange, usually with black spines and head capsule, although these are variable, as well. General form as in *C. janais*. *Pupa*—as in *C. janais*. The larvae feed in large aggregations and usually devastate the hostplant. In the United States, the larvae are commercial pests of sunflowers. See also Neck (1977).

Adult: Extremely variable, usually with many subspecies names that are not very useful, since all forms can be found in the same populations. The variations include the presence, reduction, or absence of the orange patch on the HW upperside; and the presence, reduction, or absence of the yellow patch on the HW underside, and its attendant colors. In general, *lacinia* may be recognized by the spots on the FW upperside (usually white), which are large and form a band. Compare with *C. janais* and *C. poecile*.

Habits: Occurs commonly from sea level to 1,400 m on both slopes, in association with open second-growth areas, and very common in cattle pastures. Usually found in abundance along roadsides, pastures, and all waste places. Both sexes visit a variety of flowers, which include *Lantana, Verbena, Asclepias, Turnera, Epidendrum radicans*, and numerous weedy Asteraceae. In Guanacaste, *C. lacinia* is present throughout most years, but is especially abundant at the beginning of the rainy season. At such times, literally thousands of individuals may cover the various flowers in pastures, and the males can cover a puddle in the road. In Guanacaste, the form *quetala* is usually most abundant, and to a lesser extent other forms. The form *saundersi* is rare in Costa Rica, and usually found in the Atlantic lowlands. The genetics and analysis of various polymorphisms are found in Neck (1974), along with its ecology as it occurs in Texas.

Genus **THESSALIA** Scudder, 1875

These small butterflies are recognized by their checkered orange and brown pattern. The genus ranges from the western United States through Central America, and into South America as far south as Colombia and Venezuela. My treatment here differs from that of Higgins (1960) by elevating one of the subspecies to full species rank.

Hostplants in the United States are in the Scrophulariaceae, but none of the tropical species or populations has been reared. The larvae are velvety and have many very short spines, a fleshy lateral line, and a smooth head capsule. The pupae are apparently similar to *Chlosyne* but more streamlined.

In Costa Rica, *Thessalia* is found from sea level to about 1,200 m elevation, always in association with disturbed areas, especially along the coastlines. Both sexes feed on flower nectar, and the males visit mud and urine. There is little known of their biology in the tropics. In Costa Rica and Panama we have populations that are transitional to the South American forms, as well as one species that appears endemic.

Thessalia ezra
(Hewitson, 1864)

FW Length: 16-20 mm **Plate 29**
Range: Costa Rica and Panama
Hostplant: Unknown
Early stages: Unknown
Adult: Distinguished by the wide brown wing margins on the upperside and the configuration of yellow spots on the FW. See *T. theona*.
Habits: Occurs as rare individuals from sea level to 1,000 m on both slopes, in association with open ground, pastures, and coastal vegetation. Flies in direct sunlight with a weak fluttery flight, just above the ground-level vegetation. Individuals tend to stay associated with a small patch of vegetation throughout the day, and in general are local in areas that have abundant weedy flowers. This species is rare in collections, but appears to be present throughout the year, especially in the Meseta Central.

Thessalia theona
(Ménétriés, 1855)

FW Length: 17-22 mm **Plate 29**
Range: Southern United States, south to Panama
Hostplant: *Castilleja* (Scrophulariaceae) in United States
Early stages: (Howe 1975) Body dark velvet brown with many white dots on the dorsum; dorsal midline black; lateral line fleshy yellow with black spots; head capsule orange or yellow, covered with black hairs.
Adult: Distinguished by the extensive orange checkering on the upperside and pearly medial area on the HW underside. See *T. ezra*.
Habits: Occurs locally from sea level to 1,200 m on the Pacific slope, in association with disturbed forest, second growth, and open pastures. Its habits are very similr to *T. ezra*, although it tends to be somewhat more abundant. Present throughout the year along the coastline and during the rainy season on the mainland. Uncommon in collections from Costa Rica.

Tribe **PHYCIODINI** Higgins, 1981

Identification of the species in the tribe Phyciodini (Higgins 1981) is, on the whole, a difficult enterprise. Historically, the species that occur in Costa Rica and the rest of Central America were treated within the confines of two genera (*Phyciodes* and *Eresia*), with many species, subspecies, and subgeneric groupings (Godman and Salvin 1882, Hall 1928-1930, Forbes 1945). All of these workers used configuration of the male genitalia in their analyses. As presently interpreted by Higgins (1981), the species in Costa Rica are now divided into five genera, and many of the old subgenera and subspecies have been elevated to generic and specific status, all based upon apparent differences of the male genitalia. Although this important revision has synthesized a large quantity of information, it is my feeling that future work may bring about re-aggregation of certain species and genera maintained by Higgins.

There are problems with Higgins' revision: 1. There may not be sufficient differences between taxa whose genitalia and color patterns are very similar (such as *Anthanassa, Eresia*). If the classification is based upon genitalia, and these are similar, what then defines the species? 2. A number of the species do not have female specimens that are associated with the male specimens. Hence, comparisons between populations or "species" from different areas in Central America are not possible. To me this reduces the level of critical resolution considerably. 3. Finally, some of the females appear to be polymorphic, and their matching with males is not satisfactory, although this is mostly because of lack of material. But this, too, is a problem yet to be overcome by accurate field studies.

With these points in mind, I follow the arrangement of Higgins (1981), and hope that future workers will be able to produce a clearer picture of the relationships and status of the species in this group. Because in my observations of Costa Rican butterflies I have concentrated mainly on forest-inhabiting species, I am unable to form strong opinions about the various taxa in open fields and pastures. Clearly, there is much left to be done.

The tribe Phyciodini is found only in the Americas, ranging from Canada south through the United States, Central and South America, and the West Indies. Most of the species are dull-colored, small, live in fields and pastures, and are confusingly similar. One group enters into Batesian mimicry complexes that have ithomiine, heliconiine, and *Actinote* species as models. The greatest local diversity of the tribe occurs in Central America, and the tribe is well represented in Costa Rica.

Hostplant relationships are poorly known, but Acanthaceae, Asteraceae, and Urticaceae have been recorded for some of the genera. The larvae have short, bristly spines, and some show affinities to *Thessalia* by having fleshy protuberances. All of the species appear to feed gregariously, although there is so little known about the life cycle patterns that it is impossible to be sure. Research on the basic life cycles and natural history of this group of butterflies is badly needed; such studies are the only way to answer questions of polymorphisms in *Eresia*, separation of similar species of *Anthanassa*, and evaluation of generic rankings of the group as a whole.

Genus **ANTHANASSA** Scudder, 1875

All of the butterflies in this genus are small and can be recognized by the excavated forewing margin, somber coloration, and fine, undulate lines on the hindwing margin. *Anthanassa* contains species in which the sexes are monomorphic, dimorphic, or the female polymorphic. Identification of some species can be trying, and close attention must be paid to small dots and lines on both wings. There is confusion over the proper identity of certain species, and the interested reader is referred to the introduction to *Phyciodes* by Godman and Salvin (1883) for a perceptive summary of the problems in the group. *Anthanassa* ranges from the southern United States throughout Central and South America and the West Indies. Of the twenty-five species in the genus, at least eleven occur in Costa Rica.

From what is known of the early stages of temperate species. Asteraceae appear to be important as hostplants. The larvae apparently show similarities to *Thessalia*, although none of the Costa Rican species has been reared.

In Costa Rica and, as far as I am aware, throughout its range, all species of *Anthanassa* occur in open pastures and disturbed habitats, and none enters the forest. Adults feed on nectar, and the males are known to visit wet sand and urine. This group is completely unstudied in all mainland Neotropical habitats, even though it occurs at all elevations in Central America.

Anthanassa drusilla lelex
(Bates, 1864)

FW Length: 15-18 mm **Plate 30**
Range: Mexico through Central America to western South America. **Subspecies:** Mexico to Panama
Hostplant: Unknown
Early stages: Unknown
Adult: Color variable, but marking usually pale orange to white; HW upperside has a fine, usually short, undulate line between the marginal wavy line and the discal bar on the HW upperside, which is very noticeable on the HW underside; basal one-third of HW upperside often has reddish markings; FW underside has an orangish patch on distal margin. See *A. ptolyca* and *A. phlegias*.
Habits: Occurs commonly from sea level to 1,000 m on the Atlantic slope, in all pasture-like habitats.

Anthanassa ptolyca
(Bates, 1864)

FW Length: 14-16 mm **Plate 30**
Range: Mexico to Venezuela
Hostplant: Unknown
Early stages: Unknown
Adult: Distinguished from *A. drusilla* by not having the double undulate lines on the HW upperside, and smaller. See *A. drusilla*.
Habits: Although recorded from Nicaragua and Venezuela, it has not been reported from Costa Rica. I included it here as a distinctly possible resident that may well be found with further collecting.

Anthanassa ardys
(Hewitson, 1864)

FW Length: 16-19 mm **Plate 30**
Range: Southern Mexico to Colombia
Hostplant: Unknown
Early stages: Unknown
Adult: Markings range from white to cream, and are variable in size. Distinguished from other species by: curved shape of the HW medial band, which is best seen on the underside; underside suffused with a purple cast; distal margin of HW underside has a dark area; spots on HW distinctly separate on the underside. See *A. drusilla* and *A. ptolyca*.
Habits: Occurs commonly in all fields and pastures from sea level to 1,500 m on both slopes, and is probably the most commonly seen spe-

cies. Both sexes visit flowers of weedy Asteraceae.

Anthanassa phlegias
(Godman and Salvin, 1901)
FW Length: 17-18 mm **Not illustrated**
Range: Honduras and Costa Rica
Hostplant: Unknown
Early stages: Unknown
Adult: Upperside markings deep orange; similar in pattern to *A. drusilla*, but distinguished by the deeply excavated FW margin; no fine undulate line on HW upperside, as in *A. drusilla*; HW underside has a gray discal band that is expanded near costa and bordered basally by a dark red-brown.
Habits: Very rare in collections: in Costa Rica known only from Peralta and Zent District in the Atlantic lowlands.

Anthanassa dora
(Schaus, 1913)
FW Length: 20-21 mm **Plate 30**
Range: Costa Rican endemic (?)
Hostplant: Unknown
Early stages: Unknown
Adult: Described and still known only from the female sex, which is distinguished from the female of all other species by the curved medial line, which is pale orange distally. I do not agree with Higgins (1981), who asserts this is an abberation of *A. otanes*, nor do I think that it belongs with *A. nebulosa*. In my opinion, it is either a distinct species of which the male is as yet unknown or, more likely, a female form of *A. sosis*. Compare with female *A. sosis*.
Habits: The female *dora* is known in Costa Rica only from Volcan Poas, Volcan Irazu, and the Cordillera de Talmanca above 2,800 m elevation. I have collected it visiting flowers of *Senecio megaphylla* along the Pan American highway and along rivers in the interior of the Talamancas, southeast of Cerro Chirripo. It seems most likely that this is a form of *A. sosis* or a sibling species because of the curved medial line and the overlap of habitats. This butterfly is rare in collections.

Anthanassa sosis
(Godman and Salvin, 1878)
FW Length: 16-20 mm **Plate 30**
Range: Costa Rica to Colombia
Hostplant: Unknown
Early stages: Unknown
Adult: Upperside black with indistinct cream to white spots; HW with three fine wavy submarginal lines in male, two in female; HW underside marbled brown and gray; FW underside has narrow reddish brown margin. *Female*—curved medial line and two distinct submarginal spots on the FW upperside. See *A. dora*.
Habits: Known only from montane habitats above 2,000 m on both slopes. This species and *A. dora* are the only *Anthanassa* that occur in Costa Rican collections above 2,500 m. *A. sosis* needs to be reared in order to ascertain whether it is distinct from *A. dora*.

Anthanassa atronia
(Bates, 1866)
FW Length: male 16-18 mm, female 19-21 mm **Plate 30**
Range: Mexico to Panama
Hostplant: Unknown
Early stages: Unknown
Adult: Sexes dimorphic. *Male*—almost uniformly dark on upperside; HW underside overshot with purplish and with many indistinct wavy lines; HW distal margin reddish brown; FW underside has dark brown discal area. *Female*—variable; distinguished by the conspicuous white postmedial band, or the markings may be yellowish.
Habits: Recorded from 600 to 1,000 m on both slopes. On the Pacific slope it is only reported from San Mateo. Uncommon in collections.

Anthanassa otanes sopolis
(Godman and Salvin, 1878)
FW Length: 17-20 mm **Plate 30**
Range: Guatemala and Costa Rica
Hostplant: Unknown
Early stages: Unknown
Adult: Sexes dimorphic. *Male*—HW upperside has entire discal area dull black; FW upperside has orange markings. *Female*—variable, distinguished from *A. atronia* by yellow-orange markings and the rusty brown on the HW discal area.
Habits: Known in Costa Rica only from a few specimens collected on Volcan Poas. Its habits and status are unknown.

Anthanassa crithona
(Salvin, 1871)
FW Length: 16-19 mm **Plate 30**
Range: Nicaragua to Panama
Hostplant: Unknown
Early stages: Unknown
Adult: Distinguished from all other species by the orange band that runs from the costa to tornus on the FW. See *A. fulviplaga*.
Habits: Occurs from 800 to 2,000 m on all wet montane slopes throughout the country, but

especially common in the Cordillera de Talamanca and Cordillera Central above 1,500 m. Frequently found along forest and riparian edges. Both sexes visit flowers of weedy Asteraceae.

Anthanassa fulviplaga
(Butler, 1872)
FW Length: 16-19 mm **Plate 30**
Range: Costa Rica and Panama
Hostplant: Unknown
Early stages: Unknown
Adult: *Male*—HW upperside dull brown; FW upperside has a short orange bar; FW underside has black medial area. *Female*—has no black on the FW underside; FW has an orange band. See *A. crithona.*
Habits: Occurs from 800 to 2,500 m on both slopes, in association with cloud forest habitats. Found along forest edges and road cuts that have tall forest vegetation on either side, always in association with streams, rivers, and wet places. Common.

Anthanassa tulcis
(Bates, 1864)
FW Length: 14-16 mm **Plate 30**
Range: Southern United States to Panama
Hostplant: Unknown
Early stages: Unknown
Adult: Similar to *A. drusilla* but distinguished by its smaller size; upperside darker with less reddish; underside overshot with yellow.
Habits: Occurs from sea level to 1,000 m on the Pacific slope, in pastures and highly disturbed, open forest habitats. Commonest during the rainy season in June and July.

Genus **MICROTIA** Bates, 1864

This genus contains a single species that is separated from other close relatives by the atrophied inner margin of the hindwing and by the configuration of the genitalia. It is easily recognized by the black and orange color pattern, and cannot be confused with anything else. The genus ranges from the extreme southern tip of Texas through Mexico to Costa Rica.

The hostplant relationships, larvae, and pupae are unknown. In Costa Rica, this seasonal species can be extremely abundant in some years, and is found in association with dry, open pastures.

Microtia elva
Bates, 1864
FW Length: 12-17 mm **Plates 29**
Range: Southern United States, south to Costa Rica
Hostplant: Unknown
Early stages: Unknown
Adult: Immediately distinguished by the orange bands on brown ground color.
Habits: Occurs from sea level to 1,000 m on the Pacific slope, in association with pastures and second growth. Although present throughout the year, it is most common during the rainy season, during which time it can be extremely abundant. The males sometimes cover cow dung and puddles in the roads. Both sexes visit a variety of weedy Asteraceae. It is rare to find this species in association with rain forest habitats except in associated pasture lands.

Genus **ERESIA** Boisduval, 1836

These butterflies are of moderate size with obviously elongate forewings, dimorphic sexes, and most have mimetic color patterns. Taxonomically, some of the Costa Rican species need critical reexamination because of the variation (as one would expect in a mimetic species) in the *alsina-eutropia-melaina* group, and because of the lack of association of the sexes. The genus ranges from Mexico throughout Central and South America, and reaches its greatest diversity in Costa Rica and Panama.

There is but a single complete life history known, and one oviposition record. From these records we know that at least Urticaceae and Acanthaceae are used as hostplants. The larvae are bristly, not unlike *Chlosyne*, and are gregarious feeders. More work on the life cycles is needed to separate some of the taxa and to examine the idea that some taxa are polymorphic.

In Costa Rica, the genus is found from sea level to 1,700 m elevation, with the majority of the species occurring in montane forests. Some of the species have well-defined models that fly in the same habitat, while others seem to converge on a general ithomiine pattern. The adults feed on flower nectar, but little is known about their habits. The females usually fly around midday, in light gaps and riparian edges, whereas the males of some species fly only during the morning, along forest edges.

Eresia clara

Bates, 1864

FW Length: male 17-19 mm, female 20-24 mm **Plate 30**

Range: Mexico, through Central and South America, to Brazil

Hostplant: Unknown

Early stages: Unknown

Adult: Distinguished by the broad white HW medial band and elongate wing shape.

Habits: Occurs locally from sea level to 500 m on both slopes, in association with rain forest habitats, and occasionally in montane regions. Usually found along shaded forest edges that have adjacent low vegetation, in small populations. Occasionally, I have seen small groups of males visiting wet sand along river banks. The females fly during midday, and both sexes fly low to the ground, wandering over the vegetation. Both sexes visit flowers of *Justicia* and various weedy Asteraceae. Commonest during the dry seasons.

Eresia coela

Druce, 1874

FW Length: male 20-22 mm, female 23-25 mm **Plate 30**

Range: Costa Rica and northeastern Panama

Hostplant: *Justicia* (Acanthaceae)

Early stages: *Egg*—yellow, laid in clusters of 30 to 80 on small isolated plants, in light gaps and along riparian edges.

Adult: Sexes dimorphic. *Male*—distinguished by the black wing margins and pale orange ground color. *Female*—FW black with large white spots; FW apex rounded; HW upperside reddish orange with thin black margins. See *E. poecillina*.

Habits: Occurs from 50 to 500 m, entirely confined to the Atlantic slope, and commonest at the base of the mountains of the Cordillera Central and Talamanca. Encountered as solitary individuals along forest edges and in light gaps. Males fly in more direct sunlight, whereas females stay in the forest understory. The male flies with a brisk, flutter-sail wing beat, whereas the female has a floppier flight that better mimics the ithomiine models (*Hyposcada virginiana, Napeogenes peredia*). Although present throughout most of the year, it is most common at La Selva and Carrillo during the dry seasons. I have no flower records for this species.

Eresia alsina

Hewitson, 1869

FW Length: male 25-26 mm, female 28-30 mm **Plate 29**

Range: Nicaragua and Costa Rica

Hostplant: *Pilea pittieri* (Urticaceae)

Early stages: (Young 1973*c*; as *E. eutropia*) *Egg*—creamy yellow, pear-shaped, laid on new leaves in clusters of 30 to 70. *Mature larva*—body dark green, covered with many finely branched orange spines (three pairs per segment); a sprinkling of white spots on dorsum; head capsule and all legs orange. *Pupa*—greenish brown with blotches of light brown on wingpads; overall appearance shiny. The larvae feed gregariously and apparently match the color of the hostplant leaves. If disturbed, the larva drops off the plant and coils into a tight ball with the spines projecting outward. The larvae rest on the host near the base and feed day and night.

Adult: Sexes dimorphic. *Male*—FW squarely elongate, orange from base to tornus; three oblique black bars on FW; the basal-most FW bar tapers to a thin line as it enters the tornus; HW orange with narrow black distal margins. *Female*—similarly marked, FW broadly rounded. See *E. eutropia* and *E. melaina*.

Habits: Occurs from 300 to 1,000 m on the Atlantic slope in association with montane wet forest habitats. Usually found as solitary individuals, but occasionally abundant. Both sexes fly low to the ground along forest and riparian edges, always in association with wet areas and shade. Both sexes exhibit the flutter-sail wing beat. The females oviposit only on the young leaves of the hostplant, which are dark red and contrast with the green of the mature leaves. Due to the confusion between *E. eutropia* and *E. melaina*, more observations are needed. This species (*alsina*) is especially common at Colonia del Socorro and Carrillo.

Eresia eutropia

Hewitson, 1874

FW Length: male 22-24 mm, female 27 mm **Plates 30** and **50**

Range: Costa Rica(?), Panama, and western Colombia

Hostplant: Unknown

Early stages: Unknown

Adult: Sexes dimorphic. *Male*—differs from *E. alsina* by not having the FW bar tapering as it enters the tornus, but wide and continuous with the generally black FW margin. *Female*—similarly marked but with rounded FW and wide black HW costa. Compare with *E. alsina* and *E. melaina*.

Habits: Occurs around 1,000 m on the Pacific slope, associated with the slopes of Volcan Chiriqui in the San Vito area. This may be a polymorphic species that produces what is known as the species *E. melaina*. Further field observation are needed to clarify this.

Eresia melaina

Higgins, 1981

FW Length: 25-27 mm **Plate 50**

Range: Costa Rica(?), Panama, Colombia

Hostplant: Unknown

Early stages: Unknown

Adult: Sexes dimorphic. *Male*—FW black with reduced yellowish markings; the species character (Higgins 1981) is the prominent, isolated spots just above the FW tornus; HW margin narrowly black. *Female*—FW darker and similarly marked. Compare with *E. alsina* and *E. eutropia*.

Habits: At present it is unknown whether this species is in Costa Rica or if it is separate from *E. eutropia*. Further observations are required to establish its specific rank; the individuals in Plate 50 were all collected in the same microhabitat within five days, and all were freshly emerged. This suggests that *E. melaina, E. alsina*, and *E. eutropia* may be conspecific forms, and that *E. melaina* cannot be maintained as a separate species.

Eresia sticta

Schaus, 1913

FW Length: 26-28 mm **Plate 30**

Range: Costa Rican endemic

Hostplant: Unknown

Early stages: Unknown

Adult: Sexes dimorphic. *Male*—FW black with many small white dots; HW has medial area orange and heavy black margins. *Female*—similarly marked but with rounder wings. See *E. poecilina* and *Napeogenes peredia*.

Habits: Occurs from 100 to 800 m on the Atlantic slope, in association with the Carrillo Belt, and sympatrically with its mimetic model, *Napeogenes peredia hemisticta*. Encountered as rare solitary individuals in the forest understory, associated with light gaps. Both sexes have the flutter-sail flight behavior, are very good mimics, and fly only during the morning. Rare in collections.

Eresia poecilina

Bates, 1866

FW Length: male 25-27 mm, female 28 mm **Plate 30**

Range: Costa Rica and Panama

Hostplant: Unknown

Early stages: Unknown

Adult: Sexes dimorphic. *Male*—similar to *E. sticta*, but FW spots are larger, especially across the medial area, and HW has more orange on the disc; HW underside usually has a violet overcast. *Female*—FW spots larger, wings more rounded. Compare with *E. sticta* and *Napeogenes peredia*.

Habits: Occurs from 100 to 800 m on the Atlantic slope, sympatrically with *E. sticta* and *Napeogenes peredia*. While on the wing, it also can be mistaken for *Callithomia hezia*. Uncommon, moderately rare in collections; habits are similar to those of *E. sticta*.

Eresia nigripennis

Salvin, 1869

FW Length: male 26-28 mm, female 30-31 mm **Plate 29**

Range: Costa Rica, Panama(?)

Hostplant: Unknown

Early stages: Unknown

Adult: Sexes dimorphic. *Male*—distinguished from all other similar species by the square FW apex, conspicuously scalloped HW margin, and by the pearly sheen to the HW underside. See *E. alsina, E. eutropia, E. melaina*, and *E. poecilina*.

Habits: Occurs locally at 500 to 1,000 m on the Atlantic slope, with a distribution that appears to be confined along the Cordillera Central. Found in association with cloud forest habitats as solitary individuals that sail along forest and riparian edges. Active only during the morning; flies when the weather is cloudy. Its mimetic models are probably *Olyras* and some of the *Pteronymia* species. Uncommon and local.

Eresia mechanitis

Godman and Salvin, 1878

FW Length: male 26-28 mm, female 27-30 mm **Plate 30**

Range: Nicaragua to Panama

Hostplant: Unknown

Early stages: Unknown

Adult: Sexes dimorphic. Distinguished from similar species by the black bar across the disc of the HW, and the underside washed with pale orange. The male has a more elongate FW.

Habits: Occurs from sea level to 1,000 m on both slopes, in association with rain and wet forest habitats. On the Pacific slope it is concentrated around the San Vito, but has a wider elevational distribution on the Atlantic slope. Flies low to the ground along forest edges and in second growth, always in bright sunlight. Both sexes visit flowers of *Lantana* and various weedy Asteraceae. Commonest during the dry seasons. As the specific name implies, it is a mimic of certain ithomiine species, including *Mechanitis*.

Genus **CASTILIA** Higgins, 1981

This genus is composed of small butterflies whose forms encompass both mimetic and nonmimetic patterns, and show a variety of wing shapes. The genus is characterized by the male genitalia (Higgins 1981), and there is no way to separate it from *Eresia, Anthanassa*, or *Janatella* except by dissection. The genus ranges from Mexico south to the eastern slope of the Andes. Of the thirteen species in *Castilia*, four occur in our area.

Little has been published on the life histories, but the Costa Rican species are known to use Acanthaceae. The larvae are covered with dense bristles, feed gregariously, and have fleshy protrusions, like *Thessalia*.

In Costa Rica, the genus is found from the lowland rain forests to the high mountain regions. Adults feed on flower nectar, but little is known of their population biology. One of our species may be endemic, whereas the others are wide-ranging in Central America.

Castilia eranites

(Hewitson, 1857)

FW Length: 21-23 mm **Plate 30**

Range: Mexico to Colombia and Venezuela

Hostplant: *Odontonema, Justicia* (Acanthaceae)

Early stages: *Egg*—white, with broad base, laid in a loose cluster of 30 to 80. Some eggs are laid on top of others. Early instars skeletonize the leaves, leaving only the cuticle covered with webs and frass.

Adult: Sexes dimorphic. *Male*—distinguished by the dark orange ground color and broad black margins; black bar on HW upperside set near distal margin; HW underside has the black bar broken into spots that are bordered by white. *Female*—FW apex black with scattered yellow spots. See *Eresia coela* and *Eresia mechanitis*.

Habits: Widespread and common from sea level to 1,400 m on both slopes, in all forest types except the dry, deciduous Guanacaste habitats and swamp forest. On the Pacific slope, its distribution is from San Mateo southward. Commonly found along forest edges and in second growth, flying in direct sunlight. The flight is a rapid zigzag and the butterfly frequently settles on low vegetation. When perching, males open and shut their wings while slowly turning the body around. The males patrol in the morning over patches of low vegetation with a wandering, circular flight. The females oviposit around midday, and once a plant has been selected for oviposition, a female may sit for up to thirty minutes laying a single egg cluster. Present throughout the year in most habitats and commonest during the dry seasons. Both sexes visit flowers of *Justicia* and other weedy Acanthaceae and Asteraceae.

Castilia fulgora

(Godman and Salvin, 1878)

FW Length: 14-16 mm **Plate 30**

Range: Costa Rican endemic

Hostplant: Unknown

Early stages: Unknown

Adult: Looks like an *Anthanassa* species. FW margins excavated; separated from all similar species by the two large orange spots on the FW upperside and the orange medial band on the HW upperside.

Habits: Occurs as rare, solitary individuals from 700 to 1,600 m on the Atlantic slope of the Cordillera Central, mostly on the slopes of Volcan Irazu, Poas, and Turrialba. I have found this species in Carrillo along roadsides visiting flowers of *Clibaedium*, and males on wet spots on the ground. Rare in collections.

Castilia ofella

(Hewitson, 1864)

FW Length: 18-20 mm **Plate 30**

Range: Guatemala to Colombia, Venezuela, and Trinidad

Hostplant: *Justicia, Aphelandra* (Acanthaceae)

Early stages: *Mature larva*—body black with four soft, opaque, wedge-shaped protuberances on each segment; each protrusion is armed with many fine bristles; venter white; head capsule amber with two false black eyes. The larvae feed gregariously in groups of twenty to thirty.

Adult: Distinguished from *C. myia* by having an isolated white spot in the FW cell; distal margin of the HW underside with several white triangular crescents. See *C. myia*.

Habits: Occurs locally from 100 to 1,200 m on both slopes, in all disturbed forest habitats except the lowland dry forest in Guanacaste. Flies along rivers and in second growth in bright sunshine, and will enter the forest along wide trails and in large light gaps. Males visit wet sand, and both sexes visit flowers of weedy Asteraceae.

Castilia myia

(Hewitson, 1874)

FW Length: 15-18 mm **Plate 30**

Range: Mexico to Panama

Hostplant: *Justicia* (Acanthaceae)

Adult: Distinguished from *C. ofella* by having

the white portion of the medial band isolated as a rounded spot on the FW; FW underside has black on median and orange at base. *Note*: I do not regard those specimens with a grayer base to the forewing (*griseobasalis* Röber, 1913) as a distinct species. Contrary to Higgins (1981), both forms occur in Costa Rica. Perhaps the early stages will shed light on the problem.

Habits: Occurs from sea level to 1,000 m on the Atlantic slope, in disturbed forest and second-growth habitats, often in abundance. Common and widespread.

Genus **JANATELLA** Higgins, 1981

These are small butterflies that bear a strong resemblance to some of the *Castilia* species, but are recognized by never having an excavated forewing margin, and always having wide white bands. The genus ranges from Nicaragua south to Surinam and the island of Trinidad. There are but three species in the genus, one of which occurs in our area.

Janatella leucodesma

(Felder and Felder, 1861)

FW Length: 16-19 mm **Plate 30**

Range: Nicaragua to Venezuela and Trinidad

Hostplant: Unknown

Early stages: Unknown

Adult: Wing shape rounded; heavy dark margins have a broad white medial area; HW has white spots at cell end near costa. See *Dynamine theseus* and *D. agacles*.

Habits: Occurs from sea level to 600 m on both slopes, in association with rain forest habitats. Encountered as locally abundant populations along forest and riparian edges, and occasionally in the forest interior. Both sexes are very active during sunny mornings and incessantly "jump" from one plant to the next. Both sexes visit flowers of weedy Asteraceae. Common.

Genus **TEGOSA** Higgins, 1981

These small butterflies are recognized by the ovate wingshape and the nondescript, buff-colored underside. The genus ranges from southern Mexico throughout Central America, and as far south as Peru and Argentina in South America. Of the fourteen species in *Tegosa*, most of which are entirely South American, two occur in our area.

In general, there is little known about any aspect of the biology of this genus. One wide-ranging species is known to feed on Asteraceae and has larvae that are similar to those described for *Thessalia*.

Tegosa anieta anieta

(Hewitson, 1864)

FW Length: 14-16 mm **Plate 29**

Range: Mexico to Venezuela and Trinidad

Hostplant: *Mikania, Vernonia* (Asteraceae)

Early stages: Undescribed

Adult: Distinguished from all other species by the orange ground color with narrow dark margins and FW cell bar.

Habits: Widespread and locally common on both slopes in all forest habitats from sea level to 1,400 m, except the Pacific dry forest. Found along rivers and in swampy areas, where it can be extremely common. Flies only in bright sunshine, and is associated with second-growth vegetation. There are numerous subspecies described in relation to the amount of dark brown on the wing margins (see Higgins 1981), but such variation appears in most populations in Costa Rica.

Tegosa nigrella

(Bates, 1866)

FW Length: 14-15 mm **Plate 29**

Range: Guatemala and Costa Rica

Hostplant: Unknown

Early stages: Unknown

Adult: Distinguished by the heavy black wing margins and the washed-out underside coloration. The only form known to occur in Costa Rica has white bands (*niveonotis*), but in Guatemala the insect may have yellow bands, or have the bands almost totally obscured.

Habits: Rare, and known from very few localities in Costa Rica, all of which are on the Atlantic slope: Peñas Blancas, La Cinchona, Juan Viñas, Cachi. I collected it once in July along the road to La Cinchona. Very rare in collections.

Subfamily **DANAINAE**

The butterflies in this subfamily are extremely varied in appearance, but may be recognized by several generally shared characters. The antennae are without scales, and the forelegs are greatly reduced. Additionally, the males often have obvious black androconial patches on the hindwing or have extrusible abdominal hair pencils. The best current reference to this predominantly Old World subfamily is Ackery and Vane-Wright (1984). This exemplary work deals with all 157 species worldwide, and provides an extensive reference section to their biology. The interested reader is referred to this book. In Costa Rica we have three genera and six species, all widely distributed throughout Central America.

The hostplants for the New World danaid butterflies include Asclepiadaceae, Apocynaceae, Caricaceae, Moraceae, and perhaps Loganiaceae and Theophrastaceae. The larvae are striped with conspicuous colors, without spines, and usually have one or more pairs of motile tubercles, and may be similar to some Ithomiinae (i.e., *Aeria, Melinaea*). The pupae vary from thimble shaped to roughly spindle shaped, are usually green or yellow, and may be spotted with metallic gold, as in *Danaus*.

Work on danaines has provided most of the hard information about mimicry, ecological chemistry, and butterfly pheromones and their influence on courtship. The classic experiments of J. Brower (1958), which showed that birds could learn to avoid the color pattern of a distasteful species, and that a mimic species gained protection even if it was palatable, were carried out with *Danaus*. These experiments led to the field of ecological chemistry (Brower 1969), where it was unequivocally shown that secondary compounds in plants were used by certain butterflies for their own chemical defense against predators. These results were further elaborated to show that even if the hostplants fed upon did not contain poisons, the resultant palatable *Danaus* benefited by being an "automimic" (or Browerian mimic) of those individuals that were poisonous (Brower and Moffit 1974). A summary of butterfly chemical defenses may be found in Brower (1984).

The danaines are known to utilize pyrrolizidine alkaloids gathered by adults from certain plants. These chemicals are essential precursors for the male sex pheromones (Meinwald et al. 1969). The use of pyrrolizidine alkaloids by danaines, a trait they share in common with the closely related subfamily Ithomiinae, is thought to have an integral role in the evolution, mimicry, and even chemical defenses of some danaines (Boppré 1978, 1984).

Although danaines are extremely important in Batesian mimicry complexes in the Old World, and in one instance in the New World temperate regions, there is relatively little Batesian mimicry in Central America. Indeed, of the six species in Costa Rica, two are most certainly Müllerian mimics of ithomiines, the three species of *Danaus* may be a Müllerian complex unto themselves, and one species fits no mimicry pattern at all in the New World. As far as I am aware, no classic Batesian mimicry system occurs involving the danaines of Central America.

Perhaps the most spectacular insect migrations that have been documented are those of the Monarch butterfly. Individuals from as far north as Canada are known to migrate thousands of miles south to a communal roosting area to pass the winter in Mexico (Urquhart 1976, Brower et al. 1977). These same butterflies will then return to the northern areas in the spring, laying eggs on hostplants during the return migration, and their offspring will migrate to Mexico the following year. The Central American members of *Danaus* are not known to migrate and, in Costa Rica, it seems the populations are sedentary. There remains much to learn even about the best known butterfly in the world, *Danaus plexippus*.

Genus **DANAUS** Kluk, 1802

In the New World all the butterflies in this genus are recognized by their brown-orange coloration, black wing-margins, and white spotting on the forewing. The males bear a small androconial patch on the dorsal surface of the hindwing and a pair of short abdominal hair pencils. Prior to courtship the abdominal hair pencils are extruded and passed into the pocket like androconial patches on the hindwings, where biochemical interactions are thought to occur. The now activated hair pencils are later passed over the antennae of the female during courtship, which quiets her in preparation for mating. (Note: *D. plexippus*, although it has this "equipment," does not seem to use it.) The genus *Danaus* is pantropical, and in the New World is distributed from Canada throughout North, Central, and South America, the West Indies, and is even found on Cocos Island off the coast of Ecuador.

The hostplants of *Danaus* are various genera of the Asclepiadaceae and perhaps some genera of Apocynaceae and Loganiaceae. The larvae of the Neotropical species are all without spines, have the body white or pale green with black and yellow rings, an unadorned head capsule, and bear several motile segmental tubercles. The general morphology of the larvae recalls the ithomiine genera *Melinaea* and *Aeria*.

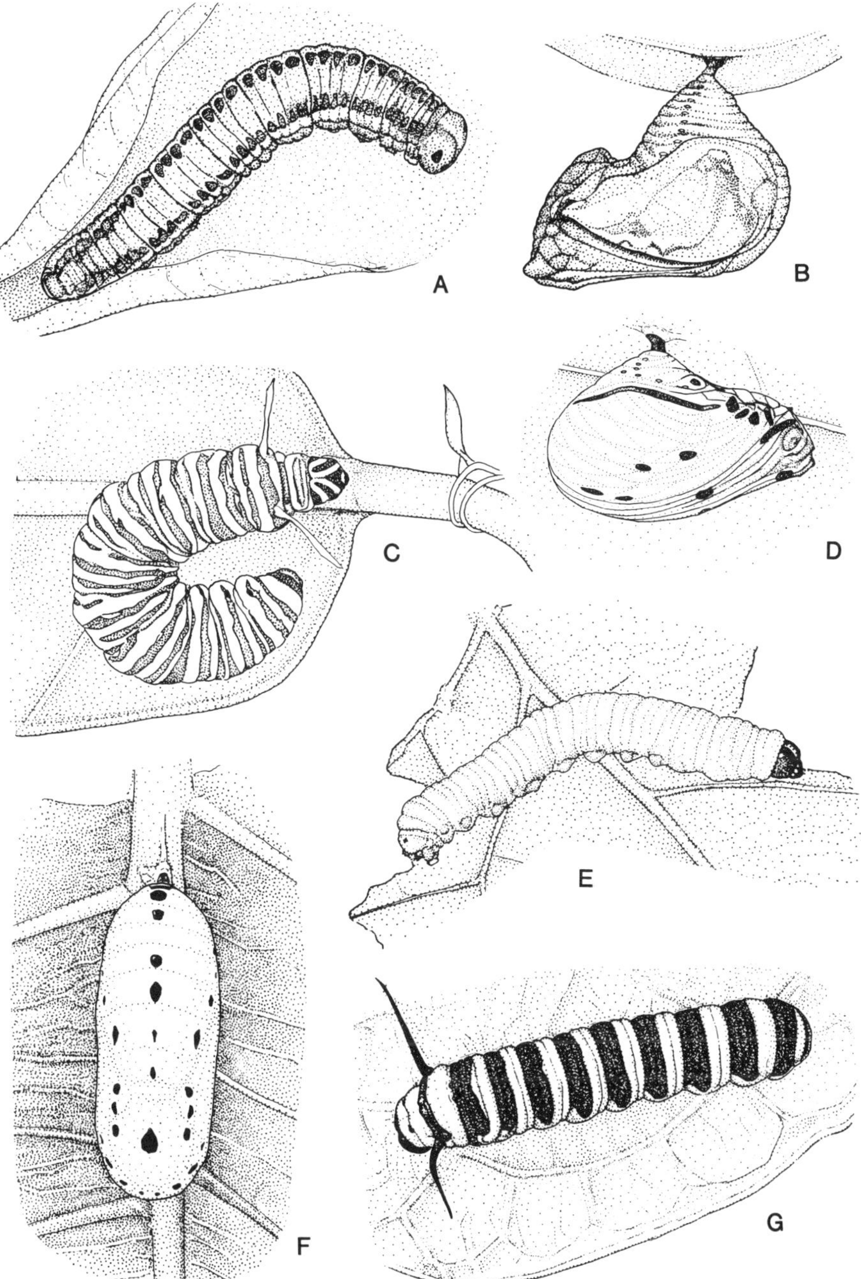

FIGURE 26. Larvae and pupae of the Nymphalidae: Danainae and Ithomiinae. A: *Greta nero* mature larva; B: *Greta nero* pupa; C: *Melinaea lilis imitata* mature larva; D: *Melinaea scylax* pupa; E: *Thyridia psidii melantho* mature larva; F: *Lycorea cleobaea atergatis* pupa; G: *Lycorea cleobaea atergatis* mature larva (drawings by J. Clark).

The pupae are thimble shaped, green, and have several golden spots on the abdominal segments.

In Costa Rica there are three *Danaus* species, all of which are found in open areas, from sea level to over 2,000 m. One important unanswered question about *Danaus* biology is whether or not adults from Central America have the same distasteful properties as the North American populations. The Central American populations are not models for mimicry complexes.

Danaus plexippus

(Linnaeus, 1758)

FW Length: 41-48 mm **Plate 33**

Range: Throughout North, Central, and South America, West Indies, Cocos Island, Philippines, Australia, Sulawesi, Moluccas, New Guinea, and as a rare migrant to Western Europe.

Hostplant: *Asclepias curassavica*, other *Asclepias* spp, *Matelea* (Asclepiadaceae)

Early stages: *Egg*—white, barrel shaped, laid singly. *Mature larvae*—ground color lemon green with rings of black along on the interfaces of the segments; each segment has a white band in the middle; there are four fleshy motile tubercles (two on the thorax, two on the posterior), of which the anterior two are longest; head capsule green with shiny black stripes on the sides and face. *Pupa*—pale green, barrel shaped, tapering abruptly at the head and cremaster; black cremaster; gold spotting on wingpads.

Adult: Very distinct, cannot be confused with anything else in Central America (see Plate 33). The Costa Rican populations differ from the migratory North American population by not having the FW margin excavated.

Habits: Widespread and common in all open areas on both slopes, from sea level to 2,500 m. Especially common in pasturelands above 1,500 m, where its hostplant is an abundant weed. Unlike many other butterfly species, the Guanacaste populations do not show reproductive diapause during the dry season. They stay close to rivers where the hostplants also occur as reproductive individuals. In a few feeding experiments with caged magpie jays, I found that individuals taken from Guanacaste populations in the early wet season are readily eaten by the birds, whereas individuals taken from populations later in the year are not.

Danaus gilippus thersippus

Bates, 1863

FW Length: 38-46 mm **Plate 33**

Range: Southern United States to Panama

Hostplant: *Asclepias, Sarcostemma* (Asclepiadaceae)

Early stages: (Emmel and Emmel 1973) *Egg*—pale green, laid singly. *Mature larva*—body whitish violet with adjacent stripes purple, reddish brown, and yellow; head capsule has two white rings on the face. *Pupa*—similar to *D. plexippus* but slightly more slender, and whitish green.

Adult: Distinguished from *D. eresimus* by having a postmedial row of white spots on the FW that runs from cell to tornus, and the black veins on HW underside are often bordered with white. See *D. eresimus*.

Habits: Widespread and common in all open areas from sea level to 1,500 m. Almost invariably found flying with *D. plexippus*.

Danaus eresimus montezuma

Talbot, 1943

FW Length: 36-40 mm **Plate 33**

Range: Southern United States to Amazon Basin. **Subspecies:** Costa Rica and Panama

Hostplant: *Asclepias, Calotropis, Cynanchum* (Asclepiadaceae); *Spigelia* (doubtful) (Loganiaceae)

Early stages: (M. Fountaine, unpublished drawings British Museum [Natural History]) *Mature larva*—basically yellow-green with fine black rings; eight pairs of white diamonds on dorsum and three single ones where the filaments arise; three pairs of motile black filaments on dorsum, arising from: behind head, behind thorax, and about one-fifth of the way anterior to anal segment, respectively; side has an indistinct black line; venter black; head capsule (indistinct in drawing) appears to be black with yellow rings around its circumference.

Adult: Similar to *D. gilippus* but distinguished by not having the postmedial row of white spots on FW and without white scaling along the black HW veins. See *D. gilippus*.

Habits: Occurs from sea level to 1,000 m on both slopes, in open areas and second-growth habitats, and decidedly more common on the Pacific slope. Of the three *Danaus* species in our area, this species is the least common and is usually encountered as solitary individuals. It differs in flight behavior by flying a little higher above the ground, and is faster and more wary than the other species.

Genus **LYCOREA** Doubleday, 1847

The butterflies in this genus are recognized by their elongate wing shape (which converges upon the Ithomiinae), naked antennae, and in the males, conspicuous abdominal hair pencils (Fig. 6). In the past, the genus *Ituna* was separated from *Lycorea* (due to general color pattern and venation), but has recently been made synonymous under *Lycorea* (Ackery and Vane-Wright 1984). The genus ranges from Mexico throughout Central and South America, and is composed of three or four species, two of which occur in our area.

The hostplants for the genus are in the Moraceae and Caricaceae. The larvae are white with black rings and have a pair of motile filaments behind the head. The pupae are somewhat elongate, pale yellow or green and have black spots on the wing pads (Fig. 26). The larvae of this genus, like *Danaus*, show similarities to the ithomiine genera *Melinaea* and *Aeria*.

The species are all mimetic and either converge upon the tiger-striped patterns of the Ithomiinae and the genus *Heliconius*, or are semi-transparent and show remarkable resemblance to the ithomiine genera *Eutresis* and *Olyras* in Central America, and *Thyridia* in South America. The mimicry is of sufficient precision and plasticity that there are numerous subspecies that follow changes along a north-south gradient, "tracking" the subspecies of the ithomiine species. It is presumed, but unproved, that these butterflies are truly unpalatable to all birds. However, P. Chai informs me that caged jacamars will very often eat *L. cleobaea*, suggesting that it is palatable at least to specialized predators.

Lycorea cleobaea atergatis

Doubleday, 1847

FW Length: 44-51 mm **Plate 33**

Range: Mexico to Peru. **Subspecies:** Mexico to Colombia

Hostplant: *Carica papaya, Jacaratia* (Caricaceae); *Ficus* (Moraceae); *Asclepias curassavica* (Asclepiadaceae)

Early stages: *Egg*—white, laid singly on underside of leaf. A female usually lays several eggs on the same plant. Early instar larvae cut a ring into the leaf tissues and wait for about an hour before feeding. Later instars may cut entire leaf veins, as has been described under *Melinaea*. This presumably prevents mobilization of defensive plant compounds. *Mature larva*—body white with narrow black rings and black anal claspers; two black spots on wingpads and abdomen (Fig. 26).

Adult: Distinguished from tiger-striped species of ithomiines and heliconiines by having short yellow antennae; HW margin slightly scalloped; HW margin has a row of white spots. See *Melinaea lilis* and *Heliconius ismenius*.

Habits: Occurs from sea level to 1,400 m on both slopes in all habitats except open areas. On the Pacific slope I have found this species to be less common in rain forest habitats where the comimics *Melinaea* and *Heliconius* lack hindwing bars. Pacific slope populations also have a high incidence of beak marks. Males perch during the morning in the subcanopy and chase other tiger-striped butterflies, occasionally with the hair pencils extruded (Fig. 6). Females oviposit during midday in all microhabitats, including open areas. The scales on the wings are very tough and many individuals retain clear outlines of bird-beak marks.

Lycorea ilione albescens

(Distant, 1876)

FW Length: 49-56 mm **Plate 33**

Range: Mexico to Brazil. **Subspecies:** Central America

Hostplant: *Ficus* (Moraceae)

Early stages: Similar to those described for *L. cleobaea*

Adult: Distinguished from the very similar, semi-opaque ithomiine *Eutresis* by the large size and short antennae, and by the behavior of the males, which immediately evert their hair pencils upon being handled.

Habits: Occurs from 500 to 1,500 m on both slopes, but chiefly found on the Pacific in association with a variety of forest habitats. Encountered as uncommon solitary individuals along forest edges, and not infrequently in open areas, including the streets of San José. The males visit flowers of *Senecio, Eupatorium,* and *Neomirandia,* from which they presumably obtain pyrrolizidine alkoloids. In the past, this species was placed in the genus *Ituna*.

Genus **ANETIA** Hübner, 1819

This curious genus contains five species that have been placed among the nymphalines, heliconiines, satyrines, brassolines, and are now correctly placed with the danaines (see review in Ackery and Vane-Wright 1984). The genus has an unusual center of distribution, the West Indies, where some islands have endemic species. There is a single species in the mainland Neotropics, and it is confined to Central America. The single species in our area is easily recognized by its general coloration.

There is an often quoted, but doubtful, hostplant record from Cuba that gives *Jaquinia* (Theophrastaceae) as a host for the Cuban species. There are no descriptions of the early stages, and any information would be very useful.

The Central American species is restricted to wet montane areas, but all other species apparently inhabit more arid areas. There is virtually nothing known about the biology of the entire genus.

Anetia thirza insignis
(Salvin, 1869)

FW Length: 39-48 mm **Plate 33**

Range: Mexico to Panama. **Subspecies:** Costa Rica and Panama

Hostplant: Unknown: *Metastelma*(?) (Asclepiadaceae)

Early stages: I have seen one oviposition on a small scandent vine with opposite leaves and milky sap. The egg was crystaline white and laid singly.

Adult: Distinguished by the maroon and black maculations on the base of the FW upperside and a white band across the HW upperside, which is an excellent field character.

Habits: Occurs locally from 900 to 2,600 m on both slopes, in association with cloud forest habitats, with its distribution in Costa Rica centered in the Cordillera de Talamanca. Although seldom common, the populations in the Valle de Copey, which occur in a rainshadow, show marked seasonality. During February to April and into May, there are usually very few individuals to be seen, whereas later in the year there may be an abundance. At this locality, females are in reproductive diapause during the dry season. Usually found as solitary individuals along rivers and forest edges in bright sunshine. While on the wing, both sexes weave in and out of the vegetation and are extremely wary. The males are frequently seen visiting flowers of *Senecio megaphylla.*

Subfamily **ITHOMIINAE**

This highly diverse group of butterflies has been considered a separate family (Fox 1956) or as a subfamily of the Nymphalidae (Ehrlich 1958*a*; Kristensen 1976). The key references to the Central American ithomiines are Fox (1940, 1956, 1960, 1967, 1968), D'Almeida (1978), Mielke and Brown (1979), Haber (1978), and Brown (1977). In the present work I have followed the systematic arrangement of Fox (1968) and have modified his treatments where appropriate.

The Ithomiinae, which are entirely Neotropical, are closely related to the danaines via the monobasic Tellervinae, with which they share similarities of adult and larval morphology (Ackery and Vane-Wright 1984). This can readily be appreciated from the larvae of *Aeria, Melinaea,* and *Tithorea.* It is of interest that in the Old World the Danainae have somewhat similar species diversity to the Ithomiinae of the Neotropics (see section on diversity).

The Neotropical Ithomiinae range from Mexico through Central and South America, reaching their greatest diversity on the eastern slope of the Andes. In Central America the commonest ithomiine color patterns are clear-winged, translucent amber, or tiger-striped. The males of all species bear long androconial scales (quite hairlike) on the costal area of the hindwing. These scales are exposed during courtship and when displaying on a lek. The ithomiines have weak antennal clubs, small eyes in relation to the thorax, and long, slender abdomens. All of the Costa Rican species have a characteristic fluttery flight with deep wing beats, and this flight behavior distinguishes the subfamily in the field. With a little care, it is easy to distinguish the ithomiines from their mimics in this way.

In Costa Rica some of our species may be confused with *Heliconius, Lycorea,* or *Dismorphia.* However, confusion more often arises between the genera and species of the Ithomiine themselves, and in order to identify them correctly, a fair amount of time needs to be spent studying these butterflies. In particular, close attention must be paid to the venation of the hindwing to distinguish between the genera. *Always* check the hindwing venation before commiting a determination to paper. The illustrations in Figure 27 should prove helpful. Once the genus has been determined, it will be easy to use the characters in the text, along with the color plates, to determine the species correctly. After working with this group of butterflies, even the most skeptical will believe in mimicry.

The hostplant relationships in the Ithomiinae are mainly with the Solanaceae, and to a limited extent with the Apocynaceae. Although a major portion of the hostplant records for the Costa Rican species are reported in Haber (1978) and supplemented by DeVries (1985*a*), the vast majority of species have never had their early stages described in detail. The larvae are typically naked, some have lateral projections arising near the venter, and some have motile filaments arising near the head, which recall the danaines. The larvae are generally translucent green and rather dull, but some have bright colors (Fig. 26). Depending on the species, larvae may feed gregariously or

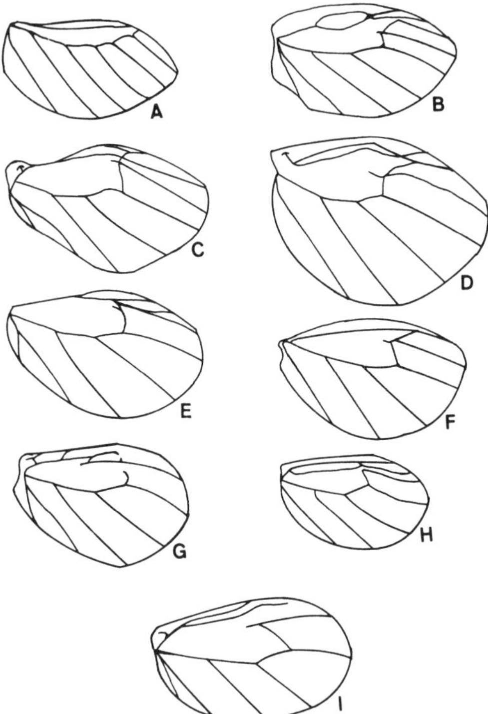

FIGURE 27. Hindwing venation of selected genera of Ithomiinae. A: *Napeogenes*; B: *Ithomia*; C: *Oleria*; D: *Dircenna*; E: *Greta*; F: *Pteronymia*; G: *Hypoleria*; H: *Pseudoscada*; I: *Heterosais*. The hindwing costa are normally covered by the forewing. The configuration of the veins at the end of the cell and apex will provide the information necessary to determine the genus (drawings by P. J. DeVries).

as solitary individuals, and many species cause characteristic feeding damage. Some species eat small round holes in the leaf tissue, whereas others may consume the entire plant. A number of the Costa Rican species oviposit on the perimeter of old feeding damage holes. The pupae vary in shape, but most have a chrome silver or gold coloration that gives the pupae the appearance of water drops when seen in the field. This reflective coloration of the pupae provides yet another similarity to the Danainae.

With few exceptions, the ithomiines are forest inhabitants, and observing the phantomlike flight of the clear-winged species in the forest understory leaves little doubt in one's mind as to where these butterflies have evolved. In Costa Rica ithomiines may be found in every habitat. The highest diversity of species is in the mid-elevational forest belts between 600 and 1,500 meters.

Migration up and down elevational gradients in Costa Rica is common for almost every species. The migrations are triggered by changes in the seasons or changes in local weather patterns. For this reason, it is possible to find over 80 percent of the total Costa Rican species in a rural backyard in San José. Given that the majority of our species are very mobile, it can be appreciated how difficult it would be to define or delimit the habitat for a given species—they are constantly on the move.

The ithomiines are among the few butterflies known to form mating displays that can correctly be termed leks. A lek is a communal display or aggregation of males which attract females to the display to mate. Such leks were known to the early naturalists, and are common in all forest areas, especially along streams. An ithomiine lek can be composed of numerous species and genera. As demonstrated by Haber (1978), the lek is initiated by males sitting on leaves and exposing the androconial hairs to release a pheromone. The male of each species is attractive to both males and females of its own species, plus some other species and genera. The other species release their pheromones, which attract still other species. Hence, after the course of a few days a lek may contain numerous different species. Lek areas that have been used for a long time have the greatest number of species in them. (For more information see Haber 1978, and Gilbert 1969*a*.)

The ithomiine pheromones are derived from pyrrolizidine alkaloids that the males collect from plant sources (Pliske et al. 1976), and it is generally thought that the males are obligated to obtain these alkaloids in order to mate. Female ithomiines may assess the alkaloid content of a courting male and choose to mate with the male with the greatest quantity. The female may aquire pyrrolozidine alkaloids via the spermataphore of the male and gain defensive chemicals through mating (see below). In Costa Rica the major plant sources highly attractive to ithomiine males are *Heliotropium, Tournefourtia,* and *Myosotis* (Boraginaceae) and *Eupatorium, Neomirandia,* and *Senecio* (Asteraceae). It is good field practice always to carry some dead Boraginaceae. By hanging bits of these plants along a trap line it is possible, over the course of several days, to get a very good estimate of which ithomiine species occur there. The males of most species and both sexes of other species avidly visit these baits within an hour of placing them in the forest. However, some species are not attracted to the baits at all (e.g. *Hyposcada, Eutresis*).

Of all Neotropical butterflies, the ithomiines are perhaps the most important models for mimicry complexes. Over a century ago, naturalists who knew nothing of ecological chemistry were aware that the ithomiines were distasteful to vertebrate predators. This awareness led to the development of mimic theory (Bates 1862; Müller 1879). The distasteful properties of the ithomiines are thought to be derived from larval feeding on the Solanaceae, a family commonly known as the deadly nightshades. This plant family contains a wide variety of very poisonous chemicals that have been used throughout history as sources of medicines and poisons. Recently, however, it has been demonstrated that the pyrrolizidine alkaloids (not found in the Solanaceae) acquired by adult feeding can be considered a defense against predators (Brown 1984). So it may well be that the males that so eagerly seek the alkaloids for their pheromones may in fact be using these chemicals for two purposes: one of love, the other of being obnoxious. For the use of pyrrolizidine alkaloids for defense and mating see also the summaries in Boppré (1984) and Edgar (1984).

For nutrition, both sexes feed on flower nectar. However, in addition to flowers, the females of certain species feed on fresh bird droppings. This type of feeding has been best documented in *Melinaea*, which, in some areas of Costa Rica, feed on the bird droppings of antbirds and antwrens that are associated with army ant swarms. It is thought that such feeding allows the females to obtain a rich source of nitrogen for their eggs, much as *Heliconius* females use pollen (Ray and Andrews 1980).

Genus **EUTRESIS** Doubleday, 1847

The two species that enter our area are recognized by the amber and translucent color patterns, the moderately large size, and the presence (in males) of only one androconial patch. The genus is separated from the similar genus *Olyras* by differences in venation, androconial patches, and genitalia. *Eutresis* ranges from Costa Rica to South America and contains a few species, all which are involved in mimicry with the danaine genus *Lycorea* and other ithomiines.

There is nothing known of the hostplants or early stages. It would be of considerable interest to publish any life history information of *Eutresis* because of its possible link with the Danainae.

In Central America all of the species inhabit cloud forest habitats and are never abundant. Both Costa Rican species are frequently observed sailing, with a characteristic flight, over chasms. Unlike many ithomiine genera, *Eutresis* is not known to visit plants that contain pyrrolizidine alkaloids.

Eutresis dilucida

Staudinger, 1885

FW Length: 47-49 mm **Plate 33**

Range: Costa Rica and western Panama

Hostplant: Unknown

Early stages: Unknown

Adult: Distinguished from similar species by the transparent triangle in the FW cell, with the apex of the triangle at the FW costa; HW transparent patches narrow and heavily bordered in amber. See *E. hypereia* and *Lycorea ilione*.

Habits: Occurs from 900 to 1,800 m on both slopes, in association with all forest habitats, and occasionally seen in the streets of San José during migrations. Encountered as solitary individuals sailing across the forest canopy during the early morning, just after sunrise. The males perch in the subcanopy at forest edges and patrol small areas around the perch. Both sexes visit flowers of emergent *Inga* trees. This species is uncommon but widespread in Costa Rica.

Eutresis hypereia theope

Godman and Salvin, 1877

FW Length: 42-45 mm **Plate 33**

Range: Costa Rica to Ecuador. **Subspecies:** Costa Rica and Panama

Hostplant: Unknown

Early stages: Unknown

Adult: Distinguished by the square transparent spot in the FW cell, followed by a triangle that runs from the cell margin to the tornus; transparent patches in the HW are wide and bordered narrowly in amber. See *E. dilucida* and *Lycorea ilione*.

Habits: Occurs from 900 to 1,600 m on both slopes, in association with forest habitats. The flight behavior is similar to that described for *E. dilucida* but, although the two species are often found in the same habitats, this species is encountered less frequently.

Genus **OLYRAS** Doubleday, 1847

The two species in this genus that enter our area are separated from the genus *Eutresis* by having a heavy scaling to the forewing, two androconial patches, and a slightly more acute forewing apex. *Olyras* contains only three species, all of which are considered to be of Central American origin.

The hostplants and early stages are unknown; the host may prove to be either Solanaceae or Apocynaceae. Like *Eutresis*, this genus is found in cloud forest habitats and individuals are seldom abundant. However, unlike *Eutresis*, *Olyras* visit sources of pyrrolizidine alkaloids.

Olyras crathis staudingeri

Godman and Salvin, 1897

FW Length: 46-49 mm **Plate 33**

Range: Costa Rica to Ecuador. **Subspecies:** Costa Rica and Panama

Hostplant: Unknown

Early stages: Unknown

Adult: Similar to *Hyaliris excelsa* but distinguished by the large size, acute FW apex, and black HW margin without white spots on the HW underside.

Habits: Occurs from 700 to 1,800 m on both slopes in association with all forest habitats. Most frequently encountered as solitary individuals flying at the canopy level of the forest in ravines or along rivers. Both sexes visit flowers of *Inga* trees, and occasionally both will visit sources of pyrrolizidine alkaloids. Although never common, this species is present in all suitable forest habitats throughout the year.

Olyras insignis insignis

Salvin, 1869

FW Length: 45-48 mm **Plate 33**

Range: Costa Rica to Ecuador. **Subspecies:** Costa Rica and Panama

Hostplant: Unknown. Upon several occasions in Parque Braulio Carrillo, I have watched (with binoculars) females oviposit upon a canopy vine with medium-sized leaves, but I have never been able to collect the plant.

Early stages: Unknown

Adult: Distinguished by the large translucent areas on both wings that have a yellow cast, especially the HW. *Note*: G. B. Small has collected a few specimens near San Vito de Java that have the HW disc entirely reddish. It remains to be seen if this represents a distinct subspecies.

Habits: Occurs in local populations from 500 to 1,800 m on both slopes in all forest habitats along the Cordillera Central and Talamanca. Just after dawn, individuals of this species fly in the forest canopy, especially in ravines or along rivers. The yellow on the HW disc is easily seen with binoculars. The males are occasionally taken at pyrrolizidine alkaloid sources, and both sexes visit flowers of *Inga* trees. I have found this butterfly to be most abundant during the dry season. Although not uncommon, this species is poorly represented in Costa Rican collections.

Genus **TITHOREA** Doubleday, 1847

Our two species in this genus are recognized by having acute forewing apices, being heavily scaled, and generally looking like *Heliconius* butterflies. The male has two androconial patches. The genus ranges from Mexico to South America, and in South America there are a number of subspecies.

The hostplants for the genus are Apocynaceae. The larvae are striped black and white and bear motile filaments, like the danaines.

Tithorea harmonia helicaon

Godman and Salvin, 1879

FW Length: 36-39 mm **Plate 34**

Range: Mexico to Brazil. **Subspecies:** Nicaragua to Panama

Hostplant: *Prestonia* (Apocynaceae)

Early stages: Undescribed

Adult: Distinguished by the black line on the HW cutting across the discal area, and the dorsal part of the abdomen being orange. See *Heliconius ismenius* and *Melinaea scylax.*

Habits: Restricted to the Pacific slope, in association with deciduous forest habitats, from sea level to 1,300 m. Encountered as solitary individuals flying in the forest understory. Both sexes visit flowers of *Psychotria, Hamelia,* and *Chomelia.* In the lowland Guanacaste forest, this species is present throughout the year but at very low population levels during the dry season. *T. harmonia* is much less common than *T. tarricina,* which probably reflects its restricted habitat preference.

Tithorea tarricina pinthias

Goldman and Salvin, 1879

FW Length: 38-44 mm **Plate 34**

Range: Mexico to Brazil. **Subspecies:** Nicaragua to Panama

Hostplant: *Prestonia portabellensis* (Apocynaceae)

Early stages: (Muyshondt et al. 1976) *Mature larva*—pale green, narrowly ringed in shiny blackish-brown; head capsule has a white triangle on the face; two anterior motile filaments. *Pupa*—elongate, chrome-colored, with black markings on the wingpads and abdomen.

Adult: Distinguished by the black FW with yellow spots; the black HW border intrudes into the orange discal area and forms a toothlike shape at the cell end. See *Callithomia hezia* and *Heliconius hecale.*

Habits: Occurs from sea level to 1,500 m in all forest areas, except those that have a strong dry season. The flight is slow and fluttery, and while flying, the butterfly pauses and glides much like its comimic, *Heliconius hecale.* For a few hours each morning, males perch about two meters above the ground in small light gaps or along forest edges. The female oviposits from late morning until early afternoon, usually on plants in light gaps. The body and wings of this species are tough and resilient, retaining clear bird-beak or lizard jaw marks without losing pieces of the wing. Both sexes visit flowers of *Hamelia, Psychotria, Eupatorium, Epidendrum panniculatum,* and various sources of pyrrolizidine alkaloids. This species is present in almost all habitats throughout the year.

Genus **MELINAEA** Hübner, 1816

In general appearance, the butterflies in this genus look like *Heliconius* but are recognized by having smaller eyes and the androconial hairs between the wings. The genus ranges from Mexico through Central and South America, with most of the species occurring on the eastern slope of the Andes. In Central America there are three species, two of which occur in Costa Rica.

In Central America the hostplants belong to the Solanaceae, of which the genera *Markea* and *Juanaloa* are important. The larvae resemble those of *Tithorea* and certain danaine species (Fig. 26). In most instars, the larvae cut the leaf veins before eating the plant tissues, presumably to prevent secondary chemicals from being mobolized to the area where the larva is feeding. The pupa is compressed into a squat J shape and bears no traces of silver or gold (Fig. 26).

In Costa Rica, *Melinaea* is found in all forest habitats up to 1,500 m elevation. Although Brown (1977) considers the Costa Rican members of the genus all under the species name *ethra,* I follow Fox (1960), and consider them two separate species because of genitalic differences. They fly together in the Meseta Central, and there are no intergrades between them; future studies can concentrate on the genetics or ecology to examine what differences there are between the two. To this end it is worth noting that *Melinaea* make excellent greenhouse animals if provided with nectar, hostplants, and a source of pyrrolizidine alkaloids.

Melinaea ethra lilis

Bates, 1864

FW Length: 44-47 mm **Plate 34**

Range: Mexico to the Amazon. **Subspecies:** Guatemala to Panama

Hostplant: *Markea neurantha* (Solanaceae)

Early stages: *Egg*—white, laid singly on the underside of leaves. Females generally lay several eggs on the same plant; *Markea* is a hemiepiphytic shrub. *Mature larva*—body white, ringed by dark lines of magenta on each segment; area behind the head pale orange-pink, which forms a slight indentation in the white of the body; the first segment bears two whiplike filaments that are black on the anterior surface and white on the posterior surface; the filaments are motile, and twitch when the larva walks; head capsule black with a white triangle on the face, having its apex fused to a lateral white line on the head, then running to the base of the mandibles (Fig. 26). *Pupa*—suspended and having the overall appearance of a wooden shoe; abdomen compressed and body held parallel to the surface of the pupation site; pale green with fine black lines on the wingpads and head; cremaster black. *Note*: the young instars have a characteristic feeding habit: they cut small circles from the leaf undersurface, wait a short time, and then feed on the leaf tissues within the circle. Mature larvae will cut across leaf veins and tissue before feeding. From this damage it is possible to estimate the number of larvae that have fed on a plant.

Adult: Distinguished from similar species by the small head, long yellow antennae, and the black inner margin of the HW. See *Heliconius ismenius* and *Lycorea cleobaea*.

Habits: Occurs from sea level to 1,300 m, mainly on the Atlantic slope, but some populations occur in the Meseta Central remnant forests, and it is very occasionally taken in the lowlands of the deciduous forest (probably transients). In the field this species is easily confused with *Heliconius ismenius telchinia* unless one can observe the size of the head. It is also commonly placed in collections with *Heliconius*. In the field it is not uncommon, although it is usually encountered as solitary individuals. The males are active from early morning until before midday, when they maintain perches in light gaps about ten meters above the ground. During their perching time, males chase other tiger-striped butterflies. The female becomes active at midday and is most frequently seen in the understory or subcanopy searching for oviposition sites. In some lowland localities, the females will follow army ant swarms (*Eciton* species) and feed on the fresh droppings of the antbirds that associate themselves with army ant raiding swarms. During these times the females will venture into open areas. Both sexes visit flowers of *Cephaelis, Hamelia, Psychotria, Inga, Lantana*, and *Warsczewisczia*. In the Atlantic lowlands, this species is present throughout the year but in greatest abundance during the dry season.

Melinaea scylax

Salvin, 1871

FW Length: 42-45 mm **Plate 34**

Range: Costa Rica to Colombia

Hostplant: *Juanaloa mexicana, Markea neurantha* (Solanaceae)

Early stages: Similar to those described for *M. ethra*, but the larvae have narrower white banding on the head capsule, and the motile filaments are somewhat shorter. The pupa is as described for *ethra* (Fig. 26).

Adult: Distinguished from similar species by the pale, irregular FW band; FW has a round yellow spot in the tornus; HW has no black median band. See *M. ethra, Heliconius ismenius*, and *Tithorea harmonia*.

Habits: Occurs from sea level to 1,200 m on the Pacific slope, in association with wet forest habitats. Occasionally found in the Meseta Central and the Guanacaste forests during the rainy season, probably as transients. The habits are similar to those described for *M. ethra*, with the exception that the hostplant in the field is as yet unknown. On the Osa Peninsula this species is most abundant during the dry season, but is generally common in all lowland Pacific rain forest habitats.

Genus **THYRIDIA** Hübner, 1816

The various problems surrounding the correct name for this genus are discussed in Fox (1968), who decided to use the name *Xanthocleis*. However, in his zeal to get the name correct, he got it wrong (Lamas 1973). The reader should be aware that the butterflies have been written about under several generic names.

The single species that occurs in Central America is recognized by the black forewing bearing several transparent spots, and the hindwing disc, which always bears a black spot at the end of the cell. The genus ranges from Mexico to the Amazon Basin, where there are apparently several species.

The hostplant for our species is *Cyphomandra* (Solanaceae). The larvae are naked, without filaments or dorsal tubercles, and semi-transparent on the venter (Fig. 26). The pupa is elongate and colored chrome-silver.

In Costa Rica these butterflies are found in all wet forest habitats up to 1,500 meters in elevation.

Thyridia psidii melantho

(Bates, 1866)

FW Length: 39-44 mm **Plate 34**

Range: Mexico to the Amazon. **Subspecies:** Mexico to Panama

Hostplant: *Cyphomandra hartwegii* (Solanaceae)

Early stages: *Egg*—white, laid singly on the underside of leaves. The female may take up to an hour investigating a hostplant before ovipositing. *Mature larva*—body colored a powdery green-blue; venter transparent with the tracheae visible; eight short yellow lateral tubercles project horizontally at the interface of the venter and the sides; each proleg has a shiny black square on the outside; head capsule black with prominent white lines across the face that follow the ecdysal sutures (Fig. 26). The prepupa changes color to a purple body with the area above the prolegs dull yellow, and the posterior two tubercles white. *Pupa*—similar in shape to *Mechanitis*, but more silver and with many fine black striations.

Adult: Occurs from sea level to over 1,500 m throughout the country, in association with disturbed forest habitats. Most frequently encountered as solitary individuals flying along forest edges during the early mornings. Its flight behavior is very characteristic, with deep wing beats, almost closing at each beat. Once seen, the flight serves as a good field character. The female oviposits from morning until midday on hostplants in direct sunshine. Males visit sources of pyrrolizidine alkaloids. Although seldom abundant, this species is present throughout the year in all habitats except the Guanacaste lowland forest. Both sexes visit flowers of *Lantana, Hamelia, Inga*, and *Carica*.

Genus **MECHANITIS** Fabricius, 1807

The butterflies in this genus show an extraordinary amount of geographical variation. Among the five species currently recognized, there are fifty-two subspecies that can be distinguished with a reasonable degree of accuracy (Brown 1977). In Costa Rica there are three species, one with two subspecies. The genus is defined on the basis of its venation, but even monographers rely on a "gestalt" to recognize the genus. In our area, the butterflies can all be recognized by having elongate forewings, a tiger-striped pattern, and each species has a characteristic marking at the forewing tornus. The genus ranges from Mexico to the Amazon Basin (where the greatest proliferation of subspecies occurs).

The hostplants are in the Solanaceae, of which the genus *Solanum* is most important. All the Costa Rican species seem to feed on several different species of the plant. The larvae are gregarious and can be very colorful, having a characteristic skirt of lateral projections arising at the base of the prolegs. The pupae are elongate and colored silver.

All of the Central American species are quite common in disturbed areas, and hence are frequently seen near human habitations. They occur in virtually all habitats from sea level to over 1,800 meters. Perhaps the most successful species is *M. isthmia*, which occurs in forests or in stark open areas recently clearcut for timber or burned for pasture. By sheer abundance I would guess that *Mechanitis* is an extremely important component in the tiger-striped mimicry complexes, and has most likely been an important factor in their evolution (Brown 1977). There is, however, little known of the ecological chemistry of *Mechanitis*. All of the species in Costa Rica migrate up and down mountains during the changes of the seasons. The males avidly visit sources of pyrrolizidine alkaloids and form semi-permanent leks in light gaps and along watercourses in the forest.

Mechanitis lysimnia doryssus

Bates, 1864

FW Length: 34-38 mm **Plate 34**

Range: Mexico to Venezuela. **Subspecies:** Mexico to Panama

Hostplant: *Solanum* (Solanaceae)

Early stages: *Egg*—white, barrel shaped, laid in clusters of ten to fifty. *Mature larva*—pale green streaked with yellow; lateral papillae well developed, one per segment; head capsule pale yellow without markings. The larvae feed gregariously and can completely defoliate the hostplant. *Pupa*—elongate, silver, with black and brown lines along the wingpads and abdomen; the thoracic area is produced into a bump; cremaster black and curved ventrally.

Adult: Two subspecies. Both can be distinguished from similar species by a black comma mark on the FW upperside just above the tornus; yellow FW bands are broad; there is usually a square black spot on the FW cell. Subspecies *doryssus* is found throughout the country and has similar sexes. The subspecies *labotas* Bates, 1864 has slightly dimorphic sexes and has been named on the basis of the female sex, which has a "clean" HW discal area (see Plate 34). This latter subspecies is found in the lowland forests around the Osa Peninsula. Compare with *M. menapis* and *M. polymnia*.

Habits: Common and widespread throughout the country, from sea level to 1,500 m in all wet forest habitats, and occasionally in the lowlands of Guanacaste during the rainy season. Frequently encountered in small groups, flying with other species of *Mechanitis*. The habits are very similar to those of *M. polymnia*, except that it does not as readily leave the confines of the forest. Both sexes visit a wide variety of flowers, and the females visit fresh bird droppings.

Mechanitis polymnia isthmia

Bates, 1863

FW Length: 34-38 mm **Plate 34**

Range: Mexico to the Amazon. **Subspecies:** Mexico to Panama

Hostplant: *Solanum* (Solanaceae). All hostplants are hirsute woody shrubs and vines occurring in second-growth habitats.

Early stages: *Egg*—small, white, barrel shaped, laid in clusters of ten to forty. *Mature larva*—body pale green with very prominent lateral papillae, each of which has a black dot at the base. The larvae are gregarious. *Pupa*—similar to that described for *lysimnia*, only reflective gold.

Adult: This highly variable species may always be distinguished by the isolated round spot (not a comma) in the tornus of the FW upperside, present in both sexes. See *M. lysimnia* and *M. menapis*.

Habits: This is the commonest and most widespread ithomiine species in Costa Rica, occurring from sea level to 1,500 m in virtually all habitats. Unlike its congeners, this species will fly in direct sunshine across open areas, as well as in the shade of the forest, and is frequently seen in the streets of all major Costa Rican cities. *M. polymnia* is persistent throughout the year in all habitats.

Mechanitis menapis saturata

Godman and Salvin, 1901

FW Length: 38-41 mm **Plate 34**

Range: Mexico to Ecuador. **Subspecies:** Mexico to Panama

Hostplant: *Solanum hispidum, S. torvum*, other *Solanum* (Solanaceae)

Early stages: *Egg*—white, laid in clusters of thirty to eighty. *Mature larva*—body pale yellow; lateral tubercles swollen at their bases, with the lateral portion yellow and the distal part white, and a black spot at the base of each tubercle; head capsule gray with two black spots on the face. The larvae feed gregariously. *Pupa*—similar to *M. lysimnia* but with more black on the head and wingpads.

Adult: Distinguished by having the FW apex black and the yellow FW bands narrow.

Habits: Occurs from 700 to 2,000 m, on both slopes, in all forest habitats. Encountered as solitary individuals in the shade of the understory or forest edge, rarely in open areas. Females oviposit in the morning, until early afternoon, on young hostplants along forest edges. Both sexes visit flowers of *Inga, Senecio*, and *Eupatorium*.

Genus **SCADA** Kirby, 1871

The butterflies in this genus are all small, semitranslucent, and characterized by a distinctive venation (Fox 1967). The single Central American species is recognized by its feeble flight and color pattern. The genus ranges from Nicaragua to the Amazon Basin, and contains about ten species. The hostplants for the Central America species are all *Solanum* (Solanaceae), and the early stages are in need of description.

Scada zibia xanthina

(Bates, 1866)

FW Length: 21-24 mm **Plate 34**

Range: Nicaragua to Peru. **Subspecies:** Nicaragua to Panama

Hostplant: *Solanum siparunoides, S. enchylozum* (Solanaceae)

Early stages: *Egg*—white, tiny, laid singly on the developing leaves of hostplants occurring in forest light gaps.

Adult: Distinguished by the tiny size, semitransparent color, and the black wing borders with white spots on both upper and underside. A good field character is the feeble flight. See *Aeria eurimedia* and *Oleria zelica*.

Habits: Occurs from sea level to 600 m on the Atlantic slope, in primary rain forest. Encountered as solitary individuals flying low to the ground in deep shade. The females oviposit around midday. I have found this species to be most abundant during the dry seasons, but it is present in most habitats throughout the year. During the early morning, both sexes visit flowers of *Cephaelis* and *Psychotria*. Usually found in very local populations, at low densities.

Genus **NAPEOGENES** Bates, 1862

This genus is recognized by its distinctive hindwing venation (Fig. 27). The color patterns range from transparent to tiger-striped, and *Napeogenes* is important in Müllerian mimicry complexes throughout the Neotropics. For example, in Costa Rica our species can be confused with *Callithomia, Dircenna, Ithomia, Hypothyris*, and *Eresia*, and other genera as well. The genus ranges from Mexico to the Amazon Basin, and although there are numerous species, only three occur in Costa Rica.

The hostplants of importance are in the genera *Solanum* and *Lycianthes*. The early stages are incompletely known and are in need of description. The Costa Rica species are all forest inhabitants, and include subspecies that are endemic to Costa Rica.

Napeogenes cranto paedaretus

Godman and Salvin, 1878

FW Length: 31-33 mm **Plate 34**

Range: Costa Rica to Peru. **Subspecies:** Costa Rica and Panama

Hostplant: Unknown

Early stages: Unknown

Adult: This species must be distinguished from other amber-winged ithomiines by the configuration of the HW venation (Fig. 27). The HW is elliptical and curves toward the distal margin. See *Dircenna, Pteronymia*, and *Ithomia xenos*.

Habits: Occurs from 700 to 1,600 m on both slopes along the Cordillera de Talamanca. This rare species is encountered as solitary individuals, always in areas of heavy rainfall, and usually flying at the subcanopy level. In flight it resembles *Ithomia xenos* to a remarkable degree, but with practice it can be determined on the wing. This species appears to be intolerant of areas of extensive disturbance. The males infrequently visit sources of pyrrolizidine alkaloids.

Napeogenes peredia hemisticta

Schaus, 1913

FW Length: 20-30 mm **Plate 34**

Range: Costa Rica to Colombia. **Subspecies:** Costa Rica

Hostplant: Unknown

Early stages: Unknown

Adult: Distinguished from similar species by the rounded FW apex, which bears many densely clustered yellow spots; base of FW always orange-brown. See *Callithomia hexia* and *Eresia sticta*.

Habits: Occurs from sea level to 800 m on the Atlantic slope in association with the Carrillo Belt. Encountered as uncommon, solitary individuals in primary forest. During the early morning, the males perch in the subcanopy, within the deep shade of the forest. I have never seen more than one male perching in any area, and they are rarely taken at pyrrolizidine alkaloid sources. When flying, the yellow spots on the FW appear fused, making it difficult to separate from *Eresia sticta*. *N. peredia* is easily separated while flying from *Callithomia hezia* by having a deeper wing beat and less gliding flight. Both sexes visit flowers of *Cephaelis* during the early morning. Neither sex is active after midday. This species is very local, and uncommon in Costa Rican collections.

Napeogenes tolosa amara

Godman, 1899

FW Length: 27-29 mm **Plate 34**

Range: Mexico to Colombia. **Subspecies:** Nicaragua to Panama

Hostplant: *Solanum, Lycianthes* (Solanaceae)

Early stages: *Egg*—white, laid singly on the underside of leaves of hostplants ranging from juvenile to mature plants.

Adult: Distinguished by the yellow hourglass figure in the FW cell; yellow spots on the FW are large and irregular; the HW is slightly angular; the spotting is variable. See *Hypothyris euclea*.

Habits: Occurs from sea level to 1,500 m, throughout the country, in all forest habitats except the dry forest of Guanacaste. This species is quite common and usually found flying with *Hypothyris euclea*. The males are frequently found in multispecies leks. Both sexes visit a variety of flowers, especially those of the Rubiaceae and various Asteraceae.

Genus **HYPOTHYRIS** Hübner, 1821

The butterflies in this genus are morphologically very similar to *Hyalyris*, a fact that has generated a good deal of taxonomic argument in the literature (Fox and Real 1971). Although there are quite a few species in *Hypothyris*, most of them are entirely South American, with only two species in our area. The genus is separated from *Napeogenes* (which it resembles) by the venation, but the two species in our area are recognized by their distinct color patterns.

The hostplants for the genus are in the Solanaceae, of which *Solanum* is most important for the Central American species. The larvae are smooth, without the lateral tubercles of *Mechanitis*, are brightly colored, and are gregarious feeders. The pupae are compressed and colored reflective gold. The early stages are similar to those of *Hyalyris*.

In Costa Rica the butterflies in *Hypothyris* occur in all habitats below 1,500 m and one species (*euclea*) is one of the most frequently encountered of the ithomiine species. Both of our species exhibit seasonal migration along elevational gradients. The common species, *H. euclea*, may show very pronounced seasonal abundance (Young 1979), which has been correlated with hours of sunshine. The males visit sources of pyrrolizidine alkaloids.

Hypothyris euclea valora

(Haensch, 1909)

FW Length: 29-33 mm **Plate 34**

Range: Mexico to Brazil. **Subspecies:** Mexico to Panama

Hostplant: *Solanum rugosum, S. umbellatum* (Solanaceae)

Early stages: (Young 1977*b*) *Egg*—white, laid singly or in clusters of 40 to 90. *Early instars*—whitish green without any distinctive markings. *Mature larva*—dorsum black with many white spots along the midline; venter and anal segment white; prolegs translucent green; head capsule shiny black with a white band across the face. The larvae feed gregariously and are capable of defoliating the hostplants. The caterpillars leave only skeletal veins. *Pupa*—compressed, with roundly produced wingpads; overall coloration reflective golden amber, with little ornamentation. The defoliation of a *S. rugosum* plant is apparently sufficient to reduce the production of flowers and fruits for several seasons.

Adult: Distinguished by the subapical band of the FW being a zigzag shape, just outside the cell; a black triangle in the FW cell has its apex directed basad; HW usually has a black medial band, but it may be absent in some southern populations. The markings on the FW are usually yellow, but occasionally white in populations in the lowland Atlantic rain forests.

Habits: Occurs from sea level to 1,400 m, in association with forest habitats of varying quality, throughout the country. Although most abundant on the Atlantic slope, it is a permanent resident in Pacific slope wet forest, and occasionally individuals are found in the Guanacaste dry forest as a result of migrations. In some areas of the Atlantic lowlands, this species shows remarkable monthly fluctuations in abundance (Young 1979). In the Meseta Central, the fluctuations correspond to the change of wet to dry season and vice versa. The females oviposit from morning until early aftenoon on hostplants along forest edges and in light gaps. Both sexes visit flowers of *Inga, Cephaelis*, and *Psychotria*. This species is very common and is present in almost every habitat throughout the country.

Hypothyris lycaste callispila

(Bates, 1866)

FW Length: 32-36 mm **Plate 34**

Range: Mexico to Colombia. **Subspecies:** Costa Rica and Panama

Hostplant: *Solanum torvum* (Solanaceae)

Early stages: All of the early stages are very similar to those of *H. euclea.*

Adult: Distinguished by the broadly black FW with an elongate orange triangle along the inner margin; a short yellow bar crosses the FW cell; HW has black margins and black spots near end of cell, which may vary in size from a small spot to a medial band. This species is variable. See *Ithomia celemia, Hypothyris euclea*, and various *Eresia* species.

Habits: Occurs from 300 to 1,600 m on both slopes, in association with montane forest habitats. Usually encountered as solitary individuals in the forest understory and during migrations, occasionally in disturbed forest in the Meseta Central. This species is local and uncommon.

Genus **ITHOMIA** Hübner, 1816

The butterflies in this genus are easily recognized by the distinctive venation of the hindwing (Fig. 27) and, in the males, a raised blister on the costa of the hindwing underside corresponding to the location of the androconial patch (an excellent character). Since there is essentially no sexual dimorphism, the females can be matched to the males. The colors range from transparent to tiger-striped and all the species are involved in mimicry complexes. *Ithomia* ranges from Mexico south throughout South America, and reaches its greatest diversity in the Amazon Basin.

The hostplants of importance to the Central American species include *Solanum, Acnistus, Lycianthes, Witheringia*, and *Capsicum*. The larvae are without filaments, rather squat, greenish, and have small lateral projections. The pupae are compressed, as in *Melinaea*, but somewhat more elongate and chrome-colored. There have been no detailed life histories published to date.

In Costa Rica, *Ithomia* ranges from sea level to over 2,000 m, and although primarily composed of forest species, it occurs in virtually all habitats at one time of the year or another. Most of our species are known to migrate seasonally, and the males of all species visit sources of pyrrolizidine alkaloids. In the Meseta Central some species can become very common in coffee plantations, due to the use of the hostplant *Acnistus* as a shade tree.

Ithomia bolivari

Schaus, 1913

FW Length: 22-24 mm **Plate 35**

Range: Costa Rica and Panama

Hostplant: Unknown

Early stages: Unknown

Adult: Distinguished by the heavy black wing borders on the upperside; prominent white FW band; deep reddish brown underside; and yellow base of the HW. See *I. diasa* and *I. terra.*

Habits: Occurs from sea level to 700 m on the Atlantic slope in association with the Carrillo Belt. This species is only found in primary rain forest habitats and is apparently endemic to the foothills of the mountains of the Carrillo Belt, south to Bocas del Toro in Panama. This uncommon species is very local, and is most abundant during the dry season in June and July.

Ithomia patilla

Hewitson, 1853

FW Length: 24-26 mm **Plate 35**

Range: Mexico to Panama

Hostplant: *Witheringia, Lycianthes* (Solanaceae)

Early stages: *Egg*—white, laid singly on the underside of leaves. *Mature larva*—dull yellow-green without markings; body squat, fatter posteriorly; above the prolegs there is a lateral row of warty, yellow-spotted protrusions; head capsule pale yellow-green with black eye-like patterns on the face. At rest the larva curls into a semicircle adjacent to the holes cut into the leaf by the larval feeding.

Adult: Distinguished from similar species by the reddish brown on the HW upperside border, heavily black FW bar and distal end of cell, no distinct cell bar, and at least one spot on HE HW apex. See *Oleria paula.*

Habits: One of the most common of the clear-winged ithomiines in Costa Rica. It occurs from sea level to 1,600 m throughout the country. Commonly encountered in all habitats except the very dry forest in northern lowland Guanacaste, where it is occasional. Small patches of remnant and second-growth forest will support large populations of this butterfly. Both sexes visit flowers of *Inga, Lantana, Hamelia, Psychotria*, and a variety of Asteraceae.

Ithomia diasa hippocrenis

Bates, 1866

FW Length: 23-26 mm **Plate 35**

Range: Nicaragua to Colombia. **Subspecies:** Nicaragua to Panama

Hostplant: *Witheringia, Lycianthes* (Solanaceae)

Early stages: Undescribed

Adult: Distinguished primarily by the black bar in the FW cell, which is always distinct (*I. patilla* rarely has a faint one); HW border is black on the upperside; usually there are three white spots on the FW and HW apices on the underside. See *I. bolivari* and *I. patilla.*

Habits: Occurs commonly from sea level to 1,400 m on the Atlantic slope, in association with montane forest habitats and occasionally on the Pacific slope in mountain passes. This species reaches greatest abundance during the dry seasons, and is uncommon during the wet. Both sexes visit flowers of *Psychotria, Cephaelis, Hamelia, Inga, Lantana*, and various Asteraceae.

Ithomia heraldica

Bates, 1866

FW Length: 30-32 mm **Plate 35**

Range: Nicaragua to Panama

Hostplant: *Witheringia riparia, Acnistus arborescens* (Solanaceae)

Early stages: *Egg*—white, laid singly; the female almost always lays more than two per plant. *Mature larva*—ground color and general morphology much like *I. patilla*, but with three wrinkles across each segment, and the head markings and lateral warts are not as prominent.

Adult: Distinguished by the semi-transparent coloration. Cannot be confused with anything else.

Habits: Occurs from sea level to 1,600 m, on both slopes, in habitats ranging from primary rain forest to second growth. This species is most abundant in coffee plantations, where *Acnistus* is used as a shade tree or as an ornamental shrub. In contrast, in natural undisturbed forest habitats, where only its native hostplant *Witheringia* is present, *I. heraldica* is not at all common. This species is frequently observed visiting fresh bird droppings in the forest; I have not seen it follow army ant swarms. Both sexes visit flowers of *Lantana, Stachytarpheta, Impatiens*, and a wide variety of other plants.

Ithomia celemia plaginota

Butler and Druce, 1872

FW Length: 30-33 mm **Plate 35**

Range: Costa Rica to Venezuela. **Subspecies:** Costa Rica and Panama

Hostplant: *Witheringia riparia* (Solanaceae)

Early stages: Undescribed

Adult: Distinguished by the black spot in the FW cell and a black isosceles triangle at the distal end of the cell; HW underside frequently has a black medial spot. See *Hypothyris euclea.*

Habits: Occurs from sea level to 900 m, only in Pacific slope rain forest habitats. Usually encountered along riparian edges or forest understory in deep shade. While on the wing, it resembles *Hypothyris euclea* and *Eresia eutropia.* This species is not common in our area except in local populations along the Golfo Dulce side of the Osa Peninsula, and in some of the remnant forest near Quepos.

Ithomia xenos

(Bates, 1866)

FW Length: 31-34 mm **Plate 35**

Range: Costa Rica and Panama

Hostplant: *Witheringia, Acnistus* (Solanaceae)

Early stages: Undescribed

Adult: This is the only amber-colored *Ithomia* in Central America. Best distinguished by the venation and the HW "blister" in the males. See *Napeogenes cranto.*

Habits: Occurs from 800 to 2,000 m on both slopes, in association with cloud forest habitats, but also in the Meseta Central coffee plantations during the wet seasons. Both sexes fly at the canopy or subcanopy level in association with the comimetic *Dircenna* species. This species was exceedingly common along the road from San José to Carrillo for over three years (1979-1982), most likely because of the mild disturbances of the roadcut and the abundance of Asteraceae flowers. It is a common visitor of *Senecio megaphyla* in the montane areas and *Lantana* in the Meseta Central.

Ithomia terra vulcana

Haensch, 1909

FW Length: 22-25 mm **Plate 35**

Range: Costa Rica to Bolivia. **Subspecies:** Costa Rica and Panama

Hostplant: Unknown

Early stages: Unknown

Adult: Distinguished by the heavy scaling at the end of the HW cell, which is black on the upperside and rich reddish on the underside (this character is best seen from underneath); there is no yellow at the base of HW as in other species, and the raised blister on the HW costa of the male is black. See *I. diasa* and *I. bolivari.*

Habits: Occurs from 1,000 to 2,000 m on both slopes in association with mountain passes and rain shadow habitats. It is distributed chiefly in the Cordillera de Talamanca. This species flies low to the ground and is more fluttery than other *Ithomia* species. Most frequently encountered along forest edges and along trails that are heavily shaded, although the males enter the bright sunshine to visit pyrrolizidine sources during the morning. This species is uncommon in Costa Rican collections, is very local and rarely encountered. It appears that this butterfly, unlike its Costa Rican congeners, does not migrate seasonally.

Genus **HYALYRIS** Boisduval, 1870

As mentioned under *Hypothyris*, this genus and the former are extremely similar in adult morphology and early instars. *Hyalyris* is characterized by the venation and by the "sum of little differences" (Fox and Real 1971). Although there are quite a few species in South America, only one species enters our area.

The hostplant for our species is *Solanum*; the larvae are very similar to those of *Hypothyris*. In Costa Rica the genus is confined to the mid-elevation cloud forest habitats.

Hyalyris excelsa decumana

(Godman and Salvin, 1878)

FW Length: 38-41 mm **Plate 34**

Range: Costa Rica to Peru. **Subspecies:** Costa Rica to Colombia

Hostplant: *Solanum accrescens, S. lanceifolium* (Solanaceae)

Early stages: Similar to those of *Hypothyris euclea* in all stages, but larger.

Adult: Distinguished by the black FW with large transparent spots on the distal half, and the anterior half of the HW has a shiny opalescent area on the underside, especially noticeable in the male. See *Olyras crathis.*

Habits: Occurs from 800 to 1,800 m on both slopes, in association with cloud forest habitats. It is also present in overgrown coffee plantations and remnant riparian forest in the Meseta Central. Most frequently seen flying in the canopy or the subcanopy of the forest or sailing across breaks in the forest along forest edges. The males perch and patrol in small light gaps about ten meters above the ground from early morning until midday. The females oviposit on hostplants occurring in the forest understory, usually associated with light gaps. Both sexes visit flowers of *Inga* and various composites. This species is present throughout the year at most elevations, but is usually very local and hence overlooked.

Genus **AERIA** Hübner, 1816

This genus is represented in Central America by a single species, easily recognized by its black and yellow wings. The genus ranges from Mexico to South America and includes about three species. *Aeria* shows affinities to the Danainae on the basis of hostplant relationships and larval morphology.

The hostplants are various species of *Prestonia* (Apocynaceae). In general form, the larvae are similar to those of *Melinaea*, only smaller, and show the danaine-like fleshy filaments behind the head. The pupa is reflective gold and shaped not unlike *Melinaea*.

In Costa Rica *Aeria* is found in all forest habitats below 2,000 m that do not experience a strong dry season. Nothing has been published on the population biology of any species.

Aeria eurimedia agna

Godman and Salvin, 1879

FW Length: 22-25 mm **Plate 35**

Range: Mexico to Colombia. **Subspecies:** Nicaragua to Panama

Hostplant: *Prestonia portabellensis* (Apocynaceae)

Early stages: (Young 1978*a*) *Egg*—white, laid singly on the underside of young leaves. *Mature larva*—body black with blue-white rings encircling the segments; venter black; anal plate and area behind head orange; two black fleshy filaments arise from behind the head; head capsule ovoid, and glossy orange. Larvae cut leaf veins in older leaves to stop the flow of milky sap, then feed on the leaf tissues after waiting a short time. The young leaves are acceptable without this "surgery." *Pupa*—elongate J-shaped, reflective gold; wingpads bordered in black with a thick red line in middle of wings; antennae, legs, and spiracles black; various small black spots on abdomen and thorax; head bifid. Eclosion takes place during the morning.

Adult: Distinguished from similar species by nontranslucent yellow and black wing areas; HW upperside has no marginal row of white spots; there is a red collar behind the head. See *Scada zibia* and *Oleria zelica*.

Habits: Occurs from sea level to 800 m on both slopes, in association with wet forest habitats. Commonly encountered as solitary individuals flying in deep shade close to the ground, usually near water courses. Although I have never found this species to be abundant, it is present in most forest habitats throughout the year. Both sexes visit flowers of *Psychotria* and *Cephaelis* during the mornings, and individuals may feed at the same flower for up to fifteen minutes at a time.

Genus **HYPOSCADA** Godman and Salvin, 1879

The butterflies in this genus are recognized by their opaque black and brown wings and, in the males, the possession of a single long androconial patch. The genus ranges from Mexico to the Amazon Basin and is composed of about eight species, one of which occurs in Central America. These butterflies behave quite differently from most other ithomiine species. The flight pattern, the apparent nonuse of pyrrolizidine alkaloid sources, and a very peculiar hostplant raises some questions as to its systematic position within the subfamily Ithomiinae.

The only hostplant record for *Hyposcada* suggests that the larvae feed on Gesneriaceae (Haber 1978), a strange plant family for any butterfly. Unfortunately there are no published descriptions of the early stages or any other information that sheds light on what the larvae or pupae look like. Because of the unusual nature of both the butterfly and the hostplant, it is important to confirm or reject the Gesneriaceae record and to describe the early stages.

In Costa Rica *Hyposcada* is found in a wide variety of forest habitats, except for the deciduous forest of Guanacaste. Individuals are generally active throughout the day, in the deep shade of the forest understory. Nothing has been published on the population biology of any *Hyposcada* species.

Hyposcada virginiana evanides

(Haensch, 1909)

FW Length: 32-35 mm **Plate 35**

Range: Mexico to Colombia. **Subspecies:** Nicaragua to Panama

Hostplant: *Columnea consanguinea, C. grata, Drymonia conchocalyx* (Gesneriaceae). These hostplant records are from Haber (1978), and since they represent oviposition records (Haber, personal communication), they require confirmation.

Early stages: Unknown

Adult: Distinguished by the black FW apex sprinkled with white spots, red-brown base of FW and disc of HW. Somewhat variable. See *Eresia poecilina* and *E. melaina.*

Habits: Occurs from sea level to 1,200 m on both slopes in association with wet forest habitats. Individuals fly in deep shade amid the understory vegetation. The males do not visit sources of pyrrolizidine alkaloids, a somewhat anomalous behavior for the subfamily. Both sexes visit flowers of *Psychotria, Malvaviscus,* and *Hamelia.* This species is a common member of the rain forest community and is present, throughout the year, in all suitable forest habitats.

Genus **OLERIA** Hübner, 1816

This genus is easily recognized by the distinctive hindwing venation (Fig. 27). It ranges from Mexico through Central and South America, and has its greatest diversity in the Amazon Basin. In Costa Rica there are four species, all but one of which has transparent wings. In South America the genus shows a great diversity of color patterns.

The hostplants of importance in Costa Rica belong to *Solanum* and *Lycianthes* (Solanaceae). The larvae are green, rather nondescript, and the pupae are J-shaped and either pale green or reflectively colored.

In Costa Rica the genus occurs from sea level to 3,000 m, and is present in all habitats that have some forest cover. All of the species appear to migrate seasonally, and most are commonly found in the Meseta Central throughout the year.

Oleria zelica pagasa

(Druce, 1875)

FW Length: 25-27 mm **Plate 35**

Range: Costa Rica to Ecuador. **Subspecies:** Costa Rica and Panama

Hostplant: *Solanum evolvifolium* (Solanaceae)

Early stages: (Young 1974*f*) *Egg*—white, laid singly, and quite large for the body of the adult. *Mature larva*—all instars are cryptic and generally drab gray-green, with many wrinkles on each segment; head capsule shiny black and somewhat small for the size of the larva. *Pupa*—pale green with almost no markings, short and strongly humped on the dorsum.

Adult: Distinguished by the heavy black wing margins; FW apex has translucent yellow bars and white spots; white spots on the HW upperside. See *Aeria eurimedia* and *Scada zibia.*

Habits: Occurs locally from sea level to 1,200 m, on both slopes, usually in association with primary rain forest but occasionally found in the deciduous forest (migrants?). Encountered as solitary individuals in deep shade and, in my experience, always in association with watercourses. Although considered rare, it can be quite common during the dry seasons in lowland rain forest habitats. Both sexes visit flowers of *Psychotria, Cephaelis,* and *Turnera,* and the males are often seen visiting flowers of *Eupatorium* and other pyrrolizidine alkaloid sources. I have not observed this species involved in the leks of other ithomiine species.

Oleria vicina

(Salvin, 1869)

FW Length: 26-29 mm **Plate 35**

Range: Costa Rica and northern Panama

Hostplant: *Solanum trizygum, Lycianthes multiflora* (Solanaceae)

Early stages: Undescribed

Adult: Distinguished by the separate white spots on the FW; brown wing margins; FW apex not heavily scaled, and FW has a faint cell bar. See *Greta nero.*

Habits: Occurs commonly in all montane habitats above 1,000 m, including open second growth. During cloudy weather individuals fly in open areas and along forest edges or in the forest during sunny days. Both sexes quite commonly visit flowers of *Senecio megaphylla,* notably along the PanAmerican highway. At certain times of the year this species is attacked by ectoparasitic ceratopogonid midges, which feed from the wing veins and eyes. The female butterflies oviposit from morning until early afternoon. This species is very common and present throughout the year.

Oleria rubescens

(Butler and Druce, 1872)

FW Length: 24-26 mm **Plate 35**

Range: Mexico to Panama

Hostplant: *Solanum siparunoides* (Solanaceae)

Early stages: *Egg*—white, laid singly, although a female will almost always lay more than one egg on the same plant.

Adult: Very similar to *O. paula,* but distinguished from it by having a very distinct black bar through the FW cell, and the black on the FW not as dark.

Habits: Occurs from 800 to 1,500 m on both slopes, in association with forest habitats; chiefly distributed along the Cordillera de Talamanca and Cordillera Central. This common species is frequently seen in the streets of San José and other major cities. Both sexes visit a variety of garden flowers, while the males avidly visit pyrrolizidine alkaloid sources.

Oleria paula

(Weymer, 1884)

FW Length: 23-26 mm **Plate 35**

Range: Mexico to Panama

Hostplant: *Lycianthes multiflora* (Solanaceae)

Early stages: Undescribed

Adult: Distinguished from *O. rubescens* by having a heavy black FW apex that has a straight inner edge; FW bar distinctly white; FW cell usually has no bar, although in some specimens there may be a faint one. Compare with *O. rubescens.*

Habits: Occurs fro n sea level to 1,200 m on both slopes in association with forest habitats. Unlike *O. rubescens,* this species is apparently restricted to the lowlands and midelevations. Although present in many habitats, it is much less common than *O. rubescens,* and flies only in the forest understory and occasionally along forest edges during the morning. Populations on the Osa Peninsula have a fairly distinct FW bar that may cause some errors in identification if caution is not exercised.

Genus **CERATINIA** Hübner, 1816

The butterflies in this genus are all semi-translucent and possess various color patterns; none is clear-winged. The genus ranges from Mexico to South America, where it reaches its greatest diversity. In Central America there is a single species that cannot be confused with any other butterfly. The hostplants of *Ceratinia* are in the genus *Solanum* (Solanaceae), and the larvae and pupae are quite similar in appearance to those of *Oleria.*

Ceratinia tutia dorilla

(Bates, 1864)

FW Length: 26-30 mm **Plate 35**

Range: Nicaragua to Amazon Basin. **Subspecies:** Nicaragua to Venezuela

Hostplant: *Solanum antillarum,* other *Solanum* spp (Solanaceae)

Early stages: *Egg*—white, laid singly. *Mature larva*—pale translucent green; lateral lines run from head to anus and converge at the anal segment; the lines are colored yellow and blue, and look like a string of beads; head capsule green with a white crown that bears two black spots over the ocelli. *Pupa*—abdomen compressed; body amber colored with silver wingpads, held horizontally.

Adult: wings colored a mixture of translucent black and orange. Highly variable (almost no two are alike) and it cannot be confused with anything else in Central America.

Habits: Occurs from sea level to 1,000 m on both slopes, in association with rain forest habitats. Encountered as solitary individuals in the forest understory. The flight of this species is characteristically weak and fluttery. Individuals are often found in association with leks of *Mechanitis polymnia.* Both sexes visit flowers of assorted Rubiaceae growing in the forest understory. Although seldom abundant, this species is found in all lowland rain forest habitats.

Genus **CALLITHOMIA** Bates, 1862

The butterflies in this genus are all medium sized and have translucent wings. The genus ranges from Mexico through Central and South America, reaching its greatest diversity in the Amazon Basin. In Central America there are three species, two of which enter our area. One of the Costa Rican species appears to be endemic and may be on the verge of extinction, due to habitat destruction. Although there are no published hostplant records or life histories for any species, one of the Costa Rican species is known to oviposit on *Solanum.*

Callithomia hezia hezia

(Hewitson, 1853)

FW Length: 33-36 mm **Plate 35**

Range: Mexico to Colombia. **Subspecies:** Nicaragua to Panama

Hostplant: (Haber 1978) *Solanum sanctae-clarae* (Solanaceae)

Early stages: I have collected several eggs from an ovipositing female, which laid single white eggs on an unidentified subcanopy woody vine.

Adult: Immediately distinguished by the angular and produced black FW margin, which has many well-spaced yellow spots; distal one-third of HW black. See *Tithorea tarricina* and *Heliconius hecalesia.*

Habits: Occurs from sea level to 1,000 m on both slopes in association with rain forest habitats. Encountered as solitary individuals flying in the understory or the subcanopy. While on the wing, individuals resemble *Tithorea tarricina* or *Heliconius hecalesia.* On the Pacific slope in habitats near the Osa Peninsula, this species can be very abundant. In the early morning, both sexes visit flowers of *Lantana, Hamelia, Psyguria,* and *Stachytarpheta* growing along forest edges or in open areas. The males avidly visit sources of pyrrolizidine alkaloids and are known to carry the pollinia of the orchid *Epidendrum panniculatum.* During the dry seasons in some years this species can be moderately common in the Meseta Central, along rivers and in coffee plantations.

Callithomia hydra megaleas

Godman and Salvin, 1898

FW Length: 30-34 mm **Plate 35**

Range: Costa Rica to Colombia. **Subspecies:** Costa Rican endemic

Hostplant: Unknown

Early stages: Unknown

Adult: In general appearance similar to a translucent *Melinaea scylax,* only smaller; yellow spotting on the FW elongated; antennae yellow; FW underside has two or three white spots; HW margin narrowly black with several white spots in the apex and on the anal margin. See venation for positive determination.

Habits: This extremely rare species is known from a very few Costa Rican specimens, all taken on the Pacific slope coastal areas from San Mateo, south to the mainland portion of the Osa Peninsula. This butterfly is (was?) probably an indigenous faunal element of the transitional forest that during the last century extended from Puntarenas to the legendary forests of Bugaba, Panama. Since this forest type has been destroyed by heavy agricultural use during the last fifty years, little, if any, is extant in primary condition today. Perhaps this species still survives in Parque Nacional Carrara, but there seems little chance of it surviving into the next century. Because of its rarity, any observations on adult or early stage biology should be published.

Genus **DIRCENNA** Doubleday, 1847

The butterflies in this genus are recognized by all having transparent amber-colored wings, a distinctive venation (Fig. 27), and yellow antennae. The genus ranges from Mexico to South America, and reaches its greatest diversity in the Andes. In Costa Rica there are only four species.

The hostplants in Costa Rica are all second-growth *Solanum* species. The larvae are naked, without protuberances, and are rather dull. The pupae are similar to those of *Oleria,* except that they are reflective gold.

The genus is involved in extensive mimicry complexes throughout its range, especially at higher elevations. In Costa Rica one species occurs in the lowland forests, the rest are montane. All of the Costa Rican species migrate seasonally and can be quite common in the Meseta Central.

Dircenna chiriquensis

Haensch, 1909

FW Length: 41-45 mm **Plate 35**

Range: Mexico to Panama

Hostplant: Unknown

Early stages: Undescribed

Adult: Extremely similar to *D. klugii* but larger, with somewhat darker margins and HW discal areas. The genitalia of the two species are distinct (Fox 1968).

Habits: Occurs from 800 to 2,000 m on both slopes, in association with cloud forest habitats. Encountered as solitary individuals flying with other *Dircenna* species. The males avidly visit pyrrolizidine alkaloid sources and are frequently observed visiting flowers of *Neomirandia, Senecio,* and *Eupatorium*; the latter is also visited by females. Both sexes visit flowers of *Inga, Hamelia,* and *Impatiens.* Although present throughout the year in most montane habitats, it is seldom abundant.

Dircenna relata

Butler and Druce, 1872

FW Length: 32-38 mm **Plate 35**

Range: Nicaragua to Panama

Hostplant: *Solanum torvum, S. umbellatum* (Solanaceae)

Early stages: (Young 1973*b*) *Egg*—white, laid singly, but female usually lays several eggs on the same plant. *Mature larva*—Pale green-white and covered with pale yellow warts and black dots; in general appearance, very short and squat; head capsule pale green with slight pubescence.

Adult: Distinguished from all other Costa Rican Dircenna species by having a smoky black FW; the FW apex in the male is elongate; HW apex and anal angle more acute than in other species; the female has the disc of the HW tawny colored. See *D. klugii* and *D. chiriquensis.*

Habits: This common and widespread species occurs from 800 to 2,000 m on both slopes, in virtually all forest habitats, and also in open areas associated with the higher elevations. The species is a familiar migrant in the Meseta Central, and in some years individuals can be extremely abundant.

Dircenna klugii

(Geyer, 1837)

FW Length: 35-38 mm **Plate 35**

Range: Mexico to Panama

Hostplant: *Solanum* (Solanaceae)

Early stages: Mature larva essentially the same as *D. relata*, but the black warts on the dorsum are more pronounced and the headcapsule is shiny green and without pubescence.

Adult: Very similar to *D. chiriquensis*, only smaller and with different genitalia. See *D. chiriquensis.*

Habits: Occurs from 600 to 1,800 m on both slopes, in a wide variety of forest and second-growth habitats. This is perhaps the most common *Dircenna* species in Costa Rica and is frequently seen near all forms of human habitation. Perhaps this success is due to its ability to utilize a wide variety of *Solanum* species as hostplants.

Dircenna dero euchytma

(Felder and Felder, 1867)

FW Length: 35-38 mm **Plate 35**

Range: Mexico to Brazil. **Subspecies:** Central America

Hostplant: *Solanum ochraceo-ferrugineum* (Solanaceae)

Early stages: Undescribed

Adult: Distinguished by the black borders of both wings, the black spot in the FW cell, and lack of black markings on the FW inner margin.

Habits: Occurs from sea level to 1,000 m on both slopes, in association with all forest habitats except the deciduous forests of Guanacaste. This is the only *Dircenna* in Central America that inhabits the lowlands. Encountered as solitary individuals in the forest understory, usually along streams or in light gaps. Although seldom abundant, this species is present throughout the year in most areas. The males visit pyrrolizidine alkaloid sources and are known to carry the pollinia of the orchid *Epidendrum panniculatum*. Both sexes visit flowers of *Inga, Psychotria*, and *Lantana*.

Genus **GODYRIS** Boisduval, 1870

The ten or so species in this genus are recognized by their venation and color patterns. In Central America our species are sexually dimorphic, but a number of the South American species are monomorphic. The genus ranges from Mexico to the Amazon Basin, with most species occurring on the eastern slope of the Andes. Two species occur in Central America.

The hostplants of the Central American species are *Solanum* and *Cestrum*. The larvae are rather nondescript, and the pupae are similar to those of *Dircenna*. In Costa Rica the genus occurs in lowland forests and occasionally gets into montane areas below 1,000 m. The pollinia of the orchid *Epidendrum panniculatum* are carried by both sexes.

Godyris zavalata sorites

Fox, 1968

FW Length: 33-36 mm **Plate 35**

Range: Mexico to Ecuador. **Subspecies:** Costa Rica and Panama

Hostplant: *Solanum brenesii* (Solanaceae)

Early stages: (Young 1974*e*) *Egg*—white, slightly conical, laid singly. *Larvae*—all instars are colored virtually the same: body naked, pale translucent green, with the last segments swollen and paler green than the rest of the body; the tracheal system and gut can be seen through the body wall; each spiracle surrounded with yellow; head capsule shiny yellow. *Pupa*—translucent green with tiny black spots on the head and wingpads, and yellow spiracles.

Adult: Sexes dimorphic. *Male*—has yellow HW disc. *Female*—wide black HW border and small marginal white spots on FW upperside; HW disc reddish brown. Compare with *G. zygia.*

Habits: Occurs from sea level to 900 m on the Atlantic slope in association with rain forest habitats. Encountered as solitary individuals flying in the shade of the understory. Both sexes visit flowers of subcanopy-sized *Inga* trees. At elevations below 300 m this species is abundant during the dry seasons, and almost entirely absent during the rainy seasons.

Godyris zygia
(Godman and Salvin, 1877)
FW Length: 32-34 mm **Plate 36**
Range: Costa Rica and Panama
Hostplant: *Cestrum nocturnum* (Solanaceae)
Early stages: Undescribed
Adult: Sexes dimorphic. *Male*—discal area on the HW yellow and orange. *Female*—HW border narrowly black; FW margin without or with few white spots. Compare with *G. zavaleta*.
Habits: Occurs from sea level to 1,200 m on the Pacific slope, in association with all forest habitats except the Guanacaste forest. Occasionally seen in the Meseta Central. Individuals behave similarly to *G. zavaleta*. It is unclear whether the two *Godyris* species are distinct, and a study of the early stages may well help clarify this question.

Genus **GRETA** Hemming, 1934

The butterflies in this genus are recognized by the venation of the HW (Fig. 27), and all of the Central American species have transparent wings. The genus ranges from Mexico through Central and South America, with a few occurring in the West Indies. In older literature, many of the species were placed in the genus *Hymenitis*.

In Costa Rica the genus *Cestrum* (Solanaceae) is the most important hostplant. The larvae are without projections and are generally unadorned with colors. The pupae are all colored a beautiful chrome-silver, and look like small mirrors; hence the Costa Rican name "espejitos."

In Costa Rica the members of this genus are very prone to migration, especially *G. oto*, and are found in virtually all habitats. At high elevations individual butterflies are often attacked by ceratopogonid midges, which feed on hemolymph of the wing veins or the eyes.

Greta oto
(Hewitson, 1954)
FW Length: 28-30 mm **Plate 36**
Range: Mexico to Panama
Hostplant: *Cestrum lanatum, C. standleyi* (Solanaceae)
Early stages: *Egg*—white, laid singly, but the female usually lays several on the same plant. *Mature larva*—pale green and naked; a broad, chalky, white-green dorsal band with a lateral line of yellow on either side and a dark green stripe between the yellow lines; head capsule green with black sides. *Pupa*—compressed abdomen with a bowed thorax; chrome colored, with cremaster and edge of wingpads red.
Adult: Immediately distinguished by the heavy black FW apex and a distinct white FW band that is visible while butterfly is on the wing.
Habits: Occurs from 500 to 1,600 m on both slopes, in association with disturbed forest habitats; very occasionally found in the lowland Guanacaste forest. One of the commonest clear-winged species in Costa Rica; individuals are often seen flying across open areas or visiting a variety of garden flowers in the Meseta Central. This species is present throughout the year, but population fluctuates from abundance to rarity from month to month. F. G. Stiles has recorded one individual that traveled over forty kilometers within a twenty-four-hour period, and on average, individuals travel about twelve kilometers a day during the migrations (F. G. Stiles, unpublished). These data indicate that *G. oto* travels long distances during an individual's lifetime.

Greta nero
(Hewitson, 1854)
FW Length: 29-31 mm **Plate 36**
Range: Mexico to Panama
Hostplant: *Cestrum standleyi* (Solanaceae)
Early stages: (Young 1972*e*) *Egg*—white, laid singly. *Mature larva*—body pale green with a double dark green dorsolateral stripe; spiracles bordered by yellow lines; head capsule yellow-green with two black spots on the sides that look like eyes. The larvae feed and rest on the dorsal surface of the leaf and construct a silk-lined semitube at the leaf tip (see Fig. 26).
Adult: Distinguished by the wide wing margins, and a heavy FW cell bar bordered by white; veins in the HW are covered with scales; the margins and veins range from black to reddish brown. See *G. anette* and *G. andromica*.
Habits: Occurs from 600 to 2,000 m on both slopes, in association with all forest habitats. Although primarily a forest species, in habitats above 1,500 m individuals will fly in open areas during periods of cloudy weather. In the Meseta Central this species is commonly found in patches of secondary forest and coffee plantations.

Greta anette
(Guérin-Ménéville, 1844)
FW Length: 30-32 mm **Plate 36**
Range: Mexico to Panama
Hostplant: Unknown

Early stages: Unknown

Adult: Variable. Some individuals are quite similar to *G. nero*, whereas others are similar to *G. polissena*. It is distinguished, however, by the narrow wing margins, scaling on the upperside margins, and veins that are usually reddish brown. FW cell bar narrow; on the HW, where the radial veins meet the distal margin, they form triangles, with the apex of each triangle centered on a vein. Compare with *G. nero* and *G. polissena*.

Habits: Occurs commonly from 800 to 2,000 m on both slopes, in association with cloud forest habitats. Although often found flying together with *G. nero*, this species does not occur in as low an elevation as the latter.

Greta andromica lyra

(Salvin, 1869)

FW Length: 26-28 mm **Plate 36**

Range: Guatemala to Peru. **Subspecies:** Guatemala to Panama

Hostplant: *Cestrum* (Solanaceae)

Early stages: *Mature larva*—body translucent whitish green; there is a pale yellow, indistinct dorsal midline with a darker yellow lateral stripe on either side of midline that runs from head to anus; venter translucent green; head capsule shiny green with two black spots on crown and two black spots on the lower portion of the frons.

Adult: Distinguished from similar species by the wide FW bar, usually no reddish brown on the upperside, and the strongly bowed vein M2 in the FW. Compare with *G. nero*.

Habits: Occurs from 800 to 1,800 m on both slopes, in association with cloud forest habitats. Flies in association with the entire complex of *Greta* species that occur in Costa Rica. Most frequently encountered along water courses.

Greta polissena umbrana

(Haensch, 1909)

FW Length: 26-29 mm **Plate 36**

Range: Costa Rica to Brazil. **Subspecies:** Costa Rica and Panama

Hostplant: *Cestrum nocturnum, C. fragil* (Solanaceae)

Early stages: Undescribed

Adult: This is the most transparent-winged *Greta* species in Costa Rica. The margins are extremely narrow and darkly scaled; FW bar narrow; white band bordering FW cell very narrow. See *G. anette*.

Habits: Occurs in all cloud forest habitats above 900 m on both slopes. Encountered far less often than other *Greta*, although it can be very common locally. Individuals fly in the forest along rivers, and often form large aggregations in light gaps. The males visit a variety of Asteraceae flowers, along forest and riparian edges. On bright sunny days, individuals are almost invisible when flying. The females oviposit from morning until late afternoon.

Genus **HYPOLERIA**
Godman and Salvin, 1879

This genus is composed of small butterflies recognized by the configuration of the hindwing venation (Fig. 27). The males have two patches of androconial scales on the hindwing. In Costa Rica there is only one species, and it can only be confused with *Pseudoscada*.

The hostplant for this genus in Costa Rica is *Solanum* (Solanaceae). The early stages are fairly nondescript and resemble those of *Oleria*.

Hypoleria cassotis

(Bates, 1864)

FW Length: 25-27 mm **Plate 36**

Range: Mexico to Panama

Hostplant: *Solanum* (Solanaceae)

Early stages: (Young 1977*b*) *Egg*—white, slightly ovoid, laid singly on the underside of leaves. *Larvae*—all instars are light green and semi-translucent, and have a wrinkled appearance; head capsule pale green. The larvae feed inside of silken tents and rest in a J shape inside the tents. *Pupa*—pale green with gold and silver areas on abdomen, wingpads, and mesothorax; head bifid with small black spots.

Adult: Distinguished by the following combination of characteristics: size small; interior edge of wing margins even; FW cell bar and white band separated by a transparent area; in males, a small (often blackish) blister on the underside of the HW margin (like *Ithomia*). See *Pseudoscada utilla*.

Habits: Occurs from sea level to 1,000 m on both slopes, in association with all forest habitats except the Guanacaste forest. Individuals fly low to the ground in deep shade, usually in light gaps or along trails. Both sexes visit flowers of various Asteraceae. This species is easily overlooked, although it can be quite common in most areas.

Genus **PSEUDOSCADA** Godman and Salvin, 1879

The butterflies in this genus are recognized by the venation of the hindwing (Fig. 27), and the males have a single androconial patch on the hindwing. These small butterflies range from Nicaragua to the Amazon Basin, where most of the species occur. In Central America there are two species, only one of which occurs in our area. The females, especially, are often confused with *Hypoleria.* There has been nothing published on the hostplants or early stages.

Pseudoscada utilla pusio

(Godman and Salvin, 1877)

FW Length: 21-23 mm **Plate 36**

Range: Nicaragua to Colombia. **Subspecies:** Nicaragua to Panama

Hostplant: Unknown

Early stages: Unknown

Adult: Distinguished from *Hypoleria cassotis* by the HW venation, rounded FW apex, an obvious transparent space between the dark FW apex and the subapical white band, and richer brown underside coloration. Compare with *H. cassotis.*

Habits: Occurs from sea level to 700 m, principally on the Atlantic slope, in association with rain forest habitats, especially in swampy areas. In general habits this species is similar to *Hypoleria cassotis*, but it is much less common and is in general little known.

Genus **EPISCADA** Godman and Salvin, 1879

The butterflies in this genus are extremely similar in appearance to *Pteronymia*, from which it must be distinguished by the genitalia and minute details of the venation. The genus ranges from Mexico to the Amazon Basin, where the greatest number of species occur. In Central America there is but a single species, and it can be separated from *Pteronymia* by characteristics of the head (see Fig. 28).

The important hostplants of the Central American species are in the genus *Solanum.* The larvae are smooth, lightly marked, and are gregarious feeders. The pupa is like that of *Pteronymia.*

In Costa Rica the genus is confined to montane areas above 1,000 m, and is always found in association with other clear-winged species; it is a confusing mimicry complex. The males frequently visit sources of pyrrolizidine alkaloids. Both sexes are attacked by ceratopogonid midges that attach themselves to the wing veins and the eyes to feed on hemolymph.

Episcada salvinia

(Bates, 1864)

FW Length: 25-27 mm **Plate 36**

Range: Mexico to Panama

Hostplant: *Solanum antillarum* (Solanaceae)

Early stages: *Egg*—white laid in clusters of fifty to seventy on the underside of leaves. *Mature*

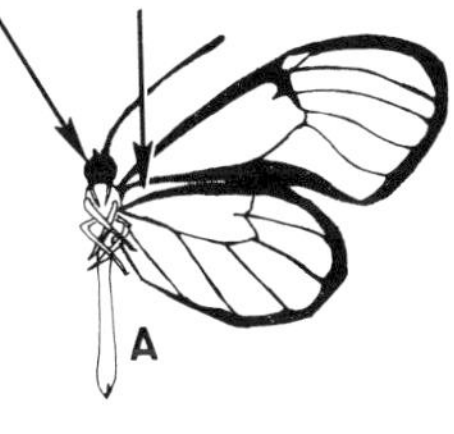

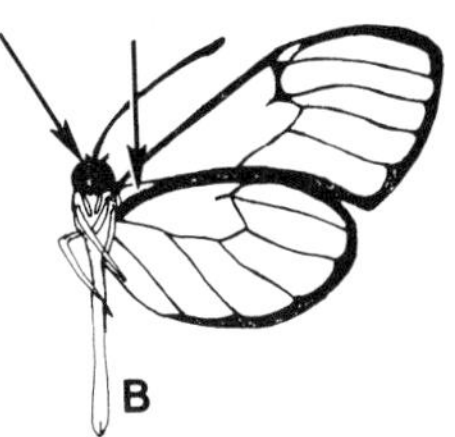

FIGURE 28. A: *Episcada salvinia*; B: *Pteronymia simplex.* Note the differences between the size of the head and the length of the silver bar on the hindwing costa (arrows). See text for further explanation (drawings by P. J. DeVries).

larva—dark green with a lateral stripe of whitish green bordered by dark green along the dorsal edge; head capsule shiny black; body without papillae. The larvae feed in groups and show synchronization in feeding, resting, and molting. *Pupa*—abdomen compressed, body held horizontally, chrome-colored, with brown highlights on the antennae and proboscis.

Adult: Extremely similar to *Pteronymia simplex*, but distinguished by having the head less than or equal in width to the thorax; on the HW there is a narrow gray costal margin extending from the wing base to the cell, or just short of it, easily seen against the reddish color of the costa (Fig. 28). Compare with *Pteronymia simplex*.

Habits: Occurs in all montane forest habitats above 1,000 m. Almost always found in association with *Pteronymia simplex*, an example of incredibly precise mimicry. Populations of this species are generally common in all forest habitats except those that have been heavily disturbed. Both sexes visit a variety of Asteraceae flowers, and both are attacked by ceratopogonid midges.

Genus **PTERONYMIA**
Butler and Druce, 1872

A diverse group of butterflies that show a great deal of pattern variation between species, *Pteronymia* is recognized by the distinctive venation of the hindwing (Fig. 27). The only group that these butterflies can be confused with are the species in *Episcada*, and in the Central American fauna this is only true of one case. Of the thirty or so described species, just under one-half are found in Costa Rica; the remainder are South American.

The hostplant genera that are important for the Central American species include *Solanum, Lycianthes*, and *Cyphomandra*, all in the Solanaceae. The larvae and the pupae are generally nondescript and resemble those of *Hypoleria*.

In Costa Rica the genus occurs from sea level to the highest mountain peaks, and in every habitat type except the lowland deciduous forest of Guanacaste. The genus contains some rare and little-known species, some which have endemic Costa Rica subspecies. The males of every species visit sources of pyrrolizidine alkaloids, and many are known to carry pollinia of the orchid *Epidendrum panniculatum*. As far as I am aware, almost all of the Costa Rican species are known to migrate seasonally, and many of them are familiar sights in the streets of San José during the change of seasons.

Pteronymia donata
Haensch, 1909

FW Length: 26-28 mm **Plate 36**

Range: Costa Rica and Panama

Hostplant: Unknown

Early stages: Unknown

Adult: Distinguished by the translucent amber ground color; distal one-third of FW black has a marginal row of yellow spots; FW has a translucent yellow band running from costa to inner margin. See *Pteronymia agalla*. *Note*: Costa Rican individuals have the FW band narrower than do those from Panama, and should probably receive subspecific status.

Habits: Although common in Panama, this species is known only from a few individuals collected in Costa Rica. All of the specimens were taken on the Pacific slope of the Meseta Central, near Finca El Rodeo, during the dry season. This species flies with *P. agalla*, and while on the wing, the two species are very similar. This species is rare and in need of study.

Pteronymia artena artena
(Hewitson, 1854)

FW Length: 27-30 mm **Plate 36**

Range: Mexico to Ecuador. **Subspecies:** Costa Rica and Panama

Hostplant: *Lycianthes* (Solanaceae)

Early stages: *Egg*—white, laid singly on the undersides of leaves. The larvae and pupae are undescribed.

Adult: Distinguished by the large head, which is wider than the thorax; elongate FW apex; FW costa reddish brown from base to end of cell; margins and wing veins black. See *P. simplex*.

Habits: Occurs from 600 to 1,800 m on both slopes, in association with all wet forest habitats. On the Atlantic slope, however, there appear to be two forms of this species: one has a head that is slightly smaller than or equal to the width of the thorax. It is conceivable that there is more than one species involved, something that might be resolved by careful comparison of larva and adult ecology. Both of these forms of *artena* fly in the shade of the forest, or along edges during the mornings, and the males are known to carry the pollinia of the orchid *Epidendrum panniculatum*. Quite common in all forest habitats above 1,000 m elevation.

Pteronymia fulvescens
Godman and Salvin, 1879
FW Length: 25-28 mm **Plate 36**
Range: Costa Rica and western Panama
Hostplant: *Solanum brenesii* (Solanaceae)
Early stages: Undescribed
Adult: In general appearance, a translucent, smoky amber color, but the character that separates it from all other similar species is the yellow antennae. See *Pteronymia fulvimargo, P. notilla*, and *P. fumida.*
Habits: Occurs locally from 800 to 1,800 m on both slopes, in association with forest habitats that are influenced by rain shadows, or that are somewhat drier than the surrounding areas (such as Valle de Copey and Las Alturas). In such areas this species can be rather common, although, judging by the number in collections, it is infrequently collected. Individuals are usually observed flying in the subcanopy of the forest and have a characteristic jerky, gliding flight. Males perch during the mornings in light gaps about ten meters above the ground, and chase other butterflies until early afternoon. Both sexes visit flowers of *Inga, Hamelia*, and *Lantana*. Occasionally this species is seen in the streets of San José, probably migrants from the populations that occur in the surrounding mountains.

Pteronymia notilla
Butler and Druce, 1872
FW Length: 23-27 mm **Plate 36**
Range: Costa Rica to Colombia
Hostplant: *Solanum brenesii, S. arboreum* (Solanaceae)
Early stages: (Young 1974*d*) *Egg*—white, laid singly. *Mature larva*—head capsule shiny black; dorsum of body black with a central white stripe running the entire length; venter yellow; bright yellow collar behind the head; last segment yellow with a black anal plate. *Pupa*—abdomen compressed and entire pupa colored reflective gold.
Adult: Sexes dimorphic. *Male*—similar to *P. fulvescens* and *P. fulvimargo* but with black antennae; HW with an even, black margin; no dark orange scaling on posterior margin of HW. *Female*—FW smoky black with submarginal and medial translucent spots; dark bar at end of FW cell; HW discal area semi-opaque orange. See *P. fulvescens* and *P. fulvimargo.*
Habits: Occurs from 800 to 2,000 m on both slopes, in association with all forest habitats. A very common and sometimes abundant species, which flies in the forest or along edges from early morning until early afternoon. During the changes of the seasons, this species undergoes wild fluctuations of abundance in areas of the Meseta Central. Both sexes visit flowers of various Asteraceae and of *Inga.*

Pteronymia fulvimargo
Butler and Druce, 1872
FW Length: 27-30 mm **Plate 36**
Range: Costa Rica and western Panama
Hostplant: Unknown
Early stages: Unknown
Adult: Distinguished by having black antennae, and the posterior margin of the HW upperside has a conspicuous, semi-opaque orange submarginal band. Compare with *P. fulvescens, P. notilla*, and *P. fumida.*
Habits: Occurs from 800 to 1,600 m on both slopes in association with cloud forest habitats, especially along the Cordillera Central and Talamanca. During the morning, this uncommon species is encountered as solitary individuals flying at the subcanopy level. The males visit sources of pyrrolizidine alkaloids.

Pteronymia agalla
Godman and Salvin, 1879
FW Length: 23-26 mm **Plate 36**
Range: Costa Rica and Panama
Hostplant: *Solanum brenesii* (Solanaceae)
Early stages: Undescribed
Adult: Similar to *P. donata* but distinguished from it by the black bar at the distal end of the FW cell, and the yellow FW band, which does not run to the inner margin.
Habits: Occurs from sea level to 1,200 m on the Pacific slope in association with disturbed forest habitats. Individuals fly along forest edges, in open gallery forest, or in full sunshine. Both sexes visit a variety of flowers that are mainly second-growth weeds. Encountered as local populations during the rainy season, and not present as adults in the dry season. Occasionally found as a migrant in the Meseta Central. In general this species is uncommon, although during the early rainy season, some areas near the Osa Peninsula have populations that may exist at high densities.

Pteronymia parva
(Salvin, 1869)
FW Length: 19-23 mm **Plate 36**
Range: Costa Rica and Panama
Hostplant: Unknown
Early stages: Unknown
Adult: Distinguished from the similar *P. cotytto* by the heavy bar in the FW cell; the black FW apex is narrower and has its inner margin excavated, not straight at the interface of black

and transparent areas. Compare with *P. cotytto*.

Habits: Occurs from sea level to 800 m on the Atlantic slope, in primary rain forest habitats. Individuals fly low to the ground in the deep shade of the understory, usually near or in swampy areas. Although it is considered common in Costa Rica (Fox 1968), I have seldom found this species, and then only as rare individuals during June and July. Because of its small size and fondness for deep shade, this butterfly is probably easily overlooked.

Pteronymia cotytto

(Guerin, 1844)

FW Length: 20-24 mm **Plate 36**

Range: Mexico to Panama

Hostplant: Unknown

Early stages: Unknown

Adult: Distinguished from *P. parva* by having the inner margin of the black FW apex straight at the interface of the transparent area, not excavated. Compare with *P. parva*.

Habits: I have never seen any authentic museum or field specimens of this butterfly from Costa Rica, despite literature records (Fox 1968). I am informed by G. B. Small that in Panama this species is confined to the lowland Pacific dry forest. If it occurs in Costa Rica it should have a similar habitat preference.

Pteronymia fumida

Schaus, 1913

FW Length: 29-31 mm **Plate 36**

Range: Costa Rica to Colombia

Hostplant: Unknown

Early stages: Unknown

Adult: In general appearance, similar to a large *P. notilla* or, as Fox (1968) decided, *P. fulvescens*. Although there is doubt as to the status of this species, I have seen a number of specimens that all have the diagnostic doubled silver spots between the radial veins on the HW distal margin and yellow antennae, as originally described by Schaus (1913).

Habits: There are few specimens of this species in existence, and only two are Costa Rican; they came from the Carrillo Belt. Any observations or records should be reported.

Pteronymia lonera

(Butler and Druce, 1872)

FW Length: 31-34 mm **Plate 36**

Range: Costa Rica and western Panama

Hostplant: *Cyphomandra hartwegii* (Solanaceae)

Early stages: *Egg*—white, laid singly on young leaves; the female usually lays several eggs on the same plant. *Mature larva*—black and white striped with a shiny black head capsule and two black anterior filaments; not unlike *Melinaea*. *Pupa*—abdomen compressed with an elongate body, and colored silver and gold. *Note*: the early stages of this species are unusual for the genus (Haber 1978).

Adult: Distinguished by the black base of the FW and smoky black distal half, which bears translucent spots; discal portion of the HW opaque orange in female; the male has HW disc semi-transparent.

Habits: Occurs from 1,000 to 1,800 m on both slopes in association with wet and cloud forest habitats. Encountered as rare solitary individuals, usually flying at the subcanopy level. Males perch along forest edges or in light gaps from late morning until early afternoon, making numerous sorties from the same perch. The females oviposit at midday, on hostplants occurring along forest edges and in light gaps. Both sexes visit flowers of *Inga* trees. This species is uncommon in Costa Rican collections, and I have never found it abundant anywhere in Costa Rica.

Pteronymia simplex simplex

(Salvin, 1869)

FW Length: 24-29 mm **Plate 36**

Range: Mexico to Panama. **Subspecies:** Costa Rica and Panama

Hostplant: *Solanum* (Solanaceae)

Early stages: *Egg*—white, laid singly on the underside of leaves. The female usually lays several eggs on the same plant. *Mature larva*—similar to that described for *P. notilla*, except less ornately colored.

Adult: Distinguished from the extremely similar *Episcada salvinia* by having the head as wide as or wider than the thorax; the reddish costa of the HW underside has a fine gray line that extends from the base to the middle of the cell, but never beyond the cell (see Fig. 28).

Habits: Occurs in all forest habitats above 1,000 m, and usually in association with *Episcada salvinia*. Occasionally found in abundance along riparian edges within the forest. This species is commonly found in the Meseta Central during ithomiine migrations. Both sexes visit a variety of flowers in the Asteraceae, and the males avidly visit sources of pyrrolizidine alkaloids. Common.

Genus **HETEROSAIS** Godman and Salvin, 1880

The butterflies in this genus are recognized by their distinctive hindwing venation (Fig. 26), which is the most reduced of all the ithomiine genera. The genus ranges from Nicaragua to the Amazon Basin, and contains three species. There are two species in Central America, one of which occurs in Costa Rica.

None of the species has been reared, and nothing is known of their population biology.

Heterosais edessa nephele

(Bates, 1862)

FW Length: 29-31 mm **Plate 36**

Range: Costa Rica to Bolivia. **Subspecies:** Nicaragua to Panama

Hostplant: Unknown

Early stages: Unknown

Adult: Distinguished by the venation of the HW (Fig. 26); in general appearance it looks like *Greta andromica*, but is redder on the underside and the HW looks smaller and out of proportion to the FW.

Habits: Occurs from sea level to 800 m on the Atlantic slope, in association with rain forest habitats. Encountered as solitary individuals flying low to the ground in the forest understory, especially near swampy areas. I have found this species to be somewhat local; it is most common during the rainy seasons, especially in the Valle de Turrialba.

Subfamily **MORPHINAE**

The butterflies in this subfamily are some of the most spectacular of all butterflies. As considered here, the Morphinae is entirely Neotropical, although upon analysis of all genera in the Nymphalidae, the subfamily may be found to contain more genera, some of which could occur in the Old World tropics. Members of the Morphinae are found from Mexico through Central and South America, with the greatest number of species in the Amazon Basin. Although Le Moult and Real (1962) recognized over seventy species in the genus *Morpho* alone, the entire subfamily probably contains fewer than half that number. In Central America there are ten species, all of which occur in Costa Rica. Major references for the Morphinae include: D'Abrera (1984), DeVries et al. (1985), Ehrlich (1958*a*), and LeMoult and Real (1962).

The hostplants of the Morphinae are in the families Arecaceae, Poaceae, Fabaceae, Menispermaceae, Mimosaceae, and Sapindaceae. The eggs are unusual among all nymphalid butterflies in being hemispherical (Fig. 30), and are generally laid singly, although some of the South American species may lay eggs in clusters. The larvae are quite colorful and hirsute; the head capsule bears many stiff hairs, and the last body segment bears two caudal tails that attain considerable length in some genera (Figs. 29, 30). The pupae are suspended, and range in shape from ovoid in the genus *Morpho* to somewhat elongate and angular in *Antirrhea* and *Caerois* (Fig. 29).

In general, members of the Morphinae are all lowland forest species, although a few occur in the high montane regions of the Andes, and others occur in extremely dry areas of Mexico and the western slope of the Andes. The adults of all species feed exclusively upon the juices of rotting fruits or fungi; none visits flowers. In all of the Neotropics there are few sights more spectacular than watching the lazy flight of a male *Morpho cypris* or close relative lazily sail above the canopy of the rain forest or along a river on a brilliantly sunny day. No one can fail to be moved, and for this reason the genus *Morpho* has become hunted for commerce. Oddly enough, the biology of the Morphinae is poorly known, even though the group includes some of the most sought-after butterflies in the world.

Genus **ANTIRRHEA** Boisduval, 1870

The *Antirrhea* butterflies are easily recognized by their angular hindwing shape, large eyes, and generally uniform underside pattern. The males possess a peculiar arrangement of androconial brushes on the overlapping portions of the forewings and hindwings, and an androconial patch of specialized scent scales of the upperside of the forewings. Some species possess an additional set of abdominal scent brushes on the inside of the male claspers: a total of three functional systems (Vane-Wright 1972; DeVries et al. 1985). The genus ranges from Guatemala south to the Amazon Basin and southern Brazil; the greatest number of species occur on the eastern slope of the Andes. Of the twenty or so species in *Antirrhea* (D'Abrera 1984), only three occur in Costa Rica.

The larvae apparently feed entirely upon palms, although few of the species have been reared. The eggs are hemispherical and resemble those of *Morpho*. The larvae of the Costa Rican species are hairy, red and yellow, have a hairy red capsule, and differ from the larvae of

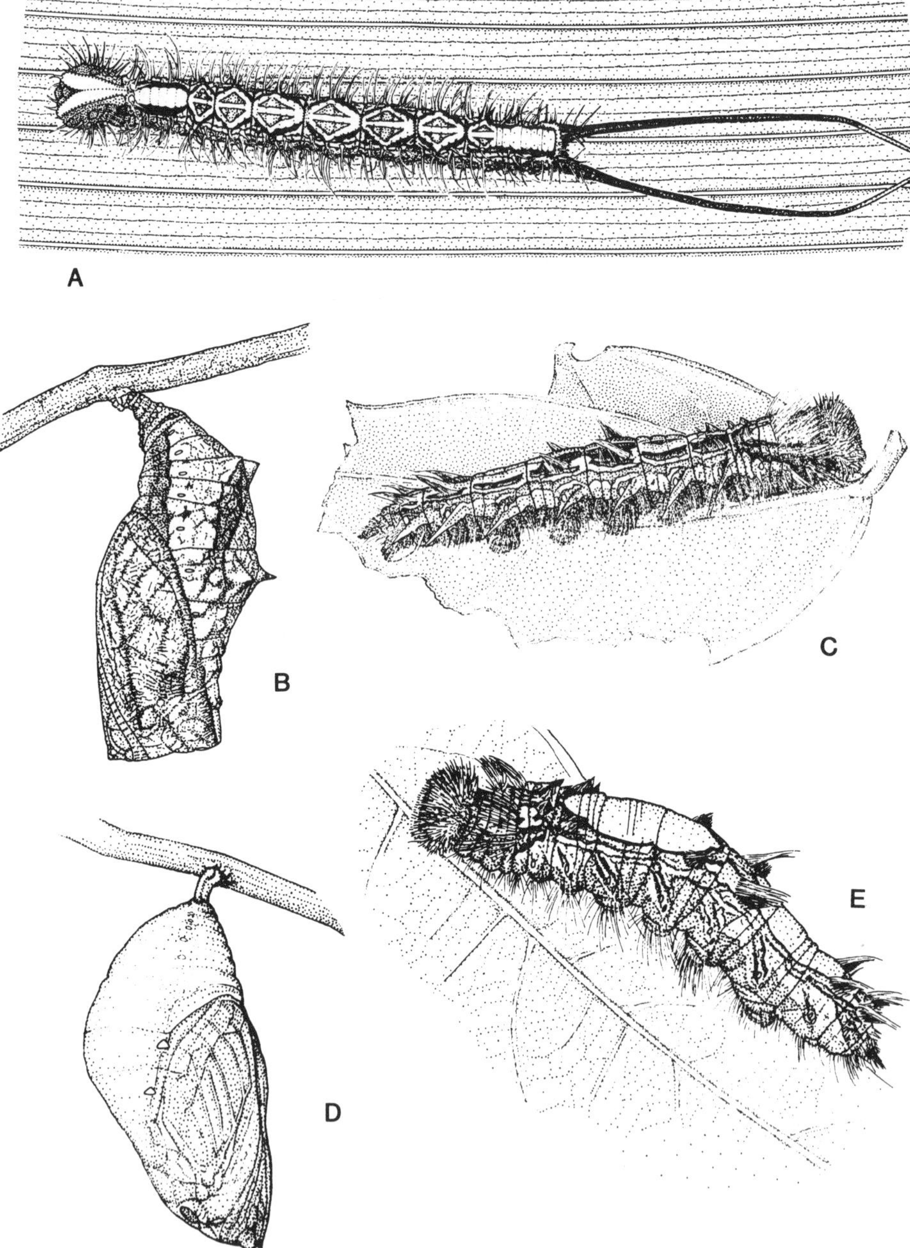

FIGURE 29. Larvae and pupae of the Nymphalidae: Morphinae. A: *Antirrhea pterocopha* recently molted mature larvae; B: *Antirrhea pterocopha* pupa; C: *Morpho peleides* mature larva; D: *Morpho amathonte* pupa; E: *Morpho amathonte* mature larva (drawings by J. Clark).

Morpho by having a pair of long whiplike caudal tails (Fig. 29).

The adults inhabit deep forest shade, and seem especially common in areas of swamp forest. Although the flight is not fast, individuals easily avoid capture by gliding along the forest floor through dense vegetation. Both sexes feed on moldy or rotting fruits and fungi that litter the forest understory. Some species appear to return to the same place to feed on consecutive days. Nothing is known about predators or parasites of *Antirrhea*, or how long adults may live. One very interesting study would be to observe how the males coordinate all of the scent brushes during courtship displays (see Plate 37, where the brushes are exposed), and how the female reacts to what must certainly be a spectacular display.

Antirrhea pterocopha

Godman and Salvin, 1868

FW Length: 47-54 mm **Plate 37**

Range: Costa Rica and western Panama

Hostplant: *Calypterogyne* (Arecaceae)

Early stages: (DeVries et al. 1985) *Egg*—pale green hemispherical, with a slight broken line on the lid. *First instar*—dull reddish with caudal tails as long as the body, and which are flattened distally; head capsule red with plumose hairs and a forked epicranium. *Mature larva*—head capsule reddish with a cream V shape on the face; head tapers to epicranium, which bears two forks; sides of head have red hairs. Body: dorsum with seven diamond-shaped marks, each with two internal triangles, and separated by a cream dorsal midline; diamonds are finely delimited in black; two creamy rectangles (one behind head, the other on the last segment) outlined in black; two long, whiplike tails with white tips about three-fourths length of body; sides finely mottled yellow, dark green, and white, and bearing a dense mat of white, recurved hairs (Fig. 29). *Pupa*—pale yellow; head and wingpads greenish brown; last abdominal segment and cremaster dark brown; abdomen has a number of triangular protuberances on dorsum interspersed with brown patches (Fig. 29). The larvae feed only on older leaves that are covered with epiphylls, and eat the leaf tissue between the veins. The larval damage is very distinct: rectangular holes are eaten from the main leaf blade, seldom at the leaf edge.

Adult: Sexes dimorphic. *Male*—HW upperside has a yellow patch near apex and reflective blue on inner margin. *Female*—FW upperside has a violet medial band; HW has yellowish distal margins.

Habits: Occurs from 700 to 1400 m on the Atlantic slope in the Carrillo Belt, in association with the tropical wet–premontane transition forest. Its known distribution is from Virgen del Socorro to the Reventazon Valley. Encountered in ones or twos in the deep shade of the forest along streams, where the butterflies fly low to the ground and frequently settle on low vegetation at the base of tree trunks. I have found that most individuals rest at the base of tree trunks during the early mornings, which may indicate that they sleep in these locations. The flight behavior of *A. pterocopha* differs from other species by being more docile; other species tend to glide through the forest understory. Unlike many species of butterflies, the females are well represented in collections and are frequently seen in the field. This is perhaps due to the fact that they are often found in male-female pairs. On finding an individual of one sex, I have, with surprising frequency, found one of the other sex after looking around for a few minutes. It has been my experience that populations are very localized along certain streams, but are totally absent in the forest twenty meters away. This suggests to me that there is probably very little movement between population areas. It also seems apparent to me that this species does not cross areas that have been clear-cut, and it is found only in undisturbed cloud forest. The only item I have observed the adults feeding upon is fungi associated with rotting wood.

Antirrhea miltiades

(Fabricius, 1793)

FW Length: 45-50 mm **Plate 37**

Range: Guatemala to the Amazon Basin

Hostplant: *Geonoma longivaginata* (Arecaceae)

Early stages: (DeVries et al. 1985) *Mature larva*—similar in general shape and morphology to *A. pterocopha*, but differing as follows: ground color reddish; sides finely irrorated with small black spots; dorsal pattern has diamond shapes, but the shapes appear as arrowheads that have the points directed to the posterior; there is a prominent yellowish inverted V shape on the face. *Pupa*—similar to *A. pterocopha*. The larvae are solitary eaters, feeding only on old mature leaves and resting along the midrib of the leaf.

Adult: Distinguished by the white patch on the HW, which can be seen from both upper- and underside. See *A. tomasia*.

Habits: Occurs locally from sea level to 400 m on the Atlantic slope, in association with swampy rain forest habitats. Usually encountered as solitary individuals gliding across the

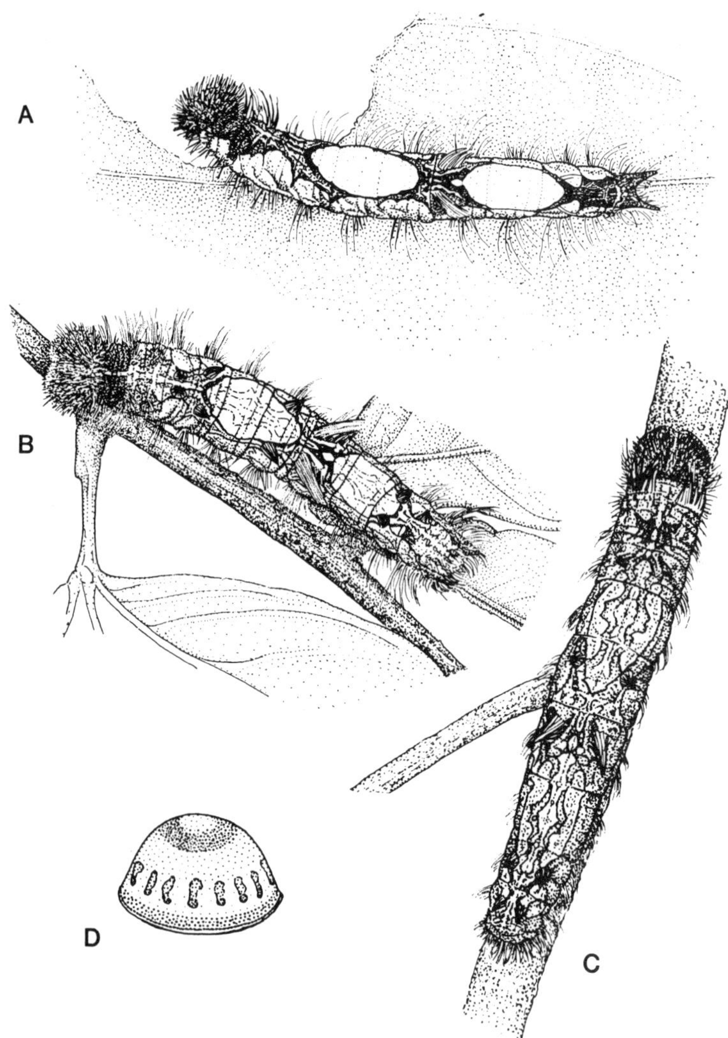

FIGURE 30. Larvae and egg of the Nymphalidae: Morphinae. A: *Morpho cypris* fourth instar larva; B: *Morpho cypris* early color phase of fifth instar larva; C: *Morpho cypris* color phase of mature larva; D: *Morpho cypris* egg (drawings by J. Clark).

forest floor. The males perch on low vegetation along trails and stream sides during the early mornings, and it seems that the same males generally perch in the same area over a period of several weeks. The females are seldom seen. During late morning, individuals are mostly males. In addition to palm fruits, both sexes will feed on fungi growing on rotting wood, and very occasionally rotting bananas. This species is most abundant in areas of extensive swampy forest like Tortuguero and the Llanura de Santa Clara. Generally present throughout the year, and commonest during the dry seasons.

Antirrhea tomasia
Butler, 1875
FW Length: 47-50 mm **Plate 37**
Range: Costa Rica and western Panama
Hostplant: Unknown
Early stages: Unknown
Adult: Distinguished by the entirely dark brown HW upperside, occasionally with a small white dot near cell end; HW underside has two distinct ocelli (one large, one small) within an elongate white patch near tornus. See *A. miltiades*.
Habits: Occurs from sea level to 500 m on the Pacific slope, in association with rain forest habitats centered around the Osa Peninsula, but ranging as far north as the remnant patches of forest in the Valle de Parrita. In my experience a rare species, usually found along ridge tops and hillsides deep within the forest. I have seen it feed only a few times, once on fungi and once on rotting bananas. This has been considered to be a subspecies of *miltiades* by some, but I am considering it a full species because of its restricted distribution. The early stages are as yet unknown. Rare in collections.

Genus **CAEROIS** Hübner, 1816

The butterflies in this genus are easily recognized by the elongate, almost falcate forewing apex and the prominent tail on the hindwing. Although closely related to *Antirrhea*, it can be distinguished by the placement of the tufts of androconial hairs on the underside of the forewing inner margin. There are but two species in *Caerois*, one of which occurs in our area. The genus ranges from Costa Rica to Ecuador.

The hostplant relationships indicate that the palm family Arecaceae is important, but the South American species *C. chorinaeus* can apparently feed upon sugar cane (Poaceae)—a record that requires confirmation. The eggs are hemispherical, as in *Morpho* and *Antirrhea*, and the larvae show a clear relationship to *Antirrhea* by possession of the long, whiplike tails (DeVries et al. 1985). The pupa is more similar to *Antirrhea* than to *Morpho* by having flared wingpads and an angular shape.

In Costa Rica it is found only in areas of swampy lowland rain forest, and is in general very rare. The adults feed on the juices of rotting vegetation and fruits, but in general are little known.

Caerois gerdrudtus
(Fabricius, 1793)
FW Length: 40-52 mm **Plate 40**
Range: Costa Rica to Ecuador
Hostplant: *Socratea durisima* (Arecaceae)
Early stages: *Egg*—hemispherical, pale greenish brown. *Mature larva*—in general shape similar to *Antirrhea*; sides and venter are pale green; dorsum has a connected series of rounded, reddish diamond shapes, which is in turn surrounded by an area of yellowish green; caudal tails are pale green and sparsely covered with dark hairs; head capsule is reddish brown, covered with very fine hairs; epicranium has a series of six short reddish horns bordered with yellow, all of which are densely packed together and curve anteriorly. The pupa is gray-green mottled with black spots, and is in general similar to *Antirrhea*, but rounder. The larva feeds on a mature leaf and cuts rectangular sections from inside the leaf blade or margin. The green larva and pupa blend perfectly into this waxy underside of the hostplant leaves.
Adult: Upperside has a dark violet cast and a large orange ocellus at the FW apex.
Habits: Occurs from sea level to 600 m on both slopes, in association with swamp forest. On the Atlantic slope, it is most abundant in Tortuguero and the Llanuras de Santa Clara; on the Pacific, it occurs in areas around the Osa Peninsula. Encountered as rare, solitary individuals in the deep shade of swamps. Both sexes fly weakly, close to the ground, and are extremely cryptic when resting on low vegetation on the ground. I have only found this species by stumbling into individuals during walks in the forest. Rare in Costa Rican collections and little known.

Genus **MORPHO** Fabricius, 1807

In many respects, the genus *Morpho* is the classic Neotropical group of butterflies, simply because alive or dead these insects demand attention. The brilliant coloration, found mostly in males, is entirely structural. The colors range from pure white to azure, to an intense, almost transparent blue-violet. The females are less colorful, and some lack any trace of reflective coloration. The genus shows a great diversity of size, ranging from the small *M. portis* to the enormous *M. hecuba*, which may have a forewing length of over 150 millimeters. Curiously, although in some species the wing length may be enormous, the body size may be relatively small. The small-bodied species fly by gliding on air currents, like kites. As body size in relation to wing length increases, the insects spend more energy utilizing typically floppy wing beats. The genus *Morpho* ranges from Mexico to South America, and has the greatest number of species in the Amazon Basin. All six of the Central American species occur in Costa Rica, and are represented by four species groups (*hecuba, polyphemus, achilles,* and *rhetenor*), each with distinct colorations and dimorphisms.

The Fabaceae and Mimosaceae are important host plants for certain Central American species. In South America, some species are reported to feed on Erythroxylaceae, Sapindaceae, Bignoniaceae, Menispermaceae, and Poaceae. The hostplant relationships for Central America are summarized by Young (1978*b*, 1982*a*) and Young and Muyshondt (1973). The eggs of *Morpho* are hemispherical and have a broken ring of red or brown around the so-called lid. The larvae are characteristically hairy, bright red and yellow, have an almost triangular head capsule covered with stiff hairs, and the last segment has a short bifid tail (Figs. 29, 30). The larvae bear eversible glands near the first set of legs, which give off a volatile odor when the larva is molested, much like the glands of brassoline and charaxine larvae (see Young 1982*a*). In addition, during a study of larvae of *Morpho*, I found that all instars of *M. peleides, M. amathonte*, and *M. cypris* secrete a drop of clear fluid after molting from a dorsal pore on the thorax. The fluid is gathered on the plumose head hairs and then combed into the various tufts of hairs along the body (DeVries 1985*c*). The function of this fluid and why it is applied to the hair tufts is unknown. As far as is known, the Central American species are solitary feeders, but in South America some species feed in large aggregations. The Central American species take from 90 to 120 days to develop from egg to adult.

In Costa Rica, the genus is found in all forest habitats from sea level to 1,800 meters, with the greatest concentration of species in the mid-elevational forests of the Atlantic slope. Two of our species show very restricted distributions (*M. granadensis* and *M. polyphemus*), and represent South American and Mexican faunal elements. Males and females are active at different times of day and occupy different microhabitats. The males are more obvious as they patrol up and down rivers and forest edges. Females are seen less often because they tend to stay in the forest, and are less conspicuously colored. Coloration and behavior of the males has probably evolved for male-male interactions. Males commonly chase and interact with each other, females do not. An old collector's trick to lure a male *Morpho* is to wave a blue silk scarf at a male passing overhead. The response is usually instantaneous; the male dives down to investigate and hover above the lure. The female shows no response. Although observations like these are known from everywhere in the Neotropics, there has been no experimental work on male-male interactions (Vane-Wright 1984). It seems fundamental to the question of why butterflies are so brightly colored, and the genus *Morpho* seems an excellent place to start.

The adults feed entirely on rotting fruits and sap flows from wounds in trees and vines. When feeding, the cryptic underside makes these insects almost invisible. The contrast between upper and underside coloration has led Young (1971*a*) to postulate that the contrast serves as a defense (see also Silberglied 1984). Such contrast, it is reasoned, surprises a predator and allows the butterfly to escape. It is also suggested that the contrast is more difficult to follow with the eye, and hence enhances the escape. Besides crypsis and contrasting coloration, a seemingly slow flight behavior, which can immediately change into a wild swooping one, also must be added to the defenses of *Morpho*. This is easily demonstrated to anyone who takes a swing at one with a butterfly net and misses; there is no second chance.

Factors affecting mortality of *Morpho* are not well understood. It is known that birds will feed on adults, larvae, and pupae, yet there are no estimates which indicate how important this type of predation is. The larvae are preyed upon by tachnid flies as well as chalcid and braconid wasps, and these predators are probably very important in reducing populations of *Morpho*. Perhaps one of the more unusual parasitoid attacks known in butterflies are tachnid fly larvae that live in the abdomen of female *Morpho theseus* (DeVries 1979*b*) in Costa Rica. The effect upon reproduction and how the fly larvae get into the host is unknown.

It has been suggested that individuals of

some *Morpho* species, where the larvae feed on several hostplants, may be distasteful and involved in automimicry (Young and Muyshondt 1973). Although it is true that some hostplant genera of *Morpho* contain alkaloids and potent toxins, there is no evidence that *Morpho* butterflies are unpalatable to predators, and this idea needs examination in detail. Indeed, in Costa Rica several flycatcher species and two species of jacamars readily pursue, catch, and eat *Morpho peleides, M. amathonte,* and *M. cypris,* as direct observation, feeding experiments, and fallen wings under the perches of jacamars will attest.

Like all large showy insects, *Morpho* has gained popularity in the hands of commercial insect dealers. The most recent revision of the genus (Le Moult and Real 1962) chiefly emphasizes splitting taxa, but has some reasonable subgeneric divisions and much distributional data, which may ultimately prove useful. I have followed the arrangement of Fruhstorfer (1912) because the names are well established in the biological literature. I have in some cases disregarded form names, or have added them as notes in passing.

Morpho theseus aquarius

Butler, 1872

FW Length: 68-75 mm **Plate 39**

Range: Mexico to Peru. **Subspecies:** Costa Rica to Colombia

Hostplant: Unknown

Early stages: Unknown

Adult: Upperside pearly gray; HW margin slightly dentate; underside has a reddish brown cast; populations from near Volcan Chiriqui in the Cordillera de Talamanca are whiter, and washed out on the underside. Distinguished from *M. polyphemus* while on the wing by the reddish underside.

Habits: Occurs from sea level to 1,800 m on both slopes, in association with wet and rain forest habitats. In Guanacaste it is found only in the mountains. The males are commonly seen flying high above the forest canopy, along gorges and rivers, and have a very characteristic jerky flight that resembles a falling leaf. During the mornings the males actively patrol breaks in the forest canopy. Not infrequently, in the presence of a female this results in a follow-the-leader procession. During courtship, the male hovers over the female while she is flying along, and this courtship will continue over long distances. I have never seen a pair *in copula*. Both sexes visit rotting fruits that are along ridge tops, but seemingly ignore fruits in valleys and bottomlands. Common in all mid-elevational forests; most abundant from June to July and then again in September to November. Populations on the Pacific slope of the Cordillera de Talamanca are commonest during February.

Morpho polyphemus catarina

Corea and Chacon, 1984

FW Length: 75-80 mm **Plate 39**

Range: Mexico to Costa Rica. **Subspecies:** Nicaragua and Costa Rica

Hostplant: *Paullinia pinata* (Sapindaceae); *Inga* (Mimosaceae) in El Salvador

Early stages: (Young and Muyshondt 1972) *Egg*—pale green with a brownish broken line on lid, laid singly. *Early instars*—body gray-brown with fine lines of yellow bordered by black; two prominent yellow-green patches on dorsum; sides covered with silver-brown hairs; dorsum with eight tufts of reddish brown and purplish hairs; head capsule brown, covered with a dense mat of silver-brown hairs. *Mature larva*—body generally pale brown with pale green dorsal patches; hairs on sides and dorsum are shorter and give the impression that the body is smoother and more cryptic than previous instars. *Pupa*—pale green, ovoid, with yellow spiracles; cremaster bluish green; head obviously bifid, with the tips red.

Adult: Distinguished from all other species in Central America by being almost pure shining white on upper and underside. Costa Rican specimens are larger than those from further north.

Habits: Until recently, this species was unknown from Costa Rica. It has been recorded from the mountains of Guanacaste near Parque Rincon de la Vieja in association with the Pacific slope premontane transition belt forest during the months of September to December. I have not seen the species myself, and am indebted to I. Chacon and R. Canet for the following observations. Males fly along the forest canopy or along river beds with a flight not unlike *M. theseus*. These males show spiraling interactions when two or more come together, and they chase other species of white butterflies, as well, especially *Appias drusilla* and *Ascia josepha*. The principal activity times are from 9 a.m. until 2 p.m., when both sexes feed on rotting fruits placed along forest edges. The high velocity of the winds coming over from the Atlantic slope apparently batter these insects about to a great degree, and most males have pieces of the wings missing. It is unclear whether this species has always been present, or whether it has recently dispersed from further north. The larvae and hostplants of the Costa Rican populations are as yet unknown, as are the limits of its distribution in Costa Rica. Rare in Costa Rican collections.

Morpho peleides limpida
Butler, 1872

FW Length: 64-78 mm **Plate 38**

Range: Mexico to Colombia and Venezuela. **Subspecies:** See "Habits" below

Hostplant: *Macharium, Pterocarpus, Lonchocarpus, Platymiscium, Swartzia, Dalbergia, Mucuna* (Fabaceae); (in Trinidad) *Paragonia* (Bignoniaceae)

Early stages: (Young and Muyshondt 1973) *Egg*—pale green with a reddish broken line on the lid, laid singly. *Mature larva*—early instars conspicuously yellow and red, but in the fifth instar the dorsum and sides are colored with fine brown, red and black lines; two conspicuous yellowish patches on the dorsum have reddish lines in the middle; body and sides covered with reddish brown and whitish hairs; these hairs are tufted in the dorsolateral regions (Fig. 29); head capsule reddish brown, covered on the corona with a dense mat of reddish hairs and sparsely covered on the remainder of the head. *Note:* larvae in Guanacaste usually lack red and yellow entirely, but are patterned with fine lines of gray and pale brown. *Pupa*—pale green, ovoid, head slightly bifid, with a few golden spots on the spiracles.

Adult: Distinguished from the similar *M. granadensis* by always having pupillate eyespots on the HW underside; has varying amounts of blue. The subspecies *limpida* is found on the Atlantic slope and on the Pacific slope as far south as San Mateo. From San Mateo up to the Meseta Central, populations have almost entirely brown uppersides with only a small amount of blue on the FW. Further south and into the lowlands of Panama is the so-called subspecies *marinita*, which has the basal portion of the wings brown and the blue reduced to bands. The underside is always variable with regard to the eyespots.

Habits: Occurs from sea level to 1,800 m on both slopes, in association with all forest habitats. This is the commonest species in Central America, and its floppy, zigzag flight along rivers and forest edges and through coffee plantations is a familiar sight. The males patrol from early morning until midday, and females are usually active only during midday, when they are seen weaving in and out of vegetation. The scent hairs adjacent to the male claspers can be extruded with gentle pressure, and smell like vanilla. The female is generally larger, has a wider black margin, and has a circular plate terminating the last abdominal segment. The sharp cut-off line at San Mateo, where the forms change, would provide an excellent means of looking at the genetics of the blue versus brown forms. It is unclear why all-blue forms are not found south of San Mateo, nor why brown forms are not found north of this area. As far as I can detect, there is no difference between the larvae or the hostplants. Commonest on the Pacific slope during the rainy seasons, except on the Osa Peninsula, where it is most abundant during the end of the rainy season. On the Atlantic slope it is commonest during the dry seasons, and each habitat along the elevational gradient has different times of abundance. It is present throughout the year in all habitats.

Morpho granadensis polybaptus
Butler, 1874

FW Length: 62-77 mm **Plate 38**

Range: Nicaragua to Ecuador. **Subspecies:** Nicaragua to Panama.

Hostplant: *Macharium seemani* (Fabaceae)

Early stages: (Young 1982*a*) Almost identical to the red and yellow larvae of *peleides*, but with small differences in head structure and placement of the body hairs. *Pupa*—same as *M. peleides*.

Adult: Entirely blue above; HW has short dentations on margin; underside has no pupils in the eyespots; ground color darker and with white lines and striations on the basal half. See *M. peleides*.

Habits: Confined to the Atlantic slope, from 200 to 600 m, in association with the Carrillo Belt. Usually found as rare solitary individuals flying with *M. peleides*. With practice it can be distinguished from *peleides* while on the wing by having a lighter blue sheen on the wings and by flying in shadier microhabitats. Although both sexes feed on rotting fruits, this species is seldom attracted to rotten bananas. Rare in collections. I have only found it to be present in the Carrillo Belt during February and March and then again in July and August, always as rare individuals. Reasons for its restricted distribution are postulated in Young (1982*a*) and should be examined in greater detail in future studies.

Morpho cypris
Westwood, 1851

FW Length: male 62-68 mm, female 73-79 mm **Plate 40**

Range: Nicaragua to Colombia

Hostplant: *Inga marginata* (Mimosaceae)

Early stages: *Egg*—laid singly, although the female may lay numerous eggs on the same plant; similar in appearance to the egg of *M. peleides* but with a row of red vertical lines encircling the widest portion (Fig. 30). *Early instars*—larvae 1 to 4 are similar to *M. amathonte*, except the body is almost entirely yellow with some red lines on the dorsum and sides; the head bears bushy, bright red hairs, and the last segment bears obvious red caudal tails (Fig. 30). Rests on the underside of leaves. *Mature larva*—early fifth instars have two large yellow ovals on the dorsum with many fine red and gray-brown lines between the ovals and along the sides; head capsule has short gray-brown hairs. As the larva matures it loses all traces of yellow, and eventually becomes densely covered with very fine brownish green lines that render the larva wonderfully cryptic. Rests on woody stems and almost melts into the background coloration (Fig. 30). *Pupa*—similar to *M. amathonte*, but with a single large white spot on the thorax.

Adult: Sexes dimorphic. *Male*—intense chrome blue on upperside with a whitish medial band. *Note*: populations from near Volcan Chiriqui in the Cordillera de Talamanca have a wider band and have been named *bugaba*. *Female*—two forms: one has a wide yellowish medial band and blue-black borders, the other, which appears to be common in Costa Rica, has a wide medial band but with blue, as in the male (form *cyanites*).

Habits: Occurs from sea level to 800 m on both slopes, in association with undisturbed rain forest habitats. The males patrol high above the forest canopy along rivers from 10:30 a.m. to 1:00 p.m., and rigidly adhere to this schedule. Depending on the angle of the sun, the reflection off the blue scaling may give the impression of a blue orb floating above the ground, an impression enhanced by very few wingbeats. The sight of this sailing blue orb against a rain forest background is truly one of the most stunningly beautiful in the Neotropics. A result of being one of the most brilliantly colored insects in the world has been the species' commercial persecution at the expense of natural history studies; its biology is essentially unknown. In Costa Rica the females are very rarely seen. The few times I have seen them were during late afternoon, high in the forest canopy, weaving in and out of the foliage; once I observed oviposition during the late morning. Although both sexes feed undoubtedly on rotting fruits, it is seldom taken at baits placed on the forest floor or in the canopy. Commonly observed, but infrequently collected.

Morpho amathonte

Deyrolle, 1860

FW Length: male 73-78 mm, female 81-87 mm **Plate 39**

Hostplant: *Pterocarpus officionale* (Fabaceae)

Early stages: *Egg*—essentially the same as *M. peleides*; first instar larvae are similar to *M. peleides* but are entirely reddish. *Mature larva*—similar in shape to *M. peleides* but more squat and thicker; no yellow on body at all; dorsum has two large patches of lime green; sides mottled dull red with a green overcast; hairs on dorsum tufted in both red and white; head capsule pale red and sparsely hairy (Fig. 29). *Pupa*—similar to *M. peleides* and *M. cypris* in shape but without any markings except for transparent areas near spiracles (Fig. 29).

Adult: Sexes dimorphic. *Male*—upperside entirely azure blue except for FW costa and apex. *Female*—upperside has wide brown margins; FW has two rows of white spots. Underside of both sexes washed with reddish brown, and eyespots reduced.

Habits: Occurs commonly from sea level to 800 m on both slopes, in association with rain forest habitats, and occasionally found above 800 m in montane forest during dry seasons. Males are active, patrolling along forest edges and rivers, during the early mornings, soon after sunrise. About mid-morning, male activity lessens and both sexes feed on fallen *Ficus, Licania, Manilkara, Dipteryx, Brosimum, Spondias*, and other fleshy fruits. The females actively search for oviposition sites at midday, invariably in swampy areas, and have a very distinctive floppy flight. In early afternoon, the males have a short burst of activity. Just before dusk, both sexes slowly flutter along ridge tops in the forest and settle on the undersides of leaves to sleep. This species is common and widespread in all rain forest habitats and is present throughout the year.

Subfamily **BRASSOLINAE**

The butterflies in this subfamily are among the largest species in the Neotropics. Closely related to the Satyrinae, all genera (except *Narope*) are recognized by having conspicuous ocelli on the underside; the eyes appear to have an alternating pigmentation of light and dark lines, and the males have well-developed androconial tufts of the wings and on the sides of the abdomen. Although Ehrlich (1958*a*) placed the brassolines in the Morphinae, Fruhstorfer (1912) suggested they were more closely related to the Old World Amathusinae. Evidence from early stages suggests that the relationships of these three groups are uncertain (DeVries et al. 1985). Although there are a great many dubious names for some of the genera, access to major references will be found in Fruhstorfer (1912), Stichel (1909), and Blandin (1976). I have followed the overall arrangement of Fruhstorfer, but it is clear that there are still unsolved problems concerning *Caligo*, since some species will freely interbreed and make visible hybrids in the insectary, whereas, on the whole, *Opsiphanes* is poorly collected in Costa Rica. The brassolines are found only in the Neotropics and range from Mexico throughout Central and South America, with a few species on the islands of Trinidad and Tobago. The greatest number of species occurs in the Amazon Basin. The Brassolinae is composed of approximately twelve genera, nine of which occur in our area.

As larvae, the brassolines feed entirely on monocots, of which Arecaceae, Musaceae, Heliconiaceae, Poaceae, and Bromeliaceae have been demonstrated to be important. Eggs of all brassolines are round, smooth or sculptured, and are laid singly or in clusters. In all but one genus (*Brassolis*), the larvae have elaborate head horns along the sides of the head, many of which are recurved and knobbed. The larvae all have bifid caudal tails that may attain a considerable length (Figs. 31, 32); again, the exception is *Brassolis*, which has a reduced tail. The larvae may have soft pseudospines on the dorsum, or be smooth. Most larvae have an eversible neck gland that is probably used for defense against ants or parasites; however, it is not known if all larvae have this trait. The pupae show a diversity of shapes that range from rounded and squat, as in *Opsiphanes* and *Caligo*, to long and slender as in *Eryphanis*, or the remarkable pupa of *Dynastor* (Figs. 31, 32), which looks like the head of a poisonous snake.

Unlike most Neotropical butterflies, certain brassolines have become economically important crop pests in some areas. *Brassolis* larvae can apparently totally defoliate individual coconut palms in plantations, and *Caligo* can be an important banana pest. Economic studies on *Caligo* have demonstrated that if banana plantations are left unsprayed, an outbreak of *Caligo* larvae was quickly diminished to negligible population levels by the normal parasite communities that build up on the *Caligo* larvae. If the crops are repeatedly sprayed, the parasites are destroyed, and the *Caligo* larvae then do very well and can destroy banana crops (Harrison 1962). A further study on *Caligo* described the only known case of phoresy in butterflies (Malo 1961). This study showed that egg parasites (family Trichogrammatidae) cling to the wing margins of *Caligo* and parasitize the *Caligo* eggs when they are laid. These tiny parasites cling to the wings of both male and female butterflies, and hence become transferred during mating; they thus have a way of always being able to find *Caligo* eggs. In banana plantations in Ecuador, there are up to eight different parasitic insects that use the early stages of *Caligo* as hosts (Malo and Willis 1961).

In Costa Rica, brassolines occur in all forest habitats from sea level to 1,800 meters, with the greatest concentration of species in the mid-elevation forests of the Atlantic slope. For the most part, all species are active at dawn and dusk, although in deep forest shade some species are active during the day. There is some evidence that *Brassolis* and *Narope* are active nocturnally. All species apparently feed on rotting fruits, but some of the rarer species never appear to visit fruits in traps. I have found that most *Caligo* species carry mites at the base of the proboscis during certain periods of the year, much like those found on *Morpho*. It is unknown if these mites have an effect on the butterflies. In the insectary, I have kept *Caligo memnon* and *C. eurilochus* from five weeks to three months, but there are no data on longevity in the field.

Although the males of all brassoline species have well-developed scent organs, there is nothing published on how these organs are used (see section under *Caligo*). When alive, some species emit a smell of vanilla or other sweet cloying odors.

As in the Satyrinae, there is no evidence that any species of brassoline is unpalatable to predators. Their defenses may include crepuscular flight, coupled with large "tear-away" wings and very fast flight. For defensive patterns, see the section under *Caligo*.

Although the Brassolinae have been extremely popular with collectors for many years and are by no means uncommon in any Neotropical habitat, there is little known about their biology in the field. Armed with about ten traps and a little patience, mark/release/recapture studies coupled with insectary work could tell us a lot about the longevity, territoriality, and mating habits of these interesting butterflies.

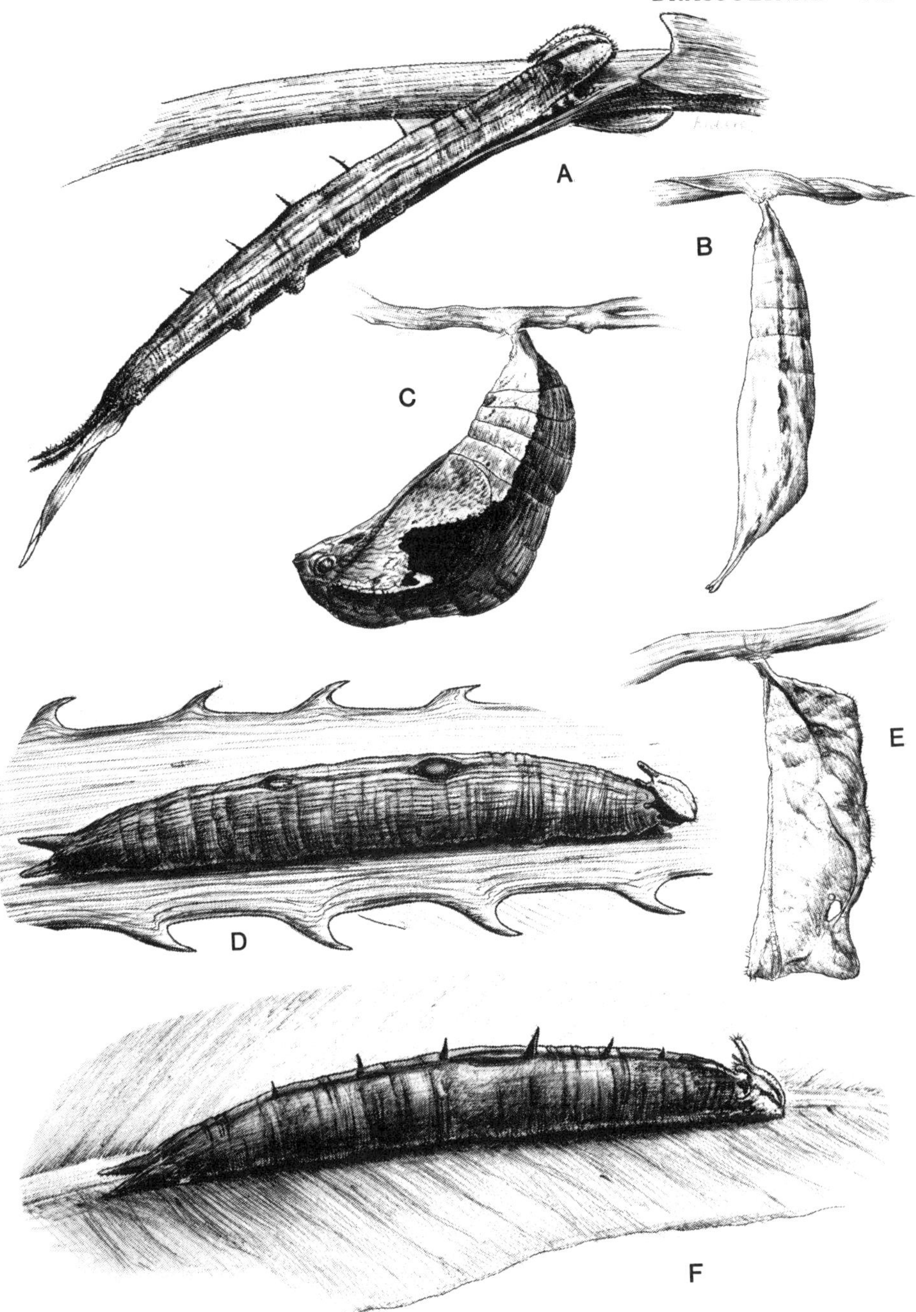

FIGURE 31. Larvae and pupae of the Nymphalidae: Brassolinae. A: *Eryphanis polyxena lycomedon* mature larva; B: *Eryphanis polyxena lycomedon* pupa; C: *Dynastor darius stygianus* pupa; D: *Dynastor darius stygianus* mature larva; E: *Caligo memnon* pupa; F: *Caligo memnon* mature larva (drawings by R. Cubero).

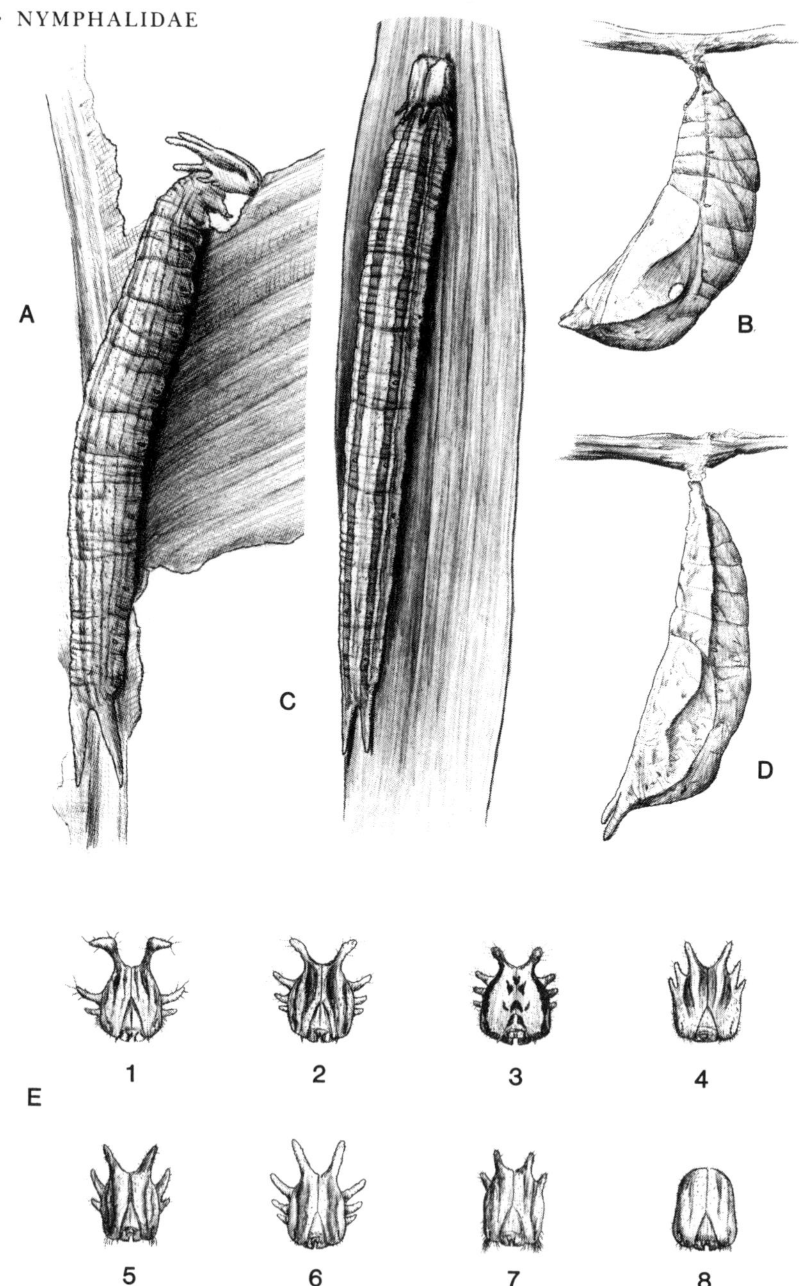

FIGURE 32. Larvae and pupae of the Nymphalidae: Brassolinae. A: *Opsiphanes tamarindi* mature larva; B: *Opsiphanes tamarindi* pupa; C: *Catoblepia orgetorix championi* mature larva; D: *Catoblepia orgetorix championi* pupa; E: frontal views of head capsules: 1. *Caligo atreus*, 2. *Caligo memnon*, 3. *Dynastor darius*, 4. *Eryphanis aesacus buboculus*, 5. *Catoblepia orgetorix*, 6. *Opsiphanes* "*bogotanus*," 7. *Opsiphanes cassina*, 8. *Brassolis* sp (drawings by R. Cubero).

Genus **BRASSOLIS** Fabricius, 1807

The butterflies in this genus differ greatly from all other brassolines by having a very stout body, short palpi, and a relatively small head. In general appearance, *Brassolis* butterflies can be mistaken for moths. The genus ranges from Guatemala south throughout the Amazon Basin and contains about five species, one of which occurs in Central America.

The hostplants of *Brassolis* are all palms, and the larvae live gregariously in silken bags. The general appearance of the larva is not unlike that of a large skipper butterfly (Hesperiidae); they are without protuberances, having a large head and a constricted neck area. The pupae are curved and rounded, showing affinities to *Dynastor* by the resemblance to a snake head. The larvae of some species are considered important pests of coconut (*Cocos nucifera*), and have been the subject of some economic work (Dunn 1917).

In Costa Rica the genus is found only along the Atlantic coast and in general is very rare. There is no information on the adult feeding habits of any species. The adults are active either at dusk or during the night.

Brassolis isthmia

Bates, 1864

FW Length: 48-50 mm **Plate 41**

Range: Guatemala to Colombia

Hostplant: *Cocos nucifera* (Arecaceae)

Early stages: (Dunn 1917) *Egg*—round, white, laid in clusters of 150 to 300, cemented together with a clear mucilage that later turns brown. *Mature larva*—cylindrical, thickest in the middle, tapering to either end; body dark brown with three yellow longitudinal stripes (one dorsal, one on either side) running the entire length of the body, and each bordered by two fine dark stripes; dorsal stripe has lighter outer margins and the middle is freckled with pale dots; body covered with fine white and dark hairs (Fig. 32); head capsule large, flat-faced, dark brown with reddish corona, and pale sides; head covered with hairs. In general appearance, the constricted neck region makes the larva look like a skipper (Hesperiidae). The larvae are gregarious nocturnal feeders, and rest during the day in a silken bag made from numerous leaflets sewn together, lined with silk, which forms a funnel that can be four feet in length. The silken bags normally contain about 400 larvae, but as many as 2,000 have been found in a single bag. The larvae are able to completely defoliate entire trees, and the aggregations are composed of several instars (indicating multiple female egg clusters). The larvae apparently suffer no parasitism by wasps or flies, but are eaten by birds, lizards, and are killed by a fungus. The pupae, on the other hand, are attacked by sarcophagid and tachinid flies, and various parasitic hymenoptera.

Adult: Distinguished from all other species by the small head; upperside dark brown with semi-falcate FW apex; FW has a pale yellow band.

Habits: In Costa Rica this species occurs rarely, from sea level to 300 m, on the Atlantic slope in association with coconut palms, primarily along the coast. Dunn (1917) reports that the species is very common in Panama and that adults are seasonal, appearing in May-June and then again from late October until early December. The adults are apparently commonly observed flying at night or in late evening, but there is no information on adult feeding. They do not visit rotting fruits placed in traps. Why this species is rare in Costa Rica is a puzzle, since *Cocos nucifera* grows abundantly on both coastlines. I have seen individuals of this species once. They were flying around a street lamp near the city of Limon at night.

Genus **DYNASTOR** Doubleday, 1849

The three species in this genus are easily recognized by the robust thorax, broadly rounded wings, and a uniform underside pattern. The genus ranges from Mexico to the Amazon Basin, with one species in Central America.

The hostplants are all in the family Bromeliaceae, both epiphytic and terrestrial. The larvae show strong affinities to *Opsiphanes*, with a stout bifid tail, smooth body, and a massive head capsule that bears a corona of prominent horns (Figs. 31, 32). The larvae all have an eversible prothoracic gland that gives off a pungent smell. The pupae are among the most curious of all butterflies: they resemble to a great degree the head of a *Bothrops* snake (Viperidae) (Fig. 31).

Little is known of the biology of the adults; there are no observations on feeding behavior. In Costa Rica the genus is active at dusk or dawn; during the day, the adults are frequently found in association with a larval hostplant.

Dynastor darius stygianus
Butler, 1872

FW Length: 51-57 mm **Plate 41**

Range: Mexico to the Amazon Basin. **Subspecies:** Guatemala to Ecuador

Hostplant: *Aechmea, Bromelia, Ananas* (Bromeliaceae)

Early stages: (Aiello and Silberglied 1978*a*) *Egg*—round, green turning gray or cream, laid singly. Early instars have a densely hairy head capsule and long whiplike tails that bear terminal setae. *Mature larva*—body dark green with fine longitudinal dark brown and green lines along dorsum and sides, blending perfectly with the hostplant leaf; two oval spots on dorsum composed of concentric rings of red, brown, and blue that look like leaf scars; head capsule reddish with cream on the face; a corona of eight stout horns that are inflated at the tips and bear long hairs; caudal tails stout at base and reddish brown in color: prothoracic gland pink to red with a pungent polystyrene to pineapple smell, depending on the hostplant. *Pupa*—looks like a light and dark brown snake head, complete with scales, pits and eyes (Figs. 31, 32).

Adult: Distinguished from all other species by the rounded wing shape; dark brown to black on upperside with large white spots across the FW. The underside coloration is pinker and the FW white spots smaller on the Atlantic slope.

Habits: Occurs from sea level to 1,000 m on both slopes, in all forest and second-growth habitats where a suitable hostplant occurs. In urban areas, where the hostplants are used as fence rows or cultivated in gardens, individuals are seen flying along these fence rows and gardens at dusk or dawn. This species is much more common than one would suspect by its representation in collections. The larvae are not uncommon at most times of the year, but adults probably go unnoticed because they do not visit rotting fruits.

Genus **OPSIPHANES**
Doubleday, 1849

The butterflies in this genus, when treated by Fruhstorfer (1912), contained a number of taxa that he considered as subgenera. I have followed Stichel (1909), who originally considered *Opsiphanes* a separate genus. The genus is recognized by the slightly excavated forewing margin, brown upperside with prominent medial band, and the tendency to have equal or larger forewings than hindwings. The males bear erectile androconial tufts on the hindwing inner margin and near the cell. Additional scent organs are found on the sides of the abdomen. All of the species have very robust bodies, large heads, and thickly scaled wings. *Opsiphanes* ranges from Mexico throughout Central and South America, and Trinidad and Tobago. There are roughly thirteen species in the genus, six of which occur in Costa Rica. However, careful collecting will undoubtedly reveal more species in our area.

The hostplants include Arecaceae, Heliconiaceae, and Musaceae. The eggs are round and laid singly. The larvae are similar to *Caligo*, with large heads and bifid tails, but differ by not having pseudospines on the dorsum, and the head horns are directed backward and have the tips acute, not clubbed. Although this has not been examined in detail, some larvae of *Opsiphanes* apparently lack the prothoracic gland seen in other related genera (Fig. 32). The pupae are streamlined and approach the shape of *Brassolis* (Fig. 32). The larvae of some species are minor pests on coconut and banana plants, and have been subject to biological control (Harrison 1962). The larvae are parasitized by tachinid flies and chalcid wasps.

The adults are all crepuscular and are most frequently seen in the evening. In Costa Rica, the genus occurs from sea level to about 2,000 meters and, depending on the species, may fly in the forest understory, canopy, or occur only in open second-growth vegetation. All of the species feed on rotting fruits, and many are easily trapped with bananas or mangoes. The stout probosces are able to pierce the soft skin of fruits, and no doubt play a role in allowing some species to feed on fruits still in the forest canopy. The base of the proboscis of many species is often packed with mites, whose effect upon the insect is unknown. There are no studies available that give good estimates of the life spans of any species.

Opsiphanes tamarindi tamarindi
(Felder, 1861)

FW Length: 42-52 mm **Plate 41**

Range: Mexico to Amazon Basin. **Subspecies:** Mexico to Panama

Hostplant: *Heliconia* (Heliconiaceae); *Musa* (Musaceae)

Early stages: (Young and Muyshondt 1975) *Egg*—usually laid on the stem or dead leaf blades of the hostplant. *Mature larva*—body pale green with fine pale orange parallel stripes; prominent bifid tails; head capsule lemon yellow with two lavender stripes on the face; four pairs of coronal horns of differing lengths (largest on epicranium, smallest most anteriorly placed) of which the largest are salmon colored with black tips; all horns have a granulate surface; general shape of the head is square (Fig. 32). *Pupa*—variably colored pale green or brown (Fig. 32). The larvae often feed on small plants in the rain forest and on larger ones where there is second growth. The larvae are attacked by tachinids and chalcids.

Adult: Sexes slightly dimorphic. Distinguished from all other species by a dirty yellow FW band in males (paler in females); distal half of HW upperside has a reddish blush that extends to tornus. Compare with *O. bogotanus*.

Habits: Common and widespread from sea level to 1,200 m, on both slopes. This species occurs in all forest and second growth where there is no pronounced dry season, but is occasionally found in lowland areas of Guanacaste. It is generally more common in second-growth areas where there are abundant *Heliconia* thickets, but it occurs as uncommon solitary individuals in primary rain forest. Frequently seen at dusk near human habitations, where both sexes feed on rotting fruits and occasionally dung.

Opsiphanes bogotanus
Distant, 1875

FW Length: 41-58 mm **Plate 43**

Range: Costa Rica to Colombia

Hostplant: Palms

Early stages: Undescribed

Adult: Distinguished from *O. tamarindi* by having a brighter and wider orange FW band in the males; FW margin more excavated and apex more acute; HW margin somewhat more undulate; female has FW band white and more jagged. Compare with *O. tamarindi* and *O. cassina*.

Habits: Occurs from 700 to 1,600 m on both slopes, in association with cloud forest habitats. It is rare, little known, and may represent a high elevational form of *O. tamarindi*. Both sexes visit rotting bananas.

Opsiphanes quiteria quirinus
Godman and Salvin, 1881

FW Length: male 43-48 mm, female 52-56 mm **Plate 42**

Range: Guatemala to Amazon Basin. **Subspecies:** Guatemala to Panama

Hostplant: Palms

Early stages: (Miles Moss, unpublished drawing, British Museum [Natural History]) *Larva*—body dark green, with a broad dull yellow dorsal stripe that runs from head to tips of caudal tails, bordered on either side with black stripes; head capsule tan with four orange, black-tipped horns on epicranium, the middle two of which each has a black spot at the base; four dull red bands on face; mandibular area dark brown.

Adult: Sexes slightly dimorphic. This species is distinguished from all others by the dentate HW margins and the complex series of brown and black lines that form the general underside pattern. See *O. tamarindi* and *O. bogotanus*.

Habits: Occurs locally, from 500 to 1,800 m on both slopes, in association with cloud forest habitats. On the Pacific slope it is found above 1,000 m along the Cordilleras, and is commonest in the Cordillera de Talamanca in the San Vito area. In general, specimens are rare in Costa Rican collections, and the species is rarely seen in nature. Both sexes visit rotting fruits along forest edges.

Opsiphanes invirae cuspidatus
Stichel, 1904

FW Length: male 43-48 mm, female 52-56 mm **Plate 42**

Range: Honduras to Amazon Basin. **Subspecies:** Honduras to Costa Rica

Hostplant: Palms

Early stages: (Miles Moss drawings, British Museum [Natural History]) *Mature larva*—body pale green to yellow with two fine red lines running from head to anus, divided by a blue center; caudal tails brown with black tips; head capsule pale brown with a corona of eight horns; face has four dark lines.

Adult: Distinguished from the similar *O. cassina* by the entire FW band, which is not split at the FW costa. See *O. cassina*.

Habits: Occurs from sea level to 600 m on the Atlantic slope in association with rain forest habitats. Moderately rare in Costa Rican collections; I have only taken it in traps in the rain forest canopy.

Opsiphanes cassina fabricii
(Boisduval, 1870)

FW Length: 36-40 mm **Plate 42**

Range: Mexico to Amazon Basin. **Subspecies:** Mexico to Panama

Hostplant: *Acrocomia vinifera, Cocos nucifera, Bactris* (Arecaceae)

Early stages: (Young and Muyshondt 1975) *Early instars*—body pale green or cream with conspicuous dorsal midline; head capsule densely hairy. *Mature larva*—body green with yellow longitudinal stripes; bifid tails brown;

head capsule brown with white area on middle of face; three to four pairs of horns; area around mandibles has a conspicuous "moustache" (Fig. 32). The larvae rest on the midrib of the leaves or inside a folded leaflet sewn together with silk. They are parasitized by tachinids and braconids.

Adult: Distinguished from the similar *O. invirae* by the FW band, which is split at the costa by the intrusion of a short black bar. See *O. invirae*. *Note*: the subspecies *O. cassina chiriquensis* Stichel, 1904 also occurs in our area; it has the FW band washed out.

Habits: Common and widespread throughout the country, from sea level to 1,400 m on both slopes. Commonest in areas of second growth, and the only *Opsiphanes* species that apparently can tolerate the severe dry season in lowland Guanacaste. Frequently seen at dusk in the streets of San José, flying around tall palms, or along beaches where coconut palms grow. In Guanacaste, individuals are found resting on the underside of palm fronds during the day. Although present throughout the year in most habitats, it is most common on the Pacific slope during the rainy season, and during the dry seasons on the Atlantic. Both sexes visit rotting and overripe fruits in the forest understory and the forest canopy, and have the same mites at the base of the proboscis as *O. tamarindi*.

Genus **OPOPTERA** Aurivilius, 1882

Similar to *Opsiphanes*, but recognized by the thinly scaled wings, small head, slender body, and brushy palps. There are two subgroups within the genus: those species with well-developed androconial organs in or near the hindwing cell, and one species that lacks these. The genus includes six species, and ranges from Costa Rica to Brazil and Bolivia. One species occurs in our area, and it is the one without androconial organs.

Opoptera staudingeri

(Godman and Salvin, 1894)

FW Length: 41-45 mm **Plate 43**

Range: Costa Rica and western Panama

Hostplant: *Chusquea* (Poaceae)

Early stages: *Egg*—white, round, finely ribbed, laid in small clusters of two to five. Early instars are pale yellow-green with two dark green lines on the dorsum; two short brown caudal tails; head capsule black with many fine hairs; two short head horns on epicranium. *Mature larva*—body pale green with fine brown lines on the dorsum; dorsal midline brown with a thickened area bordered by yellow; tails red-brown; head capsule cream-brown with a conspicuous "moustache" near the mandibles; epicranium has two large pointed horns, which are black and rough, with many fine hairs, and the black descends down the face to the mandibles; a pair of lateral horns are cream with black tips; face has a red inverted V on the suture lines. *Pupa*—unusually long, round, and slender for a brassolid; head bifid; cremaster very stout, slightly curved, with teeth on the ventral surface; ground color tan with many fine longitudinal brown striations that give the pupa the appearance of a bamboo stem; a long metallic gold stripe runs from the third segment to the head, where it merges with the bifid horns.

Adult: Distinguished by the yellow-orange medial FW band that runs into the HW marginal band; upperside has a reflective violet cast. See *Catoblepia orgetorix*.

Habits: Occurs locally in cloud forest habitats on both slopes, from 700 to 1,800 m, mainly around the Cordillera Central. When disturbed during the day its flight is weak and similar to that of a large *Taygetis*. During the day individuals perch in dense vegetation next to tree trunks or near large rotting logs. They become active at dusk but are very rarely seen. I have occasionally found individuals feeding on rotting bananas placed on the forest floor near streams and rivers. Rare in Costa Rican collections.

Genus **CATOBLEPIA** Stichel, 1902

This genus is similar to *Opsiphanes* and only weakly separated from it by the elongate wing cells in the male and the general wing shape. *Catoblepia* is recognized by the forewing bands, wing shape, reddish brown underside ground color, and prominent ocelli. The males have a well-developed androconial tuft in the HW cell. I am following Bristow (1981) in the arrangement presented here, but with reservation as to the distinctness of *Catoblepia* from *Opsiphanes*. The genus ranges from Nicaragua to the Amazon Basin and contains nine species, two of which occur in Costa Rica.

From unpublished drawings of Miles Moss in the British Museum (Natural History) and rearings in Costa Rica it appears that the larva is virtually identical to *Opsiphanes* (Fig. 32). In Costa Rica the genus is found only on the Atlantic side. The adults feed on rotting fruits, but the genus is poorly known.

Catoblepia orgetorix championi
Bristow, 1981
FW Length: male 48-50 mm, female 51-55 mm **Plate 44**
Range: Nicaragua to Ecuador. **Subspecies:** Nicaragua to Costa Rica
Hostplant: Various palms (Arecaceae)
Early stages: Undescribed, but see Fig. 32
Adult: *Male*—distinguished from similar species by the produced FW apex; ocelli on underside very distinctive. *Female*—FW upperside has a violet cast; FW band whitish violet; HW has a wide golden yellow band. See *Opoptera staudingeri.*
Habits: Occurs from sea level to 500 m on the Atlantic slope, in association with primary rain forest habitats. Encountered as rare, solitary individuals in the forest understory. In my experience, individuals do not readily come to rotting bananas, but will feed on the fallen fruits of *Dipteryx* and *Welfia*. Rare in Costa Rican collections.

Catoblepia xanthicles xanthicles
(Godman and Salvin, 1881)
FW Length: 50-53 mm **Plate 44**
Range: Costa Rica and Panama to Bolivia. **Subspecies:** Costa Rica to Panama
Hostplant: Unknown
Early stages: From a squeezed egg I report the following data: *Egg*—pale green. *First instar*—black, fuzzy head; body white with two long red stripes on dorsum; two long, black caudal tails. The larva refused to eat five different species of palms I offered it.
Adult: Distinguished from *C. orgetorix* by having the HW upperside entirely brown; males have the androconial tuft positioned above the HW cell; neither sex has HW marginal band.
Habits: This rare species is reported from lowland rain forest habitats on both slopes, but is known only from a few specimens. In September 1984 I collected one female specimen that flew into a building at Sirena, Parque Corcovado, after dark.

Genus **SELENOPHANES** Staudinger, 1887

The maintenance of *Selenophanes*, like *Catoblepia*, as a genus apart from *Opisphanes* is probably oversplitting. I am, however, following Bristow (1982), who feels Stichel's genera should be maintained. There are only three species in the genus, all of which are rare. The genus as it occurs in our area is recognized by the elongate forewing apex, a jagged forewing band, and a very conspicuous androconial patch on the hindwing of the male.

The hostplants and larvae are unknown, but from the description by Bristow (1982) the pupa of *Selenophanes* seems similar to *Eryphanis*.

Selenophanes josephus josephus
(Godman and Salvin, 1881)
FW Length: male 40-44 mm, female 56 mm **Plate 44**
Range: Guatemala, Panama, and Colombia. **Subspecies:** Guatemala
Hostplant: Unknown
Early stages: Unknown
Adult: Distinguished from all other similar species by the jagged yellowish FW band; males have a prominent triangular androconial patch posterior to the HW cell.
Habits: As yet unknown in Costa Rica, but its distribution in Guatemala and Panama suggests that it will turn up as our fauna becomes better known.

Genus **ERYPHANIS** Boisduval, 1870

Large butterflies recognized by the elongate hindwing and two elongate ocelli on the median of the hindwing underside. The genus ranges from Mexico throughout Central and South America in rain forest habitats. Of the six species in the genus, two occur in our area.

The larvae feed on bamboo, are roughly square-shaped in cross-section, have five very fine pseudospines on the dorsum, well-developed caudal tails, and a square head capsule that bears two short horns. The pupae are long, slender, and have the head produced into two appressed points that are almost the length of the body. From these life history characters it is easy to form a transition to *Caligo*, except that the pupa resembles the satyrine genus *Dioriste* and certain other high-elevation satryine genera (Figs. 31, 32).

In South America the genus is apparently quite common, and has roughly the same habits as *Caligo*. The adults are crepuscular forest insects that feed on rotting fruits. In Costa Rica the genus occurs from sea level to 1,800 m, and is in general rare and poorly known.

Eryphanis polyxena lycomedon
(Felder, 1862)

FW Length: 56-62 mm **Plate 44**

Range: Guatemala to Amazon Basin. **Subspecies:** Guatemala to Colombia

Hostplant: Bamboo (Poaceae)

Early stages: *Mature larva*—pale brown with a lighter brown lateral line; five very thin fine black bristles along dorsum; two long narrow caudal tails that are covered with fine hairs; head capsule pale brown, square, bearing six short recurved horns, the top two being the largest (Figs. 31, 32). *Note*: the Costa Rican larvae appear very different from those described by Fruhstorfer (1912), who states that the body is greenish red with white stripes. *Pupa*—long and slender, pale brown, with the head produced into two projections (Fig. 31). The larvae feed nocturnally, and are exceedingly cryptic when they rest on the stem and dead leaf sheaths of the hostplant.

Adult: Sexes dimorphic. *Male*—purple cast on FW and HW inner margin. *Female*—reflective blue at bases of both wings; FW has yellow submarginal band. Both sexes have pale brown underside. See *E. aesacus.*

Habits: Occurs from sea level to 1,200 m on both slopes, in association with wet forest habitats. Absent from Guanacaste. Encountered as rare, solitary individuals in deep shade, threading in and out of the vegetation. Most frequently found along riparian edges. Both sexes are easily baited with rotting bananas.

Eryphanis aesacus buboculus
(Butler, 1872)

FW Length: male 61-64 mm, female 68-73 mm **Plate 45**

Range: Mexico to Amazon Basin. **Subspecies:** Costa Rica to Colombia

Hostplant: Palms (Arecaceae)

Early stages: Undescribed, but see Fig. 32

Adult: Sexes dimorphic. *Male*—similar to *E. polyxena* on upperside, but has a longer scent patch on HW inner margin. *Female*—reflective blue on upperside, with a conspicuous FW yellow, marginal band. Both sexes are distinguished by the configuration of the medial ocelli on the HW underside and the rich ground color. See *E. polyxena.*

Habits: Occurs from 700 to 1,800 m on both slopes, in association with cloud forest habitats. Generally distributed along the Atlantic, but only found on the Pacific slope from Valle de Copey south. Rarely seen in nature, this insect flies when it is almost dark, and is not commonly taken at banana baits. Occasionally attracted to lights after dark.

Genus **CALIGO** Hübner, 1816

The butterflies that compose this genus are the giants of the Neotropics. They are mostly somber colored on the upperside and are immediately recognized by the large ocelli on the hindwing underside, from whence comes the common name "owl butterflies." The genus ranges from Mexico to South America, where the greatest diversity is found in the Amazon Basin. There are two groups within *Caligo*, based on presence or absence of an androconial tuft on the shiny hindwing inner margin. Correct determination depends upon paying close attention to the presence or absence of this structure. I have followed Stichel (1909) in the taxonomic treatment of the species. There are seventeen species in the genus, five of which occur in Costa Rica.

The major hostplants of *Caligo* are in the Heliconiaceae, Marantaceae, Musaceae, and to a limited extent, Arecaceae and Cylanthaceae. Since *Musa* is an introduced plant, grown in extensive monocultures, and used by *Caligo*, the latter can become a crop pest of economic importance. As a result, there have been a number of studies on its population ecology and biological control (see Harrison 1962, Malo 1961, Malo and Willis 1961). On native hostplants (*Heliconia*) it has been noted that the insect communities that feed on these plants grow slowly. Initially, it was thought that the slow growth was due to high tannin content of the leaves. Recently, it has been shown that there is very little tannin in *Heliconia* leaves and that slow growth is probably related to low nitrogen content (Auerbach and Strong 1981).

The eggs of *Caligo* are round and laid either singly or in small or large groups by the same female. The larvae are highly gregarious, and aggregations may contain tiny first instars feeding alongside mammoth sixteen-gram fifth and sixth instar larvae, who exhibit no cannibalism. In general shape, the larvae are similar to *Opsiphanes* but differ distinctly by having a row of soft pseudospines on the dorsum; all have an eversible prothoracic gland, and the head capsule is adorned with a corona of clubbed horns (Figs. 31, 32). In one experiment, I found, much to my surprise, that a raiding column of army ants (*Eciton birchalli*) refused to attack a *Caligo* larva, even when it was placed next to a large grasshopper that was eagerly being dismantled by the ants. This could perhaps be attributed to a chemical defense emitted by the prothoracic gland, and needs serious investigation. The pupae of *Caligo* are large, stocky, and without many projections (Figs. 31, 32). The best description of a *Caligo* life cycle is Casagrande (1979).

Caligo is a genus of the lowland rain forests, and few species occur above 1,600 m elevation. Most species in Costa Rica are found below 1,000 m. The adults are most active at dawn and dusk, although in well-shaded rain forest habitats individuals will feed during the day. From studies on fruit-feeding butterflies at La Selva, I have found no indication that *Caligo* ever flies in the forest canopy.

Although there have been no studies on natural populations, under laboratory conditions individuals are known to live up to five weeks (Malo and Willis 1961). The adults all feed on rotting fruits and are easily baited with bananas. Like its relatives in the Brassolinae and Morphinae, *Caligo* is often found with infestations of mites adhering to the base of the proboscis. As in other genera, there is nothing known about the biology of this interaction or the mites' effects upon the *Caligo*.

To explain the presence of the large ocelli on the hindwing underside of *Caligo*, Stradling (1976) proposed the idea that the ocelli and the dark area surrounding them have been the result of a mimicry based on a tree frog that rests on tree trunks where *Caligo* is often seen. This tree frog is apparently distasteful to predators. While owls and their eyes are certainly not the selective force behind the ocelli on *Caligo*, I feel that the most plausible explanations for the ocelli are still a resemblance to large vertebrate eyes (Blest 1957) or as target areas for direct predator attacks. Clearly, more research is needed in this area of pattern evolution.

Since there is nothing written on the courtship of *Caligo*, I will briefly describe my field and insectary observations. At dusk, males are commonly observed to patrol along forest edges, ridge tops, and along rivers, a behavior that I assume is related to precourtship and mate location. In the insectary, a virgin female is chased relentlessly until she alights with the wings folded over the back. The male hovers over her for a few moments, and if she does not move, he alights behind her with his wings folded. He then flutters his wings slightly while hopping forward until beside her. During this hopping movement, his abdomen is curved to the side and his claspers are fully open. It usually takes several tries, but eventually the genital openings meet and coupling ensues. Once coupled, the male and female face opposite directions. If the male is unsuccessful in attempts to copulate, he hovers over the female, dipping down and up in a rhythmic fashion, and the process is repeated. Although the scent organs in *Caligo* have been described in detail (see refs. in Boppré 1984), the chemistry and behavioral ecology are unknown.

My favorite story about *Caligo* concerns some phoretic egg parasites of the family Trichogrammatidae. These tiny wasps (consider that thirty may emerge from a single host butterfly egg) cling to the anal margin of the hindwing of both male and female *Caligo* and are transported from place to place. Although the biology is not completely understood, the wasps apparently wait until the female *Caligo* is laying her eggs and then leave the butterfly and parasitize the freshly laid eggs (Malo 1961). A significant proportion of *Caligo* eggs are killed by these wasps, and they can certainly be considered major predators in some *Caligo* populations. The effects of parasites on *Caligo* populations in banana plantations have been demonstrated by Malo and Willis (1961), and have served as a good example of what harmful effects the spraying of insecticides on crops may have on the natural predator community.

Caligo oileus scamander

(Boisduval, 1870)

FW Length: 72-83 mm **Not illustrated**

Range: Guatemala to Amazon Basin. **Subspecies:** Central America

Hostplant: *Heliconia* (Heliconiaceae)

Early stages: Undescribed

Adults: This is the only Costa Rican species without androconial tufts on the HW inner margin. Compared to similar species, it has a longer and more elongate FW apex; upperside has a pale yellow cast; HW gray blue; underside has a prominent dark area surrounding the medial ocellus, which runs from costa to inner margin (like *Eryphanis*); distal margin of HW lighter than base. See *C. memnon* and *C. illioneus*

Habits: The status of this species in Central America is not well known. I have only found it in lowland Atlantic rain forest up to about 700 m. In collections it has often been confused with *C. illioneus* and *C. memnon.*

Caligo illioneus oberon

Butler, 1870

FW Length: 65-77 mm **Plate 46**

Range: Costa Rica to Amazon Basin. **Subspecies:** Costa Rica and Panama

Hostplant: *Heliconia* (Heliconiaceae); *Musa* (Musaceae)

Early stages: Undescribed

Adult: Male has androconial tuft; upperside has reflective blue on median of both wings;

FW upperside has two yellowish submarginal bands; ocellus on HW underside has dark area surrounding it. See *C. oileus* and *C. eurilochus.*

Habits: Occurs from sea level to 400 m on the Atlantic slope, in association with rain forest habitats; distributed mostly at the base of the Cordillera Central and Talamanca. Commonest during July and August; rare during the remainder of the year.

Caligo memnon memnon
(Felder and Felder, 1866)

FW Length: 68-78 mm **Plate 46**

Range: Mexico to Amazon Basin. **Subspecies:** Central America

Hostplant: *Heliconia* (Heliconiaceae); *Musa* (Musaceae)

Early stages: Undescribed, but see Fig. 31.

Adult: Distinguished from all other species by the extensive yellow flush on the FW median; FW margins dark; FW underside has small submarginal ocelli; male has hair tuft. See *C. oileus* and *C. illioneus.*

Habits: Occurs from sea level to 1,400 m on the Pacific slope as a common species, but is much rarer on the Atlantic slope. This is the only *Caligo* species able to tolerate the severe Guanacaste dry seasons. It can live in severely disturbed agricultural habitats, but is apparently unable to tolerate rain forest. Persistent throughout the year, but commonest during the rainy season.

Caligo eurilochus sulanus
Fruhstorfer, 1904

FW Length: 77-91 mm **Plate 45**

Range: Guatemala to Amazon Basin. **Subspecies:** Guatemala to Panama

Hostplant: *Heliconia* (Heliconiaceae); *Calathea* (Marantaceae); *Musa* (Musaceae)

Early stages: (Malo and Willis 1961) All those after the first instar are generally similar. *Mature larva*—dark brown; six dark brown pseudospines on dorsum, the longest on segments 2-7; legs red, prolegs brown; head capsule dark tan with eight horns, dorsal ones curved outward, lateral ones curved backward; oblong patch on face from eyes to base of horns.

Adult: The largest Costa Rican species, distinguished by the gray-blue base of wings on upperside; underside has ocellus isolated in a grayish underside. See *C. illioneus* and *C. oileus.*

Habits: Widespread and common from sea level to 1,600 m on both slopes, in association with wet forest habitats. It does not occur in the deciduous forest habitats of Guanacaste. Occasionally a pest on bananas. In the insectary, *C. eurilochus* and *C. memnon* hybridize freely, and the progeny look like *C. eurilochus.*

Caligo atreus dionysos
Fruhstorfer, 1912

FW Length: 73-85 mm, **Plate 46**

Range: Mexico to Peru. **Subspecies:** Costa Rica and Panama

Hostplant: *Heliconia* (Heliconiaceae); *Musa* (Musaceae); Cyclanthaceae

Early stages: Mature larva similar to *C. eurilochus*, but body tan with many fine striations on dorsum, centered near the middle segments; five short pseudospines on dorsum; red dots along sides near spiracles; head capsule tan with fine vertical striations (Fig. 32).

Adult: Immediately distinguished by the purple upperside and the broad yellow HW marginal band.

Habits: Occurs from sea level up to 1,300 m on both slopes, in association with rain forest habitats and dense second growth. Widespread on the Atlantic slope, but found from San Mateo south on the Pacific slope, presumably because this species is intolerant of the Guanacaste dry season. I have observed courtship upon a number of occasions: the male circles around a female while both are flying (all of these observations were in large treefalls). This spectacular species is very easily identified on the wing.

Genus **NAROPE** Westwood, 1849

The eight species in this genus are all dull brown and very small for brassolines, lack the typical ocelli of the group, have well-developed androconial organs, and in general look more like the genus *Anaea* (Charaxinae) than a brassoline. The genus ranges from Mexico to the Amazon Basin. One species occurs in our area.

The single species that has been reared feeds on bamboo, and the larva is typically brassoline-like with six head horns and two caudal tails. In general, there is next to nothing known about the habits of any *Narope* species.

Narope cyllastros testacea
Godman and Salvin, 1878

FW Length: 29-32 mm **Plate 41**

Range: Mexico to Amazon Basin. **Subspecies:** Mexico to Panama

Hostplant: Bamboo

Early stages: *Egg*—from a squeezed egg: white

with concentric red circles, and highly sculptured. *Mature larva*—(Müller 1886) body gray-brown with reddish stripes; two widely spaced caudal tails; head capsule brown with a black spot in the middle of face that sends two stripes toward the horns and two more to the mandibles; corona of six horns that are directed backwards. *Pupa*—brown, black, and yellow, stout with posterior segments rounded, and a slight central ridge that is divided into three humps.

Adult: Similar in general appearance to a dull brown *Anaea*, but distinguished by the alternating dark and light pigmentation of the eyes, an acute FW apex; males bear a shiny patch on the HW costa and a scent patch between the wings.

Habits: I have only seen specimens from sea level to 1,200 m on the Pacific slope, but the species should be looked for on the Atlantic slope. The specimens I have collected have either been at rotting bananas after dusk, or at candlelight after dark. At dusk the males perch about four to ten meters above the ground along trails, streams, and forest edges, and chase each other in a way reminiscent of *Adelpha*. It is rare in Costa Rican collections and very seldom seen in the field.

Subfamily **SATYRINAE**

The butterflies embraced by this subfamily are, for the most part, readily distinguished from all other groups of the Nymphalidae by being colored brown with a conspicuous development of the ocelli on the underside of the wings. The underside patterns of the Satyrinae come closest to the ground plan for primitive nymphalids derived by Schwanwitsch (1924). The satyrines have delicate, thinly scaled wings, and with few exceptions, the bases of the veins of the forewing are inflated and form a "bubble" that is easily seen. This character holds for most Satyrinae throughout the world, except for a few species where it is presumed to be lost; a few genera of nymphalines also have this character (presumably by convergence). Although the subfamily as a whole has the upperside of the wings colored dull brown, the Neotropical fauna exhibits white, blue, orange, and silver colors, and some species are almost transparent.

The geographical distribution of the Satyrinae ranges from the Arctic through temperate and tropical regions, and many oceanic islands. In the Neotropics, satyrines occur in all habitats in which there is vegetation, from sea level to the highest mountains of the South American Andes. Because of the enormous range of habitats, the Neotropics has the greatest diversity of satyrines in the world. Throughout this great diversity, however, the satyrines maintain their distinctive appearance and peculiar flight behavior.

The higher classification of the Satyrinae, as currently understood, is based primarily upon the work of Ehrlich (1958*a*) and Miller (1968). There are, however, points yet to be clarified at the higher level (Vane-Wright 1972, DeVries et al. 1985), a task that should involve close scrutiny of the early stages as well as the adult morphology. The arrangement of certain species and genera in the present work has been a problem, due to our incomplete knowledge of Neotropical satyrines as a whole. The genus *Euptychia* was at one time the catch all genus for most of the lowland species, and its homogeneity was questioned long ago (Godman and Salvin 1888, Weymer 1910). Based largely on his study of the Bolivian fauna, Forster (1964) split *Euptychia* into numerous new genera based on differences in the male genitalia, establishing many genera to accommodate single species. These genera, however, were never adequately differentiated and, as a result, are impossible to apply to extra-Bolivian species without revising the entire Neotropical subfamily, a task beyond the scope of the present work. I have treated the Costa Rican genera in a conservative manner, employing *Euptychia* for a peculiar group of species (*sensu* Singer et al. 1983), and have for the most part ignored the genera erected by Forster (1964).

The hostplants of Neotropical Satyrinae are mostly grasses and bamboos (Poaceae), but also include Marantaceae, Arecaceae, Cyperaceae, all of which are monocots; and Selaginellaceae and Neckeraceae (club-mosses and mosses). As far as is known, there are no satyrines anywhere in the world that feed on dicotyledonous plants. Their hostplants are generally thought to lack the diversity of secondary chemicals that are found in other plant groups. The lack of secondary compounds may reflect the universal palatability of satyrines to vertebrate predators, a fact initially stated by Scudder (1889) and easily tested by anyone with a caged bird and access to live satyrines. A related fact is that among the Neotropical satyrines, unlike some Old World tropical genera, most species are quite drab and there are almost no examples of mimicry. This could be related to their universal palatability (hence no Müllerian mimics in other groups), or it could be that the Neotropical Satyrinae are unable to follow a tiger-striped pattern of ithomiine or heliconiine models due to constraints of a different developmental ground plan (hence no Batesian mimics among the Satyrine). Although secondary plant chemistry apparently plays little role in deterring satyrine larvae from feeding on grasses, most larvae grow very slowly. This is probably due to the high silica content of many grasses which, although not toxic, probably reduces digestibility. Silica gives the characteristic rough feel to grass and, as most people know, can easily slice into human skin.

Among the grass-feeding satyrines, there appears to be little host specificity (Singer and Ehrlich 1986). However, more studies are needed to compare different species and microhabitats, to examine whether this is a general pattern. In some species, ovipositing females have been demonstrated to be unresponsive to the presence of conspecific eggs on a potential hostplant, and oviposit as though there were no eggs on the plant at all (Singer and Mandracchia 1982). These findings should be compared with field study because in nature there are rarely more than two eggs laid on the same plant.

The eggs of all Satyrinae are round, with a slightly flattened base, and can be smooth or vertically ribbed. The eggs are usually laid singly, either on or off the hostplant. Species that oviposit off the hostplant may deposit eggs on associated plants or dead vegetation, or simply drop eggs on patches of hostplant from the air (e.g., *Cissia hermes*). The larvae of all satyrines have a bifid tail that can be obvious or greatly reduced. The body never has spines, but is covered with tiny tubercles or granulations. The head capsule may either be round or have two head horns that vary in prominence (Figs. 33, 34, 35). The larvae are very sluggish and can seldom be incited to anything like a quick movement. If molested while on the hostplant, a larva simply falls off and behaves like a piece of wood. As far as I am aware, satyrine larvae all have an eversible neck gland near the first set of legs. Unlike other butterflies, some Neotropical satyrines have only four larval instars, yet even so, these larvae grow very slowly. Consider that *Cissia confusa*, a small butterfly, may take two months or more to develop from egg to adult. There is but a single example of gregarious feeding and pupation known from the neotropical satyrines, *Megeuptychia antonoe* (Fig. 34), although some high elevational species (*Dioriste, Manataria*) may be gregarious feeders as early instar larvae.

The pupae of the Satyrinae are usually suspended, or, as in *Chloreuptychia*, held at 90 degrees to the ground, like a flag (Figs. 33, 34, 35). No Neotropical species are known to have subterranean pupae, as found in some European satyrine species. The general shape of the pupa is rounded, without spines or projections, as in the nymphalines, but may have the head produced into long, tightly appressed tubes as in *Dioriste*.

Almost all satyrine species fly near the ground, and most stay completely in the shade of the forest during much of the day. There are two general ways in which satyrines fly: most have a characteristic bouncy flight (as if on a string), like *Cissia*, whereas in the genera *Pierella* and *Cithaerias*, they glide over the ground like leaves floating in a stream. A few species like *Manataria* and *Drucina* fly very fast and nimbly, like some nymphaline genera. The bouncy flight behavior is best seen during courtship, when the male and female coordinate their wing beats, rising and falling in unison in a small light gap in the forest.

The courtship behaviors for the Neotropical species are essentially unknown. From studies on the European grayling, *Hipparchia*, Tinbergen et al. (1942) showed that courtship is a complicated and highly ritualized behavior that can be broken into component parts. In another European study, Davies (1978) demonstrated that small light gaps are high quality resources for satyrid males. The light gaps are vigorously defended against intruding males and are courtship arenas to attract females. Although both of these studies may have bearing upon our Neotropical fauna, there are no comparable studies for New World species. The different androconial organs found in our Neotropical satyrines (e.g., *Pierella, Taygetis, Cissia, Megeuptychia, Bia*) suggest a rich diversity of courtship behavior.

Although the majority of the satyrine species are found close to the ground, some species are known to ascend into the rain forest canopy, and may be more common in the upper levels of the forest (DeVries 1985*b*). The studies of Adams (1973) have shown that the high-elevation species in the tribe Pronophilini exhibit striking ecological zonation on an elevational gradient in the mountains of Colombia. In our Costa Rican fauna, many species are restricted to specific vegetation types (e.g., *Dulcedo, Taygetis banghassi, Lymanopoda*), but the ecological reasons for such restriction is unknown.

As adults, all satyrines feed on rotting fruits in various stages of decay, but fungi associated with decaying matter also seem to play an important part in their diet. Few species, except those at high elevations, feed on flower nectar with any regularity. Although such a diet is generally thought to

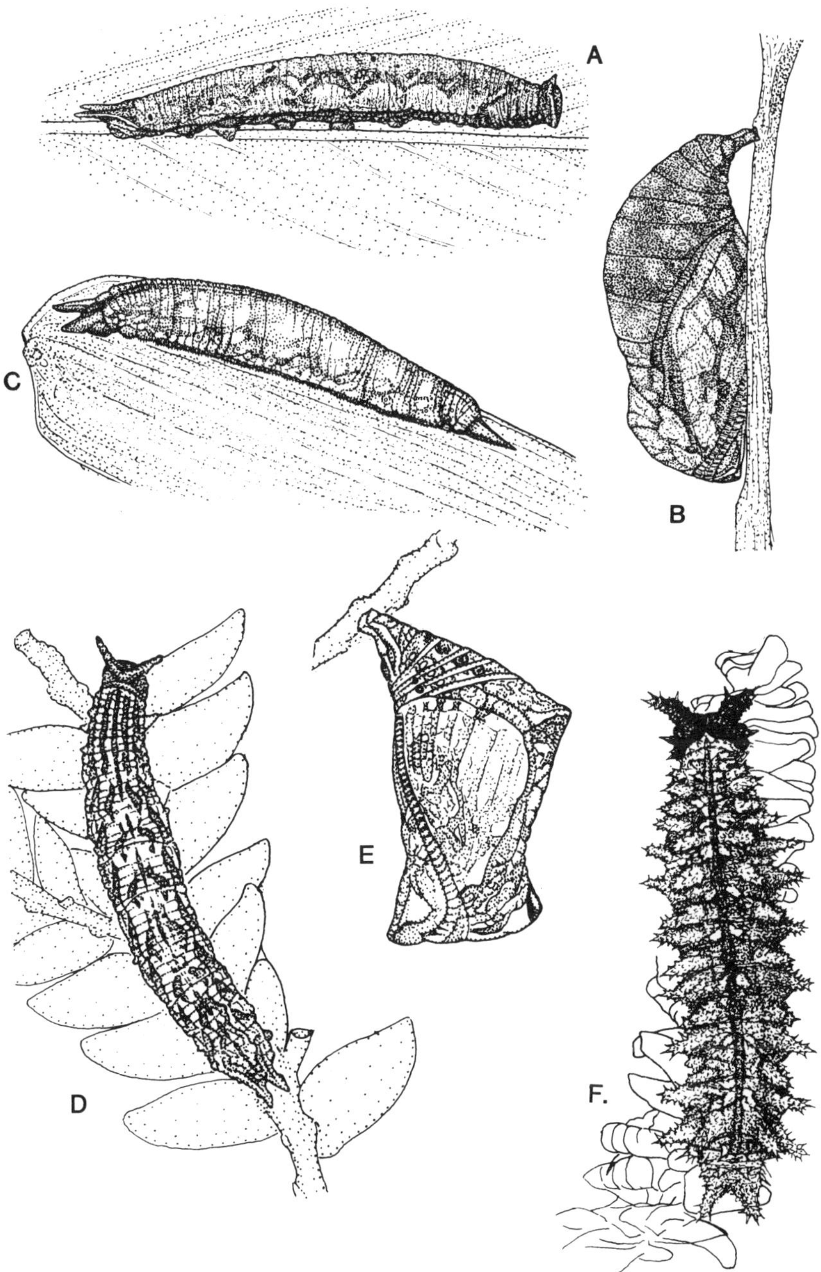

FIGURE 33. Larvae and pupae of the Nymphalidae: Satyrinae. A: *Pierella helvetia incanescens* mature larva; B: *Pierella helvetia incanescens* pupa; C: *Taygetis andromeda* mature larva; D: *Euptychia westwoodi* mature larva; E: *Euptychia westwoodi* pupa; F: *Euptychia insolata* mature larva (drawings by J. Clark).

be inferior to a diet of flower nectar, rotting fruits and fungi may be more nutritious than previously thought (DeVries, 1985*d*). For example, M. C. Singer and I kept an individual of *Cissia hesione* in the insectary for six months, and it fed only upon banana or tomatoes that were occasionally replenished. The butterfly eventually died from being trodden upon, so it was impossible to say how much longer it might have lived. Such pieces of information suggest that "frail" satyrines may live much longer in the field than has been supposed, and further work on life span and nutrition should prove to be very interesting.

Genus **CITHAERIAS** Hübner, 1819

The butterflies in this genus are recognized by their largely transparent wings; a blush of red, yellow, or blue on the hindwing; and a single ocellus on the hindwing. The genus ranges from Mexico through the Amazon Basin. There are roughly ten species in *Cithaerias*, only one of which occurs in Central America.

There is nothing known of the hostplants or early stages. The adults are found only in deep shade of the forest understory, where they appear to glide across the forest floor. Both sexes visit decomposing fungi and rotting fruits.

Cithaerias menander

(Drury, 1782)

FW Length: 30-33 mm **Plate 47**

Range: Mexico to Colombia

Hostplant: Unknown

Early stages: Unknown

Adult: Distinguished by the rose-colored HW that bears a single ocellus. See *Haetera macleannania*.

Habits: Occurs from sea level to 1,000 m on both slopes, in association with rain forest habitats, and occasionally up to 2,000 m on the Pacific slope in rain shadow valleys. Encountered as solitary individuals in the forest, flying low to the ground. The males appear to stay within a confined area, usually a small light gap, for several weeks at a time. Some areas in the forest almost invariably have a male in them. Even after a male is removed, within a day or so, another will take its place. I have occasionally found small groups of up to six individuals all perched on low vegetation in light gaps, and the individuals in these small groups also stay near such an area for weeks at a time. Both sexes feed on rotting fruits and decomposing fungi, and are highly attracted to moldy palm fruits on the forest floor. Common throughout the country and present throughout the year in all areas that do not show a marked dry season.

Genus **HAETERA** Fabricius, 1807

The butterflies in this genus are similar to *Cithaerias*, but can be recognized by their larger size, the presence of two ocelli on the hindwing, and often the presence of a tiny lobe on the hindwing margin. The genus ranges from Costa Rica to the Amazon Basin. Of the four species in the genus, one occurs in our area.

The hostplants and early stages are unknown. The habits of the adults are similar to those of *Cithaerias*.

Haetera macleannania

Bates, 1965

FW Length: 36-39 mm **Plate 47**

Range: Costa Rica to Panama

Hostplant: Unknown

Early stages: Unknown

Adult: Distinguished from similar species by the large size and the presence of two ocelli on the HW. See *Cithaerias menander*.

Habits: This very rare species occurs locally from sea level to 300 m on the Atlantic slope in rain forest habitats associated with the base of the Cordillera Central and Talamanca, with most material known from the Llanura de Santa Clara near Guapiles. I have not seen this species alive, but I am informed by R. Hesterberg that its habits are similar to *Cithaerias*.

Genus **DULCEDO** d'Almeida, 1951

The butterflies in this genus are recognized by having transparent wings, as in *Cithaerias*, but they have no reddish hindwing coloration, the wing shape is rounded, and all markings are brown. The genus ranges from Nicaragua to Colombia, and contains a single species.

The hostplants are palms, and the early stages show similarities to *Taygetis*. The larvae have a short bifid tail arising near the dorsum. The butterflies are found only in lowland rain forest areas; they feed on rotting fruits and are very local.

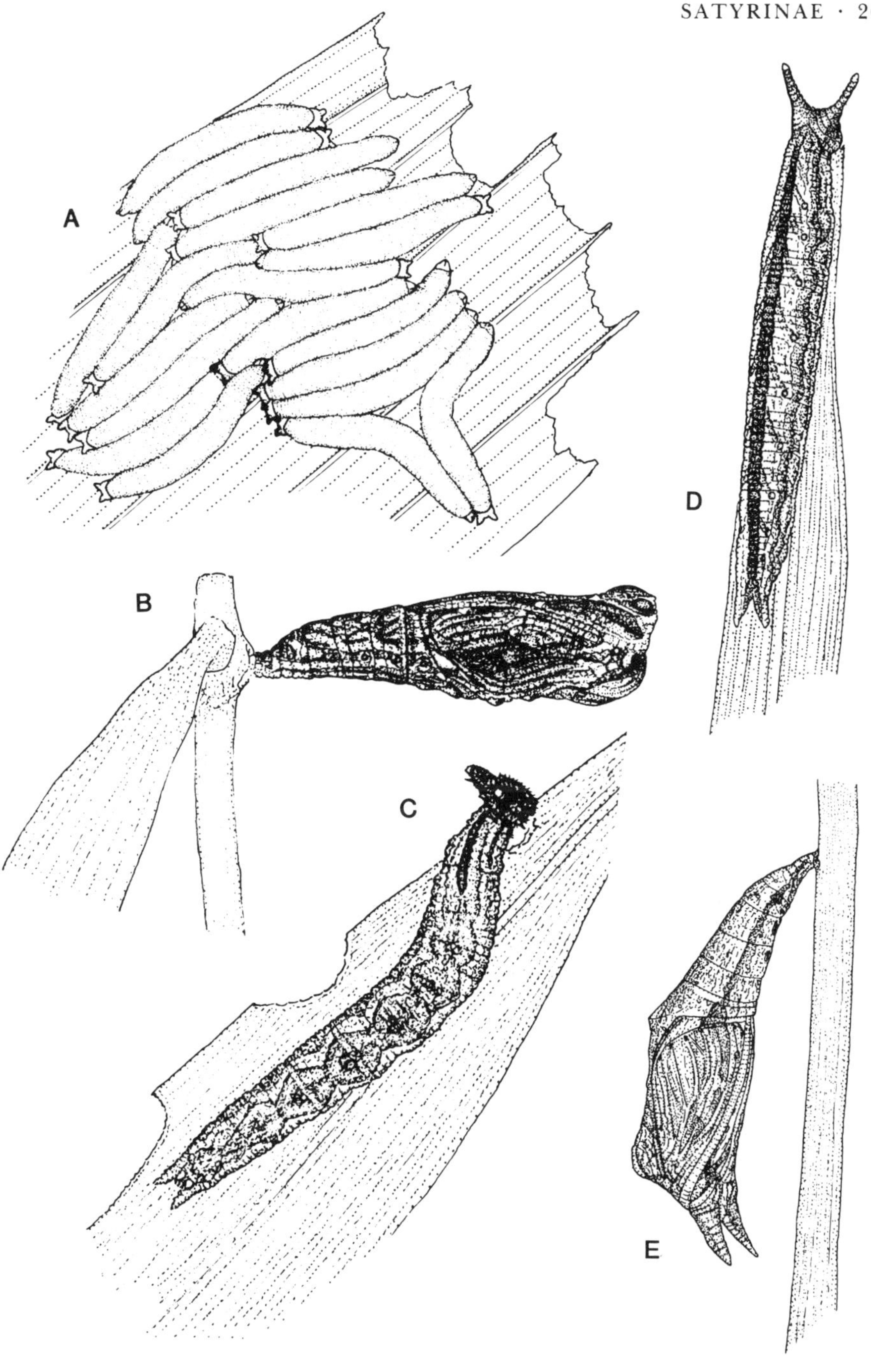

FIGURE 34. Larvae and pupae of the Nymphalidae: Satyrinae. A: *Megeuptychia antonoe* mature larvae; B: *Chloreuptychia arnaea* pupa; C: *Chloreuptychia arnaea* mature larva; D: *Cissia alcinoe* mature larva; E: *Cissia alcinoe* pupa (drawings by J. Clark).

Dulcedo polita
(Hewitson, 1869)
FW Length: 30-35 mm **Plate 47**
Range: Costa Rica to Colombia
Hostplant: *Geonoma, Welfia* (Arecaceae)
Early stages: *Egg*—white, smooth, laid singly on seedlings. *Mature larva*—body translucent yellow-brown, highly ornamented with fine longitudinal and transverse red lines; dorsal midline dark red-brown, broken by seven brown squares: sides have four reddish brown lines; area above prolegs slightly flared, forming a skirt; last segment bears two buff-colored tails born high up on the dorsum; head capsule black, granulate, and bears two or three round bumps on the epicranium.
Adult: Distinguished by the transparent wings with brown markings. This species has been placed by some authors in the genus *Callitaera*.
Habits: Occurs locally from sea level to 400 m on the Atlantic slope, in association with swamp forest habitats, especially palm swamps. Flies in the deep shade of the forest understory and is seldom found in light gaps in the forest. The females oviposit around midday and are frequently seen flying around tree trunks, ascending the tree for several meters, returning to the ground, flying off a short distance, then returning to the same tree and repeating the behavior. Although usually found as solitary individuals, small feeding aggregations are common on the fungus-infected fruits of *Welfia* that litter the forest floor. Although considered very rare (as it is in collections), I have found it common in localized swamp forests and present throughout the year.

Genus **PIERELLA**
Herrich-Schäffer, 1865

The butterflies in this genus have a wing shape similar to *Cithaerias* but are brown, have color on the hindwing distal area, and the males have an androconial tuft on the inner margin of the hindwing near the tornus. The genus ranges from Mexico throughout Central and South America, with the greatest diversity in the Amazon Basin. Of the twelve to fifteen species in *Pierella*, only two occur in our area.

The hostplants for the genus are in the Heliconiaceae and Marantaceae. The egg is round, smooth, and laid singly, usually on seedling or sapling plants. The larvae are dull brown with short bifid tails. The head capsule is large, flat-faced, and bears two bumps on the epicranium (Fig. 33).

In Costa Rica the genus occurs from sea level to about 1,500 m, and is mostly confined to areas of wet forest. The adults feed on rotting fruits and decomposing fungi, and can be extremely common. There are no studies on life span or reproduction. I have found that individuals do not survive well in the insectary.

Pierella helvetia incanescens
Godman and Salvin, 1877
FW Length: 32-39 mm **Plate 47**
Range: Mexico to Colombia. **Subspecies:** Nicaragua to Panama
Hostplant: *Heliconia* (Heliconiaceae); *Calathea* (Marantaceae)
Early stages: *Mature larva*—body dark, dirty brown covered with dark lines on dorsum and sides; seven tiny black bumps on dorsum; body constricted behind the head, forming a neck; head capsule dark brown with a reddish black face; entire head granulate; epicranium has two stubby horns (Fig. 33). When not feeding, the larva rests on the stem of the plant with the face to the ground, which gives it the appearance of being part of the stem.
Adult: Distinguished by the red distal area on the HW.
Habits: Occurs from sea level to 1,400 m on both slopes, in association with wet forest habitats. Found frequently along trails and light gaps where there are patches of *Heliconia*. In the morning, both sexes bask in the sun with the wings held open, usually in small light gaps. Certain areas in particular habitats seem always to have a few individuals in them at any time of the year. Such areas are usually light gaps. Both sexes visit rotting fruits and decomposing fungi. Common.

Pierella luna luna
(Fabricius, 1793)
FW Length: 33-39 mm **Plate 47**
Range: Mexico to Colombia. **Subspecies:** Nicaragua to Colombia
Hostplant: *Heliconia* (Heliconiaceae)
Early stages: Very similar to *P. helvetia*; the larva is more greenish and the head capsule usually has a red face.
Adult: Upperside is brown, and the male has a greenish cast on the HW.
Habits: Occurs from sea level to 1,400 m on both slopes, in association with wet forest habitats. The habitat is essentially the same as for *P. helvetia*, but *P. luna* is associated more with second growth, and is able to tolerate drier conditions as well as reach a greater altitude

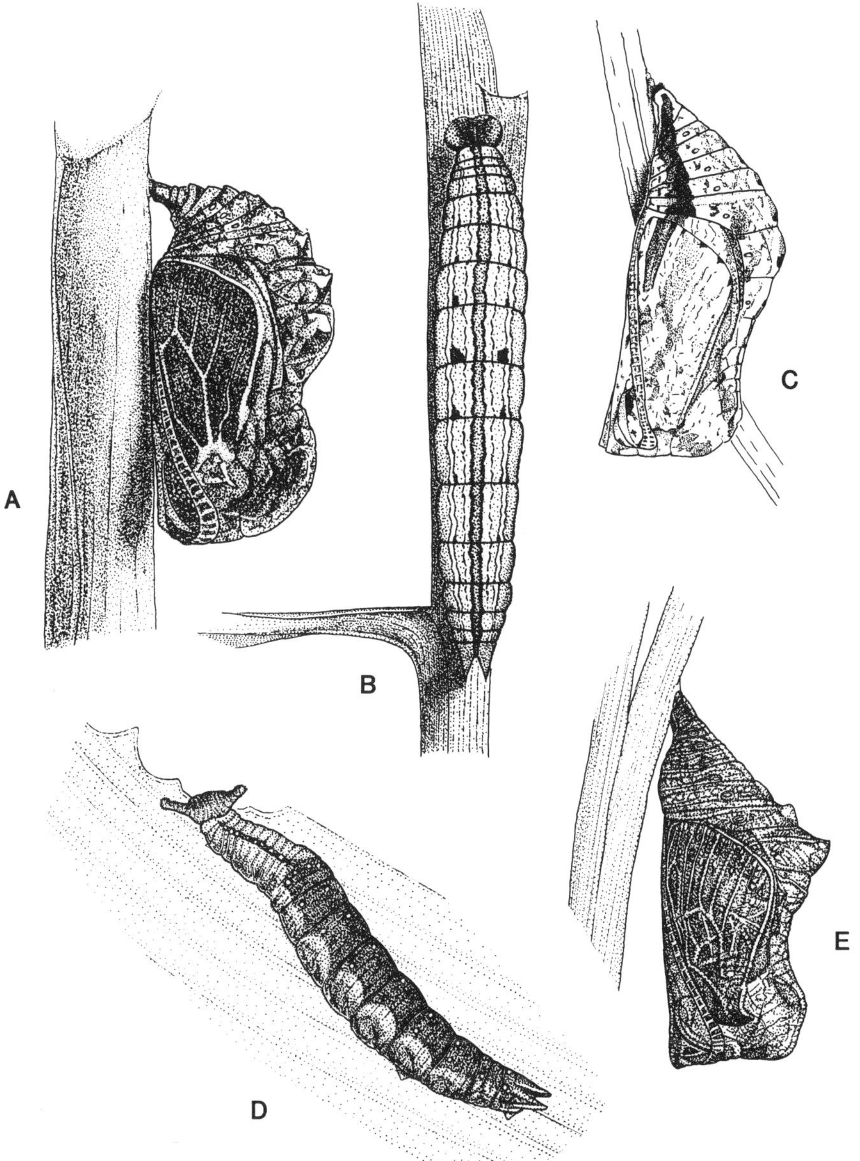

FIGURE 35. Larvae and pupae of the Nymphalidae: Satyrinae. A: *Cissia labe* pupa; B: *Cissia labe* mature larva; C: *Cissia gomezi* pupa; D: *Cissia confusa* mature larva; E: *Cissia usitata* pupa (drawings by J. Clark).

on the Pacific slope. Present in all appropriate habitats throughout the year.

Genus MANATARIA Kirby, 1900

Although the systematic placement of this genus is uncertain (Miller 1968), its species are easily recognized by their medium size, rounded hindwings, and conspicuous white bands on the forewing. The genus ranges from Mexico to Bolivia and contains two or three species, of which only one occurs in our area. Its closest relatives are thought to be the *Neorina* species that occur in the Indo-Australia region. However, *Manataria*'s systematic position requires study to confirm this.

Although the hostplants have not been substantiated, M. Serrano (personal correspondence) informs me that in El Salvador he has reared it on bamboo. Of the larvae, there is nothing recorded.

In Costa Rica, the genus occurs in all habitats from sea level to 2,800 meters. This is because in Costa Rica *Manataria* migrates from the lowlands to the highlands. Migration usually takes place at dusk and dawn, and I have seen individuals flying even late at night. Both sexes are attracted to rotting fruits and can be trapped in the forest canopy, understory, and in open areas. During migrations, the females are without developed eggs. There is nothing known about the destination of the migrating individuals, or whether migration takes place every year or only every few years.

Manataria maculata
(Hopffer, 1874)

FW Length: 40-45 mm **Plate 47**
Range: Mexico to Brazil
Hostplant: Bamboo (Poaceae)
Early stages: Undescribed
Adult: Upperside dark with white band of spots on FW; HW underside mottled with many obscured ocelli. The female tends to be lighter in color.
Habits: Migratory, but principally occurs from sea level to 2,500 m on the Pacific slope, in all habitats. There are great fluctuations in abundance from year to year, but it becomes very abundant in montane regions during July and August. The flight activity (including migration) is mostly at dawn and dusk, but I have seen large numbers of individuals flying through mountain passes while I was driving along the Pan American highway in early evening. During July and August, individuals are not infrequent after dark at lights in the Meseta Central. While flying, this species does not behave like a satyrine, but resembles some fast, strong-flying nymphaline. Common.

Genus ORESSINOMA Westwood, 1851

This genus is separated from other Neotropical satyrines by not having the base of the costa swollen, but the median and submedian veins are swollen. It is easily recognized by the wing shape, longer than broad, and all species are white and thinly scaled. The genus ranges from Costa Rica to the Andes in Bolivia and contains about three species, one of which occurs in our area.

The hostplants are in the Cyperaceae, and the early stages are similar to *Cissia hermes*. In Costa Rica it is found only in montane rain forest and cloud forest habitats. The adults feed on rotting fruits and decomposing fungi.

Oressinoma typhla
Westwood, 1851

FW Length: 23-28 mm **Plate 47**
Range: Costa Rica to Bolivia
Hostplant: *Cyperus lazulae* (Cyperaceae)
Early stages: *Egg*—pearly green, round, laid singly on isolated patches of the hostplant. First instars are green with a shiny black head capsule. *Mature larva*—body green, covered in small granulations; dark green dorsal midline runs from head to anus; four dark green lateral lines; head capsule smooth, pale green, and round.
Adult: White with dark wing margins; underside has silver streaks.
Habits: Occurs from 700 to 1,700 m on the Atlantic slope, in association with cloud forest, mainly in the Carrillo Belt. The slow and gliding flight is reminiscent of a tiny *Morpho thesus*. When alarmed, individuals can fly quite fast, and then resemble *Leptophobia aripa*, which flies in the same habitat. Encountered in local populations, always in association with the hostplant and swampy or standing water. In courtship, the male flies above the female in synchrony until the female has landed, the male hovers above her for a few moments, and then lands beside her. Upon landing he touches his antennae to hers while rapidly vibrating his wings, and eventually copulation follows. The males perch on low vegetation as-

sociated with patches of the hostplant and dart out to fly in unison with anything white that flies by. Courtship takes place during the morning. Females are active at midday, and are usually encountered as solitary individuals searching for oviposition sites. Both sexes feed on rotting fruits, fungi associated with rotten wood, and occasionally on dung. This species is not rare in Costa Rica, but is extremely local and known from a very few localities.

Genus **CYLLOPSIS** Felder 1869

The butterflies in this genus are all small, brown on the upperside, and are recognized by metallic silver or gold spots on the hindwing underside. The systematics of the genus have been revised by Miller (1974), who has been followed here. The genus ranges from North America through Mexico as far south as Panama in Central America, and has most species in Mexico. Of the twenty-five species in *Cyllopsis*, six occur in our area; three of them are endemic to the Talamancan fauna.

The hostplants are grasses and bamboos in the family Poaceae. The first life history (and the most complete to date) is found in Edwards (1897), which agrees well with some of the species I have reared in Costa Rica. The eggs are round and laid singly. The larvae have strongly forked head capsules, with the forks directed forward. The pupa of some of the Costa Rica species differ from those illustrated by Edwards (1897) by having the head area produced into a long point.

The butterflies in Costa Rica are all montane species and associated with bright open areas. Some species are present throughout the year; others appear to be highly seasonal. Both sexes feed on rotting fruits and occasionally visit flowers. Although some species are not widespread in Costa Rica, they can be locally very abundant.

Cyllopsis hedemanni hedemanni
Felder, 1869

FW Length: 20-25 mm **Plate 47**

Range: Mexico to Panama. **Subspecies:** Mexico to Panama

Hostplant: Unknown

Early stages: Unknown

Adult: Distinguished by the small lobe on the HW margin; few silver markings; the female often has a reddish blush on the HW upperside. *Note:* In the past, the name *vetones* Godman and Salvin was applied to the Costa Rican populations.

Habits: Occurs from 1,000 to 2,000 m on the Pacific slope in most open habitats, but also on the Atlantic slope in rain shadows that have a marked dry period. Individuals fly along forest edges and in the forest understory when there is bright sunlight. Encountered as solitary individuals. Both sexes visit flowers of *Mikania* and feed on rotting fruits. The flight period is from February to April, but also at various dry periods throughout the year.

Cyllopsis rogersi
(Godman and Salvin, 1878)

FW Length: 18-20 mm **Plate 47**

Range: Costa Rican endemic; Panama (?)

Hostplant: *Chusquea* (Poaceae)

Early stages: *Egg*—pale green, smooth, laid singly along the stems or leaves of the hostplant.

Adult: Distinguished by the large HW ocellus that bears an internal silver crescent. The ocellus shows through to the upperside.

Habits: Occurs from 1,000 to 2,300 m on both slopes, in association with cloud forest habitats, especially in mountain passes. Individuals fly amid thickets of bamboo that grow along rivers and streams. During sunny mornings the males perch on the bamboo and chase other satyrine butterflies, but are not faithful to their perches. Females oviposit whenever there is sunshine. Both sexes feed on rotting vegetation and associated fungi. Although rare in Costa Rican collections, this species is usually abundant in localized areas.

Cyllopsis philodice
(Godman and Salvin, 1878)

FW Length: 21-23 mm **Plate 47**

Range: Costa Rica and western Panama

Hostplant: *Chusquea* (Poaceae)

Early stages: *Egg*—same as those of *C. rogersi.*

Adult: Distinguished by the golden yellow band on the HW and two ocelli on the HW underside. The yellow is much fainter on the female. See *C. argentella.*

Habits: Occurs commonly from 1,000 to 3,000 m on both slopes, in association with montane wet and cloud forest habitats that have extensive areas of *Chusquea.* Males fly rapidly in and out of the bamboo thickets, chasing each other in wild loops and zigzags through the vegetation. The female is less exuberant and tends to remain within the thickets of hostplant. Both sexes feed on rotting fruits and fungi. This species is highly characteristic of Talamancan habitats above 2,000 m.

Cyllopsis argentella
(Butler and Druce, 1872)
FW Length: 17-21 mm **Plate 47**
Range: Costa Rica and Panama
Hostplant: *Chusquea* (Poaceae)
Early stages: Early instars are similar to mature larvae, except that they are gregarious. *Mature larva*—body pale green with two yellow lateral lines running from head to anus; between the lines is a fine rufous line; last segment has two short tails; head capsule pale green with two stout, pale brown head horns, each of which has a yellow line at its base. *Pupa*—yellow-brown, the color of dead bamboo; overall appearance like a monkey in a dunce cap with a long spike arising from the head.
Adult: Distinguished by the two small ocelli on the HW underside and a silver S mark above and below the ocelli. See *C. rogersi.*
Habits: Occurs from 900 to 2,000 m on both slopes, in cloud forest habitats and always in association with *Chusquea* thickets. The flight is very bouncy, and follows the contour of the vegetation. Males perch in sunny spots and chase other satyrine butterflies, and are somewhat faithful to the same perch for a few hours. Both sexes feed on rotting fruits and fungi. Very common throughout the country.

Cyllopsis pephredo
(Godman, 1901)
FW Length: 15-18 mm **Plate 47**
Range: Mexico to Panama
Hostplant: Unknown
Early stages: Unknown
Adult: Small; HW rounded; overall very thinly scaled. HW margin undulate with two elongate ocelli on the margin. See *C. hilaria.*
Habits: This uncommon, highly seasonal species occurs from 1,000 to 1,200 m in the Mestea Central. Its flight period follows immediately after the first rains in June and July, and then a small subsequent brood occurs in August. Both sexes are active during dawn and dusk, and fly in open areas and pastures; it is not infrequently found in gardens in San José. Both sexes feed on juices of rotting fruits and fungi, and are very attracted to compost heaps. This species is rare in collections.

Cyllopsis hilaria
(Godman, 1901)
FW Length: 15-20 mm **Not illustrated**
Range: Mexico to Panama
Hostplant: Unknown
Early stages: Unknown
Adult: Similar to *C. pephredo* but distinguished from it by a dark androconial patch on the FW upperside; silver spotting on HW underside very reduced; and an additional discal band is strongly diverted basad at vein M3. Compare with *C. pephredo.*
Habits: This species is known in Costa Rica from a single specimen in the United States Museum of Natural History from Volcan Poas.

Genus **TAYGETIS** Hübner, 1918

Although there has been little disagreement as to which butterflies belong in this genus, there is also little to separate this group from other satyrine genera. In general, the butterflies in *Taygetis* are medium to large in size, all are dull brown or gray on the upperside, and they are usually conspicuously marked with ocelli on the underside; but even these generalities are variable. There is no satisfactory revision that adequately defines *Taygetis.* I have not used the genera *Satyrotaygetis, Postaygetis, Pseudodebis*, or *Taygetina*, as erected by Forster (1964), because they are based solely upon minor differences in the male genitalia, and because Forster did not define the genera. The genus *Taygetis* ranges from Mexico throughout Central and South America, and is also found on Trinidad and Tobago. There are roughly twenty-seven species in *Taygetis*, seventeen of which occur in our area. A forthcoming revision by L. D. Miller should sort out many of the problems.

There is very little known about the host plant relationships and the early stages. The few species that have been reared feed on Poaceae and have typical satyrine larvae: caudal tails, smooth body, and a forked head capsule that recalls certain brassoline genera (Fig. 33). The larvae are apparently solitary feeders.

In Costa Rica, *Taygetis* is found from sea level to 1,800 m, with most of the species found at mid-elevations. The majority inhabit the shaded forest understory and seldom fly in bright sunshine. Other widespread species are found in open second growth and primary rain forest. The genus exhibits a diversity of activity periods that ranges from being limited to dawn and dusk, to flying throughout the day, to some that may be nocturnal. Both sexes visit juices of rotting fruits and sap flows from wounds in trees and woody vines. In Guanacaste during the dry season, several of our species are attacked by mites that attach themselves to the wing veins and the mouth parts, a relationship with unstudied consequences. The longevity and population biology are unstudied for the entire genus, although it appears from casual observations that some species are sedentary and may live several months at least.

Taygetis mermeria excavata
Butler, 1868

FW Length: 45-52 mm **Plate 47**

Range: Mexico to Brazil and Bolivia. **Subspecies:** Costa Rica and Panama

Hostplant: Grass

Early stages: (Miles Moss drawings in British Museum [Natural History]) *Pupa*—similar in shape to *T. andromeda*, but somewhat longer and with the wingpads flaired.

Adult: Distinguished by the large size, gray upperside, and the acute FW apex. The underside coloration is variable.

Habits: Occurs from sea level to 1,200 m on the Pacific slope in association with deciduous forest habitats, or second growth that is dry for a major portion of the year. Encountered as uncommon solitary individuals, usually early in the morning, late in the day, or at lights after dark. During the day, individuals rest at the base of tree trunks and are reluctant to fly if disturbed. Both sexes visit rotting fruits.

Taygetis virgilia rufomarginata
Staudinger, 1888

FW Length: 37-41 mm **Plate 47**

Range: Mexico to Brazil. **Subspecies:** Central America

Hostplant: Bamboo

Early stages: (Müller 1886) *Mature larva*—body green with yellow longitudinal stripes; short, rolled-up caudal tails; body has fine pubescence.

Adult: Distinguished from all other species by the dentate HW margins and the rufous margin on the HW upperside.

Habits: Occurs from 300 to 1,000 m on both slopes, in association with tropical wet and premontane wet forest habitats, although especially common in the Valle de Turrialba. Encountered as solitary individuals in the deep shade of the forest understory; when alarmed, they dart through the densest vegetation. Both sexes feed on rotting fruits. In my experience, this species is always very local and never abundant.

Taygetis celia keneza
Butler, 1870

FW Length: 28-33 mm **Plate 47**

Range: Nicaragua to Brazil and Bolivia. **Subspecies:** Nicaragua to Colombia

Hostplant: Unknown

Early stages: Unknown

Adult: Distinguished from similar species by the three undulating medial lines on the FW underside, which are shaded brown basally; HW underside has yellowish spots near ocelli and on median. See *T. andromeda*.

Habits: Occurs from 100 to 700 m on the Atlantic slopes, in association with rain forest habitats. Uncommon, flies in dense shaded areas, and both sexes visit rotting fruits. Rare in Costa Rican collections.

Taygetis andromeda
(Cramer, 1779)

FW Length: 33-37 mm **Plate 48**

Range: Mexico throughout Central and South America

Hostplant: *Olyra, Acroceras, Panicum* (Poaceae)

Early stages: *Egg*—round, smooth, laid singly. *Mature larva*—body pale green with many longitudinal stripes, several of which form composite dorsolateral bands that are a paler green than the ground color; anal segment has two short caudal tails; head capsule bicolored: face pale brown, basal half green as in the body; two stout horns on epicranium that are projected slightly forward; shafts of horns and side of head have several granular warts (Fig. 33; see also Young 1984). *Pupa*—pale green; abdomen slightly curved; head bifid; wing pads slightly flared and brown; some spots of black and yellow dusted on the thorax and head.

Adult: Distinguished from similar species by the straight medial line that cuts the FW and HW in half, with the basal portion of both wings dark brown with a purple cast; FW distal margin often has a yellow cast; highly variable. See *T. celia, T. godmani*, and *T. salvini*.

Habits: Widespread and common in all habitats from sea level to 1,400 m, on both slopes. Persistent throughout the year in Guanacaste, but females are often in reproductive diapause. Flies in open sunshine and occasionally in primary rain forest, although generally a second-growth species. Both sexes visit rotting fruits, dung, and decomposing fungi.

Taygetis xenana godmani
Staudinger, 1888

FW Length: 30-35 mm **Plate 47**

Range: Costa Rica to Amazon Basin. **Subspecies:** Costa Rica and Panama

Hostplant: Grass

Early stages: (Miles Moss drawings in British Museum [Natural History]) *Pupa*—similar to *T. andromeda*.

Adult: Distinguished from similar species by

the produced FW apex; underside has dark brown basal half of both wings and dark brown distal margins; medial area gray-violet. See *T. andromeda* and *T. salvini.*

Habits: Occurs from sea level to 600 m on the Pacific slope, in association with wet and rain forest habitats, and occasionally in the Guanacaste deciduous forest along rivers during the rainy season. Very rare in Costa Rican collections; I have only found it upon a few occasions, always at rotting fruits.

Taygetis kerea

Butler, 1879

FW Length: 24-27 mm **Plate 47**

Range: Guatemala to Paraguay

Hostplant: Unknown

Early Stages: Unknown

Adult: Small, and could be confused with some *Cissia* species; distinguished by the scalloped HW margin; golden yellow patches on HW underside along medial area; ocelli on HW margin indistinct. See *Cissia satyrina, C. gigas,* and *C. gulnare.*

Habits: Occurs from sea level to 800 m on the Pacific slope, in association with deciduous forest habitats. Common in Guanacaste during the early rainy season (June-July) and diminishes in abundance until rare in the dry season. Both sexes feed on rotting fruits of *Guazuma, Spondias,* and other forest trees. Persistent throughout the year but, during the dry season, populations become localized in river beds. Individuals are attacked by mites during the dry season.

Taygetis salvini

Staudinger, 1888

FW Length: 28-31 mm **Plate 47**

Range: Costa Rica to Colombia

Hostplant: Unknown

Early stages: Unknown

Adult: Sexes slightly dimorphic; distinguished by the wide rufous margin on the HW underside, which is most conspicuous along the dentate margin; basal half of HW underside is darker brown (mostly in male); a submedial reddish line is bordered on either side by yellow. See *T. andromeda* and *T. zimri.*

Habits: Occurs very locally from 200 to 1,000 m on both slopes, in association with montane wet and tropical wet forest habitats. Usually found in the deep shade of the forest but will feed on rotting fruits at forest edges. Uncommon in Costa Rican collections.

Taygetis zimri

Butler, 1870

FW Length: 27-30 mm **Plate 48**

Range: Guatemala to Colombia

Hostplant: Unknown

Early stages: Unknown

Adult: Distinguished from all other species by the irregular yellowish medial band on the FW and HW underside; color variable. See *T. salvini.*

Habits: Occurs from 100 to 700 m on the Atlantic slope, in association with tropical wet and premontane wet transition forest, mostly along the Carrillo Belt. Uncommon, very local, and encountered as solitary individuals along riparian edges. Both sexes visit rotting bananas and fly at dawn and dusk. This species is rare in Costa Rican collections.

Taygetis banghassi

Weymer, 1910

FW Length: 31-34 mm **Plate 50**

Range: Costa Rica and Bolivia

Hostplant: Unknown

Early stages: Unknown

Adult: This unusual species is distinguished by the convex FW margin; both FW and HW cells have a diffuse yellow spot; underside has a violet cast; there are whitish submargins to both wings. See *Narope cyllastros.*

Habits: This peculiar species is known only from montane Bolivia and Costa Rica. In our area it occurs at La Estrella de Cartago at 1,700 m and then again above Moravia de Chirripo at 1,600 m, both localities being classified as premontane rain forest. I have found it in association with a delicate bamboo, *Rhypidocladum maxonii,* which is apparently itself a rare species. The butterflies are fairly torpid and reluctant to fly during the day, and must be flushed from the shady understory where individuals rest at the bases of trees. When disturbed, an individual flies a short distance and then settles at the base of another tree. Until very recently, this species was unknown from anywhere but Bolivia, and its occurrence in Costa Rica may be of biogeographical interest.

Taygetis penelea

(Cramer, 1779)

FW Length: 26-29 mm **Plate 48**

Range: Costa Rica to the Amazon Basin

Hostplant: Unknown

Early stages: Unknown

Adult: Distinguished by the yellowish band on the HW underside that runs from base to submargin.

Habits: Apparently extremely rare in Costa Rica. I have never seen it in the field but include it here because of several specimens in the British Museum (Natural History) collected by C. Lankester from an unspecified locality in Costa Rica. Additionally, it is known to occur on the Pacific slope lowland rain forest in Panama, near David.

Taygetis lineata

(Godman and Salvin, 1880)

FW Length: 27-30 mm **Plate 48**

Range: Costa Rica to Colombia

Hostplant: Unknown

Early stages: Unknown

Adult: Distinguished from all other species by the dark brown underside and a white medial line that traverses both wings.

Habits: Known in Costa Rica only from several specimens (in The British Museum [Natural History]) taken by C. Lankester at Las Concavas, near Cartago, and hence very rare.

Genus **EUPTYCHIA** Hübner, 1816

Although *Euptychia* has been used in the past as a blanket genus for most small Neotropical satyrine species that have rounded hindwings, I am using the name only for those species that show a particular suite of hostplant affinities and larval characters (see below), and have a characteristically delicate, semi-transparent appearance (Singer et al. 1983). The genus ranges from Mexico through to the Amazon Basin, where there is the greatest number of species. I estimate there are approximately fifteen species in the genus, although because the adults are very similar and the life histories are largely unknown, this number is probably a conservative estimate. In Costa Rica there are at least six species.

The hostplant relationships are with the Selaginellaceae and at least one species of moss in the Neckeraceae (Singer et al. 1983). The egg is round, smooth, and laid singly. The larvae are green, and bear fleshy tubercles that make the larvae amazingly similar in appearance to their hostplants (Fig. 33). The pupae are best described as a "monkey in a duncecap" with eyes, nose, and moustache on the face (Fig. 33). Although the chemistry of the mosses and Selaginellaceae is unusual, as far as is known *Euptychia* is completely palatable to vertebrate predators.

In Costa Rica, the genus is found from sea level to 1,400 m, but is mainly a lowland rain forest group. All species are weak fliers, feed on rotting fruits, and tend to stay close to the hostplant. From cultures kept in insectary conditions, I estimate that the adults live about five weeks. To what extent parasitoids and predators effect the early stages is unknown, but the larvae are killed by tachinid flies and braconid wasps, and some are carried off by predaceous ants.

From observations with binoculars on the rain forest canopy at Finca la Selva, I noticed that some species ascend into the canopy at dusk and then descend to the forest floor the following morning. This was quite surprising, since they are always found low to the ground during the day. In other observations I found no evidence that *Euptychia* feed on rotting fruits in the canopy, but they are easily attracted to fruits in the understory.

Euptychia jesia

Butler, 1869

FW Length: 13-15 mm **Plate 48**

Range: Mexico to Colombia

Hostplant: *Selaginella horizontalis* (Selaginellaceae)

Early stages: *Mature larva*—always found on the underside of the stems; body green, mottled with shades of light and dark green on dorsum; dorsum has many stubby warts; dorsal midline composed of a series of dark green V shapes that have the arms directed to the posterior and the apex interrupted by a narrow dark green line; head capsule green with two short granulate horns and two black lines that run from the top of the horns, across the face, to the base of the mandibles. *Pupa*—mottled dark and light brown; overall appearance like a monkey in a duncecap that has the eyes crossed, a low pointed nose, and a puckered mouth. The larvae are solitary feeders, but it is common to find different instars on the same plant. The larvae feed only on the small leaves and the reproductive parts.

Adult: Distinguished from similar species by the black on FW upperside that is dark and clear-cut as it enters the cell. Also, this is the smallest species. See *E. westwoodi* and *E. mollis.*

Habits: Occurs from sea level to 500 m on both slopes in association with all wet forest habitats, but commonest in rain forest. Always found in association with the hostplant in small populations of ten to twenty individuals. The females oviposit around midday. After ovipositing, the female perches a short distance away from the hostplant and rests with the wings open. After a few moments, she flies to another plant to lay another egg, and the process is repeated, usually about five times in succession. Common, and present throughout the year in all rain forest habitats.

Euptychia westwoodi

Butler, 1866

FW Length: 16-20 mm **Plate 48**

Range: Mexico to Panama

Hostplant: *Selaginella arthriticum* (Selaginellaceae)

Early stages: Larva like *E. jesia* but differing distinctly by the dorsal pattern composed of diamond shapes bordered by a fine white line; head capsule dull green with the two head horns colored black (Fig. 33). *Pupa*—similar to *E. jesia* but greenish, and the eyes of the "monkey face" are not crossed (Fig. 33). Compare with *E. jesia*.

Adult: Similar to *E. jesia* but distinguished by the black on the FW apex being indistinct and blending into the white below the FW cell; larger wing span. Compare with *E. jesia*.

Habits: Occurs from sea level to 500 m on both slopes in association with rain forest habitats, usually sympatrically with *E. jesia*. It is similar in habits to the preceding species, but is less common and most abundant during the brief dry spells that occur during the Atlantic slope rainy season. On the Pacific slope it is uncommon and local.

Euptychia mollis

Staudinger, 1875

FW Length: 20-23 mm **Plate 48**

Range: Costa Rica and Panama

Hostplant: *Selaginella horizontalis* (Selaginellaceae)

Early stages: Similar to *E. westwoodi* but distinguished by larger size; diamond pattern on dorsum is bordered on either side by a dark green zigzag line; head capsule green with green horns that are black-tipped; the black tip of the horns continues as a fine line to base of head. *Pupa*—pale green, highlighted along the edges of wing pads and first abdominal segment in brown; the monkey face has a longer nose than that of *E. westwoodi*, and the eyes are crossed.

Adult: Distinguished by the larger size; upperside washed in pearly gray; HW underside has an oblong yellow area that surrounds the marginal ocelli; FW underside has reddish submarginal line that is in line with subapical ocellus. See *E. molina*.

Habits: Occurs from sea level to 600 m on both slopes, in association with primary rain forest habitats. Encountered as rare solitary individuals in deep shade or during midday in light gaps. It is rare in Costa Rican collections and its affinities to *E. molina* are uncertain.

Euptychia molina

(Hübner 1818)

FW Length: Unknown from type; probably as in *E. westwoodi* **Not illustrated**

Range: Costa Rica to Colombia

Hostplant: *Selaginella* (Selaginellaceae)

Early stages: The larva is similar to *E. westwoodi* except that the dorsal tubercles and head horns have blue tips.

Adult: Although the type of *E. molina* is lost, the illustration in Hübner (1818) differs from similar species by having a distinctly sharp black FW margin, and HW upperside has a clear undulating black submarginal band. I am including this species, even though it is not established what the name refers to, because in the montane Atlantic slope regions of the Carrillo Belt, I have reared one specimen of what I believe to be this species. The larva is different from other species and this is the only *Euptychia* I have found in association with cloud forest. Its true affinities should become apparent when the biologies of all the Costa Rican species have been studied.

Euptychia insolata

Butler and Druce, 1872

FW Length: 17-21 mm **Plate 48**

Range: Costa Rica and Panama

Hostplant: *Neckeropsis undulata* (Neckeraceae)

Early stages: *Egg*—White, round, and shiny, laid singly on mosses growing on tree trunks. *Mature larva*—body green, looking like moss; dorsum has ten pairs of fleshy tubercles that in turn bear tiny bristles; along various areas of the dorsum and sides there are red-brown areas at the segmental interface; head capsule dull black with two large, stout horns that bear accessory spikes on the shafts and tips; epicranium has a dull brown patch; top of epicranium has a white line; each side of head has three flat spines (Fig. 33). *Pupa*—similar to *E. molis* but smaller and with more sprinkling of brown and black spots.

Adult: Sexes dimorphic: male dull brown above, female generally white above; distinguished from all similar species by the large ocellus on the HW tornus. The size of the large ocellus is variable.

Habits: Occurs from sea level to 700 m on both slopes, in association with primary rain forest habitats. Encountered as solitary individuals flying in deep shade or during midday in light gaps. The female flies around midday, fluttering up and down tree trunks or old moss-covered treefalls looking for suitable oviposition sites. Both sexes visit rotting fruits. I have found it most commonly in the rainy seasons.

Euptychia hilara

(Felder, 1867)

FW Length: 20-23 mm **Plate 48**

Range: Nicaragua to Colombia

Hostplant: Unknown

Early stages: Unknown

Adult: Distinguished from all other species by the yellow discal area on the FW underside; upperside is pale brown.

Habits: I have never seen this in the field. It is represented in the British Museum (Natural History) by a few specimens from Costa Rica without specific locality data. It has been taken in Chontales, Nicaragua, and will probably be found on the Atlantic slope of Costa Rica.

Genus **CHLOREUPTYCHIA** Forster, 1964

The butterflies in this genus are recognized by the reflective blue on the hindwing upperside and an elongated forewing. The genus ranges from Mexico through to the Amazon Basin and is composed of about six species, one of which occurs in our area.

The hostplants are all Poaceae. The larvae have stout head horns that bear auxillary spines on them, and the pupae are held horizontally to the ground and at 90° angle to the pupation surface (Fig. 34).

In Costa Rica the butterflies occur in lowland rainforest, and are quite common throughout the country.

Chloreuptychia arnaea

(Fabricius, 1777)

FW Length: 19-23 mm **Plate 48**

Range: Mexico to Colombia

Hostplant: *Eleusine, Oplismenus, Ichnanthus* (Poaceae)

Early stages: *Egg*—round, shiny white, laid singly. *Mature larva*—body mottled dark brown and light brown; dorsum has a broad band that is formed by a series of diamond shapes; sides uniformly brown; venter dark brown and prolegs pale brown; head capsule black with two distinctive horns that are slightly branched at the tips and white at the extremities (Fig. 34). *Pupa*—elongate mottled dark brown, tapering toward the cremaster and chopped off at the head. The newly eclosed pupa has the head directed toward the ground, but upon hardening, the entire pupa is held out horizontally (usually off a grass stem) (Fig. 34).

Adult: Distinguished from all other species by the reflective blue on the upperside of the HW. There is variation in the size of the largest HW ocellus; Pacific slope individuals have the largest ocellus, Atlantic slope individuals have intermediate ones, and the Meseta Central have the smallest.

Habits: Occurs from sea level to 900 m on both slopes, in association with rain forest and tropical-wet forest habitats. In the Meseta Central, some populations occur along rivers and in remnant patches of forest. Individuals fly in the understory along sunlit trails and in light gaps. Females oviposit during the late afternoon on isolated clumps of hostplants, usually at the base of trees. The eggs are often parasitized by trichogrammatid wasps. The butterflies are persistent throughout the year in rain forest habitats, although they can be very local. Both sexes feed on rotting fruits.

Genus **MEGEUPTYCHIA** Forster, 1964

This genus monobasic is separated by the male genitalia, and is further distinguished by having gregarious larvae and pupae (Fig. 34). The genus ranges from Mexico throughout Central and South America.

Megeuptychia antonoe

(Cramer, 1779)

FW Length: 29-34 mm **Plate 48**

Range: Mexico to Amazon Basin

Hostplant: *Callathea lutea* (Marantaceae)

Early stages: *Egg*—yellowish, laid in clusters of thirty to forty-five. *Mature larva*—body pale yellow, like the hostplant leaves, with a short bifid tail, and essentially no markings on the rough yellowish skin; head capsule yellowish with two widely spaced horns, which may have sooty black tips (Fig. 34). The larvae feed and molt gregariously in all stages, and behave like small *Caligo* caterpillars. *Pupa*—golden yellow or red-brown, rounded and compact without ridges or ornaments. Pupation takes place in gregarious masses.

Adult: Looks like a large *Cissia gomezi* but the ground color is brown, the HW margin is not scalloped, all the HW ocelli are of approximately equal size.

Habits: Occurs from sea level to 700 m, on both slopes. Encountered as solitary individuals in the forest understory, but is one of the most common canopy species on the Atlantic slope (DeVries, 1985*b*). Individuals feed entirely on rotting fruits in the canopy, and are collected in the understory very occasionally, never at fallen fruits.

Genus **CISSIA** Doubleday, 1848

The genus *Cissia* is used here for a heterogeneous group of butterflies that are generally small and brown, and were at one time all placed in the genus *Euptychia*. I have ignored the many genera proposed by Forster (1964) because they are based on dubious characteristics, and none of the genera are defined. A discussion of *Cissia* is found in Singer et al. (1983). The genus ranges from the southern United States throughout Mexico, Central and South America, and the West Indies and Trinidad, with the greatest species diversity in the Amazon Basin. In Costa Rica, the genus is well represented and includes a number of rare and endemic species.

The hostplants of *Cissia* include Poaceae, Arecaceae, and Marantaceae, the eggs are round, and laid singly on or off the hostplant. The larvae all have short bifid tails, are without projections on the body, and the head capsule usually has two epicranial horns, although they are greatly reduced in some species. The pupae are for the most part stocky, with a short bifid head, and short projections on the abdomen (Figs. 34, 35). Unlike most butterflies, many *Cissia* species have only four larval instars.

In Costa Rica, *Cissia* occurs from sea level to 1,800 meters throughout the country. Although primarily a forest genus, some species have radiated into the extensive open areas created by agriculture. Although field studies have not been carried out on *Cissia*, one individual of *C. hesione* lived in an insectary for over four months, and other species have lived, on average, two or three months. These data are surprising because it has been widely assumed that small satyrine butterflies would live a few weeks at most. Clearly, the rotting fruits and fungi that these butterflies feed on must contain sufficient nutrients to provide them with a considerably better diet than is normally supposed (DeVries, 1985*d*).

The adults are preyed upon by large robber fly species (Asilidae), some which appear to be specialists on small butterflies in the forest understory. The larvae are attacked by braconid wasps, and a single larva may sustain up to twenty-five parasites. There is also a record of a healthy tachinid fly (*Eumasiscera*) that emerged from a larva of *C. confusa* without killing the butterfly (DeVries 1984). The eggs are parasitized by trichogrammatid and scelionid wasps.

Cissia similis

(Butler, 1866)

FW Length: 20-23 mm **Plate 48**

Range: Mexico to Colombia

Hostplant: Grasses (Poaceae)

Early stages: *Mature larva*—body pale brown with many fine, dark brown lines running from head to caudal tails; mid-lateral section has an indistinct dark brown area running from penultimate to fifth proleg; two dark spots above prolegs 4-5; head capsule pale brown with short, bicolored horns. *Pupa*—similar in shape to *C. confusa*, pale brown with dark brown on venter and wingpads, and isolated spots on abdomen.

Adult: Similar to *C. usitata* but distinguished by the FW apex, which is truncated; HW margin dentate; HW upperside has a single ocellus with a blue pupil; no yellow between the two major ocelli on the HW. *Note*: the HW ocelli vary with elevation and dry season; in higher and drier areas the pupils in the ocelli become less distinct. See *C. usitata*.

Habits: Widespread and common from sea level to 1,000 m on the Pacific slope, in deciduous forest habitats. Individuals fly in the forest understory, along forest edges, and occasionally in open areas. In Guanacaste this species is most abundant during the rainy season (June-August), and becomes less abundant as the dry season progresses. Individuals are persistent throughout the year, but females in some areas of Guanacaste stay in reproductive diapause during the height of the dry season. Both sexes feed on fruits of *Ficus*, *Brosimum*, *Spondias*, and *Guazuma*.

Cissia usitata

(Butler, 1866)

FW Length: 18-21 mm **Plate 48**

Range: Mexico to Colombia

Hostplant: *Eleusine* (Poaceae)

Early stages: *Mature larva*—body pale pinkish brown with a regular dark brown dorsal midline; each segment has four brown spots; a distinct dorsolateral line of three colors: a red-brown center line, bordered on either side by pale brown, which is in turn bordered by black; head capsule mottled brown and black with two rounded head horns; area between the horns has a white midline; frons has two distinct spots that give the appearance of a cat face. *Pupa*—dark brown; angular and tapered toward the cremaster; two lobes on thorax; head area truncate with an angular protuberance on dorsum (Fig. 35).

Adult: Similar to *similis*, but distinguished by the round FW apex; HW margin never dentate; HW upperside has one or more ocelli on margin, all with double pupils; HW underside has metallic silver between two largest ocelli. See *C. similis*.

Habits: Occurs from sea level to 700 m on both slopes, in association with rain forest and wet forest habitats. Commonest on the Atlantic slope, and found on the Pacific slope only in rain forest from Quepos to the Osa Peninsula. Frequently found along forest edges or in associated second-growth areas. Essentially the ecological replacement of *similis* in rain forest habitats.

Cissia confusa

(Staudinger, 1888)

FW Length: 22-25 mm **Plate 48**

Range: Mexico to Colombia

Hostplant: *Iriartia, Genoma* (Arecaceae), *Panicum* (Poaceae), *Calathea* (Marantaceae)

Early stages: (Singer et al. 1983) *Egg*—white, laid singly on the hostplant. *Mature larva*—body brown with a dark brown dorsal midline that is slightly expanded in the middle of body; segments 1-3 usually paler than other segments; segments 4 to the anal segment have a diamond pattern along either side of midline; segments 4-10 have two white spots located at the constrictions of the diamond pattern; head capsule brown (as the body) with two widely spaced, distally curved, dull black horns that are covered in granulations; tips of horns pale brown; mandible black (Fig. 35). *Pupa*—mottled black and pink, with the pink along the abdomen. *Note:* both larval head capsule and body vary slightly in shade of brown; some are very dark. Larvae feed singly, usually on seedlings or isolated plants on the forest floor. When at rest, the larva sits on the stem or the midrib of the leaf.

Adult: Distinguished from similar species by the single marginal line (not two) in the HW tornus as it meets the inner margin; medial band on HW curves sharply to meet the inner margin. Compare with *C. labe, C. joycae, C. pseudoconfusa, C. gomezi, C. terrestris*, and *C. drymo*.

Habits: Occurs from sea level to 1,000 m on both slopes in association with tropical-wet and rain forest habitats, and does not enter the deciduous forest on the Pacific slope. Encountered as solitary individuals in the deep shade of the forest understory and subcanopy. Present throughout the year in lowland rain forest, but not abundant.

Cissia pseudoconfusa

Singer, DeVries, and Ehrlich, 1983

FW Length: 19-22 mm **Plate 48**

Range: Mexico to Panama

Hostplant: *Panicum* (Poaceae)

Early stages: (Singer et al. 1983) The larva differs from *confusa* by having light brown body highly mottled with dark brown; dorsal midline dull blackish brown with a wide diamond pattern surrounding the midline; two dull black spots per segment at the lateral apexes of each diamond shape; sides of body have a broad, indistinct, dull back band; spiracles black; head capsule dark brown with two black granulate horns; epicranium and tips of horns light brown. *Pupa*—dark or light brown but never with pink, as in *C. confusa*.

Adult: Distinguished from similar species by the two marginal bands along the HW tornus as they meet the inner margin; HW shape angular, not rounded. Compare with *C. confusa, C. labe, C. terrestris, C. drymo*, and *C. gomezi*.

Habits: Occurs from sea level to 700 m on both slopes, in association with a variety of habitats that range from primary rain forest to moist, disturbed deciduous forest. The habits are similar to *C. confusa*, but this species is much more common and it also is found in the forest canopy.

Cissia labe

(Butler, 1870)

FW Length: 20-23 mm **Plate 48**

Range: Mexico to Ecuador

Hostplant: *Paspalum, Ichananthus* (Poaceae)

Early stages: (Singer et al. 1983) *Egg*—yellowish, laid on dead vegetation associated with clumps of the hostplant. *Mature larva*—body medium brown with a slight orange cast; prominent dark brown dorsal midline running from head to anus; some larvae have four very dark brown dorsolateral spots; head capsule highly granulate brown with the head horns reduced to epicranial bumps (Fig. 35). *Pupa*—dark brownish purple to almost black, marked with striations of light brown; shape compact and rounded (Fig. 35).

Adult: Distinguished from all other species by the prominent reddish square in the HW tornus and no ocellus on inner margin. The female is paler on the upperside and has an ocellus near the tornus. Compare with *C. palladia.*

Habits: Occurs from sea level to 1,200 m on both slopes, in association with all forest types except dry deciduous forest. Encountered as solitary individuals along forest edges or in large light gaps. Both sexes feed on rotting fruits and decomposing fungi. The female oviposits during late morning until midday, typically where the grasses are in tall clumps. The female alights and drops down into the grass and lays eggs on dead leaves, twigs, or the ground. Most abundant during the dry seasons, although seldom common.

Cissia palladia

(Butler, 1866)

FW Length: 16-19 mm **Plate 48**

Range: Nicaragua to Brazil, Trinidad

Hostplant: Grasses (Poaceae)

Early stages: (Singer et al. 1983) *Egg*—pale yellow with fine striations. *Mature larva*—body medium brown with an alternating pattern of light and dark rectangles; head capsule very rough and granulate with similar head horns as seen in *C. labe* and *C. terrestris.*

Adult: Distinguished from similar species by the submarginal line on the HW that ends in a square and is immediately followed by a tiny ocellus on the inner margin. See *C. labe* and *C. terrestris.*

Habits: Occurs very locally from 300 to 800 m on the Pacific slope, in association with premontane moist forest. Rare in Costa Rica, known only from the remnant forests near Atenas.

Cissia joycae

Singer, DeVries, and Ehrlich, 1983

FW Length: 20 mm **Plate 48**

Range: Costa Rica

Hostplant: Unknown

Early stages: Unknown

Adult: Similar to *C. pseudoconfusa* but distinguished by the single submarginal line in the HW tornus; HW ocelli are set further from the margin; FW medial band is angled at the cell near the costa. See *C. pseudoconfusa.*

Habits: This very rare species is known from two specimens from Costa Rica, one of which was taken in the rain forest canopy at Finca La Selva. Nothing is known of its distribution or habits.

Cissia terrestris

(Butler, 1866)

FW Length: 17-20 mm **Plate 48**

Range: Nicaragua to Amazon Basin

Hostplant: Unknown

Early stages: Unknown

Adult: Distinguished by the irregular metallic markings between the two largest HW ocelli; HW tornus with a single submarginal line. See *C. confusa.*

Habits: I have seen no authentic Costa Rican material, but collections from Nicaragua and David, Panama, suggest that this species will be found as our fauna becomes better known.

Cissia drymo

(Schaus, 1913)

FW Length: 22 mm **Plate 48**

Range: Costa Rica

Hostplant: Unknown

Early stages: Unknown

Adult: Distinguished from similar species by the FW upperside having a reddish orange blush; HW margin scalloped; HW submarginal lines as in *C. agnata*; medial and postmedial lines reddish. See *C. agnata* and *C. gomezi.*

Habits: This rare and very beautiful species is known only from two specimens collected near Guapiles on the Atlantic slope. I have never seen it alive.

Cissia agnata

(Schaus, 1913)

FW length: 25-27 mm **Plate 48**

Range: Costa Rica

Hostplant: Unknown

Early stages: Unknown

Adult: Distinguished by the pale gray ground color; prominent red-brown rectangle at the HW inner margin; ocelli ringed in pale yellow; HW margin dentate. See *C. libye* and *C. gomezi.*

Habits: Occurs from 100 to 400 m on the Atlantic slope, in association with primary rain forest habitats. Encountered as solitary individuals during late morning until midday, in light gaps. I have only found it during the dry seasons around the Rio Sucio, Guapiles, and Finca la Selva. Rare in collections.

Cissia gomezi

Singer, DeVries, and Ehrlich, 1983

FW Length: 20-23 mm **Plate 48**

Range: Costa Rica

Hostplant: Grass (Poaceae)

Early stages: (Singer et al. 1983) *Mature larva*—body orange with darker dorsolateral stripes and a series of V shapes connecting the stripes; head capsule amber with two long head horns that project forward in a straight line, much like *C. alcinoe* or *Dioriste. Pupa*—pale brown with fine striations of darker brown, a thick latero-ventral line on abdomen, and in general shape elongate (Fig. 35).

Adult: Distinguished from similar species by the reddish gray cast to the underside ground color; HW underside similar to *C. agnata* but with only two prominent ocelli and a set of indistinct yellow areas between them; two submarginal lines at the HW tornus. See *C. agnata* and *C. drymo.*

Habits: This rare species is known from four specimens from Costa Rica, one of which was reared from a larva on the Osa Peninsula, at Sirena in Parque Corcovado; the others are without precise data.

Cissia libye

(Linnaeus, 1767)

FW Length: 22-24 mm **Plate 48**

Range: Mexico to Amazon Basin

Hostplant: *Panicum* (Poaceae)

Early stages: *Mature larva*—body pale brown with a regular dorsal midline that is bordered on either side with pale brown; two spots on the posterior edge of each segment located dorsolaterally; entire body has many fine striations that form a lateral band; head capsule pale brown with two short, roundly triangular horns that project slightly forward and have a brown band running from tip to base of head. *Pupa*—similar to *C. confusa* except almost entirely black.

Adult: Distinguished by the blue-gray cast to the ground color; prominent HW marginal ocelli; HW margins scalloped. See *C. agnata* and *C. tiessa.*

Habits: Widespread and common, from sea level to 1,200 m on both slopes, in all second-growth forest habitats. Flies along forest edges, in thickets, and occasionally in open areas. Individuals are persistent throughout the year in all habitats.

Cissia gigas

(Butler, 1866)

FW Length: 27-30 mm **Plate 48**

Range: Mexico to Panama

Hostplant: Unknown

Early stages: Unknown

Adult: Similar to *C. satyrina* but distinguished by the darker brown color; ocelli on HW underside prominently developed; no metallic spotting between the HW ocelli. See *C. satyrina, C. tiessa, C. libye.*

Habits: Occurs from 800 m to 1,400 m on both slopes, mainly along the Cordillera de Talamanca. Flies in forest understory, usually with *C. satyrina*, but is a much less common species. Both sexes feed on rotting fruits.

Cissia satyrina

(Bates, 1865)

FW Length: 26-30 mm **Plate 48**

Range: Mexico to Panama

Hostplant: Grass (Poaceae)

Early stages: *Mature larva*—similar to the larva of *C. libye* but pale yellow-brown; fewer striations on body, and head capsule has better developed horns. *Pupa*—similar to that of *C. gomezi.*

Adult: Distinguished by the reddish brown ground color; ocelli on HW underside reduced; metallic spots present between the ocelli on the underside. *Note*: Butler uses the name *incerta* to refer to specimens with an orange-red patch on the FW and more metallic markings. See *C. gigas* and *C. tiessa.*

Habits: Common and widespread in all forest habitats, from 800 to 1,800 m on both slopes. Individuals fly in the forest understory and can be abundant during the dry seasons. Both sexes feed on rotting fruits and are most active during morning hours.

Cissia tiessa

(Hewitson, 1869)

FW Length: 27-30 mm **Plate 48**

Range: Nicaragua to Ecuador

Hostplant: Unknown

Early stages: Unknown

Adult: Distinguished from similar species by the reddish ground color with silver-gray bands (in which the ocelli are set). See *C. gigas* and *C. libye.*

Habits: Occurs very locally, from 100 to 600 m on the Atlantic slope, in primary rain forest habitats. Encountered during the morning as solitary individuals in deep shade, usually perched on moss-covered tree trunks. I have never collected this species at rotting fruits, in either the understory or the canopy. Rare in Costa Rican collections.

Cissia metaleuca

(Boisduval, 1870)

FW Length: 18-20 mm **Plate 48**

Range: Mexico to Brazil

Hostplant: Grasses (Poaceae)

Early stages: *Egg*—white, round, laid singly. *Mature larva*—body bright green with two short caudal tails; head capsule shiny black with two short epicranial horns. *Pupa*—pale green, roundly elongate, similar to *C. hesione.*

Adult: Distinguished by the single white band on the underside that traverses both wings. See *C. hesione.*

Habits: Occurs from sea level to 1,000 m on both slopes, in wet and rain forest habitats. Flies along forest edges and in light gaps, as solitary individuals. Most abundant during the dry season, but seldom common. Both sexes visit fruits of the Araceae.

Cissia hesione

(Sulzer, 1776)

FW length: 18-21 mm **Plate 48**

Range: Mexico to Ecuador

Hostplant: *Eleusine* (Poaceae)

Early stages: *Egg*—black, laid singly. *Mature larva*—body bright green with two caudal tails; head capsule green with red epicranial horns. *Pupa*—pale green, smooth, head not bifid.

Adult: Distinguished by having two white bands on the underside that traverse both wings. See *C. metaleuca*.

Habits: Widespread and commoon, from sea level to 1,200 m on both slopes in all forest habitats except the lowland Guanacaste deciduous forest. Frequently encountered in small populations in old second growth or along forest edges. Both sexes are active during the morning until late afternoon. The females oviposit on isolated grasses growing at the bases of trees.

Cissia renata

(Cramer, 1782)

FW Length: 22-26 mm **Plate 48**

Range: Mexico to Ecuador

Hostplant: Grasses (Poaceae)

Early stages: *Mature larva*—body pale brown; wide dorsal midline composed of fine dark lines, and the midline bears a spot in the middle of segments 4-9; a black zigzag line on either side of the midline has white outer margins; head capsule pale brown, round, with two rounded bumps on epicranium and two black spots on top of head.

Adult: Distinguished by the drab underside coloration and the ocelli reduced to black dots.

Habits: Occurs from 100 to 1,800 m on the Pacific slope in all habitats except the Guanacaste lowland forest, and on the Atlantic slope above 700 m in drier ecotones. This species is most common at higher elevations, and seems to be transitory in the lowland forests. At higher elevations, it is frequently found in abundance along forest edges and in second growth. Both sexes visit rotting fruits and mammal dung, and are active whenever there is bright sunshine.

Cissia gulnare

(Butler, 1870)

FW Length: 18-22 mm **Plate 48**

Range: Costa Rica to Colombia

Hostplant: Unknown

Early stages: Unknown

Adult: Distinguished by the zigzag submarginal line on the underside of both wings; HW underside has three black ocelli with white pupils. See *C. alcinoe*.

Habits: Very rare throughout its range, and known in Costa Rica only from a few specimens from the San Mateo area, on the Pacific slope in premontane belt transition forest.

Cissia alcinoe

(Felder, 1867)

FW Length: 18-21 mm **Plate 41**

Range: Costa Rica to Bolivia

Hostplant: Grasses (Poaceae)

Early stages: *Mature larva*—similar to that described for *C. gomezi* except that the ground color is pale yellow brown and the V shapes are narrower. The head capsule also has shorter head horns (Fig. 34). *Pupa*—pale brown with fine striations, abdomen elongate; head elongately bifid (Fig. 34). *Note*: this pupa is unusual for *Cissia* but quite similar to those in the genus *Dioriste*.

Adult: Similar to *C. hermes* and *C. calixta*, but distinguished by the slightly excavated FW margin; HW medial bands are relatively straight; HW ocelli have double pupils. See *C. calixta* and *C. hermes*.

Habits: Occurs from sea level to 600 m on both slopes, in association with primary rain forest habitats, and on the Pacific it appears to be restricted to area adjacent to the Osa Peninsula. Encountered as solitary individuals in light gaps and along forest edges; occasionally, during the dry seasons, in small populations of up to ten individuals that fly in the forest understory. In my experience this is not a common species, and seems to be seasonal and local. Both sexes visit rotting fruits and decomposing fungi, and are active whenever there is bright sunshine.

Cissia calixta

(Butler, 1877)

FW Length: 17-20 mm **Plate 41**

Range: Costa Rica to Ecuador

Hostplant: *Cyperus lazulae* (Cyperaceae)

Early stages: *Mature larva*—body grass green, slightly granulate, and similar to *hermes*; two short caudal tails arise from high on the body and are held above the substrate; head capsule green, round, granulate, with two black spots on the face. *Pupa*—as in *C. hermes*.

Adult: Distinguished by the two ocelli on the HW underside, of which the one in the apex is larger; HW medial line wavy. See *C. alcinoe* and *C. hermes*.

Habits: Widespread and common in all habitats, from 800 to 3,000 m on both slopes. This species is basically the high elevational replacement of *C. hermes*, and is also found where there is second growth. In some areas along the Pan American highway, this species can be extremely common. Both sexes are active whenever there is sunshine, and are most common around water sources and in swampy areas. Both sexes visit rotting fruits, dung, and decomposing fungi.

Cissia hermes

(Fabricius, 1775)

FW Length: 16-20 mm **Plate 41**

Range: Southern United States throughout the Neotropics

Hostplant: Grasses (Poaceae)

Early stages: *Mature larva*—body pale green without distinctive markings; sides produced slightly over the prolegs, forming a skirt; entire body covered in fine white granulations; head capsule round, covered with granulations, entirely green. *Pupa*—mottled green or brown with an overall appearance like a grass stem; a double ridge of small undulations on dorsum; head area not bifid but squarely produced.

Adult: Distinguished from similar species by small size; HW medial lines always wavy; HW has a small black ocellus in tornus; ocelli have single pupils. *Note*: dry season specimens may have the underside pattern "washed out," and the ocelli may appear only as black dots. See *C. alcinoe* and *C. calixta*.

Habits: Widespread and common throughout the country from sea level to 1,500 m, in all habitats. Most common in pastures and other open areas, but occasionally found as rare individuals in forest light gaps. In Guanacaste this species can be exceedingly common during the rainy seasons along roadsides and forest edges. Large populations are persistent throughout the year in all habitats. Both sexes feed on rotting fruits, dung, carrion, and occasionally on flower nectar.

Cissia polyphemus

(Butler, 1866)

FW Length: 24-30 mm **Plate 41**

Range: Costa Rica to Colombia and Ecuador

Hostplant: *Chusquea* (Poaceae)

Early stages: *Mature larva*—body dark emerald green with a short bifid tail; head capsule light green with two short, triangular head horns. *Pupa*—dark brown with the same shape as *C. confusa*.

Adult: Distinguished by the dark brown ground color and the single black ocellus, with a single white pupil, on the HW underside.

Habits: Occurs in all forest and old second-growth habitats, from 800 to 2,500 m. Individuals are frequently found along forest edges, flying in and out of *Chusquea* thickets with a characteristic bouncy flight. Most common during dry seasons, but persistent throughout the year in most habitats.

Genus **AMPHIDECTA** Butler, 1867

The butterflies in this genus are recognized by the square forewing apex and the hindwing margin, which is undulate and elongated at the anal margin. The genus ranges from Costa Rica to the Amazon Basin and is composed of three species, one of which enters our area. Nothing is known about the hostplants or early stages.

Amphidecta pignerator

Butler, 1867

FW Length: 31-33 mm **Plate 49**

Range: Costa Rica to Amazon Basin

Hostplant: Unknown

Early stages: Unknown

Adult: Immediately distinguished by the FW apex, the white spots on the FW underside, and the produced HW anal margin.

Habits: Rare in Costa Rica. I have seen few specimens, all from the Pacific slope betweeen Esparza and Parrita. All of the specimens collected within the last few years have been either from inside buildings or from lights at night. I have never seen it alive.

Tribe **PRONOPHILINI**

The remaining Costa Rica satyrine genera all fall within the entirely Neotropical tribe Pronophilini (originally named by Reuter, 1896). As defined in Miller (1968), the butterflies in this tribe have "the hindwing crossvein M1-M2 produced distad at M2 and a fused vein (without a cell?) throughout its length." Upon examination of a number of genera, I have found these characters do not hold up; they are found in other tribes as well. The pronophilines are, however, a cohesive group of Neotropical satyrines. In our area, all occur at high elevations and can be recognized by their general wing shape, hairy thorax, and coloration. The tribe has its greatest number of genera and species in the mountains of South America, and comparatively few in Central America. The pronophilines in Central America show two areas of diversity, one in Guatemala and the other along the Cordillera de Talamanca in Costa Rica.

For the most part, the hostplants and early stages of the tribe are unknown, but in Costa Rica at least, partial life histories of some species have been worked out. Of the larvae that are known, all have long, pointed head horns and feed on the *Chusquea* species that are so common in the Neotropical mountains. The larvae may be either solitary or gregarious.

In Colombia the adults exhibit zonation on an elevational gradient (Adams 1973). Probably this also occurs in Costa Rica, but has yet to be studied. Adults will feed on flower nectar, dung, rotting fruits, and decomposing fungi. Populations of some species can be very local, and in Costa Rica, represent some of the rarest species in our butterfly fauna.

Genus **DRUCINA** Butler, 1872

The butterflies in this genus are recognized by the elongate forewing and the broad hindwing. The palpi are very long and hairy. There are three species in the genus, two being Central American and the other Andean. The genus ranges from Guatemala to Bolivia, and the three species do not overlap in their distributions.

The hostplants are unknown, but will probably be found to be bamboos. This butterfly genus is entirely montane and occurs only in cloud forest habitats.

Drucina leonata

Butler, 1872

FW Length: 40-45 mm **Plate 49**

Range: Costa Rica and Panama

Hostplant: Unknown

Early stages: Unknown

Adult: Distinguished by the wing shape and the spots on the FW upperside. The female may have the spots indistinct and coalesced.

Habits: Occurs locally, from 900 to 2,000 m on both slopes, in cloud forest habitats. The flight is fast and very nymphalid-like, with the butterflies taking to the wing and then abruptly landing, like *Eunica*. When settled, the forewing is folded down into the hindwing, and the insect almost becomes invisible. Frequently found along rivers and roadcuts on the Atlantic slopes to Volcan Poas and Irazu, but generally rare in other areas. Within the forest, individuals rest at the base of moss-covered trees. When disturbed, they fly up and settle again at the base of another tree. Both sexes feed on the juices of rotting fruits and mammal dung. In the Carrillo Belt, this species is present throughout the year, and although it is most commonly seen on bright, sunny days, individuals will fly in a slight drizzle.

Genus **DIORISTE** Thieme, 1906

The butterflies in *Dioriste* are recognized by having a dark brown ground color and a jagged, creamy yellow patch on the upperside. It was at one time united with *Oxeoschistus*, and is clearly close to it on the basis of the adult morphology. The genus ranges from Mexico to the Andes and is composed of about four species, three of which occur in Costa Rica.

The hostplants are all bamboos (Poaceae). The eggs are laid in small clusters or singly. The larvae are gregarious in early instars, but later appear to be solitary feeders. The head capsule bears two large triangular horns that project forward. The pupae are slender at the cremaster, square at the body, and have a very long and slender bifid head, much like *Eryphanis*.

In Costa Rica the genus is entirely montane, ranging from 700 to over 2,000 m, in all forest habitats. All of the species appear to be very local, and are always found in association with bamboo thickets. Adults feed on rotting fruits and decomposing fungi. Nothing is known about their courtship or population biology.

Dioriste tauropolis

(Westwood, 1850)

FW Length: 35-40 mm **Plate 49**

Range: Mexico to Panama

Hostplant: Unknown

Early stages: Unknown

Adult: Similar to *D. cothon*, but differs by the sharply dentate yellow patch on the HW upperside, which is also seen on the underside; FW underside has three marginal spots. See *C. cothon*

Habits: Occurs from 900 to 1,700 m on both slopes, in association with cloud forest and wet forest habitats. Individuals fly in well-shaded areas, darting in and out of bamboo thickets with a characteristic bouncy flight. On the Pacific slope and in the Meseta Central, this species is most common during the rainy season. Both sexes feed on rotting fruits and fungi, and are active at dusk and dawn. Common.

Dioriste cothon
(Salvin, 1869)
FW Length: 29-33 mm **Plate 49**
Range: Costa Rica and western Panama
Hostplant: *Chusquea* (Poaceae)
Early stages: *Mature larva*—body pale brown with four dark lines on the thorax; two long caudal tails; head capsule pale brown with two long, stout horns on the epicranium that project forward and are slightly curved outward at the tips. *Pupa*—similar to *D. cothonides*.
Adult: Similar to *D. tauropolis* but smaller; four yellow spots on the FW underside at the margin; large yellow patch on the HW upperside is not dentate. See *D. tauropolis*.
Habits: Occurs very locally from 1,200 to 1,800 m in isolated populations in the Meseta Central and the Cordillera de Talamanca. It has been considered a subspecies of *D. tauropolis* (with which it flies), but the genitalia are different and the size and the pattern are constant. A comparison of the early stages will shed further light on the problem of whether the two are separate species or not. In habits, it is similar to *D. tauropolis*.

Dioriste cothonides
(Grose-Smith, 1896)
FW Length: 33-35 mm **Plate 49**
Range: Costa Rica and Panama
Hostplant: *Chusquea* (Poaceae)
Early stages: *Mature larva*—body pale brown with short dark lines on the dorsum just behind the head, and then again on the posterior third; the dorsum has many white spots; two long caudal tails with reddish tips; head capsule tan, with two long horizontally held horns that curve outward at the tips; mandibles are dark brown. *Pupa*—straw yellow with two long, thin head horns of bright yellow, which are tightly appressed; generally tapered at either end with wingpads outlined in brown.
Adults: Distinguished from similar species by the reddish brown upperside of the HW and the larger size.
Habits: Occurs from 1,400 to 2,000 m on both slopes, in association with mountain passes and rain shadow valleys, mostly along the Cordillera de Talamanca and Central. I have found it most often on the slopes of Volcan Barva and in the Valle de Copey. Encountered as uncommon solitary individuals flying along water courses in dense bamboo thickets. Individuals frequently settle on the ground (near or inside the thickets), with the forewing tucked down into the hindwing. I have no information on feeding habits. It is rare in collections.

Genus **OXEOSCHISTUS** Butler, 1862

Medium-sized butterflies recognized by an orange band traversing both wings on the upperside, an undulate hindwing margin, and a produced forewing apex. The genus ranges from Mexico to the Andes in Bolivia. All species are montane and very nymphalid-like in appearance. There are nine species in *Oxeoschistus*; about half are Central American, and two occur in our area.

The early stages are as yet unknown, although I have found females ovipositing on *Chusquea* (Poaceae) in Costa Rica. The adults are not common in Costa Rica, although apparently in certain South American localities they can be very abundant.

Oxeoschistus euriphyle
Butler, 1872
FW Length: 32-37 mm **Plate 50**
Range: Costa Rica and Panama
Hostplant: Unknown
Early stages: Unknown
Adult: Distinguished by the pale yellow-orange on the upperside, which is dotted with ocelli; underside is similar to that of *Dioriste*.
Habits: Occurs from 900 to 2,000 m on both slopes, in association with bamboo thickets in cloud forest habitats. Individuals fly along water courses and closely follow the contours of the bamboo thickets. Flies with *O. puerta submaculatus* on the Atlantic slopes of the Meseta Central.

Oxeoschistus puerta submaculatus
Butler, 1874
FW Length: 33-39 mm **Plate 49**
Range: Costa Rica to Colombia. **Subspecies:** Costa Rica and Panama
Hostplant: *Chusquea* (Poaceae)
Early stages: *Egg*—white, round, laid singly on the internodes and dead leaf sheaths of the hostplant. The female will lay several eggs on the same plant.
Adult: Distinguished by the brown-orange band that traverses both wings and ends broadly on the HW tornus. See *O. euriphyle*.

Habits: Occurs from 800 to 2,400 m on both slopes in mountain pass, cloud forest habitats, especially along the Cordillera Central. Individuals fly in the forest along rivers and trails, and in ravines in association with large patches of *Chusquea*. Both sexes feed on rotting fruits and are active whenever there is sunshine. Populations are local, but in mountain passes this species is usually found in abundance.

Genus **ERETRIS** Thieme, 1905

The butterflies in this genus resemble *Cissia* or certain *Pedaliodes* but are recognized by the distinct excision or notch on the hindwing inner margin at the tornus. The only other group of New World satyrine to have this excision on the hindwing is *Calisto* (see Munroe 1950), a pronophiline genus confined to the West Indian islands (Brown and Heinman 1972). The genus *Eretris* ranges from Guatemala to South America, where the greatest diversity is found in the Andes. In Central America there are three or possibly four species, whereas there are at least fifteen species in South America.

The hostplants are probably all bamboos, although there are almost no observations on the early stages of this genus. Throughout its range, *Eretris* occurs at high elevations. In Central America, the genus shows a great deal of endemism, some species being extremely rare and local. The adults feed on fruits, flower nectar, and decomposing fungi. Nothing is known about their longevity or population biology but, in Costa Rica, I have seen populations go extinct when the bamboos (hostplants?) flower and die. It seems likely that the movement of the hostplant thickets through flowering and dying is of major importance in determining the distributions of some species.

Eretris hulda

(Butler and Druce, 1872)

FW Length: 23-25 mm **Plate 49**

Range: Costa Rica and Panama

Hostplant: Unknown

Early stages: Unknown

Adult: Distinguished by the flush of reddish orange on the HW underside, often with some ochre; HW has two ocelli in the tornus. Variable.

Habits: Occurs commonly from 1,600 to 3,200 m on both slopes in montane rain forest and paramo habitats, always in association with *Chusquea* thickets. Frequently found in abundant populations where individuals dart in and out of the vegetation along rivers, and in bright sunny areas. During the mornings the males become active first, and spend the first few hours of daylight perching on low vegetation with the wings open. Later in the morning, both sexes are active, feeding on *Miconia* and *Smilacena* and other fleshy fruits. This is the most common *Eretris* species in Costa Rica, and is especially abundant along the Cordillera de Talamanca.

Eretris suzannae

DeVries, 1980

FW Length: 24-27 mm **Plate 49**

Range: Costa Rica and western Panama

Hostplant: *Chusquea* (Poaceae)

Early stages: (DeVries 1980*a*) *Egg*—pearly green, smooth, laid singly on the terminal spine of the leaves. First instar larvae are pale green with a round, shiny, black head capsule.

Adult: Distinguished by the ocelli on the HW underside, of which the apical and tornal are the largest; the female has an ocellus on the HW upperside.

Habits: Occurs from 900 to 1,400 m on the Atlantic slope in the Carrillo Belt, associated with premontane rain forest. Occasionally found in large, local populations in association with the hostplant, but most often found as solitary individuals. As in the other species, individuals fly in and out of the *Chusquea* thickets in bright sunshine. Males chase any brown butterfly that is in the area. The females oviposit at any time of the day while it is sunny. After ovipositing, the female rests in a sunny spot with the wings open for a few minutes, and then lays another egg, and the process is repeated. Both sexes feed on the juices of fleshy fruits that are on the ground or still on the plants, or on fungi associated with rotting wood, and on flowers of *Satyrium*. Colonies go extinct after the hostplant flowers (every five years or so), a factor that probably strongly influences the distribution of the species. In established colonies, this species is present throughout the year.

Eretris subrufescens

(Grose-Smith, 1895)

FW Length: 21-24 mm **Plate 49**

Range: Costa Rica(?), Colombia

Hostplant: Unknown

Early stages: Unknown

Adult: Distinguished by the distinct reddish brown HW margin on the underside; HW underside has a row of equal-sized ocelli, with white pupils.

Habits: Described from a single specimen labeled "Costa Rica," which I believe to be erroneous. Common in Colombia.

Genus **PEDALIODES** Butler, 1874

The butterflies in *Pedaliodes* range from small to medium-sized, are mostly dull brown, and usually have an undulate hindwing margin. The systematics are poorly understood, and there will be much work to do in sorting out the numerous species and generic names. I have not utilized the genera erected by Forster (1964). The genus *Pedaliodes* is distributed from Mexico to South America, and is found only in montane regions. There are apparently well over one hundred species in *Pedaliodes*, most of which are found in the Cordilleras of Colombia and the Andes of Peru and Bolivia. In Central America there are six species, all of which occur in our area. The ecological analog of *Pedaliodes* in the temperate zones of both New and Old World is the genus *Erebia*.

Although there are no published life histories for any species, the hostplant relationships appear to be entirely with the bambusoid grasses, of which *Chusquea* is important. The egg is round and laid singly on or off the hostplant, the larvae and pupae of some species are similar to *Cissia*.

In Central America the species range from those that are very common and found in all appropriate habitats, to some species that are very rare or extremely local, and represent large range disjunctions from South America. The adults feed on rotting fruits, mammal dung, and fungi associated with dead vegetation. In the Cordillera de Santa Marta of Colombia, Adams (1973) showed that species of *Pedaliodes* are stratified along an elevational gradient, and some species are confined to a narrow elevational band. Furthermore, this same study indicated a very high degree of endemism within connected mountains. There are no estimates on longevity or aspects of early-stage biology for any species.

Pedaliodes perperna

(Hewitson, 1862)

FW Length: 26-32 mm **Plate 49**

Range: Costa Rica and Panama, Colombia and Venezuela

Hostplant: *Rhipidocladum maxonii* (Poaceae)

Early stages: *Egg*—white, laid singly and haphazardly on stems, leaves, and associated vegetation near the hostplant.

Adult: Distinguished from similar species by a large, black ocellus on the FW tornus, visible on both sides; HW slightly undulate, without a tooth; FW underside has a reddish blush surrounding the ocellus. See *P. petronius* and *P. ereiba*.

Habits: Occurs locally from 1,300 to 1,800 m on both slopes, in rain shadow valleys located in premontane wet and rain forest. Individuals fly close to the ground along trails and in light gaps. Males are very active during sunny mornings, perching on low vegetation and chasing other brown butterflies. The females are active from late morning until early afternoon, but I have found them associated only with clumps of the hostplant. Both sexes feed on rotting fruits and fungi. This species is uncommon in Costa Rican collections. In the field, small populations in the Cordillera de Talamanca are most abundant from February to May.

Pedaliodes petronius

(Grose-Smith, 1900)

FW Length: 36-40 mm **Plate 49**

Range: Costa Rica and Colombia

Hostplant: Unknown

Early stages: Unknown

Adult: Similar to *P. perperna* but distinguished by the larger size; FW underside has a wide tan margin; ocelli do not show on the upperside; HW margin dentate, with a produced tooth. See *P. perperna* and *P. ereiba*.

Habits: This rare species is known only from the Atlantic slope, from 800 to 1,000 m in the forest near Moravia de Chirripo. Although there were several specimens labeled "Costa Rica" in the British Museum (Natural History), it was only in 1982 that I. Chacon found a colony in the Talamancas, confirming beyond doubt its occurrence in Costa Rica. I have been told that it flies along the forest edges in bright sunshine, low to the ground, like *P. perperna*. Of interest is that this species was previously known only from the mountains of Colombia.

Pedaliodes dejecta

(Bates, 1865)

FW Length: 26-30 mm **Plate 49**

Range: Mexico to Panama and Colombia

Hostplant: *Chusquea* (Poaceae)

Early stages: *Mature larva*—pale brown and similar in pattern and shape to *Cissia libye*. *Pupa*—similar to *Cissia gomezi*.

Adult: Similar to *P. manis*, but distinguished by

the smear of reddish on the FW underside; HW medial line is roundly angled; HW has indistinct black ocellus with a single white pupil. See *P. manis.*

Habits: Widespread and common, from 800 to 2,500 m on both slopes in all second growth, forest edges, and open habitats. Most abundant in association with premontane rain forest habitats, but enters the drier forests on the Meseta Central.

Pedaliodes manis

(Felder and Felder, 1867)

FW Length: 24-28 mm **Plate 49**

Range: Costa Rica to Venezuela

Hostplant: Unknown

Early stages: Unknown

Adult: Similar to *P. dejecta* but distinguished by smaller size; underside overcast with a faint reddish blush; HW medial line runs from costa to outside cell, then angles sharply, without many undulations, to the inner margin; never has an ocellus on the HW, but only a faint white spot. Compare with *P. dejecta.*

Habits: Occurs from 700 to 2,000 m on both slopes along the Cordillera Central and Talamanca. This species has been considered a variation of *P. dejecta*, but the genitalia are distinct (M. Adams, personal communication).

Pedaliodes ereiba cremera

Godman and Salvin, 1878

FW Length: 34-38 mm **Plate 49**

Range: Costa Rica to Colombia. **Subspecies:** Costa Rica and Panama

Hostplant: *Chusquea* (Poaceae)

Early stages: *Egg*—white, round, laid singly at the clustered bases of the leaves where they join the stem.

Adult: Distinguished by the wide reddish orange band on the FW, visible on both sides; HW has three ocelli, one large followed by two smaller ones. See *P. petronius.*

Habits: Occurs locally from 1,600 to 2,500 m on both drainages in the Cordillera Central and Talamanca, in association with cloud forest habitats. Encountered as solitary individuals flying along the borders of river vegetation where there is a profusion of *Chusquea*. Individuals frequently settle on bare ground. This species is rare in collections, and I have never seen it abundant in nature.

Pedaliodes triaria

Godman and Salvin, 1878

FW Length: 27-30 mm **Plate 49**

Range: Costa Rica and Panama

Hostplant: Unknown

Early stages: Unknown

Adult: Distinguished from all other species by the orange band on the FW and part of the HW. This character is easily seen in the field.

Habits: Occurs from 1,600 to 3,200 m on both slopes in association with montane rain forest habitats, mostly along the Cordillera de Talamanca. The flight is fast and is reminiscent of *Adelpha*. During the morning, males perch along forest edges and in light gaps, from three to ten meters above the ground, and chase passing butterflies. Females are active around midday. Both sexes are only active in bright sunshine. Individuals feed on rotting fruits and visit flowers of *Miconia* and *Fuschia*. I have found this species to be very local in nature and uncommon in collections.

Genus **CATARGYNNIS** Röber, 1892

The butterflies in this genus are all medium-sized and have very hairy eyes, long palpi, and the underside highly mottled. In general, the genus bears a resemblance to *Oxeoschistus*. The genus ranges from Guatemala to the Bolivian Andes, where most of the species occur. There are about fifteen *Catargynnis* species, three of which occur in Central America. There are no published accounts of the hostplants or early stages, but I have upon several occasions watched one of our species oviposit on *Chusquea*.

All species occur in high montane forest to paramo habitats. Nothing is known of the adult biology of any species, and all appear to be rare. M. Adams (personal communication) has found altitudinal stratification or zonation in several species in Colombia.

Catargynnis rogersi

(Godman and Salvin, 1878)

FW Length: 32-36 mm **Plate 50**

Range: Costa Rica and western Panama

Hostplant: *Chusquea* (Poaceae)

Early stages: *Egg*—round, pearly white, laid singly on the stems and leaf axils.

Adult: Distinguished by the reddish yellow band, with a number of large brown spots on the FW, HW underside has a postmedial band of ocelli and a row of silvery spots to either side. See *Oxeoschistus puerta submaculatus.*

Habits: Occurs locally from 900 to 2,000 m on both slopes, in association with montane rain forest habitats. Most frequently found flying along rivers that are choked with *Chusquea*. The flight is bouncy, and individuals zigzag through the vegetation. Females oviposit from late morning to early afternoon, whenever there is bright sunshine. In the Talamancas, this species is most abundant during February and March, although it is persistent throughout the year.

Catargynnis dryadina
Schaus, 1913

FW Length: 37-41 mm **Plate 50**
Range: Costa Rica and western Panama
Hostplant: Unknown
Early stages: Unknown
Adult: Distinguished by the dull gray-brown upperside and the submarginal row of spots on the FW.
Habits: This rare species occurs on both slopes in forest habitats above 2,600 m, mainly in the Cordillera de Talamanca. The flight is very fast and nymphalid-like, and individuals fly along forest edges or at the forest canopy level. I observed one individual on Volcan Turrialba that rested in the canopy of a tree for over twenty-four hours without moving. During this period the weather was alternately sunny and cloudy, and it only moved when I dislodged it by throwing a stick into the branches of the tree. While at rest, the forewing is tucked into the hindwing, and the underside pattern renders the butterfly almost invisible against tree bark. I have very seldom seen this species, and it is very rare in collections. Most museum specimens have been collected from Volcan Irazu and Volcan Turrialba.

Genus **PRONOPHILA**
Doubleday, 1849

All of the butterflies in this genus are medium sized, have rounded wing shapes, and usually possess a conspicuous band of yellow or white on the forewing. The genus ranges from Costa Rica to South America, where it reaches its greatest diversity in the mountains of Colombia and the Bolivian Andes. There are about fifteen species of *Pronophila*, one of which occurs in Central America.

There is nothing known about the hostplant relationships or early stages of any species, although bamboo would certainly be a place to look. All of the species are high montane and occur in association with bamboo thickets.

Pronophila timanthes
Salvin, 1871

FW Length: 40-44 mm **Plate 50**
Range: Costa Rica to Ecuador
Hostplant: Unknown, but almost certainly a bamboo
Early stages: Unknown
Adult: Immediately distinguished by the large size, brown upperside, and the row of elongate orange spots on the FW.
Habits: Locally abundant from 900 to 3,000 m (on both slopes) in cloud forest habitats, always associated with bamboo thickets. Males patrol flyways within patches of bamboo or forest interior, and use the same routes on a daily basis. The patrolling males thread their way in and out of the vegetation, and their floppy, floating wing beats recall those of *Morpho.* In the Cordillera de Talamanca this species is most abundant during March and April.

Genus **LYMANOPODA**
Westwood, 1851

The butterflies in this genus are recognized by the narrow forewing and oblong hindwing. The genus is mostly Andean, with about thirty-five species. Two species are found in Central America, one in Guatemala and the other in Costa Rica.

Nothing is known about their hostplants or early stages. In Costa Rica, our species has the sexes dimorphic, is found only on the highest mountains, and is very rare.

Lymanopoda euopis
Godman and Salvin, 1878

FW Length: 24-27 mm **Plate 50**
Range: Costa Rican endemic
Hostplant: Unknown
Early Stages: Unknown
Adult: Sexes dimorphic. *Male*—distinguished by the row of black ocelli that traverse both wings on the upperside; HW underside has a row of oblong ocelli; and a ground color of warm brown. *Female*—upperside has a wide ochraceous band; underside ground color pale yellow-brown.
Habits: Occurs locally from 2,000 to 3,000 m on both slopes, in association with montane wet forest. Individuals fly very close to the ground in wet grassy areas along forest edges. The males will settle on muddy areas associated with grassy patches, and fly only in bright sunshine. The females fly in sunny or foggy weather during late morning. This species is local, never abundant, and rare in collections.

APPENDIX I

THE MAJOR COLLECTING LOCALITIES IN COSTA RICA

The following localities are listed by province and represent the best-collected sites in Costa Rica. The elevation for montane areas and the latitude/longitude bearings are approximated. For example, in Parque Corcovado the single coordinate point will locate the general area but is not meant to impose boundaries.

In some areas, more than one life zone is included. Those instances separated by a hyphen are a series, whereas those separated with a comma indicate the separate life zones indicated. The life zones are taken from Holdridge Life Zone system map of Costa Rica printed by the Tropical Science Center, San José, Costa Rica. Each number refers to a distinct life zone, as follows: 1. tropical dry forest, 2. tropical dry forest, moist province transition, 3. tropical moist forest, 4. tropical moist forest, prehumid province transition, 5. tropical moist forest, premontane belt transition, 6. tropical wet forest, 7. tropical wet forest, premontane belt transition, 8. premontane moist forest, 9. premontane wet forest, basal belt transition, 12. premontane wet forest, rain forest transition, 13. premontane rain forest, 14. lower montane moist forest, 15. lower montane wet forest, 16. lower montane rain forest, 17. montane wet forest, 18. montane rain forest, 19. subalpine rain paramo.

An asterisk (*) indicates a locality worked extensively by William Schaus; most museums have Schaus material from these areas. Useful references for Costa Rican geography and locality descriptions are: Blutstein *et al.* (1970), Holdridge (1967), and Noriega (1923).

ALAJUELA PROVINCE

Locality	*Elevation (meters)*	*Latitude/Longitude*	*Life Zone*
Abangares		10°15n–85°00w	2
Atenas	500	9°58n–84°23w	8
Cariblanco	850	10°16n–84°10w	7
Colonia Blanca	500	10°50n–85°10w	6
Colonia Virgen del Socorro	700	10°14n–84°12w	7
La Cinchona	1,300	10°13n–84°09w	13
Lago Hule	900	10°15n–84°14w	7
Laguna	1,600	10°13n–84°24w	7
La Libertad	600	10°50n–85°05w	7
Parque Volcán Poas	2,000–2,700	10°12n–84°15w	16,17
San Mateo		9°56n–84°31w	5
San Miguel	400	10°19n–84°09w	7
Zarcero	1,700	10°11n–84°32w	14
San Ramon		10°05n–84°39w	3

CARTAGO PROVINCE

Locality	*Elevation (meters)*	*Latitude/Longitude*	*Life Zone*
Chitaria	500	9°57n–83°36w	6
Curridibat	1,400	9°55n–84°02w	8
Cachi	1,100	9°50n–83°48w	10
Estrella	1,600	9°48n–83°57w	15
Juan Viñas*	1,300	9°54n–83°45w	15
La Carpintera	1,850	9°53n–83°58w	15

CARTAGO PROVINCE (*cont.*)

Locality	*Elevation (meters)*	*Latitude/Longitude*	*Life Zone*
La Suiza	800	9°51n–83°37w	10
Moravia de Chirripo	1,000	9°52n–83°25w	10
Orosi	1,300	9°48n–83°51w	13
Platanillo	1,100	9°50n–83°33w	10
Redondo		9°59n–83°58w	12
Tapanti	1,400	9°46n–83°48w	13
Tres Ríos*	1,400	9°54n–83°58w	12
Tuis*	1,200	9°51n–83°35w	13
Turrialba	600	9°54n–83°41w	11
Parque Volcán Irazu	2,800–3,400	9°58n–83°53w	17-18
Volcán Turrialba	2,800–3,400	10°02n–83°46w	17-18

GUANACASTE PROVINCE

Locality	*Elevation (meters)*	*Latitude/Longitude*	*Life Zone*
Arenal	700	10°29n–84°53w	10
Cañas	100	9°14n–83°25w	2
Libano	300	10°25n–85°01w	3
Parque Rincon de la Vieja	700–1,800	10°55n–85°22w	10-13
Parque Santa Rosa	0–100	10°57n–85°37w	2-3
Taboga	80	10°20n–85°13w	1
Tilaran	600	10°28n–84°59w	5

HEREDIA PROVINCE

Locality	*Elevation (meters)*	*Latitude/Longitude*	*Life Zone*
Barba	1,200	10°04n–84°07w	10
Finca la Selva	50–100	10°26n–83°59w	11
Chilamate	100	10°26n–84°02w	6
Magsaysay	200	10°25n–84°03w	6
San José de la Montana	1,500	10°03n–84°08w	10
Volcán Barba	2,500–3,000	10°08n–84°06w	16-17

LIMON PROVINCE

Locality	*Elevation (meters)*	*Latitude/Longitude*	*Life Zone*
Amubri	200	9°31n–82°56w	11
Bribri	100	9°38n–82°47w	11
Cairo*	100	10°07n–83°31w	11
Fila Bugu	1,200–1,400	9°26n–83°09w	13
Guapiles*	150–300	10°13n–83°46w	6
Kichuguecha	500	9°30n–83°05w	13
Florida*	200	10°05n–83°33w	6
Limon*	0–50	10°00n–83°02w	11
Parque Cauhita	0–50	9°44n–82°50w	3
San José Cabecar	500–700	9°25n–83°17w	13
Siquirres	100	10°06n–83°30w	11
Sixaola*	100	10°06n–83°30w	11

LIMON PROVINCE (*cont.*)

Locality	*Elevation (meters)*	*Latitude/Longitude*	*Life Zone*
Toro Amarillo	350	10°13n–83°47w	6
Parque Tortuguero	0–50	10°35n–83°50w	6
Zent District	0–100	10°02n–83°16w	4

PUNTARENAS PROVINCE

Locality	*Elevation (meters)*	*Latitude/Longitude*	*Life Zone*
Barranca	100	9°59n–84°43w	10
Esparta	100	9°59n–84°40w	3
Las Alturas	1,500–1,700	8°56n–82°51w	12
Las Mellizas	1,500	8°52n–82°45w	10
Miramar	200	10°06n–84°44w	3
Monte Verde	1,300–1,600	10°06n–83°26w	13-16
Parque Corcovado	0–600	8°32n–83°37w	7,13,16
Paso Real	700	8°59n–83°15w	3
Río Piedras Blancas	100	8°46n–83°12w	12
Punta Quepos	0–50	9°27n–84°09w	12
Rincon	0–100	9°55n–84°13w	6
San Vito	1,100–1,300	8°47n–83°00w	13
Santa Eleana	1,000–1,200	10°18n–84°48w	14
Ujarras	800	10°13n–83°02w	3
Villa Neily	550	8°37n–82°57w	6

SAN JOSÉ PROVINCE

Locality	*Elevation (meters)*	*Latitude/Longitude*	*Life Zone*
Bajo La Hondura	1,600	10°04n–84°00w	13
Cascajal	1,700	9°54n–84°38w	15
Copey	2,000–2,600	9°39n–83°54w	15
Desamparados	1,000	9°54n–84°04w	8
Division	2,800	9°28n–83°43w	16
Hacienda el Rodeo	600	9°55n–84°16w	8
El Empalme	1,800	9°44n–83°52w	15
Escazu	1,000	9°51n–84°10w	8
Guatuso	1,300	10°42n–84°50w	8
La Gloria	500	9°45n–84°24w	11
Madre Selva	2,700	9°40n–83°50w	17
Parque Braulio Carrillo	300–2,700	10°05n–83°58w	6,7,13,17
Parque Chirripo	2,800–3,850	9°29n–83°30w	17,18,19
San José	1,200	9°52n–84°07w	8
Villa Mills	2,800–3,000	9°33n–83°42w	18

APPENDIX II

LARVAL HOSTPLANT RELATIONSHIPS

The following is a list (by butterfly family and subfamily) of hostplant families they are known to feed on. Details of plant genera are found in the species accounts of the butterflies.

Family Papilionidae

Subfamily Papilioninae

Aristolochiaceae: *Parides, Battus*
Annonaceae: *Eurytides*
Apiaceae: *Papilio*
Hernandiaceae: *Papilio*
Lauraceae: *Papilio*
Piperaceae: *Papilio*
Rutaceae: *Papilio*

Family Pieridae

Subfamily Dismorphiinae

Mimosaceae: *Dismorphia, Lieinix*

Subfamily Pierinae

Brassicaceae: *Ascia, Leptophobia*
Capparidaceae: *Ascia, Itaballia, Pieriballia, Perrhybris*
Loranthaceae: *Catasticta, Hesperocharis, Pereute, Melete*
Tropaeolaceae: *Leptophobia*

Subfamily Coliadinae

Bignoniaceae: *Aphrissa*
Caesalpinaceae: *Aphrissa, Anteos, Eurema, Pheobis*
Fabaceae: *Eurema, Phoebis*
Simaroubaceae: *Eurema*
Zygophyllaceae: *Kricogonia*

Family Nymphalidae

Subfamily Nymphalinae

Acanthaceae: *Anartia, Siproeta*
Burseraceae: *Eunica*
Ericaceae: *Adelpha*
Euphorbiaceae: *Biblis, Callicore, Catonephele, Dynamine, Eunica, Ectima, Hamadryas, Haematera, Myscelia*
Melastomaceae: *Adelpha*
Rubiaceae: *Adelpha*
Sapindaceae: *Epiphile, Callicore, Nica, Pyrrhogyra, Temenis, Diaethria*
Tiliaceae: *Adelpha*
Turneraceae: *Euptoieta*
Ulmaceae: *Diaethria, Adelpha, Hypanartia*
Verbenaceae: *Adelpha*

Subfamily Melitaeinae

Acanthaceae: *Chlosyne*
Amaranthaceae: *Chlosyne*
Compositae (= Asteraceae): *Anthanassa, Tegosa*
Urticaceae: *Eresia*

Subfamily Acraeinae

Compositae (= Asteraceae): *Actinote*

Subfamily Heliconiinae

Passifloraceae: *Agraulis, Dione, Dryadula, Dryas, Eueides, Heliconius, Philaethria*
Turneraceae: *Eueides*

Subfamily Danainae

Asclepiadaceae: *Danaus, Lycorea*
Apocynaceae: *Danaus*
Caricaceae: *Lycorea*
Moraceae: *Lycorea*

Subfamily Ithomiinae

Apocynaceae: *Aeria, Tithorea*
Solanaceae: *Dircenna, Episcada, Hypothyris, Hypoleria, Hyaliris, Ithomia, Callithomia, Ceratinia, Greta, Mechanitis, Melinaea, Napeogenes, Oleria, Pteronymia, Scada, Thyridia*

Subfamily Apaturinae

Ulmaceae: *Doxocopa*

Subfamily Charaxinae

Erythroxylaceae: *Agrias*
Euphorbiaceae: *Anaea, Memphis, Hypna*
Flacourtiaceae: *Siderone, Zaretis*
Lauraceae: *Memphis, Archaeoprepona*
Mimosaceae: *Prepona*
Piperaceae: *Consul, Zaretis*

Subfamily Morphinae

Arecaceae (= Palmae): *Antirrhea, Caerois*
Fabaceae: *Morpho*
Mimosaceae: *Morpho*

Subfamily Brassolinae

Arecaceae: *Brassolis, Opsiphanes*
Bromeliaceae: *Dynastor*
Cyclanthaceae: *Caligo*
Heliconiaceae: *Caligo, Opsiphanes*
Poaceae: *Eryphannis, Opoptera, Selenophanis*

Subfamily Satyrinae

Arecaceae: *Cissia, Dulcedo, Pierella*
Cyperaceae: *Cissia, Oressinoma*
Heliconiaceae: *Pierella*
Marantaceae: *Cissia, Pierella, Megeuptychia*
Neckeraceae: *Euptychia*
Poaceae: *Cissia, Cyllopsis, Dioriste, Eretris, Catargynnis, Pedaliodes, Taygetis*
Selaginellaceae: *Euptychia*

APPENDIX III

SYSTEMATIC CHECKLIST OF COSTA RICAN BUTTERFLIES

The following is a checklist of the butterflies treated in this book. A name followed by ?? indicates that there is some question as to the validity of the name or whether or not this taxon occurs in Costa Rica. A name followed by ** indicates that there may be an alternative systematic arrangement for this group. In both instances the reader is advised to look up the taxon in the text for an explanation. Comb. nov. indicates a new combination of names (e.g., *Cissia similis*).

Family Papilionidae

Subfamily Papilioninae

Parides
- *photinus* (Doubleday)
- *alopius* (Godman and Salvin)??
- *dares* (Hewitson)??
- *montezuma* (Westwood)
- *sesostris zestos* (Gray)
- *childrenae childrenae* (Gray)
- *lycimenes lycimenes* (Boisduval)
- *erithalion sadyattes* (Druce)
- *iphidamas iphidamas* (Fabricius)
- *arcas mylotes* (Bates)

Battus
- *polydamas polydamas* (Linnaeus)
- *belus varus* (Kollar)
- *laodamas rhipidius* (Rothschild and Jordan)
- *lycidas* (Cramer)
- *crassus* (Cramer)

Papilio
- *polyxenes stabilis* Rothschild and Jordan
- *thoas nealces* Rothschild and Jordan
- *cresphontes* (Cramer)
- *astyalus pallas* Gray
- *androgeus epidaurus* Godman and Salvin
- *anchisiades idaeus* Fabricius
- *isidorus chironis* Rothschild and Jordan
- *rhodostictus rhodostictus* Butler and Druce
- *torquatus tolmides* Godman and Salvin
- *ascolius zalates* Godman and Salvin
- *birchalli godmani* Rothschild and Jordan
- *victorinus vulneratus* Butler
- *cleotas archytas* Hopffer
- *garamas syedra* Godman and Salvin

Eurytides
- *pausanias prasinus* (Rothschild and Jordan)
- *phaon* (Boisduval)??
- *euryleon clusoculis* (Butler)
- *ilus* (Fabricius)
- *branchus* (Doubleday)
- *philolaus* (Boisduval)
- *epidaus epidaus* (Doubleday)
- *agesilaus eimeri* (Rothschild and Jordan)
- *protesilaus dariensis* (Rothschild and Jordan)
- *marchandi panamensis* (Oberthür)
- *lacandones lacandones* (Bates)
- *calliste olbius* (Rothschild and Jordan)
- *orabilis* (Butler)

Family Pieridae

Subfamily Dismorphiinae

Pseudopieris
- *nehemia* (Boisduval)

Enantia
- *licinia marion* Godman and Salvin
- *melite amalia* (Staudinger)

Lieinix
- *cinerascens* (Salvin)
- *viridifascia* (Butler)
- *nemesis* (Latreille)

Patia
- *orise sororna* (Butler)

Dismorphia
- *eunoe desine* (Hewitson)
- *crisia lubina* Butler
- *lua costaricensis* (Schaus)
- *zaela oreas* Salvin
- *zathoe pallidula* Butler and Druce
- *amphiona praxinoe* (Doubleday)

Subfamily Pierinae

Hesperocharis
graphites Bates
crocea Bates
costaricensis Bates

Archonias
tereas approximata Butler
eurytele Hewitson

Melete
florinda (Butler)
isandra (Boisduval)

Leodonta
dysoni (Doubleday)

Pereute
charops (Boisduval)
cheops Staudinger

Catasticta
nimbice bryson Godman and Salvin
theresa Butler
flisa (Herrich-Schaffer)
teutila flavomaculata Lathy and Rosenberg
cerberus Godman and Salvin
strigosa actinotis (Butler)
prioneris hegemon Godman and Salvin
sisamnus sisamnus (Fabricius)

Appias
drusilla (Cramer)

Leptophobia
aripa (Boisduval)
caesia tenuicornis (Butler and Druce)

Itaballia
demophile centralis Joicey and Talbot
pandosia kicaha Reakirt

Pieriballia
mandela noctipennis (Butler and Druce)

Perrhybris
lypera (Kollar)
pyrrha (Fabricius)

Ascia
monuste (Linnaeus)
josephina josepha (Godman and Salvin)
limona (Schaus)

Subfamily Coliadinae

Zerene
cesonia centralamericana (Röber)

Anteos
clorinde Godart
maerula Fabricius

Kricognia
lyside Godart

Phoebis
rurina (Felder)
philea philea (Linnaeus)
argante (Fabricius)
agarithe Boisduval
sennae (Linnaeus)
trite (Linnaeus)

Aphrissa
statira (Cramer)
boisduvalii (Felder)

Eurema
proterpia (Fabricius)
mexicana (Boisduval)
salome (Felder)
xanthochlora (Kollar)
gratiosa (Doubleday and Hewitson)
boisduvaliana (Felder)
dina westwoodi (Boisduval)
albula (Cramer)
nise (Cramer)
lisa (Boisduval and Conte)
nicippe (Cramer)
daira (Godart)
elathea (Cramer)

Family Nymphalidae

Subfamily Charaxinae

Agrias
aedon rodriguezi Schaus
amydon philatelica DeVries

Prepona
dexamenus Hopffer
gnorima Bates
lygia Fruhstorfer
omphale octavia Fruhstorfer

Archaeoprepona
camilla (Godman and Salvin)
demophon centralis Fruhstorfer
demophoon gulina Fruhstorfer
meander amphimachus (Fabricius)
phaedra (Godman and Salvin)

Siderone
marthesia (Cramer)
syntyche Hewitson

Zaretis
ellops (Felder)

itys (Cramer)
callidryas (Felder)

Hypna
clytemnestra clytemnestra (Cramer)

Consul
fabius cecrops (Doubleday)
electra (Westwood)
panariste jansoni (Salvin) Comb. nov.

Anaea
aidea (Guérin-Ménéville)

Memphis
titan peralta (Hall)
eurypyle confusa (Hall)
ryphea ryphea (Cramer)
chrysophana (Bates)
glycerium (Doubleday)
aureola (Bates)
lankesteri (Hall)
herbacea (Butler and Druce)
ambrosia (Druce)
beatrix (Druce)
proserpina (Salvin)
chaeronea indigotica (Salvin)
centralis (Röber)
xenocles (Westwood)
arginussa eubaena (Boisduval)
niedhoeferi (Rotger, Escalante, and Coronado)
morvus boisduvali (Comstock)
lyceus (Druce)
elara (Godman and Salvin)
laura laura (Druce)
oenomais (Boisduval)
artacaena (Hewitson)
pithyusa (Felder)
forreri (Godman and Salvin)
orthesia (Godman and Salvin)
cleomestra (Hewitson)
aulica (Röber)

Subfamily APATURINAE

Doxocopa
clothilda (Felder)
pavon (Latreille)
callianira (Menetries)
felderi (Godman and Salvin)
cherubina (Felder)
cyane (Latreille)
excelsa (Gillot)
laure (Drury)
plesaurina (Butler and Druce)

Subfamily LIBYTHEINAE

Libytheana
carinenta mexicana Michener

Subfamily NYMPHALINAE

Colobura
dirce (Linnaeus)
dircoides (Sepp)??

Tigridia
acesta (Linnaeus)

Historis
odius (Fabricius)
acheronta (Fabricius)

Baeotus
baeotus (Doubleday)

Smyrna
blomfildia datis Fruhstorfer
karwinskii (Hübner) ??

Pycina
zamba zelys Godman and Salvin

Biblis
hyperia (Cramer)

Mestra
amymone Menetries

Hamadryas
februa ferentina (Godart)
glauconome glauconome (Bates)
feronia farinulenta (Fruhstorfer)
guatemalena guatemalena (Bates)
ipthime ipthime (Bates)
fornax fornacalia (Fruhstorfer)
amphinome mexicana (Lucas)
arinome ariensis (Godman and Salvin)
laodamia saurites (Fruhstorfer)

Panacea
procilla lysimache Godman and Salvin

Ectima
rectifascia Butler and Druce

Myscelia
cyaniris cyaniris (Doubleday)
leucocyana smalli Jenkins
pattenia Butler and Druce

Dynamine
agacles Dalman
theseus Felder
ate (Godman and Salvin)
salpensa Felder
hecuba Schaus
hoppi gillotti Hall Comb. nov.
chryseis Bates
sosthenes Hewitson
thalassina Boisduval
mylitta (Cramer)
glauce Bates
dyonis Hubner

*Marpesia***
petreus (Cramer)
coresia (Godart)
chiron (Fabricius)
alcibiades (Staudinger)
merops (Boisduval)
marcella (Felder)
iole (Drury)
berania (Hewitson)

Eunica
tatila caerula Godman and Salvin
monima modesta Bates
malvina Bates
mygdonia Godart
mira Godman and Salvin
norica Hewitson
caresa Hewitson
venusia Felder and Felder
excelsa Godman and Salvin
augusta Bates
alcmena amata Druce
pomona Felder

Temenis
laothoe agatha (Fabricius)
pulchra Hewitson

Epiphile
adrasta Hewitson
orea plusios Godman and Salvin
eriopis devriesi Jenkins
grandis Butler

Nica
flavilla canthara Doubleday

Pyrrhogyra
neaerea hypsenor Godman and Salvin
otolais otolais Bates
crameri Aurivillius
edocla aenaria Fruhstorfer

Catonephele
mexicana Jenkins and de la Maza (= *nyctimus* Westwood?)
numilia esite (Felder)
orites Stichel
chromis godmani Stichel

Nessaea
aglaura aglaura (Doubleday)

Haematera
pyramus thysbe Doubleday

Cyclogramma
pandama Doubleday

Diaethria
eupepla (Godman and Salvin)
anna (Guérin-Ménéville)
marchalii (Guérin-Ménéville)
astala (Guérin-Ménéville)

Callicore
lyca aerias (Godman and Salvin)
brome (Boisduval)
atacama manova (Fruhstorfer)
faustina (Bates)
texa titania (Salvin)
patelina (Hewitson)
pitheas (Latreille)
peralta (Dillon)
pacifica bugaba (Staudinger)

Perisama
barnesi Schaus

Adelpha
melanthe Bates
zalmona sophax Godman and Salvin
salmoneus salmonides Hall
boreas opheltes Fruhstorfer
stilesiana DeVries and Chacon
leucophthalma (Latreille)
zina Hewitson
justina lacina (Butler)
cytherea marcia Fruhstorfer
cocala lorzae Boisduval
heraclea (Felder)
boeotia boeotia (Felder and Felder)
erymanthis Godman and Salvin
delinita uta Fruhstorfer
basiloides (Bates)
iphiclus (Linnaeus)
erotia (Hewitson)
lerna aeolia (Felder)
phylaca (Bates)
naxia (Felder and Felder)
ixia leucas Fruhstorfer
leuceria (Druce)
tracta (Butler)
demialba (Butler)
diocles (Godman and Salvin)
celerio Bates
fessonia Hewitson
zea paraeca Bates
serpa sentia Godman and Salvin
felderi Boisduval

Hypanartia
lethe (Fabricius)
godmani (Bates)
kefersteini (Doubleday)
arcaei (Godman and Salvin)

Siproeta
epaphus epaphus (Latreille)
stelenes biplagiata (Fruhstorfer)
superba eunoe Fox and Forbes

Anartia
fatima Godart
jatrophae (Linnaeus)

Vanessa
virginiensis Drury
cardui (Linnaeus)

Junonia
evarete (Cramer)

Hypolimnas
misippus (Linnaeus)

Euptoieta
hegesia hoffmanni Comstock
claudia poasina Schaus

Subfamily ACRAEINAE

Actinote
leucomelas (Bates)
anteas (Doubleday)
guatemalena (Bates)
melampeplos Godman and Salvin
lapitha (Staudinger)

Subfamily HELICONIINAE

Philaethria
dido (Linnaeus)

Dryadula
phaetusa (Linnaeus)

Dione
juno (Cramer)
moneta poeyii Butler

Agraulis
vanillae (Linnaeus)

Dryas
iulia (Fabricius)

Eueides
aliphera (Godart)
lineata Salvin
lybia olympia (Fabricius)
lybia lybioides Staudinger
vibilia vialis Stichel
procula vulgiformis Butler and Druce
isabella (Cramer)

Heliconius
doris (Linnaeus)
charitonius (Linnaeus)
melpomene rosina Boisduval
cydno galanthus Bates
cydno chioneus Bates
pachinus Salvin
erato petiverana Doubleday
hecalesia formosus Bates
hecale zuleika Hewitson
ismenius telchinia Doubleday
ismenius clarescens Butler
clysonymus montanus Salvin
sara fulgidus Stichel
sara theudela Hewitson
sapho leuce Doubleday
hewitsoni Staudinger
eleuchia eleuchia Hewitson

Subfamily MELITAEINAE

Chlosyne
janais (Drury)
hippodrome (Geyer)
melanarge (Bates)
gaudealis (Bates)
narva (Fabricius)
erodyle (Bates)
poecile (Felder)
lacinia (Geyer)

Thessalia
ezra (Hewitson)
theona (Menetries)

Anthanassa
drusilla lelex (Bates)
ptolyca (Bates)
ardys (Hewitson)
phlegias (Godman and Salvin)
dora (Schaus)??
sosis (Godman and Salvin)
atronia (Bates)
otanes sopolis (Godman and Salvin)
crithona (Salvin)
fulviplaga (Butler)
tulcis (Bates)

Microtia
elva Bates

Eresia
clara Bates
coela Druce
alsina Hewitson
eutropia Hewitson
melaina Higgins??
sticta Schaus
poecilina Bates
nigripennis Salvin
mechanitis Godman and Salvin

Castilia
eranites (Hewitson)
fulgora (Godman and Salvin)
ofella (Hewitson)
myia (Hewitson)

Janatella
leucodesma (Felder and Felder)

Tegosa
anieta anieta (Hewitson)
nigrella (Bates)

Subfamily Danainae

Danaus
plexippus (Linnaeus)
gilippus thersippus Bates
eresimus montezuma Talbot

Lycorea
cleobaea atergatis Doubleday
ilione albescens (Distant)

Anetia
thirza insignis (Salvin)

Subfamily Ithomiinae

Eutresis
dilucida Staudinger
hypereia theope Godman and Salvin

Olyras
crathis staudingeri Godman and Salvin
insignis insignis Salvin

Tithorea
harmonia helicaon Godman and Salvin
tarricina pinthias Godman and Salvin

Melinaea
ethra lilis Bates
scylax Salvin

Thyridia
psidii melantho (Bates)

Mechanitis
lysimnia doryssus Bates
polymnia isthmia Bates
menapis saturata Godman and Salvin

Scada
zibia xanthina (Bates)

Napeogenes
cranto paedaretus Godman and Salvin
peredia hemisticta Schaus
tolosa amara Godman

Hypothyris
euclea valora (Haensch)
lycaste callispila (Bates)

Ithomia
bolivari Schaus
patilla Hewitson
diasa hippocrenis Bates
heraldica Bates
celemia plaginota Butler and Druce
xenos (Bates)
terra vulcana Haensch

Hyalyris
excelsa decumana (Godman and Salvin)

Aeria
eurimedia agna Godman and Salvin

Hyposcada
virginiana evanides (Haensch)

Oleria
zelica pagasa (Druce)
vicina (Salvin)
rubescens (Butler and Druce)
paula (Weymer)

Ceratinia
tutia dorilla (Bates)

Callithomia
hezia hezia (Hewitson)
hydra megaleas Godman and Salvin

Dircenna
chiriquensis Haensch
relata Butler and Druce
klugii (Geyer)
dero euchytma (Felder and Felder)

Godyris
zavaleta sorites Fox
zygia (Godman and Salvin)

Greta
oto (Hewitson)
nero (Hewitson)
anette (Guérin-Méneville)
andromica lyra (Salvin)
polissena umbrana (Haensch)

Hypoleria
cassotis (Bates)

Pseudoscada
utilla pusio (Godman and Salvin)

Episcada
salvinia (Bates)

Pteronymia
donata Haensch
artena artena (Hewitson)
fulvescens Godman and Salvin
notilla Butler and Druce
fulvimargo Butler and Druce
agalla Godman and Salvin
parva (Salvin)
cotytto (Guérin)
fumida Schaus

lonera (Butler and Druce)
simplex simplex (Salvin)

Heterosais
edessa nephele (Bates)

Subfamily MORPHINAE

Antirrhea
pterocopha Godman and Salvin
miltiades (Fabricius)
tomasia Butler

Caerois
gerdrudtus (Fabricius)

Morpho
theseus aquarius Butler
polyphemus catarina Corea and Chacon
peleides limpida Butler
peleides marinita Butler
granadensis polybaptus Butler
cypris Westwood
amathonte Deyrolle

Subfamily BRASSOLINAE

Brassolis
isthmia Bates

Dynastor
darius stygianus Butler

Opsiphanes
tamarindi tamarindi (Felder)
bogotanus Distant
quiteria quirinus Godman and Salvin
invirae cuspidatus Stichel
cassina fabricii (Boisduval)
cassina chiriquensis Stichel

Opoptera
staudingeri (Godman and Salvin)

Catoblepia
orgetorix championi Bristow
xanthicles xanthicles (Godman and Salvin)

Selenophanes
josephus josephus (Godman and Salvin)

Eryphanis
polyxena lycomedon (Felder)
aesacus buboculus (Butler)

Caligo
oileus scamander (Boisduval)
illioneus oberon Butler
memnon memnon (Felder and Felder)
eurilochus sulanus Fruhstorfer
atreus dionysos Fruhstorfer

Narope
cyllastros testacea Godman and Salvin

Subfamily SATYRINAE

Cithaerias
menander (Drury)

Haetera
macleannania Bates

Dulcedo
polita (Hewitson)

Pierella
helvetia incanescens Godman and Salvin
luna luna (Fabricius)

Manataria
maculata (Hopffer)

Oressinoma
typhla Westwood

Cyllopsis
hedemanni hedemanni Felder
rogersi (Godman and Salvin)
philodice (Godman and Salvin)
argentella (Butler and Druce)
pephredo (Godman)
hilaria (Godman)??

Taygetis
mermeria excavata Butler
virgilia rufomarginata Staudinger
celia keneza Butler
andromeda (Cramer)
xenana godmani Staudinger
kerea Butler
salvini Staudinger
zimri Butler
banghaasi Weymer
penelea (Cramer)
lineata (Godman and Salvin)

Euptychia
jesia Butler
westwoodi Butler
mollis Staudinger
molina (Hübner)
insolata (Butler and Druce)
hilara (Felder)??

Chloreuptychia
arnaea (Fabricius)

Megeuptychia
antonoe (Cramer)

Cissia
similis (Butler) Comb. nov.
usitata (Butler) Comb. nov.

confusa (Staudinger)
pseudoconfusa Singer, DeVries, and Ehrlich
labe (Butler)
palladia (Butler)
joycae Singer, DeVries, and Ehrlich
terrestris (Butler) Comb. nov.??
drymo (Schaus)
agnata (Schaus)
gomezi Singer, DeVries, and Ehrlich
libye (Linnaeus) Comb. nov.
gigas (Butler) Comb. nov.
satyrina (Bates) Comb. nov.
tiessa (Hewitson) Comb. nov.
metaleuca (Boisduval) Comb. nov.
hesione (Sulzer) Comb. nov.
renata (Cramer) Comb. nov.
gulnare (Butler) Comb. nov.
alcinoe (Felder) Comb. nov.
calixta (Butler) Comb. nov.
hermes (Fabricius) Comb. nov.
polyphemus (Butler) Comb. nov.

Amphidecta
pignerator Butler

Drucina
leonata Butler

Dioriste
tauropolis (Westwood)
cothon (Salvin)
cothonides (Grose-Smith)

Oxeoschistus
euriphyle Butler
puerta submaculatus Butler

Eretris
hulda (Butler and Druce)
suzannae DeVries
subrufescens (Grose-Smith)??

Pedaliodes
perperna (Hewitson)
petronius (Grose-Smith)
dejecta (Bates)
manis (Felder and Felder)
ereiba cremera Godman and Salvin
triaria Godman and Salvin

Catargynnis
rogersi (Godman and Salvin)
dryadina Schaus

Pronophila
timanthes Salvin

Lymanopoda
euopis Godman and Salvin

BIBLIOGRAPHY

Ackery, P. R. 1984. Systematic and faunistic studies on butterflies. Symp. R. Entomol. Soc. Lond. 11: 9-21.

Ackery, P. R., & R. I. Vane-Wright. 1984. Milkweed butterflies: their cladistics and biology. London: British Museum (Natural History), Entomology.

Adams, M. J. 1973. Ecological zonation and the butterflies of the Sierra Santa Marta, Colombia. J. Nat. Hist. 7: 699-718.

Adams, M. J., & G. I. Bernard. 1977. Pronophiline butterflies of the Sierra Nevada de Santa Marta, Colombia. Syst. Entomol. 2: 263-281.

Aiello, A. 1984. *Adelpha* (Nymphalidae): deception on the wing. Psyche 91: 1-45.

Aiello, A., & R. Silberglied. 1978*a*. Life history of *Dynastor darius* (Lepidoptera: Nymphalidae). Psyche 85: 331-345.

———. 1978*b*. Orange bands, a simple recessive in *Anartia fatima* (Nymphalidae). J. Lepid. Soc. 32: 135-137.

Alexander, A. J. 1961*a*. A study of the biology and behavior of the caterpillars, pupae, and emerging butterflies of the subfamily Heliconiinae in Trinidad West Indies. Part I. Some aspects of larval behavior. Zoologica N.Y. 46: 1-24.

———. 1961*b*. A study of the biology and behavior of the caterpillars, pupae, and emerging butterflies of the subfamily Heliconiinae in Trinidad, West Indies. Part II. Moulting, and the behavior of pupae and emerging adults. Zoologica N.Y. 46: 105-123.

Arms, K., P. Feeny, & R. C. Lederhouse. 1974. Sodium: stimulus for puddle behavior by tiger swallowtail butterflies, *Papilio glaucus*. Science 185: 372-374.

Auerbach, M. J., & D. R. Strong. 1981. Nutritional ecology of *Heliconia* herbivores: plant fertilization and alternate hosts. Ecol. Monogr. 51: 63-83.

Baker, R. R. 1984. The dilemma: when and how to go or stay. Symp. R. Entomol. Soc. Lond. 11: 279-295.

Barcant, M. 1970. Butterflies of Trinidad and Tobago. London: Collins.

———. 1981. Breeding experiments with *Morpho peleides insularis* (Lepidoptera: Nymphalidae) in Trinidad, W.I. J. N.Y. Entomol. Soc. 88: 80-88.

Bates, D. M. 1935. The butterflies of Cuba. Bull. Mus. Comp. Zool. (Harvard) 78: 63-258.

Bates, H. W. 1862. Contributions to an insect fauna of the Amazon Valley, Lepidoptera: Heliconidae. Trans. Linn. Soc. Lond. 23: 495-566.

Beebe, W., J. Crane, & H. Flemming. 1960. A comparison of eggs, larvae, and pupae in fourteen species of heliconiine butterflies from Trinidad, W.I. Zoologica N.Y. 45: 111-154.

Belt, T. 1874. The Naturalist in Nicaragua. London: John Murray.

Benson, W. W. 1972. Natural selection for Müllerian mimicry in *Heliconius erato* in Costa Rica. Science 176: 936-939.

———. 1978. Resource partitioning in passion vine butterflies. Evolution 34: 493-518.

Benson, W. W., & T. C. Emmel. 1972. Demography of gregariously roosting populations of the nymphaline butterfly *Marpesia berania* in Costa Rica. Ecology 54: 326-335.

Benson, W. W., K. S. Brown, & L. E. Gilbert. 1976. Coevolution of plants and herbivores: passion flower butterflies. Evolution 29: 659-680.

Berenbaum, M. 1981. Furanocoumarin distribution and insect herbivory in the Umbelliferae: plant chemistry and community structure. Ecology 62: 1234-1266.

———. 1983. Coumarins and caterpillars: a case for coevolution. Evolution 37: 163-179.

Blandin, P. 1976. La distribution des Brassolinae (Lep.: Satyridae). Faits et problemes. In H. Descimon (ed.), Biogeographie et evolution en amerique tropicale, pp. 161-218. Paris: Publ. Lab. Zool. de l'Ecole Norm. Sup., No. 9.

Blest, A. D. 1957. The function of eyespots in the Lepidoptera. Behaviour 11: 209-256.

Blutstein, H. I., L. C. Anderson, E. C. Betters, J. C. Dombrowski, & C. Townsend. 1970. Area Handbook for Costa Rica. Washington, D.C.: U.S. Government Printing Office.

Boggs, C. L., & L. E. Gilbert. 1979. Male contribution to egg production: further evidence for transfer of nutrients at mating in butterflies. Science 206: 83-84.

Boggs, C. L., J. T. Smiley, & L. E. Gilbert. 1981. Patterns of pollen exploitation by *Heliconius* butterflies. Oecologia 48: 284-289.

Boppré, M. 1978. Chemical communication, plant relationships and mimicry in the evolution of danaid butterflies. Entomol. Exp. Appl. (Amsterdam) 24: 64-77.

———. 1984. Chemically mediated interactions between butterflies. Symp. R. Entomol. Soc. Lond. 11: 259-275.

Borror, D. J., & D. M. DeLong. 1971. An Introduction to the Study of Insects, 3rd edition. New York: Holt, Rinehart & Winston.

Bowers, M. D. 1981. Unpalatability as a defensive strategy of western checkerspot butterflies (*Euphydyas* Scudder, Nymphalidae). Evolution 35: 367-375.

Bristow, C. R. 1981. A revision of the brassoline genus *Catoblepia* (Lepidoptera: Rhopalocera). Zoo. J. Linn. Soc. 72: 117-163.

———. 1982. A revision of the brassoline genus *Selenophanes* (Leidoptera: Rhopalocera). Zoo. J. Linn. Soc. 76: 273-291.

Brower, J.V.Z. 1958. Experimental studies of mimicry in some North American butterflies, part 3. *Danaus berenice* & *Limenitis archippus floridensis*. Evolution 12: 273-285.

Brower, L. P. 1969. Ecological chemistry. Sci. Amer. 220: 22-29.

———. 1984. Chemical defences in butterflies. Symp. R. Entomol. Soc. Lond. 11: 109-133.

Brower, L. P., & J.V.Z. Brower. 1964. Birds, butterflies, and plant poisons: a study in ecological chemistry. Zoologica N.Y. 49: 137-159.

Brower, L. P., J.V.Z. Brower, & J. M. Corvino. 1967. Plant poisons in a terrestrial food chain. Proc. Nat. Acad. Sci. 57: 893-898.

Brower, L. P., W. H. Calvert, L. E. Hendrick, & J. Christian. 1977. Biological observations on an overwintering colony of monarch butterflies (*Danaus plexippus*: Danaidae) in Mexico. J. Lepid. Soc. 31: 232-242.

Brower, L. P., & O. M. Moffit. 1974. Palatability dynamics of cardenolides in the monarch butterfly. Nature 249: 280-283.

Brown, F. M. 1929. A revision of the genus *Phoebis* (Lepidoptera). Am. Mus. Novit. 368: 1-22.

———. 1931. A revision of the genus *Aphrissa*. Am. Mus. Novit. 454: 1-14.

Brown, F. M., & B. Heineman. 1972. Jamaica and Its Butterflies. London: E. W. Classey Ltd.

Brown, K. S. 1977. Geographical patterns of evolution in Neotropical Lepidoptera: differentiation of the species of *Melinaea* and *Mechanitis* (Nymphalidae, Ithomiinae). Syst. Entomol. 2: 161-197.

———. 1981. The biology of *Heliconius* and related genera. Ann. Rev. Entomol. 26: 421-456.

———. 1984. Adult-obtained pyrrolizidine alkaloids defend ithomiine butterflies against a spider predator. Nature 309: 707-709.

Brown, K. S., & W. W. Benson. 1975. West Colombian biogeography: notes on *Heliconius hecalesia* and *H. sapho* (Nymphalidae). J. Lepid. Soc. 29: 299-212.

Brown, K. S., A. J. Damman, & P. Feeny. 1981. Troidine swallowtails (Lepidoptera: Papilionidae) in southeastern Brazil: natural history and foodplant relationships. J. Res. Lepid. 19: 199-226.

Brown, K. S., P. M. Sheppard, & J.R.G. Turner. 1974. Quaternary rufugia in tropical America: evidence from race formation in *Heliconius* butterflies. Proc. R. Soc. Lond. *B* 187: 369-378.

Brues, C. T. 1924. The specificity of food-plants in the evolution of phytophagous insects. Am. Nat. 58: 127-144.

Calvert, W. H., L. E. Hendrick, & L. P. Brower. 1979. Mortality of the monarch butterfly (*Danaus plexippus* L.) due to avian predation at five overwintering sites in Mexico. Science 204: 847-851.

Carpenter, G.D.H. 1942. Observations and experiments in Africa by the late C.F.M. Swynerton on wild birds eating butterflies and the preferences shown. Proc. Linn. Soc. Lond. 154: 10-46.

Casagrande, M. M. 1979. Sobre *Caligo beltrao* (Illinger). I. Taxonomia, biologia, morfologia das fases imaturas e distribuciones espacial e temporal (Lepidoptera, Satyridae, Brassolinae). Rev. Bras. Biol. 39: 173-193.

Chai, P. 1985. Responses of rufous-tailed jacamars (*Galbula ruficauda*) to butterflies in a tropical rainforest. Ecology (in press).

Chermock, R. L. 1950. A generic revision of the Limenitini of the world. Am. Midl. Nat. 43: 513-569.

Chew, F. S. 1975. Coevolution of pierid butterflies and their cruciferous foodplants. I. The relative quality of available resources. Oecologia 20: 117-127.

———. 1977. Coevolution of pierid butterflies and their cruciferous foodplants. I. The relative quality of available resources. Oecologia 20: 117-127.

———. 1977. Coevolution of pierid butterflies and their cruciferous foodplants. II. The distribution of eggs on potential foodplants. Evolution 31: 568-579.

———. 1980. Foodplant preferences of *Pieris* caterpillars (Lepidoptera). Oecologia 46: 347-353.

———. 1981. Coexistence and local extinction of two pierid butterflies. Am. Nat. 118: 655-672.

Chew, F. S., & R. K. Robbins. 1984. Egg laying in butterflies. Symp. R. Entomol. Soc. Lond. 11: 65-79.

Clark, A. H. 1947. The interrelationships of the several families grouped within the butterfly superfamily Nymphaloidea. Proc. Entomol. Soc. Wash. 49: 148-149.

———. 1949. Classification of butterflies with the allocation of the genera occurring in North America north of Mexico. Proc. Biol. Soc. Wash. 61: 77-81.

Clark, J.F.G. 1974. Presidential address for 1973, the national collection of Lepidoptera. J. Lepid. Soc. 28: 181-204.

Coen, E. 1983. Climate. In D. H. Janzen (ed.), Costa Rican Natural History, pp. 35-46. Chicago: University of Chicago Press.

Collenette, C. L., & G. Talbot. 1928. Observations on the bionomics of the Lepidoptera of Matto Grosso, Brasil. Trans. R. Entomol. Soc. Lond. 76: 391-416.

Common, I.F.B., & D. F. Waterhouse. 1981. Butterflies of Australia. London: Angus & Robertson.

Comstock, J. A., & L. Vasquez. 1961. Estadios de los ciclos biologicos en lepidopteros Mexicanos. Ann. Inst. Biol., U.N.A. Mexico 31: 349-448.

Comstock, W. P. 1961. Butterflies of the American Tropics: The genus Anaea, Lepidoptera, Nymphalidae. New York: Am. Mus. Nat. Hist.

Cook, M., K. Frank, & L. P. Brower. 1971. Experiments on the demography of tropical butterflies. I. Survival rate and density in two species of *Parides*. Biotropica 3: 17-20.

Corbet, A. S., H. M. Pendlebury, & J. N. Eliot. 1978. The Butterflies of the Malay Penninsula. 3rd ed. Kuala Lumpur: Malayan Nature Society.

Cordell, G. A. 1981. Introduction to Alkaloids. New York: J. Wiley & Sons.

Cottrell, C. B. 1984. Aphytophagy in butterflies: its relationship to myrmecophily. Zoo. J. Linn. Soc. 80: 1-57.

Cowan, C. F. 1970. Annototiones Rhopalocerologicae. 1970: 1-70, Berkhamsted: the author.

D'Abrera, B. 1981. Butterflies of the Neotropical Region, Part I. Papilionidae & Pieridae. Melbourne: Lansdowne.

———. 1984. Butterflies of the Neotropical Region, Part II. Danaidae, Ithomiidae, Heliconidae & Morphidae. Victoria: Hill House.

D'Almeida, R. F. 1965. Catologo dos Papilionidae Americanas. Soc. Brasil. Entomol.

———. 1978. Catologo dos Ithomiidae Americanos (Lepidoptera). Curitiba, Brazil.

Davies, N. B. 1978. Territorial defence in the speckled wood butterfly (*Pararge aegeria*): the resident always wins. Anim. Behav. 26: 138-147.

de la Maza, J., & G. B. Small. 1979. Descripcion del macho de *Epiphile grandis* Butler (Nymphalidae). Rev. Soc. Mex. Lepidopterol. 4: 57-60.

Dempster, J. 1984. The natural enemies of butterflies. Symp. R. Entomol. Soc. Lond. 11: 97-104.

Denis, J.N.C.M., & M. Schiffermüller. (1775). Systematisches Verzeichniss Schmetterlindge. Vienna.

Descimon, H. 1976. Biogeographie, mimetisme et speciation dans le genre *Agrias* Doubleday (Lep.: Nymphalidae: Charaxinae). Publ. Lab. Zool. de l'Ecole Norm. Sup. (Paris) 9: 307-344.

DeVries, P. J. 1978. Apparent lek behavior in Costa Rican *Perrhybris pyrrha* (Lep.: Pieridae) from the Osa Peninsula. J. Res. Lepid. 17: 142-144.

———. 1979*a*. Pollen feeding in rainforest *Battus* and *Parides* (Papilionidae) butterflies in Costa Rica. Biotropica 11: 237-238.

———. 1979*b*. Occurrence of fly maggots in adult *Morpho theseus* (Lep.: Morphinae) females from Costa Rica. Brenesia 16: 223.

———. 1980*a*. Description, natural history and distribution of a new species of *Eretris* from Costa Rica (Satyridae). J. Lepid. Soc. 34: 146-151.

———. 1980*b*. The genus *Agrias* (Lepidoptera: Nymphalidae: Charaxinae) in Costa Rica: Description of a new subspecies of *Agrias amydon*, new records, and natural history observations. Brenesia 17: 295-302.

———. 1982. The case of *Perrhybris lypera* (Pieridae) and the Lauraceae: hostplant record or assumption? J. Lepid. Soc. 36: 229-230.

———. 1983. Checklist of butterflies. In D. H. Janzen (ed.), Costa Rican Natural History. pp. 654-678, 703-704, 722-723, 729-732, 741-742, 751-752, 754-755. Chicago: University of Chicago Press.

———. 1984. Butterflies and Tachinidae: does the parasite always kill its host? J. Nat. Hist. 18: 323-326.

———. 1985*a*. Hostplant records and natural history notes on Costa Rican butterflies (Papilionidae, Pieridae, & Nymphalidae). J. Res. Lepid.

———. 1985*b*. Species stratification by rainforest butterflies in Costa Rica: canopy and understory habitats. Unpublished manuscript.

———. 1985*c*. The life cycle and natural history of *Morpho cypris* (Morphinae) in Costa Rica. Unpublished manuscript.

———. 1985*d*. Pollen and rotting fruit in the diet of tropical butterflies. Unpublished manuscript.

DeVries, P. J., & I. A. Chacon. 1981. A new species of *Adelpha* (Nymphalidae) from Parque Nacional Braulio Carrillo, Costa Rica. J. Res. Lepid. 20: 123-126.

DeVries, P. J., I. J. Kitching, & R. I. Vane-Wright. 1985. The systematic position of *Antirrhea* and *Caerois*, with comments on the higher classification of the Nymphalidae (Lepidoptera). Syst. Entomol. 10: 11-32.

Dethier, V. G. 1970. Chemical interactions between plants and insects. In E. Sandheimer & J. B. Simeone (eds.), Chemical Ecology, pp. 83-102. New York and London: Academic Press.

Dillon, L. S. 1948. The tribe Catagrammini (Lepidoptera: Nymphalidae) Part I. The genus *Catagramma* and allies. Reading (Pennsylvania) Public Museum Science Publication 8: 1-133.

Downey, J. C., & A. C. Allyn. 1975. Wing scale morphology and nomenclature. Bull. Allyn Mus. 31: 1-32.

Dunlap-Pianka, H. 1979. Ovarian dynamics in *Heliconius* butterflies: correlations among daily oviposition rates, egg weights, and quantitative aspects of oögenesis. J. Insect Physiol. 25: 741-749.

Dunlap-Pianka, H., C. L. Boggs, & L. E. Gilbert. 1977. Ovarian dynamics in heliconiine butterflies: programmed senescence versus eternal youth. Science 197: 487-490.

Dunn, L. H. 1917. The coconut-tree caterpillar (*Brassolis isthmia*) of Panama. J. Econ. Entomol. 10: 473-488.

Dyar, H. G. 1912. Descriptions of the larvae of some Lepidoptera from Mexico. Proc. Entomol. Soc. Wash. 14: 54-58.

Edgar, J. 1984. Parsonsieae: ancestral larval foodplants of the Danainae and Ithomiinae. Symp. R. Entomol. Soc. Lond. 11: 91-93.

Edwards, W. H. 1868-1897. The Butterflies of North America. 3 vols. Philadelphia: Am. Entomol. Soc.

Ehrlich, P. R. 1958*a*. The comparative morphology, phylogeny, and higher classification of butterflies (Lepidoptera: Papilionoidea). Kansas Univ. Sci. Bull. 39: 305-370.

———. 1958*b*. The integumental anatomy of the monarch butterfly *Danaus plexippus* L. (Lepidoptera: Danaidae). Kansas Univ. Sci. Bull. 39: 1315-1349.

Ehrlich, P. R. 1984. The structure and dynamics of butterfly populations. Symp. R. Entomol. Soc. Lond. 11: 25-40.

Ehrlich, P. R., & A. H. Ehrlich. 1982. Lizard predation on tropical butterflies. J. Lepid. Soc. 36: 148-152.

Ehrlich, P. R., & L. E. Gilbert. 1973. Population dynamics and structure of the tropical butterfly *Heliconius ethilla*. Biotropica 5: 69-82.

Ehrlich, P. R., & P. H. Raven. 1965. Butterflies and plants: a study in coevolution. Evolution 18: 586-608.

Eisner, T. 1970. Chemical defense against predation in arthropods. In E. Sondheimer & J. B. Simeone (eds.), Chemical Ecology, pp. 157-217. New York and London: Academic Press.

Eisner, T., & Y. C. Meinwald. 1965. Defensive secretion of a caterpillar (*Papilio*). Science 150: 1733-1735.

Eltringham, H. 1910. African Mimetic Butterflies. Oxford: Clarendon Press.

Emmel, T. C., & J. F. Emmel. 1973. The butterflies of southern California. Nat. Hist. Mus. Los Angeles Co. Sci. Series 62: 1-148.

Emsley, M. 1963. A morphological study of imagine Heliconiinae (Lep.: Nymphalidae) with a consideration of the evolutionary relationships within the group. Zoologica N.Y. 48: 85-130.

———. 1964. The geographical distribution of the color pattern components of *Heliconius erato* and *Heliconius melpomene* with genetical evidence for the systematic relationships between the two species. Zoologica N.Y. 49: 245-286.

Espenshade Jr., E. B. (ed.). 1966. Goode's World Atlas. 12th ed. Chicago: Rand McNally & Co.

Evans, H. C. 1982. Entomogenous fungi in tropical forest ecosystems: an appraisal. Ecol. Entomol. 7: 47-60.

Feltwell, J., & M. Rothschild. 1974. Carotenoids in thirty-eight species of Lepidoptera. J. Zool. Lond. 174: 441-465.

Fisher, R. A. 1930. The Genetical Theory of Natural Selection. Oxford: Clarendon Press.

Forbes, W.T.M. 1939. Revisional notes on the Danainae. Entomol. Am. 19: 101-140.

———. 1943. Revisional notes on the Danainae (Supplement). J. N.Y. Entomol. Soc. 51: 296-304.

———. 1945. The genus *Phyciodes* (Lepidoptera: Nymphalinae). Entomol. Am. 24: 139-207.

Forster, W. 1964. Beitrage zur Kenntnis der Insecktenfauna Boliviens XIX. Lepidoptera III, Satyridae. Veroff. Zool. Staatssamml. Munchen 8: 51-188.

Fox, R. M. 1940. A generic review of the Ithomiinae. Trans. Am. Entomol. Soc. 66: 161-207.

———. 1956. A monograph of the Ithomiidae (Lepidoptera). Part I. Bull. Am. Mus. Nat. Hist. 111: 1-76.

———. 1960. A monograph of the Ithomiidae (Lepidoptera). Part II, the tribe Melinaeini, Clark. Trans. Am. Entomol. Soc. 86: 109-171.

———. 1967. A monograph of the Ithomiidae (Lepidoptera). Part III, the tribe Mechanitini, Fox. Mem. Am. Entomol. Soc. 22: 1-190.

———. 1968. Ithomiidae (Lepidoptera: Nymphaloidea) of Central America. Trans. Am. Entomol. Soc. 94: 155-208.

Fox, R. M., & A. C. Forbes, 1971. The Butterflies of the genera *Siproeta* and *Metamorpha* (Lepidoptera: Nymphalidae). Ann. Carnegie Mus. 43: 223-247.

Fox, R. M., A. W. Lindsey, H. K. Clench, & L. D. Miller. 1965. The butterflies of Liberia. Mem. Am. Entomol. Soc. 19: 1-438.

Fox, R. M., & H. G. Real. 1971. A monograph of the Ithomiidae (Lepidoptera) Part IV, the tribe Napeogenini, Fox. Mem. Am. Entomol. Inst. 15: 1-368.

Fracker, S. B. 1915. The classification of lepidopterous larvae. Ill. Biol. Monogr. 2, No. 1. 2nd rev. ed. 1930.

Friden, F. 1958. Frass-drop Frequency in Lepidoptera. Uppsala: Almqvist & Wiksells Boktryckeri Ab.

Fruhstorfer, H. 1912-1916. Aegeronia, Brassolidae, Prepona, Morpho, Adelpha, Agrias. In A. Seitz (ed.), The Macrolepidoptera of the World, vol. 5. Stuttgart: Alfred Kernen.

Futuyma, D. J., & M. Slatkin (eds.). 1983. Coevolution. Sunderland, Mass.: Sinauer Associates.

Gentry, A. H. 1982. Patterns of neotropical plant species diversity. Evol. Biol. 15: 1-84.

Gilbert, L. E. 1969*a*. Some aspects of the ecology and community structure of ithomid butterflies in Costa Rica. In O.T.S Coursebook, 1969. San José, Costa Rica.

Gilbert, L. E. 1969*b*. On the ecology of natural dispersal: *Dione moneta* in Texas (Nymphalidae). J. Lepid. Soc. 23: 117-185.

———. 1971. Butterfly-plant coevolution: has *Passiflora adenopoda* won the selectional race with heliconiine butterflies? Science 172: 585-586.

———. 1972. Pollen feeding and reproductive biology of *Heliconius* butterflies. Proc. Nat. Acad. Sci. 69: 1403-1407.

———. 1975. Ecological consequences of a coevolved mutualism between butterflies and plants. In L. E. Gilbert & P. H. Raven (eds.), Coevolution of Animals and Plants, pp. 210-240. Austin: University of Texas Press.

———. 1976. Postmating odor in *Heliconius* butterflies: a male contributed antiaphrodisiac? Science 193: 419-420.

———. 1977. The role of insect-plant coevolution in the organization of ecosystems. In Comportement de insects et mileau trophique., V. Labyrie, ed., Coll. Int. C.N.R.S. 265: 399-413.

———. 1979. Development of theory in the analysis of insect-plant interactions. In H. Horn, R. Mitchel, & G. Stairs (eds.), Analysis of Ecological Systems, pp. 117-154. Columbus: Ohio State University Press.

———. 1983. Coevolution and mimicry. In D. Futyuma & M. Slatkin (eds.), Coevolution, pp. 263-281. Sunderland, Mass.: Sinauer Associates.

———. 1984. The biology of butterfly communities. Symp. R. Entomol. Soc. Lond. 11: 41-54.

———. 1985. Ecological factors which influence migratory behavior in two butterflies of the semi-arid shrublands of South Texas. In M. A. Rankin, ed., Migration: Mechanisms and adaptive Significance. Contributors in Marine Science Suppl. 28 (in press).

Gilbert, L. E., & M. C. Singer. 1975. Butterfly ecology. Ann. Rev. Ecol. Syst. 6: 365-397.

Godman, F. A., & O. Salvin. 1879-1901. Insecta, Lepidoptera, Rhopalocera. Biologia Centrali Americana. Vols. I, II, III. London.

Haber, W. 1978. Evolutionary ecology of tropical mimetic butterflies (Lepidoptera: Ithomiinae). Ph.D. dissertation, Univ. of Minnesota.

Hall, A. 1928-1930. A revision of the genus *Phyciodes* Hubn. (Lepidoptera: Nymphalidae). Bull. Hill Mus., Witley (as supplements to Vols. 2-4), pp. 1-205.

———. 1938. On the types of *Adelpha* (Lepidoptera: Nymphalidae) in the collection of the British Museum. Entomology 51: 184-187, 208-211, 232-235, 257-259, 284-285.

Hancock, D. L. 1978. Phylogeny and biogeography of the Papilionidae. Masters thesis, University of Queensland.

———. 1983. Classification of the Papilionidae (Lepidoptera): a phylogenetic approach. Smithersia 2: 1-48.

Harmsen, H. 1966. The excretory role of pteridines in insects. J. Exp. Biol. 25· 1-13.

Harrison, J. O. 1962. Factors affecting the abundance of Lepidoptera in banana plantations. Ecology 45: 508-519.

Harvey, D. J. 1983. Actinote leucomelas. In D. H. Janzen (ed.), Costa Rican Natural History. Chicago: University of Chicago Press.

———. 1985. Observations on the systematics and biology of three species of *Junonia* (Nymphalidae) in Florida and the Bahamas. (Unpublished manuscript).

Hemming, F. 1937. Hübner, A Biographical Account of the Entomological Works of Jacob Hübner. 2 vols. London.

———. 1967. The generic names of the butterflies and their type species (Lepidoptera: Rhopalocera). Bull. Br. Mus. (Nat. Hist.) Entomol., Suppl. 9: 509 pp.

Hennig, W. 1966. Phylogenetic Systematics. Urbana: University of Illinois Press.

Higgins, L. G. 1960. A revision of the Melitaeine genus *Chlosyne* and allied species (Lepidoptera: Nymphalinae). Trans. R. Entomol. Soc. Lond. 112: 381-467.

———. 1981. A revision of the genus *Phyciodes* Hubner and related genera with a review of the classification of the Melitaeinae (Lepidoptera: Nymphalidae). Bull. Brit. Mus. (Nat. Hist.) Entomol. 43: 77-243.

Hoffmann, C. C. 1940. Catalogo sistematico y zoogeografico de los lepidopteros mexicanos. Ann. Inst. Biol. U.N.A.M. 11: 639-739.

Holdridge, L. R. 1967. Life Zone Ecology. Rev. ed. San José, Costa Rica: Tropical Science Center.

Honda, K. 1983. Defensive potential of the components of the larval osmeterial secretion of papilionid butterflies against ants. Physiol. Entomol. 8: 173-179.

House, H. L. 1973. Digestion and nutrition. In M. Rockstein (ed.), Physiology of Insecta 5: 1-120.

Howe, W. H. 1975. The Butterflies of North America. New York: Doubleday.

Hübner, J. 1818. Zuträge zur Sammlung exotisher Schmettlinge, 1. Augsburg.

Huxley, J. S. (ed.). 1940. The New Systematics. London: Clarendon Press.

Janzen, D. H. 1967. Why mountain passes are higher in the tropics. Am. Nat. 101: 233-249.

———. 1973*a*. Sweep samples of tropical foliage insects: effects of seasons, vegetation types, elevation, time of day, insularity. Ecology 54: 687-708.

———. 1973*b*. Comments on host-specificity of tropical herbivores and its relevance to species richness. In V. H. Heywood (ed.), Taxonomy and Ecology, pp. 201-211. New York and London: Academic Press.

———. 1980. When is it coevolution? Evolution 34: 611-612.

———. 1983*a* (ed.). Costa Rican Natural History. Chicago: University of Chicago Press.

———. 1983*b*. *Ehrblichia odorata* Seem. (Turneraceae) is a larval hostplant of *Eueides procula vulgiformis* (Nymphalidae: Heliconini) in Santa Rosa National Park, Costa Rica. J. Lepid. Soc. 37: 70-77.

———. 1985. Mimicry among caterpillars. Unpublished manuscript.

Jenkins, D. W. 1983. Neotropical Nymphalidae I. Revison of Hamadryas. Bull. Allyn Mus. 81: 1-146.

———. 1984. Neotropical Nymphalidae II. Revision of Myscelia. Bull. Allyn Mus. 87: 1-64.

———. 1985*a*. Neotropical Nymphalidae III. Revision of Catonephele. Bull. Allyn Mus. 92: 1-65.

Jenkins, D. W. 1985*b*. Neotropical Nymphalidae IV. Revision of Ectima. Bull. Allyn Mus. 95: 1-30.

———. 1986. Neotropical Nymphalidae V. Revision of Epiphilo. Bull. Allyn Mus. 101: 1-70.

Jordan, C. T. 1981. Population biology and hostplant ecology of caper-feeding pierid butterflies in northeastern Mexico. Ph.D. dissertation, Univ. of Texas–Austin.

Jordan, K. 1907-1913. Papilionidae; Acraeinae. In A. Seitz (ed.), The Macrolepidoptera of the World, vol. 5. Stuttgart: Alfred Kernen.

Killip, E. P. 1938. The American species of Passifloraceae. Publ. Field Mus. Nat. Hist. (Bot.) 19: 1-613.

Kitching, I. J. 1984. The use of larval chaetotaxy in butterfly systematics, with special reference to the Danaini (Lepidoptera: Nymphalidae). Syst. Entomol. 9: 49-61.

Klots, A. B. 1928. A revision of the genus *Eurema* Part I. New World species, morphology, and phylogeny. J. N.Y. Entomol. Soc. 36: 61-76.

———. 1929*a*. The genus *Anteos* Hubner (Lepidoptera: Pieridae). Bull. Brooklyn Entomol. Soc. 24: 134-142.

———. 1929*b*. A revision of the genus *Eurema* Hubner. Entomol. Am. 9: 99-171.

———. 1933. A generic revision of the Pieridae (Lepidoptera). Entomol. Am. 12: 139-242.

———. 1951. A Field Guide to the Butterflies. Boston: Houghton Mifflin Co.

Krieger, R. I., P. Feeny, & C. F. Wilkinson. 1971. Detoxification enzymes in the guts of caterpillars: an evolutionary answer to plant defenses. Science 172: 579-581.

Kristensen, N. P. 1976. Remarks on the family-level phylogeny of butterflies (Insecta, Lepidoptera, Rhopalocera). Z. Zool. Syst. Evolutionsforsch. 14: 25-33.

Lamas, G. 1973. Taxonomia e evolucao dos generos *Ituna* Doubleday (Danainae) e *Patitia* gen. n., *Thyridia* Hubner e *Methona* Doubleday (Ithomiinae) (Lepidoptera: Nymphalidae). Ph.D. dissertation, Univ. São Paulo, Brazil.

———. 1979. Los Dismorphiinae (Pieridae) de Mexico, America Central, y las Antillas. Rev. Soc. Mex. Lepidopterol. 5: 1-38.

Lankester, C. H. 1918. Costa Rican butterflies. Entomol. News 30: 216.

Lane, R. P. 1984. Host specificity of ectoparasitic midges on butterflies. Symp. R. Entomol. Soc. Lond. 11: 105-108.

Lederhouse, R. C. 1982. Territorial defense and lek behavior of the black swallowtail butterfly, *Papilio polyxenes*. Behav. Ecol. Sociobiol. 10: 109-118.

———. 1983. Population structure, residency and weather related mortality in the black swallowtail butterfly, *Papilio polyxenes*. Oecologia 59: 307-311.

LeMoult, E., & R. Real. 1962. Les Morpho d'Amerique de Sud et Centrale. Novit. ent. (Suppl.): 1-296.

Leston, D., D. S. Smith, & B. Lenczewski. 1982. Habitat diversity and immigration in a tropical island fauna: the butterflies of Lignum Vitae Key, Florida. J. Lepid. Soc. 36: 241-255.

Longino, J. T. 1985. The biology of *Heliconius hewitsoni* (Lepidoptera: Nymphalidae) in Costa Rica: hostplant characteristics, oviposition, larval behavior, and natural enemies. Unpublished manuscript.

Mallet, J.L.B., & J. T. Longino. 1982. Hostplant records and descriptions of juvenile stages of two rare *Eueides* (Nymphalidae). J. Lepid. Soc. 36: 136-144.

Malo, F. 1961. Phoresy in *Xenufens* (Hymenoptera: Trichogrammatidae) a parasite of *Caligo eurilochus* (Lepidoptera: Nymphalidae). J. Econ. Entomol. 54: 465-466.

Malo, F., & E. R. Willis. 1961. Life history and biological control of *Caligo eurilochus*, a pest of bananas. J. Econ. Entomol. 45: 530-536.

Mayr, E. 1969. Principles of Systematic Zoology. New York: McGraw-Hill.

Mayr, E., E. G. Linsley, & R. L. Usinger. 1953. Methods and Principles of Systematic Zoology. New York: McGraw-Hill.

Meinwald, J., Y. C. Meinwald, & P. H. Mazzonlin. 1969. Sex pheromones of the queen butterfly: chemistry. Science 164: 1174-1175.

Michener, C. D. 1942. A generic revision of the Heliconiinae (Lepidoptera: Nymphalidae). Am. Mus. Novit. 1197: 1-8.

———. 1943. Some systematic notes on the Libytheidae. Am. Mus. Novit., No. 1232.

Mielke, O., and K. S. Brown. 1979. Supplemento ao Catologo dos Ithomiidae Americanas. Parana, Brazil: Curitiba.

Miller, L. D. 1968. The higher classification, phylogeny, and zoogeography of the Satyridae (Lepidoptera). Mem. Am. Entomol. Soc. 24: 1-174.

———. 1974. Revision of the Euptychini (Satyridae) 2. *Cyllopsis* R. Felder. Bull. Allyn Mus. 20: 1-98.

Mosher, E. 1969. Lepidoptera pupae, five collected works on the pupae of North American Lepidoptera. East Lansing: Entom. Reprint Specialists.

Morton, A. C. 1984. The effects of marking and handling or recapture frequencies of butterflies. Symp. R. Entomol. Soc. Lond. 11: 55-58.

Moss, M. A. 1919. The Papilios of Para. Novitates Zool. 26: 295-319.

———. 1933*a*. The gregarious sleeping habits of certain Ithomiine and Heliconine butterflies in Brazil. Proc. R. Entomol. Soc. Lond. 7: 66-67.

———. 1933*b*. Some generalisations on *Adelpha*, a neotropical genus of nymphalid butterflies of the group Limenitidi. Novitates Zool. 39: 12-20.

Müller, F. 1879. *Ituna* and Thyridia; a remarkable case of mimicry in butterflies (translated by R. Meldola). Proc. Entomol. Soc. Lond., pp. 20-29.

Müller, W. 1886. Sudamerikanische Nymphalidenraupen: Versuch eines naturlichen systems der nymphaliden. Zoologische Jahrbucher (Jena) 1: 417-678.

Munroe, E. 1950. The systematics of *Calisto* (Lepidoptera: Satyridae) with remarks on the evolution and zoogeography of the genus. J. N.Y. Entomol. Soc. 58: 211-240.

———. 1953. The phylogeny of the Papilionidae. Proc. 7th Pacific Sci. Congr. Auckland (1949) 4: 83-87.

———. 1961. The classification of the Papilionidae (Lepidoptera). Can. Entomol. Suppl. 17: 1-51.

Munroe, E., & P. R. Ehrlich. 1960. Harmonization of concepts of the higher classification of the Papilionidae. J. Lepid. Soc. 14: 169-175.

Murawski, D. A., & L. E. Gilbert. 1986. Pollen flow in *Psiguria warscewiczii*: a comparison of *Heliconius* butterflies and hummingbirds. Oecologia (in press).

Muyshondt, A. 1973*a*. Notes on the life cycle and natural history of butterflies of El Salvador Ia. *Catonephele numilia esite* (Nymphalidae: Catonephelinae). J. N.Y. Entomol. Soc. 81: 164-174.

———. 1973*b*. Notes on the life cycle and natural history of butterflies of El Salvador IIa. *Epiphile adrasta adrasta* (Nymphalidae: Catonephelinae). J. N.Y. Entomol. Soc. 81: 214-223.

———. 1973*c*. Notes on the life cycle and natural history of butterflies of El Salvador III. *Temenis laothoe liberia* (Nymphalidae: Catonephelinae). J. N.Y. Entomol. Soc. 81: 224-233.

———. 1973*d*. Notes on the life cycle and natural history of butterflies of El Salvador IV. *Pseudonica flavilla canthara* (Nymphalidae: Catonephelinae). J. N.Y. Entomol. Soc. 81: 234-242.

———. 1973*e*. Notes on the life cycle and natural history of butterflies of El Salvador I. *Prepona omphale octavia* (Nymphalidae). J. Lepid. Soc. 27: 210-219.

———. 1974*a*. An unusually long pupal stage of *Battus polydamas polydamas* L. (Papilionidae). J. Lepid. Soc. 28: 174-175.

———. 1974*b*. Notes on the life cycle and natural history of butterflies of El Salvador IV. *Anaea (Memphis) eurypyle confusa*. J. Lepid. Soc. 28: 306-314.

———. 1974*c*. Notes on the life cycle and natural history of butterflies of El Salvador V. *Pyrrhogyra hypensor* (Nymphalidae: Catonephelinae). J. N.Y. Entomol. Soc. 82: 163-172.

———. 1975*a*. Notes on the life cycle and natural history of butterflies of El Salvador VI. *Anaea (Memphis) pithyusa* (Nymphalidae). J. Lepid. Soc. 29: 168-176.

———. 1975*b*. Notes on the life cycle and natural history of butterflies of El Salvador V. *Anaea (Memphis) morvus boisduvali* (Nymphalidae) J. Lepid. Soc. 29: 32-39.

———. 1975*c*. Notes on the life cycle and natural history of butterflies of El Salvador VIa. *Diaethria astala* Guerin (Nymphalidae: Callicorinae). J. N.Y. Entomol. Soc. 83: 10-18.

———. 1976*a*. Notes on the life cycle and natural history of butterflies of El Salvador VII. *Archaeoprepona demophon centralis* (Nymphalidae). J. Lepid. Soc. 30: 23-32.

———. 1976*b*. Notes on the life cycle and natural history of butterflies of El Salvador VIII. *Archaeoprepona antimache gulina, Siderone marthesia, Zaretis callidryas*, and *Consul electra* (Nymphalidae). J. Lepid. Soc. 30: 159-168.

Muyshondt, A., & A. Muyshondt, Jr. 1974. Gregarious seasonal roosting of *Smyrna karwinskii* in El Salvador (Nymphalidae). J. Lepid. Soc. 28: 224-229.

———. 1975*a*. Notes on the life cycle and natural history of butterflies of El Salvador Ib. *Hamadryas februa* (Nymphalidae-Hamadryadinae). J. N.Y. Entomol. Soc. 83: 157-169.

———. 1975*b*. Notes on the life cycle and natural history of butterflies of El Salvador IIb. *Hamadryas guatemalena* Bates (Nymphalidae-Hamadryadinae). J. N.Y. Entomol. Soc. 83: 170-180.

———. 1975*c*. Notes on the life cycle and natural history of butterflies of El Salvador IIIb. *Hamadryas amphinome* L. (Nymphalidae-Hamadryadinae). J. N.Y. Entomol. Soc. 83: 181-191.

———. 1975*d*. Notes on the duration of the pupal stage of some swallowtails of El Salvador. Entomol. Rec. 87: 45.

———. 1976. Notes on the life cycle and natural history of butterflies of El Salvador Ic. *Colobura dirce* L. (Nymphalidae: Coloburinae). J. N.Y. Entomol. Soc. 84: 23-33.

———. 1978. Notes on the life cycle and natural history of butterflies of El Salvador IIc. *Smyrna blomfildia* and *S. karwinskii* (Nymphalidae). J. Lepid. Soc. 32: 160-174.

———. 1979. Notes on the life cycle and natural history of butterflies of El Salvador IIc. *Historis odius* and *Coea acheronta* (Nymphalidae-Coloburinae). J. Lepid. Soc. 33: 112-123.

Muyshondt, A., A. Muyshondt, Jr., & P. Muyshondt. 1976. Notas sobre la biologia de lepidopteros de El Salvador I. Rev. Soc. Mex. Lepidoptrol. 2: 77-90.

Muyshondt, A., A. M. Young, & A. Muyshondt, Jr. 1973. The biology of the butterfly *Dione juno huascama* (Nymphalidae: Heliçoniinae) in El Salvador. J. N.Y. Entomol. Soc. 81: 137-151.

Nahrstedt, A., & R. H. Davis. 1981. The occurrence of the cyanoglucosides Limarin and Lotaustralin, in *Acraea* and *Heliconius* butterflies. Comp. Biochem. Physiol. 68*B*: 575-577.

———. 1983. Occurrence, variation and biosynthesis of the cyanogenic glucosides Linamarin and Lotaustralin in species of the Heliconiini (Insecta: Lepidoptera). Comp. Biochem. Physiol. 75*B*: 65-73.

Neck, R. W. 1974. Ecological genetics of a larval color polymorphism in the butterfly genus *Chlosyne*. Ph.D. dissertation, Univ. of Texas–Austin.

———. 1977. Foodplant ecology of the butterfly *Chlosyne lacinia* (Geyer) (Nymphalidae). J. Res. Lep. 16: 69-74.

Nielsen, E. T. 1961. On the habits of the migratory butterfly *Ascia monuste* L. Biol. Meddr. 23: 1-81.

Noriega, F. F. 1923. Diccionario Geografico de Costa Rica. San José, Costa Rica: Imprenta Nacional.

Norris, M. J. 1936. The feeding habits of the adult Lepidoptera, Heteroneura. Trans. R. Entomol. Soc. Lond. 85: 61-90.

Ohsaki, N. 1979. Comparative population studies of three *Pieris* butterflies *P. rapae, P. melete* and *P. napi*, living in the same area. I. Ecological requirements for habitat resources in the adult. Res. Popul. Ecol. 20: 278-296.

Oldroyd, H. 1958. Collecting, Preserving and Studying Insects. New York: Macmillan.

Opler, P. A., G. W. Frankie, & H. K. Baker. 1976. Rainfall as a factor in the release, timing, and synchronization of anthesis by tropical trees and shrubs. J. Biogeogr. 3: 231-236.

Opler, P. A., & G. O. Krizek. 1984. Butterflies East of the Great Plains. Baltimore and London: Johns Hopkins University Press.

Owen, D. F. 1966. Predominantly female populations of an African butterfly. Heredity 21: 443-451.

———. 1971. Tropical Butterflies. Oxford: Clarendon Press.

Owen, D. F., & D. O. Chanter. 1969. Population biology of tropical African butterflies. Sex ratio and genetic variation in *Acraea encedon*. J. Zool. Lond. 157: 345-374.

Papageorgis, C. 1975. Mimicry in neotropical butterflies. Amer. Sci. 63: 522-532.

Pasteur, G. 1982. A classificatory review of mimicry systems. Ann. Rev. Ecol. Syst. 13: 169-199.

Pianka, E. R. 1966. Latitudinal gradients in species diversity: a review of concepts. Am. Nat. 100: 33-46.

Pliske, T. E., J. A. Edgar, & C. C. Culvenor. 1976. The chemical basis of attraction of ithomiine butterflies to plants containing pyrrolizidine alkaloids. J. Chem. Ecol. 2: 255-262.

Pliske, T. E., & T. Eisner. 1969. Sex pheromone of the queen butterfly: biology. Science 164: 1170-1172.

Poulton, E. B. 1908. *Essays on Evolution*. Oxford: Clarendon Press.

Rausher, M. D. 1978. Search image for leaf shape in a butterfly. Science 200: 1071-1073.

———. 1979. Egg recognition: its advantage to a butterfly. Anim. Behav. 27: 1034-1040.

Ray, T., & C. C. Andrews. 1980. Ant butterflies: butterflies that follow army ants to feed on antbird droppings. Science 210: 1147-1148.

Reuter, E. 1896. Uber die palpen der Rhopaloceren. Acta. Soc. Scientiarum Fennicae 22: 1-577.

Riley, N. D. 1975. A Field Guide to the Butterflies of the West Indies. London: Collins.

Robbins, R. K. 1981. The "false head" hypothesis: predation and wing pattern variation of lycaenid butterflies. Am. Nat. 118: 770-775.

Rosenthal, G. A., & D. H. Janzen (eds.). 1979. Herbivores: Their Interaction with Secondary Plant Metabolites. New York and London: Academic Press.

Ross, G. N. 1963. Evidence for lack of territoriality in two species of *Hamadryas*, Nymphalidae. J. Res. Lepid. 2: 241-246.

———. 1964*a*. Life history studies on Mexican butterflies I. Notes on the early stages of four papilionids from Catemaco, Vera Cruz. J. Res. Lepid. 3: 9-18.

———. 1964*b*. Life history studies on Mexican butterflies III. Nine Rhopalocera (Papilionidae, Nymphalidae, Lycaenidae) from Ocotol Chico, Vera Cruz. J. Res. Lepid. 3: 207-229.

———. 1975-77. An ecological study of the butterflies of the Sierra de Tuxla in Vera Cruz, Mexico. J. Res. Lepid. 14: 103-124, 169-188, 233-252; 15: 41-60, 109-128, 185-200, 225-240; 16: 87-130.

Rothschild, M. 1971. Speculations about mimicry with Henry Ford. In

R. Creed (ed.), Ecological Genetics and Evolution, pp. 202-233. London: Oxford Univ. Press.

———. 1972. Secondary plant substances and warning coloration in insects. Symp. R. Entomol. Soc. Lond. 6: 59-83.

Rothschild, W., & K. Jordan. 1906. A revision of the American papilios. Novitates Zool. 13: 411-752.

Rydon, A.H.B. 1971. The systematics of the Charaxidae (Lepidoptera: Nymphaloidea). Entomol. Rec. 83: 219-233, 283-287, 310-316, 336-341, 384-388.

Salt, G. 1935. Experimental studies in insect parasitism. III. Host selection. Proc. R. Entomol. Soc. *B* 177: 413-435.

———. 1937. Experimental studies in insect parasitism. V. The sense used by *Trichogramma* to distinguish between parasitized and unparasitized hosts. Proc. R. Entomol. Soc. *B* 122: 57-75.

Schaus, W. 1884. [untitled]. Papilio 4: 101.

———. 1913. New species of Rhopalocera from Costa Rica. Proc. Zool. Soc. Lond. 24: 339-367.

Schwanwitsch, B. N. 1924. On the ground-plan of the wing-pattern in nymphalids and certain other families of the rhopalocerous Lepidoptera. Proc. Zool. Soc. Lond. 1924: 509-528.

———. 1926. On the modes of evolution of the wing-pattern in nymphalids and certain other families of the rhopalocerous Lepidoptera. Proc. Zool. Soc. Lond. 1926: 493-508.

Scudder, S. H. 1889. The Butterflies of the Eastern United States with Special Reference to New England. Vols. 1-3. Cambridge, Mass.

Seitz, A. (ed.). 1907-1924. The Macrolepidoptera of the World. Vol. 5. Stuttgart: Alfred Kernen.

Sepp, J. 1828-1848. Surinaamsche Vlinders. Amsterdam: J. C. Sepp en Zoon.

Shapiro, A. M. 1980. Egg load assessment and carryover diapause in *Anthocharis* (Pieridae). J. Lepid. Soc. 34: 307-315.

———. 1981. The pierid red-egg syndrome. Am. Nat. 117: 276-294.

———. 1984. Experimental studies on the evolution of seasonal polyphenism. Symp. R. Entomol. Soc. Lond. 11: 297-307.

Shields, O. 1967. "Hilltopping": an ecological study of summit congregation behavior of the butterflies of a southern Californian hill. J. Res. Lepid. 6: 69-178.

Silberglied, R. E. 1977. Communication in the Lepidoptera. In T. A. Sebeok (ed.), How Animals Communicate, pp. 362-402. Bloomington: Indiana University Press.

———. 1984. Visual communication and sexual selection among butterflies. Symp. R. Entomol. Soc. Lond. 11: 207-223.

Silberglied, R. E., A. Aiello, & G. Lamas. 1979. Neotropical butterflies of the genus *Anartia*: systematics, life histories, and general biology. Psyche 86: 219-260.

Simpson, G. G. 1945. The principles of classification and a classification of mammals. Bull. Am. Mus. Nat. Hist. 85: 1-350.

Singer, M. C. 1983. Multiple host use by a phytophagous insect population. Evolution 37: 389-403.

———. 1984. Butterfly-hostplant relationships: host quality, adult choice and larval success. Symp. R. Entomol. Soc. Lond. 11: 81-88.

Singer, M. C., P. J. DeVries, & P. R. Ehrlich. 1983. The *Cissia confusa* species group in Costa Rica and Trinidad. Zoo. J. Linn. Soc. 79: 101-119.

Singer, M. C., & P. R. Ehrlich. 1986. Diversity and specificity among grass-feeding butterflies. J. Res. Lepid (in press).

Singer, M. C., P. R. Ehrlich, & L. E. Gilbert. 1971. Butterfly feeding on a lycopsid. Science 172: 1341-1342.

Slansky, F. 1978. Utilization of energy and nitrogen by larvae of the imported cabbage worm, *Pieris rapae*, as affected by parasitism by *Apanteles glomeratus*. Environ. Entomol. 7: 179-185.

Smiley, J. T. 1978. Plant chemistry and the evolution of host specificity: new evidence from *Heliconius* and *Passiflora*. Science 201: 745-747.

Smith, D.A.S. 1976. Phenotypic diversity, mimicry and natural selection in the African butterfly *Hypolimnas misippus* L. (Lepidoptera: Nymphalidae). Biol. J. Linn. Soc. 8: 183-204.

Smith, K. M. 1967. Insect Virology. New York & London: Academic Press.

Sneath, P.H.A., & R. R. Sokal. 1973. Numerical Taxonomy. San Francisco: W. H. Freeman.

Snodgrass, R. E. 1961. The caterpillar and the butterfly. Smithsonian Misc. Colls., Vol. 143, No. 6.

Sokal, R. R. and P.H.A. Sneath, 1963. The Principles of Numerical Taxonomy. San Francisco: W. H. Freeman.

Southwood, T.R.E. 1978. Ecological Methods. New York: Halsted Press.

Stichel, H. 1909. Brassolidae. Das Tierreich 25: 1-244.

———. 1939. Nymphalidae III; Charaxinae II. In F. Bryk (ed.), Lepidopterorum Catalogus. 30: 375-794.

Stradling, D. J. 1976. The nature of the mimetic patterns of the brassolid genera *Caligo* and *Eryphanis*. Ecol. Entomol. 1: 135-138.

Swihart, C. A. 1971. Colour discrimination by the butterfly *Heliconius charitonius*. Linn. Anim. Behav. 19: 156-164.

Swihart, C. A., & S. L. Swihart. 1970. Colour selection and learned feeding preferences in the butterfly *Heliconius charitonius*. Linn. Anim. Behav. 18: 60-64.

Swynerton, L.F.M. 1926. An investigation into the defences of the butterflies of the genus *Charaxes*. III. Inter. Entomol. Kongress Zurich Band 2: 478-506.

Tinbergen, N. 1958. Curious Naturalists. London: Country Life.

Tinbergen, N., B.J.D. Meeuse, L. K. Boerema, & W. W. Varossieau. 1942. Die Balz des samfalters, *Eumenis* (= *Satyrus*) *semele*. Z. Tierpsychol. 5: 182-226.

Turner, J.R.G. 1971. Studies on Müllerian mimicry and its evolution in burnet moths and heliconid butterflies. In E. R. Creed (ed.), Ecological Genetics and Evolution. Oxford: Blackwell.

———. 1977. A bibliography of *Heliconius* and the related genera. Stony Brook, N.Y.: SUNY-Stony Brook Prog. Ecol. Evol., Contr. 151.

———. 1984. Mimicry: the palability spectrum and its consequences. Symp. R. Entomol. Soc. Lond. 11: 141-161.

Tuxen, S. L. (ed.). 1970. Taxonomist's Glossary of Genitalia of Insects. 2nd ed. Copenhagen: Munksgaard.

Tyler, H. A. 1975. The Swallowtail Butterflies of North America. Healdsburg, Calif.: Naturegraph.

Urquhart, F. A. 1976. Found at last: the monarch's winter home. Nat. Geogr. Mag. 150: 160-173.

Vane-Wright, R. I. 1972. Precourtship activity and a new scent organ in butterflies. Nature 239: 338-340.

———. 1976. A unified classification of mimetic resemblances. Biol. J. Linn. Soc. 8: 25-56.

———. 1979. The colouration, identification and phylogeny of *Nessaea* butterflies (Lepidoptera: Nymphalidae). Bull. Brit. Mus. (Nat. Hist.) Entomol. 38: 27-56.

———. 1980. On the definition of mimicry. Biol. J. Linn. Soc. 13: 1-6.

———. 1981. Mimicry and its unknown ecological consequences. In P. H. Greenwood (ed.), The Evolving Biosphere, pp. 157-168. New York: Cambridge Univ. Press.

———. 1984. The role of pseudosexual selection in the evolution of butterfly color patterns. Symp. R. Entomol. Soc. Lond. 11: 251-253.

Vane-Wright, R. I., & P. R. Ackery (eds.). 1984. The Biology of Butterflies. Symp. R. Entomol. Soc. Lond. 11: 1-429.

Vane-Wright, R. I., P. R. Ackery, & R. L. Smiles. 1977. The polymorphism, mimicry and hostplant relations of *Hypolimnas* butterflies. Biol. J. Linn. Soc. 9: 285-297.

Vinson, S. B., & G. F. Iwantsch. 1980. Host regulation by insect parasitoids. Q. Rev. Biol. 55: 143-165.

Waldbauer, G. P., & J. G. Sternberg. 1975. Saturniid moths as mimics: an alternative explanation of attempts to demonstrate mimetic advantage in nature. Evolution 29: 650-658.

Waller, D. A., & L. E. Gilbert. 1982. Roost recruitment and resource utilization: observations on a *Heliconius charitonia* L. roost in Mexico (Nymphalidae). J. Lepid. Soc. 36: 178-184.

Watt, W. B. 1968. Adaptive significance of pigment polymorphisms in *Colias* butterflies. I. Variation of melanin pigment in relation to thermoregulation. Evolution 22: 437-458.

Weatherston, J., J. E. Percy, L. M. MacDonald, & J. A. MacDonald. 1979. Morphology of the prothoracic defensive gland of *Schizura concinna* (J. E. Smith) (Lepidoptera: Notodontidae) and the nature of its secretion. J. Chem. Ecol. 5: 165-177.

Weymer, G. 1910. Satyridae. In A. Seitz (ed.), The Macrolepidoptera of the World, vol. 5. Stuttgart: Alfred Kernen.

Wickler, W. 1968. Mimicry in Plants and Animals. London: World Univ. Library.

Wiley, E. O. 1981. The Theory and Practice of Phylogenetic Systematics. New York: John Wiley & Sons.

Williams, C. B. 1930. The Migration of Butterflies. Edinburgh and London: Oliver & Boyd.

Young, A. M. 1971*a*. Wing coloration and reflectance in *Morpho* butterflies as related to reproductive behavior and escape from avian predators. Oecologia 7: 209-222.

———. 1971*b*. Mimetic associations in natural populations of tropical papilionid butterflies I. Life history and structure of a tropical dry forest breeding population of *Battus polydamas polydamas*. Rev. Biol. Trop. 19: 211-240.

———. 1972*a*. The ecology and ethology of the tropical nymphaline butterfly *Victorina epaphus* I. Life cycle and natural history. J. Lepid. Soc. 26: 155-170.

———. 1972*b*. Mimetic associations in natural populations of tropical butterflies II. Mimetic interactions of *Battus polydamas* and *Battus belus*. Biotropica 4: 17-27.

———. 1972*c*. A contribution to the biology of *Itaballia caesia* (Pierinae) in a Costa Rican mountain ravine. Wasmann J. Biol. 30: 43-70.

———. 1972*d*. Notes on the life cycle and natural history of *Dismorphia virgo* (Lepidoptera: Pieridae: Dismorphinae). Psyche 79: 165-178.

———. 1972*e*. On the life cycle and natural history of *Hymenitis nero* (Lepidoptera: Ithomiinae) in Costa Rica. Psyche 79: 284-294.

———. 1973*a*. Notes on the life cycle and natural history of *Parides arcas mylotes* (Papilionidae) in Costa Rican premontane wet forest. Psyche 80: 1-22.

———. 1973*b*. The life cycle of *Dircenna relata* (Ithomiidae) in Costa Rica. J. Lepid. Soc. 27: 258-267.

———. 1973*c*. Notes on the biology of *Phyciodes (Eresia) eutropia* (Lepidoptera: Nymphalidae) in a Costa Rican mountain forest. J. N.Y. Entomol. Soc. 81: 87-100.

———. 1973*d*. Note on the biology of the butterfly, *Heliconius cydno* (Lepidoptera: Heliconiinae) in Costa Rica. Wasmann J. Biol. 31: 337-350.

———. 1974*a*. On the biology of *Hamadryas februa* (Lepidoptera: Nymphalidae: Nymphalinae) in Guanacaste, Costa Rica. Zeit. Angew. Entomol. 75: 380-393.

———. 1974*b*. Further observation on the natural history of *Philaethria dido dido* (Lepidoptera: Nymphalidae: Heliconiinae). J. N.Y. Entomol. Soc. 82: 30-41.

———. 1974*c*. Notes on the natural history of a rare *Adelpha* butterfly (Lepidoptera: Nymphalidae) in Costa Rican high country. J. N.Y. Entomol. Soc. 82: 235-244.

———. 1974*d*. Notes on the biology of *Pteronymia notilla* (Ithomiidae) in a Costa Rican mountain forest. J. Lepid. Soc. 28: 257-268.

———. 1974*e*. On the biology of *Godyris zaveleta caesiopicta* (Lepidoptera: Nymphalidae: Ithomiinae). Entomol. News 85: 227-238.

———. 1974*f*. A natural history account of *Oleria zelica pagasa* (Lepidoptera: Ithomiidae) in a Costa Rican mountain rainforest. Stud. Neotrop. Fauna 9: 123-140.

———. 1975*a*. Observations on the life cycle of *Heliconius hecale zuleika* (Hewitson) in Costa Rica. Pan-Pac. Entomol. 51: 76-85.

———. 1975*b*. Leakage of *Morpho theseus* (Lepidoptera: Nymphalidae) into the northeastern lowlands of Costa Rica. Brenesia 6: 59-67.

———. 1976*a*. Notes on the life cycle of the butterfly *Hypanartia kefersteini* (Nymphalidae: Nymphalini) in Costa Rica. Brenesia 9: 61-69.

———. 1976*b*. Notes on the biology of *Hypothyris euclea* (Lepidoptera: Nymphalidae: Ithomiinae) in Costa Rica. Pan-Pac. Entomol. 53: 104-113.

———. 1977*a*. Studies on the biology of *Parides iphidamas* (Papilionidae: Troidini) in Costa Rica. J. Lepid. Soc. 31: 100-108.

———. 1977*b*. Notes on the biology of the butterfly *Hypoleria cassotis* (Bates) (Nymphalidae: Ithomiinae) in northeastern Costa Rica. Brenesia 10: 97-108.

———. 1978*a*. The biology of *Aeria eurimedea agna* (Nymphalidae: Ithomiinae) in Costa Rica. J. Kansas Entomol. Soc. 51: 1-10.

———. 1978*b*. Studies on the interactions of *Morpho peleides* (Morphidae) with Leguminosae. J. Lepid. Soc. 32: 66-74.

———. 1979. Weather and regulation of *Hypothyris euclea* (Lepidoptera: Nymphalidae: Ithomiinae) populations in northeastern Costa Rica. J. Lepid. Soc. 33: 68-69.

———. 1980. Notes on the behavioral ecology of *Perrhybris lypera* (Pieridae) in northeastern Costa Rica. J. Lepid. Soc. 34: 36-47.

———. 1982*a*. Notes on the natural history of *Morpho granadensis polybaptus* Butler (Lepidoptera: Nymphalidae: Morphinae) and its relation to that of *Morpho peleides limpida* Butler. J. N.Y. Entomol. Soc. 90: 35-54.

———. 1982*b*. *Perrhybris lypera* (Pieridae) feeding on Lauraceae: a response to DeVries. J. Lepid. Soc. 36: 230-232.

———. 1984. Natural history notes for *Taygetis andromeda* (Cramer) (Satyridae) in eastern Costa Rica. J. Lepid. Soc. 38: 102-113.

Young, A. M., L. M. Cook, & E. W. Thomason. 1976. Population structure of the tropical butterfly *Heliconius charitonius*. J. Anim. Ecol. 45: 851-863.

Young, A. M., & A. Muyshondt. 1972. Biology of *Morpho polyphemus* in El Salvador. J. N.Y. Entomol. Soc. 80: 18-42.

———. 1973. The biology of *Morpho peleides* in Central America. Caribb. J. Sci. 13: 1-49.

———. 1975. Studies on the natural history of Central American butterflies in the family cluster Satyridae-Brassolidae-Morphidae III. *Opsiphanes tamarindi* and *Opsiphanes cassina* in Costa Rica and El Salvador. Stud. Neotrop. Fauna 10: 19-56.

INDEX

Italicized numbers refer to an illustration on that page.